A Companion to
Faulkner Studies

A Companion to Faulkner Studies

Edited by Charles A. Peek
and Robert W. Hamblin

GREENWOOD PRESS
Westport, Connecticut • London

Library of Congress Cataloging-in-Publication Data

A companion to Faulkner studies / edited by Charles A. Peek and Robert W. Hamblin.
    p. cm.
    Includes bibliographical references (p.) and index.
    ISBN 0–313–32030–6
    1. Faulkner, William, 1897–1962—Criticism and interpretation—Handbooks, manuals, etc. I. Peek,
Charles A. II. Hamblin, Robert W.
PS3511.A86Z758   2004
813′.52—dc22   2004010392

British Library Cataloguing in Publication Data is available.

Library of Congress Catalog Card Number: 2004010392
ISBN: 0–313–32030–6

First published in 2004

Greenwood Press, 88 Post Road West, Westport, CT 06881
An imprint of Greenwood Publishing Group, Inc.
www.greenwood.com

Printed in the United States of America

The paper used in this book complies with the
Permanent Paper Standard issued by the National
Information Standards Organization (Z39.48–1984).

10   9   8   7   6   5   4   3   2   1

Copyright Acknowledgments

Excerpts from *The Faulkner Journal* were reprinted with permission.

We dedicate this *Companion* to our companions,
Faulkner readers and scholars.
It is especially for Jim Campbell and the late Bill Shaver,
who called clearly and often for a book like this one.

Contents

Preface

AIM

For several years now, we have engaged in many conversations with scholars, teachers, and readers of Faulkner, in which they have voiced the need for a "companion" work, one that would rehearse how critics have read Faulkner over the years, digest the major critical approaches that have been brought to bear on his work, and apply some of those approaches, either as sample readings or as continuations of work already done.

In many circles, the words *criticism* and *critical* have taken on pejorative senses of being negative and carping. Their proper use refers to the disciplined study of acts of imagination. The purpose of such criticism, of the critical eye, is to illumine works of art. One critic is said to have described the task of criticism as the creation of little works of art in honor of greater works of art. That is the sense in which we introduce to you 13 critical stances that illumine Faulkner's writing, each in its own way, each with its own many and varied practitioners, each constructing a small work of art in honor of the great American novelist, William Faulkner. And, of course, by Faulkner and Faulkner's writing, we mean his imagination, his observation, his historic moment, his craft, and the material processes by which his works receive and reach readers.

With the success of *A William Faulkner Encyclopedia,* Greenwood Press gave serious consideration to a volume such as this and asked us to undertake its planning and completion. As with the former work, we set about to enlist authors we knew to be competent, reliable, and insightful, seeking a mix of well-established and rising scholars and a range of contexts within which these authors go about their own reading, teaching, and scholarship. We looked only for evidence of their capacity for undertaking a contribution in their particular field of criticism and asked each to work within the following simple parameters:

- Presentation of a definition of their particular approach and the terms relevant to it.
- Consideration, from their given perspective, of as much as is relevant from the whole body of Faulkner's novels, short fiction, essays, poems, screenplays, speeches, and letters.
- An overview of the significant extant scholarship written from this approach.
- In-depth referencing of the critical works most important to their perspective.
- An accounting of what this approach has yielded for Faulkner studies.
- Citation of bibliographical entries of extant criticism.
- Personal views and original ideas concerning the approach and its usefulness.

We did not ask of them that the 13 essays printed in this volume closely resemble the others in style or structure; in fact, it is our belief that a particular approach shapes the style and structure of its presentation. Hence, the 13 chapters here bear not only the personal stamps of their authors but also the unique signatures of the approach itself. Nor, given that the borders among the approaches are porous and tentative constructions, did we seek to eliminate all repetition. Some may read the book from cover to cover—it is our hope that such a reading would be highly rewarding for scholar and general reader alike; but many may read some chapters but not others, or even sections of chapters. Hence, for most readers, we feel the repetition will be minimal.

The audience for the resulting chapters is that same audience that prompted the book in the first place; it will help readers to read, critics to criticize, and students to study. In a very profound sense, no matter how long we have been about the business of reading, teaching, or writing about Faulkner, we all remain students of his works. Like all students, our study is improved by dialogue, through reading or conversation. This book is a contribution to that dialogue.

METHOD

Many, though not all, of the chapters contain their own endnotes, in which you will find not only explanatory material but also numerous references to sources. The works cited have been collected into a section of bibliographic references, except where authors chose to give full bibliographic information in the text or endnotes to their chapters. The bibliography also contains short listings of scholarly roundups, films, and handbooks.

Similarly the definitions of pertinent critical terms are collected into an alphabetized Glossary whose terms are bold-faced in the text of the appropriate chapter(s). In addition to a thorough cross-referencing index, there are within the text of each chapter points at which a further discussion of a theme in another chapter is indicated by the notation "[see chapter . . .]." For some contributors, you will find most references to works cited within the text itself; for others, most are in the endnotes. Since in reading the chapters you will find readily apparent which are which, this does not seem to us to present any difficulty in further pursuing lines of thought or references. Whether in the text, the notes, or the bibliography, the style is generally MLA or CMS. Habits in this matter are beginning to differ widely among scholars, and we made only minimal attempts to regularize them for this book. After the Selected Bibliography and Index, you will find brief biographical details about each of the authors.

In general, the meaning of our title has driven our method: the book is meant to become a companion for you in the joys and struggles of reading Faulkner. We have therefore endeavored to make the book as companionable as we knew how. To do so, wherever possible, the chapters are jargon-free, in the plain language of the literate reading public. When specialized terms are required, there is the aid of the Glossary. Individually and in their variation, the styles of expression are engaging and lucid. Within the presentations, points to be made are illustrated as well as stated. In the choice of authors for each presentation, we sought to avoid any conflict of interest but to encourage definite ideas about and commitments to approaches.

On rare occasions, when, in the process of editing, we became aware of a source pertinent to a chapter, we added it to the other references in the text of the chapter or in the chapter's endnotes. No substantive changes were made in any chapter without the author's express permission.

Acknowledgments

We must first acknowledge our 13 contributors. Each of them has worked tirelessly to achieve the goals of this book, and they have all put up with and accommodated a barrage of suggested editorial revisions—some small and some not—designed to give the book a sense of cohesiveness, thoroughness, and accuracy. They have been a highly refreshing and rewarding group with whom to work.

And, of course, we thank Greenwood for yet another opportunity to work in our chosen field, to be of some assistance to folks who read, teach, or write about Faulkner as much, if not more, than we do. Our publisher has been immensely helpful.

Thanks are due to Kaye Hamblin and Nancy Peek: all authors will know what their loved ones suffer in the course of a major production. Each gifted in her own right, they have been as supportive as any could be.

We thank, too, the University of Nebraska at Kearney and Southeast Missouri State University for their support of us as scholar-teachers and their particular support of this project, despite the difficult stresses of an era of budget cutting at both institutions. This includes our thanks to Bobby J. Meyer who, upon completion of his M.A., assisted in the final editing, during which time the Index, the Selected Bibliography, the Glossary, and indeed the final structure of the book took shape.

Thanks to other scholars and teachers who suggested to us names of those who might make solid contributions to the book. Thanks as well to them and other colleagues for their encouragement of the idea for this book and for their support as boosters of our own confidence in our ability to complete the ambitious project we had undertaken.

We would also like to thank the following student assistants who helped with the final indexing and proofing of the volume: Ndeye Fatou Ba, Clara Blanken-biller, Erica Chu, Gary Dop, Taffnee Faimon, Jeff Gerdes, Tory Hooton, Michael Johnson, Amanda Maryott, Jodi Meyer, Jace Pittman, Paul Powell, John Ross, David Salyer, Micah Torgrimson, and Lynn Watson.

Mostly, we thank you, the readers, for investing at least your curiosity and in some cases even your trust in us. We hope you find the book a rewarding companion.

1

Mythic and Archetypal Criticism

Robert W. Hamblin

Any consideration of the role of **myth** and **archetype** in Faulkner's work must examine two related but quite distinct aspects of mythic practice. The first involves an author's use of mythological plots, characters, and themes in writing his or her own novels, stories, poems, or plays. In this essay this approach will be identified by the name given it by T. S. Eliot—"the **mythical method.**" The second approach concerns an author's invention of an original set of characters, places, events, and beliefs that, taken together, create the semblance and signif- icance of ancient myth. Modern examples of such authorial myths include the visionary works of William Butler Yeats, the Poictesme novels of James Branch Cabell, the "Myth of America" poetry of Hart Crane, the Narnia novels of C. S. Lewis, and the symbolic fantasies of J.R.R. Tolkien. Over the decades scholars have found both of these classifications of myth relevant to Faulkner. His works have been carefully analyzed in relation to ancient myths, specifically Greco- Roman and Christian; and he has been heralded for creating, in his extended series of interlocking novels and stories, a mythical world of his own, the one now universally known as Yoknapatawpha.

THE MYTHICAL METHOD

In 1923, in his extraordinarily prescient review of James Joyce's *Ulysses,* T. S. Eliot gave a name to a relatively new literary trend that would become increas- ingly prominent in the years and decades to come. Eliot asserts that in using Homer's narrative of the epic journey of Ulysses in *The Odyssey* as the frame- work for the twentieth-century story of Leopold Bloom, "Mr. Joyce is pursuing a method which others must pursue after him. . . . It is a method for which the horoscope is auspicious. Psychology . . . , ethnology, and *The Golden Bough* have concurred to make possible what was impossible even a few years ago. Instead of narrative method, we may now use the mythical method."[1]

As Eliot defines the term, "the mythical method" involves an author's "manipulating a continuous parallel between contemporaneity and antiquity," the purpose being to provide "a way of controlling, of ordering, of giving a shape and a significance to the immense panorama of futility and anarchy which is contemporary history" (483). Clearly, Eliot saw the use of myth as one means of understanding and resisting the chaotic conditions dramatized by World War I. While other writers, including Faulkner, would direct the application of myth away from the political and philosophical agenda of Eliot, the fact remains that Eliot correctly identified the literary technique that would come to dominate the practice of writers of his, and the next, generation.

Eliot could write so knowingly about Joyce's use of the mythical method, of course, because Eliot himself was employing the same principle in his work. *The Waste Land,* published one year earlier than his review of Joyce's novel, similarly draws heavily upon mythic sources, as Eliot explains in the copious footnotes to the poem. Eliot specifically cites Jessie L. Weston's study of the Grail legend, *From Ritual to Romance,* and Sir James George Frazer's *The Golden Bough* as major influences upon his poem. Just as Weston and Frazer sought to demonstrate that many aspects of Western civilization have actually evolved from pagan rituals and beliefs, so Eliot merged the Christian myth of death, burial, and resurrection with corresponding details from primitive vegetation myths. Woven into these blended myths are also quotations from or allusions to nearly three dozen authors representing various historical epochs. All such elements, mythic and literary, become for the narrator of Eliot's poem "fragments" to be "shored against [the] ruins" (l. 431) of contemporary chaos.

As Eliot notes in his review of *Ulysses,* recent developments in psychology and anthropology had laid the foundation for the mythical method of writing. In his reference to psychology, Eliot was undoubtedly alluding to the pioneering work of Sigmund Freud and Carl Jung, both of whom were engaged in analyzing the role of the subconscious mind in human behavior. Indeed, Freud's utilization of the term *Oedipus complex,* applying the actions in Sophocles' ancient play to the behavior of certain patients, parallels Joyce's reprise of Homeric materials. Even more than Freud, Jung would become crucial to the development of mythic literary practice because of his insistence, in a significant extension of Freudian theory, that individuals possess not only a personal but also a **"collective" unconscious,** or "racial memory," in which are stored "archetypes" that embody the memories and experiences of the entire human race. According to Jung, these archetypes, which he calls "primordial images," have supplied the characters, situations, symbols, and themes of stories from primitive societies onward throughout history. Examples of archetypes may be found in the symbolism typically associated with such images as water (creation, purification, redemption), circles (wholeness, unity), gardens (paradise, fertility), and various colors (red: blood, sacrifice; green: hope, progress; black: evil, melancholy, death; white: purity, innocence), as well as such universal character types as the Innocent, the Serpent, the Great Mother, the Wise Old Man, the Hero, the Trickster, and the Scapegoat. Writers being individuals in whom the working of the collective unconscious is particularly strong, these archetypal symbols, motifs, and character types will naturally find expression in literary works, quite independent of the conscious awareness or intention of the writers themselves.[2]

While Jung's theory of the collective unconscious provides one of the major underpinnings of the mythical method, giving it a psychological and even pseudo-scientific validity, it is important to recognize that writers and critics quickly broadened the definition of "archetype" to include cultural and conscious—as well as personal and unconscious—derivatives of older materials. It is this wider definition that Eliot alludes to in his mention of the importance of ethnology and *The Golden Bough*. Here his reference is almost certainly to the Cambridge Hellenists, an influential group of British scholars, including F. M. Cornford, Gilbert Murray, and Jane Harrison, as well as Frazer, who were busily applying recent anthropological findings to the examination of the mythic and ritualistic origins of Greek drama. Their aim was to discover the essential and universal truths of existence buried, like treasures in ancient tombs, in the narratives embraced by early cultures.

A conscious (or at least semiconscious) use of literary archetypes would be further explored by Maud Bodkin, a British psychologist and literary critic whose *Archetypal Patterns in Poetry: Psychological Studies of Imagination* represents another important contribution to the development of mythic criticism. Bodkin applied Jung's theories to wider cultural and linguistic considerations. For Bodkin, archetypes are located not so much within the individual consciousness as in "the common nature lived and immediately experienced by the members of a group or community." While not denying a "biological inheritance" of archetypes, Bodkin argues for a "social inheritance" as well, one that is passed down from generation to generation through language and the recycling of narrative and poetic patterns.[3]

This idea of a "social inheritance" best interpreted by anthropologists and archaeologists explains the importance to Eliot and other mythic writers and critics of Frazer's *The Golden Bough*. An encyclopedia (eventually comprising 12 volumes) of primitive man's beliefs and practices, *The Golden Bough* documents Frazer's notions of how the superstitions and magic rituals of prehistoric cultures evolved into the religious practices of the civilized, Christian world. Specifically, Frazer investigated the practice of primitive societies in ritualistically slaying an aging king, thought to be divine, and replacing him with a younger, more vigorous successor. Only by so doing, the ancients believed, could the vitality and health of their culture be ensured. In such primitive concepts, Frazer argued, could be found the origins of the basic tenets of Judeo-Christian theology, as well as many modern secular behaviors such as hero worship and scapegoating. Perhaps the most famous literary expressions of Frazer's notions are the uses of the Fisher King motif in Eliot's *The Waste Land*

and Hemingway's *The Sun Also Rises* and of the scapegoat motif in Shirley Jackson's "The Lottery," but one has only to place the text of Faulkner's "The Bear" alongside Frazer's chapter on "Killing the Sacred Bear" to understand the relevance of Frazer to Faulkner studies as well.

Predictably in a culture heavily influenced by Judeo-Christian thought, biblical myths have provided especially fruitful material for writers seeking to import older narratives into their contemporary works. This pattern is clearly illustrated by such works as Thomas Mann's *Joseph and His Brothers,* Robinson Jeffers's *Tamar,* Archibald MacLeish's *J. B.,* Thornton Wilder's *The Skin of Our Teeth,* and John Steinbeck's *East of Eden,* as well as in several works by Faulkner.

As demonstrated by Eliot's allusions in *The Waste Land* to earlier writers such as Dante, Chaucer, Spenser, Shakespeare, and Goldsmith, and to even more recent authors such as Baudelaire, the mythical method quickly came to embrace the use of any literary predecessor (particularly authors of classics well known to the reading public) a writer would find useful to his or her purposes. Thus the mythical method may be understood to apply not only to such works as Eugene O'Neill's retelling of the classical myths of Oedipus (*Desire Under the Elms*) and Agamemnon (*Mourning Becomes Electra*) or Robert Bly's employment of an ancient folk tale in *Iron John* but also to such literary adaptations and restatements as Joseph Conrad's use of Dante's *Inferno* in *Heart of Darkness,* Robert Penn Warren's recycling of Shakespeare's *Julius Caesar* and Milton's *Paradise Lost* in *All the King's Men,* William Golding's ironic employment of island utopias from Sir Thomas More's to R. M. Ballantyne's in *Lord of the Flies,* and Jane Smiley's retelling of *King Lear* in *A Thousand Acres.* The process is ongoing, of course, so that by now Faulkner's texts have also become a "mythic" pattern for later writers: *The Sound and the Fury,* for example, provides much of the design for William Styron's *Lie Down in Darkness,* and Graham Swift's *Last Orders* is modeled on *As I Lay Dying.*

Building upon the psychological theories of Freud, Jung, and Bodkin; the anthropological materials provided by Frazer and the other Cambridge Hellenists; and the literary practice of Joyce, Eliot, and others, a number of influential thinkers and critics have applied and extended the tenets of mythic literary theory. Joseph Campbell, in *The Hero with a Thousand Faces* and the multivolume *Masks of God,* greatly expanded comparative mythology to include studies of Indian, Eskimo, Australian, and Oriental as well as Greek and Christian stories, finding in all of them the same recurring myths and archetypes, especially that of the "monomyth," the story of the hero's journey, initiation, and return that, according to Campbell, supplies the single pattern that undergirds all mythic structures. Northrop Frye, in his seminal *Anatomy of Criticism,* argues that the seasonal cycles of the year stand as archetypes for the major literary genres: spring for comedy, summer for romance, fall for tragedy, and winter for irony. Frye has been particularly influential in incorporating literary antecedents as myth, calling attention to the "reverberating significance, in which every literary work catches the echoes of all other works of its type in literature, and so ripples out into the rest of literature and thence into life."[4] Claude Lévi-Strauss, the generally acknowledged founder of structuralism, is equally important as a mythic theorist. His *Structural Anthropology* seeks to identify the basic structural features in myth ("mythemes") that are comparable to the fundamental components of language (for example, phonemes and morphemes) identified by structural linguists such as Ferdinand de Saussure. Like other myth critics, Lévi-Strauss is concerned to decode the essences that are embedded within all narratives.

All of the individuals cited above would tend to agree that the aim of mythical and archetypal criticism is "to see beneath the surface of 'story' to essential and lasting concerns of the human race, to recognize the repetitions of man's history and the commonality of the human condition throughout man's life, and to realize the craftsmanship of the author in weaving his creation with the very stuff of all men's lives."[5] As this observation reveals, the mythic writer or critic is primarily concerned with two principal aspects of life and literature: universality and repetition. The two characteristics are mutually dependent: the same old stories are told over and over again because they are universally true, and one knows that they are true because they are repeated in all times and places.[6]

FAULKNER AND THE MYTHICAL METHOD

While Faulkner seems to have had little direct involvement with the works or ideas of Freud, Jung, or any of the mythic or archetypal critics except Eliot, he clearly identified with the basic principles of the mythic approach to literature. On at least one occasion, Faulkner discussed the symbolic aspects of his work in language that almost exactly parallels Jung's notion of the collective unconscious. "What symbolism is in the books," Faulkner told one interviewer, "is evidently instinct in man, not in man's knowledge but in his inheritance of his old dreams, in his blood, perhaps his bones, rather than in the storehouse of his memory, his intellect" (Meriwether and Millgate 126). More often, however, Faulkner spoke of artistic genesis in language resembling Maud Bodkin's theory of socially embedded archetypes. The writer, Faulkner said, "collects his material all his life from everything he reads, from everything he listens to, everything he sees, and he stores that away in a sort of filing cabinet" (Gwynn and Blotner 116). Speaking of the Christian elements in his fiction, Faulkner explained, "The Christian legend is part of any Christian's background, especially the background of a country boy, a Southern country boy. . . . I grew up with that. I assimilated that, took that in without even knowing it" (Gwynn and Blotner 86). It is such statements as these that lead many readers to identify the role of Quentin Compson in *Absalom, Absalom!* with the function of the artist.

If Faulkner tended to agree with the mythic critics regarding the genesis of a writer's work, he was similarly persuaded of their opinions concerning the universals and repetitions of human history. This latter point explains Faulkner's tendency to downplay his regionalism, his Southernness. For Faulkner, regionalism was only a means to a greater end. He wrote to Malcolm Cowley:

I'm inclined to think that my material, the South, is not very important to me. I just happen to know it, and dont have time in one life to learn another one and write at the same time. Though the one I know is probably as good as another, life is a phenomenon but not a novelty, the same frantic steeplechase toward nothing everywhere and man stinks the same stink no matter where in time. (Cowley, *Faulkner-Cowley* 14–15)

At Virginia he said: "I feel that the verities which these [characters] suffer are universal verities. . . . And in that sense there's no such thing as a regional writer" (Gwynn and Blotner 197). At West Point, just weeks before he died, Faulkner reiterated this point: "The writer is simply trying to use the best method he possibly can find to tell you a true and moving and familiar old, old story of the human heart in conflict with itself for the old, old human verities and truth, which are love, hope, fear, compassion, greed, lust" (Fant and Ashley 59).

Given the developing interest in myth and its literary uses among the writers and thinkers of Faulkner's generation, as well as his own statements on the subject, it is not at all surprising that a considerable amount of criticism has been devoted to Faulkner's use of myth. A number of early reviewers, most notably Evelyn Scott, who produced an insightful monograph to accompany the publication of *The Sound and the Fury,* and André Malraux, who wrote the preface for the French edition of *Sanctuary,* called attention to Faulkner's affinity with ancient myths, both Greco/Roman and Christian, and later critics would develop these parallels in greater depth. During the 1950s, when Faulkner's international reputation as a Nobel laureate encouraged scholars to emphasize the universality of his work, mythic criticism provided a highly useful approach. The publication of *A Fable* in 1954 gave further impetus to mythic approaches to Faulkner. Even those reviewers who disliked the book (and there were many) could not ignore the centrality of the Christ myth to Faulkner's novel of modern warfare.

A sampling of criticism from this period attests to the large number of critics who were finding mythic approaches relevant to Faulkner's work. Carvel Collins, in a series of insightful essays, analyzed Freudian and Christian elements in *The Sound and the Fury,* Jungian features in "The Bear," and Demeter-Persephone parallels in *As I Lay Dying.* Maurice E. Coindreau called attention to the underlying mythic structures of *The Wild Palms.* Walton Litz, Ilse Dusoir Lind, and Beekman Cottrell discussed the biblical aspects of *Go Down, Moses, Absalom, Absalom!,* and *Light in August.* R.W.B. Lewis grouped Isaac McCaslin with numerous other American Adams who represent the loss of innocence in the garden of the New World. Marjorie Ryan treated the Shakespearean parallels in *The Sound and the Fury,* and C. N. Stavrou argued that the Promethean myth is prominent in Faulkner's work.

The mythic approach continued to be a major thrust of Faulkner criticism in the 1960s. Robert M. Slabey noted parallels with Frazer's slain gods and Jung's mandala in *Light in August* and with the Greek god Hermes in *Sanctuary.* Kathryn G. Gibbons found influences of Frazer and Jung in the Quentin section of *The Sound and the Fury.* John B. Vickery examined the use of the scapegoat in "Dry September," and Donald M. Kartiganer linked *Absalom, Absalom!* to Frazer's god-kings who struggle with the issues of progeny and succession. Biblical parallels received extensive treatment. Lewis P. Simpson discussed Ike McCaslin and Temple Drake in relation to the Eden myth, while James M. Mellard traced the biblical patterns in *Go Down, Moses.* James Dean Young, Francis L. Kunkel, and Ignace Feuerlicht, among others, analyzed the Christ figures in various Faulkner works. Literary antecedents were also considered. For example, Cecil D. Eby Jr. argued that *The Hamlet* is a reworking of Washington Irving's "Legend of Sleepy Hollow," while Slabey, Mary Jane Dickerson, and Ida Fasel explored Faulkner's various uses of *The Waste Land.* James Guetti linked *Absalom, Absalom!* to works by Melville and Conrad. Thomas L. McHaney argued that Faulkner may have drawn some of the details in *The Sound and the Fury* from Robinson Jeffers's *Tamar.*

The year 1968 may be taken as the zenith of Faulkner mythic criticism, since that year saw the publication of three important books on the topic. Richard P. Adams, who thought it highly probable that Faulkner had read both Joyce's *Ulysses* and Eliot's review of the book, devoted a good portion of his influential study, *Faulkner: Myth and Motion,* to a discussion of mythic elements in Faulkner's works, including, to name only a few, the Fall from Eden and the Grail legend in *Sanctuary;* the epic journey in *As I Lay Dying;* fertility goddesses, Christ, and Buddha in *Light in August;* classical tragedy, medieval romance, and the Gothic novel in *Absalom, Absalom!;* and the Passion Week of Christ, Freudian psychology, and Shakespeare's *Macbeth* in *The Sound and the Fury.* As Eliot had understood Joyce, Adams sees Faulkner's work as a dramatization of the tension between the order and stability of myth and the instability and motion of the actual life process.

Walter Brylowski's *Faulkner's Olympian Laugh: Myth in the Novels,* which remains one of the most thorough explorations of Faulkner's use of myth and archetype, identifies four different levels of myth in Faulkner's work. The first and simplest, highly prominent in the early novels, is the employment of allusion and analogy, as observed in the numerous references in *Soldiers' Pay* to Jove, Atalanta, Narcissus, Niobe, Atthis, Christ, and other mythological figures. The second level is the use of myth as the controlling feature of plot, as in Faulkner's use of the scapegoat motif in the story of Joe Christmas. The third level, what Brylowski calls the "mythic mode of thought," is based on Ernst Cassier's discussions of myth as symbolic form and is defined by Brylowski as "the spiritual activity of the individual seeking to create a configuration of reality, an activity that is determined by laws other than the rational-empiric."[7] Brylowski includes in this mode numerous Faulkner narrators, such as those who recreate the Thomas Sutpen story, as well as Faulkner the author—all of whom share an instinctive need to create myths in the attempt to capture a truth that lies beyond facts and empirical analysis. The fourth level of myth found by Brylowski is the use of a "myth of the South" that factors into Faulkner's creation of Yoknapatawpha. This aspect of Faulkner's utilization of myth will be discussed in greater detail toward the end of this present essay.

David Noble's *The Eternal Adam and the New World Garden* is in part a rejoinder to R.W.B. Lewis's *The American Adam*. Noble, too, finds the Adam and Eve threads crucial to Faulkner (and many other American writers); but instead of Lewis's innocent Adam before the Fall, Noble concentrates on the error-prone, guilt-ridden, postlapsarian Adam. Central to Noble's analysis are *Sanctuary* and *Light in August*.

From the 1970s onward, mythic interpretations of Faulkner have been gradually pushed into the background by emerging new interests—feminist [chapter 9], multicultural [chapters 2 and 7], race/class/gender [chapters 2, 7, and 13], postmodern [chapter 6], New Historical [chapter 7], and postcolonial [chapter 10], to mention only a few of the most dominant approaches. Nevertheless, even in this radically changed critical environment, mythic studies continue to appear, although most of these merely repeat or gloss themes and sources already treated by previous critics. Because of space limitations, attention will be given here only to book-length studies that significantly extend the mythical method to the interpretation of Faulkner's works.

One such work is Lynn Gartrell Levins's wide-ranging *Faulkner's Heroic Design: The Yoknapatawpha Novels*. Levins finds parallels in Faulkner's novels with the ancient epic, Greek tragedy, biblical myth, the medieval chivalric romance, and other literary traditions. The journey of the Bundren family to bury Addie, for example, "evokes the voyage to the land of the dead undertaken by Odysseus, Aeneas, and Dante."[8] In similar fashion, Lucius Priest and his companions in *The Reivers* cross Hell Creek to descend into the Memphis "underworld." Thomas Sutpen is linked not only with King David of the Old Testament but also with Oedipus, Faust, and the Gothic villain. Quentin Compson, Gail Hightower, the Tall Convict, Harry Wilbourne and Charlotte Rittenmeyer, Ike Snopes, and Gavin Stevens reprise the sacrificial actions of medieval knights-errant in the service of chivalry and courtly love. In all of these cases, Levins insists, Faulkner is "not parodying traditional literary modes by focusing on the diminution of legend and myth" but rather stressing the "heroic proportions" of his characters and events (3).

Donald Kartiganer, in *The Fragile Thread: The Meaning of Form in Faulkner's Novels,* quarrels with approaches such as Levins's (and even with Eliot's use of the concept of the mythical method in relation to Joyce's *Ulysses*), arguing that the high modernists like Faulkner never intended their works to eventuate in an achieved final "order" or aesthetic unity but rather to present a fragmentation and dislocation of form that forfeits and denies clear interpretation or resolution. Novels like *The Sound and the Fury* and *As I Lay Dying* dramatize "the quality of an emerging form, of fragments in the act of trying to generate an intelligible order." Kartiganer's emphasis here is upon *trying to* instead of *intelligible order.* Moreover, Kartiganer argues, the "achieved design" of the two novels that he considers Faulkner's greatest, *Light in August* and *Absalom, Absalom!,* is hardly a "design" at all in the traditional sense of the term but rather one that is "always on the verge of collapse," a pattern intended to reflect not order but "a constant becoming."[9] Kartiganer believes that Faulkner applies the mythical method as defined by Eliot, that is, in the service of order triumphing over chaos, only in the novels beginning with *The Hamlet*—and, in Kartiganer's view (as well as that of many other critics), these are Faulkner's weakest novels.

In *Faulkner's Apocrypha:* A Fable, Snopes, *and the Spirit of Human Rebellion,* Joseph R. Urgo, like Kartiganer, challenges a too-narrow interpretation of the mythical method. Urgo significantly expands Faulkner's use of biblical materials by arguing that the Apocrypha was also a major influence. For Urgo, drawing upon the etymological meaning of *apocrypha* as a "hidden" or "subversive" narrative, Faulkner's statement that he created his art "by sublimating the actual into apocryphal" (Meriwether and Millgate 255) means that he was writing a noncanonical, antiauthoritarian narrative that refutes and rejects traditional, accepted ideas. Instead of (or, more accurately, alongside) the "mythical county" of Cowley and the New Critics with its entrenched views of history and reality, Urgo posits an "apocryphal county" that incorporates alternate, wholly "other" interpretations of that same history and reality. While this apocryphal dimension, Urgo contends, is discernible in all of Faulkner's works, it is only in the 1950s that the fiction makes a dramatic shift toward radical rebellion. Whereas such early characters as Horace Benbow, Quentin Compson, and Joe Christmas prove incapable of engaging in purposeful human action within society, Faulkner's later protagonists—most notably the corporal and the runner in *A Fable* and Flem and Mink Snopes in the Snopes trilogy—seek to wrest control of their own destinies by actively opposing the forces (war and poverty, respectively) that threaten to enslave them. In like manner, *The Reivers* is a "heretical" book in which the young (Lucius Priest) and the dispossessed (Boon Hogganbeck and Ned McCaslin) engage in "stealing guns, stealing cars, stealing horses, *stealing experience and meaning* [Urgo's emphasis] from those who control these icons of power and authority."[10]

One of the most ambitious and provocative recent treatments of Faulkner's use of myth is Virginia Hlavsa's *Faulkner and the Thoroughly Modern Novel,* which argues that the 21 chapters in *Light in August* are consciously modeled on the 21 chapters of the Gospel of John, supplemented with additional parallels with Frazer's *The Golden Bough.* Thus, according to Hlavsa, Joanna Burden is John the Baptist/Diana, Joe Christmas is Jesus/Dionysus, Lena Grove is Mary/Isis, Lucas Burch is Judas/Osiris, Byron Bunch is Joseph/Adonis, and Gail Hightower is Pilate/Hippolytus. The extensive structural parallels that Hlavsa finds between novel and gospel are intriguing, if sometimes forced. For example, the arrival of the pregnant Lena Grove in chapter 1 is paired with John's opening announcement of the coming of "the Word" and the proclamations of John the Baptist. Chapter 8 of Faulkner's novel, with its account of Bobbie the prostitute, corresponds to chapter 8 of the gospel, which records the story of the adulterous woman. And the deaths of both Christ and Christmas occur in chapter 19 of the respective works. Even Hlavsa admits to "perhaps a tendency to overstate," and many readers might think she has done just that in linking Joanna Burden's initials with those of John the Baptist and the inverted initials of Gail Hightower with the Holy Ghost. Still, as Hlavsa insists, and meticulously documents, "the correspondences are there";[11]

and her book unquestionably demonstrates how thoroughly Faulkner's narrative strategies may be analyzed in relation to the mythical method.

As noted previously, several critics have examined Faulkner's works in relation to Jungian archetypes, yet, surprisingly, David Williams's *Faulkner's Women: The Myth and the Muse* remains the only book-length study devoted exclusively to an archetypal approach. Williams analyzes Faulkner's characterizations of the Great Goddess. According to Williams, Faulkner's men, with few exceptions, are characterized by "a preference for martyrdom over life, a commitment to the ruthlessly logical justice of men, and a revulsion from bitchery, from menstruation and sap-flowing trees."[12] Thus Faulkner's Christ figures are predominantly victims or impotent failures. Faulkner's women, on the other hand, are "primal heirs of life and moment" (4). While Williams traces this elevation of the feminine principle (Jung's anima) throughout Faulkner's work, he argues that only *The Sound and the Fury, As I Lay Dying, Sanctuary,* and *Light in August* present "full and uniform . . . incarnations of the goddess" (xv). Caddy Compson and Dilsey are, respectively, the Madonna and the Pietà; Addie Bundren is both "blood-generating madonna" and "blood-shedding priestess" (109); Temple Drake is "the profaned temple" (127); Lena Grove is the Great Mother. For Williams, these embodiments of the feminine archetype represent Faulkner's efforts, not altogether conscious, to reclaim a sacred and numinous reality that has been enervated and nearly eradicated by the patriarchal spirit of Western civilization.

THE INITIATION MOTIF

Faulkner's fondness for mythic correspondences is nowhere more apparent than in his use and reuse of the "initiation" motif. Like Dickens, time and again Faulkner returns to the fate of innocence in a tragic world. "I am telling the same story over and over," Faulkner wrote to Cowley, "which is myself and the world" (Cowley, *Faulkner-Cowley* 14); and he observed of his use of the stream image in *The Sound and the Fury,* "I saw that [the] peaceful glinting of that branch was to become the dark, harsh flowing of time sweeping [Caddy] to where she could not return."[13] As in the works of Milton and Blake, innocence and experience represent the essential oppositions in Faulkner's world. Consistent with the ironic pattern of the mythical method, however, Faulkner usually excludes from his "monomyth" of initiation any type of heroic return or triumph (the Lena Grove story in *Light in August* and the Lucius Priest narrative in *The Reivers* are notable exceptions). In Faulkner's world the Fall is seldom fortunate.

"That Evening Sun" stands as the prototype of Faulkner's many treatments of initiation.[14] Faulkner develops his theme by ironically juxtaposing the adult world of sex (including adultery and prostitution) and of death (including suicide and anticipated murder) with the ignorance and innocence of children. These contrasting extremes come together, though only barely, in the person of Quentin, the oldest child and narrator of the story. In Quentin's characterization Faulkner dramatizes the moment when childhood innocence gives way to the beginnings of mature perception and understanding. Quentin's initiation thus serves to bridge the opposing worlds of innocence and awareness and, further, to foreshadow the impending fate of the other children.

The adult world of "That Evening Sun" is a tragic one permeated with real and imagined evil. In Mr. Stovall's abuse of Nancy; in Jesus' expressed antagonism toward white men; in Nancy's promiscuity, drug addiction, and paranoia; in Mr. Compson's indifference to Nancy's possible fate; and in Mrs. Compson's selfishness, one perceives a problematic world in which man's inhumanity to man and a propensity to violence pervade both individual and societal relations. Though the starkness of these details is somewhat muted by the limited perspective of the child-narrator's viewpoint, the reader can hardly miss the bleakness of the situation. Without question the overriding tenor of the story is one of hopelessness and despair.

Jesus, Nancy's husband, personifies the sinister threat that hovers over all the characters of the story. Appropriately, Jesus exists primarily as an abstraction. His one brief appearance, "with his razor scar on his black face like a piece of dirty string" (Faulkner, *Collected Stories* 292) and his vengeful remarks about white men, while supporting the identification of Jesus with evil, hardly account for the degree of fear and repulsion that the other characters feel toward the man. Faulkner makes Jesus (his name, by the way, is one of the clearest examples of irony in all of Faulkner's works) more than a wronged black man harboring revenge; he becomes an unseen but unavoidable presence, a spectral figure linked with forebodings of doom. Significantly, Nancy identifies him with Satan: "He say I done woke up the devil in him" (294–95).

The children have strict instructions to stay away from Jesus. As Quentin observes, "We would stop at the ditch, because father told us to not have anything to do with Jesus . . . and we would throw rocks at Nancy's house until she came to the door" (290). Mrs. Compson objects to her husband's willingness to "leave these children unprotected, with that Negro about" (294). However, all such attempts to shield the children are bound to fail. When Dilsey, the regular housekeeper, becomes ill, Nancy enters the Compson household, bringing with her Jesus and all he symbolizes.

If Jesus is the personification of a general and pervasive evil, Caddy serves as the principal embodiment of childhood innocence. Throughout the narrative she constantly displays ignorance and naïveté—as well as a compulsive curiosity—about the adult situation. "Off of what vine?" "Talking what way?" "Let what white men alone? How let them alone?" "Slit whose belly, Nancy?" "All right from what, Nancy? Is Jesus mad at you?" "What's the matter with you, Nancy?" "What, Father? What's going to happen?" (292 ff.) All such questionings dramatize a child's inability to penetrate or comprehend the world of adults.

Only Quentin among the children comes to discern something of Nancy's pitiful plight. There are three instances in the story that suggest Quentin's unique understanding, limited though it be, of Nancy's dilemma. The first occurs early in the narrative when Nancy, in acknowledgment of Quentin's being the oldest child, attempts to justify her behavior to him: "I aint nothing but a nigger. . . . It aint none of my fault" (293). The second is found in the scene in which Quentin clarifies for a miscomprehending Caddy the nature of Nancy's desperate prayer: "It's the other Jesus [that is, not her husband] she means" (297). Finally, and most importantly, toward the end of the story, after he has viewed the disabling effect of Nancy's fear and paranoia, Quentin asks, "Who will do our washing now, Father?" (309). Like the other children, Quentin is a long way from being an adult in this story; but, appropriately for the oldest child, he is the youngster who comes closest to understanding Nancy's predicament.

Viewing "That Evening Sun" as an initiation story about childhood innocence invites a further consideration of the title of the story. As various critics have noted, the title seems to derive from the lyrics of W. C. Handy's "St. Louis Blues": "I hate to see that evenin' sun go down / 'Cause that man of mine done left this town" [Cf. chapter 13]. Linked with Nancy, the title is highly ironic, since Nancy's blues result from her fear, even conviction, that her man has *not* left her town. But the title surely relates to the children as to Nancy; and the opening line of the title's source, "I hate to see that evenin' sun go down," fairly echoes Faulkner's regret, expressed many times but perhaps most poignantly in his reference to Caddy and the stream imagery (quoted previously), concerning the inevitable fate of childhood innocence.[15]

Faulkner's narratives of initiation take many different forms, and not all of them involve children. *Soldiers' Pay,* Faulkner's contribution to the Lost Generation novel, traces the painful adjustment that Donald Mahon and other soldiers must make in returning to a homeland largely unaffected by the tragic experiences of war. *Sartoris* extends the Lost Generation motif to make Bayard Sartoris's story representative of the displacement of a traditional, rural society (symbolized by the horse and the hunt) by a modern, mechanized society (symbolized by the airplane and the automobile). *The Sound and the Fury,* which continues the initiation of the Compson children begun in "That Evening Sun," and *As I Lay Dying* both register a growing cynicism and disillusionment concerning familial relationships—brother-sister, child-parent, and husband-wife. *Sanctuary* and its sequel, *Requiem for a Nun,* trace the Fall experiences of Temple Drake, an Ole Miss student who must cope with both rape and confinement in a Memphis brothel—and with her own willful collusion in her tragic circumstances. In *Light in August* Joe Christmas is initiated into, and destroyed by, a Southern society ruled by excessive Puritanism and racial bigotry. Racial conflicts also provide the context of the coming-of-age stories of Thomas Sutpen, Isaac McCaslin, and Chick Mallison in *Absalom, Absalom!, Go Down, Moses,* and *Intruder in the Dust. The Unvanquished* traces the maturation process of Bayard Sartoris. *If I Forget Thee, Jerusalem* (*The Wild Palms*) presents disillusioning experiences in relation to dual quests for romantic love and human freedom. The Snopes trilogy follows the destructive influences of the Snopes clan upon Frenchman's Bend and Jefferson. *A Fable* recounts the crucifixion of a Christ figure who tries to stop a war. Not insignificantly, Faulkner's last novel, *The Reivers,* returns to the treatment of childhood, recounting the initiatory experiences of the 11-year-old Lucius Priest during his first trip to Memphis.

BIBLICAL MYTH AND *THE SOUND AND THE FURY*

Though Faulkner takes the title of his most famous novel from the well-known speech by Macbeth and seems almost certainly to derive certain aspects of the characterization of Quentin Compson from Hamlet, the central myths employed in *The Sound and the Fury* are biblical. There are two such myths and, probably not coincidentally, they are the most universally recognized stories in the Bible—the Garden of Eden story from the older testament and the story of Christ's passion from the newer.

The only direct allusion to the Eden story appears in Quentin's several recollections of the hymn sung at Caddy's wedding, "The Voice That Breathed O'er Eden." This song, which celebrates "the pure espousal" of Adam and Eve, serves as an ironic and painful reminder to Quentin of his sister's dishonor and arranged marriage with Herbert Head, in Quentin's view a cheat and "blackguard" (2nd Norton ed., 71). But Quentin's remembrance of the wedding hymn is only one of several Eden parallels within the novel.

Quentin tells his father the confession of incest is an attempt "to isolate [Caddy] out of the loud world." Mr. Compson replies, "you are not thinking of finitude you are contemplating an apotheosis in which a temporary state of mind will become symmetrical above the flesh" (112). Such statements, along with Quentin's various stratagems (such as his avoidance of clocks and shadows) to escape the reality of time, reveal that Quentin desires to void the actual world of mutability and evil and inhabit an ideal world of timeless perfection and perpetual innocence: in short, he wishes to convert his "fallen" world into the idyllic state of Eden. In *The Sound and the Fury,* as in so much of Western literature and thought, this prelapsarian ideal is symbolized by the prepuberty of childhood. This provides one explanation of why Faulkner chose to open his novel with the Benjy section. With its predominant emphasis upon a long-lost past and its focus on the timeless, innocent (that is, time-less and uncomprehending) mind state of a mentally retarded person, the Benjy section becomes an appropriate analogue to Eden before the Fall. However, as the reader begins to perceive not far into the Benjy narrative—and knows beyond a shadow of a doubt in reading the Quentin section—this world has been destroyed and continues to exist only in the nostalgic memories of the various participants.

The key incident in the Benjy section, one that epitomizes childhood innocence but at the same time foreshadows the fall into awareness that will occur as the children grow older, is the scene in which Caddy climbs a pear tree to look through the parlor window to view her grandmother's funeral. Faulkner identified this scene as the genesis of the novel: "It began with a mental picture. I didn't realize at the time it was symbolical. The picture was of the muddy seat of a little girl's drawers in a pear tree where she could see through a window where her grandmother's funeral was taking place and report what was happening to her brothers on the ground below" (Meriwether and Millgate 245).

As Melvin Backman, one of the first critics to discern the extent of the Eden parallels in the novel, points out, the pear tree in this episode becomes the forbidden tree of knowledge.[16] In this connection, one is struck by the serpent imagery in the passage that appears just prior to Caddy's climb up the tree: "A snake crawled out from under the house. Jason said he wasn't afraid of snakes and Caddy said he was but she wasn't and Versh said they both were" (24). Then, displaying the curiosity and courage of Eve in the garden, and ignoring Versh's reminder that her father had warned her to avoid "that tree," Caddy climbs the forbidden tree while the other children watch "the muddy bottom of her drawers" (25). Caddy's soiled panties, of course, foreshadow her later sexual promiscuity that stains the Compson family honor. But the stain also symbolizes original sin, which Faulkner (like Hawthorne and indeed a host of writers since Augustine) chooses to identify with carnal experience. As though to underscore this association, Faulkner has Dilsey chase Caddy out of the tree with the reprimand, "You, Satan" (29). Later, after trying unsuccessfully to clean the mud from Caddy's clothes, Dilsey comments, "It done soaked clean through onto you" (48). It is hardly surprising that this episode, fusing a child's discovery of the fact of death with a foreshadowing of the loss of virginity, contained for Faulkner the very essence of the novel. In its widest application of meaning, *The Sound and the Fury* is a retelling of the loss of Eden, of humanity's recurring initiation into the tragic certainties of life.

Faulkner's use of the Christ story in *The Sound and the Fury* is more direct and thus more obvious than his use of the Eden story. Faulkner alerts the reader to the centrality of the Christ myth by means of the chapter headings for the three present-tense sections of the novel: April 6, 7, and 8, 1928, as the reader eventually discovers, fall on Good Friday, Holy Saturday, and Easter Sunday. While the reader might not become aware of this fact until the Dilsey section, and while many of the Christian allusions and parallels might escape notice on a first reading of the book, reexamination of Faulkner's text reveals a plethora of Christian elements distributed through each of the four sections.

Benjy's section contains numerous references to Christmas, and Benjy, 33 years of age, may be viewed as an innocent though impotent Christ figure, scourged and victimized in a fallen world. Quentin—who frequently alludes to Christ, partakes of a Last Supper (June 2, 1910, fell on a Thursday, the day of the week commonly associated with Christ's last meal with his disciples), is captured by a mob and taken before a magistrate, and pours out his anguished soul to his father—is also an impotent Christ, distinguished like Benjy by his suffering but incapable of transforming his experiences into any positive results. His death effects no resurrection. Jason, from his own point of view, is also something of a Christ figure, a scapegoat persecuted by Jews and others, and misunderstood and "crucified" by the world. Jason's distresses on Good Friday—his headache, the flat tire, his failure to catch Miss Quentin with the carnival showman, his financial loss in the stock market—take place at the same time of day as Christ's execution. In reality, though, Jason is anti-Christ. Dilsey, the moral and ethical center of the novel, says of him, "I dont put no devilment beyond you" (117); and the description of his "close-thatched brown hair curled into two stubborn hooks, one on either side of his forehead" (174) suggests popular caricatures of Satan. Moreover, Jason sarcastically ridicules Easter, spitefully saying to his mother, "You never resurrected Christ, did you?" (174); and he openly curses and defies God, imagining himself as "dragging Omnipotence down from his throne" (190).

In depicting the Compson brothers as various types of pseudo-Christ figures, Faulkner is inverting the older heroic myth for ironic purposes, as Joyce does with the Homeric materials in *Ulysses*. That such is Faulkner's intent becomes evident in the description of the Easter worship service in section four. In a church tackily adorned with shabby ornaments, the Reverend Shegog, an "undersized" and "insignificant looking" (182) man, preaches a sermon that ironically counterpoints the tragedy of the Compsons. The preacher opens with a grim reminder of the endless human pilgrimage toward death, already depicted in the novel by the deaths of Damuddy, Roskus, Quentin, and Mr. Compson: "Dey passed away in Egypt, de swingin chariots; de generations passed away" (184). Shegog goes on to describe Jesus as the innocent child victimized by the world—and to identify his fate with the children who are present in this congregation: "Look at dem little chillen settin dar. Jesus wus like dat once. . . . de little Jesus. I hears de angels singin de peaceful songs en de glory; I sees de closin eyes; sees Mary jump up, sees de sojer face:. . . . We gwine to kill yo little Jesus!" (184).

Both of these themes—the passing away of the generations and the Slaughter of the Innocents (that is, innocence)—are embodied in the experience of the Compsons. Dilsey, appearing to recognize the parallel, reacts with compassion and grief: weeping, she observes, "I seed de beginnin, en now I sees de endin" (185). This remark, repeated several times as a choral refrain, applies Jesus' claim to be "Alpha and Omega, the beginning and the ending" (Revelation 1:8) to a human situation of failure and loss. So obsessed seems Dilsey with the final Compson disintegration that one suspects she does not even hear the Reverend Shegog's concluding remarks, stressing the traditional Easter message of resurrection and joy. If she has heard, the testament of faith and hope has brought her little consolation in her distress. Preoccupied as she is with the dissolution of the Compson family, Dilsey finds little cause to celebrate on this particular Easter Day.

That Shegog's final affirmation is intended ironically is further underscored by the hateful actions of Jason on this day. Just as Caddy's wedding is juxtaposed with Damuddy's funeral in the Benjy section, the Easter church service is undercut by Jason's vengeful pursuit of his niece and the money she has taken in her flight. While Shegog preaches of Christ's resurrection, Jason is cursing God and the churches he passes. The preacher's references to the soldiers seeking to kill the infant Jesus are counterpointed with Jason's vision of himself leading a troop of soldiers against the Almighty. While Dilsey sits with the rejected and suffering Benjy in church, Jason is violently attacking a stranger in a neighboring town.

The contrast between Jason's satanic behavior and Dilsey's genuine faith and compassion suggests that Dilsey is the authentic Christ figure in the novel. Significantly, she possesses a keen awareness of evil, recognizing its existence not only in Jason but also in others, even those in her own family. "Lemme tell you somethin, nigger boy," she says to Luster, "you got jes es much Compson devilment in you es any of em" (172). However, unlike Benjy, who is incapable of coping with the evil of the world, or Quentin, who seeks to escape it, or Jason, who succumbs to it, Dilsey actively combats evil. "Git on back to hell, whar you belong at," she commands the jaybirds (168); and she rebukes Frony for objecting to Benjy's being brought into the Negro church (181). Her role as intermediary "savior" is evident not only in her protection of Benjy but also in her intervention in the feud between Jason and Miss Quentin. "She came hobbling between us, trying to hold me again," Jason narrates. "'Hit me, den,' she says, 'ef nothin else but hittin somebody wont do you. Hit me,' she says" (116). Dilsey is, quite literally, the suffering servant; but unlike the pseudo-Christs of the novel, she is able to transcend her suffering to embody the Christian virtues of love, compassion, and forgiveness.

Nevertheless, sadly, one must recognize that such virtues seem to have little practical effect upon the world that Dilsey inhabits. The Compson family unit is past saving (though some readers find some small consolation—and even hints of an empty tomb—in the escape of Miss Quentin from Jason's angry clutches), and Jason's final act of venting his rage and frustration on the helpless Benjy and the youthful Luster adds a disturbing note to the ending of the novel. The reader cannot fail to notice that it is Jason, and not Dilsey—Satan, not Christ—who controls the final scene by physically attacking Luster and Queenie. From the final perspective of the novel, that of Benjy—who has earlier been identified by Mr. Compson with universal human tragedy ("the sequence of natural events and their causes which shadows every mans brow even benjys" [112])—the violently enforced order described in the final phrases—"as cornice and façade flowed smoothly once more from left to right, post and tree, window and doorway and signboard each in its ordered place" (199)—ends the novel on a very problematic note. Jason's actions mock the poetry of these lines, just as he has earlier mocked God.

In discussing the design of the original dust jacket of *The Sound and the Fury,* Faulkner indirectly characterized the conflict of the novel as "the powers of darkness and of light wrestling, struggling" (Gwynn and Blotner 262). While Faulkner characteristically left ambiguous the ultimate resolution of that conflict, there can be little doubt that in the immediate context of the Compsons' experience, the powers of darkness have prevailed. In this regard the observation of Wilbourne in *If I Forget Thee, Jerusalem* may be applied to the ending of *The Sound and the Fury:* "Because [love] cant last. There is no place for it in the world today. . . . We have eliminated it. It took us a long time, but man is resourceful and limitless in inventing too, and so we have got rid of love at last just as we have got rid of Christ" (115). Like Joyce and Eliot before him, Faulkner has applied an old myth ironically, as a tragic reminder of what is missing, or at least diminished, in the modern world.

THE CHRIST STORY AND *A FABLE*

Faulkner's most ambitious use of the mythical method is to be found in *A Fable,* published in 1954. Conceived in Hollywood during the mid-1940s, labored at for more than a decade, called by Faulkner his "big book" (Blotner, *Selected Letters* 328 ff.) and by Random House his "crowning achievement" (dust-jacket flap), *A Fable* has been generally regarded as Faulkner's hugest novelistic failure. Lawrance Thompson's judgment is typical: "Perhaps the worst artistic fault is that the allegorical skeleton sticks through the flesh unpleasantly, and the characters come too near to being types who seem created too largely for purposes of illuminating the thinly-concealed allegorical meaning."[17] As more sympathetic critics have argued, however, such negative judgments are mistaken, deriving largely from a misunderstanding of Faulkner's intention in his application of Christian myth.

A Fable merges the Christ story into the account of an obscure French corporal who leads a mutiny during the latter stages of World War I. This soldier, who is born in a stable and is the illegitimate son of the supreme commander of the Allied Forces, gathers around himself a squad of 12 disciples and travels with them throughout the front lines encouraging both French and German troops to lay down their arms. For a brief time it appears that the idealistic scheme of the corporal and his followers will succeed, as the refusal of one French regiment to attack leads to a temporary cessation of fighting all across the battlefront. However, the corporal and the other rebellious soldiers are arrested, and high-level Allied and German commanders conspire to ensure the resumption of the war.

On Thursday of this modern-day Passion Week, the jailors serve a meal to the corporal and his squad. They have been imprisoned because Polchak, a fellow soldier, has betrayed the corporal into the hands of the authorities. Another companion, appropriately named Pierre Bouc, denies his leader. Following the reenactment of the Last Supper, the corporal is called away to a private meeting with his father, the supreme commander. From a point overlooking the city of Paris, in a scene that recalls both Christ in the Garden of Gethsemane and Satan's temptation of Christ in the wilderness, the old marshall offers the corporal secret passage to safety. The corporal, however, refuses the offer, and returns to his cell. The next day he is tied to a post between two criminals and executed by a firing squad. When he is shot, he falls into a coil of barbed wire—Faulkner's equivalent of the crown of thorns. Following the execution, the corporal's half sisters, Marthe and Marya, claim the body for burial on the family home site; but shortly after the burial an artillery shell hits the area, destroying any trace of the corporal's grave or body.

After the war some soldiers are assigned to locate an unidentified corpse to be placed in the Unknown Soldier's tomb under the Arc de Triomphe. Ironically they unwittingly secure the body of the disgraced corporal and deliver it to Paris, to lie under the eternal flame as the symbol of the heroic sacrifice made by a common soldier for all humanity. In addition to this natural type of "immortality," the corporal also lives on in the memory and example of the British runner, a Saul-turned-Paul-type disciple whose defiance of the military in the concluding scene of the novel perpetuates the message and actions of the doomed corporal.

As noted earlier, most reviewers and critics panned *A Fable* mercilessly, and, despite the author's and publisher's pride in it, the novel quickly found its way to the bottom of the list of Faulkner's works. And the critics unwilling to leave it there have been few indeed, for example, Dayton Kohler, Heinrich Straumann, Keen Butterworth, Noel Polk, Joseph R. Urgo, Richard Godden. On occasion, invited lecturers at the annual Faulkner and Yoknapatawpha Conference have admitted, sometimes even boasted, that they have never bothered to read the novel.

While it is not necessary to defend the novel as an artistic success in order to demonstrate that it clearly shows Faulkner's fondness for biblical myth, it is arguable that an accurate understanding of the nature and function of the mythical method would serve to refute most, if not all, of the objections to the work. First of all, readers should recognize that they are reading a post–World War II novel that is set during World War I and uses the Passion Week of Christ as an analogue for twentieth-century events and issues. As Urgo properly notes, "The corporal . . . is not a *symbolic* Christ, nor is the story an *allegory* based in the life of the historical Jesus."[18] In other words, *A Fable* is not about Christ, or even primarily World War I, but rather the world situation as Faulkner saw it in the late 1940s and early 1950s. In addition, readers must remember that the technique of the mythical method, as Eliot defined it, requires the old myth to be inverted, thereby creating an ironic contrast to the contemporary application. Arguments, therefore, that Faulkner's handling of the Christ story is inconsistent with New Testament accounts are quite beside the point. If readers and critics would take more seriously Faulkner's explanation of his design and purpose, they would understand that the novel is a modern fable and not a literal retelling of the life and death of Christ. As Faulkner explained in a 1944 letter to Robert Haas,

> The argument is (in the fable) in the middle of that war, Christ (some movement in mankind which wished to stop war forever) reappeared and was crucified again. We are repeating, we are in the midst of war again. Suppose Christ gives us one more chance, will we crucify him again, perhaps for the last time.
>
> That's crudely put; I am not trying to preach at all. But that is the argument: We did this in 1918; in 1944 it not only MUST NOT happen again, it SHALL NOT HAPPEN again. i.e. ARE WE GOING TO LET IT HAPPEN AGAIN? now that we are in another war, where the third and final chance might be offered us to save him. (Blotner, *Selected Letters* 180)[19]

As Faulkner already knew from the repetitions of history and the old myths, the answer to that question is Yes. Unlike the gospel accounts, Faulkner's narrative does not end with a divine miracle of resurrection. The ending of *A Fable* is just as ironic and no more hopeful than that of *The Sound and the Fury*. "I am not laughing," the old soldier says in the final lines. "What you see are tears" (437).

There are numerous clues planted in the text of *A Fable* that fix the present tense of the narrative in the post–World War II era, and, coincidentally, these are no less accessible than the ones that orient Benjy in the present tense in *The Sound and the Fury*. Among such clues are the direct quotations from Faulkner's 1950 Nobel Prize acceptance speech and allusions to the Marshall Plan, atomic-bomb shelters, and house trailers. There are also passages like the following, which seems far more descriptive of totalitarian regimes like Hitler's and Stalin's and Franco's than of the Axis powers during World War I:

> "Bah," the corps commander said again. "It is man who is our enemy: the vast seething moiling spiritless mass of him. Once to each period of his inglorious history, one of us appears with the stature of a giant, suddenly and without warning in the middle of a nation as a dairymaid enters a buttery, and with his sword for paddle he heaps and pounds and stiffens the malleable mass and even holds it cohered and purposeful for a time. But never for always, nor even for very long: sometimes before he can even turn his back, it has relinquished, dis-cohered, faster and faster flowing and seeking back to its own base anonymity." (30)[20]

The military, however, merely substitutes one type of anonymity for another; and it is against all faceless anonymity and in defense of individual freedom that the corporal raises his rebellion and sacrifices his life. This is the conflict, in Faulkner's view, in the secular, political, and militaristic modern world that finds its analogue in Christ's struggle against the religious and cultural establishment of his day.

Readers who approach *A Fable* as a retelling of the New Testament story of Christ are understandably perplexed and even offended by many of Faulkner's alterations in the biblical narrative,[21] perhaps most of all by the fusion of the God figure of the novel—the supreme commander—and Satan. Adding to the confusion of this pairing is the fact that it is the satanic figure, the Tempter, who voices the sentiments of Faulkner's Nobel Prize speech: "Oh yes, he will survive . . . [he later adds "prevail"] because he has that in him which will endure even beyond the ultimate worthless tideless rock freezing slowly in the last red and heatless sunset" (354). Such ambiguous attribution of moral and ethical values is hardly biblical, but it is very much the context of the modern world. Cold War readers should have been better able to recognize their contemporary world in the pages of Faulkner's novel; today's readers—post-Vietnam, post-Watergate, post-Clinton, postterrorism, post-Worldcom—can hardly fail to recognize theirs.

THE MYTH OF YOKNAPATAWPHA

While Faulkner clearly employed the mythical method by borrowing materials from ancient stories in creating his own fiction, he was also keenly aware that he was inventing his own all-embracing "myth" of people, places, and events in an imaginary Mississippi county he called Yoknapatawpha. It is this inventive, *myth-making* dimension of his art that he had in mind when he spoke of "sublimating the actual into apocryphal" and of creating "a cosmos of [his] own." "I like to think of the world I created," Faulkner continued, "as being a kind of key-stone in the Universe; . . . if it were ever taken away, the universe itself would collapse" (Meriwether and Millgate 255). The same intent is captured in the signature Faulkner added to one of his maps of Yoknapatawpha: "William Faulkner, sole owner & proprietor" (*Absalom* back flyleaf).

Critics have long debated the point at which Faulkner became consciously aware of the overall design of his Yoknapatawpha narratives. It is indisputable that early on, following the advice of Sherwood Anderson, he recognized the literary potential in his "little postage stamp of native soil" (Meriwether and Millgate 255) and that, almost as soon, he began recycling characters like Horace Benbow, Gavin Stevens, Quentin Compson, the Sartorises, and the Snopeses. Nevertheless, the idea of a highly integrated series of novels and stories spanning several historical epochs and presenting a select number of overarching themes (somewhat on the order, Faulkner said, of Honoré de Balzac's *Comédie humaine*) seems to have been a product of Faulkner's later life and career. George Marion O'Donnell is generally credited with being the first scholar to call attention to an interlocking pattern in Faulkner's works. O'Donnell's 1939 essay, "Faulkner's Mythology," subsequently challenged as being too reductive, interprets Faulkner's novels as recurring treatments of a Southern ethical tradition (symbolized by the Sartorises) being threatened and overrun by an amoral modernism (represented by the Snopeses). But O'Donnell's approach, despite his title, was more allegorical than mythological. The notion that Faulkner was deliberately creating a myth of the South seems primarily (some would say solely) the product of Malcolm Cowley's compilation of *The Portable Faulkner* in 1946.

The promotional blurb on the dust jacket makes clear Cowley's intent in selecting and organizing more than 700 pages from Faulkner's various works: "the saga of Yoknapatawpha County, 1820–1945, being the first chronological picture of Faulkner's mythical county in Mississippi. . . . " In his introduction to the volume, Cowley argued that Faulkner's work presents "a mythical kingdom" that should be viewed as "an organic unity."[22] Cowley's selection of materials, dating from antebellum and Civil War times through the closing of the frontier and the rise of the poor whites to the racially torn modern South, is chosen to present Faulkner as "an epic or bardic poet in prose, a creator of myths that he weaves together into a legend of the South" (23).

Early readers and reviewers of *The Portable Faulkner* could not know what Cowley would reveal two decades later in *The Faulkner-Cowley File:* that Faulkner had at first been reluctant to accept Cowley's suggestions about a con-trolling design in his books, particularly one that purported to be "a legend of the South," but that he gradually acceded to Cowley's thesis and eventually even cooperated in the project by supplying a new "Appendix" to *The Sound and the Fury* for inclusion in the text and by drawing a revised map of Yoknapatawpha County to be printed inside the front and back covers of the volume. More sig-nificantly, one may argue, once the idea of a Southern "saga" or "legend" had been planted in Faulkner's mind, and long after the appearance of Cowley's book, Faulkner seized opportunities to create missing pieces of the pattern. For example, the historical interchapters of *Requiem for a Nun,* the pseudoautobiographical essay "Mississippi," and even such political and cultural essays as "On Privacy" and "Address to the Delta Council" strike one as attempts to fill in gaps in the mythohistorical chronicle suggested by Cowley.

Following Cowley's lead (and perhaps Faulkner's own endorsement of Cowley's project), other scholars emphasized the mythic quality of Faulkner's work, particularly as it related to the history of the American South. Irving Howe's influential study defines Faulkner's "Southern myth" as "the fate of a ruined homeland," pitting Faulkner's "pride in the past against his despair over the present."[23] Other critics, including Robert Penn Warren, Carvel Collins, William Van O'Connor, Hyatt H. Waggoner, and Richard P. Adams, questioned a too-close identification of Faulkner's works with the South, arguing that Faulkner's myth is not regional but universal.

These last critics were right, of course; and they had the advantage in the ongoing debate because Faulkner agreed with them. On numerous occasions (and as he initially tried to inform Cowley), Faulkner sought to explain that the actual South, both historical and contemporary, was a microcosm, a synecdoche, for a larger Faulknerian cosmos. For example, in 1955 in Manila he stated:

> I think that the setting of a novel is just incidental, that the novelist is writing about truth;. . . . I doubt if environment or country can be enough inspiration to write a book about, that the writer is simply using the tool which he knows. I write about American Mississippi simply because that is what I know best. (Meriwether and Millgate 202)

Faulkner undoubtedly felt that he had already explained all of this in "The Bear," if readers had only paid closer attention. There he presents a detailed overview of Southern history but makes it unequivocally clear that that history is representative of a far broader experience. "Dispossessed of Eden," the refrain that runs throughout part four of the story, expresses the central theme of the narrative; and that theme is applied to a series of situations that range from the personal to the universal. [See also chapter 13 for a discussion of the theme of dispossession in *The Sound and the Fury.*] At the simplest level, "The Bear" presents the initiation of a young woodsman, Isaac "Ike" McCaslin. The deaths of Sam Fathers, Old Ben, and Lion and the corresponding disappearance of the wilderness expose Ike to the tragic realities of time and change and loss, of life's defeats and limitations. Simultaneously, Ike discovers sin and guilt when he reads in the old family ledgers of his grandfather's miscegenation, incest, and inhumanity. Through this double initiation, Faulkner intensifies Ike's loss of childhood innocence and his emergence into adult awareness and responsibility.

To extend this bildungsroman [see also chapter 13] beyond the individual and the immediate, Faulkner places Ike's story within a framework of symbolic allusions and parallels. The pattern of the work may be diagrammed as a series of five concentric circles, with the inner one representing Ike's personal experience and the succeeding ones symbolizing, in order, the Southern experience, the American Dream, European history, and the archetypal Eden myth. Thus, in its broadest allegorical application, "The Bear" becomes an interpretation of the history of humanity. Ike sees all of history as a continual rise and fall of empires, each founded on romantic dreams of permanence and perfection, and each in its turn falling prey to human folly and weakness.[24] This view accounts for the many historical and biblical allusions within the work—not only to the discovery of America and the settlement of the Old South but also to the rise and fall of the Roman Empire, the destruction of Noah's world by flood, the quest of the Hebrews for Canaan, and, most importantly, the loss of Eden. The history of humanity—all nations and cultures—is a cyclical reenactment of the loss of Eden and the quest to reclaim the garden experience in some "promised land" of the future. Thus caught between a lost Eden and a dreamed-of Canaan, human beings exist in a paradoxical state of ambition and failure, hope and memory: like old L.Q.C. McCaslin, they are "capable of anything any height or depth" (*Go Down, Moses* 282).

While Yoknapatawpha presents, in its detailed record of people and events, an essentially tragic view of human history, in another important respect Faulkner's invented cosmos makes an altogether affirming statement. This characteristic of Faulkner's myth, the product of what might be termed his religion of art, posits the maker of Yoknapatawpha as an imitator of God, the divine creator, and the world thus created, that is, the art, as immortal. Much of the critical commentary on Faulkner's mythology concerns Yoknapatawpha as *mimesis,* a copy of the actual world, whether Southern, American, or universal. Faulkner, however, more typically spoke of his fictional creation as *poesis,* emphasizing not the end result but the act of creativity itself. For Faulkner, Yoknapatawpha is only secondarily a mirror of objective reality; it is first and foremost an imaginary process, a fleshing out of the artist's genius and inner vision.

For this reason, Faulkner tended to subordinate the mimetic aspects of Yoknapatawpha. "The artist's prerogative," he once said, "is to emphasize, to underline, to blow up facts, distort facts in order to state a truth" (Gwynn and Blotner 282). Such has always been the case with the best writers, Faulkner insists. As he has Julius say in *Mosquitoes,* "Dante invented Beatrice, creating himself a maid that life had not time to create, and laid upon her frail and unbowed shoulders the whole burden of man's history of his impossible heart's desire" (280). "There's probably no tribe of Snopeses in Mississippi or anywhere else outside of my own apocrypha," Faulkner stated (Gwynn and Blotner 282). Concerning the characters and events in "The Bear," he said, "There's a case of the sorry, shabby world that don't quite please you, so you create one of your own, so you make Lion a little braver than he was, and you make the bear a little more of a bear than he actually was" (Gwynn and Blotner 59). Not altogether joking, he claimed that in the creation of his characters in *Flags in the Dust,* he had "improved on God who, dramatic though He be, has no sense, no feeling, for theatre" (Blotner, 1974 *Faulkner* 532). In his later years this association of the maker of Yoknapatawpha with the divine creator would become a staple of his public appearances. As he told the students at Virginia, "I think that any writer worth his salt is convinced that he can create much better people than God can" (Gwynn and Blotner 118). The Nobel Prize speech contains a veiled allusion to the god of the Genesis story in Faulkner's description of his own "life's work" as an endeavor "to create out of the materials of the human spirit something which did not exist before" (Meriwether 119). Jean-Paul Sartre once remarked that, to the youth of France, "Faulkner is a god" (Blotner, 1974 *Faulkner* 1187); and, though not in the way the French meant, that is precisely the way Faulkner thought of himself in relation to Yoknapatawpha.[25] He was quite in character when he referred to his artistic creation as "a cosmos of [his] own" and identified himself as the "sole owner & proprietor."

Not only, in neoromantic fashion, does Faulkner imbue the artist with divinity, but he also insists, as a logical corollary, that the product of that creativity may earn for its creator a type of immortality. Such is certainly Faulkner's expressed hope for Yoknapatawpha. Writing, Faulkner said on numerous occasions, was his way of "saying No to death" (*Faulkner Reader* ix); and he wrote to Joan Williams, "That's the answer, the reason for it all, the one and only way on earth you can say No to death: the best, the strongest, the finest, the most enduring: to make something" (Blotner, 1974 *Faulkner* 1461). "Since man is mortal," Faulkner told Jean Stein, "the only immortality possible for him is to leave something behind him that is immortal since it will always move. This is the artist's way of scribbling 'Kilroy was here' on the wall of the final and irrevocable oblivion through which he must someday pass" (Meriwether and Millgate 253). Faulkner's most eloquent statement on the immortality of art is his foreword to *The Faulkner Reader,* in which he writes: "Some day [the author] will be no more, which will not matter then, because isolated and itself invulnerable in the cold print remains that which is capable of engendering still the old deathless excitement in hearts and glands whose owners and custodians are generations from even the air he breathed and anguished in; if it was capable once, he knows that it will be capable and potent still long after there remains of him only a dead and fading name" (ix). Such sentiments partly explain why Faulkner regarded Keats's "Ode on a Grecian Urn," which likewise celebrates and yearns for artistic immortality, as one of the greatest poems ever written.

These sentiments also suggest why Faulkner so frequently places within his work what might be termed "art surrogates," physical objects that have survived the passing of time and "live on" for later generations. The monument erected over John Sartoris's grave, the slipper that Benjy loves, the hunting horn that Ike McCaslin preserves and passes on, and (at the communal level) the Jefferson courthouse and jail as described in *Requiem for a Nun*—these are only a few such objects that have proven impervious to time. Sometimes, significantly, these objects take the form of a written text, as in the case of the letter Judith Sutpen gives to Quentin Compson's grandmother, or the old ledgers Ike McCaslin reads in the plantation commissary, or the signature Cecilia Farmer scratches into the jailhouse window—all such texts "speaking, murmuring, back from, out of, across from, a time as old as lavender, older than album or stereopticon, as old as daguerreotype itself" (*Requiem* 254). Each of these art surrogates symbolizes Faulkner's expressed belief that "the aim of every artist is to arrest motion, which is life, by artificial means and hold it fixed so that 100 years later when a stranger looks at it, it moves again since it is life" (Meriwether and Millgate 253).[26]

Faulkner's views on the divinity of the author and the immortality of art properly belong to the realm of myth because such views are long-cherished, heroic, idealistic imaginings that are clearly beyond the boundaries of all that is known about time and history—as unreal and visionary as any fictional character, place, or event. Longinus is certainly right in his observation that "Time is fleeting," but the first half of his aphorism, "Art is long," is more problematic. The vast majority of authors and works do not outlast the pitiless parade of decades and centuries, and there is no guarantee that Faulkner will continue to prove one of the exceptions. Indeed, some readers, teachers, and critics already want to dismiss Faulkner's works as dated and irrelevant. As Ian Hamilton has recently demonstrated, many esteemed authors, including a surprising number of twentieth-century poets who were considered great during their lifetimes, have lost their fight against oblivion.[27] But all such observations merely serve to prove that Faulkner's exalted views of art and the artist are mythic, reaching, like all myths, beyond empirical fact and logic to embrace, as Faulkner put it, "the whole history of the human heart" (Gwynn and Blotner 144). As a chronicle of repetitious and unresolved human experience, Yoknapatawpha may be a tragedy, but as an artistic creation it is a human comedy that is very nearly divine. And it is just such polarities that comprise the myth of Yoknapatawpha.

CONCLUSION

Recent critics such as feminists, deconstructionists, and neo-historicists have persuasively argued the political nature of all literary discourse, even those approaches that purport to be apolitical.[28] Without question the "mythical method" is similarly based upon a number of presuppositions about human nature, institutions, and experience. That human beings share an identical psyche; that all national, regional, and local differences are ultimately subsumed into oneness; and that history is inevitably cyclic, ever repeating the past, are views that, no longer privileged as absolute, have fallen out of critical fashion; and there can be little doubt that the will to believe such "truths" was prompted at least in part, as Eliot understood and enunciated, by a felt need to restore unity and order to a modern world that seemed to be moving toward chaos. In this regard the study of myth and its literary applications in the first half of the twentieth century may be paralleled with concomitant searches for one-world government and a single, worldwide language. Like these other dreams of universal unity, the mythical method would come to be viewed as seriously flawed and dated, not the Truth it claimed to be but merely another "truth" among many. Nevertheless, the fact remains that it provided the underlying theory and working materials for the generation of writers who are arguably the best that the twentieth century produced. And Faulkner, as evidenced by his own statements as well as by his literary practice and achievement, must be counted as one of the movement's most ardent and accomplished members.

NOTES

1. T. S. Eliot, "Ulysses, Order and Myth," *Dial* 75 (November 1923): 483. For Eliot's own use of "the mythical method," see The Waste Land *and Other Poems* (San Diego: Harcourt, 1955).

2. For a good summary of Freud's and Jung's influence on literature, see Wilfred L. Guerin and others, *A Handbook of Critical Approaches to Literature,* 3rd ed. (New York: Oxford University Press, 1992), 118–26, 166–71.

3. Maud Bodkin, *Archetypal Patterns in Poetry: Psychological Studies of Imagination* (New York: Vintage Books, 1958), 19, 23.

4. Northrop Frye, *Fables of Identity: Studies in Poetic Mythology* (New York: Harcourt, Brace and World, 1963), 37.

5. David J. Burrows and others, eds., *Myths and Motifs in Literature* (New York: Free Press, 1973), xiii.

6. For a good recent demonstration of these principles, see David Leeming, *Myth: A Biography of Belief* (Oxford: Oxford University Press, 2002).

7. Walter Brylowski, *Faulkner's Olympian Laugh: Myth in the Novels* (Detroit: Wayne State University Press, 1968), 14.

8. Lynn Gartrell Levins, *Faulkner's Heroic Design: The Yoknapatawpha Novels* (Athens: University of Georgia Press, 1976), 2.

9. Donald M. Kartiganer, *The Fragile Thread: The Meaning of Form in Faulkner's Novels* (Amherst: University of Massachusetts Press, 1979), xv, xviii.

10. Joseph R. Urgo, *Faulkner's Apocrypha: A Fable, Snopes, and the Spirit of Human Rebellion* (Jackson: University Press of Mississippi, 1989), 27.

11. Virginia V. James Hlavsa, *Faulkner and the Thoroughly Modern Novel* (Charlottesville: University Press of Virginia, 1991), 208.

12. David Williams, *Faulkner's Women: The Myth and the Muse* (Montreal: McGill-Queen's University Press, 1977), 4.

13. William Faulkner, *The Sound and the Fury,* 2nd Norton Critical ed. (New York: W. W. Norton, 1994), 222.

14. What follows is a condensation of my article, "Before the Fall: The Theme of Innocence in 'That Evening Sun,'" *Notes on Mississippi Writers* 11 (Winter 1979): 86–93.

15. See Faulkner's comment to Buzz Bezzerides about Jill's childhood: "It's over very soon. . . . This is the end of it. . . . She'll grow into a woman" (Blotner, 1974 *Faulkner* 1169). Note, too, Charles A. Peek, "'Handy' Ways to Teach 'That Evening Sun,'" in *Teaching Faulkner: Approaches and Methods,* ed. Stephen Hahn and Robert W. Hamblin (Westport, CT: Greenwood Press, 2001), 53–57.

16. Melvin Backman, *Faulkner: The Major Years: A Critical Study* (Bloomington: Indiana University Press, 1966), 19.

17. Lawrance Thompson, *William Faulkner: An Introduction and Interpretation,* 2nd ed. (New York: Holt, Rinehart and Winston, 1967), 13.

18. Urgo, 95.

19. Faulkner's view of this matter did not change over the decade of composition of the novel. See, for example, his remarks at the University of Virginia (Gwynn and Blotner 27).

20. A remarkably similar passage, which is a description of Hitler, appears in *Battle Cry,* the unproduced screenplay Faulkner wrote in 1943. See Louis Daniel Brodsky and Robert W. Hamblin, *Faulkner: A Comprehensive Guide to the Brodsky Collection,* Vol. 4: *Battle Cry* (Jackson: University Press of Mississippi, 1985), 252–54.

21. Faulkner is not the only writer who has been taken to task for such "errors." Consider the response of much of the Christian community to Andrew Lloyd Webber and Tim Rice's musical *Jesus Christ, Superstar* and Nikos Kazantzakis's *The Last Temptation of Christ.*

22. Malcolm Cowley, ed., *The Portable Faulkner* (New York: Viking, 1946), 5, 24.

23. Irving Howe, *William Faulkner: A Critical Study,* 2nd ed. (New York: Vintage Books, 1962), 27, 29.

24. With regard to the dialogue between Ike McCaslin and Cass Edmonds, some critics side with Ike, others with Cass. It is important to note, however, that Ike and Cass do not disagree on the nature of history, but rather on what the appropriate response to that history should be—Ike arguing for renunciation, Cass for engagement.

25. Interestingly, Faulkner also referenced the divine in his remarks about James Joyce's *Ulysses* and *Finnegans Wake:* "That was a case of a genius who was electrocuted by the divine fire" (Gwynn and Blotner 53).

26. For a more detailed treatment of Faulkner's denial of death, see Robert W. Hamblin, "'Saying No to Death': Toward William Faulkner's Theory of Fiction," in *"A Cosmos of My Own"*: *Faulkner and Yoknapatawpha, 1980,* ed. Doreen Fowler and Ann J. Abadie (Jackson: University Press of Mississippi, 1981), 3–35.

27. Ian Hamilton, *Against Oblivion: Some Lives of the Twentieth-Century Poets* (New York: Viking, 2002).

28. Concerning this last point, see Lawrence H. Schwartz, *Creating Faulkner's Reputation: The Politics of Modern Literary Criticism* (Knoxville: University of Tennessee Press, 1988).

2

Historical Criticism

Theresa M. Towner

I began to think about what a man's dying really means: his story is lost. Bits and pieces of it remain, but they are all secondhand tales and hearsay, or cold official records that preserve the facts and spoil the truth. . . . The gaps in the stories of the famous are filled eventually; overfilled. Funeral eulogies become laudatory biography, which becomes critical biography, which becomes history, which means everyone will know the facts even if no one knows the truth. But the gaps in the stories of the unknown are never filled, never can be filled, for they are larger than data, larger than deduction, larger than induction. Sometimes an attempt is made to fill them; some poor unimaginative fool, calling himself an historian but really only a frustrated novelist, comes along and tries to put it all together. And fails.

—David Bradley, *The Chaneysville Incident* (1981)

It's just incredible. It just does not explain. Or perhaps that's it: they dont explain and we are not supposed to know. We have a few old mouth-to-mouth tales; we exhume from old trunks and boxes and drawers letters without salutation or signature . . . ; we see dimly people. . . . [Y]ou bring them together in the proportions called for, but nothing happens; you re-read, tedious and intent, poring, making sure that you have forgotten nothing, made no miscalculation; you bring them together again and again nothing happens.

—William Faulkner, *Absalom, Absalom!* (1936)

William Faulkner's career as a writer of fiction is certainly "known" in every sense of Bradley's word. His work has been translated into the languages of the world's most powerful cultures and into the dialects of the more obscure; criticism devoted to that work has now outpaced that of every other writer except Shakespeare; one or two Faulkner novels make it onto every "Top 100 Novels" list ever produced; the academy continues to offer Faulkner courses; the high-school kids still read "A Rose for Emily" or "Barn Burning" when they get to American literature. In the midst of such diverse populations, we find more frequently than any other pedagogical aid the lens of historically informed criticism focused on Faulkner and his texts. In search of Faulkner's meaning and determined to make him give it up, readers reach most often for history—a record of "real" events and "real" methods of research and interpretation that, should we succeed in applying them, will reveal what the text "really means" by what it says.

I can make that claim with confidence because, as a prominent guide to literary theory explains, "Historical theory and criticism embraces not only the theory and practice of literary historiographical representation but also other types of criticism that, often without acknowledgment, presuppose a historical ground or adopt historical methods in an ad hoc fashion." "Very frequently," it continues, "what is called literary criticism, particularly as it was institutionalized in the nineteenth century and even up to the late twentieth century, is based on historical principles" (Groden and Kreiswirth 382–83). These principles stem from Giambattista Vico's assertion, in the 1725 volume *New Science,* that we can best know any given thing by studying its origins, but we can only know for certain those things that we ourselves have made and that, consequently, we have recorded in language. Vico's "new science" was history, the science from which all others spring. For well over the next 200 years, literary criticism was literary history.

Criticism of Faulkner's work followed that path as well and took some interesting historical detours of its own. When the Faulkner industry started in earnest in the 1950s, following the release of the Viking Press's *The Portable Faulkner* and the Swedish Academy's awarding of the Nobel Prize in literature to Faulkner, academic critics were interested for the most part in the general themes and recurrent patterns in the fiction—particularly in the Yoknapatawpha stories and novels [see chapter 13]. Journalists were interested in Faulkner's status as a Southerner in a time of great national racial turmoil. The early readings advanced by the academy thus tried to find and demonstrate the history of Faulkner's county, while the news and op-ed writers of the day tried to locate Faulkner himself in the historical matrix of his country. Even when new kinds of literary criticism seemed to challenge historicist approaches, their methods often relied upon historical means; the same general pattern appears in Faulkner studies. Therefore, when John Paul Russo reminds us that formalist, psychological, modernist, and New Critical methods all still "lean on historical premises or . . . require a historically determined fact to build a case" (Groden and Kreiswirth 386), we understand too that Faulkner studies in those disciplines owe many and varied debts to historical theory and criticism. While pioneering Faulknerians like Cleanth Brooks and Michael Millgate elevated Yoknapatawpha and modernism, for instance, other critics shored up their efforts by collecting primary texts and documents that seemed to illustrate the primacy of that thematic vision: they produced editions of Faulkner's letters, essays, speeches, classroom sessions, and interviews. They also began to produce biographies and other biographical materials, the subject of another essay in this volume [see chapter 4] that also speaks to the pervasiveness of the historical model in Faulkner studies. And further suggesting the complexity of this model, Faulkner criticism itself now has a history with which the erstwhile professional student of Faulkner must contend. That history has as many prejudices, unspoken assumptions, misreadings, blind alleys, and loopholes as any other sustained attempt to make sense of texts in context of the times in which they were produced as well as in those in which they are read.

Given the scope of historical criticism, my task in this chapter is both to describe history in Faulkner's work and to suggest how a range of historical methodologies can reveal as well as obscure his texts. In order to do so, I examine the primary historical events that affected Faulkner as they appear in his fiction, the critical commentary on those primary events, and 3 important cultural constructs in his work. These avenues also produce a working history of Faulkner criticism as it has evolved over the last 60 years. All of these efforts share the working definition of historical criticism advanced by Russo—namely, criticism that takes history as its subject, and criticism that depends upon historical premises, methods, or historically determined facts to build its case.

PRIMARY HISTORICAL EVENTS

By far the most striking features of the historical landscape in Faulkner's lifetime were wars. His great-grandfather, William Clark Falkner, served in the army of the Confederacy; stories about that man and his war filled Faulkner's childhood and youth. As a young man, Faulkner faked documents, an accent, and his own life history to join the Royal Flying Corps so that he might serve in the Great War. As a middle-aged man, he talked of serving in the Second World War and wrote letters of support to members of his family who actually did serve. His Nobel Prize address expressed his great trepidation at the prospect of a nuclear apocalypse: "There are no longer problems of the spirit. There is only the question: When will I be blown up?" (Meriwether 119). To recount every one of Faulkner's references to actual wars, battles, or combatants would simply be to rehearse his entire body of work; what follows, then, is a description of the works in which the three major wars in Faulkner's life figure most prominently.

As early as his very first novel, *Soldiers' Pay* (1926), the toll exacted on men and women by the Great War emerges as primary in Faulkner's imagination. At the center of the action sits Donald Mahon, the terribly disfigured pilot, and around him wheels a constellation of caregivers and rivals. Joe Gilligan and Margaret Powers help Donald home to his father, a rector in a small Georgia town who refuses to accept the seriousness of Donald's condition. Like all of the returning soldiers, Joe is psychologically wounded as Donald is physically; Mrs. Powers represents this lost generation's educated women, whom war has rendered unable to love. Donald's fiancée, Cecily, is the other sort of woman produced by the war—the teasing flapper who tries to dance and romance away all memory of unpleasant things. *Flags in the Dust,* the first Yoknapatawpha novel (published as *Sartoris* in 1929), describes the intertwined lives of the twins Bayard and John Sartoris, Narcissa and Horace Benbow, Byron Snopes, the twins' grandfather (also named Bayard), and the elder Bayard's Aunt Jenny. The latter two survived the Civil War and Reconstruction and still suffer from that legacy, as do their black servants; John dies in the Great War, and Bayard and Narcissa suffer from his loss as well as their own postwar psychological burdens. In *As I Lay Dying* (1930), we discover that Darl Bundren was "in France at the war" and brought home a pornographic kaleidoscope (254). *Light in August* (1932) contains an extended description of Reverend Gail Hightower's childhood, which he spent spellbound by stories of how many Yankees his grandfather allegedly killed during the Civil War; Hightower has given his entire life over to the process of moving to and living in Jefferson, where his grandfather died in a silly raid on a chicken house. His dying realization that his own wife died because of his obsession reflects Faulkner's understanding that war is just as hard on women at home as on men at the front.

Perhaps the most famous of the primary historical events in Faulkner's fiction is the Civil War as it appears in *Absalom, Absalom!* (1936). The title refers to a biblical battle between King David and his estranged son Absalom and to David's grief upon hearing of Absalom's death; Faulkner's novel recounts how three very different narrators try to figure out one historical fact: shortly before Christmas in 1865, Henry Sutpen shot and killed Charles Bon. The Civil War also provides the master narrative for *The Unvanquished* (1938), in which Bayard Sartoris (the grandfather in *Flags in the Dust*) sees how his grandmother copes with wartime economic reality and how the recently emancipated slaves and their former enslavers cope with Reconstruction. *Go Down, Moses* (1942) examines the tangled familial and race relations born in slavery, further complicated by the Civil War and Reconstruction, and still poisoning the years as America headed into World War II. Certainly the most infamous of the novels primarily concerned with war is *A Fable* (1954), the book that Faulkner often described as his "magnum o" but which most reviewers regard with the same scorn Norman Podhoretz voiced: "*A Fable* might not be Faulkner's worst book; one would have to reread *Pylon* to make a definitive judgment, and I personally could not face the ordeal" (243). The fable asks, most simply, what people would do if Christ reappeared on earth—this time with the express purpose of stopping the Great War itself. It answers with the despairing realization that he would just be crucified all over again, and this time by "*all the scarlet-and-brazen impregnability of general staffs*" (857). The First World War becomes a comic setting for Montgomery Ward Snopes's commercial ambitions in *Sanctuary* (1931) and *The Town* (1957). In *The Mansion* (1959), Linda Snopes Kohl, who with her husband volunteers for the Spanish civil war, works in a defense plant during World War II, in which Charles Mallison serves and becomes a prisoner of war.

Faulkner's short stories make even more extensive use of wartime settings and themes than do the novels, and not infrequently Faulkner puts war to comic uses there. The Civil War figures in stories like "My Grandmother Millard and General Bedford Forrest and the Battle of Harrykin Creek," in which Bayard Sartoris's cousin Melisandre gets a husband and the husband gets a new name. World War I gives John Sartoris comic opportunity in "All the Dead Pilots" even as his life draws to a sad ending; Faulkner puts that war to eerie effect in "The Leg," when a young American begs his dead friend to find and bury his amputated limb and then suffers an attempt on his life when the leg apparently develops a new body for itself. The Great Depression, aftermath of one world war and prelude to the next, spawns the humor of "Shingles for the Lord": Solon Quick is so furious at the WPA for insisting on its workers' complete unemployment that he reduces all of his financial dealings to "work units" and bargains with those for Res Grier's hunting dog. Of course, the short stories also contain exemplary tragic and ironic performances set during wartime. Captain Bogard of "Turnabout" is so outraged at the military's wasting of human life that he recklessly bombs a château in which the brass convene to strategize; "Ad Astra" describes the psychological wasteland into which the soldiers fall after the Armistice in 1918; "Two Soldiers" is the first-person account of a little boy's attempt to join his brother in the army headed for Japan in 1942. When we look at war in Faulkner's fiction, then, we see comedy, tragedy, irony, as well as terrible sadness and pain, like the "wounded man's gibberish" in "Crevasse," "meaningless and unemphatic and sustained" (*Collected Stories* 474).

The early Civil Rights movement of the 1950s and the Cold War in which the nation was simultaneously engaged also marked Faulkner's life and work. He was recruited in various ways for both efforts, and his responses managed to alienate people on all sides of all of the issues. For instance, when he was asked by the women of the Civil Rights Congress (CRC) to comment on the upcoming execution of Willie McGee, convicted of raping a white woman, he came out so strongly in McGee's favor that the editor of the Memphis *Commercial Appeal* "thought it would hurt Faulkner." However, he also said that he thought the CRC women were being "used." His revised statement drew the public fury of "a prominent Baptist minister" as well as the district attorney, "who declared that Faulkner either was 'seduced by his own fictitious imaginations [*sic*] or has aligned himself with the Communists'" (Blotner, 1984 *Faulkner* 539). I don't think the Communists would have taken him. In Manila in 1955, he told a group of journalists that "in the world today. . . . is one ideology against a simple natural desire of people to be free" (Meriwether and Millgate 199). He added that "the Russian authors that I have read today are propagandists"—not a comment designed to make the Kremlin happy, but offered to the credit of the oppressed Russian artists. He said he was "convinced" that these artists were working in secret and that their talent would "someday . . . come to light" (Meriwether and Millgate 206). (In the 1960s, Alexander Solzhenitsyn did indeed "come to light," winning the Nobel Prize for literature in 1970.) Neither did Faulkner's public comments of the 1950s champion any of Eisenhower's agendas. In fact, he publicly criticized the People-to-People program for relegating individuals to "opposite opposed arbitrary factional regimented group[s]" (Meriwether 161). And in a speech to UNESCO, he positioned all artists firmly against both sides of the Cold War:

Mr. Khrushchev says that Communism, the police state, will bury the free ones. He is a smart gentleman, he knows that this is nonsense since freedom . . . is the cause of all his troubles in his own country. But if he means that Communism will bury capitalism, he is correct. That funeral will occur about ten minutes after the police bury gambling. Because simple man, the human race, will bury both of them. That will be when we have expended the last grain, dram and iota of our natural resources. But man himself will not be in that grave. The last sound on the worthless earth will be two human beings trying to launch a homemade space ship and already arguing about where they are going next. (Meriwether 167)

Even though he repeatedly professed to "believe that 'I, Me' is more important than any government or language" (Meriwether 166), in his fiction and his nonfiction alike, Faulkner always stood firmly inside history.

CRITICAL COMMENTARY ON FAULKNER AND HISTORY

The very first reviews and criticism of Faulkner's fiction are historically informed. As Frederick Hoffman observes, Faulkner's first reviewers were primarily either "humanists" or "leftists," both of whom "sought a virtue of statement in literature and were much distressed when they failed to see it" ("Introduction" 2). These readers excoriated Faulkner throughout the 1930s, with a few exceptions; one, Oscar Cargill, even hoped that Faulkner would, in a sequel to *The Hamlet,* "come to terms with his protagonist" to reveal "the wherefores of the Bilbos and the Huey Longs" (Hoffman, "Introduction" 5). That reviewer, like the leftists and humanists, wanted Faulkner to write history even as he overlooked the history that Faulkner actually wrote. In contrast to those readers, George Marion O'Donnell [see chapters 1 and 13] read Faulkner in 1939 as "a traditional moralist" whose greatest "principle is the Southern social-economic-ethical tradition which Mr. Faulkner possesses naturally, as a part of his sensibility" ("Faulkner's Mythology" in Hoffman and Vickery 82). O'Donnell was the first to set Faulkner inside Southern history, and the tradition of reading Faulkner as "naturally" imbued with historical sensibility because he was Southern persists even today.

In his introduction to Viking's *The Portable Faulkner,* Malcolm Cowley both read the real William Faulkner historically and argued for a historical reading of his fiction. He claimed that Faulkner had returned to Oxford, Mississippi, after the Great War to apprentice himself in fiction writing "while at the same time he was brooding over his own situation and the decline of the South." Such efforts allowed Faulkner "first, to invent a Mississippi county that was like a mythical kingdom, but was complete and living in all its details; second, to make his story of Yoknapatawpha County stand as a parable or legend of all the Deep South" (Cowley, "Introduction" vii–viii).

The effect of *The Portable Faulkner* on Faulkner's career cannot be overestimated. Joseph Urgo calls the volume "a rescue mission which was, perhaps, among the more timely in the history of American literature." As Cheryl Lester does, Urgo points out that the critical acclaim resulting from the *Portable* "almost to a voice [sang] Cowley's tune" and in doing so "produced an author who would come to be understood as a Southern mythmaker, the clearest voice in the Southern literary renaissance, a gentle, pipe-smoking conservative and a brooding, self-educated, moralist anomaly in American letters who was sadly neglected in his own country and badly treated by those people in Hollywood who took advantage of his need for money" (*Faulkner's Apocrypha* 6). With Cowley, then, the historical way to read Faulkner became the most popular way to read him.

Reviewing the *Portable* for the *New Republic,* Robert Penn Warren averred that "the sense of the past is crucial in Faulkner's work," and he praised Cowley for tracing the "history" of Yoknapatawpha County, as though that place really did exist anywhere else other than in Faulkner's language ("William Faulkner" in Hoffman and Vickery 110). I will have more to say on the subject of Faulkner's critical reputation later, but it is important to invoke it here because the tendency to read Faulkner's life historically and to look for the history of his county has produced some invaluable work on the subject of Faulkner and history itself—the kind of "primary events" sketched in the first section of this chapter.

The most sustained investigation into the family and regional history surrounding Faulkner is Joel Williamson's *William Faulkner and Southern History.* Williamson has thoroughly researched not only the writer's paternal great-grandfather, the Confederate colonel who served as a model for Colonel John Sartoris, but also the ancestors on his mother's side of the family, who receive far less critical attention. Williamson also offers evidence of a "shadow family" of black Falkners descended from William Clark Falkner and his slave Emeline Lacy (25, 64–66). Williamson traces these complicated relations carefully and builds his historical cases well, but he is less conversant with the conventions of literary criticism, so the sections of his book that try to apply historical cases to Faulkner's fiction do not do so convincingly. His history is unexceptionable, his criticism unexceptional. Don Doyle, a historian based at Vanderbilt University, spent nearly 20 years in the various phases of researching *Faulkner's County: The Historical Roots of Yoknapatawpha.* "The more I read of his 'apocryphal' and 'actual' county (as he once distinguished them)," Doyle begins, "the more I admired his achievement not only as a writer but also as a historian—an interpreter of the past" (xii). Although his book is in many ways interdisciplinary, Doyle resists what he calls "practicing literary criticism without a license" (17) and instead divides his study into 10 substantial chapters that eloquently document the history of Lafayette County, Mississippi. He also provides a clear analysis of how Cowley's reading of Faulkner and the South produced a "romantic view of Southern history. . . . romanticizing the Sartorises of the Old South and demonizing the Snopeses of the New South" (16). Doyle's genuine history provides an essential corrective to the faux history of Faulkner and Yoknapatawpha that ran so rampant in early criticism and still mars the discipline, and he offers compelling recreations of the names, dates, and mysteries of what really happened in Faulkner's county. Richard Godden, in essays and in his groundbreaking book *Fictions of Labor*, undertakes work not unlike Doyle's. Godden scrupulously renders the details of the labor history he considers relevant to Faulkner's fiction, and this vantage point produces new visions of works we thought we understood [see chapter 7].

The list of essays treating Faulkner's multivalenced relationship to and treatment of history is as extensive as Williamson's, Doyle's, and Godden's books are intensive. Since 1974, for example, the University of Mississippi has hosted a conference on the general subject of **Faulkner and Yoknapatawpha,** and the very first of the published presentations from that conference is David Sansing's "History of Northern Mississippi." It is a romantic attempt to mythologize the state and its inhabitants as tragic dreamers, to a person: "Remember, that we dreamed of empire, and when those dreams were laid waste on the fields of Antietam and Vicksburg and Gettysburg, we fantasized" (21). From this ostensible attempt to praise Faulkner as an accurate historian of the North Mississippi consciousness, one can move through the rest of the volumes of annual conference proceedings to find a wonderful array of historical criticism. Several of those volumes are particularly concerned with primary events. *The South and Faulkner's Yoknapatawpha: The Actual and the Apocryphal,* edited by Evans Harrington and Ann J. Abadie, contains Daniel Aaron's "The South in American History" (which, again, opens the volume); Michael Millgate's "Faulkner and History" as well as his "Reflections" on "Faulkner and the South"; and Shelby Foote's thoughts on "Faulkner and War." The 1977 conference found Lewis Simpson arguing that Faulkner had assumed a "godlike power paradoxically to create a sacramental cosmos out of his particular experience of the historicism of consciousness" ("Sex and History" 68). This conference's status increased among scholars at the same time the second generation of full-fledged Faulkner scholars began to make their mark on the profession. Calvin Brown, James Hinkle, Thomas McHaney, Noel Polk, and James Gray Watson joined the platform with Millgate and Joseph Blotner, Faulkner's primary biographer, to produce excellent work that brought contemporary theory and practice to history in Faulkner's texts, most extensively in *Fifty Years of Yoknapatawpha,* edited by Doreen Fowler and Ann J. Abadie. The European Faulknerians soon joined these scholars in Oxford, and the volumes of the conference proceedings reflect an increasingly global perspective on Faulkner and history (see, for instance, *Faulkner: International Perspectives,* edited by Doreen Fowler and Ann J. Abadie). In the 1980s and 1990s this historical interest appears consistently in various examinations of topics within the admittedly wide scope of historical criticism; the essays in *New Directions in Faulkner Studies,* edited by Doreen Fowler and Ann J. Abadie, and *Faulkner and Ideology, Faulkner in Cultural Context,* and *Faulkner at 100,* all edited by Donald Kartiganer and Ann J. Abadie, are for the most part solidly grounded in a commitment to revisit Faulkner's relation to primary historical events. What has changed since Sansing's reverential look at Mississippi in 1974 is the willingness—even eagerness—among scholars to find limitations in Faulkner's views and representations of history. Yet alongside this corrective streak also runs an equally strong impulse to find out how much cultural history

Faulkner knew and how he incorporated that knowledge into his work. The most recent volume of conference proceedings contains a gem of such research. "'A-laying there, right up to my door': As American *As I Lay Dying*" is Charles Peek's description of how the Good Roads movement in the South joins up in the novel with "a piety plagued by doubt" to show us that "there is more to life than the world" (128, 132).

A similarly exhaustive source of historically informed essays is the *Faulkner Journal,* which began production in 1985 under the co-editorship of James Carothers and John Matthews. Their initial description of the journal's mission serves as a pointed example of John Paul Russo's definition of historical criticism's reach: "The editors welcome original scholarship and criticism, notes, queries, anecdotes, and other types of commentary aimed at extending our understanding of Faulkner's world." In nearly 20 years of production, the journal has expanded our understanding by contributing to our knowledge of the primary events in Faulkner's own life (including his recipe for barbeque sauce), his work (the first issue began with the first publication of a poem dating from 1921—a satirical piece called "Elder Watson in Heaven"), and his world (the fourth issue examined Faulkner's complex relationship with the military and included Joseph Fant's recollections of Faulkner's visit to West Point). The *Faulkner Journal* has been an important launching point for essays that either prompted or were excerpted from important works in progress on Faulkner and history. For instance, Kevin Railey's [see chapter 4] "Paternalism and Liberalism: Contending Ideologies in *Absalom, Absalom!*" was a tantalizing glimpse of his *Natural Aristocracy: History, Ideology, and the Production of William Faulkner.*

Mississippi Quarterly's annual Faulkner number concludes the roster of important and ongoing sources of essays concerned with Faulkner and history of all kinds. Recently in those pages, W. Kenneth Holditch added to his history of New Orleans during the time Faulkner lived there; James Mellard fleshed out his evolving theories of Faulkner's contribution to "the construction of modernism" ("Something" 478); David Newman offered an apology for the maligned New Critics and, in the process, a much-needed caution about the "gaps" and "unacknowledged and absolutely necessary community of interests" among **cultural-studies** [see chapter 7] critics (499). Cheryl Minnick added an invaluable update of Judith Bryant Wittenberg's catalog of **feminist** and **gender studies** [see chapters 7, 8, and 9] treatments of Faulkner.

Two other projects seeking to explicate Faulkner's use of history might seem capriciously chosen but deserve mention here. One project is a scholarly enterprise, the other Faulkner's own. A new series of books from the University Press of Mississippi seeks to comment on how Faulkner used what he knew—all kinds of history chief on the list. The *Reading Faulkner* volumes seek "to provide, for new readers and for old hands, a handy guide not just to the novel's allusions, chronologies, Southernisms, and difficult words, but also to its more difficult passages" (Polk, Series Preface 8). At this writing, volumes have appeared on *The Sound and the Fury, Sanctuary, Light in August,* and *The Unvanquished; As I Lay Dying, Absalom, Absalom!,* and *Collected Stories* are under contract. The series adds appreciably to other annotation projects, first and chief among them Calvin Brown's *A Glossary of Faulkner's South.* The other project relevant to the present discussion is the famous map of Yoknapatawpha County. On two occasions, Faulkner produced maps of his fictional county that obviously reflect the contours of Lafayette County. The first map, in his handwriting, appeared in the endpapers of *Absalom, Absalom!* The second he helped to produce for *The Portable Faulkner;* he added slightly to the 1936 version, and Random House had "the lettering done as his is not very legible" (Cowley, *Faulkner-Cowley* 63). These maps are just plain fun to look at; Blotner reports that Faulkner liked to do that, too (1984 *Faulkner* 371). More seriously, however, they can be read as extra, even anomalous attempts to locate the products of his imagination on the page in a different, perhaps more expressly "historical" way. They certainly catch Faulkner in the act of creating a primary historical document, and that document has received some illuminating attention. Elizabeth Duvert's "Faulkner's Map of Time" does a fine job of discussing the map's history in criticism until 1986. She then extends that discussion to argue that "the map becomes an icon of Faulkner's vision of landscape as spatialized time," and her argument is grounded in the historical: "Place becomes synonymous with event; landscape becomes history; and the map of Yoknapatawpha, Faulkner's image of reality as shaped by the history of place" (14). Gabrielle Gutting is the map's most assiduous scholar. She has argued that Faulkner was a highly skillful mapmaker, "an artist who knew the secrets of map-making well enough to apply them both in fiction and in reality" ("Mysteries" 89). Her *Yoknapatawpha: The Function of Geographical and Historical Facts in William Faulkner's Fictional Picture of the Deep South* convincingly describes Faulkner's map as evidence of "Faulkner's conception of space and time as equally important factors [in] determining both man's reality and the fictional representation of human life" (5).

Faulkner studies were enriched and problematized by Neil McMillen and Noel Polk's publication of an early letter of Faulkner's to a newspaper on the subject of lynching. The letter has not attracted a great deal of attention. Not many critical works have appeared that treat Faulkner's relationship to either the Civil Rights movement or the cold war extensively—the great exception being Lawrence Schwartz's *Creating Faulkner's Reputation: The Politics of Modern Literary Criticism.* When it appeared in 1988, it generated controversy among traditional Faulknerians because it argues that Faulkner's rise to literary eminence was due at least as much to cultural pressure and marketplace realities as to Faulkner's skill. "Earlier efforts to launch Faulkner met with failure until the demands of the Cold War propagated a new aestheticism" in "the most powerful nation on earth," Schwartz writes; "no more than any other historical event was [Faulkner's reputation] 'inevitable'" (6–7). His book is must-reading in historical criticism; critics now cite his arguments as established fact rather than opinion. I find that an interesting historical phenomenon in itself, which allows commentators to assert rather than examine literary history. Catherine Kodat's fascinating inquiry into *A Fable,* for instance, is marred by its claims that "the architects of U.S. cultural diplomacy appropriate[d] modernism as uniquely expressive of American freedom and autonomy" and that "Faulkner's willing (even eager) participation in this co-opting of modernist negation is well-documented" (94). Kevin Railey's *Natural Aristocracy* also reads Faulkner's fiction as a product of cultural forces, as does Michael Kreyling in *Inventing Southern Literature.* True enough, as far as that goes, but Faulkner goes further than culture. Indeed, as Susan Donaldson demonstrates, he frequently wrote powerful cultural critiques in very unlikely places. She argues that while revising stories originally published in the *Saturday Evening Post* for use in his novel *The Unvanquished,* Faulkner wrote "to undermine the easy assumptions and unified reading habits usually underlying the Civil War fiction" appearing in the pages of that magazine and "exposed the circumscribed nature of [the *Post*'s] expectations" ("Dismantling" 193–94). Deborah Cohn builds a case for Faulkner as a cultural force himself; she reads him as an important historical fact in the writing lives of Caribbean and Latin American writers. The subtitle to the first chapter of *History and Memory in the Two Souths* ("neighboring spaces and the search for meaning in difficult pasts") actually informs every line of her provocative study. While many studies of race and politics and Faulkner exist, of which I shall have more to say in the next section, few consider Faulkner's nonfiction and speeches in this context. My own *Faulkner on the Color Line* joins Noel Polk, Joseph Urgo, and Charles Reagan Wilson in trying to fill in some of those gaps. Polk has maintained a consistent interest in Faulkner as a public man, arguing that "his political engagement in the fifties seems to me a thoroughly admirable, courageous, and direct response to the racial and historical morality of his own fiction" ("Force" 60). For his part, Wilson provides the kind of penetrating detective work so vital to complete literary history. In his description of how Faulkner criticized the American Way that Kodat and others assume he willingly promoted, Wilson cites seven things that Faulkner believed "had become shibboleths" in America, complete with capital letters: "Security," "Subversion," "Anti-Communism," "Christianity," "Prosperity," "The American Way," and "The Flag." "One could hardly imagine," he continues, "a more incisive, rigorous, thorough critique" than that, which "suggest[s] Faulkner would not have been a likely sunny spokesman for the well-scrubbed and cheerful Father Knows Best America of that decade" (158–59).

CULTURAL CONSTRUCTS IN FAULKNER

In the last 15 or 20 years, historical criticism of Faulkner has turned almost exclusively to examinations of race, class, gender, and other political and sociological phenomena. This seems to be due in part to a kind of **New Historicist** backlash against the **New Critics** and their insistence on the primacy of the text as an independent aesthetic unit; we believe now that literature does not—indeed cannot and should not—exist or be examined in a vacuum [see chapters 3, 5, and 7]. As Thomas McHaney's work on what Faulkner read during his intellectually formative years indicates, Faulkner didn't believe in the windowless

room of the mind; he read newspapers and followed sports and talked to his bud-
dies in hunting camp; his work all breathes a wondering awareness of the world
around him ("What Faulkner"). That's one quality that makes reading him so
much fun, such an endless process of discovery in reading as it must have been
for him in writing. Moreover, he knew that the various institutions created by
man were not natural and spontaneous, nor were they necessarily always carefully planned improvements to our fate and condition. He never stopped interrogating his world, and the questions he asked and couldn't answer fully provide
historical criticism with chances to examine both his culture and our own. In the
space of this subsection, I will explore three of the most important avenues
taken by criticism examining cultural constructs in Faulkner: race, ethnicity, and
the wilderness.

   Polk is on record arguing that race in Faulkner's work is "a mask for gender"
issues and that "only four of his nineteen novels, and barely three of his over a
hundred short stories, are 'about' race" (*Children* 234). He admits to swimming
against the critics on this one, but he does help make my point about the culturally constructed nature of such categories as race and gender. Biology makes a
male, but what makes a human male a "man" differs in time and place; language, itself the descriptor of status and the instrument of its change, is similarly
gendered and racialized, often in ways we don't recognize, understand, or sometimes even care about. I think Faulkner was interested in how "race" worked
from the beginning of his career as a prose artist. *New Orleans Sketches* contains
a piece called "Sunset" that juxtaposes the sad final days of a rural black man
with a newspaper's uncomprehending account of his slaughter by the National
Guard (76–85). *Soldiers' Pay* and *Mosquitoes* (1927) represent rather than interrogate their characters' ingrained racism, but *Mosquitoes* does contain what
Michel Gresset describes as one of Faulkner's "self-portraits," in which the
novel's sexpot describes him as "a little kind of black man" and as "crazy"
(116–17). *Flags in the Dust* has a full complement of black characters serving
in various capacities on the Sartoris plantation. One of them has served in the
Great War. *The Sound and the Fury* surrounds the Compson family past and
present with black folks, and Faulkner investigates Quentin and Jason's brands
of racism intently indeed. Even when there would seem to be no reason for a
black character to appear, one does, or for any character's language to be racialized, Faulkner racializes it. In *As I Lay Dying,* the only appearance of black characters serves to reveal the Bundrens' tenacious clinging to one another as family
and to highlight their belief in their superiority to non-Bundrens; in *Sanctuary,*
as Popeye gropes Temple during the night at the Old Frenchman's Place, she
imagines him as "a nigger boy" in order to exert some kind of control over her
own terror (219). In *If I Forget Thee, Jerusalem* (1939), Harry Wilbourne casually tells Charlotte Rittenmeyer that in his job testing people for venereal dis-
ease, all he needs is enough light to tell what color his patients are. The oddest
place to find a black citizen of Yoknapatawpha would have to be in a three-man
assassination squad for a French general of the Great War, but there Philip
Manigault Beauchamp is, in *A Fable,* in what Joseph Urgo might call the third

"eruption" of Mississippi into that text ("Where" 101). Mink Snopes's self-delusion is never more apparent in *The Hamlet* (1940) than when he wonders if his jailers will feed the black prisoners before they feed him, his racism never more pernicious than when he questions the presence of a bereaved black mother in a makeshift veterans' church in *The Mansion.* Faulkner's great novels and short stories that obviously concern race and its enormous presence in the American psyche—*Light in August, Absalom, Absalom!, Go Down, Moses, Intruder in the Dust* (1948), "Dry September," "Wash," and "That Evening Sun"—have made his reputation. Those not as overtly concerned with the topic still never look far away from it.

Studies of Faulkner and racial issues date to the 1970s, and a few works appeared in the 1980s that attempted to sort out race relations in the fiction. In *Go Slow Now: Faulkner and the Race Question,* Charles Peavy was the first to try to understand both Faulkner's nonfictional commentary and his fictional portraits. Lee Jenkins's *Faulkner and Black-White Relations* tried to psychoanalyze the man and the work, whereas James Snead focused on "the linguistic supports of an immoral social system" (x). Other pioneers in the study of Faulkner and race include Darwin Turner, Thadious Davis, Erskine Peters, and Eric Sundquist. Among landmark books are Davis's *Faulkner's "Negro,"* which finds a series of traceable patterns in Faulkner's treatment of black characters, and Sundquist's *Faulkner: The House Divided,* which argues that "Faulkner's best work reflects a turbulent search for fictional forms in which to contain and express the ambivalent feelings and projected passions that were his as an author and as an American in the South" (x). Of these scholars, only Davis continues to revisit Faulkner.

After the explosion of new literary theories of race in the 1980s came new applications in Faulkner studies during the 1990s. These new theories often invigorated, and certainly changed the terms of, critical debate. We began to look at Faulkner's black characters differently and to examine how we were looking and why, and we also began to interrogate Faulkner as a racial subject involved in the process of creating both the Other and a Self. Philip Weinstein has been most insistent and most successful in his examinations of race, subjectivity, identity, and cultural politics. His *Faulkner's Subject* concludes gracefully that:

> Reading him, we undergo again the strangeness of our being in culture. There can be no agential reshaping of our practices, no refocusing of our optics, until we measure how penetrated we are by arrangements we did not invent and do not control. To engage Faulkner's cosmos is to experience a compelling subjective desire . . . for mastery—and to recognize in the fate of that desire a remapping of our place in culture, culture's place in us. (165)

Weinstein joins a great many critics interested in Faulkner's literary relationship with African American writers (see his *What Else But Love?,* Craig Werner's "Minstrel Nightmares," the essays in Carol Kolmerten and others' *Unflinching Gaze,* and Evelyn Jaffe Schreiber's *Subversive Voices*). Other critics have mastered the language of the debate in order to advance rather timeworn agendas.

Karl Zender, for instance, has taken up the "new methodologies" in order "to articulate a middle-of-the-road alternative to the dominant postmodern approaches" to Faulkner (*Faulkner* xiv). He argued in *The Crossing of the Ways* that Faulkner had a "backward-turning imagination" that increasingly required his attention "for both internal and external reasons": internal, because "the libidinal subject matter of his earlier art . . . was receding into inaccessibility"; external, because "his other great subject matter— . . . his native region—was also disappearing" (100–101). In the recent *Faulkner and the Politics of Reading,* he maintains that during the 1950s Faulkner had "internal and external" reasons for his "withdrawal from referential specificity": internal, by "resisting not just a midlife waning of sexual energy but the passing of a traditional, patriarchal understanding of male sexual privilege"; external, because of "an inability to envision . . . the postwar spread of mass culture as democratizing power" (152). More productive approaches to Faulkner and race occur when the critic's new vocabulary and focus are aimed at Faulkner's texts in demonstrable historical context, as they are in Polk's *Children of the Dark House.* Of "Pantaloon in Black" from *Go Down, Moses,* Polk suggests that Faulkner confronts more than one racial stereotype:

> Most have accepted that Faulkner wrote "Pantaloon" to force white readers to go behind the stereotype of a black man. He is also asking us to look behind the stereotype of the Southern lawman, even as Nub Gowrie's heartbreak forces Chick Mallison behind the stereotype of Beat Four rednecks [in *Intruder in the Dust*]: we who have eagerly seen Rider as a misunderstood human being have been unable to see the white man as equally human. The deputy is trying to make sense of his actual experience of Rider, which has made that magnificent black man something devastatingly different from the stereotype he has always presumed to think he knows: perhaps this deputy is also somebody devastatingly different from the redneck we have all presumed to know. (240)

In a similar effort to set Faulkner in context, Peter Nicolaisen argues that Faulkner had an ongoing intellectual discussion with the political thought of Thomas Jefferson. Their "affinity," he says, "seems to be based on an awareness that the great democratic experiment in America might have a dark underside" and "a sense of despair over the issue of race" even though both were willing to take on its burden (78). Nicolaisen and Polk join a diverse array of critics interested in the various ways that Faulkner represents and challenges whiteness (see Martha Banta, Cedric Gael Bryant, Minrose Gwin, Theresa Towner, and Linda Wagner-Martin). Race theory has cut a brand-new door in the reading room marked "Faulkner," and as we learn more about its descendant—postcolonial theory—I expect even more entryways to open there.

Ethnicity, as Werner Sollors demonstrates, is a trickier business than race to analyze and explain. Like race, ethnicity is based on a contrast. "In the modern world," Sollors says, "the distinction often rests on an antithesis between individuals (of the nonethnically conceived in-group) and ethnic collectivities (the out-groups)"; and "what is often called 'race' in the modern United States is perhaps the country's most virulent ethnic factor." Sollors is riffing on the constructedness of these categorizations, but he pauses to explain the commercial moment in history that brought us ethnicity as a deployed agent in the culture wars:

> Together with nationalism . . . ethnicity has spread with particular intensity since the times of the American and French Revolutions and remained a powerful force in political history ever since. Whereas the aristocracy organized its rule by direct and personal knowledge and family relationships that notably transcended national and linguistic boundaries, bourgeois power was dependent upon a shared interest among people who might never meet but who could feel connected through literature: hence newspapers, broadsides, manifestoes, popular songs, as well as plays, poems, epics, and novels have played important roles in sustaining feelings of belonging—the need for which the bourgeois era exported to the far corners of the earth. Ethnicity and ethnocentrism may thus be described as modern Europe's and North America's most successful export items. (288, 289)

When we think of William Faulkner as both a consumer and creator of such things as Sollors claims help to generate and maintain ethnic identities, we are on new ground indeed. Faulkner once wrote a letter to Malcolm Cowley that suggests the South itself might be an ethnic, not merely a geographical, entity, complete with its own ethnic history. He said that before the Civil War, "there was no literate middle class to produce a literature," and during the war "the South was too busy" to do so and afterwards had to "stop trying to be pre 1861 barons and become a middle class [and] began to create a literature" (Blotner, *Selected Letters* 216). Clearly, Charles Reagan Wilson and William Ferris, the editors of the massive *Encyclopedia of Southern Culture,* base their ongoing work on that premise. George Pozetta, introducing the "Ethnic Life" chapter of that volume, sketches the historical circumstances of ethnic life within the South and predicts that in the future "cultural and ethnic minorities will play a greater rather than a lesser role in molding the cultural fabric of the region" (404). There are 37 entries in that chapter, ranging from Highland Scots to Cajuns to Syrians to Lumbees. Faulkner's work accurately reflects that diversity. His Compsons, for example, descend from Highland Scots. His Tall Convict lives for a time in the bayous of southern Louisiana and partners up with a "cajan," who in turn tries to warn him of the impending dynamiting of the levees at New Orleans— historical fact and cultural disaster for the rural Cajuns in order to save the property of the Creoles in the city, both of which realities Faulkner got right in *If I Forget Thee, Jerusalem. New Orleans Sketches,* Faulkner's earliest efforts in prose narrative and characterization, contain a black longshoreman, an Italian cobbler, and characters named Jean-Baptiste, Juan Venturia, and Tony the Wop.

The ethnic groups that Faulkner treated most frequently, however, were the Native Americans displaced by the white settlers and their black slaves. All of the stories in "The Wilderness" section of *Collected Stories* concern these folks. "Red Leaves," perhaps the best-known story, describes the ritual hunt for a dead chief's slave. "A Courtship" and "Lo!" are comic exercises in romance and politics, respectively; and "A Justice" uses initial humor to conceal the sad racial realities surrounding Sam Had-Two-Fathers's birth. Sam Fathers himself is a vital character in *Go Down, Moses.* When Byron Snopes wires his four wild children by a Jicarilla Apache woman to his cousin Flem, we have a discomfiting end to *The Town* during which Chick seems to want us to laugh even as Faulkner wants us to understand the limits of Chick's narrative perspective. Faulkner often claimed that Yoknapatawpha's very name is an Indian word meaning, "water runs slow through flat land" (Gwynn and Blotner 74). Even though Don Doyle has explained that Faulkner wasn't entirely accurate on this point—"Yoknapataw-pha" during Faulkner's time was widely understood to mean "split [or divided] land" and so had more sinister connotations for its citizens than Faulkner's defi-nition (24–25, 387 n. 2)—the point significant to the present discussion is Faulkner's naming of his county with an Indian word rather than a European one. Curiously, given Faulkner's returns to his Indians, not much criticism has exam-ined these stories. One book exists: Lewis Dabney's *The Indians of Yoknapataw-pha,* which corrects some of the faulty impressions created by Elmo Howell on the subject of how well Faulkner knew Indian culture. More recently, Howard Horsford, Arthur Kinney, and Lothar Hönnighausen have visited the subject, with different degrees of success. Horsford documents Faulkner's general ignorance on the subject of pre–Civil War Indian life, and Kinney takes up what I hope is the beginning of another, longer line of inquiry. In "Faulkner's Other Others," he begins to analyze the role of Indians according to Toni Morrison's model in *Play-ing in the Dark.* The stories in which they appear "use Indians to comment on something else" (197), which is usually the process by which what Sollors and Morrison would describe as the "in-group's" struggles with ethnic presences. The essays by Kinney and Hönnighausen complement each other very nicely. Hön-nighausen demonstrates that Faulkner's "rewriting in 'Lo!' of a dark chapter of the history of the South in the grotesque manner of the regional tall-tale tradition shows . . . that his aim was not Edenic nostalgia but satire, not facile Rousseauist affirmation but the exploration of a historical dilemma and its traces in the recesses of the human soul." The Indian stories of "The Wilderness" section of *Collected Stories* are in this view evidence of "Faulkner's commitment to *rewrite*—in the sense of recover and come to terms with—both the black and the Indian history of Yoknapatawpha" (337). Hönnighausen's essay also cites the events of "Mountain Victory" as aftermath of the Indian removal from the South. The white protagonist of that story has a mixed racial and ethnic background that demonstrates also a certain fluidity of class structures on the antebellum Missis-sippi frontier. His name is Saucier Weddel, son of Choctaw chief Francis Weddel, son in his turn of a Choctaw woman and a "French émigré" named Francois Vidal. On his way home after the South's surrender, Weddel runs squarely into the present-tense class of poor whites in Tennessee. His mixed ethnicity and his wealthy background repel the men in the household as surely as they attract the woman there, and the clash kills him and very probably his black manservant as well. The story is a subtle examination of how class barriers and race lines, which ethnic identities should cross and subsume, in fact had rigidified in the American South to such an extent that mixed ethnicity was to white folks evidence of racial inferiority and by definition taboo.

As Hönnighausen notes, Faulkner's placement of his Indians in "The Wilderness" reveals the modernist's interest in looking for the origins of the human story and comparing it to the fragmented present. I think, more significantly, that "The Wilderness" section of *Collected Stories* calls attention to the disappearance of wilderness itself—and not because of the influx of white people and white ways, but because of any human habitation of the natural landscape at all. Readers of the Indian stories have regularly read them as evidence that association with the white man corrupted the native peoples. The discussion between two warriors in "Red Leaves" about what to do with excess numbers of black slaves, for example, often appears in evidence of that view. The five Civilized Nations in the Southeast were so called because they adopted African chattel slavery; what more historical evidence seems necessary to document the reading that equates race-based slavery with moral corruption? Now, however, scholarship has shown us that chattel slavery is common, even likely, in all cultures that go to war. Faulkner's Indian stories make a provocative bridge between obvious cultural constructs like race and ethnicity and less apparent ones like the disappearance of the truly wild from the earth itself: at the moment man appears to document the presence of wilderness, it ceases to be wild and instead becomes another part of another narrative written by man. As Henry Nash Smith argues in his critique of Frederick Jackson Turner's "frontier hypothesis" of American history, this narrative of the wilderness is endemic in the American imagination: "[Thomas] Jefferson's agrarian ideal proves to be virtually identical with the frontier democracy that Turner believed he had discovered in the West. To imagine an ideal so vividly that it comes to seem actual is to follow the specific procedure of poetry" (255).

Wilderness, then, is not the same as life in nature. "Wilderness" is the great Other in the human mind, perhaps the ultimate cultural construct because its presence defines an absence of culture just as culture blots out wilderness (see Polk, "The Force"). Critics have been discussing Nature in Faulkner from the get-go, giving him credit for loving things natural and for equating them with moral goodness. Early on, Millgate, for instance, credited Caddy Compson's status as a "natural leader" and noted how "she is persistently associated with such elemental things as the fire, the pasture, the smell of trees, and sleep" (*Achievement* 97). Cleanth Brooks claimed that *The Hamlet* "keeps our attention upon the body of his world—its sights, smells, and sounds, the gestures and postures, the quality of the folk community which is so far removed from our own that it seems simple to the point of fabulousness, and yet which is in its essence so thoroughly and humanly ourselves that we continue to believe in it and find ourselves reflected in it" (*Yaknapatawpha Country* 189). The lack of self-consciousness with which Brooks moves from "the body" of the world to the community that inhabits it helps me to make my point: *any* human community creates, displaces, and destroys wilderness simply by being itself. I think that's what Faulkner was getting at when he claimed that the human race would destroy both capitalist and communist ideologies by destroying first all of our natural resources (Meriwether 167).

Environmentally informed modern-day criticism seems to address the same concern. Judith Wittenberg, writing on *Go Down, Moses* (the work of Faulkner's that generates the greatest share of nature commentary), says that novel's "conceptual scope . . . is impressive, because its rich and provocative treatment of racial, class, and gender issues is splendidly amplified by its consideration of the interrelationship of the human problems with basic questions concerning not only land ownership—most vividly apparent in Isaac McCaslin's radical gesture of repudiation—but also the very essence of the connections between human beings and the natural environment" (49). To account somehow for the work of a man who loved the paradoxical idea of wilderness, who loved being out-of-doors as often as he could, and who loved too the symbolists and early modernists was the task of speakers at the 1996 Faulkner and Yoknapatawpha Conference. Donald Kartiganer described the contradictory demands of that task: "every imaginative conception of nature is just that, an *imagined* perspective that cannot help but reflect the culturally informed mind that is its source. Still—and this is the argument for the very existence of an environmental imagination—there is the possibility of mind relinquishing some of the force of its own sovereignty, giving itself up, as it were, to that which is *not itself,* while still remaining, as it must, an imagining presence" (Kartiganer and Abadie, *Natural World* x–xi). And both man and the natural world create—another similarity carrying the likelihood of destruction in it like an ambivalent seed. The accomplished critic Lawrence Buell described both at this conference when he cited wilderness encroaching on the abandoned Doane's Mill of *Light in August* as "a version of a typical insight in Faulkner's work of a special intensity to subtropical Southern nature that potentially gives it as much power over its human inhabitants as vice versa" (in Kartiganer and Abadie, *Natural World* 5). Thomas McHaney notes in the same volume the sexualized language that Faulkner uses to describe key moments in both plots of *If I Forget Thee, Jerusalem:* "the juxtaposition . . . is stunning, and it does not allow us to forget, or abstract, either nature or human affairs" (42); and Mary Jo Dondlinger suggests that certain "resourceful people can navigate cultural constraints" placed upon their physical selves (124). What the variety of approaches today to Faulkner and wilderness will yield remains for us all to see, but I'm encouraged that readers seem ready to re-envision rather than merely to rehash it.

My first reaction upon being contacted as a potential contributor to this volume was to hope that the required length of the chapter was a misprint. Somewhere near the end of the research process, I began to feel like Huck Finn, who if he'd a knowed what a trouble it was to make a book wouldn't a tackled it and ain't agoing to no more. I bring this essay to a close rather than conclude it, for I have learned that not only is the answer to one critic's question—"Faulkner Criticism: Will It Ever End?"—a resounding "NO, in thunder," historical criticism in particular keeps expanding. It has, I have learned, astonishing reach and hybridity. It morphs to live. Following André Bleikasten's lead, I believe this resilience and productivity are traceable to the fact that "language is the historian's medium no less than the novelist's." Scholars still debate the very terms of the discussion (see Joseph Turner, for example). As Bleikasten explains:

In a fiction, even a realistic fiction, events are produced by and in discourse; they have no reality prior to their telling, even though they are presented as if they did, and the novelist is not required to provide proof of what his novel asserts. Historical discourse, on the other hand, is assumed to bear upon a real and verifiable referent; it is expected to tell us, not what might have occurred or could possibly occur, but what actually occurred . . . and to establish the truthfulness of its narrative through carefully checked and judiciously assessed documentary evidence.

The validity of a historical text can be tested against extra-textual material; fiction must be self-validating. But we have also to consider that no fiction is ever pure fiction. . . . Both fictional and historical discourse build on our empirical knowledge of the world, and both are also alike in lacking a tangible referent. If the former's is known from the start to be imaginary, the latter's is lost or at any rate fading: the events the historian is concerned with have vanished irrevocably into the past, and in most cases their human agents are dead. To repeat one of Faulkner's statements: "There is no such thing as *was*—only *is*." A past event is, in the last resort, as unreal as an imagined one. Like fiction, history is discourse about something that is not actually there, and, with both, it takes imagination to fill the gap. ("The Novelist" 344, 345)

Thanks to William Faulkner, we have beautiful shapes to fill those lacks, gorgeous and moving wordsymbols of perishable and fragile life. We know, as David Bradley would say, the stories of the famous and the unknown alike—the Bundrens and Mallisons and Snopeses and De Spains and Old Hets, whether they ever have a name or not. The young woman who visits Isaac McCaslin in his tent in "Delta Autumn" lives as fully for us as does Cecilia Farmer, who etched her name in a pane of window glass for time itself to read: *"Listen, stranger; this was myself: this was I"* (*Requiem* 649).

Like us, they are history.

3

Formalist Criticism

D. Matthew Ramsey

"Formalism" is, in the current critical climate, something of a dirty word, and it's a bum rap. Few critics, in my experience, identify themselves as formalists. For many, to describe a critical (or artistic) work as formalist (often preceded by "cold" or "empty") is to dismiss it as anachronistic, unhistorical, devoid of cultural or human significance. Yet such an understanding of formalism fails to take into account the complexity and range of those approaches that try to account for the effects of a work by looking at its smaller parts. Formalist criticism rarely, if ever, looks at the work in a total cultural, historical, or biographical vacuum. And it is an unassailable fact that formalist approaches to literary analysis have had a major impact on the rise of William Faulkner's status within and outside the Anglo-American academy—most notably through New Criticism, while more recent offshoots of formalism such as poststructuralism and deconstruction have both enlivened and, at times, placed that status in jeopardy. The significant impact of formalism on Faulkner studies justifies offering an overview of the most important and/or compelling critical works devoted to approaching Faulkner's texts from a formalist perspective.

Not surprisingly, handbooks and histories of literary criticism don't necessarily agree on what schools of thought should actually be considered formalist. For the sake of convenience, I have created some admittedly arbitrary categories, since few critics fit snugly within any one interpretive paradigm, any more than Faulkner himself does. These critical works all take as a methodological given the attention paid to formal aspects of the texts, but such a definition can, of course, be applied to any critical approach; in some respects, then, the issue is one of emphasis or degree. I have tried to limit my scope to those studies which emphasize the **form** of the work and the ways the work's parts contribute to its overall effect, keeping in mind that the distinction between form and content is blurry at best, as is that between form and style.

Formalism has been defined, theoretically speaking, as finding meaning and value in the text itself and, accordingly, regarding matters such as context, reception, or biography as extraneous. In practice, few followers of formalist methodology disregard *all* factors outside the realm of form and style. What formalists do look for are structural relationships and patterns in words, phrases, sentences, and larger units of discourse. This is what ties together such seemingly incompatible approaches as New Criticism, structuralism, poststructuralism, deconstruction, narratology, and Bakhtinian readings. I have chosen these as the most important categories within formalism for Faulkner studies, keeping in mind that many other critical approaches make use of formalist methods and that the terms formalism and form have come to be considered old hat, or even relatively useless, within some critical circles.[1] It is hard to ignore the importance, however, of these various formalist approaches, particularly in the field devoted to an author so interested in style, narrative complexity, structure, gaps and surplus, and the power of the sentence.

NEW CRITICISM AND RELATED FORMALISMS

Many critics have noted the importance **New Criticism** has had for the "resurrection" of Faulkner's literary prestige, as well as the ways in which Faulkner's reputation reinvigorated New Criticism itself.[2] I have placed those critics who are explicitly identified as New Critics alongside those who are not but whose methods and attitudes resemble those of practitioners of New Criticism. The most famous of the New Critics who dealt in detail with Faulkner is Cleanth Brooks, and recent literary studies have been reassessing the strengths and weaknesses of Brooks's New Critical approach.[3] New Criticism, in its reverence for the autonomy of the "verbal icon," has often been attacked both for its disdain of historical context in the production and reception of literary texts and for its elitism (favoring "high" culture over more popular or genre-based forms of literature). The New Critics are often dismissed for focusing on form (with its negative connotations) and ignoring human experience, and for subtly advocating a conservative, even reactionary, political ideology to thousands of undergraduates under the rubric of "objectivity." Wesley Morris, a vocal opponent of New Criticism and of Faulkner scholars' continuing reliance on New Critical principles, argues, "A central tenet of New Critical formalism—the exclusion from literary interpretation of any concerns with social history, influence, biography, intentionality, and representationalism—serves, conveniently, to repress the Agrarian origins of New Critical aesthetics" (Morris and Morris 66).

Cleanth Brooks is an obvious target for such attacks, particularly given his influence on Faulkner criticism. Although more famous perhaps for his 1947 treatise on poetry, *The Well-Wrought Urn,* Brooks dedicated much of his later career to Faulkner, with mixed results. As Frederick Crews (no advocate of "theory-based" criticism) puts it in his defense of the critic, many have "hitched a ride on an anti-Brooks bandwagon that began rolling in the later 1970s. Brooks-bashing has by now become a standard substitute for thought in politically self-righteous Faulkner studies."[4] Crews notes that, although outdated, Brooks's *William Faulkner: The Yoknapatawpha Country* (1963) is the work many of us still pull off the shelf to help us make sense of "Faulkner's bewildering social world" (73). Brooks wrote several book-length studies of Faulkner—including *William Faulkner: Toward Yoknapatawpha and Beyond* (1978); *William Faulkner: First Encounters* (1983); and *On the Prejudices, Predilections, and Firm Beliefs of William Faulkner* (1987)—but most critics agree that *The Yoknapatawpha Country* is particularly important for Faulkner studies.

In this study of most of the more "important" novels, Brooks's New Critical methodology is clearly evident in his skilled close readings, his attention to structure and form (including the "mythical" nature of Faulkner's world [see chapter 1]), his preference for irony and paradox, his suggestion that the "real" South and Faulkner's South are very different places, and ultimately, in his assignation of value and worth for the literary object. "Faulkner's Savage Arcadia: Frenchman's Bend" begins by describing *The Hamlet* as an introduction to "a strange and special world" (*Yoknapatawpha Country* 167). Brooks is often attacked for his attempts to distance Faulkner's South from the South he knows, but as we can see, this does not suggest a purely "objective" or "coldly unhuman" take on the form and function of the novel's parts.

What many New Critics (including Malcolm Cowley) do with Faulkner, however, is to mythologize or allegorize the novels through a close reading of the descriptions, style, and narrative. In his discussion of the horse-trading scene, for instance, Brooks attends to the description of one of the wild ponies:

> There is the realistic and matter-of-fact detail—the sound of hooves drumming on the solid earth—but the detail is associated with a creature that seems in no way earthbound, but rather wraithlike, "bodiless, without dimension." Devices of this sort, used constantly throughout *The Hamlet,* build up the sense of the marvelous and almost supernatural quality of beings and happenings in a remote, entranced world. (170)

He goes on to emphasize the "mythic atmosphere," which depends on "a special heightening of characters and incidents—a heightening achieved directly by the author through his own description and narration, or else indirectly through letting the reader see the characters and events as mirrored in the imagination of a Labove or a Ratliff" (170).

This is intelligent criticism, and it's hard to see why one might object to this reading. But when Brooks begins to point out structural relations and allegorical content, we can begin to see why many "ideological" critics have some trouble with his New Critical approach:

> Thus the impotent Flem, who is pure single-minded acquisitiveness, and Eula, who is the unself-conscious and almost mindless personification of the fecundity of nature, are almost like goddess and ogre, a positive and a negative power, and

the yoking of them together takes on the quality of an allegorical event. What keeps the story from becoming transparent allegory, and thus a too bald commentary on the modern scene, is the richness of detail and the sheer power of fact which locate these two creatures in a community that is still close enough to nature to have nymphs and trolls walk within it and not so self-conscious as to have to rationalize them out of existence. (172)

Brooks tends not only to push allegorical readings throughout *The Yoknapatawpha Country,* but in doing so he often ends up making somewhat facile, or disturbing, assumptions about characters. Throughout his reading, Eula "becomes the archetypal feminine," a vital element in this "sardonic Horatio Alger story" (174), and only in passing does he note that this misogynist attitude towards Eula might come from a particular narrative perspective—Eula is mindless and fecund "at least in the eyes of the young fanatic Labove, and in a sense she becomes such for the whole community" (172).

This is what is both exciting and distressing about the New Criticism practiced by Brooks—his close readings reveal fascinating and compelling aspects of the text, such as the notion that Eula's *seeming* "mindlessness" comes from the perspective of the male community, but he immediately forgets such complications and establishes her as an element within an allegorical/mythological framework. Does this mean the allegory is actually being *established* through Labove's perspective, and that we readers, with ironic distance, recognize this? Is this Labove's allegorical framework?

Detractors of New Criticism emphasize the lack of emphasis on "human experience" in these close readings of "the text itself," but when we look at what Brooks and company are actually doing, these are far from cold or empty analyses. While Brooks might, in the opinion of some, overemphasize myth and allegory, or reveal his own pastoral/agrarian nostalgia, ultimately he does *not* suggest, as is so often asserted, a Faulkner disconnected from his own world or ours. The chapter on *The Hamlet* concludes: "Flem, Eula, and Ike, then, mark some of the boundaries of the total human experience which *The Hamlet* undertakes to explore. . . . They are not exhibits in a freak show. They are there to tell us about ourselves" (191). Brooks's nuanced, compelling, sometimes reactionary readings are admittedly replete with disturbing assumptions about gender, race, and sexuality, but arguably no more so than those of his contemporaries.

Another extremely important book-length study of Faulkner's novels that came out of the same New Critical tradition—without explicitly claiming the name New Critical (Brooks didn't really use the term very often either)—is Olga W. Vickery's *The Novels of William Faulkner: A Critical Interpretation* (1959). Less burdened by misogyny and devotion to the agrarian ideals of many of the New Critics, this study similarly covers most of the major novels, and also attempts to delineate patterns within Faulkner's body of work. Vickery focuses on the "formal and technical experimentation" (156) found in the novels, with an eye to how the novels seek to balance oppositions in order to suggest theme. Vickery is also more appreciative than Brooks or Cowley of Faulkner's non-Yoknapatawpha works. In the chapter on *The Wild Palms* entitled "The Odyssey of Time," she attempts to find a pattern of connection between the two inter-locking narratives, "Old Man" and "Wild Palms":

> The total meaning of the book is derived from a recognition of the three possible ways in which the stories are related. Regarded as parallel, each is concerned with the relationship between the individual, society, and nature, and between freedom and order. In both, the same pattern of confinement, flight, and capture is devel-oped though in different contexts. Juxtaposed, the two narratives obviously mod-ify and influence the reader's interpretation of either one. A too facile admiration of the noble savage in the "Old Man" is prevented by recognition of the greater sensitivity and potentialities of the lovers in "Wild Palms," with the result that the literary shibboleths of primitivism and romanticism are both placed in a truer per-spective. (156)

As with Brooks, we see an impulse towards finding larger patterns, although Vickery tends to emphasize "theme" more than other New Critical approaches [see chapter 13]. And like those of Brooks, these readings tend toward allegory and/or universality and away from historical/cultural specificity: "And finally, taken together, the two stories transcend the peculiarities of a specific time and place as described in each and depict that cyclic movement of culture which Faulkner has explored from various points of view in all his major works" (163). Vickery's close reading juxtaposes the passivity of the Tall Convict with the active nature of Harry and Charlotte, suggesting that "Old Man" meanders and has fewer abrupt shifts and "sudden, jerky flights" (163) than "Wild Palms," thus replicating the passivity/activity of the characters.

Like her New Critical counterparts, Vickery is interested in the "larger unity" and patterns of *The Wild Palms:*

> All its characters are caught in a double trap set by time. Thus, both Harry and Charlotte are conscious of being confined within the circle of human life. They have only a limited number of years before death plunges them into oblivion. The structure of their section of the novel repeats this circle, for it both begins and ends in the small Mississippi town and also follows their departure from and return to New Orleans. (165)

She ends up arguing that the novel is, in effect, about "balance" itself, the balance "between man, nature, and society, between reason and emotion, between an excess of order and chaos . . . [that] ensures man's freedom and dignity" (166).[5]

Throughout this study, Vickery takes a close look at the distinct parts of the novels and analyzes the ways they order our experience of reading, which then opens up more questions about how we make sense of the world around us in terms of "perception, language, and time" (240). More so than Brooks, Vickery sees pattern making and allegory as *potentially* harmful—"When an individual translates a personal ideal into a formula or a pattern of behavior, he falsifies experience and substitutes private conviction for truth" (246). Clearly, Brooks and Vickery are both opposed, in New Critical fashion, to relativistic approaches to interpretation, and there is in both a somewhat rigid notion of what the inter-pretive process actually entails. But while Vickery is perhaps prone to over-thematize, to seek unity where in fact there may be none, hers is another important assessment of the body of Faulkner's work, one impossible to imagine without the New Critical/formalist methodology being employed throughout literary studies at the time.[6]

STRUCTURALISM

A natural extension of many of the methodological assumptions of New Criticism's search for a text's meaning, **structuralism** is in theory more dedicated to the systematic elaboration of the rules and constraints that work to make the generation of meaning possible and has played an important role in the development of Faulkner studies. As a revolt against literary history and biographical criticism, and with its close attention to details of language and form, it is, like New Criticism, a return to the text. Structuralism focuses more, though, on establishing scientific methodological models and tracing linguistic patterns, even as structuralist approaches to literature tend to examine literary conventions and devices more generally, seeking to understand how texts are organized and how patterns and devices function to create meaning. This impulse ties it closely to other theories covered in this chapter, particularly deconstruction and narratology. Structuralism as a vibrant school of literary criticism has more or less disappeared—critics now rarely identify themselves as structuralists—but the methodologies continue to be important in narratology as well as poststructuralism and deconstruction.

One of the earliest structuralist works devoted, albeit obliquely, to Faulkner is Wesley Morris's *Friday's Footprint: Structuralism and the Articulated Text* (1979). Heavily indebted to Lévi-Strauss, Roland Barthes, Noam Chomsky, and Jacques Derrida among others, Morris attempts to negotiate several critical impasses within literary criticism, which he perceives as wracked by the "fragmentation of modern theory in our post-romantic world" (xi) and "endless debates over the adequacy of various interpretive methodologies" (xii). As a sample text to test out his theories of literary interpretation and his own "literary **hermeneutics**," Morris focuses on several stories from *Go Down, Moses,* though his main emphasis is on literary theory. The result is an interesting, complicated, jargon-laden work—understandably so—which does not add a great deal to our understanding of *Go Down, Moses,* nor does it seem intended to do so, though it does perhaps implicitly underline the continuing appeal and challenges of Faulkner's work to formalist critics.

John N. Duvall's *Faulkner's Marginal Couple: Invisible, Outlaw, and Unspeakable Communities* (1990) is also influenced by several different strands of literary theory, including deconstruction and poststructuralism, but is more clearly focused on Faulkner, elucidating a particular dilemma—the relationships between men and women, between individual and community, in Faulkner's texts—and how responses to these novels and stories have in part been dictated by the state of Faulkner studies itself. Duvall proceeds to note the necessity to deconstruct the "Agrarian influence on Faulkner studies," as well as to use structuralism and semiotics in order to reassess the concept of the "Faulknerian community." It is interesting to note how many structuralist and poststructuralist critics feel the need to "kill the Father" in the form of Cleanth Brooks, so large is the shadow he casts. Following suit, Duvall notes that Brooks "uses the term *community* in *William Faulkner: The Yoknapatawpha Country* as though its meaning were innocent and transparent. . . . Brooks's valorization of community carries a heavy ideological burden" (7). In order to rethink Faulkner's communities, Duvall makes use of A. J. Greimas's "conception of reciprocal communication as an exchange constituting a contract" and Roman Jakobson's "communication model outlined in 'Linguistics and Poetics'" (xiv). In using Greimas's narrative semiotics, Duvall is able to investigate, through the categories of "destinator" (that which destines) and "destinatee," the "possibilities for narrative action," particularly concerning the relationships between men and women in Faulkner's fiction (xv).[7]

In his attempts to explore Faulkner's seeming misogyny, Duvall finds unity among many (if not all) of Faulkner's works: "In the Faulkner novels that I see as a unit, male characters who act as destinators to female characters often do so by condemning female sexuality" (xv). The sexist/misogynist attitudes found in many of Faulkner's works such as *Light in August, Sanctuary, Pylon,* and *Absalom, Absalom!* are thus deflected onto an "ideological structure [Duvall] designate[s] the patriarchal destinator," which can, according to Duvall, be either male or female (xv–xvi).

Such categories allow Duvall to identify patterns within Faulkner's oeuvre. For example, explaining how the seemingly unconventional relationship between Roger, Jack, and Laverne in *Pylon* is "normalized" by the community, he suggests, "As is also the case in *Light in August* and *The Wild Palms,* the community is able to use narrative as a strategy of containment, denying the alternative formation its radical potential by reading it back into paradigms they can understand and judge" (93). Such a reading suggests a real potential on the part of a structuralist approach for rethinking standardized interpretations of Faulkner's works, while at the same time begging the question of whether critics sometimes find the pattern they're looking for (a possibility Duvall himself tacitly acknowledges). Although Duvall's book stresses structuralism, its mixture of deconstruction, poststructuralism, and feminist and biographical criticism typifies the tendency of most critics to formulate methodologies that do not follow just one particular line of theoretical inquiry but might be more accurately called pluralistic and poststructuralist.

DECONSTRUCTION AND POSTSTRUCTURALISM

Given its close affinities to New Criticism, particularly in the emphasis on close reading and the autonomy of the text, and the complex nature of Faulkner's texts, it is small wonder that **deconstruction** has proven a very popular critical methodology for Faulkner studies. Few critics today call themselves deconstructionists, but many make use of the concepts behind deconstruction without explicitly identifying their work as such and would likely be more comfortable with the label of **poststructuralism.** Deconstruction in its "purest" form (best represented in the works dating from the 1980s) is often attacked as showy and interested only in a virtuoso display by the practitioner. In this, it also resembles New Criticism. A full definition is impossible, but roughly, deconstruction is described as the critical activity that draws out the contradictory logics of sense and implication within the text, exposing the extent to which all that was consciously excluded from the text, all that was pushed to the margins, was in fact necessary to its organization. Derridean deconstruction (named for the leading deconstructionist, Jacque Derrida) undercuts the binary structures on which logocentric thought is presumed to be based—inside/outside, reality/appearance, subject/object, beginning/ending, black/white, masculine/feminine, conscious/ unconscious, presence/absence, speech/writing—destabilizing dualisms by disrupting the illusion of priority which coalesces around one of the terms.

Unlike New Criticism and structuralism, deconstruction involves a close reading of texts in order to demonstrate that any given text has irreconcilably contradictory meanings, rather than being a unified, logical whole. Deconstruction arose as a response to structuralism and formalism more generally. Deconstructors question the New Critical hierarchy of figures and the distinctions upon which hierarchical valuations are based, as well as the plausibility that a complete understanding of the literary work is possible. Deconstruction assumes conflicts and ambiguities are irreconcilable, embedded as they are within the text itself, and rejects the notion of a literary text being unified from beginning to end.

The fullest expressly deconstructive study within Faulkner studies is undoubtedly John T. Matthews's *The Play of Faulkner's Language* (1982), which features close readings of several texts, including *The Sound and the Fury, Absalom, Absalom!, The Hamlet,* and *Go Down, Moses.* Matthews sets out to "show that Faulkner's major fiction elevates fabrication over representation, confronts the loss of the original idea and subject, makes writing a kind of mourning (as it produces the very insufficiencies it seeks to overcome), and celebrates the playfulness of writing in the space (or play) between the written and the written about" (9). Critics have long noted Faulkner's acknowledgment, in such places as Addie's chapter in *As I Lay Dying,* of the inadequacy of language itself, and Matthews uses this as his jumping-off point. Derrida inspires *The Play of Faulkner's Language,* yet Matthews clearly holds onto the notion of "meaning."

In his chapter on *The Hamlet,* "Rites of Play," Matthews identifies the decentered "play of systems" in the novel:

> Such slippages and decenterings permit play in *The Hamlet,* where games playing structures society. Ratliff comes to understand that the centers of meaning in the community are strictly arbitrary; they lack contact with the origins of authority or truth. Nature, the supernatural, romantic love, finance, law, and language—all potential "grounds" for human society—are exposed as systems of play that float around missing centers. Such play produces sense and coherence by organizing conventions of exchange, opportunities for intimacy, and various economies of

lack and substitution. But they are not centered, they do not signify prior or hidden sources of authority, and they prove defenseless against Flem Snopes's patently lawful exploitation of them. (163)

For Matthews, this lack of a center calls into question typical readings of the novel as nostalgic for a pre-Fallen South: "*The Hamlet* displays a world unalterably established on the discourses of society; there are no natural centers from which to measure the fall into civilization" (164). Throughout, Matthews offers nuanced, close readings of gaps, repetitions, and binaries, always attentive to the language itself. In fact, this study suggests just how close deconstruction and New Criticism can actually be. One major difference here is what the critics do with the sense of community in Faulkner—Brooks no doubt would have serious reservations about the lack of "natural centers," but would find much to be admired in Matthews's reading. And Matthews, while explicitly objecting to Brooks's "campaign to establish the facts of *Absalom*," does not feel the need to spend much time tearing down the old man of Faulkner criticism.

Deconstruction, as one of the major threads running throughout poststructuralism, inevitably helps shape many different approaches to literary study, but most critics prefer to identify their work as poststructuralist in nature and deconstructive in method. One of the most important collections of essays that includes deconstructive and poststructuralist approaches to Faulkner is *Faulkner's Discourse: An International Symposium* (1989), which contains the influential work done during the 1987 International Faulkner Symposium. In these short essays, a wide range of poststructuralist theories and approaches are applied to many of Faulkner's canonical and noncanonical works. In his introduction, editor Lothar Hönnighausen identifies the major threads running throughout Faulkner studies at the time, noting the "great criticism" of Cleanth Brooks alongside Derrida and Foucault. It is interesting to observe how Hönnighausen seeks to distance this collection from formalism and, more specifically, New Criticism, while maintaining a tacit recognition of the formalist roots at the heart of the poststructuralist project. Noting the range of critical approaches found in the collection, he finds a thread running throughout, "a refusal to limit the critical effort to the textual surface after the manner of the New Critics" (xiv).

The table of contents of *Faulkner's Discourse* reads like a who's who of poststructuralist Faulkner critics—included are essays by Philip M. Weinstein, James A. Snead, François Pitavy, Jacques Pothier, Matthews, Richard Godden, Judith Wittenberg, Noel Polk, Ilse Dusoir Lind, Karl F. Zender, Sonja Basic, Stephen M. Ross, André Bleikasten, Michel Gresset, Thomas L. McHaney, and Gerhard Hoffman.

In "Roland Barthes Reads *A Fable*," Noel Polk uses Barthes's notion of mythical language as a system of signs—most clearly expressed in his *Mythologies*—to interrogate the ways Faulkner is able to "undertake to explore the signs—portraits, images, gestures, words—by which the unstated assumptions, the myths, of our culture are perpetuated" (109). Polk does not limit himself to the performatives of Faulkner's literary texts alone, however, and in poststructuralist style manages to analyze Faulkner's performance in Stockholm as well:

Faulkner's troublesome Nobel Prize speech also articulates a myth which Faulkner likewise understands as a myth, and that, to use Barthes's terms, he deliberately made *that* myth, that speech, "the departure point for a third semiological chain, to take its signification as the first term of a second myth" . . . the second myth, in this case, is *A Fable*. . . . Thus Faulkner becomes Barthes's "reader of myths," who has focused "on the mythical signifier as on an inextricable whole made of meaning and form." (116)

Several poststructuralist critics make use of structuralist and narratological methodologies in order to question the privileging of certain Faulkner texts over others, and this has been one of the most important aspects of the poststructural project in Faulkner studies. Polk's attempt to rescue *A Fable* from its relative critical obscurity is a good example of this healthy impulse to interrogate the canonical and noncanonical status of Faulkner's texts. Other infrequently discussed texts in the collection include *The Reivers,* "Carcassonne," and "Beyond." Not surprisingly, however, the great number of essays focus on that most postmodern [see chapter 6] of texts, *Absalom, Absalom!,* and the collection is invaluable for providing a variety of different approaches to this one novel.

There are also many important book-length poststructuralist studies of Faulkner, including Ralph Flores's *The Rhetoric of Doubtful Authority* (1984), Wesley Morris and Barbara Alverson Morris's *Reading Faulkner* (1989), John E. Bassett's *Visions and Revisions: Essays on Faulkner* (1989), Minrose C. Gwin's *The Feminine and Faulkner: Reading (Beyond) Sexual Difference* (1990), Richard C. Moreland's *Faulkner and Modernism: Rereading and Rewriting* (1990), and Philip M. Weinstein's *Faulkner's Subject: A Cosmos No One Owns* (1992). Several others are noted in the chapter on postmodernism in this volume [see chapter 6]. Although critics sometimes attack elements of these works as narrow deconstructive exercises or as cumbersomely theory-heavy, they all make productive use of deconstruction and poststructuralist ideas to bring new life to Faulkner studies. It is hard to imagine that Faulkner's texts would have achieved the level of institutional prominence they held in the 1960s and 1970s without New Criticism—it is even harder to imagine Faulkner studies remaining "relevant," not to say as compelling, without poststructuralism.

NARRATOLOGY

As I have been stressing throughout this chapter, all of these formalist strands are interrelated, and **narratology** owes a debt to all of the approaches to literary study previously discussed. Narratology relies on close textual analysis, coupled with an emphasis on linguistic and rhetorical figures within the text. Like their New Critical and structuralist counterparts, narratologists tend to look for patterns of narrative techniques within the corpus of Faulkner's work. With its emphasis on questions of point of view, narrative perspective, and rhetorical devices, narratology clearly has much to offer Faulkner criticism, and Faulkner studies has been deeply enriched by the plethora of narratological approaches on offer.

Several essays in *Faulkner's Discourse* address narratology, particularly in the section entitled "The Problem of Narration." Sonja Basic's "Faulkner's Narrative: Between Involvement and Distancing," for example, looks at the notion of narrative distancing in several texts, including *The Sound and the Fury, Light in August, Absalom, Absalom!,* "Old Man," and *The Hamlet.* One particularly valuable aspect of narratology is its tendency to question the standard valuations placed on Faulkner's novels. In this particular case, Basic favorably compares the critically popular (because, in part, of its postmodern aspects) *Absalom, Absalom!* to the *seemingly* less interesting *The Hamlet:*

> *The Hamlet* . . . is not a step backward, towards a more traditional realism. On the contrary, it brings Faulkner closer to some aspects of postmodernism: in its insistence on the process of narration, for example, on what has been called fabulation, and on the juxtaposition of vastly different narrative modes and styles, which amounts to arbitrariness, as well as in those roller-coaster plunges between the sublime and the trivial, which amount to melodrama and kitsch. All these elements are not only formal or structural abstractions: they contribute directly to the creation of Faulkner's world and to the production of meaning in his novels. (148)

Narratologists such as Basic attempt to identify particular narrative strategies in an author's works, an effort that distinguishes narratology from those theories—such as deconstruction and structuralism—that are more suspicious of the notion of authorial control or, to use a term taken from film theory, **auteurism.** Basic concludes, "By showing that Faulkner experimented continually and obsessively with various degrees and kinds of telling . . . I have singled out one of his important strategies for undermining narrative authority. An awareness of this strategy should help us to understand the problematic, profoundly ironic tenor of his discourse" (148). Such statements underline the investment for Basic and narratology more generally in the notion of Faulkner as an author whose narrative strategies can be identified and interpreted in terms of their effects and their intentionality.[8]

In one of the more engaging of the book-length narratological studies, Hugh M. Ruppersburg's *Voice and Eye in Faulkner's Fiction* (1983) makes point of view the major focus of examination, suggesting that the real power of Faulkner's works lies therein: "Faulkner employs [point of view] in a way more complex, more convoluted and involuted, than any other successful novelist of the English language. Readers who fail to recognize its importance may seriously misunderstand his art, his artistry" (5). Ruppersburg finds connections in terms of point of view between four "representative" novels, two canonical works—*Absalom, Absalom!* and *Light in August*—and two "neglected" texts—*Pylon* and *Requiem for a Nun.* In the study, Ruppersburg repeatedly works to relate narrative point of view with thematic concerns. For example, his reading of *Pylon* emphasizes the same type of concern with community versus individual we see in Brooks and Duvall:

> One way *Pylon* symbolizes theme is through contrasting two or more distinctly isolated character perspectives. In *Light in August* character perspectives overlap and

intersect, creating a pervasive community consciousness which helps define the individual. No overlapping occurs in New Valois, thus no communal consciousness. The typical New Valoisian perceives himself only from his own viewpoint. . . . Contrasting character perspectives—isolated centers of consciousness—provide the basic structure for at least two chapters. (72)

Ruppersburg constantly draws comparisons between different novels, once again establishing the sorts of patterns and connections we have seen so many critics interested in illuminating, but also keeping in mind more worldly cultural and social concerns as well: "*Pylon* may be Faulkner's most unusual, atypical book. But it explores themes which remained of interest to him throughout his career—isolation, economic exploitation, the powerlessness of language, the individual in conflict with his environment" (80). Interestingly, Ruppersburg is not particularly concerned with ultimately upending the typical hierarchy of Faulkner's oeuvre—he concludes that despite its interesting narrative experimentation, *Pylon* "does not measure up" (80) to *Absalom, Absalom!* or *Light in August* or *Go Down, Moses.*

Narratological critics who devote full-length studies to Faulkner's works tend to operate in this way: they distinguish particular textual features that speak to point of view, narration, and rhetorical tropes, and they typically thematize and often make culturally/historically/socially relevant these narrative features, finding patterns within several texts, connections between seemingly disparate stories and novels. Narratology has allowed Faulkner studies to attend more systematically to perspective and narrator without sacrificing thematic or social import and, more than other formalist approaches, foregrounds the importance of audience reception in the production of meaning. Although many such studies continue to look at the text as an object that does not necessarily change depending on its viewer, narratology remains an important and productive strand within Faulkner criticism. Some of the most important studies in this area include Joseph W. Reed Jr.'s *Faulkner's Narrative* (1973), John T. Irwin's *Doubling and Incest/Repetition and Revenge: A Speculative Reading of Faulkner* (1975), Arthur F. Kinney's *Faulkner's Narrative Poetics: Style as Vision* (1978), Donald M. Kartiganer's *The Fragile Thread: The Meaning of Form in Faulkner's Novels* (1979), and Stephen Ross's *Fiction's Inexhaustible Voice: Speech & Writing in Faulkner* (1989).

BAKHTIN AND DIALOGICS

This chapter ends by looking at the recent developments in Faulkner studies that rely on the theories of Mikhail Mikhaylovich Bakhtin because so many critics found among the other categories within formalism have turned to his writings and theories in their continuing engagement with Faulkner, and it appears that, due to the more cultural turn formalism has taken in literary studies, Bakhtin will continue to have a profound impact on Faulkner studies for years to come. It seems appropriate that Bakhtin, whose works have been picked up in our more culturally sensitive critical climate, was himself a staunch critic of formalism and structuralism in their more sterile incarnations, citing their abstraction, their failure to analyze the content of literary works, and the difficulty they find in analyzing linguistic and ideological changes.

The Bakhtinian concepts most productively applied to Faulkner studies include **heteroglossia,** the **carnivalesque,** and **dialogism.** Bakhtin saw the study of the novel as an entirely separate enterprise from that of analyzing poetry, and he criticized formalist analysis for what he perceived as a failure to acknowledge this distinction (a charge often leveled at the New Critics). As Gary Saul Morson and Caryl Emerson write:

> Bakhtin strongly believed that criticism of novels in terms borrowed from poetics tends to miss just what is most distinctive about them. For example, the richness of poetic language (the trope) is essentially different from that of the novel (dialogized heteroglossia). Other constituent features of novels, such as their special sense of temporality and psychology, have also been missed because they were approached in terms set by poetics. (in Groden and Kreiswirth 65)

There are many typical features in Faulkner's works that obviously appeal to Bakhtinian principles of language and narration, including the notion of multiple perspectives, the upending of hierarchies, the struggles with communication that threaten to destroy characters, and the emphasis on disorder and the interrogation of facile binaries. Examples of Bakhtinian readings of Faulkner include Patrick Samway's "Narration and Naming in *The Reivers,*" Millie M. Kidd's "The Dialogic Perspective in William Faulkner's *The Hamlet,*" Olga Scherer's "A Dialogic Hereafter: *The Sound and the Fury* and *Absalom, Absalom!,*" Richard Pearce's "The Politics of Narration: Can a Woman Tell Her Story in Yoknapatawpha County—Even with All Those Yarns?," and Marion Tangum's "Rhetorical Clues to *Go Down, Moses:* Who is Talking to Whom?"

Judith Lockyer's *Ordered by Words: Language and Narration in the Novels of William Faulkner* (1991) is one of the few book-length applications of Bakhtin to Faulkner studies. In it, she emphasizes the multivoiced nature of so many of Faulkner's novels:

> Not until Faulkner creates Quentin Compson and Darl Bundren does he find the power in genuine exchange. Both characters are arguably mad, driven so by their desire to construct and order an immutable reality in language, but they appear in novels that find their strength in challenging the idea of a closed narration. In *The Sound and the Fury, Absalom, Absalom!,* and *As I Lay Dying,* as well as in *Light in August,* Faulkner disarms the threat of the multivoiced world by embracing it. In these novels, Faulkner makes the act of narration a metaphor for living in the world. Listening to other voices, articulating one's own, and integrating them all into an open-ended yet coherent whole are the major preoccupations of these novels. (x)

Lockyer uses Bakhtin's notion that meaning is situational to interpret the ways Faulkner's texts present to us characters who, in seeking or believing in absolutes, are destroyed. Quentin, for example, cannot escape "the absolute word" or "authoritative discourse" and is wrecked because of it. In failing to recognize the polyvocal, dialogic nature of language and communication,

Faulkner's "men of words" (we might include Rosa Coldfield here) aspire, fruit-lessly, "to the power that absolute language holds" (xi).

Lockyer focuses on Horace Benbow, Quentin Compson, Ike McCaslin, as well as *As I Lay Dying* and *Light in August.* She ends with a compelling, and telling, reading of *Requiem for a Nun* that arguably takes us back to the mythol-ogizing and universalizing tendencies in New Criticism, but with a difference. In charting the various narrations woven throughout *Requiem,* Lockyer suggests that Faulkner's later works seek the kind of unity his earlier works found impos-sible to imagine. Late Faulkner, Lockyer argues, suggests that "language will save humans" (149). With Temple Drake's belated—and to many critics uncon-vincing—acceptance of life, Faulkner:

> constructs a novel that unfolds the history of Yoknapatawpha County in terms of humanity's moral development. Every element in the play and in the narrative contributes to Faulkner's definition of our position in a world that we have both inherited and made. . . . Ultimately, Faulkner's play-novel asserts the tenacity of human beings and the unequaled capacity of language to assert it. (148)

What might seem ideologically problematic in Faulkner's later fiction is shown by Lockyer to be explicitly traceable through the dialogic nature of the dis-course, and her Bakhtinian approach allows her to approach more extensively the question of "authorial voice" and the points at which Faulkner may, and may not, agree with his characters' assessments of the power, and insufficiencies, of language.

It is sometimes the case that Bakhtinian readings of Faulkner say more about Bakhtin than they do about the novelist—Bakhtin says X about the novel, Faulkner is doing X—but more typical is an opening up of the texts, typically those less often studied at length, to nuanced readings of narrative voice and cultural multiplicities. John T. Matthews, who has already been discussed as a poststructuralist, demonstrates in "The Autograph of Violence in Faulkner's *Pylon*" how methods usually associated with deconstruction can become pow-erful tools in approaching a text from a Bakhtinian perspective. This article also suggests how much more pressing cultural and social concerns have become within poststructuralist approaches to Faulkner's works. He begins by question-ing the typical understanding of *Pylon,* with its seemingly less complicated nar-rative, a "holiday" from his writing of *Absalom, Absalom!:* "Or might *Pylon* have forced Faulkner to realize one of the main empowering principles of his greatest novel: that all individuals are radically conditioned by the historical and material realities of their eras, and that no writer can afford to believe his char-acters have no places in their cultures or economies" (247).

Matthews's article makes use of close reading, biographical details, cultural and historical research on New Orleans and America's economic situation in the early 1930s, and attention to narrative perspective (particularly that of the reporter) in its analysis of the novel. He ends up pursuing, in poststructuralist language, "registers of meaning that elude the reporter's control," and suggests that Faulkner's novel does not share the reporter's "blindness to historical context" (251). In order to open up the text to such a reading, Matthews makes use of Bakhtin's carnivalesque, arguing that the novel appears on the surface, with all its T. S. Eliot trappings, as that pristine object arguably so beloved by the New Critics, but is actually politicized by its carnivalesque subtext: "*Pylon* rides on an interplay between this sense of imminent historical transformation [the 'desperation of the oppressed' in the early 1930s] and the celebration of the Mardi Gras festival" (252). But Matthews does not wholeheartedly endorse the attempt:

> Yet as I go on to interpret Faulkner's use of the carnivalesque in *Pylon,* I will observe that its original spirit appears deformed, though deformed in instructive ways. Ultimately we shall notice the strain of translating a medieval folk spectacle into the New Orleans of Roosevelt and Huey Long through the idiom of Joyce's and Eliot's high modernism. (253)

Matthews performs the necessary task of interrogating the relevance of Bakhtin's culturally specific theories of language and literature in interpreting Faulkner's novels, which are admittedly part of a very different tradition. The results, for Matthews, are mixed, and therein lies the strength of this mosaic of critical approaches. His article opens up *Pylon* to compelling questions about the transgressive, disruptive nature of the Roger/Jack/Laverne triangle in all its culture specificity, bearing in mind the importance of the narrative perspective in such an investigation. And through a Bakhtinian lens, Matthews sees the novel's self-parody as an expression of the admitted defeat of any real belief in social/cultural revolution: "The carnival appears in *Pylon* as the image of *lost* possibilities for self-awareness, connection, and gaiety" (266).

It is a compelling, quirky reading of a novel that has not been much appreciated, and it clearly highlights the power of what a nuanced formalist approach can achieve. Many of the critiques and studies discussed in this chapter make one want to go back and read the novels and stories again—this is one benefit of literary criticism that, sadly, is often undervalued. Identifiably formalist readings of Faulkner present many challenges, admittedly raise disturbing ideological and methodological issues, but ultimately offer interpretive possibilities not found in many other approaches to Faulkner's texts. We are all, essentially, close readers, and this in and of itself makes nearly every interpretation "formalist" in the broadest sense.

But Faulkner criticism has for decades felt it incumbent to distance itself from the taint of formalism. In the early 1980s, André Bleikasten wrote, in "For/Against an Ideological Reading of Faulkner's Novels," that attempts to draw Faulkner studies out of the shadow of New Criticism had by and large failed:

> It is wrong to say that current Faulkner criticism is more rigorously grounded in theory than it was previously. What unifies it is not theory, that is, a serviceable set of working assumptions, but a new ideological consensus, another *doxa,* a gaudy bundle of received ideas and fashionable clichés ultimately just as arbitrary and just as constraining as those of the New Criticism of the 1950s. (6)

The previous overview of formalist criticism suggests that Bleikasten might be overstating the case. Faulkner criticism certainly has its weak spots, and many articles and books are perhaps theoretically lacking in rigor, but by the 1970s and 1980s Faulkner studies was making progress, as many of the formalist (yet theoretical) texts in this chapter demonstrate. Nor is Bleikasten's blanket dismissal of New Criticism compelling. New Criticism certainly had too tight a grip on Faulkner studies in particular, but a careful reading of these critical texts themselves are hard to dismiss so easily, and still offer textured, and in most cases approachable, interpretations of Faulkner's difficult oeuvre. And as this chapter has suggested, these formalist theories of reading are interrelated, sometimes difficult to distinguish from one another, a blurring of boundaries that should be celebrated.

Bleikasten, one among many detractors of formalism, has in recent years continued to use New Criticism as the whipping boy of Faulkner studies—even as he praises the poststructuralist criticism that remains indebted to New Criticism—in his 1995 article "Faulkner and the New Ideologues": "Since the fifties, academic Faulkner criticism in America has been almost uniformly uncritical, and most of it was blandly ahistorical and apolitical. . . . There was a clear need, then, to remove Faulkner's work from the sanitary vacuum of the New Criticism and to take a sharper look at its ideological implications" (3). While it is certainly true that poststructuralism has served as a necessary corrective to the grip New Criticism has at times held on Faulkner studies, when it is done well, New Criticism (and formalism more generally) has always offered more than a clinical dissection or a scientific study performed within a "sanitary vacuum," and New Critical and formalist approaches have much to offer the Faulkner scholar.

NOTES

1. "Literary criticism is particularly prone to talk about 'form,' indeed one dominant school of criticism of a generation ago was 'Formalism.' The word 'form' has been used so widely and loosely that it is due for a rest, and students should be chary of using it; likewise 'content'" (O'Sullivan et al. 122).

2. See Lawrence Schwartz's excellent study in *Creating Faulkner's Reputation: The Politics of Modern Literary Criticism* of the political factors behind Faulkner's rebirth in the 1940s and 1950s and the ways his works and Southern "elder statesman" persona "spoke" to New Critical concerns.

3. For example, see John T. Matthews's "The Sacrifice of History in the New Criticism of Cleanth Brooks," where he offers a critique of Brooks's New Critical works and their thinly veiled Christian agrarian ideological bias. For a spirited defense of Brooks (in particular, his poetry criticism), see R. V. Young's "The Old New Criticism and its Critics." For a balanced analysis of how Brooks's readings differ not so greatly from those of deconstructionists and poststructuralists, see David Newman's "'the vehicle itself is unaware': New Criticism on the Limits of Reading Faulkner."

4. This quote comes from an exchange between Crews and John Duvall (identified as a "notorious" Brooks-basher) in the letter section of the *New York Review of Books,* 24 October 1991.

5. For a fuller formalist approach to the unity of *The Wild Palms,* see Thomas L. McHaney's *William Faulkner's* The Wild Palms: *A Study* (1975).

6. It would be impossible to list all of the New Critical/formalist critical studies devoted to Faulkner. These, however, are some of the more important book-length works within this tradition: Walter Slatoff, *Quest for Failure: A Study of William Faulkner* (1960); James Guetti, *The Limits of Metaphor: A Study of Melville, Conrad, and Faulkner* (1967); Donald M. Kartiganer, The *Fragile Thread: The Meaning of Form in Faulkner's Novels* (1979); John Pikoulis, *The Art of William Faulkner* (1982); Gail L. Mortimer, *Faulkner's Rhetoric of Loss: A Study in Perception and Meaning* (1983); Thadious Davis, *Faulkner's "Negro": Art and the Southern Context* (1983); Robert Dale Parker, *Faulkner and the Novelistic Imagination* (1985); and Dirk Kuyk Jr., *Sutpen's Design: Interpreting Faulkner's* Absalom, Absalom! (1990).

7. For an earlier Greimas-inspired approach to Faulkner, see Duvall's "Using Greimas' Narrative Semiotics: Signification in Faulkner's 'The Old People.'" Another interesting, explicitly structuralist, approach to Faulkner is Jack J. Healy's "Structuralism Applied: American Literature and its Subordination to Structure," which deals with both *Absalom, Absalom!* and *As I Lay Dying.*

8. For an earlier reading by this same author inspired by Barthes, Todorov, and Genette, see "Faulkner's Narrative Discourse: Mediation and Mimesis."

4

Biographical Criticism

Kevin Railey

A NOTE ON METHOD

Both biography and autobiography have more recently been collapsed under the title of life-writing. Influenced by the theories of postmodernism [see chapter 6], this term refers to the writing done by "subjects"—critics, biographers, and writers themselves—about the writer's life. Postmodernism has influenced us to recognize that this writing is always interpretive, whether it be the writing of a biographer or critic, or whether it be the writer writing about his own life. The notions of the self as object, on one hand, and the notion that human perception in such matters is never objective, on the other, have linked biography and autobiography in definite and interesting ways. For an essay about biographical criticism about William Faulkner, this shift opens various questions. Faulkner, of course, did not write autobiography as we have generally understood that term. In fact, he often stated his desire to be null and void as a private individual, and there are few direct references to himself or his life in his writing.[1] Critics, however, have at times investigated Faulkner through the lens of autobiography and with an assumption that art and life are intricately interwoven for the artist himself. Moreover, critics for some time have taken and used Faulkner's own statements about life and art as authoritative comments in one way or another—a long-standing method influenced by the Romantic notion that artists are seers into truth and reality. And, they have used his letters as a tool to analyze both biography and art—a move that has increased with the release of more and more Faulkner letters. So, what to include when discussing biographical criticism? In this essay I have generally included all these forms of criticism. I don't focus on biography as that term has traditionally been used, though I do discuss the prominent Faulkner biographies. I collapse the distinction between autobiography and biography and focus more generally on criticism/writing that takes as its subject the relationship between a writer's life and his art.

That said, when one begins to review Faulkner criticism to find how interpretations of his life affect opinions about the writing, one begins to realize just how deeply the interrelationships extend. On one hand, those critics whose main purpose is traditional biography often project their interpretations of personal events into their analysis of the fiction. Also, certain preconceptions and assumptions about Faulkner, ones that explain the choice of him as a worthy biographical subject, inevitably influence these critics' work. On the other, many whose main purpose is literary criticism reveal their sense that Faulkner's real life, that life which matters most, is symbolized, sublimated, or revealed only in the fiction. Moreover, all the criticism, it seems, is infused with some particular sense of the motivating forces in Faulkner's life and is deeply influenced by some particular conception of the artist that gets projected into the reading of Faulkner and his work. Almost everything, then, becomes connected to biography, to the story we tell each other and ourselves about William Faulkner and to the general conceptions we have of artists and their relationships to truth and to creativity. Thus, I will proceed down two paths that will be interwoven at various points along the way. First, I will attempt to outline, broadly, some of the understandings and conceptions of art and artists that have guided and influenced Faulkner criticism and interpretations of Faulkner's life over the years. Second, I will discuss works that can be more specifically labeled auto/biographical criticism, as a reference guide might label them, and place them in the more general narrative that has been developing about Faulkner since the beginning.

BACKGROUNDS FOR THE STORY

In his *Creating Faulkner's Reputation,* Lawrence Schwartz argues that the New Critics and the New York intellectuals crafted Faulkner's rise from near obscurity to literary prominence as they came to explain Faulkner in ways that met the dominant expectations for literature. Though he makes a convincing case, Schwartz does not discuss the ways in which this process was part of a longer and broader history. Perhaps going back as far as John Stuart Mill's discussion and interpretation of the enlivening effects of Wordsworth's poetry, this history certainly has its American origins in the late nineteenth-century debate between philologists and literary critics. In various MLA forums, literary critics such as James Russell Lowell and John Phelps Fruit argued for the aesthetic appreciation and interpretation of literature. Students needed to be trained to see the genius behind and in great books and to see literature as the autobiography of mankind. To distance themselves from philology and the philological use of biography to understand literature, these men and others called for more psychological studies of writers' lives. These studies would seek to understand the newly labeled spirit of the writer and often would seek so-called true biography in the literary text itself rather than in a direct account of the life story. These moves had the effect of pushing biography as a genre into the background and of downplaying the authority of the author. True writers, it was argued, did not really see themselves as responsible for the production of the work, and no matter how hard one studied the details of the life, it was posited, one could not get at a true understanding of the origin and meaning of the work. These mysteries could only be unraveled through the power of the sympathetic imagination of the critic. (For a discussion of the details of this process, see Ross, "Too Close.")

Articulated in the late nineteenth century, these ideas influenced and found further voice in the work of those like I. A. Richards and T. S. Eliot. They competed for dominance in the early twentieth century with ideas voiced by those like Van Wyck Brooks, on one hand, and V. L. Parrington, on the other. Nonetheless, as we well know, the absolute importance and centrality of the aesthetic critic focused on the details of the text and inspired by a sensitive imagination became established with the New Critics. By its very nature biography was relegated to a different arena within this new order. It certainly was not the domain of undergraduate study any longer, for students were prone to see everything through the personal lens, the argument went, and needed to develop more refinement and training to analyze the complexities and understand the profundities of literature. In the professional arena of scholarship, though, effects reverberated as well. After this point, biography within American literary criticism always had a distinct purpose beyond the record of the life.

Within this new order biography's purpose paralleled, it seemed, the purpose of literary criticism. It was threefold. As literary criticism's purpose was to see and to explain the order, beauty, and complexity of the literary work, the biographer's purpose was to see and to explain the coherent personality, the expressiveness, and the genius of the literary artist. As literary criticism's purpose was to see individual works of art as part of a distinct literary history, the biographer's purpose was to read the writer's life as a literary journey, influenced by writers and literature more than by other forces. Finally, as part of literary criticism's purpose was to demonstrate the value and worth of the critic, biography was also in part about demonstrating the biographer's astute and imaginative sensibility. Another influence, at times, for American biographies was for the individual life to be read as part of a broader American story. (For a discussion of this trend, see Rob Wilson, "Producing American Selves.") As will be demonstrated through the various individual discussions that follow, Faulkner biographical criticism is deeply embedded within this larger framework surrounding and enveloping American literary criticism in general. Not until the work of Judith Sensibar, where breaks are implied and hinted, and that of Richard Gray, which functions within different assumptions to a great extent, does this general framework lose its force. Even when a critic/biographer attempts to sound as objective as possible, such as with Joseph Blotner, Faulkner biographical criticism functions within a broader network of influences that work to shape it and can be said to constitute it.

"Faulkner," in fact, as we generally know him today—as both man and artist—took a while to be created, invented, and/or discovered. With rare exception, such as Evelyn Scott, George Marion O'Donnell, Warren Beck, Conrad Aiken, Robert Penn Warren, and Delmore Schwartz, Faulkner was not seen to be a worthy enough subject to be explored and discussed in professional literary circles. He was considered by most to be too derivative to deserve major critical attention, too bizarre, complex, and complicated for his own good, or too dark and perverse for public or critical attention [see chapter 13]. Though perhaps the first assessment is still justified in relation to *Soldiers' Pay* and *Mosquitoes,* the others were clearly influenced by the tenets of social realism and by attitudes toward the American South. Faulkner's now infamous inability to cope with public settings—his drinking too much in public gatherings and his posing during interviews and conversations—did nothing to help his reputation either. Hard to imagine as it is today, Faulkner's books were virtually out of print, and he was almost relegated to the dustbin of history in the early 1940s. It is hard to believe that this situation was not caused, in part, by definitions of art that Faulkner's fiction did not match and by expectations of writers and their lives that Faulkner's place of birth and life did not match either. Faulkner's *The Sound and the Fury,* the book that eventually became his quintessential expression of artistic ability, was not at first understood as a fine example of literary modernism akin to Joyce and Proust. Neither was it seen to be exploring the depths of personal, familial, and social angst in ways akin to Shakespeare. *As I Lay Dying* and *Sanctuary* only proved to many that despite his pretensions to being a technical artist Faulkner was a dark and possibly depraved creator with few redeeming traits. Enter Malcolm Cowley.

Though brief, this story of the assessments of Faulkner in the 1930s reveals how much assumptions and attitudes of readers affect their assessments. Obviously, the books themselves were the same in the 1930s as they are today, and probably critics did not just become smarter. More likely, they simply changed. Malcolm Cowley's entrance into Faulkner's life and his legacy for both Faulkner and Faulkner criticism supports this point in a couple of ways. Cowley was an integral and influential part of the generation of New Critics, who affected the entire direction of literary criticism in major ways. On one hand, these critics reacted against the Maxwell Geismar, Vernon L. Parrington, and Edmund Wilson emphasis on social concerns and content, and shifted the concerns to those of artistic complexity and invention. On the other hand, these critics were unified in their universal aversion to capitalism and business, and envisioned art as the antithesis to these phenomena. For some time thereafter, art and politics were diametrically opposite. Thus, Cowley was equipped to see Faulkner's artistic achievements in ways that previous critics were not. Most importantly, he was also able to place Faulkner's art and life into an understandable and acceptable narrative frame—a frame that became deeply influential and still reverberates today throughout Faulkner criticism. Loosely summarized, Cowley's conception came to define Faulkner as artist in terms of originality and formal inventiveness, as seer in terms of a seeker and knower of human truths, and as moralist in terms of his recognition and depiction of the negative effects of capitalism on human existence. Though the terms are used in many ways, it could be said that Cowley opened the ways for Faulkner to become a modernist with a romantic soul. Cowley was able to read Faulkner's earlier lack of success as a by-product of Faulkner's originality and genius, and he was able to see Faulkner's work as an attempt to depict the end of civilization due to the ravages of the unenlightened masses and the corrupted capitalists. He was also able to see Faulkner's work as transcending the social and extending into the metaphysical, as probing the very meanings of life. It worked (and works). Cowley's vision and the values that inspired it opened the door for a completely new appraisal of Faulkner. Though he overplayed Faulkner's part in a Lost Generation, almost all Faulkner criticism is indebted to him and his vision. Certainly, the first biographers of Faulkner are.

THE STORY

All who know Faulkner criticism know that the first "real" biography of Faulkner was Joseph Blotner's 1974 two-volume *Faulkner: A Biography.* Blotner's monumental work, though, was preceded by the work of a few other men who mined the shadowy and ingenious shape of Faulkner's life. Though preceded by Irving Howe, whose *William Faulkner* (1951) included a short appreciation of Faulkner's life, really the first of the early biographical critics was Robert Coughlan. Coughlan's book, *The Private World of William Faulkner* (1953), combined ideas from various essays he had published in *Life* magazine with general views on Faulkner's life and work. Not surprisingly, the work feels dated in 2004, but, almost shockingly, it also contains ideas that have remained commonplaces in Faulkner criticism. Here we have the assertion of the incredibly powerful influence of the Old Colonel, Faulkner's great-grandfather, on William's life (and the beginnings of a story influenced by the values of patriarchy), which remain entrenched in Faulkner scholarship. Here we have a description of Faulkner's relationship to Oxford and Mississippi as an "organic" one that inspired his best writing, which reveals the connection to a Romantic ideology. Here we have Faulkner's early development described as that of the artist as a young man, a point that again reveals the influence of a romantic ideology. Here Faulkner's inventions, Jefferson and Yoknapatawpha, are described as the most impressive feats of imagination in modern literature, ideas justifying Faulkner as a legitimate biographical subject and legitimizing Coughlan's own sensibility. And here, too, we have the story of Faulkner's fiction as being about, at least in part, a reaction against the rise of the rednecks and a longing for the old order, claims solidifying Faulkner's modernist credentials. That these are commonplaces of criticism, of course, does not make them any less true or interesting than others. That they became commonplaces only emphasizes my earlier point: romantic notions of art and artists, as perhaps best defined by M. H. Abrams's *The Mirror and the Lamp,* and the modernist theme of art as antithesis to capitalism have been deeply important in Faulkner criticism since the beginnings. They shaped the perspective from which Faulkner biography was originally written.

This move to recognize Faulkner's power as an imaginative genius and to read his development as an artist as an organic, natural, internal, and inevitable process dominated the reassessments of Faulkner in the 1950s and 1960s. Due to the very frame itself, much of this work was not biographical (or historical); it was literary analysis connecting Faulkner to literary history. There were many in this vein, the best of whom was probably Cleanth Brooks. Other critical books that included biographical explorations were Edmond L. Volpe's *A Reader's Guide to William Faulkner* (1964) and William Van O'Connor's *The Tangled Fire of William Faulkner* (1954), books that did little to affect Faulkner criticism. Their approach was mirrored but not extended by a 1973 book, *William Faulkner of Yoknapatawpha County,* by Lewis Leary. Others included Michael Millgate's *The Achievement of William Faulkner* (1963) and H. Edward Richardson's *William Faulkner: The Journey to Self-Discovery* (1969), books to which I will turn shortly. Important, too, was the work of Carvel Collins.

Collins was a Faulkner critic and biographer whose meticulous work and rich archive leaves a lasting legacy to his lifelong devotion to Faulkner. After his death Collins left a treasure trove of materials to the Harry Ransom Humanities Research Center at the University of Texas at Austin (discussed in James G. Watson, "Carvel Collins's Faulkner"). He was perhaps the first to define and characterize Faulkner as a modernist, but his legacy is in biographical criticism and editorial work. In 1958, in his "Introduction" to *New Orleans Sketches,* he offers detailed information about Faulkner's stay in New Orleans in the early 1920s and the context surrounding the writing of these sketches. He explains the Sherwood Anderson connection and presents New Orleans as a very literary, and thus influential, place in which Faulkner stayed longer than originally planned and wrote his first novel. Collins explores connections between Faulkner's acquaintances and characters in the early novels and argues that these sketches and stories foreshadow some of Faulkner's subsequent mature work. To Collins's eye, New Orleans becomes the incubator for the genesis of Faulkner's fiction.

Collins followed this work with his edition of *William Faulkner: Early Prose and Poetry* in 1962, in which he also included a biographical introduction, "Faulkner at the University of Mississippi." This introduction reveals Collins at perhaps his meticulous best when he corrects errors as he finds them in both Frederick J. Hoffman's *William Faulkner* (a forgotten book) and Millgate's *The Achievement of William Faulkner* (an influential book). This essay has little criticism, focusing on Faulkner's publication record in the university newspaper, but does again make connections between the early work and Faulkner's later fiction. Pursuing his collecting and studying of Faulkner materials, Collins went on to help secure the publication of Faulkner's *Mayday* (1976) and wrote an introduction for it. This introduction discusses the biographical details surrounding the writing of this book, originally given to Helen Baird as a gift in 1926. It also discusses the links between its themes and Faulkner's feelings for Helen and between the style and themes of this book and those of *The Sound and the Fury.* Based on a story told to him by a reliable friend, Collins even offers the possibility that Faulkner began writing *The Sound and the Fury* while in Paris in 1925, thereby very closely linking the writing of both books and offering biographical evidence that they are closely connected.

All of his work was to lead Collins, he thought, to write an extended biography. It never happened, the odds of its appearance probably decreasing significantly with Blotner's 1974 book. He did continue his work, though, and his 1981 essay, "Biographical Background for Faulkner's Helen," indicates what a Collins biography might have been; it is his most extensive essay. Collins's interesting conclusion is that Faulkner's turn away from poetry to fiction in the mid-1920s was his way of saying yes to life, to the temporal flux of life, and to his willingness to participate in that flux and to resist death. Using references to letters and fiction to argue his point, Collins sees Helen Baird as representing for Faulkner the eternal flame of regenerative life. Collins rereads the Blotner version of the relationship between Faulkner and Helen Baird as one more complicated than Faulkner pursuing and Helen being completely disinterested. Collins links Helen to Meta Carpenter Wilde, the woman with whom Faulkner had a passionate relationship while in Hollywood, and to the fictional Charlotte Rittenmeyer from *The Wild Palms* [*If I Forget Thee, Jerusalem*]. All of these women, Collins argues, represented the flame of life and passion for Faulkner, and Faulkner wrote the novel because he was both deeply attracted to Helen and Meta and deeply troubled about losing them. Implicit in these descriptions of Collins's work are the ways in which he works from the romantic/modernist paradigm even while he helps to place Faulkner within it. For Collins, all of Faulkner, his life and his work as well as his early life and later life, is of one piece. It all fits together in a tightly unified organic whole demonstrating Faulkner's imaginative genius. Nonetheless, weaving factual detail with careful and sensitive readings, Collins here exhibits the true possibilities of subtle biographical criticism. (For more about the story of Faulkner's relationship with Meta Carpenter Wilde, see her book with Orin Borsten.)

This work was followed by Collins's last essay, published posthumously, "'Ad Astra' through New Haven: Some Biographical Sources of Faulkner's War Fiction" (1992). This essay describes the ways in which the short story builds on and takes from the 10 weeks Faulkner spent in New Haven during April, May, and June of 1918. Invited there by Phil Stone in order to be absent from Oxford when Estelle got married to Cornell Franklin, Faulkner met various people in New Haven, Collins argues, that served as models for characters in the story. These characters are the officer, whose loss of an imagined wife connects to Faulkner's emotional state, the German prisoner, and the subadar from India. As always, Collins presents impeccable information, turns that information into meaningful insights into the literature, and draws general conclusions about the relationship between one Faulkner work and more general themes in other work.

Like Malcolm Cowley before him, Carvel Collins believed that art and artists have the power and ability to transcend the personal, the social, and the historical. For them the biography of writers was almost always the story of how they became writers and how they turned the personal into some more perfect and eternal form. Agreeing with T. S. Eliot, they felt that "the more perfect the artist the more completely separate in him will be the man who suffers and the mind which creates" (quoted in Collins, "Biographical" 32). In this view, history was literary history, and biography was the portrait of the artist as it was delineated in the work of those like Wordsworth and Joyce. This basic view and its duality also influenced Michael Millgate and H. Edward Richardson.

Millgate's *The Achievement of William Faulkner* is not organized around a tight interweaving of biographical data and literary analysis; nonetheless, it is an example of biographical criticism in the mode described above and an important book in many ways. Millgate begins with a biographical chapter on "The Career" and follows that with discussions of Faulkner's books and stories. The book seems most significant today in the way that it frames the basic and long-standing story of Faulkner's life on which so many Faulkner critics, including myself, were schooled. Like Coughlan, Millgate sees the seeds of Faulkner's great talent and eventual status planted very early, by his legendary and author-ial great-grandfather, and he finds them early in Faulkner's career (for Millgate, in *The Marble Faun*). For Millgate, *Sartoris/Flags in the Dust* reveals Faulkner finding his true subject, his "little postage stamp of native soil," and the inevitable step into greatness comes with *The Sound and the Fury.* Moreover, Millgate parallels this literary biography with what is now also a familiar story of Faulkner's biography. He postulates the influence of family and describes the early years of searching and posing and Phil Stone. He announces the ascension into the realm of art and presents the great, productive years of the 1930s com-plicated by Hollywood. He links the 1940s to Cowley and concludes by associ-ating the 1950s with race, public persona, and fading power. Unlike Coughlan and Cowley before him, Millgate makes a strong case that Faulkner is not a regional writer or a product of the Lost Generation. Like a growing chorus of Faulkner scholars at the time, he argues movingly for Faulkner's achievement and claims it exists in artistic prowess and moral vision. Uniquely, perhaps because of his own understanding of the great British social realist novels of the nineteenth century, Millgate does not see the second half of Faulkner's career as the serious fading of artistic power that many who follow him would. (He sees Faulkner's failing talent only revealed in *The Town* and *The Mansion*.) In these ways his book was both a product of the viewpoint that inspired it and a ground-breaking work that left its own mark on history.

To emphasize the ways in which Millgate's work, and that of those like him, was somewhat a product of its time, one need only see how his influences are revealed, on one hand, by some information in which he simply is not interested and does not pursue, and on the other hand, by information and experiences he downplays or ignores. By labeling the early years as apprentice work, as *only* apprentice work one might say, Millgate does not give them serious analytical attention—as later critics will. Millgate seems to think that this work might detract from an argument about Faulkner's greatness. By leaning heavily on Faulkner's own remarks about his loss of energy and interest in the 1950s, Mill-gate also does not look as intently on the artistic productions of these years as some have begun to do now. He also completely downplays Faulkner's drinking and by so doing does not complicate the organic-growth-to-greatness story in ways that now seem obvious. Finally, he omits virtually any discussion of Faulkner's troubled marriage and relationship with Estelle and the various affairs Faulkner had throughout his life. These topics have since opened many doors to explorations into Faulkner's attitudes, influences on his creativity, and various themes in the fiction. Millgate's emphasis is on literary history and literary biography—the ways in which the two illuminate and relate to one another. Information that might complicate the seamless unity of these realms is avoided. Many investigations into these omitted areas in Millgate stem from critics interested in psychology and psychobiography [see chapter 8]. These critics' viewpoint opened these doors, shed light into places left dark by Millgate's lens, and generally link biography and fiction in much more intimate ways. An early example of this approach is Richardson's book.

William Faulkner: The Journey to Self-Discovery (1969) shares various features with books of its time, the 1960s. Its overall approach is influenced by the negative reputation Faulkner had for some time, and its attempt is to correct certain misperceptions and misunderstandings about Faulkner the man and Faulkner the artist. At the same time, it was new, different from the work of those like Cowley and Millgate, and it introduced certain other points and ideas that too have become influential for later Faulkner critics. What was most new about Richardson's book was its combination of the aesthetic and psychological where the two approaches were meant to act as illuminating mirrors, the psychological illuminating Faulkner's work and the work itself illuminating his personal attitudes and motivations. Richardson focused exclusively and extensively on the early work, what he called the juvenilia, as a means to understand the mature artist. He thus began a trend followed later by such critics as Judith Sensibar and James Watson. He also characterizes Faulkner as being caught between the fabled past and the shabby present and argues that because of this condition Faulkner had to write himself into being. These ideas later find their way into many critics' work (Judith Sensibar, Richard Gray, Daniel Singal, Kevin Railey, James Watson). Finally, Richardson offers reasonable explanations for Faulkner's various poses during the early 1920s as aspects of his struggle to identity—an idea with which, in *William Faulkner: Self-Presentation and Performance,* Watson also agrees—and reads the personal struggle into the early work, most notably *The Marble Faun,* "Cathay," and *A Green Bough.* Richardson's book combines reasonable psychological analysis with good close reading of some of Faulkner's early work, especially the poetry. By focusing on the relationship between the mind and the work, Richardson does fit with the general framework guiding literary criticism. He essentially wants to understand and illuminate the spirit of Faulkner's work and claim that it was always there, even early in the development. However, he connects a type of biographical investigation and literary analysis in productive ways and links them much more closely than any other critic had to this point. In his preface, he extends his wish that his book might contribute to the making of a definitive biography of William Faulkner. He did not have long to wait.

Joseph Blotner's two-volume *Faulkner: A Biography* (1974) was and is a monumental work of 2,115 pages done by a friend and an admirer of William Faulkner. Every biography written after this one would have to contend with it, and none has replaced it in importance—though others have added points of view and explored in more detail previously ignored aspects of Faulkner's life. Blotner himself followed this work with a revised, updated, and condensed version, which in many ways is a better work. Blotner claims that his 1974 book is a biography of William Faulkner's works as well as of their creator. This introductory remark indicates that underneath it all Blotner feels, and perhaps knows, that the life, no matter how well and meticulously it is narrated, simply cannot explain the power and mystery and origin of the art. Despite his claims, Blotner's books are more biography than criticism, and in this regard they are grounded in the basic premises of the romantic/modernist paradigm. Blotner's critical comments are summary and descriptive in nature. The tone of both books is one of reverence and awe for Faulkner, the artist and the man.

The power of the first biography is its encyclopedic nature, its meticulous (some would say relentless) chronological rendering of the life of Faulkner's forebears and the detailed account of the long story of Faulkner's own journey. Nonetheless, Blotner always functions under the premise that Faulkner's "real" life was his writing. His first book is told from a polite, even prudish, point of view and offers little explanation for or hypothesizing about some of the more troubling events it relates. In fact, presentation, not explanation, is the predominant mode Blotner always takes. He seems unwilling to tread on Faulkner in any way that might tarnish the claim to artist, genius, and moralist. The later book offers both corrections and improvements. It deletes much—plot summaries, summaries of reviews, and irrelevant explorations into some family members' lives. It adds more interviews with and letters from people connected to Faulkner and creates a more dramatic story, especially regarding Estelle, Hollywood, Cowley's role, and Faulkner's life in the 1950s. Blotner still seems at times a hesitant narrator of the life, especially when it comes to Faulkner's relationships with women, but the second volume is much better on Estelle, Meta Carpenter Wilde, and Faulkner's other relationships with women.

In his "Monument of the Famous Writer" (1981), Dennis Petrie argues somewhat convincingly that Blotner's attempts at factual narration and objective method are types of rhetorical strategies that serve the overall function the book is designed to serve: to secure Faulkner's status and to verify Blotner's own insightful sensibility. Judith Sensibar has been in the process of revealing just how intensely the angle of vision taken by most biographers has severely downplayed Estelle Oldham's contribution to Faulkner's life. Though she does not make the claim overtly, her work verifies the influence of patriarchal values within Faulkner biographical scholarship and operating on Blotner himself. And Matthew Ramsey (see below) has revealed how omission of factual information in a book posing to be encyclopedic in its recitation of facts can serve various ideological functions—such as presenting a specific version of masculinity. Blotner's book, then, reveals both the assertive power of the romantic/modernist paradigm, placing Faulkner on the hallowed ground reserved for monumental figures, and the potentially repressive nature of this paradigm. Blotner himself would have admitted his own oversights, I suspect, and his book cannot at all be condemned for its perspective. In fact, all biographical criticism has been indebted to Blotner and will continue to be for some time it seems.

Clearly, Blotner is someone who deserves space to himself when discussing biographical criticism of Faulkner, not only for the biography itself but also for the other work he has done over the years. Two years after the first biography, he offered in "The Sole Owner and Proprietor" (1976) a shorthand version of the links he finds between Faulkner's life and art. He also published a discussion of the links between Faulkner's family and the fiction in "The Falkners and the Fictional Families" (1976). In 1980 he offered a short appreciation of Faulkner, the man, in "Did You See Him Plain?" A discussion of the possible biographical and personal sources of Faulkner's genius is offered in "The Sources of Faulkner's Genius" (1980). All of these essays are more auto/biographical in nature with little overt criticism. An essay more in the mold of biographical criticism is "William Faulkner: Life and Art" (1986). In this essay, Blotner explores women in Faulkner's life and various characterizations of women in the fiction; he also references various essays written by women about Faulkner's depictions. In 1990 Blotner returned to the Faulkner and Yoknapatawpha series to write "Faulkner and Popular Culture" [see chapter 11]. There, he explores various types of popular culture to which Faulkner was exposed as a child, connections between Faulkner and various forms of popular culture as he developed as a writer, and Faulkner's feeling about pop culture. Later, as he was turning to extensive work about Robert Penn Warren, Blotner published "William Faulkner and Robert Penn Warren as Literary Artists" (1996), in which he compared the details, similarities and differences of the two Southern writers' lives. Blotner also edited Faulkner's letters (see *Selected Letters of William Faulkner* [1977]) and teamed with Frederick Gwynn to produce *Faulkner in the University* (1959), comprised of transcripts of Faulkner's lectures and comments at the University of Virginia.

The first major work of biographical criticism to benefit directly from Blotner's work was *Faulkner: The Transfiguration of Biography* (1979) by Judith Wittenberg. Wittenberg based her story on Blotner's narrative of Faulkner's life, but she was the first to apply a rich and nuanced psychological approach to the entire career. Richardson's early work had combined psychological concerns with overt statements about the absolute necessity of close reading, and he was careful to illustrate that process. Thus, his work fit with New Critical paradigms. Wittenberg's work was obviously analytical and interpretive, but it was different. It was not wholeheartedly embraced at the time. Seemingly sensitive to the critical current, she is often quite careful to explain and justify her method. This method, psychogenesis, is concerned with the promptings from the individual's subconscious that become important for and in the creative process itself. She sees Faulkner's inner life as a living force in his art and claims that a writer's psychology ultimately has aesthetic ramifications because it helps us understand the recurrent psychological patterns in his fiction. Like others, Wittenberg reads Faulkner's writing as inspired by a sense of loss and trauma and as a means to cope with that condition. She claims that in its essence all Faulkner's work is autobiographical, and her title ultimately refers to the attempt to read Faulkner's work from beginning to end as topography of his inner being.

Wittenberg bases her approach to a certain extent on Edmund Wilson's ideas as explained in "The Wound and the Bow," and she offers a strong and viable interpretation of Faulkner's life and art. Her story articulates some common-places in Faulkner criticism only more recently questioned, such as the assertion that Faulkner's later work, after *Go Down, Moses,* lacks the power of the earlier work and that after Faulkner worked out his problems his emphasis became the desire to educate and enlighten. Wittenberg's work was also based on the assumption that Faulkner's true life was revealed in the fiction itself, where the signs and indications of the important and (importantly) invisible struggles were to be discerned. Thus, a major work of biographical criticism had ambiva-lent feelings about biography. Nonetheless, her work was a major point in the history of biographical criticism about Faulkner because her viewpoint allowed her to explore Faulkner in what were then uncharted ways.

Another major contribution around this same time was David Minter's *William Faulkner: His Life and Work* (1980)—an early glimpse of which was published in 1979 as "Faulkner, Childhood, and the Making of *The Sound and the Fury.*" Like Wittenberg's book, this one announces its intention and method as one that seeks to link Faulkner's life and work and to see them as mutually illuminating. Unlike Wittenberg's, though, this book does not announce a strictly psychological orientation. In fact, it does not announce any overt orien-tation. Nonetheless, it has one. Simply put, Minter reads Faulkner's life and development as the portrait of the artist. One wonders if he reads it this way because Faulkner himself read it this way. He relies heavily on Faulkner's own comments about his life and art, which by this point had become easily available to Minter because of previous publications of interviews, letters, essays, and early prose of Faulkner. One also wonders if Minter read it this way because this view was a prevailing manner through which to view artists and their lives. Either way, his interpretation resonated, and it was generally more favorably received at the time than Wittenberg's book.

Minter's Faulkner is deeply connected to region and an identifiable place, that home that is the South. That identification becomes associated with nature and the woods and with family and childhood. As Faulkner enters that coming-of-age moment, he realizes that he will soon lose the woods to history and soon lose his view of his family as united due to his growing awareness of the real tension between his mother and father. Thus, stepping into the future for Faulkner becomes a challenge, a consummation devoutly not to be wished. Minter reads Faulkner's life thematically in terms linking it to such literary char-acters as Hamlet and Prufrock: biography is read in terms of literary history. In his early years, before 1925, Faulkner is both a romantic nostalgically yearning for the past and a modernist despising the advent of industrialism. Like that developed by those of both eras, the answer lies in the turn to the imagination: human beings need larger participation in the life of the mind and more involvement with imagination over the mundane facts of life. For Minter, Faulkner becomes Faulkner, if you will, when he turns to that arena that is truly representative of his own true self and that allows his imagination to flourish in fertilized ground—as he does with the Yoknapatawpha works. These books reflect both the internal dimensions of Faulkner's process and the struggles with the external. The titles for Minter's chapters reveal the stages in this overall process and the romantic/modernist paradigm from which he operates: "Versions of the Artist, 1925–1926," "The Self's Own Lamp, 1928–1929," and "Three Trips to Babylon, 1932–1936."

In his 1994 biography (see below), Richard Gray stresses the ways in which history and autobiography mutually interrelate and illuminate one another. In Minter's book, clearly, biography, specifically the biography of great men, is history. In this manner he reveals the way in which he was influenced by the longstanding Romantic/Victorian influence on biography as a genre, initiated and articulated by Thomas Carlyle. This influence also partly explains the focus in Faulkner biography and criticism on Faulkner as an individual, one might say as an isolated individual. Since Faulkner is a great man, this view postulates, he is more influenced by his internal struggle and growth than by interactions with others and with the world at large. The status of genius allows transcendence of the personal, the social, and the historical. In this view, the cultural codes through which one develops identity and the conflicts one faces and resolves with forces and people in the world become more or less only background that the artist encounters and overcomes. From this set of assumptions, these forces and experiences do not, of themselves, constitute an artist. Rather, he has a core and coherent personality that become increasingly manifest as he develops. These broad assumptions explain why the main branches of Faulkner biography and criticism have been those influenced by the romantic/modernist paradigm and the psychological one—both of which focus on the individual and the artist as unique individual by nature. These are still the most operative and influential forces on biographical criticism today—though cracks in the foundation have appeared. Nonetheless, after the works described above had set the foundation, as biographical criticism of Faulkner entered the 1980s, it began to expand and explode. Faulkner had not only been established as an artist, a genius, and an ambassador; he also had become an industry.

Of course, the 1970s saw not only the publication of these major books; other work was being published as well. Jackson J. Benson published "Quentin Compson: Self-Portrait of a Young Artist's Emotions" (1971), where links implied by many between Faulkner and Estelle and Quentin's feeling in *The Sound and the Fury* were made explicit and directly. Louis D. Rubin published "William Faulkner: Discovery of a Man's Vocation" (1976), in which he links Faulkner's development as a writer to Faulkner's questions about masculinity. Charles Peavy published *Go Slow Now: Faulkner and the Race Question* (1971). This book explores comments about race, the South, and Mississippi that

Faulkner made in interviews and essays, and analyzes them in conjunction with the ways in which Faulkner explores race and black Americans in his fiction. It is an even-handed account, oddly alone in its topic and analysis for some time. It initiates a branch within biographical criticism that gets increasingly explored only many years later. Also, in the mid-1970s, Thomas McHaney published his excellent study, *William Faulkner's* The Wild Palms: *A Study* (1975). In the introduction and chapter 1, McHaney explores the biographical backgrounds to *The Wild Palms* (which has since been given the title Faulkner originally intended for it—*If I Forget Thee, Jerusalem*). He draws out the connections between this novel's context and the time period of the mid-1920s, discussing at some length the influence of Faulkner's experiences with Sherwood Anderson and Ernest Hemingway. McHaney also draws the connection, which Carvel Collins fully explores in 1981, between the feelings Faulkner had for Helen Baird and Meta Carpenter Wilde and the themes of this book. McHaney makes the case that *The Wild Palms* is a much more important book than it had been seen to be, both for its relationship to Faulkner's life and for its development of his style. He and Noel Polk have been responsible for shedding new and significant light on this book—and for getting the original title reinstated.[2]

During the 1980s, short, focused discussions accompanied the work of notable Faulkner scholars who have produced significant biographical criticism. In 1980, David Wyatt published a study about authority and authorship that includes the chapter, "Faulkner and the Burdens of the Past." Wyatt's concerns are with how a writer comes to develop authority over materials to be a self-conscious author. To this end he analyzes the weight of Faulkner's biographical past, particularly the weight of a son having to avenge an action against a father. Wyatt links Faulkner to his grandfather, J.W.T. Falkner (rather than to his great-grandfather), who did not avenge his own father's death, and claims this inaction haunted the developing author. Wyatt links the Burden genealogy in *Light in August* to that of the Sartorises in *Sartoris* in order to justify his claims, and he reads the resolution of this conflict in *The Unvanquished*. Here, Bayard Sartoris, and Faulkner, assert that symbolic and internalized actions can take the place of literal ones, that *not* doing is good and understanding is forgiveness. In this move, Faulkner fully established his authority. In 1981, Karl Zender published an article, "Faulkner at Forty: The Artist at Home." (This article became part of chapter 3 in his later book, *The Crossing of the Ways* [1989], a book not dominated by biographical criticism.) Here, he cites Faulkner's internal conflict between his artistic and social identities—much-documented in Blotner—and argues that much of it was self-imposed because of the image Faulkner had of himself. In this way, his reading of the biography differs markedly from Blotner, who mainly blames society for Faulkner's problems. Zender then claims that this internal conflict becomes externalized in the conflict between Roth Edmunds and Lucas Beauchamp in *Go Down, Moses* and is resolved with Ike McCaslin. As Ike has similarities to the later Gavin Stevens, this move also represents the symbolic avowal of Faulkner's diminishing artistic power—a point that is a major theme of Zender's book. Also in 1981, Robert Hamblin mined the interviews and essays to uncover many of Faulkner's comments about vocation; he interrelates them to scenes and aspects of the fiction to conclude that Faulkner settled on writing as the means to participate in the resistance to death and time through creativity. In the same collection in which Hamblin's essay appears, *"A Cosmos of My Own,"* Panthea Reid Broughton has a rather powerful essay, "Faulkner's Cubist Novels" (1981). In this essay Broughton complicates the conventional narrative of Faulkner's biography until this point by exploring that moment or period in which Faulkner stopped writing poetry and began writing prose. Her claim that Faulkner criticism's obsession with the transformation that produced *The Sound and the Fury* had blinded it to the one that occurred before that—why, that is, he stopped writing poetry and turned to prose. Her conclusion is that this move was inspired by Faulkner's rejection of a destructive romanticism and the embrace, which took some time to finalize, of the modernism embodied by cubism. Broughton weaves discussions of biography with close readings of Faulkner's two introductions to *The Sound and the Fury,* reveals a wide knowledge of artistic movements, and discusses a number of Faulkner novels—*As I Lay Dying* and *The Wild Palms* included. It is an original essay based on sound scholarship.

An essay similar to Broughton's in its points and conclusions, though written from an entirely different angle, is Jay Martin's "'The Whole Burden of Man's History of His Impossible Heart's Desire': The Early Life of William Faulkner" (1982). Martin takes a focused psychoanalytical approach [see chapter 8] in this essay to examine exactly the same time period in which Broughton is interested. Using both academic and personal biographies about Faulkner, Martin theorizes that the severity of Faulkner's mother and the distance from his father led to the imitative early writings in which Faulkner yearned for death rather than life. He sees the flowering of Faulkner's art, as exemplified by *Flags in the Dust* and beyond, as being related to the regaining of Estelle's love, an occurrence that reopened channels of eroticism and rekindled the optimism of Faulkner's youth. Martin offers some fascinating ideas and gives to Estelle a positive influence few others, except Sensibar, grant to her. Finally, Michel Gresset, a well-known and prolific French critic of Faulkner, published "Faulkner's Self-Portraits" (1986). In this essay he steps into a more contemporary understanding of autobiography as (just) another form of life-writing, one that is interesting but not necessarily privileged because the author wrote it. He sees self portraits as signed representations of the exchange between a subject and a subject-as-object, and explores his sense of Faulkner's self portraits. He identifies three instances of Faulknerian self portraits and traces them to two personae that emerge from the early poetry and remain constant throughout Faulkner's career: a puny figure creeping along the earth and a superbly distanced suzerain.

Other essays published during the 1980s lean more toward traditional biography but should be noted. Donald P. Duclos published "Damned Sartorises! Damned Falkners!" (1985), which draws connections between fictional and real families.[3] Louis Daniel Brodsky, a famous collector of Faulkner materials, published 2 essays. In "Faulkner's Life Masks" (1986), he explores Faulkner's lifelong concern, one might say obsession, with failure and concludes that Faulkner never quite saw his role as a writer overriding that sense of inadequacy. Then, in "Faulkner and the Racial Crisis" (1988), Brodsky publishes for the first time excerpts from a group of letters that he says help clarify Faulkner's position on Civil Rights in the late 1950s. In 1986, Carl E. Rollyson Jr. published "'Counterpull': Estelle and William Faulkner," an article that points to a growing interest in Estelle as an active agent in the Faulkner life story. Finally, Michel Gresset also published "A Public Man's Private Voice: Faulkner's Letters to Else Jonsson" (1987), a much more biographical essay than the one by Gresset described previously. He studies 24 letters Faulkner wrote to Jonsson, a woman whom Faulkner met in Sweden while there for the Nobel Prize ceremony, and analyzes their style for what they tell us about Faulkner's quality of thought.

The 1980s also saw the publication of a number of books that utilized work from the past, extended ideas and areas within Faulkner biographical criticism, and developed new approaches and perspectives. Walter Taylor's 1983 *Faulkner's Search for a South* frames Faulkner's subject as basically the story of the rednecks versus the aristocrats, as the biographers had said Phil Stone had framed it for Faulkner in the late 1920s. He also brings a significant focus to the question of Faulkner and race, one that was being explored by others outside the realm of biographical criticism. Taylor situates Faulkner's family within the context of Mississippi political history as well as its virulent history of racism, and he utilizes Faulkner's fiction, commentaries, and comments for his analysis. He argues that Faulkner's South as depicted in *Sartoris* (not, surprisingly, in *Flags in the Dust,* published in 1973) is really the South to which Faulkner felt closest and with which he identified his entire life. That assertion of the conservative nature of Faulkner's vision basically shapes all the analyses of later novels, and Taylor feels that Faulkner never really confronted the horrors and injustices of race relations in Mississippi. Taylor's book treats virtually all Faulkner's novels through *The Reivers;* it is thematic in nature, and its tone is much more decidedly critical than had been the general norm in Faulkner criticism at this point, a trend that continues today. Taylor's general view certainly is not one that assumes great artists are moral visionaries, and his book runs counter to much earlier work in Faulkner criticism that focused on aesthetic and/or moral aspects of Faulkner's fiction. That Taylor was doing something "different" seems verified by the topics explored in the 1984 publication, *New Directions in Faulkner Studies,* edited by Doreen Fowler and Ann J. Abadie. Calls for more focused studies of Faulkner's modernist aesthetics and the potential for psychological studies abound—the dominant directions in Faulkner studies as I have delineated them are still operative. There are no calls for thematic or biographical criticism. Thus, though Taylor's treatment of the novels might be seen to be a bit too thin, not formal enough, the book holds interest, I would argue, for the way it interweaves discussions of life and art throughout Faulkner's career and for its unique, perhaps even bold, treatment of its subject. (Two essays written approximately ten years after Taylor's book confirm that he was indeed unique for even forming a strong opinion about Faulkner's attitude toward race. In "Faulkner's Conflicting

Views of the Equality of Color" [1989], Reginald Martin explores interviews with and articles about Faulkner, all concerning the question of race in America, and ends with virtually no conclusion at all. Arthur Kinney's "Faulkner and Racism" [1993] explores the fictional treatments of race to try to determine Faulkner's view and concludes that Faulkner was conflicted but most likely well-intentioned.)

Another interesting book in various ways is Max Putzel's *Genius of Place: William Faulkner's Triumphant Beginnings* (1985). Putzel divides Faulkner's career into four periods: the early, initiatory (but uninteresting) period of 1918 through 1924; the most varied and significant period of 1924 through 1931; the years of 1932 through 1942, in which Faulkner wrote his greatest tragic novel and his greatest comic novel; and the declining years after 1942. In this way, he breaks with earlier critics who saw the production of *The Sound and the Fury,* rather than the move to prose generally, as the significant moment of Faulkner's career and aligns himself indirectly with Panthea Reid Broughton. At the same time, he maintains the notion that the period after 1942 shows Faulkner in his decline, a point only later critics will begin to reassess. Putzel's focus is on the second period, in which Faulkner produced the greatest amount of significant work, including both long and short fiction, and during which, he argues, Faulkner only gradually came to understand and define his place, Yoknapatawpha. He links the life experiences of this period with Faulkner's artistic experiments, traces Faulkner's exposure to poetry and literary magazines, and reads published and unpublished materials, short and long fiction in a step-by-step, chronological process as a means to uncover Faulkner's imaginative development of place. Putzel defines place as a personal merging of Faulkner's ongoing experience with the memory of early childhood and adolescence filled with intense feelings. Unlike Judith Sensibar, Putzel sees little value in the early poetry period, and, unlike a horde of Faulkner critics, Putzel feels that Faulkner's own comments about life and art are more harmful than helpful when analyzing Faulkner's work—that they are, in fact, a major source of misunderstanding. Putzel also articulates a major premise of Faulkner studies in general at this point in time and argues against it. In examining a text, he explains, most people feel that one must resist the temptation to lug in biography or other extraneous matter. But, he counters, there are moments when it seems absolutely clear that there are connections between art and life, that certain characters and situations come from keenly felt, private needs of Faulkner's own. In this move, Putzel argues against the general trend to exclude biographical justification for certain literary analytical insights. That he makes this move in such a conscious and articulated way is refreshing. He basically explains the overall context in which biographical criticism found itself, as well as the continuing motivation for its production.

Michael Grimwood also offers a full-length study in the late 1980s. His *Heart in Conflict: Faulkner's Struggles with Vocation* (1987) presents an original view about the story of Faulkner's life and art. Grimwood argues that Faulkner's vocation—his sense of himself as a man and writer—was deeply connected to the literary genre of the pastoral. This literary and pastoral identity, so to speak, enabled him to avoid being identified with the middle class and gave him a means through which to find connection to the world around him. Faulkner's relationship to the poor white and black communities of rural Mississippi was incorporated into this literary identity, and he was able to envision a unified social world. When he experienced a midlife upheaval in that social construction, Faulkner's literary power began to decline. Grimwood, like other critics, reads the decline of Faulkner's artistic output as occurring after *Go Down, Moses,* but he analyzes this decline as resulting from Faulkner's recognition of the contradictions within himself and his cultural heritage. The psychic and social pressures inherent in pastoralism as a genre were exploded, both psychologically and socially, for Faulkner in the 1940s, and he was not able to contain the effects of this explosion to create art without parody. Grimwood combines psychological theory, mostly that of Erik Erikson, with sociological analysis and biographical information to argue that Faulkner's story is essentially one of genius divided against itself. He analyzes early work such as *The Marble Faun,* "Carcassonne," and "The Leg," and combines that with readings of what he calls the anthology novels—*The Wild Palms, The Hamlet, Knight's Gambit,* and *Go Down, Moses.* Thus, though he accepts and continues the accepted story of the trajectory of Faulkner's career, he explains it differently and treats a very different range of books than is usually addressed. Grimwood also goes against the grain of much Faulkner criticism by essentially claiming that Faulkner, the great artist, was not able to form, eventually, a coherent personality.

In a prelude to the postmodern understanding of the relation between Faulkner's life and art taken by Hönnighausen (*Faulkner: Masks*), Joseph Urgo offers a compelling reinterpretation of the latter part of Faulkner's career in *Faulkner's Apocrypha: A Fable, Snopes, and the Spirit of Human Rebellion* (1989). Though not exploring details of Faulkner's biography, Urgo argues that Malcolm Cowley established the general frame for the story of Faulkner's life. Cowley, Urgo claims, canonized Faulkner as a sagacious old man with strong humanist fiber who believed in God and did not mean to drink too much. Further, this interpretation influenced Faulkner criticism to such an extent that the man's character and genius have remained mysteries to all his biographers. What all biographers have missed, Urgo argues, is that there were multiple Faulkners, many Faulkners in fact. In seeking the single authoritative definition of the man, biographers have dismissed Faulkner's guises and roles as ways for him to hide his true self. Yet, as is clearly manifested in both his life and fiction, truth for Faulkner was always a matter of perspective, a multifaceted revolving structure of stories and images all existing simultaneously. Basing his analyses on the surprisingly simple yet original insight, Urgo claims that in the later fiction Faulkner turns to creating an apocrypha—a political and ideological alternative to what he considered to be the totalitarianism of modern society. For Urgo, Faulkner's apocrypha stands as a response to the figure Cowley created, as a challenge to what was defined to be real by virtually any authority. Faulkner's quest, in fact, became centered on resisting authority, resisting the reification of

meaning, and raising the acts of interpretation and expression to moral imperatives. Besides the works referred to in his title, Urgo also offers enlightening discussion and insight about *As I Lay Dying, Go Down, Moses, Intruder in the
Dust, Pylon,* and *The Reivers.*

Reviewing Faulkner in the 1980s, one notes also the work of a few critics
whose efforts in biographical criticism extend beyond an individual work—
Judith Sensibar, Noel Polk, and James G. Watson. Sensibar began her publish-
ing career in biographical criticism about Faulkner in 1979 with "Pierrot and the
Marble Faun: Another Fragment." In the same year as her 1982 dissertation on
Faulkner, she published "William Faulkner, Poet to Novelist: An Impostor
Becomes an Artist." All of this work came to fruition in a groundbreaking work,
The Origins of Faulkner's Art (1984). On one hand, Sensibar's ideas fit with earlier and traditional ideas about Faulkner's life and art as she asserts that the
genius/artist who produced the fiction existed within the tyro apprentice who
produced the poetry. On the other hand, she explores in perceptive and unique
ways the complicated web of emotion and psychology existing at the heart of
much of Faulkner's life and art at least until the writing of *Absalom, Absalom!*
This web includes idealizations and reifications of women and love, ambivalent
or even twisted attitudes toward sexuality and women, and the distinctive effects
of various women on Faulkner. Sensibar argues that Faulkner's early life was
marked by trauma and its constellation was similar to that described in the psychoanalytical theory of the Impostor. She uses this theory and Freudian theory
to uncover relationships between Faulkner's life and the early work, focusing on
The Marble Faun, The Lilacs, and *Vision in Spring.* She discusses at length
Faulkner's relationship with his mother, interviews Faulkner's daughter Jill, and
uses quotations from Meta Carpenter Wilde to unpack Faulkner's attitudes
toward women. Ultimately, Sensibar argues that Faulkner was able to transcend
the limitations and challenges he faced as a young man/Impostor and poet only
by turning to fiction. In fiction he was able to externalize his own conflicts in his
characters, and this externalization gave him an awareness and a consciousness
he otherwise would not have developed. Through this process Faulkner found
the means to write himself into being, into history. Sensibar's work brought
attention and sophisticated analysis to Faulkner's early poetry in ways only
touched upon by Richardson's 1969 book. Her focus is on the growth of
Faulkner's mind, the definite relationship between the narrative experiments of
the poetry and the later fiction, and on the complex intertwining of life and art.
Her sense of the power of Faulkner's writing as an agent in his growth and
change is a theme influential to many, including James Watson, Jay Watson, and
in my own work. Sensibar's efforts also point to the ways in which Faulkner
struggled with definitive features of his external world, the ways these were
overdetermined by that world and his place in it, and the **agency** Faulkner
exhibited in confronting these.

Sensibar's originality and importance for Faulkner biographical criticism is
verified in the work that followed her book. In her introduction to Faulkner's
Vision in Spring (1984), she encapsulates some of her book but more pointedly

connects Faulkner's poetry to his feelings for women and attitudes about love. *Vision in Spring,* on one hand, is part of Faulkner's process to clear imaginative space for himself as he explored the forms his imagination must embrace in order to see poetry and writing as the moral substitute for physical action. On the other hand, this poetry collection is symbolic of the ongoing, lifelong relationship between Faulkner's imagination and women, revealing the importance of the imaginary re-creation of woman in language. Poetry, for Faulkner, was the language of impossible dreams, the largest of which was, perhaps, love. Sensibar followed this work with "'Drowsing Maidenhead Symbol's Self': Faulkner and the Fictions of Love" (1989). In this essay she develops even more what she argues in the introduction and what was implied in her book—her deep sense of the influence of women on Faulkner and his idea of love. Sensibar draws from interviews she had been conducting with William and Estelle's daughter Jill Faulkner Summers and from her own growing dissatisfaction with biographical treatments of the women in Faulkner's life. In a move congenial to this essay, Sensibar asserts that Faulkner studies have been dominated by the essentially romantic view of the Great (Male) American Writer. She is sensitive to the ways in which biographical criticism has been shaped by ideas about individuality and artistic genius first developed in nineteenth-century Britain and argues that this emphasis has blinded critics to the effects and importance of relationships for Faulkner and his creativity. Specifically, she explains the stereotypical version of Faulkner's relationship with Estelle and challenges it rather convincingly with fresh (feminist) insight, questions, and biographical research [see chapter 9]. She argues that there were four major women in Faulkner's life—his two "mothers," Maud Butler and Caroline Clark Barr, his wife Estelle, and his daughter Jill—who deeply influenced him. In this essay she points to questions and concerns she will continue to develop in later work and focuses on Faulkner's relationship with Estelle. She argues that the relationship was much more rich and inspirational to Faulkner than any of the biographers to date have made it appear. Rich, provocative, and grounded in sound scholarship, this work built anticipation for Sensibar's longer project, which has yet to appear. It also points to potentially fascinating directions in Faulkner biographical criticism, ones that look at the ways Faulkner's relationships with other people and with the external world shaped his life and art, a potential realized in Richard Gray's book (discussed later), especially in his discussion of *The Wild Palms.*

Sensibar again utilizes her growing awareness of the influence of women on Faulkner's development in a 1990 essay, "Faulkner's Fictional Photographs: Playing with Difference." Here, she explains the way in which the South relegated the creation of art to women, claiming that "real" men did not create art, and discusses the way this cultural paradigm influenced and was undermined by Faulkner through the use of fictional photographs. Using biographical information to develop a case that Faulkner's artistic inspirations and influences came from his grandmother, mother, and future wife, Sensibar argues that Faulkner often used photographs—his famous posing sessions—as ways to reveal the masculinity his culture demanded from him. These photos asserted an identity that allowed him to create art without suspicion or question. She extends her insights into a discussion of Faulkner's use of fictional photographs—in *The Marionettes, Absalom, Absalom!,* and *Sanctuary*—and explains how he subverted gender classifications and challenged Southern attitudes about art. Pictures allowed Faulkner to say what he wanted to say without using words. Furthering and developing her ideas yet again, Sensibar convincingly questions some traditional biographical givens—that Faulkner's great-grandfather was the major influence on him becoming an artist and that his genius flowered in somewhat of a cultural vacuum. Sensibar also moves away from that romantic/modernist paradigm by highlighting the ways in which Faulkner became the writer we know by interacting with the real conditions and the real people around him and negotiating a sense of himself within a specific time and place. She reveals how viewing Faulkner from a different perspective than one applied previously can offer rich insights indeed.

When turning to the work of Noel Polk, one turns to a critic whose life work has, essentially, been his work in Faulkner studies. I isolate here the 5 essays I think best fall into the category of biographical criticism. They begin with his work on *Sanctuary,* "Afterword" (1981) and "The Space Between *Sanctuary*" (1985). The "Afterword" to Polk's editing of the original *Sanctuary* text, published with the permission of Faulkner's daughter Jill, mainly and briefly addresses the question of Faulkner's revisions to the original. Though there are literary motivations cited, Polk also agrees with André Bleikasten's assessment that Faulkner was moving to exorcise narcissistic self-involvement in the revisions and that the later version connects more directly with Faulkner's concerns at the time, 1930, when the revisions occurred. These implications are more fully explored in "The Space Between *Sanctuary.*" As the title connotes, this essay speaks to the period between the completion of the original version and its revision 18 months later. Polk speculates that one reason Faulkner revised, had to revise, one might say, was that S*anctuary* was intolerably "close." Polk proceeds to unpack some similarities between Horace Benbow—who more dominates the original text than the revised—and Faulkner and uses Freudian theory to present some possible ways to examine these similarities [see chapter 8]. Polk argues that certain themes and concerns exposed in the original were powerful enough to find their ways into other work being written during this 18-month period. He reveals that what Faulkner cut in the revision were those sections dealing with Horace's childhood, his fantasies, his parents and his relationship to Popeye, who serves as Horace's dark twin. These incidents reveal the ways in which this book came too close for Faulkner to leave it as it had been originally written.

In "Man in the Middle: Faulkner and the Southern White Moderate" (1987), Polk discusses the "hellishly complex" topic of Faulkner and race. He explores this topic by examining the interviews, Faulkner's comments, and the fiction as others before (and after) him do. In one way Polk's comments in this essay link him to others who do not really form any opinion free from the influence of the overall attitude toward Faulkner and artists in general. These influences lead him to make some conclusions about great artists being much more complex than any one statement indicates and that Faulkner was generally a good person doing the best he could in a complicated time. These conclusions are perhaps correct, and Polk offers some good evidence for his opinion of Faulkner's personal feelings on the subject. In another way, he offers original insights and penetrating analysis. Not only does he completely criticize the attention given to Gavin Stevens in various discussions on this topic, but also he points to the unexplored possibility that Faulkner was attempting in his public statements to appeal to the blue-collar citizenry who would never connect to the modernism of the fiction. From this angle Polk offers a wonderful exposition of "Pantaloon in Black" as a story attempting to go behind the stereotype of the Southern lawman, the Southern redneck. The story becomes potentially instructive to all, including the redneck himself, when seen from this perspective. It also offers a composite of Faulkner's dual and sharp sense of how the world should be and how it actually was, a condition that is hard for any of us to imagine now. Polk's general conclusions come from his own deeper and more significantly appreciative sense of Faulkner, the man and artist, than many other critics on this subject.

Other biographical criticism from Polk comes in the 1990s. In "'Polysyllabic and Verbless Patriotic Nonsense': Faulkner at Midcentury—His and Ours" (1995) he sees Faulkner's public personae of the early 1950s as a last and failed attempt to participate in the life of people from whom he always felt alienated. Polk argues that Faulkner realizes personally what the general in *A Fable* sees—that people cling to hope naïvely and that they are enslaved by their ideological demons and want to stay that way. Thus, what seems like a contradiction in Faulkner's career—the dark early novels and the moralistic later ones—is not one at all. Tragic vision is followed by darker visions for Faulkner. Darkness is always there, and man is doomed to his own pitiful weakness. Faulkner came to the realization that he could not change that reality, Polk argues, and thus he retreats to the strictly personal realm as a shield from that darkness. In "The Artist as Cuckold" (1996), Polk explores the way in which Faulkner may have been exploiting his own psychic life in his fiction. He argues that gender issues are much more of a concern to Faulkner than racial ones and that perhaps Thomas Sutpen repudiated Eulalia Bon because she was not a virgin, rather than because she had African ancestry as has usually been assumed. To substantiate this speculation, Polk turns to the biography and Faulkner's relationship to Estelle and argues that the neurosis that so antagonized Faulkner's youth manifests itself in many instances in the fiction. In these essays, and many others, Polk offers original analyses based on meticulous readings and knowledge of Faulkner's life. As a testament to his efforts, some of his essays, including the ones discussed here in one form or another, were collected and published as *Children of the Dark House* (1996).

The 1980s also saw the advent of another significant contributor to biographical criticism, James G. Watson. Watson's publishing career about Faulkner has always taken somewhat original and unique avenues of exploration, focusing to a large extent on Faulkner's letters and what they tell us about Faulkner and his art. In "New Orleans, *The Double Dealer,* and 'New Orleans'" (1984), Watson discusses the time Faulkner spent in New Orleans during the 1920s and the writing he did there. He argues that the New Orleans sketches that Faulkner produced need to be seen as a self-conscious artistic epigraph to works of genius, and he bases part of his argument on the biographical details surrounding this writing. That quality-minded editors of *The Double Dealer* and Faulkner himself took this work seriously points to the ways in which current literary tastes, more than the sketches themselves, have affected their reception. Watson's "'But Damn Letters Anyway': Letters and Fictions" (1987), read at the Faulkner and Yoknapatawpha Conference in 1983, was a prelude to his book, *William Faulkner, Letters and Fictions* (1987). These works are based on two notions: that all writing aspiring to be literature is autobiography, and that much writing purporting to be the first-person recording of a life is self-consciously literary. Watson reads parallels among Faulkner's private letters, uses of letters in fiction, and the themes in the novels. He examines Faulkner as a private and public man and as a master of writing in both the epistolary and novel form. Writing, in general, is a means through which Faulkner both reveals and conceals his private self. For Watson, letters exist midway between life and art, and measure the personal distance between natural experience and imaginative re-creation. Watson offers astute and interesting analysis of both real and fictional letters, and makes a strong case for the importance of letters for Faulkner and his fiction. Letters serve as a means to investigate the various personae Faulkner created for himself throughout his life and as a window into the close thematic relationship between Faulkner's life and art [see chapter 13]. Though taking this new road, Watson does not change much in terms of the interpretation of Faulkner's life story. The early years, through *Flags in the Dust,* are apprentice years; the middle years are seen to be those of artistic maturity and personal struggle; and the later years, after *Go Down, Moses,* are seen to be the ones where Faulkner struggles with his role as a public figure. These are the familiar common points of Faulkner's biography. Watson's contribution, then, is not in its original insight into the interpretation of Faulkner's life trajectory—as Sensibar and Polk often offer—but the way in which his analysis argues for a much more unified vision of the relationship between life and art in terms of themes and emotional matrices. This contribution is perhaps best illustrated in the essay, repeated in chapter 5 of the book, where he investigates *Requiem for a Nun* and its relationship to Faulkner's relationships with various women. Watson does, though, offer a comprehensive account of the relationship between letters and Faulkner's canon, covering much of the early work and most of the novels through *The Mansion.*

In 1990 Watson published a short piece in the *Faulkner Journal,* "Faulkner's 'What is the Matter with Marriage.'" It briefly describes the context surrounding Faulkner's writing of the essay and reprints it. In 1992 Watson published an edited collection of Faulkner's letters, *Thinking of Home: Faulkner's Letters to His Mother and Father, 1919–1925,* using materials made available in the Harry Ransom Humanities Research Center. That same year he published "'My Father's Unfailing Kindness': William Faulkner and the Idea of Home." In this article he argues that the usual take on Faulkner's relationship with his father, one of distance and intense tension, may not have been exactly right. Analyzing these new letters, he reveals that Faulkner's father played a more active role in Faulkner's life and imagination during the 1920s than has been previously thought. Reading letters as literary texts and fiction as a discursive way to reveal images of the self, Watson crosses the boundary between New Critical readings and contemporary perspectives on life-writing. For Watson, to some extent, Faulkner has no essence but that revealed through the complex web of discursive strategies he utilizes in both epistolary and fictional modes.

Before leaving the 1980s, two biographies need to be mentioned. In 1987 Stephen Oates published *William Faulkner, the Man and the Artist,* and in 1989 Frederick Karl published *William Faulkner: American Writer.* Oates's book seems to want to be the popular version of Faulkner's life—short and readable enough for the *Reader's Digest* crowd. It offers no new information and basically no literary criticism; it is a condensed Blotner. Karl's book, on the other hand, in its length and claims appears to want to replace Blotner's biography, a grand ambition indeed. As his title reveals, Karl seeks to redefine Faulkner as a distinctly American writer, giving shape to the life story in a way that Blotner did not. This definition means for Karl that Faulkner yearned for the order of the Old South but was astute enough to recognize its racism and that he was attracted to the dynamism of modernism but was repelled by twentieth-century materialism. Thus, like many other Americans, Faulkner sought the impossible American Eden. Karl's major thrust is both contrived and believable. The details are troubling. He seems to want to confront and explain as many details as he possibly can in 1,000 pages, linking too many instances of the life directly to the fiction through psychological speculation. Many of these are stretched, and sadly, this book's weaknesses outweigh its strengths. For Karl, defining Faulkner as American means claiming that Faulkner was not, essentially, Southern—an arguable point at best and an insulting one at worst. For Karl, Faulkner's tension-packed marriage is revealed over and over again in the fiction—a simplistic and reductive point at best. For Karl, *The Hamlet* is not a good book—a comment more connected to the dictates of high modernism than to the novel's terms and links to other forms of literature. Combined with many simply factual errors, some of these more general tendencies simplify and skim Faulkner's lifework in a manner hard to comprehend in a book this long—and hard to accept when so much other good work had been published during the 1980s. Karl shares with many others the belief that the artist, in this case Faulkner, unifies all life's conflicts and all society's contradictions in the artistic enterprise. His story of Faulkner is essentially the familiar romantic/modernist version of the artist as seer, though this time the conflicts and contradictions are American ones.

By the 1990s, it seems critics often needed to announce or indicate their position about the relationship between Faulkner's life and art. At least, often, the previous work done about Faulkner's life had to be acknowledged and the critic's sense of it had to be articulated. Moreover, contemporary literary theory in many of its manifestations was making its presence felt in Faulkner criticism and Faulkner biographical criticism. The two major efforts of the decade were

Joel Williamson's *William Faulkner and Southern History* and Richard Gray's *The Life of William Faulkner.* These works contribute significantly to the ways we do and will think about Faulkner and his life.

The potential influence of Williamson's book lies in its biographical and historical efforts, and the book seems to reveal both the strengths and weaknesses of a historian's approach to Faulkner. As I have indicated, people before Williamson have mined the Faulkner biography to great lengths. Nevertheless, Williamson succeeds in bringing new information to light and in offering another credible way to perceive Faulkner. Using the historical method of research and taking from such primary sources as real-estate sales, slave sales and contracts, military reports, cemeteries and gravestones, U.S. Census Reports, and newspapers, Williamson uncovers both small, specific facts about William Faulkner as well as forms large, speculative opinions based on sound evidence. He fills a gap that few even noticed existed by tracing the maternal side of Faulkner's ancestors. He uncovers evidence pointing to the strong possibility that Faulkner's white family was/is connected to a "shadow" family originating from a liaison between the Old Colonel and Emeline Lacy Falkner, a mixed-race woman who lived with the Falkners for a time. His detailing of the many facets of Southern history, his rooting of Faulkner's family in that history, and his linking the family so tightly to Faulkner expose the view that Faulkner can be seen to be a representative Southerner in many ways (as well as a literary genius). Williamson also opens doors of perception in regards to Faulkner's habit of posing, his relationship to Meta Wilde, and the severity of his drinking. Thus, this historian offers us a Faulkner we have not really seen before. This Faulkner differs from Blotner's view of the man who organically grew into a genius by struggling with his own mind and from Karl's view of the tortured soul struggling fruitlessly to escape his Southern past and his unconscious fixations. This Faulkner is both deeply connected to a region and deeply original in his interactions with that region.

The fruits of the historian's approach end when Williamson turns to the fiction, however. Linking Faulkner's canon to 2 general themes, the ideal versus the real and nature versus modern society, Williamson offers little to nothing new regarding Faulkner's fiction. His readings suffer from plot summary and simple connections between biography and fiction—a trait he shares with Daniel Singal (discussed later in this chapter). The last 30 years or so of literary theory have taught literary critics much about the complex relationships among history, biography, and literature, but these lessons are not applied in Williamson's analyses. These same general tendencies are exhibited in Williamson's "A Historian Looks at Faulkner" (1996), a truncated version of what he discovered about the possibility of a Falkner "shadow" family. Thus, Williamson's work gives Faulkner scholars some new ways to think about and conceive Faulkner but not Faulkner's fiction. It takes Richard Gray's work to fulfill this mission.

It seems not at all surprising that a well-written and carefully documented book wholeheartedly infused with Marxist theory and a materialist understanding of reality comes from an English critic of Faulkner. Unlike America, and very much unlike Faulkner criticism, England has a long and respected tradition steeped in knowledge of historical materialism. Faulkner criticism, on the other hand, seems steeped in suspicion of it. There are still only a couple of full-length treatments of Faulkner, by Americans, influenced by this approach (for example, Myra Jehlen's and my own). Whatever the reasons, Richard Gray's *The Life of William Faulkner* (1994) proves indisputably that materialist criticism of Faulkner [see chapter 7], rooted in the ideas of Mikhail Bakhtin, Louis Althusser, Raymond Williams, and Fredric Jameson, can offer powerful ways to read and understand Faulkner's life and art, and the intimate connection between them. (The book was preceded by an essay read at the 1992 Faulkner and Yoknapatawpha Conference, published in 1995 as "On Privacy: William Faulkner and the Human Subject.") Gray comments that writing was the most important aspect of Faulkner's life. This point is central to his approach as he focuses more squarely than most biographies on the fiction as signs of the life, rather than on a relationship between the life and the art. He is much closer to Minter than to any other biographer, but he includes even more literary criticism. This approach, though, is inspired by his Bakhtinian conceptions that one's personal identity is constructed only through language, that language derives from the social world in which one exists, and that artistic identity is revealed by the ways in which one both accepts and resists that language. In other words, for Gray, Faulkner as man and artist is **overdetermined** but not imprisoned by the language world in which he was situated and immersed.

This condition is then exemplified in careful and insightful readings of all of the novels, in which Gray reveals the ways Faulkner's texts are both symptoms and diagnoses of those symptoms and the way they enact as well as depict the problems that arise in them. The earlier texts, through *Flags in the Dust/Sartoris,* are closely allied to the past, to the symptoms, to enacting problems and concerns in the world as it came to Faulkner in early twentieth-century Mississippi, and this tendency is repeated in *The Unvanquished.* The best novels, from *The Sound and the Fury* to *Go Down, Moses,* exhibit the dual tendency described above and hit the highest mark for novels—being polyphonic. Taken from Bakhtin, this term refers to the way in which novels have the unique power and ability to allow multiple voices to exist in tension and harmony, in ways that exhibit the nature of different voices existing simultaneously within society at large. Beyond that possibility, authors can add discourse that reveals the power relations and the moral relations among these voices, and in this overall manner they exhibit their authorial voice or persona—the life, that is, of William Faulkner.

Gray's book links with some others' views about Faulkner's life and art and the various themes that run through and create that story; yet, in the final analysis, this book seems almost always original. Gray does discuss the early, poetry years and the early novels, through *Flags in the Dust/Sartoris.* He reads into them themes that carry over into the later fiction, as Sensibar does, and he is sensitive to the various poses and guises Faulkner adopted during these years, as many critics are. These years are read as years in which Faulkner's own voice was dominated by the voices of others, by voices of the past, combined with hints of rebellion and frustration with the limitations of the past. Gray is not opposed to claims that at times Faulkner was not able to outrun the influences of his time and place. That is, he is not glued to the notion that genius always has the power to transcend biography and history. He points to places where Faulkner reveals the racist and sexist views of the world in which he existed. At the same time, Gray clearly and convincingly argues for the ways in which Faulkner was powerfully aware of the limited interpretations of human life within the South and the ways in which he analyzed these in vivid and moving detail. These analyses become that much more powerful in Gray's interpretation because of the ways in which he reveals the intensity of the conflict within Faulkner and thereby reveals the incredible effort and courage Faulkner exhibits when he analyzes so intently. Faulkner's honesty did not allow him to take easy paths, and he was driven by his art to seek and reveal the truth. Though that truth, as is revealed by Gray, was never one-sided, its multifaceted nature as depicted in Faulkner never matched the typical view in society. In Gray's interpretation, Faulkner defies the easy categories into which the hoipoiloi thrust life, and he defies, too, the perhaps too-easy categories into which critics have placed him. For Gray, Faulkner's art is exemplified at its best by a rich depiction of the multiple voices existing within society combined with a rich array of authorial voices questioning, probing, and testing the morality of those voices. Gray reveals especially well how this process works in Faulkner's exploration of race in *Light in August, Absalom, Absalom!,* and *Go Down, Moses.*

Gray follows a similar path when discussing Faulkner's attitude toward women. He shows how Faulkner's attitudes toward women were deeply influenced by patriarchal influences of the South, as well as the ways Faulkner attempted constantly to analyze those attitudes to find new ways of forming relationships and experiencing the world. The subtlety of Gray's approach is revealed in the way in which he does not feel compelled to answer this question one way or the other, once and for always. The truth is much more complicated than that, and the various ways in which Faulkner interacted with these issues and the various ways he answered certain questions and resolved certain tensions at particular points are explored as the life and art dictate. A revealing discussion is his treatment of *The Wild Palms.* Like Singal, Gray sees the biographical connection to Charlotte Rittenmeyer. Like Collins, Gray sees the way in which Charlotte links to Faulkner's feeling for Meta Carpenter and Helen Baird. And like Collins and Sensibar, he sees that these relationships reveal much of Faulkner's own attitudes toward women, sexuality, and the needs women satisfied for him. Uniquely, he reads the entire question of romance and love for Faulkner as always being connected to the pull to be seen as "a man" with social and financial power and the pull to live life truly by feeling deeply, sincerely, and passionately. He convincingly argues that Faulkner felt driven by both of these dual pressures and that the fiction reveals not just a personal conflict at one point in the life but a continual conflict caused by Faulkner's personal and cultural milieu. This conflict is answered differently at different moments and is never resolved.

Like many others, Gray feels that Faulkner's fiction changes during and after *Go Down, Moses.* He explains this change, though, in keeping with his own theoretical terms. The later books do not necessarily lose artistry and significance for Gray. There are, he claims, situations, scenes, and characters that reveal Faulkner at his best throughout, but these books begin to lose the polyphonic nature of the earlier novels and become more univocal and declamatory in nature. Faulkner was, Gray argues, driven increasingly to make statements, to educate and edify. Thus, the nature of his writing changed. The possibility of the novelistic discourse being dominated by voices from the past remained, as *The Unvanquished* and *Intruder in the Dust* reveal, but even when Faulkner broke from these influences, the later works tended toward the declamatory and away from the polyphonic. Autobiography is history, Gray concludes, and his book is based on a deep knowledge of both Faulkner biography and American history. Gray's book demonstrates how a thorough grounding in contemporary theory can elucidate in brilliant detail the complicated literary process that involves but is not imprisoned by the personal and cultural milieu in which an author lived and struggled.

These influential works were joined in the 1990s by other biographical criticism that had a more-limited focus. In 1990, Louis J. Budd published "Playing Hide and Seek with William Faulkner: The Publicly Private Artist." Budd's essay questions the established biographical mantra of Faulkner's desire for privacy (based mostly on his comments to Cowley when developing *The Portable Faulkner*). Budd traces the many ways Faulkner participated in gaining publicity of one sort or another, quotes various people on Faulkner's desire for publicity, and analyzes Faulkner's role in interviews. In general he questions Faulkner critics who took Faulkner at his word rather than looking at the overall history and record. In 1994 Thomas Moser published "Faulkner's Muse: Speculations on the Genesis of *The Sound and the Fury.*" In keeping with Sensibar's claim about the influence of Estelle on Faulkner's life and mind, Moser argues that Estelle was crucial to the creation of Caddy Compson and, more, that she always served as the muse behind Faulkner's creativity. Moser discusses at length Faulkner's relationship to Estelle before and after her marriage and presents Faulkner's various reactions to Estelle's pregnancies and children. He argues that Faulkner desperately loved Estelle and the brotherly-sisterly relationship they had had their whole lives and that he was forever deeply wounded by her desertion of him. He then turns his attention to the writing from 1918 to 1927, discussing "The Lilacs," *The Marble Faun, Marionettes, Vision in Spring, Soldiers' Pay, Mosquitoes, Father Abraham,* and finally *The Sound and the Fury.* He connects the writing of *Father Abraham* more closely to Faulkner's life at the time than any other critic, and he argues that this fragment reveals Faulkner's acceptance of an abiding truth—the chief source of his creativity and his muse's most significant act was to have belonged to another and borne a child, then to have returned.

Daniel Singal's *William Faulkner: The Making of a Modernist* (1997) is both interesting and frustrating. Singal had published some of his thoughts about Faulkner in "William Faulkner and the Discovery of Evil," which appeared in *The War Within: From Victorian to Modernist Thought in the South, 1919–1945* (1982). This new book adds substantially to those ideas while keeping its main line of argument. As the title suggests, the book presents the main struggle of Faulkner's life as a conflict between shedding values from a Victorian past and accepting those of a modernist present. Many have seen a definitive struggle in Faulkner's life and art and labeled it in terms appropriate for their argument. And many have seen Faulkner's quest as one of identity and one that required writing to bring it to fruition. In these regards, Singal's work falls into line with a long list of Faulkner scholars. He also reads the trajectory of the life and career in familiar ways, claiming that Faulkner's genius is first revealed in *The Sound and the Fury* and that he experienced diminishing powers during and after the writing of *Go Down, Moses.* For the most part, he explores and assesses novels in ways familiar to all Faulkner scholars. A few aspects of this work do stand out, however. Singal strongly asserts the radical nature of *Light in August* and its critique of race in America. He gives *The Wild Palms* a central place in Faulkner's intellectual career, linking Charlotte Rittenmeyer to Faulkner himself in their quest for a modernist identity. And, he argues that Faulkner's diminishing powers were caused by nerve damage brought on by his drinking. The book reveals that Singal has a sound knowledge of the main directions of Faulkner scholarship, and it offers some provocative discussion of texts. It does, however, suffer in some places from reductive discussions of texts and a rather too-easy connection between life and art in others. To say that *The Wild Palms* was written solely because of Faulkner's experiences with Meta Carpenter Wilde, for example, discounts the ways its themes seem significant to Faulkner's life at least since he met Helen Baird (as Carvel Collins had demonstrated). To say that Charlotte Rittenmeyer is a biographical character is also, on one hand, easy to say, and on the other, to offer only a limited point, denying the full complexity of the characterization and its relation to Faulkner's life. To argue, as Singal does, that Faulkner's great-grandfather, the Old Colonel, lurks almost everywhere and forever in Faulkner's work seems a bit overstated.

A number of books also included a chapter of biographical analysis whose conclusions are then infused into and connected to analyses of the fiction. In 1996 Philip Weinstein published *What Else But Love?,* a book exploring both Faulkner and Toni Morrison. Though not much of a contribution to biographical criticism in general, Weinstein's chapter entitled "Personal Beginnings: Mammies and Mothers" offers an approach it seems he has mastered. He reads Faulkner's creation of Dilsey through Faulkner's relationship with Caroline Barr as well as through his own relationship with the black nanny with whom he grew up. Using his own life as inspiration, Weinstein claims that Faulkner's perception and his depiction of race relations are rooted in the necessary duality of the relationship he had with Callie Barr. This duality leads to a portrait that reveals affection but superiority, love but inequality, and intimacy but alienation all combined. Ultimately, the portrait is as compelling in what it sees as in what it misses. Expressing complicated ideas in a clear and coherent manner, appreciating and assessing Faulkner, revealing that Faulkner was both "like us" and "much better than us," Weinstein offers, as usual, a provocative and worthwhile look at Faulkner (and in this case, at Morrison as well).

Updating the psychoanalytical approach taken by many, Doreen Fowler [see chapter 8] adds a Lacanian reading of Faulkner's life and art in *Faulkner: The Return of the Repressed* (1997). In her preface and introduction, "Faulkner's 'Heart in Conflict,'" Fowler carefully details her approach. She explains that for her, and Lacan, the traumatic entry into language and identity creates a conflict within any subject between Desire and Law, between an imaginary unity with the mother and the prohibition and separation symbolized by the father. She proceeds then to trace this tension in Faulkner's life, claiming that the well-known disguises and stylized relationships Faulkner had with people, even those in his family, reflected a psychic disjunction that is universally experienced and universally repressed. Grounding her ideas very much in the biographical insights of Minter, Fowler then analyzes Faulkner's relationships with women, with men, his drinking, and his attitude toward death in these Lacanian terms. Not really using Lacan to explain Faulkner but rather revealing how both were exploring universal human experiences, Fowler brings years of interest in Faulkner and Faulkner scholarship to bear in a new and enlightening approach. Her book reveals one of the ways that theories influencing literary criticism in general do not necessarily reduce the literary experience itself. She proceeds to discuss what have been called the major novels, focusing on gender [see chapter 9] and race [see chapters 2 and 13] as the arenas of the repressed.

What might be the most postmodern [see chapter 6] reading of the relationship between Faulkner's life and art is Lothar Hönnighausen's *Faulkner: Masks and Metaphors* (1997). Hönnighausen begins his book with a biographical chapter focusing on Faulkner's well-documented role-playing in photos, letters, and interviews. Hönnighausen reads these activities, however, not as pathological or compensatory, as so many of the psychological and psychoanalytical critics do, but as essential modes of living and creating, as ways in which Faulkner explored, experienced, and coped with various conflicts he had both within himself and with the outside world. In this reading, Hönnighausen projects new directions for biographical criticism that takes this approach. A chapter on theory follows these ideas, in which he discusses the phenomena of masks and metaphors as matters of discourse, more than matters of ontology, and reads role-playing as a decisive factor in human life especially in any artistic transformation of life. He discusses the tendency within Faulkner biography and biographical criticism to present one artistic identity and to read the life as a continuous development of that identity. Against that thrust, he presents the postmodern view that refuses to see human personality as a unified entity developing organically. Rather, he sees it as a multivocal and multifaceted entity that responds to internal and external factors in a variety of ways more dependent on context and circumstance than on organic development. Drawing the connection between the fascination with masks of both the decadence movement and modernism, Hönnighausen relates Faulkner's personal connection between masks and narrative perspective. Drawing heavily on the ideas of Nietzsche, Hönnighausen relates acting as the paradigmatic expression of human nature and as central to art in the twentieth century (if not for much longer than that). Masks are the vehicles of expression in form, and they expose rather than hide meaning. This discussion brings Faulkner biographical criticism into a sphere it has yet to explore much at all. Considering the concentric circles in which Faulkner's life and art traveled, other critics will most likely follow down this path.

In my own work, *Natural Aristocracy: History, Ideology, and the Production of William Faulkner* (1999), I discuss both Faulkner's specific historical world, focusing on a history of its ideological formations, and his biography, the ways Faulkner's family and he were influenced by this world. In my chapter 2, "Faulkner's Ideology: Ideology and Subjectivity," I reveal the ways in which the South's main ideological formations, paternalism and liberalism, shaped and helped produce Faulkner and his sense of himself. Grounding my ideas in the theory of ideology as articulated by Althusser and Eagleton, I offer a materialist analysis of the terrain covered by many other critics. My conclusions, like those of others, see the turning point of Faulkner's life and career as that moment between *Flags in the Dust* and *The Sound and the Fury* when Faulkner turned to a confrontation, in my terms, with history. I discuss the major novels from *The Sound and the Fury* through *The Reivers,* exclusive of *Go Down, Moses,* and treat issues of class, race, and gender as appropriate to the text at hand. Like others, I see Faulkner's career as one implicitly involving identity, his sense of himself in the world, and as a struggle between two poles. I see *Absalom, Absalom!* as the major text and give serious attention to the Snopes trilogy as not less effective or artistic but structured differently on purpose and concerned with other issues than the earlier novels.

MOVING TO A MOMENTARY END TO THE STORY

It seems fitting to begin a discussion of twenty-first century criticism about Faulkner with the published proceedings of the Faulkner and Yoknapatawpha Conference, *Faulkner at 100: Retrospect and Prospect* (2000), edited by Donald Kartiganer and Ann J. Abadie. Though the essays in this collection are rather short due to the nature of the conference, they indicate certain directions, old and new, interesting to the history of biographical criticism. Hönnighausen condenses his ideas from *Faulkner: Masks and Metaphors* in "Faulkner, the Role-Player." He wants us to understand posing not as a disturbing psychological oddity but as a normal process of artistic and human life. Wearing masks can be seen to be shifting responses to social, psychological, and literary contexts and part of a discursive practice that uses role-playing as communicative acts and artistic strategy. Hönnighausen subtracts from this aspect of Faulkner's life any hint of psychological struggle or inner demons. In some ways, Hönnighausen comes close to Blotner by seeming to imply that a great artist always controls his personal development, but in his book this argument is more complicated than in this short essay. Polk continues a type of monumentalizing in his essay "Was Not Was Not Who Since Philoprogenitive" by claiming that first and foremost Faulkner was the man who wrote the books. Though he claims, too, that Faulkner critics pretend to talk about Faulkner when they are really talking about themselves, Polk does not push this rather provocative insight to explain how his ideas are just as much about himself as they are about the great artist. Similarly, Hans Skei argues in "'Faulkner Before Faulkner': The Early Career as a Construction in Retrospect" that the first part of Faulkner's career is only interesting in terms of how it can be said to lead to the later explosion of genius. Biography is only interesting in the ways it might help us understand individual works, argues Skei, but it can never explain the art. In this essay, we are back to 1891 and James Russell Lowell.

John Irwin takes a different direction in his essay, "Not the Having but the Wanting: Faulkner's Lost Loves." Irwin here claims that no scenario in Faulkner seemed more productive than the troubadouresque attachment that sprang from his being rejected by an idealized woman. He discusses Faulkner's relationships with Helen Baird and Meta Carpenter and Faulkner's experiences with Estelle, and shows how these were turned into scenes and books and art. He implies here a type of selfishness in Faulkner—an interpretation not often seen—since Faulkner continually chose art over love, his work over the women in his life. Irwin opens interesting doors both in terms of rereading Faulkner's choices in personally moral terms and in terms of the ways Faulkner objectified women for literary purposes. Judith Sensibar moves in a unique direction as well, continuing her development of very interesting and provocative interpretations of Faulkner's life, especially regarding his relationship with Estelle. In "Faulkner and Love: The Question of Collaboration," Sensibar argues that Faulkner's relationship with Estelle was deeply inspirational both intellectually and artistically, and goes so far as to claim that Faulkner's turn to prose was caused by his working with Estelle on her fiction. Sensibar offers a biographical and plausible explanation for a conundrum that has stumped many critics. What remains part of the mystery of a great artist becomes, for Sensibar, a definitive and momentous experience of interaction between two minds. Rather than treading on the hallowed ground traversed by so many before them, both Irwin and Sensibar open new doors of perception and offer possible direction for further inquiry and interpretation.

Others in the twenty-first century do the same. D. Matthew Ramsey's [see chapter 3] "'Turnabout' is Fair(y) Play: Faulkner's Queer War Story" (2002) represents the possibilities opened by new and different approaches; it also reveals the way in which conceptions of Faulkner's biography underlie much of Faulkner criticism in general. Focusing on the early 1930s, Ramsey presents the ways in which the recounting of Faulkner's life in Blotner represses the very real connection between Faulkner and gay culture at the time. Comparing Blotner's tales to those found in Karl and Ben Wasson, Ramsey exposes the gay identities of many of Faulkner's friends in the early 1930s—Ben Wasson and Stark Young in particular—and the nature of many of the places Faulkner was said to visit. He opens the possibility that concern for Faulkner's literary reputation and the values guiding the biographers influenced critics to overlook the ways in which Faulkner's life justified an analysis of the questioning of typical male masculinity. Ramsey then directs his attention to "Turnabout," a 1930s war story, and reads its depiction of masculinity, queering the way the story is usually read and citing the ways in which Faulkner undermines assumptions about war, masculinity, male camaraderie, and homo-sexuality. In ways similar to Judith Sensibar, Ramsey highlights how cultural val-ues have played a role in creating the Faulkner we generally know and shows how the literature can be read in even more ways than it has been previously.

In contrast to Ramsey, Theresa Towner shows how Faulkner criticism of the twenty-first century will also continue directions begun in the past. Her treat-ment of the question, "Was Faulkner a Racist?," in her fifth chapter of *Faulkner on the Color Line* (2000), is a refreshingly honest, nuanced, and well-written analysis of the relationship between Faulkner's life and art in terms of this per-plexing question. She reviews and analyzes Faulkner's public statements to find unifying themes and connects these to the artistic purposes of the later novels, especially the Snopes trilogy. Though she makes new connections between life and art, Towner concludes where many before her have: Faulkner was compli-cated, basically a good man, somewhat a product of his times and somewhat transcendent of them.

Somewhere between these two works is James G. Watson's *William Faulkner: Self-Presentation and Performance* (2000). This full-length study brings into the twenty-first century the notion shared by many that Faulkner wrote himself into being, but it takes a new approach. Linking content and themes from the works with details of Faulkner's life, Watson argues that Faulkner used self-presentation as a narrative strategy. This strategy capitalized on his experiences and his per-formance in the novels (and letters and life) and revealed the various ways he represented his various selves as they formed, were explored, and then dis-carded. Watson reads many of Faulkner's letters painstakingly to reveal autobi-ographical sources for the work, and his efforts are based not only on his own previous work but also on that of Blotner, Louis Brodsky, and Robert Hamblin in editing the letters. Watson argues convincingly for critics to reconnect the life and art in ways that some earlier critics saw as wrong-headed. His major theme is that Faulkner wrote himself into existence continually by experimenting with various versions of the self in his fiction and trying them on for size in life. His work fits in the tradition of Wittenberg in that he feels that the concerns and con-flicts, the hopes and fears, the unfolding events of Faulkner's life and their mean-ing all find form and expression in the fiction. It also fits with Watson's own earlier work in that he assumes a direct connection between discursive forma-tions and subjective identity. His book does not really add any new information to the biography, but he brings to bear a different and interesting approach to the study of Faulkner's life and art. Watson crosses the boundary between new crit-ical analysis and postmodern approaches.

Meant as a descriptive and not an evaluative comment, Faulkner biographical criticism has remained a conservative field for the most part. Since its inception, its purpose has been to move Faulkner, as a subject, into the hallowed ground of written discourse, and it has always been sensitive to conserving that hard-won status. That relative consistency, with the various exceptions noted above, bodes well for the future, I would argue, for there remains much to be said. New insights must come from new perceptions, of course, and the field of Faulkner criticism will continue to grow and be moved by these new perceptions. The overall ways in which postmodern theories have influenced Faulkner biography and the genre of biography in general are relatively slight. This trend most likely will begin to change. Judith Sensibar's work already implies that a rather commonplace habit in the work of many male biographers has occurred in the history of Faulkner biographical criticism. This work has basically been the biography of a male by men, and it has been written, as William Epstein explains about Norman Mailer and Marilyn Monroe, *over* the body of women. Surely, the stories of Faulkner's life have relegated Estelle Oldham Faulkner and other women to merely background roles, sometimes to the role of a hindrance to the production of his art. One can also see the genre of biography experience a resurrection similar to that experienced by history. Biography could turn to be a discussion about the ways in which subjects are constituted through relationships and through historical and biographical conflicts. Biography could even explore the conceptions of art and artists with which authors themselves identify and thus begin to discuss the ways that the role of art in society is also one constituted by time and place. Especially relevant to Faulkner biographical criticism would be an exploration of the role of race and racial identity in terms of writing and personal development. How Faulkner's life was shaped by the fact of his whiteness would open up various as yet unexplored areas of investigation. Finally, biography could also renounce its affiliation with the myth of the coherent personality and explore the ways in which subjects are many-sided and multifarious entities. Simon Trezise's conjectures in regard to Dickens biography pose some questions worth pursuing in these contexts. What constitutes greatness, and why should we expect the great writer to be a great man or woman? What does it mean to focus on the individual subject post-Freud, -Jung, -Saussure, -Lacan, and -Althusser? What do individual personality and artistic ingenuity mean when psychoanalysis and ideological theory open the possibility that even writers are slaves rather than masters of language? Can we reduce the process of history to an account of selected lives without regard to class, gender, race, and economic forces? Clearly, some critics have traveled down these avenues of exploration, but only a short distance.[4] Future critics, one hopes, will open the doors of exploration and of perception to chart the unseen aspects of Faulkner's life and its relation to the production of his fiction.

NOTES

1. Gresset, in "Faulkner's Self-Portraits," discusses them.

2. This matter has not yet been entirely resolved. Recently the Faulkner estate has moved to restore the title as *The Wild Palms.*

3. Duclos devoted much of his career to his work about Faulkner's family and eventually published *Son of Sorrow*, a book focused on Colonel W. C. Falkner.

4. Several authors cited in this chapter appear elsewhere in this volume as well as in *A William Faulkner Encyclopedia,* ed. Robert W. Hamblin and Charles A. Peek (Westport, CT: Greenwood, 1999) by the same editors; that volume also contains summaries of biographical and autobiographical materials.

5

Modernist Criticism

Debrah Raschke

That Faulkner is considered among the twentieth century's prominent modernists is no surprise: the studies of modernist influence on Faulkner are many.[1] Precisely how Faulkner's body of work is judged modernist, however, yields considerable debate. Part of this debate emanates from the wide range of definitions of modernism itself. Modernism has been aligned with **impressionism,** which attempts to capture the experience of fleeting moments, and with the philosophy of Henri Bergson, who defines reality as the "irreversible succession of heterogeneous states melting into one another" (Douglass 19).[2] It has also been identified with **imagism, symbolism, aestheticism, primitivism,** and **cubism.** It has been defined as being indebted to Romanticism and to Victorianism (sometimes at the same time), and linked with the death of metaphysics. It has been considered as closed, determinate, conservative, and fascist, and conversely as avant-garde, subversive, and transgressive.[3] As Vicki Mahaffey notes in "Modernist Theory and Criticism," in the "recent debates over modernism versus [**postmodernism**], the characteristic unorthodoxy of modernism has been displaced onto the postmodern," and modernism, "in motivated reversal," is "characterized as the corrupt canonized orthodoxy" (512).[4] Susan Stanford Friedman perhaps describes modernism best as "BangClash," an ongoing "definitional dissonance" (510).[5] Such definitional tensions, according to Friedman, are its lifeblood; there are, as such, many modernisms.

In spite of my predilections for expanding interpretations of modernism, I have, however, found it necessary to limit my definition for the purpose of this analysis. I begin by examining how modernism, although intertwined with the literary methods of **New Criticism** (and to a much lesser extent **structuralism**), is not tantamount to it. I then focus on modernism as an experience of loss, particularly an **epistemological loss,** which subsequently affects the construction of the self and that self's relation to others and to the communal—an interpretation that concurs with Noel Polk's assessment of *The Sound and the Fury* as the "quintessential American high modernist text" (1).[6] It is a definition, moreover, that lends itself well to a discussion of literary techniques most frequently associated with modernism. I conclude by examining how this experience of loss becomes connected with issues of gender. I then extend this definition of modernism to the blurring of boundaries that frequently accompanies this loss, a definition that invokes a postmodern modernity. I contend, though, that the instability of the self, the porous boundaries, and the lack of an Archimedean point that have formed definitions of postmodernism have always been a part of the modernist discussion; postmodernism simply provided a critical vocabulary with which to address these issues. As Jean-François Lyotard suggests, "the postmodern is undoubtedly part of the modern."[7] Richard Moreland's analysis of Faulkner's modernism in *Faulkner and Modernism* borders on a postmodernist reading of modernism in its discussion of transgression, retelling, and disruption that becomes intertwined with discussions of race, class, and gender.[8] Philip Weinstein uses Lacanian theory to illustrate his discussion of the critique of the subject.[9]

Gail Mortimer in *Faulkner's Rhetoric of Loss* emphasizes the significance of absence, as well as the speciousness of boundaries and containers that attempt to create the illusion of presence and security.[10] Charles Hannon in "Signification, Simulation, and Containment in *If I Forget Thee, Jerusalem*" suggests a blurring of the boundaries between "aesthetics" and the "lived experience of everyday life." (143)[11] Thus, the focus on modernism as an experience of loss and of shifting ground is the reading I bring to this analysis of Faulkner and his critics.

MODERNISM AS AND AS NOT NEW CRITICISM

Modernism, often to its detriment, has frequently been associated with methods of literary interpretation, in particular, with New Criticism, which dominated literary practice from the 1930s through the 1970s. For the New Critic, the "wounds of fragmentation" are bound into an aesthetic unity, or what Cleanth Brooks calls the "well-wrought urn"—the intricate interpretation of paradox and juxtaposition, of repeated image, symbol, and trope that emerges through the act of "close reading."[12] Thus, the numerous readings of Faulkner's work pertaining to how aesthetic choices create meaning have their roots in the methods of New Criticism, one of the most frequently noted being Olga Vickery's *The Novels of William Faulkner.*[13] For the New Critic, the work under scrutiny is completely autonomous and self-sufficient, its intricacies of language yielding its full meaning. It prizes, in other words, fullness and autonomy. For Weinstein, this paradigm of reading mirrors the desire for a stable self, free from the intrusiveness of the cultural Other with which so many modernist texts wrestle. In Weinstein's estimation, placing boundaries around the self represses "that intolerable sense of *being-helplessly-caught-up-in-the-Other* that Faulkner represents in the plight of Quentin Compson" (86). In fact, this act of reifying the aesthetic object as an organic whole has been read as a means of counteracting the **polysemous** self that so frequently surfeits the modern novel. Conversely, David Newman in "'the vehicle itself is unaware': New Criticism on the Limits of Reading Faulkner" attempts to revive a New Critical appreciation of Faulkner by arguing that its methods have been too narrowly conceived.[14]

To a much lesser extent, modernism has become aligned with structuralism, an association that has emerged through some postmodernist readings, which (I think mistakenly) have equated modernism with legitimatizing metanarratives (*grand récits*) that breed a stultifying homogeneity.[15] For the structuralist, the similar functioning of plots, narrative progressions, and tension reveal the **hermeneutic** or determinate meaning of an author's work.[16] Structuralism emphasizes a totality and consistent inner structure that may be best expressed through discussions of modernist architecture: the essence of the modern as "crystallization of its inner structure, the slow unfolding of its form."[17] This search for the overall structure is what Malcolm Cowley does when he claims that all of Faulkner's books in the "Yoknapatawpha saga are part of the same living pattern" (8).[18] Arthur Kinney takes a similar approach, emphasizing the "ripples of *narrative consciousness*" that "spread out through the various scenes of Faulkner's novels," which then leads us to "embrace our sense of the work *as a whole,* our *structural consciousness*" (5, italics in original).[19] As Donald Kartiganer further suggests in *The Fragile Thread,* pattern, particularly in archetypal motifs, supersedes the prolific individual images of chaos (xv).[20]

Both structuralism and New Criticism pose a paradox in their readings of modernist texts: Structuralism, which reached its zenith in the United States in the 1960s, and particularly New Criticism, which dominated literary practice from the 1930s through the 1970s, are the primary lenses through which we have read and interpreted modernism. Yet, at the same time, they have been read as reactions to modernism's preoccupations with fluidity and the abyss. As Vicki Mahaffey comments in the essay collection *The Future of Modernism,* it is a mistake to equate modernism solely with New Criticism:

> In retrospect, the so-called high modernists frequently have been lionized and belittled in succession, although more and more frequently what is being attacked in the name of modernism is not the various and elastic strands of modernist practice, but rather the dominant critical theory of the time—the New Criticism—so often confused with it. (101)[21]

This incompleteness of both New Criticism's and structuralism's methodologies is the impetus for Donald Kartiganer's *The Fragile Thread: Meaning of Form in Faulkner's Novel,* which combines both approaches in his analysis of Faulkner. In focusing on the "separate pieces" that are then reconstituted to make a "comprehensible design," New Criticism, according to Kartiganer, misses the fluidity and the fragility of the form.[22] That form, when it does emerge, is fraught with "contingency"—one that "never denies its dubious status" (xvi–xvii). In *The Sound and the Fury,* this contingent form emerges in the refusal "to allow the four distinct voices to build into a coherent narrative," and in *Light in August* and *Absalom, Absalom!* the structural "design" is "always on the verge of collapse" (xviii). As Kartiganer acknowledges, his project has affinities with such **poststructuralist** critics as Paul de Man, Ihab Hassan, J. Hillis Miller, Jacques Derrida, Edward Said, and Joseph Ridell, who, in query-ing the stability of language and form, have seen in the modernist project a richer, albeit less unified, vision. Modernism is then, at least in part, a Bergson-ian reality, a vital and perpetual motion that esapes categorization, a phenome-non which can be found in many other modernist writers (Joyce, Woolf, Conrad, Pound, Proust, Stevens). In this light, Kartiganer sees Bergson's criticism of the parsing intellect as paralleling literary modernism's attempt to shed irrelevant forms and modes (162).[23] It is, in essence, the narrative realization of Lena Grove's comment in *Light in August:* "My, my. A body does get around" (480).

MODERNISM AS EPISTEMOLOGICAL LOSS

One of the most salient interpretations of modernism has been its casting as epistemological loss, a loss of metaphysical certainty, which, in turn, has affected the definition of the subject and the subject's relationships with others and with the communal. The early twentieth century was indeed a time of flux, which was less attributable, in my estimation, to a single event than it was the result of the accumulated changes that affected the last 70 years of the nine-teenth century. Daniel Singal in *The Making of a Modernist* suggests that Faulkner is enticed by a Victorian purity and calm that he must overcome in order to become a "modernist."[24] And while I would agree that the modernist sensibility is clearly different from a Victorian one and that, as Virginia Woolf suggests, "On or about December 1910, human character changed,[25] I also see the Victorian era as a tumultuous breeding ground for what emerged as a mod-ernist sensibility in the early part of the twentieth century:[26] The construction of the railroad and the perfection of the steam engine accelerated the Industrial Revolution and the pace of communications in the early part of the century; the motor car later in the century increased even further the rapidity of communica-tion, while the expansion of empire, particularly in England, extended its breadth; meanwhile, the Reform Bills of 1832 and 1867 in Great Britain, the Civil War in the United States, and the numerous revolutions in Europe shifted economic and political power. Subsequently, individual identities founded on such power distributions were disrupted. With the beginnings of mass produc-tion and the proliferation of factories, a new relationship between the worker and the work performed was forged, giving credence to Karl Marx's comment that the worker is alienated from the process and the product of his labor, and subsequently from himself and his community.[27] Thus, in differing ways, the cultural, political, and economic shifts of the late nineteenth century threatened the very core on which many constituted their identities and their heritage.

This, however, was not all. By the middle of the nineteenth century, scientific and linguistic discoveries produced an equally powerful jolt to metaphysics and theology: The "Sea of Faith," whether located in Nature or in the theological, metamorphoses into a "melancholy, long, withdrawing roar." A "new world" was emerging, but it offered, at least in Matthew Arnold's view, "really neither joy nor love, nor light, / Nor certitude, nor peace, nor help from pain."[28] Discoveries in geology unveiled that the earth was older than previously thought; discoveries in astronomy extended the vastness of the universe; Darwin's *Origin of the Species* diminished origin; and Freud, in identifying the power of the unconscious, made individual autonomy a fantasy. It was quadruple shrinking: a smaller speck in time and space and less noble in origin, individual identity could no longer fully claim even the autonomy of control. Exegetical criticism questioned the literality of the Bible; Saussure's discoveries in linguistics challenged the verity of the word; Einstein's theory of relativity contradicted the belief in absolutes; and Bergson, in conceiving time as fluid, further subverted conceptions of a fixed identity or fixed categories as the foundation of truth. In 1895 Nietzsche declared God dead, and on December 31, 1900, Hardy greeted the prospects of the new century with a description of the "land's sharp features" as the "Century's corpse outlent."[29]

In this light, modernism is frequently depicted as emerging from a phenomenon of flux, if not loss. Ian Watt in "Impressionism and Symbolism in *Heart of Darkness*" captures well the uncertainty that characterized the early twentieth century when he contends that

> impressionism and symbolism are essentially manifestations of various general tendencies which first came to prominence in the romantic period; both are anti-traditional assertions of the private individual vision; and they both took their full shape during the epistemological crisis of the late nineteenth century, a crisis most familiar to literary history under the twin rubrics of the death of God and the disappearance of the omniscient author. (39–40)[30]

For Watt, this loss of certainty (metaphysical, theological, and aesthetic) produced a new kind of isolation in a world that no longer possessed an Archimedean point. Michael Levenson in *A Genealogy of Modernism* describes modernist consciousness as "hovering," as manifesting the "disintegration of stable balanced relations between subject and object" (22). Perry Meisel reads modernism as enacting the impossibility of origin. Bette London sees modernism as an intersection between a "crisis in narrative and cultural authority," in which conflicting cultural voices within an individual voice accentuate the instability of the self.[31] Repeatedly, within a variety of venues, modernism has been defined as manifesting an epistemological uncertainty. As Rosi Braidotti suggests, for those of us living in the twentieth century, "we are all epistemological orphans" (2).[32]

Within this context, many modernist writers address not only the problem of knowledge but also the problem of how knowledge is created and transmitted. If

the possibility for the absolute is no longer possible, then the single, authoritative vision of the omniscient author will no longer suffice. As Lily Briscoe in
Virginia Woolf's *To the Lighthouse* claims, one needs "fifty pairs of eyes to see
with" (198). Epistemological and linguistic uncertainty prevails. When Marlow
in Conrad's *Heart of Darkness* comes across the eviscerated natives digging a
hole, he sees them as "enemies," as "criminals," and then finally as simply
"unhappy natives" (154). And if language itself is seen as slippery, then the
structures it creates—metaphysical, theological, cultural—are equally tenuous.
As Michael Bell suggests, Saussure's evaluation of the linguistic sign as arbitrary in relationship to the external referent and his assessment of meaning as
relational reversed the Adamic model that assigned names and solidity of meaning to preexisting things (16).[33] Origin/truth no longer can be unequivocally
equated with the word; or as Joyce parodies in *Finnegans Wake,* "in the bugin-
ning there was the *woid*" (378).[34] To complicate matters, as many recent critics
have suggested, the point at which modernism ends and postmodernism begins
is ambiguous—a dilemma that has emerged, as well, in discussions of modernist
interpretations of Faulkner. [See chapter 6.]

EPISTEMOLOGICAL AND OTHER LOSSES IN FAULKNER

Gail Mortimer in *Faulkner's Rhetoric of Loss* comments that Faulkner's narratives are surfeited with a "preoccupation with loss," particularly in the "identity themes" that surface in his narrators and male characters. Mortimer views
Faulkner's world as a "world sustained among tensions about loss: loss of the
self, loss of control, loss of desired objects through the passage of time" (7).[35]
Objects "tend to be traces of absent things, significant less in themselves than by
virtue of what they say about absent things" (8). What is at stake then is "the
basic integrity of the self" (4). Jun Liu's discussion of teaching *The Sound and
the Fury* in relationship to Nietzsche connects this experience of loss specifically with modernism. In Liu's estimation, the "profound loss" that emerges in
the Compsons' "intrafamilial problems signify nothing metaphorically," but
instead "signify the deeper ambiguity and larger sense of loss that is modern
nihilism" (91).[36]

There is, in other words, no Archimedean point that provides a stable ground.
In Arthur Kinney's words, Faulkner's narrative poetics is "in line with those
modernist thinkers who are as concerned with how we know as with what we
know" (15). And Faulkner, like other modernists, clearly depicts the limits of
language in constructing that knowledge. Kartiganer describes this realization
as the "modernist urge to expose the illusoriness of language by freeing it from
referentiality, from the 'things' it seems to exist only to name" (169). In this
light Faulkner, in a Nietzschean fashion, "endows the symbolic image with
'supreme significance' and dissolves it" (174). There is, in John Orr's words, an
exhaustion that exemplifies the failure "to make the necessary connections
between word and thing, signifier and signified" (109).[37] Orr in *The Making of*

the Twentieth-Century Novel links Faulkner with other writers who produce a "crisis in compassion" that is linked inextricably to a "narrative seeing" no longer able to "produce a unified field of meaning" (6). Karl Zender in *The Crossing of the Ways* emphasizes this breakdown in signification by examining how sound takes precedence over the word.[38] John Bassett in *Visions and Revisions,* particularly in his treatment of an absence that surfeits both the personal and the linguistic, accentuates a modernist miscarrying of the signs (the failure of the verbal code): the sign in front of Hightower's house that no longer bears any significance for him; Doc Hines reading "signs of bitchery and abomination" in the dietician's actions; the varied responses to the state of pregnancy; and the word-labels that become mislabeling (109–113).[39] Bassett continues: "The preached word—like the prayers of McEachern and Joanna—comes to have no more relationship to any reality than Joe Christmas has, as a symbol, to the Christ-figure with whom so many critics in one way or another have connected him" (116). The ending, Bassett claims, "suggests the arbitrariness of all endings, the potential ambiguity of all signs and texts, and the textuality of experience itself" (117). In a slightly different light, Kinney suggests that although the "images are synecdoches for the narrative consciousness which they help to define," they are frequently rooted in the unconscious, thus metaphoric and inexact. When words resonate with private meanings and memories, such as Joe Christmas's associating toothpaste with sexuality, they produce a breakdown in the verbal coding (90–91). At least for most, toothpaste does not signify sexual encounter.

If, in Addie Bundren's view, words are indeed "gaps in people's lacks" (166), then the structures generated from words are even more tentative. These imposed structures and conceptions become like the trout in *The Sound and the Fury* that no one has caught for 25 years but which becomes for the boys fishing in the stream the already-caught fish, metamorphosed into its prize—first the fishing rod, then the $25.00 the fishing rod would yield, and then the horse and wagon the $25.00 would buy. This simple fishing scene reveals the airy process on which we create the building blocks of a reality that, at base, has no true foundation. Kartiganer rightly links this scene specifically to Quentin's assertion that he and Caddy committed incest—his alchemizing the word, so that language establishes the reality. However, this fishing scene is linked to the process of creating meaning and abstractions in an even more important way. In *The Sound and the Fury,* we begin with concrete pieces of reality: trees, honeysuckle, the sound of bells—the building blocks of Benjy's narrative. We then create abstractions around these concrete words and infuse them with value—virginity, sister, honor, Harvard—which is a "such a fine sound" (174). For Benjy, Caddy smells like trees (an innocence he cannot conceptualize), to Quentin she is a lost paradise, and to Jason she is a whore. In the end she becomes a photograph, lost in the conceptualizations of others.

Around such empty words, we build narratives. This is one of the main emphases of Kartiganer's *The Fragile Thread,* which stresses the fluidity of Faulkner's language and structures. In his discussion of *The Sound and the Fury,*

As I Lay Dying, Light in August, and *Absalom, Absalom!,* Kartiganer identifies a precariousness of form and structure that reveals the problem of narration and the unattainablity of truth (6).[40] In addition to the four separate monologues, *The Sound and the Fury,* for Kartiganer, yields a "sense of motion without meaning, of voices in separate rooms talking to no one" (21)—in essence the impossibility of structure and the impossibility of imposed meanings. The Benjy section yields the raw material—the untainted image, which becomes for both Quentin and Jason constructed fictions. When Benjy smells Caddy's perfume, he senses her newly discovered sexuality, and does not calm down until Caddy once again "smells like trees." In Quentin's hands, Caddy's actions metamorphose into an obsession for purity, which ultimately leads him to replace the actual events with his own fantasy of incest. In Jason's hands, Caddy's actions become tantamount to the loss of stature—to the bank job he never got. Both Quentin and Jason construct a narrative that answers the absence of Caddy—neither of them accurate. Their narratives, as so many modernist narratives, unveil the speciousness of the structures that drive both identity and belief.

In Kartiganer's estimation, *Absalom, Absalom!* follows a similar pattern in that the emerging narratives that attempt to explain Henry Sutpen's murder of Charles Bon are all personally driven, demonstrating Jacques Lacan's later assertion that language is desire.[41] The diabolic Sutpen that Rosa Coldfield invents is rooted in her own terror of sexuality and race (74); the Sutpen that Mr. Compson creates is rooted in his cynicism, in his belief that Sutpen did not murder Bon for honor but simply because everything in both their lives "conspired" that he do so (87); the narrative Sutpen, Quentin and Shreve create is rooted in both an ideality and a self-indulgence that ultimately results in their own isolation (93). Henry Sutpen himself, the object of the narrative, becomes entrapped in structures he cannot understand. Kartiganer concludes that what drives the "modern tragedy" is the "inability of one man to speak to another, some inviolable privacy at the center of that imagination and love." Borne out of absence, it "returns Bon and Henry, Quentin and Shreve, *Absalom, Absalom!,* to the wordless fact of a dumb and secret despair" (106).

Kartiganer then extends the faulty construction of the personal narrative to the larger mythic narratives, concluding that the mythic Christian structure that underlies the **diegetic** narrative (Holy Thursday, Good Friday, and Easter Sunday) bears no function at all, except that it is "irrelevant." In other words, the structure is there, but its function bears no meaning. Likewise, in *As I Lay Dying,* the mythic structure of the journey, although hardly irrelevant, is equally deflated in that it becomes "stripped of much of its meaning and dignity." In other words, the "Bundrens know the myth they follow," but in their hands the myth becomes trivialized into a desire for "an abortion, a toy train, and a set of false teeth" (180–82). Both *The Sound and the Fury* and *As I Lay Dying,* in Kartiganer's estimation, reflect a "break in expression," and both call into question not only the ordered constructions that become the obsession of the characters but also the larger mythic structures that feed them. Similarly, in *Light in August* not only is the theological structure that drives these characters faulty, but the ordering process that creates the structures is also depicted as resting on an airy nothing. Kartiganer notes this elaborate system of doubling in *Light in August*: Mr. Hines's confused identification of Lena's baby with Joe Christmas when he was a child; the Northern fanatic, Joanna Burden, and the Southern fanatic, Gail Hightower; and the comic encounter of Lucas Burch and Byron Bunch. The links are arbitrary as are the ordering and the structure. These numerous links that continue throughout the novel have very little to do with one another, except in the reader's mind, which then functions as a kind of mirror to the reader's own ordering process (64–67).[42]

If an overriding structure is impossible, so too is origin. Paul de Man in *Blindness and Insight* sees modernism as "a deliberate forgetting"—the attempt to wipe out origin in order to create a new origin (148)[43]—in essence, Pound's injunction "to make it new." It is precisely this failure of origin that underlies Peter Brooks's "Incredulous Narration: *Absalom, Absalom!*"[44] Commenting on Mr. Compson's interpretation of Charles Bon's death, Brooks notes that Mr. Compson cannot seem to find the predicate: "the proper names are there, but they refuse to accede meaning" (109)—just as Charles Bon is unable to claim his proper name: in the end, what seems to be Bon's erotic desire for Judith is Bon's unequivocal need to be recognized by the father, a recognition that never transpires (119). The name, disassociated from action, obscures origin. For Perry Meisel, this impossible search for origins exemplifies the very crux of modernity in which "proper names" become ghostly and unanchored (5). The "proper name," invariably connected to the **law-of-the-father** and paternal authority, thus becomes dislodged. And it is this proper name that then becomes exposed as a fiction in *Absalom, Absalom!* As Peter Brooks suggests, *Absalom, Absalom!* "preeminently concerns fathers, sons, generations, and line of descent," but presents "no clear authority, not even of a provisional sort, for the telling of the story, and as a result no suggestion of how to achieve mastery of interpretation" (110).[45] This dislodged authority is further amplified by Sutpen, who attempts to create a pure narrative. Humiliated as a boy when he delivers a message to a plantation house where he is barred from the front door and told to use the back one, Sutpen creates a "compensatory plot" that will "assure his place on the proper side of difference" (117). He makes a fortune in Haiti, which obscures, but does not obliterate, his poor origins. He takes a wife whom he thinks is part Spanish and part French, but who has unbeknownst to him, a trace of black blood. And even though she looks and seems white in all respects, for Sutpen, this trace threatens to undermine his whole scheme. Starting over with a new design, Sutpen finds his plans threatened again when Charles Bon emerges and demands the acknowledgment of his paternity. Origin thus is always specious. A trace of difference, invariably embedded in the dominant narrative, thus will always threaten to disrupt that narrative's purity and, subsequently, the authority, which claims its legitimacy from that purity.

These breakdowns in meanings, structure, and origin all work to undermine any coherent sense of selfhood. Philip Weinstein deals with this extensively in *Faulkner's Subject: A Cosmos No One Owns*. Focusing on the novels that emerged between 1929 and 1942, Weinstein explores the concept of selfhood as a fantasy.[46] For Weinstein, the self is produced ideologically in culture, and culture (particularly white male culture obsessed with control) emerges as a fraud. Quentin in *The Sound and the Fury* becomes a paradigm for this flawed subjectivity. Emphasizing the incomplete state that characterizes Faulknerian **stream of consciousness,** Weinstein notes that "Quentin cannot finish his thought or firm up his identity, cannot keep Dalton Ames and Father and Caddy and honeysuckle from penetrating his being, cannot keep at bay the maelstrom of sayings by his mother, Herbert, Mrs. Bland and others" (84). Quentin is "unlike characters in the nineteenth-century classical novel (who are typically passed on to us by the narrator's coherent entities, summarized organisms existing over time"); he instead "appears a moment-by-moment involuntary recorder of others' voices, a sentient receptacle wounded by the shards of their utterances" (84–85).[47] He, in other words, does not own his own identity. He becomes, like Joseph Conrad's Kurtz, "only a voice." Quentin's own words perhaps best capture this position: "Thinking I was not who was not was not who"[48]—an uncanny precursor of Lacan's revision of Descartes: "I think of what I am where I do do not think to think" (*Écrits* 166). In this light, Quentin becomes a model for the failed subjectivity that Weinstein identifies in 1929 through 1942 texts.

Jason, whose rhetorical voice is dramatically different from Quentin's, nonetheless shares his plight: he is a pastiche of clichés (121). In a similar vein, *Light in August*'s Joe Christmas is his rehearsed scripts—"culture's religious and racial insistences" (104–7). And of *Absalom, Absalom!,* Weinstein states: "Its nineteenth-century characters recede into rhetoric, becoming the objects rather than the subjects of narrational urgency" (140). For Weinstein, to privilege "individual identity" is to "fantasize a protected sacred space, the place of ourselves, which would be immune to the vicissitudes of time, space and culture" (86). It is nevertheless a false haven—one explored relentlessly by other modernist writers. Emphasizing how "rhetorical practice" creates ideology, Weinstein identifies *The Sound and the Fury* as Faulkner's initiation into modernism and sees his work after *Absalom, Absalom!* conversely as a departure from a "modernist aesthetics of shock and ideological confounding, of fissured subjectivity," as a movement toward a "conservative aesthetics of *Bildung,* of ideological bolstering" (152). Gail Mortimer makes a similar point in her discussion of a Faulknerian "character in conflict as if he or she were really two people, or split into two characteristics" (6). Mortimer continues: "Splitting things apart visually gives the illusion of their being under control; it avoids the need to cope with ambiguity." This "security of vision" is, however, a "false security" (7).

As Weinstein, suggests, Joe Christmas is "foreign to himself" and thus is "foreign to others" (106). Hardly an anomaly, this sense of isolation and disconnection is common in Faulkner work. This disjointedness is the focus of Orr's discussion of Faulkner in *The Making of the Twentieth-Century Novel.* Reading the modern novel as a failure of compassion or the inability to connect, Orr sees the absence that Caddy embodies as "the mirror of the void which the other members of the family" fail to communicate with one another: "Compassion as the lost structure of feeling highlights the family's eclipse, since such compassion could only resonate through the mythic honour or traditional form it can no longer recapture" (96). This absence of compassion, Orr argues, emerges through the absence of the other, which is mirrored in "absence of the fictional subject" and ultimately in the absence of society or the communal (16). The severing for Orr is linguistic, erotic, and communal—a wastelandic whirlpool folding in on itself into a solipsistic vacuum. Kartiganer, as well, emphasizes this isolation in Faulkner's fiction. In his discussion of *As I Lay Dying,* he notes that Darl simply cannot connect. When he attempts to burn the barn that contains the coffin and stop the journey, he "presents the fire as a piece of art, a kind of stage play at which he is only a spectator" (31). It is pure performance.

Exploring specifically Faulkner's use of sound, Karl Zender in *The Crossing of the Ways* extends this alienation to an alienation of culture. Zender notes that the old wilderness of the South resonates with an Edenic quality. Its language is yet unspoiled. However, as the "South descends into the modern age, this original unfallen language comes to be supplanted by a debased alternative" (102). Sounds, Zender notes, become increasingly inimical in Faulkner's later works. In part a response to a "vanishing world," in part a response to his more complicated views of this disappearing world, and in part a response to his views of the imagination, sound, linked with the invasiveness of modern culture, is depicted as alien and hostile. Citing the use of "amplified sound" in *Pylon* as paradigmatic example, Zender notes: By filling the airport rotunda with "the voice of the [race] announcer reverberant and sonorous, Faulkner created an image that served the rest of his career as his central metaphor for the dehumanizing and alienating power of modern culture" (19). It is indeed a resistance that is not unfamiliar in modernist literature. In Eliot's "Burial of the Dead" in *The Waste Land,* Saint Mary Woolnoth's Church bells mark not eternal time, but nine o'clock—the time of the workaday world. As the clock strikes, a crowd, portrayed as the living dead with "sighs, short and infrequent," flows into the London financial district (60–69). In Woolf's *To the Lighthouse,* as Mrs. Ramsay turns the pages of a catalog for her son James, her calm is interrupted by minor sounds that ultimately elicit a feeling of terror: The pleasant sounds of men talking and children playing give way to the usually soothing sound of the "monotonous fall of the waves on the beach," which suddenly metamorphoses into "a ghostly roll of drums" that "thundered hollow in her ears and made her look up with an impulse of terror" (16).[49]

Richard Moreland in *Faulkner and Modernism: Rereading and Rewriting* sees this breaking down of boundaries and polyphonia that most critics identify in Faulkner's middle period as emerging most poignantly in his later works, which many critics label conservative. In Moreland's estimation, it is a postmodernist opportunity for silenced voices to speak, to break through the dominant ideology that codified the South, and to produce a significant ideological disruption. The doors that have suppressed these voices have always been visible, but the voices themselves have been silenced. This is, as Moreland notes, not just a Southern problem: "The Southern plantation ideology adopted by Sutpen is an extreme form of a noted, wider American bourgeois dream of an abstract, pure freedom from place, class, history, limitation, or attachment" that emerges in Franklin, Emerson, Melville, James, and Fitzgerald (106). What cracks this purity for Moreland are the voices of the underclass in *The Hamlet,* the voices of blacks in *Go Down, Moses,* and the voices of women in *Requiem for a Nun.* Moreland's depiction of Ab's resistance in *The Hamlet*'s "Barn Burning" illustrates this well. When Ab ruins his planter's rug, he refuses to settle the dispute in the "planter way." To the contrary, he "does not want to erase and be forgiven the mark," but instead desires a "more adequate reading of the mark," which will expose the justice system (15). Ab becomes a "vandal who admires his handiwork" (135). "One may not like Ab Snopes, but one at least has to give credit to his ingenuity, as an "unpredictably resourceful subject" (138). And, in doing so, a new subjectivity of the underclass emerges. Similarly, in *Go Down, Moses,* one not only hears black voices, but Faulkner, in revisiting scenes in *Absalom, Absalom!* and by employing similar language used to characterize idealized scenes surrounding Sutpen, deflates those scenes by making them humorous. In other words, the binary oppositions break down, and through the retellings, a different story emerges.[50]

FAULKNER'S MODERNIST TECHNIQUES

Loss and, in particular, loss of certainty, authority, and identity are all themes that suffuse modernist texts. The techniques for portraying this message, though, at least in some definitions of modernism, are equally as important as the message itself. Form, in Arthur Kinney's estimation, is vision,[51] or as Peter Brooks suggests in another context, "Narrative meaning very much depends on the *uses* of narrative" ("Incredulous Narration" 110). In this light, a discussion of Faulkner's modernism would not be complete without addressing the literary techniques that, in part, create the message: **stream of consciousness, interior monologues,** the privileging of circularity over linearity, the pivotal importance of the image, the **montage** method, the blurring of boundaries between prose and poetry, the multiple narrative points of view, and the attempt to actively involve the reader in the narration.[52]

Stream of consciousness, a common modernist technique, attempts to render the consciousness of a character by recording the flow of conscious thought. Governed by the image, which becomes the catalyst for other images, memories, impressions, and emotions, stream of consciousness's prevailing mode is metonymic and fragmented, not linear. Weaving in and out of memory in a continuous flow of thought, stream of consciousness presents the potential for linking past, present, and future. In its attempts to record fleeting moments of observation, stream of consciousness embodies impressionism's attempt to capture the ephemerality of the moment and Henri Bergson's critique of time and space as faulty concepts.[53] Faulkner employs stream of consciousness in its least intrusive manifestation as a means of conveying the recurring theme that past is always present—for example, in the opening of *Flags in the Dust.* In its most disruptive manifestation, though, it serves as a means of critiquing subjectivity. As Weinstein suggests, techniques of stream of consciousness are a "powerful strategy" in creating "disunity" and disrupted subjectivities (85). Using Quentin's narrative in *The Sound and the Fury* as a model, Weinstein contends that in Quentin's inability "to consolidate what he has absorbed" and in his inability "to shape his own thoughts into the coherence of a temporal project, he is a figure in Motley"—a self in fragments (85). Thus, as Weinstein and others have suggested, techniques of stream of consciousness become inseparable from the modernist "refusal to affirm coherent selfhood through the vehicle of plot" (85).[54] They become both method and theme. Likewise, Daniel Singal traces the first seeds of this "modernist" impulse in Faulkner's local color sketches written for the *New Orleans Times-Picayune* Sunday feature, in which he identifies Faulkner's "growing belief in a universe governed by chance where the only thing a person could count on was change and impermanence," a belief that was marked by distinctive stylistic shifts: the "attempts to transcribe consciousness by means of interior monologues, to relate the same event through multiple perspectives, to juxtapose the realist and the symbolic, the prosaic and the poetic" (59).

It is the use of interior monologue, a type of stream of consciousness, however, that contributes to the radical vision of both *The Sound and the Fury* and *As I Lay Dying*. Attempting "to recreate the course and rhythm of consciousness just as it occurs in a character's mind" with minimal interference from the author, interior monologue engulfs the reader more completely into the vision of an individual character.[55] The technique accentuates motifs of isolation, what Walter Pater describes as the solitary and individual impressions that imprison us all:

> Experience, already reduced to a swarm of impressions, is ringed round for each one of us by that thick wall of personality through which no real voice has ever pierced on its way to us, or from us to that we can only conjecture to be without. Every one of those impressions is the impression of the individual in his isolation, each mind keeping as a solitary prisoner its own dream of a world. (248)[56]

The interior monologue, as well as in its more general application in stream of consciousness, becomes the foundation for creating a consciousness that, in effect, makes one a solitary prisoner in a private dream world. Darl, in *As I Lay Dying,* is one of Faulkner's most poignant examples of this. Moreover, both the techniques of stream of consciousness and the interior monologue, because of their reliance on the image and their metonymic functioning, enact what Arthur Kinney calls "visual thinking" (*Faulkner's* 90). It is a kind of thinking that frequently occurs in poetry, thus blurring the boundaries between poetry and prose, a technique that is common in many modernist texts: Joyce's *A Portrait of the Artist as a Young Man, Ulysses,* and *Finnegan's Wake;* Woolf's *To the Lighthouse* and *The Waves;* Proust's *Remembrance of Things Past;* Dorothy Richardson's *Pilgrimage;* and Rilke's *The Notebooks of Malte Laurids Brigge.*

The multiple narrative points of view (4 in *The Sound and the Fury,* 15 in *As I Lay Dying,* and 4 in *Absalom, Absalom!*) accentuate further the overall fragmentation and impossibility of certitude that distinguishes all of these novels. Philip Weinstein in "Teaching *The Sound and the Fury*" offers insightful means for teaching Faulkner within a modernist context. He suggests using Proust's "Combray" and Joyce's *Dubliners* as a means for portraying stultified time, Joyce's *Ulysses* as means of illustrating narrative revisionism, and Proust's *Remembrance of Things Past* as a means for conveying the multiplicity of selves. Likewise, in *Light in August* the multiple perspectives are more masked, but no less present. As Kartiganer suggests, the fragmentation emerges in compartmentalization of the voices of those characters who surround Joe Christmas. Joe's blackness/whiteness blends this duality into a wholeness that is nonetheless driven by motion and process, by the accumulation of fragments (43).

And finally, all of this disruption encourages the reader's active participation in the production of the narrative—what Philip Weinstein describes in *Faulkner's Subject* as performative readings. It is as well a wholeness incomprehensible to a community whose only understanding lies in compartmentalization: McEachern, Hines, and Percy Grimm are harnessed to "an implacable machine in the shape of God, carving a complex reality into the complex names of good and evil" (56). If there is a wholeness, it emerges through the act of reading. Finally, Thomas McHaney in "Faulkner and Modernism: Why Does it Matter?" underscores the importance of recognizing these modernist techniques in Faulkner's work: his maneuvering a "crisis in language," his "poetics of absence," his "architectonics of concatenation" all contribute to Faulkner's relationship with modernism.[57] In short, the techniques become a conduit for the message.

HOW TO AVERT HAVING ONE'S BONES BEING PICKED BY A WHIRLPOOL, OR, RESPONSES TO A MODERNIST WASTELAND

These literary techniques, most characteristic of Faulkner's middle period, emphasize the dissolution or the wastelandic qualities that are frequently associated with modernism. The response to this dissolution, however, has always been complicated. One response seen in many modernist writers is the attempt to create life through art. Robert Hamblin [see chapter 1] in "Saying No to Death" notes: "Faulkner's attitude toward death, and toward the time-ridden world which eventuates in death, is crucial to an understanding of his perception of himself as an artist. Confronted with death as possible annihilation, Faulkner was inclined to view art as the principal means by which man might defy time and death and achieve at least a measure of immortality" (8).[58] This sense of immortality, Hamblin contends, although persistent throughout Faulkner's work, is particularly poignant in the short story "Shall Not Perish," in which a boy becomes haunted by the museum paintings of people and places of Frenchman's Bend, of "the names of them before they were quiet enough and the names of the deeds that made them quiet enough and the names of the men and the women who did the deeds, who lasted and endured" (Faulkner, *Collected Stories*

114).[59] Here, according to Hamblin, Faulkner "pays homage to the capacity of art to both record and transcend the life it captures and, as a result, to inspire its participants to a greater awareness and understanding of the human condition" (274). What is even more important, though, as Hamblin suggests in "Carcassonne in Mississippi: Faulkner's Geography of the Imagination," is the creative process itself, in which the imagination, draped with "ambiguities and uncertainties," frees the individual from confining realistic limits (162)[60]—a perspective shared by Virginia Woolf in her essay "Mr. Bennet and Mrs. Brown." In this, both form and language become stretched to their physical limits (166). Art and the artistic process, in this sense, become alchemical. Another response, clearly connected to the impulse toward art, is the attempt to create a new myth out of the ruins (also seen in Eliot, Forster, Joyce, Lawrence, Yeats, and Woolf [see chapter 1]. For Kartiganer, *The Hamlet* represents Faulkner's first real mythic turn. Thus, myth is not only present in the novel, it attains a "level of mythic force" that wields the power to control and define lives (109), and, in this, the emphasis shifts from the individual to the community, from the individual struggle to the collective struggle that is the story of Yoknapatawpha County. It becomes a means for re-creation and atonement (132).[61]

Daniel Singal also sees modernism's dissolution in a much more positive light, as a "super integration" and as opportunity for change. In this light, he sees Faulkner as possessing two different selves, a Victorian self and a modernist self that he continually attempted to forge. "All his life Faulkner would struggle to reconcile these two divergent approaches to selfhood—the Victorian urge toward unity and stability he had inherited as a child of the southern rural gentry, [what Singal describes as the enticement of the **Cavalier** myth[62]] and the Modernist drive for multiplicity and change that he absorbed very early in his career as a self-identifying member of the international artistic avant-garde" (15). In emphasizing modernism as a "drive for multiplicity and change," Signal emphasizes a counterinterpretation to the social and metaphysical upheaval that has been its defining marks. For many, the upheaval produced a sense of loss, but for others, as Marianne DeKoven suggests, it produced a welcome opportunity for change.

The split, which Singal identifies as an oscillation between the desire for a more comfortable era and the desire to break free from the constraints of that era, is not uncommon among modernist writers, particularly in their early writing. Desiring an older and more Romantic Ireland, Yeats in "The Fisherman" yearns to write about a fisherman, who with "his sun-freckled face and grey Connemara cloth" does "not exist," and for this imagined man, he wants to write a poem as "cold / And passionate as the dawn."[63] Eliot in his early poetry uses Romantic imagery to undercut a Romanticism that he has not quite thrown off.

Singal notes a similar ambivalence in Faulkner. In discussing Faulkner's *The Marble Faun,* in which this tension is quite clear, Singal stresses that the "faun may dream of finding an ideal woman, but it remains wholly unclear whether he really *wants* to become a sensual being or whether in fact he prefers to experience life solely through the imagination" (49). In discussing the symbolist tradition in *The Marionettes,* Singal further contends that escaping from a "mundane reality" into a "dreamlike poetic landscape where absolute beauty might be found" is key (51). It is a "visionary aesthetic" that was "based on the fin de siècle assumption that art was far superior to experience, existing primarily to put us in contact, however momentarily, with a 'higher' realm that could elevate and inspire" (52).[64] According to Singal, the importance of such prose sketches as "Nympholepsy" was "not to plumb the depths of experience or make the reader aware of the endless complexities of reality, as would be the case in genuine twentieth-century modernism" (52). While I would agree here that the epiphanous experience that emerges in modernist literature is frequently accompanied by complexity and depth, the concept of the aesthetic object as conduit to a "'higher' realm' that could elevate and inspire" was common in modernist aesthetics.[65] Lothar Hönnighausen, for example, discusses Faulkner's contributions to the 1920–1921 *Ole Miss Yearbook* as highly influenced by **aestheticist** tendencies that can be seen in many modernist texts.[66]

Much of the tension Singal identifies pertains to an ambivalence toward sexuality, an "ideal of transcendent sexuality" that haunts Faulkner's poetry and his early novels such as *Soldiers' Pay* and *Mosquitoes.*[67] It is, as I see it, an ambivalence that inevitably becomes intertwined with shifts in the sex/gender system that paralleled the emergence of modernism. According to most Victorian interpretations of womanhood, women gravitated toward the spiritual and emotional side of love. Bearing vestiges of the "innocence of Paradise," women's "innocence" or "inherent purity" was seen as "an exalted state of feminine consciousness."[68] And much of the sexual ideology of the time depicted them as untroubled by desire and sexual feeling. Women, or more precisely, the "angel in the house" became the haven from rapid changes in industry, class structure, and communications that marked the latter part of the nineteenth century. Singal gives considerable attention to this issue: Faulkner himself, Singal claims, was obsessed with the "Diana-like girl"—a "transcendent image" that was "impregnably virginal" (77). Singal notes that as a character we see this in the "Diana-like girl" and in "the sister-as-mother" (Narcissa Benbow in *Flags in the Dust,* Pat Robyn in *Mosquitoes,* Caddie Compson in *The Sound and the Fury,* and Addie Bundren in *As I Lay Dying*). This obsession with purity continues in Quentin's "ironclad commitment to virginity," in his attempts to protect his real and surrogate sister, in his fantasy of the cauterizing "clean flame" that becomes his "spiritual apotheosis" in the fires of hell (123). It emerges, as well, in what Horace Benbow cannot bear in *Sanctuary:* the "image of the innocence defiled, of blackness pouring from the 'temple' of a white woman's body—an image which causes him to rush to the bathroom and vomit" (Singal 162). Singal sees these recurring motifs (both the obsession with a hard purity and Faulkner's portrayal of women) as residual nineteenth-century beliefs that continued to haunt his writing throughout his life (19). They represent, in Singal's estimation, Faulkner's nonmodernist self.

While I wholly agree that obsessions with purity plagued Victorian consciousness and while I agree as well that these obsessions mark Faulkner's texts,

I see the preoccupation with sexual tensions themselves as central to the discussion of modernism. The economic, political, and cultural shifts of the late nineteenth century that intensified an ideological longing for "the angel in the house" also paradoxically provided women with newfound opportunities that threatened to undermine this cultural fantasy. Marianne DeKoven, Bonnie Kime Scott, and Sandra Gilbert and Susan Gubar argue that the response to modernist dissolution frequently splits along gender lines [see chapter 9]. Contending that modernist formal practice enacts the terrifying appeal of the radical social change embodied in the feminist and socialist movements that marked the early part of the twentieth century, DeKoven in *Rich and the Strange* argues that the response to this change was "differently inflected for male and female modernists." In DeKoven's words, "male modernists generally feared the loss of hegemony the change they desired might entail, while female modernists feared the punishment for desiring that utter change" (4). Sandra Gilbert and Susan Gubar similarly argue that "both men and women engendered words and works which continually sought to come to terms with, and find terms for, an ongoing battle of the sexes that was set in motion by the late nineteenth-century rise of feminism and the fall of Victorian concepts of 'femininity.'"[69] For Gilbert and Gubar, this sexual tension is the defining mark of modernism; for Marianne DeKoven in *Rich and Strange* it is that which is "under erasure"; and for Bonnie Kime Scott it is that which produces a complicated web between male and female writers. What Singal reads as Faulkner's regression into a Victorian sensibility, particularly in his portrayal of women, is, as I see it, actually a defining mark of modernism. Quentin's obsession with sexual purity can be seen in Stephen Dedalus's parodied turning away from real women in *Portrait:* in his refusal to kiss E. C., in his fantasized relationship with Mercedes of *The Count of Monte Cristo,* and in his gazing at the bird-girl at the end of chapter 4 of *Portrait:* "Her eyes had called him and his soul had leaped at the call" (172). It can be seen in Marlow's proclamation in *Heart of Darkness* that women "live in a beautiful world of their own" (149). It can be seen in Eliot's Prufrock, who is horrified at arms, which "braceleted and white and bare" reveal in the "lamplight" downs of "light brown hair." What Quentin cannot bear—femininity as "the uncontrollable flow of nature," that "river of force" in which he is "helplessly caught" (Singal 121)—suggests, in a much later Joyce, the woman as river in *Finnegans Wake:* Anna Livia Plurabelle, who taking her name after the River Liffey, becomes almost synonymous with the river.

What is at stake, then, is a shifting definition of sexuality, what John Duvall identifies as the "sexual politics" of modernism.[70] In "Contextualizing *The Sound and the Fury:* Sex, Gender, and Community in Modern American Fiction," Duvall begins his essay by claiming that "a modernist theme that deserves careful scrutiny when one teaches *The Sound and the Fury* is the relationship between women and men, particularly the confusion, nervousness, and anger men express about women" (101), and then he illustrates how concerns over shifting sexual boundaries are played out in modernist themes and, in particular, in *The Sound and the Fury.* Likewise, Singal notes of Joe Christmas in *Light in*

August: "All through his life he will feel his manhood is in jeopardy," given that "masculinity for him is closely associated with autonomy—being 'hard, sufficient, potent, remorseless, strong'" (174). This tension frequently results in a kind of gender blurring both in the figure of the male character and in the women to whom he is attracted. In addition to Joe's "continuous psychological emasculation at the hands of white society," he is attracted to women whose gendered identities are similarly blurred: Bobbie Allen, who exists on the "bare margin of femininity" and Joanna Burden, who is Christmas's "mirror or double image" (175–77). In *The Sound and the Fury,* this gender reversal emerges in Caddy Compson, who, galloping to the scene of her brother's duel with Dalton Ames, finds him "passed out like a girl" (131). In *The Wild Palms,* the reversal emerges in Charlotte Rittenmeyer, an independent-minded woman who, for many critics, usurps Harry Wilbourne's masculinity (226).

Singal's *William Faulkner: The Making of a Modernist,* conjoining a personal and aesthetic reading, provides a unique perspective. However, his loose period definitions at times present difficulties. In his discussion of a nostalgia for a less-complicated time, the descriptions seem more Romantic than they do Victorian. And his definition of modernism, at times, is strained. Singal comments:

> Quentin is Faulkner during his fin de siècle stage shorn of all elements of Modernist influence; his tragic trajectory is the one Faulkner sensed might have been his own had he not encountered Eliot, Joyce, Freud, and other Modernist masters.
> . . . Quentin, by contrast, finds it impossible to determine who he is. (116)

To give a different definition, one could argue (as many critics have) that Quentin's ability to determine who he is *is* precisely what makes him a modernist figure. Quoting James McFarlane who contends that "the defining thing in the modernist mode is not so much that things fall *apart* but that they fall *together*," that the impulse is toward "superintegration" not "disintegration,"[71] Singal contends that Faulkner's "search for identity was to be found in the process of Modernist integration itself," that Faulkner creates a "provisional unity out of continuously shifting fragments" (114). It is not so much the interpretation with which I quarrel, but the singular definition of modernism, the concept that there could be *one* modernist self. The "superintegration" does in many ways characterize much of Faulkner's work; as a definition of modernism, though, it is only one of the 13 ways of looking at a blackbird.

What Singal so aptly assesses in his discussion of Faulkner and modernism is the blurring of boundaries that becomes inextricable from issues of changing notions of gender and sexuality, and the key role these conflicted issues played in the formation of Faulkner's imagination. It is this significance of this conflicted imagination that is also the subject of Karl Zender's *The Crossing of the Ways.* Focusing on how the use of sound unveils this conflict, Zender notes:

> Like most heirs of the romantic tradition, Faulkner believed that the imagination shapes our knowledge of the world. In the early part of his career, he toyed with an extreme, solipsistic form of this belief in which he ascribed to the imagination a capacity not only to shape our perceptions but also to alter external reality itself. (11)

Although Faulkner, as Zender illustrates, later incorporates the power of the world and otherness in his theories of imagination, the otherness (frequently associated with sound) elicited a hostile quality (11). Lisa Rado in "'A Perversion That Builds Chartres and Inverts Lear is a Pretty Good Thing'" in some ways conjoins Singal's and Zender's arguments.[72] Like Singal, Rado recognizes Faulkner's preoccupation with the "Diana-like girl" and recognizes, as well, his propensity for splitting himself into different characters. Like Zender, she recognizes the importance of theories of the imagination and the muse. She, thus, contends that the shifts in sexual theory that emerged at the turn of the twentieth century produced a "crisis in imagination" and a "crisis in authority" in that the female muse who so frequently inspired male writers became an androgyne. In her analysis of *Mosquitoes*'s artist Dawson Fairchild, Rado notes: "For what bothers him most about the boyish 'creatures' he sees on the streets is that they have displaced familiar, predominately male constructions of femininity—the hourglass shapes displayed on magazines, advertisements, and theater bills—with a provocative and transgressive sexual indeterminacy, thus changing the nature of female representation" (100)—and of the female muse. Moreover, the female Other of the Romantic poets becomes for the modern author an internal part of himself (108). What Zender identifies as Faulkner's initial impulse to wall out the Other, in Rado's estimation, is the struggle of the "male artist engaged in constant battle to maintain a balance between 'masculine' and 'feminine' parts of his imagination" and the attempt to avert being "subsumed or 'feminized' by the artistic enterprise" (117). In this light, intersections between gender issues and modernism become inextricable. The gender issues, thus, become part of the crisis.

What modernist criticism has yielded for Faulkner studies has indeed been multiple and diverse in form. From the associations with New Criticism there have emerged innumerable important close readings of Faulkner texts. From those readings that have focused on crises in aesthetics and crises in knowing, there have emerged key readings that place Faulkner's works and the techniques he employs at the core of a salient and intractable definition of modernism.

Robert Dale Parker in Absalom, Absalom!: *The Questioning of Fictions* calls Faulkner the "premier American modernist" and notes that "Faulkner responded deeply to the most talked about modernist narrative extravagances, from Cézanne and cubism to T. S. Eliot's *The Waste Land* and James Joyce's *Ulysses*" (7, 10).[73] From those readings that connect Faulkner's work to other modernist enterprises in literature, painting, or philosophy, there emerges an interdisciplinary enrichment. From those readings that engage a blurring of the boundaries that marks both modernism and postmodernism, there have emerged new questions and new parameters not only of modernism, but also of Faulkner's engagement with modernism. As Sanford Schwartz comments, "Modernism may be receding into the cultural past, but it seems to have found new life in the posthumous encounter with its [postmodernist] heir" (9).[74] It suggests, as Faulkner's oeuvre suggests, a continual motion. It leads to new directions, some twisting and circuitous, leading to places we do not expect. I remember after finishing a

Faulkner seminar deciding to take a reprieve by driving through the western foothills of Colorado with my mother on an old, unmarked gravel road. It was supposed to be a short excursion. But then the moon was on the right side of the car and then on the left, then on the right, and then on the left again. My mother, who has an impeccable sense of direction, said, "You know, I think we are headed for the Tetons." There were no road signs, only other unmarked intersecting roads, so I drove on. Finally, she made me flag down someone in an old pickup, coming from the opposite direction, who told us we were five miles from the Wyoming border. Theoretically, what happened that night enacted the combined, diverse modernist approaches to Faulkner: "My, my. A body does get around" (Faulkner, *Light* 480).

NOTES

1. There are numerous studies noting modernist influence. The following serves as a selection. Martin Kreiswirth in *William Faulkner: The Making of a Novelist* (Athens: University of Georgia Press, 1983) notes the influence of Houseman, Eliot, Pound, Verlaine, and Symons on Faulkner's poetry, of Aldous Huxley on *Mosquitoes,* and of an overall influence of Conrad and Joyce. André Bleikasten in *The Most Splendid Failure: Faulkner's* The Sound and the Fury (Bloomington: Indiana University Press, 1976) notes the importance of Aldous Huxley's influence in *Soldiers' Pay* and Joyce's influence in *Mosquitoes,* as well as the influence of Eliot on Faulkner's poetry. In terms of Faulkner's poetry, the symbolists, the decadents, and the imagists all emerge as influential. Richard Groden notes, in particular, the importance of the symbolists (Mallarmé, Valéry, Baudelaire, and Swinburne) on Faulkner's *A Green Bough.* See his "Lips by 'Laus Veneris,' Breasts by 'Anactoria,' Anecdote by William Faulkner," *Essays in Poetics* 14.1 (1989): 1–278. See also Lothar Hönnighausen, who in *William Faulkner: The Art of Stylization in his Early Graphic and Literary Work* (Cambridge: Cambridge University Press, 1987) emphasizes the importance of aestheticism and symbolism in Faulkner's early poetry. A. E. Elmore and Ida Fasler also address Faulkner's connections with Eliot. See A. E. Elmore, "Faulkner on the Agrarian South: Waste Land or Promised Land?" in *The Vanderbilt Tradition* (Baton Rouge: Louisiana State Press, 1991): 175–88 and Ida Fasel, "A 'Conversation' between Faulkner and Eliot," *Mississippi Quarterly* 20 (1967): 195–206. Hugh Kenner points out that although Faulkner could not be aligned with any of the formal tenets of **imagism,** his prose style does evoke parallels in spirit: where the imagists would "pare away" excess "verbiage," Faulkner would pare away "information." See Hugh Kenner, "Faulkner and the Avant-Garde," in *Faulkner, Modernism, and Film: Faulkner and Yoknapatawpha, 1978,* ed. Evans Harrington and Ann J. Abadie (Jackson: University Press of Mississippi, 1979), 188.

In terms of the fiction, Joyce is the most frequently noted influence, even though, as Michael Zeitlin notes, Faulkner claimed in a 1932 interview with Henry Nash Smith "that he had never read *Ulysses*" (63). Zeitlin goes on to argue, though, that Faulkner was quite familiar with *Ulysses* and that the force of unconscious fantasies that is so prevalent in Joyce's work influences much of his work. See "Versions of the 'Primal Scene': Faulkner and *Ulysses,*" *Mosaic* 22, no. 2 (1989): 63–77 and "Faulkner and Psychoanalysis: The *Elmer* Case," in *Faulkner and Psychology: Faulkner and Yoknapatawpha, 1991,* ed. Donald M. Kartiganer and Ann. J. Abadie (Jackson: University Press of Mississippi, 1994), 219–41. Hugh Kenner notes the Joycean traces in *The Sound in the Fury,* connecting Quentin's language patterns with Molly Bloom, Jason's with the Citizen in "Cyclops," and Benjy's with the opening of *Portrait* (25–29). See Hugh Kenner, "Faulkner and Joyce," in *Faulkner, Modernism, and Film,* 20–33. See also Gary Lee Stonum, *Faulkner's Career: An Internal Literary History* (Ithaca: Cornell University Press, 1979).

2. Paul Douglass, *Bergson, Eliot, and American Literature* (Lexington: University Press of Kentucky, 1986). Douglass here is addressing Bergson's *Creative Evolution.*

3. For an overview of a multifaceted modernism, see Astradur Eysteinsson in *The Concept of the Modern* (Ithaca: Cornell University Press, 1990). See also Bonnie Kime Scott, *Refiguring Modernism,* 2 vols. (Bloomington: Indiana University Press, 1995).

4. Vicki Mahaffey, "Modernist Theory and Modernist Criticism," in *The Johns Hopkins Guide to Literary Theory and Criticism* (Baltimore: Johns Hopkins Press, 1994), 512–15.

5. Susan Stanford Friedman further notes: "Tradition comes into being only as it is rebelled against. Definitional excursions into the meanings of *modern, modernity,* and *modernism* begin and end in reading the specificities of these contradictions" (510). See her "Definitional Excursions: The Meanings of *Modern/Modernity/Modernism,*" *Modernisms/Modernity* 8 (2001): 493–513.

6. Noel Polk, introduction to *New Essays on The Sound and the Fury* (Cambridge: Cambridge University Press, 1993). Polk notes: "Modernist criticism of *The Sound and the Fury* begins in the middle 1970s, with John T. Irwin's *Doubling and Incest/Repetition and Revenge: A Speculative Reading of Faulkner* (1975) and André Bleikasten's *The Most Splendid Failure*" (16).

7. Jean-François Lyotard, *The Postmodern Explained: Correspondence 1982–1984,* trans. Julian Pefanis and Morgan Thomas (Minneapolis: University of Minnesota Press, 1993). Most current readings of postmodernism see this postmodernism as an extension of modernism, not its opposite. See Hugh Witemeyer's essay collection, *The Future of Modernism* (Ann Arbor: University of Michigan Press, 1997).

8. Richard C. Moreland, *Faulkner and Modernism: Rereading and Rewriting* (Madison: University of Wisconsin Press, 1990).

9. Philip M. Weinstein, *Faulkner's Subject: A Cosmos No One Owns* (Cambridge: Cambridge University Press, 1992). In fact, many recent important critiques of subjectivity have emerged through the Lacanian readings of Faulkner. I have mentioned only a few key studies in this analysis, since this essay collection has a chapter on psychological criticism [see chapter 8]. I have similarly limited my discussions of gender, given the chapter on postmodernist criticism [see chapter 6]. Unless otherwise specified, all citations of Weinstein's work refer to *Faulkner's Subject.* On a further note, I read postmodernism as an extension of modernism. Postmodernism indeed is more diffuse, but many of the issues are similar—such as the failure of identity that Weinstein and Moreland address.

10. Gail Mortimer, *Faulkner's Rhetoric of Loss: A Study in Perception and Meaning* (Austin: University of Texas Press, 1983). Unless otherwise specified, all citations of Mortimer's work refer to *Faulkner's Rhetoric of Loss.*

11. Charles Hannon, "Signification, Simulation, and Containment in *If I Forget Thee, Jerusalem,*" *Faulkner Journal* 7, nos. 1–2 (1991): 133–50. See also Daniel Ferrer, *"In Omnis Iam Vocabuli Mortem:* Representation of Absence: The Subject of Representation and Absence in William Faulkner's *As I Lay Dying,*" *Oxford Literary Review* 5 (1982): 21–36 and Gerhard Hoffmann, *"Absalom, Absalom!:* A Postmodernist Approach," in *Faulkner's Discourse An International Symposium,* ed. Lothar Hönnighausen (Tübingen: Max Niemeyer Verlag, 1989), 276–92.

12. Cleanth Brooks, *The Well-Wrought Urn* (New York: Harcourt, 1927). Of those most frequently associated with New Criticism, Cleanth Brooks, Robert Penn Warren, and Allen Tate are the most noted in Faulkner studies. See for example, Cleanth Brooks, "The Narrative Structure of *Absalom, Absalom!*" *Georgia Review* 29 (1975): 366–94. In his major works on Faulkner, however, Brooks frequently abandons a totally New Critical perspective, in which the autonomous aesthetic object becomes disassociated from its author. Brooks often casts Faulkner within a humanist frame, manifesting the importance of Faulkner's personal beliefs—his wrestling with Romanticism and with a vision of good and evil (*Hidden God* 43). See respectively *William Faulkner: Toward Yoknapatawpha and Beyond* (New Haven, CT: Yale University Press, 1978) and *The Hidden God: Studies in Hemingway, Faulkner, Yeats, Eliot, and Warren* (New Haven, CT: Yale University Press, 1963). See also Robert Penn Warren, "William Faulkner," in *The Forms of Modern Fiction: Essays Collected in Honor of Joseph Warren Beach,* ed. William Van O'Connor (Minneapolis: University of Minnesota Press, 1948), 125–43. Allen Tate mostly discusses Faulkner as an agrarian within a Southern context.

13. Olga W. Vickery, *The Novels of William Faulkner: A Critical Interpretation* (Baton Rouge: Louisiana State University Press, 1992). See also H. F. Garlick, "Three Patterns of Imagery in Benjy's Section of *The Sound and the Fury*," *Journal of the Australian Modern Language Association* 52 (1979): 274–87; Michael Groden, "Criticism in New Composition: *Ulysses* and *The Sound and the Fury*," *Twentieth Century Literature* 21 (1975): 265–77; Irving Howe, *William Faulkner: A Critical Study* (Chicago: University of Chicago Press, 1951); Thomas L. McHaney, *William Faulkner's* The Wild Palms: *A Study* (Jackson: University Press of Mississippi, 1975); François Pitavy, *Faulkner's* Light in August, trans. Gillian E. Cook (Bloomington: Indiana University Press, 1973); Joseph W. Reed Jr., *Faulkner's Narrative* (New Haven, CT: Yale University Press, 1973).

14. David Newman, "'the vehicle itself is unaware': New Criticism on the Limits of Reading Faulkner," *Mississippi Quarterly* 48, no. 3 (1995): 481–99.

15. Ihab Hassan, *The Dismemberment of Orpheus: Toward a Postmodern Literature* (New York: Oxford University Press, 1982).

16. See Jonathan Culler, *Structuralist Poetics: Structuralism, Linguistics, and the Study of Literature* (Ithaca: Cornell University Press, 1975) and Claude Lévi Strauss, *Structural Anthropology*, trans. Monique Layton (New York: Penguin, 1978). Structuralism did not emerge in the United States until the 1960s; however, for at least a decade it heavily influenced interpretations of modernism.

17. Ludwig Mies van der Rohe, "Technology and Architecture," in *Programmes and Manifestoes on Twentieth-Century Architecture,* ed. Ulrich Conrads (London: Lund Humphries, 1970), 152, qtd. in Steven Connor, *Postmodernist Culture: An Introduction to Theories of the Contemporary* (Oxford: Blackwell, 1989), 68.

18. Malcolm Cowley, introduction to *The Portable Faulkner* (New York: Viking, 1949). See also Cowley, "Magic in Faulkner," in *Faulkner, Modernism, and Film*, 3–19. In a similar light, Martin Kreiswirth and André Bleikasten see in Faulkner's earlier fiction the seeds of modernist experimentation that is so frequently associated with *The Sound and the Fury, As I Lay Dying, Light in August,* and *Absalom, Absalom!* See also Stonum, *Faulkner's Career.*

19. Arthur F. Kinney, *Faulkner's Narrative Poetics: Style as Vision* (Amherst: University of Massachusetts Press, 1978). Unless otherwise specified, all citations of Kinney's work refer to *Faulkner's Narrative Poetics.*

20. Donald M. Kartiganer, *The Fragile Thread: The Meaning of Form in Faulkner's Novels* (Amherst: University of Massachusetts Press, 1979). All citations from Kartiganer's works refer to *The Fragile Thread* unless otherwise specified.

21. Vicki Mahaffey, "Heirs of Yeats: Eire as Female Poets Revise Her," in *The Future of Modernism,* ed. Hugh Witemeyer (Ann Arbor: University of Michigan Press, 1997), 101–17. Eysteinsson in *The Concept of the Modern* makes a similar point: "From a certain perspective, modernism, in its rejection of traditional social representation and in its heightening of formal awareness, would seem the ideal example of New Critical tenets and of the New Critical view of the poem as an isolated whole, whose unity is based on internal tensions that perhaps remain unresolved but nonetheless do not disturb the autonomy of the work." Eysteinsson, however, continues by emphasizing that this New Critical mode is *a* critical paradigm (one among many), and that there need be no "natural" connection between New Criticism and modernist criticism (11).

22. See also Stephen M. Ross, *Fiction's Inexhaustible Voice: Speech and Writing in Faulkner* (Athens: University of Georgia Press, 1989). Ross, in his analysis of different kinds of voices in Faulkner's work, combines structural and New Critical approaches.

23. Noting Faulkner's use of the long sentence, Paul Douglass also notes the importance of a Bergsonian fluidity in Faulkner's work. See also Ida Fasel, "Spatial Form and Spatial Time," *Western Humanities Review* 16 (1962): 223–34; Carolyn Norman Slaughter, "*Absalom, Absalom!:* 'Fluid Cradle of Events (Time),'" *Faulkner Journal* 6 (1991): 65–84; and Vickery, *The Novels of William Faulkner.*

24. Daniel Singal, *William Faulkner: The Making of a Modernist* (Chapel Hill: University of North Carolina Press, 1997). Unless specified otherwise, all references to Singal's work will be to *William Faulkner.*

25. Virginia Woolf, "Mr. Bennet and Mrs. Brown," in *Virginia Woolf: Collected Essays.* vol. 1 (New York: Harcourt, 1967), 320. Willa Cather makes a similar remark: "The world broke in two in 1922 or thereabouts" (v). See her prefatory note in *Note Under Forty* (Lincoln: University of Nebraska Press, 1988).

26. Much of the calm that Singal describes pertains to definitions of Victorian womanhood, which became one of the few perceived havens against a world that was rapidly changing.

27. See Karl Marx, "Free Human Production," in *The Writings of the Young Marx on Philosophy and Society,* ed. and trans. Loyd D. Easton and Kurt H Guddat (New York: Doubleday, 1967), 272–82.

28. Matthew Arnold, "Dover Beach." in *Victorian and Later English Poets,* ed. James Stephens, Edwin L. Beck, and Royall H. Snow (New York: American Book, 1934).

29. Thomas Hardy, "The Darkling Thrush," in *Victorian and Later English Poets,* 914.

30. Ian Watt, "Impressionism and Symbolism in *Heart of Darkness,*" in *Joseph Conrad: A Commemoration: Papers from the 1974 International Conference on Conrad,* ed. Norman Sherry (London: Macmillan, 1976), 37–53.

31. See respectively Michael Levenson, *A Genealogy of Modernism* (Cambridge: Cambridge University Press, 1984); Perry Meisel, *The Myth of the Modern: A Study in British Literature and Criticism after 1850* (New Haven, CT: Yale University Press, 1987); Bette London, *The Appropriated Voice: Narrative Authority in Conrad, Forster, and Woolf* (Ann Arbor: University of Michigan Press, 1990). As many female modernist critics have noted, however, how this epistemological uncertainty is experienced varies. For many female modernists, the uncertainty produced a sense of release and freedom. See Marianne DeKoven, *Rich and Strange: Gender, History, and Modernism* (Princeton, NJ: Princeton University Press, 1991) and Bonnie Kime Scott, *Refiguring Modernism,* 2 vols. (Bloomington: Indiana University Press, 1995).

32. Rosi Braidotti, *Patterns of Dissonance: A Study of Women in Contemporary Philosophy,* trans. Elizabeth Guild (New York: Routledge, 1991). Braidotti's discussion takes in all of the twentieth century; however, she locates the beginnings of these epistemological disruptions in modernism.

33. Michael Bell, "The Metaphysics of Modernism," in *The Cambridge Companion to Modernism,* ed. Michael Levenson (Cambridge: Cambridge University Press, 1999).

34. See Christina Froula, *Modernism Body: Sex, Culture, and Joyce* (New York: Columbia University Press, 1996).

35. See also André Bleikasten who likewise emphasizes the importance of loss in Faulkner. See his *Faulkner's* As I Lay Dying, trans. Roger Little (Bloomington: University of Indiana Press, 1973) and *The Most Splendid Failure: Faulkner's* The Sound and the Fury.

36. Jun Liu, "Nihilists and Their Relations: A Nietzschean Approach to Teaching *The Sound and the Fury,*" in *Approaches to Teaching Faulkner's* The Sound and the Fury, ed. Stephen Hahn and Arthur F. Kinney (New York: Modern Language Association, 1996), 89–95.

37. John Orr, *The Making of the Twentieth-Century Novel: Lawrence, Joyce, Faulkner and Beyond* (New York: St. Martin's, 1987). Orr's discussion here pertains to *As I Lay Dying.* See also John E. Bassett, "*Absalom, Absalom!* The Limits of Narrative Form," *Modern Language Quarterly* 46 (1985): 276–92; Patrick O'Donnell, "The Spectral Road: Metaphors of Transference in Faulkner's *As I Lay Dying,*" *Papers on Language and Literature* 20 (1984): 60–79; and Carolyn N. Slaughter, "*As I Lay Dying:* Demise of Vision," *American Literature* 61 (1989): 16–30.

38. Karl Zender, *The Crossing of the Ways: William Faulkner, the South, and the Modern World* (New Brunswick: Rutgers University Press, 1989).

39. John E. Basset, *Visions and Revisions: Essays on Faulkner* (West Cornwall, CT: Locus Hill Press, 1989).

40. Kartiganer is referencing James B. Meriwether and Michael Millgate, eds., *Lion in the Garden: Interviews with William Faulkner, 1926–1962* (New York: Random House, 1968).

41. See Jacques Lacan, *Écrits: A Selection,* trans. Alan Sheridan (New York: Norton, 1977).

42. Richard C. Moreland, in "Faulkner and Modernism," in *The Cambridge Companion to William Faulkner,* ed. Philip M. Weinstein (Cambridge: Cambridge University Press, 1995), makes a similar argument in his discussion of Hightower in *Light in August.*

43. Paul de Man, *Blindness and Insight: Essays in the Rhetoric of Contemporary Criticism* (New York: Oxford University Press, 1971), ctd. in Kartiganer (160). This obliteration of origin, as Kartiganer suggests, echoes Harold Bloom's *The Anxiety of Influence* (New York: Oxford University Press, 1973). It is in Kartiganer's words, "a clear breaking forth from history, from art, from illusion, from everything that carries over from the past [. . .]," (170).

44. Peter Brooks, "Incredulous Narration: *Absalom, Absalom!*" in *William Faulkner's* Absalom, Absalom!" ed. Harold Bloom (New York: Chelsea House Publishers, 1987), 105–27.

45. This modernist challenge to authority and to the individual and cultural father is addressed more fully in psychoanalytic criticism [see chapter 8].

46. Although the concept of the fragmented self is a familiar topic in modernist discussions, its cultural ramifications, particularly the ideological explorations of race, gender, and class, emerged later in the postmodernist reexaminations of modernism.

47. Daniel Singal takes the opposite view, arguing that it is Quentin's lack of identity that characterizes him as Victorian rather than modernist.

48. Cited in Weinstein, *Faulkner's Subject,* 83. Karl Zender makes a similar point: Voice "undermines" any hope Quentin may have of "verbal omnipotence" (*Crossing* 16–17).

49. Modernist literature's perceived tendency to resist popular culture has been a source of criticism from many postmodernist critics.

50. See for example, Charles A. Peek, "Adjusting the Apocrypha: the Thirties and Faulkner's Radical Critique of 'The Old Plantation,'" *Arkansas Review* 31 no. 1 (April 2000): 16–20.

51. This is the main premise of Kinney's *Faulkner's Narrative Poetics.*

52. Some of these techniques are obviously inextricable from one another. Commentary on Faulkner's modernist narrative techniques is too extensive to incorporate fully. What follows is a selected overview. For a general discussion of the narrative techniques applicable to modernism see Thomas E. Connolly, "Point of View in Faulkner's *Absalom, Absalom!*" *Modern Fiction Studies* 27 (Summer 1981): 255–72; Albert J. Guerard, "Faulkner: The Problems of Technique," in *The Triumph of the Novel: Dickens, Dostoevsky, Faulkner* (New York: Oxford University Press, 1976) 204–34; Bruce Kawin, "The Montage Element in Faulkner's Fiction," in *Faulkner, Modernism, and Film,* 103–26; Stephen M. Ross, "Evocation of Voice in *Absalom, Absalom!*" *Essays in Literature* 8 (1981): 135–49 and "Shapes of Time and Consciousness in *As I Lay Dying,*" *Texas Studies in Literature and Language* 16 (1974): 723–37. Guerard's discussion provides an excellent overview of Faulkner's innovations in narrative. For a discussion of stream of consciousness and interior monologue, see Carvel Collins, "The Interior Monologues of *The Sound and the Fury,*" in *The Merrill Studies in* The Sound and the Fury (Columbus: Ohio State University Press, 1970), 59–79; Robert Humphrey, "Form and Function Stream of Consciousness in William Faulkner's *The Sound and the Fury,*" in *Stream of Consciousness in the Modern Novel* (Berkeley: University of California Press, 1954), 17–21, 64–70, 104–11; Frederick Hoffman, *The Twenties: American Writing in Postwar Decade* (New York: The Free Press, 1962), 246–49; Donald M. Kartiganer, "*The Sound and the Fury* and Faulkner's Quest for Form," *ELH* 37 (1970): 613–39; Bruce F. Kawin, *The Mind of the Novel: Reflexive Fiction and the Ineffable* (Princeton, NJ: Princeton University Press, 1982), 251–72; Deiter Meindl, "Some Epistemological and Esthetic Implications of William Faulkner's Discourse," in *Faulkner's Discourse,* 149–58; and Weinstein, *Faulkner's Subject.* For techniques that emphasize isolation, see Hugh M. Ruppersburg, *Voice and Eye in Faulkner's Fiction* (Athens: University of Georgia Press, 1983) and William A. Freedman, "The Technique of Isolation in *The Sound and the Fury,*" *Mississippi Quarterly* 15 (1962): 21–26. For discussions of Faulkner's poetic techniques in his prose see Robert M. Adams, "Poetry in the Novel; or Faulkner's Esemplastic," *Virginia Quarterly* 39 (1953): 419–34; Paul R. Lilly Jr., "Caddy and Addie: Speakers of Faulkner's Impeccable Language," *Journal of Narrative Technique* 3 (1973): 170–83. See also Gary Lee Stonum's chapter "Visionary Poetics" in *Faulkner's Career,* where he argues that Faulkner's prose style emerged out of his poetics (41–61). For discussions emphasizing the merging of art and literature, see Albert Guerard, "*Absalom, Absalom!:* The Novel as Impressionist Art," in *The Triumph of the Novel,* 302–39; Ilse Dusoir Lind, "The Effect of Painting on Faulkner's Poetic Form," in *Faulkner, Modernism, and Film,* 127–48; Arthur

L. Scott, "The Myriad Perspectives of *Absalom, Absalom!*" *American Quarterly* 6 (1954): 210–20. Panthea Reid also has several articles on Faulkner's intersections with modernist art. See "Teaching *The Sound and the Fury* as a Postimpressionist Novel," in *Approaches to Teaching Faulkner's* The Sound and the Fury, 114–21; "The Scene of Writing and the Shape of Language for Faulkner When 'Matisse and Picasso Yet Painted,'" in *Faulkner and the Artist: Faulkner and Yoknapatawpha, 1993,* eds. Donald M. Kartiganer and Ann J. Abadie (Jackson: University Press of Mississippi, 1993), 82–109; and "Faulkner's Cubist Novels," in *"A Cosmos of My Own": Faulkner and Yoknapatawpha, 1980,* ed. Doreen Fowler and Ann J. Abadie (Jackson, MS: University Press of Mississippi, 1981), 59–94. For discussions that emphasize active reading, see Arthur Kinney; Donald Kartiganer; Philip Weinstein; Betty Alldredge, "Spatial Form in Faulkner's *As I Lay Dying,*" *Southern Literary Journal* 11, no. 1 (1978): 3–19; and Karen McPherson, "*Absalom, Absalom!:* Telling Scratches," *Modern Fiction Studies* 33 (1987): 431–50.

53. See Henri Bergson, *Matter and Memory* (New York: Zone Books, 1991). See also Maurice Coindreau, who connects *The Sound and the Fury* to impressionistic music in "Preface to *The Sound and the Fury,*" trans. George M. Reeves, *Mississippi Quarterly* 19 (1966): 107–15.

54. Kartiganer describes Benjy's monologue in *The Sound and the Fury* as a "series of frozen pictures" that he relives over and over again in the eternal present—as preconscious, thus distinguishing it from stream of consciousness (8–9).

55. See M. H. Abrams, *A Glossary of Literary Terms,* 4th ed. (New York: Holt, Rinehart and Winston), 187.

56. Walter Pater, "Conclusion," *The Renaissance: Studies in Art and Poetry* (New York: Macmillan, 1905).

57. Thomas L. McHaney, "Faulkner and Modernism: Why Does it Matter?" in *New Directions in Faulkner Studies: Faulkner and Yoknapatawpha, 1983,* ed. Doreen Fowler and Ann J. Abadie, (Jackson: University Press Mississippi, 1984), 37–60.

58. Robert W. Hamblin, "'Saying No to Death': Toward William Faulkner's Theory of Fiction," in *"A Cosmos of My Own": Faulkner and Yoknapatawpha, 1980,* 3–35.

59. Robert W. Hamblin, "'Like a Big Soft Fading Wheel': The Triumph of Faulkner's Art," in *Faulkner at One Hundred: Retrospect and Prospect: Faulkner and Yoknapatawpha, 1997,* ed. Donald Kartiganer and Ann J. Abadie (Jackson: University Press of Mississippi, 2000), 272–84.

60. Robert W. Hamblin, "Carcassonne in Mississippi: Faulkner's Geography of the Imagination," in *Faulkner and the Craft of Fiction: Faulkner and Yoknapatawpha, 1987,* ed. Doreen Fowler and Ann J. Abadie (Jackson: University Press of Mississippi, 1989), 148–71.

61. See, in particular, Robert W. Hamblin's discussions of Faulkner and myth in this collection [chapter 1].

62. The term was initially used to describe the lighthearted, melodious, and frequently courtly verse of a group of poets in the seventeenth century. Singal uses it to designate codes of honor in the Victorian period.

63. William Butler Yeats, "The Fisherman," in *A Collection of Poems of W. B. Yeats.* (New York: Macmillan, 1903).

64. Singal is citing Gary Lee Stonum, *Faulkner's Career.*

65. See for example Yeats, "Symbol of Poetry," in *Essays and Introductions* (New York: Macmillan, 1961), 153–64; Wallace Stevens, *The Necessary Angel: Essays on Reality and the Imagination* (New York: Vintage, 1942); and Rainer Marie Rilke, *The Duino Elegies,* trans. J. B. Lieshman and Stephen Spender (New York: Norton, 1963).

66. Commenting on Faulkner's calligraphy for the imagist anthology (noted from Robert Hamblin and Louis D. Brodsky, *Selections from the William Faulkner Collection of Louis Daniel Brodsky*), Hönnighausen contends that Faulkner "rebound and hand-lettered" the "characteristic document of Modernism in the *art nouveau* manner of his own hand-crafted books" (15). Hönnighausen extends this use of the *art nouveau* manner to Faulkner's illustrations in *The Marionettes.*

67. Singal sees *Flags in the Dust* as beginning to break out of the Cavalier myth, as becoming more "modern" in its inclinations. By employing Freudian tropes, Singal argues that Faulkner

addresses in *Flags in the Dust* the cultural pathology he perceived within himself and the South—"with its obsessive attachment to a mythic past, its repression of vital human instincts, its illusive and destructive pursuit of purity, and its incestuous close-mindedness" (112).

68. Peter T. Cominos, "Innocent Femina Sensualis in Unconscious Conflict," in *Suffer and Be Still: Women in the Victorian Age,* ed. Martha Vicinus (Bloomington: Indiana University Press, 1972), 157.

69. Sandra M. Gilbert and Susan Gubar, *No Man's Land,* vol. 1, *The War of Words.* (New Haven, CT: Yale University Press, 1988), xii.

70. John Duvall, "Contextualizing *The Sound and the Fury:* Sex, Gender, and Community in Modern American Fiction," in *Approaches to Teaching Faulkner's* The Sound and the Fury, 101–7.

71. Ctd. in Singal (10).

72. Rado argues that for Faulkner the sexual "revolution" of the early twentieth century produced a "profound crisis of artistic identity" (101). See Lisa Rado, "'A Perversion That Builds Chartres and Invents Lear Is a Pretty Good Thing': Psychic Incest and Haunted Hermaphroditism in Faulkner," in *The Modern Androgyne: A Failed Sublime* (Charlottesville: University of Virginia Press, 2000), 99–137.

73. See Robert Dale Parker, Absalom, Absalom!: *The Questioning of Fictions* (Boston: Twayne, 1991). See also Panthea Reid Broughton, "Faulkner's Cubist Novels," in '*A Cosmos of My Own': Faulkner and Yoknapatawpha, 1980,* 59–94.

74. Sanford Schwartz, "The Postmodernity of Modernism," in *The Future of Modernism,* 9–31. See also, Panthea Reid Broughton, "Faulkner's Cubist Novels," 59–94.

6

Postmodern Criticism

Terrell L. Tebbetts

William Faulkner was not a postmodernist. Neither his fiction nor his observations about his writing make him such. Both, in fact, are far more characteristic of modernism, which is addressed elsewhere in this volume [see chapter 5].

What then does postmodernism have to do with Faulkner's fiction? Perhaps this: though he learned much of his craft from the early modernist writers and used many of the tools they showed him how to use, Faulkner is much more than a modernist. We might say that just as Shakespeare is a playwright both of the Renaissance and for all ages, so is Faulkner a novelist both of the modern period and beyond it. And it is precisely postmodernism, with its differences from modernism and its critique of it, that shows us how much Faulkner himself critiques the intellectual and literary traits of modernism even as he uses them. Postmodernism, then, is the window Faulkner slips through to enter the future.

That window has five panes. That is to say, postmodern writers and critics share five intellectual assumptions that constitute what we can call the postmodern worldview. They are as follows: (1) Language cannot represent reality. Language is reality. (2) All truth is contingent rather than final, temporary rather than eternal, social rather than transcendent. (3) All authorities and hierarchies are suspect because they favor singularity over multiplicity, orthodoxy over heterodoxy. (4) Transgression is a positive act, breaking down artificial boundaries and destabilizing oppressive social and intellectual orders. (5) Human identity is relational rather than essential and thus as unstable and multiple as truth itself. Contemporary critics have considered all five of these assumptions in relation to Faulkner's fiction, turning most often to *Absalom, Absalom!* and, appropriately enough, almost always coming to different conclusions. They seem to agree, primarily, that these assumptions open up new questions and fresh understandings when they read *Absalom, Absalom!* and other major fiction with them in mind. They certainly bring Faulkner's nineteenth- and twentieth-century characters and stories into the cyber age and make it worthwhile to slip through that postmodern window with them.

LANGUAGE CANNOT REPRESENT REALITY

For the postmodernist, it is impossible to represent the real in language. After all, words, written or spoken symbols, are not the things they represent: the word *desk* is not a desk. Moreover, words are tricky: even the relatively concrete word *desk* can refer to anything from a steel-tubed student chair in a classroom to a battered oak rolltop in a home office to a polished mahogany status symbol in a center of power. The simple difficulty of specifying to which desk one is referring, multiplied enough times, leads postmodernists to declare "the failure of language to ever say what one means" (Duvall, "Postmodern" 39). Even if speakers or writers find the exact words that denote their meanings, they must still deal with the hearers/readers and the connections they make with the words. As Fredric Jameson explains, "language itself [is] an unstable exchange between its speakers" ("Foreword" xi). Though modernists might consider such issues mere difficulties to overcome with due care as they go about representing reality, postmodernists make them the center of their epistemology, their philosophy of knowledge. In his valuable treatise *The Idea of the Postmodern: A History,* Hans Bertens explains how Derridian poststructuralism has led postmodern thinkers to reject entirely the idea that "language can represent reality" and to assert the contrary, that "language constitutes, rather than reflects, the world, and that knowledge is always therefore distorted by language" (6).

Two commentators see this epistemological dilemma in typical Faulknerian compositional strategies. Although Jameson's consideration of Faulkner is relatively brief, he does bring the dilemma to bear on Faulkner's fiction as a whole in his major analysis of postmodernism, *Postmodernism, or, The Cultural Logic of Late Capitalism.* Jameson comments on how frequently Faulkner's narratives return to particular moments in the past, piling on more and more details "in an attempt to conjure" a character or an action with more representational reality than a mere "movement of sentences" can really give it (133). Through this technique Jameson sees Faulkner "exhibit[ing] a deeply-embedded foreshadowing of the necessary failure of language, which will never coincide with its object" and thus represent it adequately (133). Philip Cohen [see chapter 12], in turn, sees Faulkner's textual strategies as creating and accepting an "instability" intrinsic in language and thus necessary to his craft as a writer (177). Character and plot shift as Faulkner carries an earlier story into a novel or reprises previous material—as he moves through the Snopes trilogy, for instance.

Critics examining specific works find this failure of language to represent reality a particular concern in the Compson novels. Doreen Fowler focuses on Quentin Compson in *The Sound and the Fury* and *Absalom, Absalom!,* arguing that Quentin's crisis derives from the "dissolution" of the notion prevailing "from the Renaissance through the modern period . . . that language somehow represents meanings that exist independent of language" ("Revising" 96). Martin Kreiswirth agrees, seeing in *Absalom, Absalom!* "a serious and critical questioning of representation, . . . one of the few agreed upon hallmarks of . . . postmodernism" ("Intertextuality" 111). The use of language in the novel to tell, to contradict, and to retell the Sutpen history, he claims, creates an "instability" that finally "meddles with the process of representation itself" and convinces readers of the "impossibility" of certain knowledge (113), engaging them in the "postmodern problems of reference and representation" (115). All the language of the novel, all the telling, ultimately reveals much more about the hearts of its users than about the object it tries to represent and thus know, Thomas Sutpen. Language is more self-reflexive than representational.

To be sure, *Absalom, Absalom!* challenges the sufficiency of language in passage after passage. An important one is the speech Jason Compson attributes to Judith Sutpen when she hands Grandmother Compson the letter presumably written by Charles Bon: even when written in stone, Judith says, words are mere scratches without meaning, and "it doesn't matter" that it is so (101).[1] Another important passage, even without Judith's comment, is the letter itself, for without salutation or signature its "real" meaning will forever elude its readers. A third important passage is the language attributed to Grandfather Compson, who called language "that meagre and fragile thread" by which we momentarily connect our brief and equally unstable lives (202). Although Quentin Compson may embody what Philip Weinstein calls modernism's "raging desire to overcome" the "weakness" of language, *Absalom, Absalom!* as a whole may better embody what Weinstein calls postmodernism's "wry acceptance of irreducible linguistic conditions" ("Postmodern" 20).

Another important novel to consider in light of the postmodern problem with language and representation is *As I Lay Dying.* At one pole lies Addie Bundren with her profound distrust of language. At another lies Anse Bundren with his penchant for making reality disappear into language like a rabbit into a hat. Between these poles representing the thing and the word hang the Bundren children, twisting in the wind.

Addie Bundren utterly rejects language. She dismisses it repeatedly in her monologue, objecting to it in startlingly postmodern terms. She calls words "no good," for example, because they "don't ever fit . . . what they are trying to say" (171). Instead of words she prefers to listen to the voiceless language of the earth itself, where "the words are the deeds" (174). Instead of speaking she prefers to act; as a teacher she seems to have found the blood drawn by her switch more meaningful than any knowledge imparted in her lessons. Indeed, to Addie Bundren language is nothing more than "a shape to fill a lack" (172), a poor substitute when the act is missing, and unnecessary when it is present.

Anse Bundren gives Addie plenty of reason to reject language. He uses it to create a reality distinct from the one his deeds create. He calls himself a "hardworking man" (110), for instance, unwilling to be "beholden" (117), giving to his children "without stint" (256). Others, however, indicate that Anse never works enough to cause a sweat (17), has relied on his neighbors for so much help that they "cant quit" (33), is so lazy he hates moving (114), somehow makes others "have to help him" (192), and is so worthless he would bury his wife in a borrowed grave if only he could (240). Rather than giving to his children, he takes from them—Cash's graphophone money, Jewel's horse, Dewey Dell's abortion money, and Darl's freedom, the latter a frank exchange for the value of Gillespie's barn (232). Anse's language does not represent the real, yet neither others' observations nor his own deeds seem so real to Anse as his own self-serving, specious words.

The two other characters closest to Addie outside the family join Anse in using words to create realities separate from deeds, living in worlds as word-centered, or **logocentric,** and self-serving as Anse's. The Reverend Whitfield and Cora Tull take their reality-creating language not from the world of work but from religion. Vernon Tull observes that Whitfield's language and Whitfield's person are separate and contrasting entities: "It's like they are not the same. It's like he is one, and his voice is one" (91). Tull's comment foreshadows Whitfield's separation of his words from his deeds when he fails to confess his adultery: he feels no need to deliver his confession as long as he has "framed the words" (178), for he assures himself that God takes "the will for the deed" (179). Like Whitfield, Cora Tull talks a great deal about living according to God's will (8) and living right in God's sight (23), but Vernon Tull, again, points out how different those words are from actions. In reality, Cora would like to crowd out others before the throne of God, he says (71), and even assume the throne herself (74). Yet Cora remains as blind to the distance between words and deeds as Anse and Whitfield.

Before postmodernism, readers might take such discrepancies as simple hypocrisy, Anse and Whitfield and Cora being types of the biblical Pharisees, whited sepulchres all. Postmodernism, however, helps readers understand Faulkner's depiction of Addie's atypical and radical response to these discrepancies. Addie yearns for a reality truer and more substantial than that created by language, a totality that grounds all language and that exists before words begin and after they end. In connecting with such a totality, Addie might overcome the aloneness that marks her as strongly as her distrust of words. Addie has not found that totality in eternal verities like love, for she never experiences them. Love in particular has become just another word to fill a lack. Neither has she found that totality in a transcendent realm, which, after all, she experiences primarily in the very words she distrusts. She embodies the postmodern Lacanian view that an original but lost connection with totality (the child's connection to the mother) has been replaced by a promised but undelivered reconnection through the logocentric (word-centered) symbolic order (the cultural order, from traditional lore to established systems and institutions), which promises to connect the lone individual with a longed-for totality but is incapable of doing so. With no confidence in the power of love to connect her to a third Lacanian realm, the Lacanian Real, which exists beyond the word-centered world and cannot be approached through words, Addie must continue to live alone. Thus she chooses death over life, the grave over the Bundren home; for in the grave she literally enters the totality of the earth itself, the realm of original connection, where she will no longer bear the burden of speaking or hearing the mere words of the symbolic order so full of promise but so empty of connection. She overcomes her aloneness by connecting with the earth alone. There she grounds herself in a totality.

Readers will differ on how to take such a reading. Does the novel make the language of Anse, Whitfield, and Cora so repugnant that readers are compelled to endorse Addie's rejection of language altogether as well as the symbolic orders it describes or creates? Some might do so, but such would be a problematic truth to draw from a novel, a world itself constituted entirely of words that would by definition become false.

On the other hand, does the novel's comic structure convince readers that Addie's postmodern rejection of language is itself false? After all, the novel does culminate with the expulsion of the apparent sources of disorder, Addie's rotting body and Darl's decaying mind, and with the reestablishment of order (Anse's remarriage and the harmony of music in the long-awaited graphophone). Perhaps, but again, such a conclusion comes with its own problems, with Anse's repugnance so thoroughly established and especially with so reliable a narrator as Dr. Peabody indicating that Anse rather than Addie or Darl is the true source of disorder: "you could have stuck his head into the saw," he tells Cash, "and cured a whole family" (240).

Readers face further problems accepting either Addie's rejection of language or Anse's triumph in it when they consider the state of the Bundren children. They all have special problems with language. Until the end Cash can express himself only in figures and lists, allowing himself only the most concrete use of language, presumably as wary of it as is his mother (82–83). Darl acquires knowledge without any language at all, knowing Jewel's paternity (136) and Dewey Dell's pregnancy and Addie's death without recourse to words: "He said he knew without the words like he told me that ma is going to die without words" (27). This wordless way of knowing violates others, Dewey Dell in particular, yet ironically it also separates Darl from others, rendering him as "alone" as Addie, the community as well as his family viewing him as odd and finally, of course, isolating him in a cell as confining as his mother's grave. His words become gibberish. In her Lacanian reading of the novel, Fowler argues that Addie has made Darl into a duplicate of herself, for "Addie's revenge is to make Darl suffer the mother's endlessly reenacted fate: he is sacrificed to insure the continuance of the social order" (*Return* 62). Jewel's language separates him, as well, his most frequent word being the "goddamn" he hurls at others like stones from the high hill he and Addie alone would possess (e.g., 13, 14, 15, 18, 95, 96, 99, 145, 146, 188). Even as the family enters Jefferson, Jewel's language almost provokes a fight with a stranger. Dewey Dell is almost wordless, fanning her dying mother but saying nothing to her, staring at Dr. Peabody but not speaking, staring at Darl and others with silent looks that could kill (115), having her wishes almost forced from her by Moseley (200) and MacGowan (243), fooling even Cash as to her hatred of Darl (237)—through it all just as "alone" as her mother (58, 59). Vardaman is reiterative and sometimes so incoherent that even the levelheaded Vernon Tull has trouble understanding him (for a contrasting view, however, see Joseph Urgo, *Faulkner's Apocrypha* 58–69). How can readers pin these multiple problems with language exclusively on either Addie or Anse? They both give their children cause to fail, Addie in her postmodern rejection of language, Anse in his mendacity.

Perhaps readers should take a distinctly postmodern approach to forming their understandings and look at the **marginal** characters for insight. Vernon Tull, for instance, commands words that do seem to reflect objective reality, both inner and outer, and to connect his observations with meaning. He fills his narratives both with detailed reports of what he sees and with apparently objective (at least disinterested) evaluations of what he reports. At the Bundren house before Addie's death, he details the "gapmouthed, goggle-eyed" fish Vardaman has dropped into the dust (31), the condition of Anse's shirt and of his eyes, and Anse's stomping into his shoes and stopping before the door to Addie's room, blinking (32). In each case, seven times, he attaches an evaluation prefaced by the word "like," indicating the honesty at the heart of his connections of observation with meaning. It is "like" the fish is ashamed of its own death (31), "like" Anse hopes he "can quit trying" (32), or "like" Anse is no longer surprised at anything (33). Joined repeatedly by the connector *like,* deeds and the individuals performing them no longer exist in the "aloneness" that Addie suffers. Nor does Tull sense such aloneness. He feels connected, in fact, even to Anse Bundren, a man he knows never sweats (32) and would never move again if he could prevent it (32)—so connected that he offers to help this ultimately lazy man harvest his corn "if he gets into a tight" (33). He sees his wife with equal clarity and maintains an even stronger connection to her. For Tull, words do not just fill lacks. They connect deeds and lives and meanings like the fragile threads Compson called them.

How do such marginal characters, then, help readers comprehend the words and deeds of the major characters? One possibility opened up by Vernon Tull's connectedness is that, though Addie does embody a postmodern sense that language can neither represent the real nor connect one with the Lacanian Real, and though Anse portrays the grounds for such distrust, the novel as a whole rejects the postmodern view. To understand, after all, is not necessarily to agree.

The transformation of Cash would support such a reading. The transformation comes after the burial of Addie, as if her postmodern problem with language were buried with her. Suddenly the heretofore inarticulate Cash finds words, blossoming for the first time as a narrator, offering 2 narratives that recognize ambiguities in people and events but that nevertheless work for grounded understanding. And like Vernon Tull, Cash fills his narratives with connectors. In his first narrative, for example, he uses *but* 19 times to begin clauses, balancing the opposing views he connects as he works toward understanding in the face of ambiguity. In his final narrative he uses the conjunctions *so* (9 uses) and *and* (29 uses), piling them upon each other as he connects events and characters and meaning as firmly as Tull does with *like*. This novel, more explicitly about language than any other in the Faulkner canon, ends with this blossoming of language so full of connectors that no thought or deed stands apart either from balancing opposites or from added equals or from resulting consequences.

As I Lay Dying anticipates postmodernism's problem with language. The misuse of language so evident in Anse and Cora Tull and the Reverend Whitfield perhaps captures the commercial and political misuse of language at a time when the rise of advertising was creating a consumer nation, when the airwaves were beginning to spread political spin, and when competing economic and political systems—democratic and totalitarian, capitalistic and socialist—were at each other's throats in Europe and America. Although the novel is therefore sympathetic to Addie's postmodern response to such misuse, it nevertheless suggests that Addie—and thus the postmodernism that would adopt her stance—are wrong to hold that language merely distorts reality and makes all knowledge unreliable. *As I Lay Dying* values language, no matter how fragile its thread.

TRUTH IS CONTINGENT RATHER THAN ETERNAL, SOCIAL RATHER THAN TRANSCENDENT

Postmodernists may not approve of the move made at the end of the preceding section of this chapter. That move recognized ambiguities and tensions in coming to terms with a theme and then tried to establish a harmonizing "final" understanding of the theme. Modernists make such moves, for the writers and critics who founded modernism, practically inventing fragmentation and ambiguity, still believed that if they accumulated all their fragments they could reconcile ambiguities and finally arrive at complex yet whole truth. But not so the postmodernists. If language cannot represent the real, how can human beings hope it will lead them to any final truth?

Postmodernists see human attempts to describe and establish truth not only as futile but even as destructive, ultimately twisting and reducing reality to cram it into intellectual pigeonholes. Bertens's history of postmodernism explains the issue precisely. Postmodernists, he says, believe that modernism's search for "timeless, representational truth" subjects experience to "unacceptable intellectualizations and reductions" (5). Postmodernists hold that transcendent truth is "forever out of reach" (11), "social and provisional" truths being all humans can attain (9). Terry Eagleton agrees, describing the postmodern mind as "relativist and skeptical," suspicious of "all assured truths" (201). Many critics—Fowler, for instance—attribute this postmodern position to the influence poststructuralists like Ferdinand de Saussure and Jacques Derrida, whose work "undermines traditional conceptions of truth" that have been based on a belief in a "transcendental signifier" that "does not exist" ("Revising" 96). The position may well go back another generation or two to Nietzsche, for the absent transcendental signifier is, of course, God, who, for the purposes of postmodernism, is as good as dead.

With this same older connection in mind, Philip Weinstein describes one of the common results of seeing **contingency** as governing truth. He describes the growth of "parody" and a "Nietzschean preference for play/construction rather than truth/correspondence" ("Postmodern" 20). Postmodern writers, who consider all representations of the real to be no more than fictional to begin with, either playfully or parodically "rewrite" older texts, convinced that all of history, whether remembered or read, is no more "real" than frankly fictional texts. Their penchant for play and parody engages them in what Linda Hutcheon calls the "intertextual parody of historiographic metafiction" (125). Describing Toni Morrison's *Song of Solomon* as such **metafiction,** for example, Hutcheon sees its "utopian three-woman household" parodying the "dystopic one in Faulkner's *Absalom! Absalom!*" [*sic*] (67). In his major study of these two novelists, Philip Weinstein has seen similar connections between *Absalom, Absalom!* and Morrison's *Jazz,* particularly in the way the novels handle the "racial dynamics" of "miscegenous begetting" (*What Else* 145, 147). Postmodern critics alert to this technique might read the comedic conclusion to *As I Lay Dying,* referred to in section 1, as itself parodic. They might see the restoration of order in the marriage of the newly empowered Anse Bundren as a parody of such restorations deeply rooted in Western literature, from the *Odyssey* to Shakespeare to, say, George Eliot. Such a reading makes Anse more the "rough beast" of Yeats's "The Second Coming" than his falconer (Faulkner?), his social order deeply flawed and destructive.

But postmodern critics interested in the impossibility of truth have turned to *Absalom, Absalom!* more than to *As I Lay Dying* or the other fiction. Some have seen the novel embracing this postmodern attitude. Gerhard Hoffman, for example, has pointed to the narrative strategy of the novel, specifically to its diction, as betraying a postmodern rejection of truth. He describes a "pattern of uncertainty" and suggests that the multiple uses of "perhaps" and "maybe" point to the novel's grasp of "the fictitious state of truth" (288). Brian McHale likewise sees a movement into postmodern sensibility, especially in chapter 8, where he sees the novel abandoning modernist "questions of authority and reliability" and allowing the narrators to "*fictionalize*" history without restraint (*Postmodernist* 10), truth becoming what they make it. Fowler comes to a similar conclusion, arguing that Quentin Compson reaches a "postmodern awareness" ("Revising" 106) when he finds in the Sutpen saga not some kind of final meaning but rather the impossibility of all meaning, imaged in the "dissolution and disintegration" he witnesses at his visit to Sutpen's Hundred (105). Other postmodern critics, on the other hand, have stopped short of finding such postmodern attitudes in *Absalom, Absalom!* or elsewhere in Faulkner's work. Ihab Hassan, for instance, insists that in Faulkner relativism is "repugnant" and "the will to meaning outlasts all denials" ("Privations" 7), including the Nietzschean "will to lie" (8). In Faulkner, he asserts, belief in "universalisms," or eternal truths, prevails (8).

With the question remaining thus open, *The Sound and the Fury* is a good novel in which to test Faulkner's investment in this postmodern rejection of truth, for the two articulate Compson sons both have major problems with truth. Are their problems postmodern?

Jason is great at the sleight of tongue we now call "spin," a common post-modern substitute for truth. He claims to like working (196), for instance, and repeatedly castigates African Americans for not working, yet he spends as little of the day at his job as he can despite Earl's concern about the number of shoppers in town. He claims to respect a "good honest whore" (233) like Lorraine and to find her more honest than churchgoing women (246), yet at home he reverses positions, claiming to respect his mother as a good Christian and castigating Quentin as a "little whore" (216). He castigates Earl for suspecting that anything he doesn't understand is dishonest (229), yet he repeatedly expresses his own suspicion that the cotton market is dishonest. For Jason, truth does not exist as anything more than what is self-justifying and convenient at the moment. Truth is as provisional as the passing need. It is what he makes it.

With such an attitude toward truth, Jason is eager to attack whatever suggests that truth is something more eternal than spin. At the hardware store, when Earl confronts him over the truth about the money that bought his car, Jason sneers at Earl's conscience and contrasts it with his appetite (229). Conscience, of course, suggests a set of moral standards guiding behavior in all circumstances, Hassan's "universalisms," while appetite suggests the absence of any guide but the impulse of the moment. After his confrontation with the sheriff, who, like Earl, takes Jason's spin at something less than face value and confronts him with the truth of who really owned the missing $3,000, Jason imagines himself leading a "file of soldiers with the manacled sheriff in the rear, dragging Omnipotence down" (306). The sheriff embodies legal standards resistant to spin, and Omnipotence represents the "transcendent signifier" that postmodernism has dragged down, a knowable divinity that would establish an ultimate standard by which to judge all spin. For Jason Compson, truth is neither eternal nor transcendent. It is only provisional.

The question then becomes whether *The Sound and the Fury* embraces Jason's position. Is Jason a Nietzschean figure embracing "play" rather than truth? Is he like the frequently cited Jacob Horner of John Barth's *The End of the Road,* exhilarated by the empowering freedom of a completely open universe? Philip Weinstein helps answer this question. In discussing Jacob Horner, he focuses on the difference between traditional Western "dissimulation" and postmodern "simulation," using Dickens's Uriah Heep as an example of the former and Horner as an example of the latter. Traditional dissimulators conceal a "fullness of motive" behind hypocritical masks that are eventually ripped away; postmodern simulators, on the other hand, cheerfully offer truths about themselves and the world as guileless masks "standing in for a void" ("Postmodern" 21). Jason Compson is surely a dissimulator, a Uriah Heep rather than a Jacob Horner. He deceives no one but himself and his mother with his self-serving "provisional truths." The novel invites readers to join Earl and the sheriff in calling Jason a thief, to shout with Quentin, "You're lying" (213). It makes theft a universal evil by sending those blue jays screaming around the house on Easter morning (266, 269, 284). In folk tradition the scream of the blue jay is heard as "thief!" The novel offers the screams of these jays, then, as the voice of the universe itself, outraged at the violation of the sacred day.

For the other articulate Compson, the question of truth is more complex and more problematic. Quentin does see the void described by postmodernism; he has learned of it from his father, who embraces it. Quentin cannot get past his father's insistence on the arbitrariness of all social, intellectual, and moral orders and thus of the truths that underpin them (77). Quentin recalls Father saying that battles are never won and victories never achieved (76). He has learned that nothing matters, that no apparent faults are worth the effort of changing (78). Though he has spent a year at Harvard, he has done so recalling that its education is the "reducto absurdum of all human experience" and cannot fit his needs (76), since the greatest of thoughts represented in it are essentially dead (95). Such charges sound very much like postmodernism's charge that language distorts rather than represents reality. Indeed, Quentin echoes Addie Bundren when he describes words as mere tools people use each other with (118) and books as "ordered certitudes" with little connection to reality (125). At this level, Quentin rejects both language and all the universal truths writers have used it to describe. He has moved from modernism's difficulty of knowing to postmodernism's impossibility of knowing.

Quentin expresses the postmodern nature of his perception through his difficulty with time. Under his father's influence, he has come to see the arbitrary imposition of clock time on the fluid flow of events as an expression of the arbitrariness of all human truths (77). On the morning of his suicide, he removes the hands from his watch to assert his determination to free himself from the nagging claims of time and the systems of truth it represents. Later he enters the jeweler's shop and determines that none of the watches in the window shows the correct time in order to confirm his position that none of the world's competing systems of truth is right (84). He fixes on the trout in the country stream and the gull above the Charles River, both completely still despite the rushing flow about them (120, 121), seeing both as symbols of escape from time and thus of freedom from the demands that systems of truth make upon human life in general and, most painfully, upon his life in particular. Gull and trout are at ease with the flow of events, uninterested in imposing any kind of system upon it. They capture perfectly postmodernism's acceptance of unorganized, fluid experience.

Unlike his brother Jason, however, Quentin does not respond to the postmodern fluidity with a barrage of dissimulations worthy of Uriah Heep. But neither does he engage in Jacob Horner's playful simulations. Instead, he loathes the very position he insists on and annihilates his own life in protest against the nihilism his position implies. Having denied clock time, he turns himself into a sundial, consulting his shadow to tell the time, as if his whole being demands a system of truth despite his denial. Yet continuing to believe that all is "without relevance" or "significance," he must judge the actions of his life and thus his life itself as mere "shadows" that whisper "was not . . . was not was not" (170). He will find peace not in escape from truth but in escape from life: "I'll not be." (174). Quentin has reached the postmodern state described by Fowler, seeing life as "fluid" and "meaning" a mere "human construction" ("Revising" 106), and he finds such a life without truth to be not worth living. Just as Anse Bundren embraces the falseness of language, Quentin's brother Jason embraces the problematic nature of truth, using it to create his own dissembling truths. Just as Addie Bundren escapes the falseness of language by entering the ground, Quentin escapes the apparent absence of truth by entering the timeless fluidity of the river.

As in *As I Lay Dying,* it may be that Faulkner was able to see beyond modernism and into postmodernism without accepting the latter. Here in *The Sound and the Fury* he sees that an epistemology embracing ambiguity and paradox— a vision of the world in which the times displayed on faces of watches conflict with each other and all fall short of being THE time—can ultimately lead not only to fuller, surer and more nuanced truths but also to no truth at all. The latter state he finds intolerable. Citing Faulkner's 1955 essay on "Privacy," Hassan puts it this way: "Faulkner finds relativism repugnant" and thus portrays the postmodern view of truth "without acceding to it" ("Privations" 7–8). Hassan's idea is that Faulkner views postmodern relativism as a manipulative ideology (8), used for "self-empowerment" by those who embrace it (1). Hassan holds Faulkner to embrace a contrary position—not self-empowerment but "pure self-lessness" (16) or "self-dispossession" (18). Though Hassan does not apply this view to *The Sound and the Fury,* it might imply that Jason's self-serving dissimulations express the self-empowerment that lurks just behind postmodern playfulness, while Quentin's suicide becomes the only form of self-emptying possible in a world from which truth has disappeared and with it the possibility of dissolving the self "in the name of a vaster mystery" (16). Postmodernism, then, helps readers see what Faulkner saw before postmodernism flourished— saw but rejected.

In another interestingly postmodern move, *The Sound and the Fury* shows what it embraces in regard to truth through a marginal character—not through a Compson or its final third-person narrator but through the servant Dilsey Gibson. She is the suffering servant, a character overlooked by all the Compsons but the cornerstone of what the novel builds. She expresses precisely what Hassan says Faulkner embraces, a self-emptying into a vaster mystery. Though critics influenced by Marxism, feminism, or other theories of race, class, and gender might critique her character as an expression of the white patriarchy's self-serving desire for an accommodating black and female "Other," in doing so they miss her centrality to the novel's positive vision. Dilsey is not in the novel to serve the patriarchy. She is there to offer an alternative to the self-destructive postmodern condition of the Compsons.

The novel puts Dilsey in direct touch with Hassan's "universalisms," his "vaster mystery." In her oft-quoted comment following the Reverend Shegog's Easter sermon, Dilsey claims that she has seen the first and the last, the beginning and the end (297). She refers most directly to the Compson family, perhaps recalling its original member in Jefferson, Grandfather Compson, and certainly foreseeing the end of the Compson line there. More significantly, though, she also implies a wholeness of vision that allows her to see beyond the moment, a kind of universal vantage point beyond the social and provisional. She locates that vantage point in the transcendental realm when she responds to her daughter's objection to taking Benjy to church with her family: she assures Frony that the Lord does not care how intelligent he is (290). She speaks from that transcendental vantage point again when she replies to Frony's objection to the Reverend Shegog's stature, commenting that she has known the Lord to call stranger people than he (293). Dilsey is confident in the transcendental signifier that confirms her truths. Though postmodern readers can argue that her confidence is misled, the novel affirms Dilsey too strongly to give weight to such an ideological reading.

This is not to say that Dilsey is unaware of the many social and provisional truths swarming about the household like summer flies. To express her awareness, the novel returns to the issue of clock time so vexing to Quentin. Twice it has the Compsons' kitchen clock strike an erroneous hour, once before the Easter service and once after, and on both occasions it has Dilsey call out the correct hour. It suggests no ambiguity about the issue: Dilsey knows what time it is. How different she is from Quentin and his lamented conviction that, since no clocks can tell time correctly, there is no correct time. The novel suggests, of course, that the "wrong" hours struck by the Compson clock represent the twisted and partial truths and outright lies the Compsons live by and that the "correct" hours announced by Dilsey are the full and whole truths she lives by. Perhaps the Compsons live under *kronos,* the world's time, while Dilsey lives under *kairos,* eternal time. The point is that Dilsey lives in two realms at once. She is not removed into a transcendental realm abstracted out of experiential life, out of history, like a Thomas Sutpen caught up in his design, nor is she ground into the earth like an Addie Bundren. She is planted solidly in the realm of time and space while at the same time viewing it from a universal realm.

Interestingly, postmodernism may make its best contribution to the understanding of *The Sound and the Fury* in its power to elucidate the transcendental realm that Dilsey has contact with. The postmodern psychology of Jacques Lacan, referred to earlier, posits a realm which Lacan calls the "Real" but which lies beyond "reality" known to human beings caught up in the world of experience and its symbolic order. Fowler describes that realm as a "mystery" unknowable to those "trapped in language" (*Return* 13), a remark that connects the Lacanian realm of the Real to Hassan's view that Faulkner's vision calls for self-surrender to a "vaster mystery." Fowler also explains that the Lacanian Real "posits the possibility of meaning outside of the arbitrary cultural orderings of the symbolic order" (*Return* 13). In regard to *The Sound and the Fury,* then, Lacan might posit the existence of a Real time beyond human clock time, a Real truth beyond human truths. The realm of the Real, Fowler reports, has been associated, among other things, with "light" (*Return* 13).

And there Lacan intersects with Faulkner. The fullest expression of the nature of the transcendental realm Dilsey lives in is the Reverend Shegog's Easter sermon. The Reverend Shegog certainly uses the tool of the Lacanian symbolic order—language. His powerful and myriad "voice" captures the congregation and moves its members to the "ricklickshun en de blood of de Lamb" (295). The

voice evokes the same blood that Addie Bundren contrasts to words. Yet the
Reverend Shegog's words and the blood they evoke are not separate but are one.
The great voice proclaims that it "sees de word," and apparently the congregation does as well, answering the voice with a "Yes, Jesus!" (295). The word, language, is no longer separate from the experiential world, which is unable to
represent it or state truth about it, but is somehow palpable, one with the experiential world. And the voice and the congregation also agree that they can see the
"light" that accompanies that palpable word.

The Reverend Shegog is referring to the Christian understanding of Jesus as
the incarnate deity, God-become-human, the "Word made flesh" in the language
of the Gospel of John. His way of doing so also suggests an interesting possibility regarding the Lacanian Real. Though human beings trapped in a logocentric
(word-built) symbolic order cannot grasp or enter the Real, is it possible that a
being who inhabits the Real can leave the Real and enter the symbolic order?
That would appear to be the suggestion of the Reverend Shegog's sermon. It
would explain how Dilsey has come in contact with that "vaster mystery"—not
that she sought and found it, an impossible feat for one trapped in the symbolic
order, but that it sought her and she surrendered to it.

Evidence that the novel suggests that this is the case lies in another assertion
in the gospel that connects the Word with the figure of Jesus. Twice the Gospel
of John shows the man it describes as the Word-made-flesh promising to deliver
the "truth" to those who surrender to him. "If ye continue in my word," he promises, "ye shall know the truth" (John 8:31–32). Then when asked how those who
surrender can "know the way" (a good rendering of the postmodern question
Quentin sees but fails to answer), he asserts that he himself is "the way" and "the
truth" (John 14:5–6). The presence of the word that is seen by the Reverend Shegog's congregation and identified as Jesus implies, through this extension, that
Dilsey knows what time it is because she has surrendered to the author of time,
who may dwell in the inaccessible realm of the Real but who has chosen to bring
his "truth" into the realm of language.

Dilsey Gibson, this marginal character, then, brings together traditional Christian theology and postmodern theory. The writer of John's Gospel meets Jacques
Lacan. If Faulkner sees modernist epistemology leading to equally unacceptable
postmodern conditions—Jason's spin and Quentin's despair—he also captures
in his modernist narrative a possibility implicit in postmodern psychology—that
the Real might enter the symbolic and thus make truth knowable. It is fascinating, then, to remember that, a few years after writing *The Sound and the Fury,*
Faulkner moved into Rowan Oak—the old Shegog house.

HETERODOXY TRUMPS ORTHODOXY

The postmodern promotion of heterodoxy follows naturally from the two
beliefs discussed previously. If language is bound to fail and if truth is forever
beyond reach, then humans have no justification for insisting that a single truth
should prevail in any sphere of thought and action. Rather, humans should be

intellectually heterodox, viewing all "truths" as equally valid and equally invalid, of equal interest no matter what their source or history. So too should humans be culturally heterodox, valuing all cultures, races, ethnicities, sexes, and individuals equally no matter what "truth" they express. Thus the birth of diversity as a national ideal. Richard Ruland and Malcolm Bradbury's history of American literature captures the genealogy of heterodoxy perfectly: if we can never do any better than "project meanings" onto an "actual world" resistant to all meanings, which are "never quite perfect," then we must face "the challenge of heterodoxy," the truth that truth itself is "multiple" (372).

It is a paradox, of course, that heterodoxy has become an orthodoxy of post-modernism. Commentator after commentator agrees, though, so orthodoxy it is. Bertens writes of postmodernism's commitment to "difference, pluriformity, and multiplicity" (8), and Hutcheon uses almost the same language, describing postmodernism's interest in the "multiple, the heterogeneous, the different" (66). Hassan suggests the paradox when he compares postmodernists to worshipers and evangelists of a true god, calling them "votaries of decenterment and apostles of multiplicity" ("Privations" 2). Perhaps it is modernism, with its interest in ambiguity, which made such self-contradiction possible. Whatever its sources, orthodox heterodoxy is not only possible but also well developed, with a number of intellectual offshoots.

One of the offshoots is the rejection of authority. The intellectual progression to an antiauthoritarian position is clear enough: since one's authority derives from one's proximity to the totality of truth, when postmodernism claims that there is no ultimate truth it must also claim "that there is no ultimate authority," as Fowler puts it ("Revising" 101). Any assertion of authority, therefore, becomes a denial of the orthodox heterodoxy and thus illegitimate. Of course, suspicion of authority is as old as the Enlightenment, with its argument for governments legitimized by social contract rather than divine right and churches led by a priesthood of all believers rather than a privileged clergy. On the other hand, postmodernism's rejection of authority abandons principles guiding Western individualism from the Enlightenment through most of the twentieth century—to wit, that there are self-evident truths built into the cosmos and legitimized by its creator, the most important ones being what the West calls human rights. In the political realm, for instance, a postmodernist would have to consider that a Roosevelt or a Churchill had no more legitimate authority than a Hitler or a Stalin, a Jimmy Carter no more than a Pol Pot.

A corollary to the delegitimization of authority is the rejection of all hierarchies based on and supporting authority. Hierarchies are vertical intellectual and social structures supporting the idea and the individual with the greatest authority—as, for instance, cardinals, archbishops, bishops, and priests (each with a decreasing amount of independent authority) support the pope within the Roman Catholic Church. Fowler explains that postmodernism "maintains that there are no natural hierarchies" ("Revising" 101)—that is, none existing in nature and thus necessarily applicable to human life. And Hutcheon points out postmodernism's corresponding rejection of human social and intellectual hierarchies, as well, when she explains that postmodernism's preference for multiple and contradictory truths leads it to "reject" systems that might "conceal a secret hierarchy of values" (43). Bertens traces this desire to "undo institutionalized hierarchies" to the thought of Lacan and Michel Foucault and links it to the "feminism and multiculturalism that are now generally associated with postmodernism" (8). Authorities and hierarchies supporting them, of course, attempt to establish singularity rather than multiplicity, sameness rather than difference, orthodoxy rather than heterodoxy.

This postmodern rejection of authority and hierarchy has led to what Jameson describes as a "narrative view of 'truth' and the vitality of small narrative units at work everywhere *locally* [as opposed to] the older master-narratives of legitimation" ("Foreword" xi). Postmodernism prefers a "narrative" view of truth because the opposing "logical" view necessitates vertical thought, which either proceeds deductively from a truth with claim to universality or progresses inductively toward establishing a new truth as universal. The "narrative" view, on the other hand, allows thought to take horizontal rather than vertical routes and to move toward open rather than closed endings. At the same time, postmodernism prefers "local" narratives and rejects **"master narratives"** for the very reason the term itself implies: if a narrative is "master," it is authoritative and thus can legitimize or delegitimize various local narratives, making the many one, the multiple into versions of the single. Master narratives include canonical literary works, organizing mythologies, religious creeds, and all formative theories and texts based on them, whether political, economic, or even literary. This corollary, of course, returns to the opening paradox. The orthodox heterodoxy of postmodernism leads it to reject not only the organizing theories and texts of others but its own as well. Postmodernism cannot (or should not) become a master narrative. Yet it has become one, extending its own paradoxical self-contradiction. As this problematic postmodern stand works its way into Faulkner criticism, the fiction it encounters both opens to it and leads it out of its dilemma.

Postmodernism's interest in heterodoxy has succeeded in pushing Faulkner criticism in several new directions. While textual criticism, for example, has long had the goal of establishing the final, authoritative texts of literary works, Martin Kreiswirth has recently pointed to the textual "fissures, gaps, and discrepancies" that make determining authorial intent and establishing a "final" text entirely problematic ("Paradoxical" 165). Even more recently, Philip Cohen [see chapter 12] has upped the ante, arguing that an examination not only of Faulkner's own versions of his texts but also of "non-authorial textual process" inevitably "adds even more contradictions and instabilities to those already present" in Faulkner's versions of his texts (174). These scholars agree that postmodern textual critics must abandon the search for a single authoritative text and instead accept a multiplicity of texts. And there we have it—textual heterodoxy.

Even within any particular version of any Faulkner text, Gerhard Hoffman has noted, postmodern critics have become increasingly accepting of disorderly narratives, no longer so interested in "proving coherence" as in "acknowledging

Faulkner's conscious endeavor to leave or even establish gaps, discontinuities, breaks and contradictions in the narrative" (277). Joseph Urgo sees this narrative technique at work in *Pylon,* where he argues no "authoritative voice" confirms or rejects what "the reporter or anyone else" has to say ("Postvomiting"132). In effect, Urgo contends that the Faulknerian text sometimes denies that it possesses authority to guide readers toward any "real truth" (133). The text refuses to become a master narrative controlling the local narratives created by multiple individual voices within it and by multiple readers of it. Narration becomes heterodox.

Many critics see *Absalom, Absalom!* as Faulkner's fullest use of this postmodern narrative technique—heterodox and multiple storytelling that denies the authority of its own narrators and finally of itself. Although Urgo disagrees, seeing the occasional third-person narrator as an "authoritative voice" whose role is "to endorse the inventions made by Quentin and Shreve, affirming their" truth (132), most postmodern critics agree with Molly Hite that in a postmodern reading the novel's multiple, contradictory versions of the Sutpen saga "resist being pulled together into the 'organic' whole too often assumed to be the goal of modernist writing" (73). The narrator's "probably true enough" becomes as equivocal as the portraits of Sutpen as demon, Bon's mother as betrayed Fury, her lawyer as scheming embezzler, and even Bon as Sutpen's mixed-race son. For Hite and other postmodern critics, the reasons for Sutpen's rejection and Henry's killing of Charles Bon remain as mysterious at the end of the novel as at the beginning despite the narrator and despite Quentin's claim to have discovered the final truth in his visit to Sutpen's Hundred. Regarding the latter, they might point to the brevity of Quentin's time with Henry and Clytie and the closed circularity of his conversation with Henry, recognizing that Quentin has reached his own private despairing closure but arguing that the novel resists it. They might accuse Quentin, in effect, of attempting to establish his version of the saga as a master narrative and of tempting readers to accept it and to turn the novel as a whole into a master narrative as well. But Hite and others insist that "at the same time that readers are seduced by the claims of the story to be a supreme fiction, they are bombarded with reminders that this fiction is one of many possible, and that no version can claim final authority" (75).

The novel's postmodern narrative form dovetails with its portrait of Thomas Sutpen. When he moved with his family to Tidewater, Virginia, in his boyhood, he left the heterodox, authority-less world of the mountain wilds for the patriarchal and hierarchical world of society, where the plantation owner rules and others obey, the land "all divided and fixed and neat with a people living on it all divided and fixed and neat" (179), all according to a master narrative of race and class and gender. Finding himself brutalized by his place in that master narrative, Sutpen fights it not by tearing it down but by acceding to it, creating his personal master narrative in accord with it (his design), and rising within its hierarchy. When he divides and fixes people by race and gender, a postmodern reading would argue, he brings about his own doom, for heterodoxy inevitably trumps orthodoxy, all authority weakening and all hierarchies crumbling. The

Civil War is the trump of doom. Sutpen's effort to enter the master narrative and establish himself as an authority within it is as vain as Quentin's effort as narrator to establish an orthodox understanding of Sutpen.

Critics studying characterization in other novels have followed similar paths. When this essay offered "marginal" characters as essential to grasping the totality of *As I Lay Dying* and *The Sound and the Fury,* it followed a trail opened up by John Duvall in his study of *Faulkner's Marginal Couple.* In that work, Duvall examines couples whose unmarried relationships either reveal the oppressive basis of "normal," married relationships or offer healthier alternatives to them. He argues that in Faulkner the "different," with its power to challenge, correct, and even destroy, carries far more moral weight than the orthodox. He attempts to show that Faulkner challenges the master narrative of family and community life and makes a case for heterodox local narratives of family and community.

This interest in heterodoxy may, in general, be postmodernism's most helpful contribution to Faulkner's readers. It helps them see how consistently Faulkner's fiction values human multiplicity and criticizes authority in almost every sphere, whether religious, social, economic, or political. In particular, it consistently undermines white patriarchal authority, which it repeatedly shows denying full humanity to women and African Americans. Lucius Quintus Carothers McCaslin, for example, is a patriarch of Sutpen's mold, destroying the land he redeems from the swamp as well as the children he begets. Both of these patriarchal authorities, Sutpen and McCaslin, fail the test of acknowledging the full humanity of those they classify as Other—women and African Americans. McCaslin turns his own slave daughter Thomasina into his mistress, and Sutpen (according to Quentin) denies his mixed-race son Charles Bon and almost commands his murder. The descendents of such "authorities" who manage to survive perpetuate the white, male singularity of their fathers. Though Ike McCaslin sadly sees his grandfather's bequest of $1,000 to Tomey's Turl as an evasion of the profound truth of human multiplicity and equality across lines of race and gender, something *"cheaper than saying My son to a nigger"* (258), he joins his cousin Roth in repeating the very act as he offers Roth's lover a sheaf of banknotes and sends her away with Roth's son in her arms [see also chapter 1].

In *The Unvanquished,* by contrast, the Civil War removes the white male patriarchal authorities like John Sartoris and disrupts the hierarchy of gender and race they have kept in place. As the confining walls of the patriarchs' homes, towns, and courthouses burn to the ground, white women like Cousin Dru and Granny Millard and African Americans like Ringo find new authority within themselves and engage in political and economic and even military affairs previously reserved for the privileged white male authorities. They show, in their changes and development, how fully society has constructed race and gender to benefit the white male authorities and then confined others within the accepted forms. In truth, these characters are multiple—Granny a strategist capable of taking on an occupying army, Dru a fighter, Ringo an artist, an actor, and a decision maker.

The novel ends, however, with a moment of comedy as dark as that at the end of *As I Lay Dying.* Order returns as Bayard Sartoris begins a new era of white male authority—a less violent one, to be sure, but one that nevertheless is once again denying full participation to women and African Americans. The multiple is retreating to the single. Granny is dead, Dru is forced back into her dress, and Ringo has become a servant. A careful look at Ringo, in particular, a character who still loves Bayard but is bitter at his own remarginalization, brings the complex point home. Ringo has been unmanned—he is twice called a "boy" (212–13)—and even dehumanized, pushed back into the "herd of niggers" (207) to be driven by white males, even though he remains a fully competent man accomplishing tasks that others "would not have thought of" (213), a man Bayard says he "will never catch up with" (216). Bayard, by contrast, has room both to become "the Sartoris" (214) and "be thought well of" in society (243) and also to "live with myself" (240)—that is, both to enter the hierarchy and achieve authority within it and also to develop all of his multiple characteristics. Faulkner expresses his own bitterness in Ringo's remark to Bayard about "that white skin you walks around in" (218). *Sub regno* Sartoris, society is to be single rather than multiple, and Ringo is to be confined to a single role within it. America's Jim Crow laws are just around the corner.

Postmodern antiauthoritarian heterodoxy also opens up *Sanctuary,* perhaps Faulkner's most feminist novel. While modernist criticism tended to demonize its central character, Temple Drake, as a spoiled and self-indulgent *femme fatale,* a Siren luring men to their doom, the postmodern perspective has allowed readers to see another side of Temple. It suggests that although the ruling hierarchy may indeed have spoiled her, it has done so in its own interest, not Temple's. It helps readers consider the degree to which Temple's actions constitute her own private Civil War and her fate as sad a triumph of the reestablished authority as that presented in *The Unvanquished.*

Such a reading might start by observing how authority controls Temple and how she responds to that control. Temple acknowledges that control and sometimes accepts it; she has told the town boys that her father is a judge so many times that they mock her for it (30). At these times her father's authoritative position helps her control men lower in the hierarchy. At other times, however, Temple is eager enough to disregard her father's authority and follow her own wishes. She has slipped out with the town boys often enough that she is on probation at the university, and she breaks the rules again by leaving the train at Taylor to ride with Gowan Stevens. One question raised, then, is whether the social hierarchy, presided over by her father, Judge Drake, and encompassing the university and its rules of behavior, is interested in nurturing Temple for her sake or in merely controlling her for its own. A second question, answerable following the first, is whether Temple's increasing willingness to break the rules of the social hierarchy makes her a freedom fighter or a terrorist.

The novel begins to answer these questions when it turns Popeye into Temple's surrogate father. It makes him one in several ways. Popeye assumes a parental tone with Temple even as she sits bleeding in the car following his rape of her: "Aint you ashamed of yourself?" he demands (139). He buys her candy at Dumphries after she asks for some. He takes her to a surrogate mother, Miss

Reba, and supplies her with food, clothing, and shelter. And then, most tellingly, Temple wheedles and whines and begs him as a child would, finally calling Popeye "Daddy" (231, 236). Popeye becomes what Judith Bryant Wittenberg calls "the most pernicious 'father-figure' in Faulkner's fiction" (*Faulkner* 95). Through this pattern the novel seems to suggest that Popeye's role with Temple is equivalent to Judge Drake's role with her, that though neither "daddy" may actually have sex with her, both are keeping her for sexual exchange, for use by another male, a presumed ally, and thus are turning her into a "whore" and "raping" her through surrogates. As a top outlaw, Popeye is the mirror image of the top man of the law, Judge Drake, and thus makes evident what the other might be able to hide. My daddy the gangster and my father the judge are one and the same.

One of the characters Duvall identifies as marginal confirms such a reading. Ruby Lamar, the most "firmly married" woman in Faulkner even if she has had no wedding, defines for Temple the essential male-female relationship within the gender roles allotted by society's master narrative. With a painful mix of envy, shame, and pride, she describes a system with "real men" on top and with women reduced to "whores," crawling in the mud beneath their feet (59). Then when she recounts how her father shot down the man she chose according to her own will rather than his, she foreshadows Red's fate at the hands of "Daddy" Popeye, Popeye's fate at the hands of the law presided over by the likes of Judge Drake, and Lee's fate at the hands of the all-male jury and all-male mob that take him to be a disrupter of their sexual control of women. "We got to protect our girls," an old patriarch pronounces. "Might need them ourselves" (298). Indeed.

The language of the novel reinforces this postmodern feminist reading, especially when Temple is reunited with her family. In the courtroom the prosecutor has dramatically displayed the corncob, the instrument of the rape that has violated the holy temple, the sanctuary that family and society supposedly exist to protect. The language suggests, however, that the jury and then the mob are eager to punish its wielder not because that corncob has momentarily disrupted the master narrative of family and community life but because it reveals what Duvall calls "the paradigms of rape and prostitution" underlying that narrative (*Marginal* 60). In full consciousness of its double meaning, the novel twice describes Judge Drake as "erect" when he enters the courtroom to reclaim his daughter, and it adds that all four of Temple's brothers at the back of the courtroom are standing "stiffly erect" (288–89). Imagery joins language when, in this episode and the final one as well, Judge Drake carries a "slender black stick" (288) and rests his hands upon its "head" (317). Black is Popeye's color: he has black eyes, wears black suits, and gets called a "black man" by Temple (49). The judge thus blends with Popeye, and the cane he carries is phallic. To reinforce the phallic imagery, this father-judge sports a moustache described as a "bar" (288) and again as a "rigid bar . . . beaded with moisture" (317). The corncob has made evident what the cane and the bar express in hidden ways, the phallus and the law-of-the-father encoded in patriarchal authority and society's highly gendered master narrative.

Thus the bankruptcy of the social system throughout the novel. Horace begins by believing in the system. The novel makes his enlightenment the readers'. The church, in the form of the Baptist ladies who persuade Jefferson's hotelier to evict Ruby, exasperates Horace in its betrayal of its commission to feed the hungry and shelter the homeless. The law is even worse. If the grasping Senator Clarence Snopes makes the law, it will only aggrandize its makers. If the mendacious Eustace Graham prosecutes those who break such laws, he does so to advance himself rather than protect the weak. If the police charged with arresting lawbreakers frequent Miss Reba's in the numbers she claims (211), there is no real difference between those inside and outside the law, just as the morphing of Judge Drake and Popeye has suggested. No wonder Horace comes to see that "there is a logical pattern to evil" (221). The evil is the dehumanization of the many—the multiple, differing, heterodox mixture that is humanity. The pattern is the hypocritical, self-serving hierarchy instituted by a master narrative that carries out that dehumanization to secure and protect its own authority. How can anything but a kind of Civil War alter such organized evil?

Temple Drake, then, becomes a freedom fighter rather than a terrorist, however flawed and doomed her struggle. Yes, she leaves a trail of bodies behind her—Tommy's, Red's, Lee's, and finally Popeye's. Yes, she is directly implicated in the deaths of Red and Lee, though men do the killing in both cases. Perhaps the patriarchy has given her no option but to struggle through its agents and with its own ways and means. And, yes, Temple's struggle leads her right back into the arms of the judge. But as in *As I Lay Dying* and *The Unvanquished,* the restoration of order at the end of this novel is highly ironic. Indeed, the apparent disrupters, Popeye and Lee, have been expelled, and Horace and Temple have returned to their reunited families. But Horace has returned to a living death, his home like the jails holding Lee and Popeye before they die. "Go lock the back door," Belle tells him repeatedly (299). And Temple faces a similar death. Authority has prevailed, the mess is cleaned up, and the gendered master narrative endures. Temple sits in the Luxembourg Gardens under the authority symbolized by her father's cane and bar, beholding the dead queens on their pedestals as the year dies into winter. If "achieving closure . . . closes down the future," as Hite suggests (76), truly Temple is one of the dead queens, and it is her life that has closed down.

Postmodernism helps readers see how fully Faulkner's fiction embraced human heterodoxy decades before postmodernism articulated it. In it, courage and strength are as common in a Granny Millard and a Ringo as in a John Sartoris. Self-determination is as alluring to a Cousin Dru and a Temple Drake as to a Bayard Sartoris. And evil flourishes more fully in the Jefferson courthouse than at the Old Frenchman place.

The only catch is that Faulkner does not arrive at heterodoxy by postmodern means. He endorses *human* heterodoxy, not theoretical heterodoxy. In other words, he pleads for the full acceptance of all people not because he rejects universal truths but precisely because he believes that such acceptance *is* a universal truth. Human heterodoxy is an orthodoxy Faulkner will not trade away. It is his unabashed master narrative, a key to what Hassan calls Faulkner's richer moral and spiritual universe ("Privations" 17). Just as postmodernism can help readers see Faulkner's heterodoxy more clearly, then, Faulkner's fiction can help post-modernists retreat from what Hassan, again, calls its "sterile . . . dead-end games" (4). Faulkner puts heterodoxy on a firmer base than self-contradictory paradox.

TRANSGRESSION IS A POSITIVE ACT

Postmodern admiration of transgression flows naturally out of the positions discussed previously. If language cannot represent the real, if final truths are therefore unreachable, and if heterodoxy is therefore superior to orthodoxy enforced by authority and hierarchy, it follows that all barriers and boundaries that attempt to define and divide and arrange ideas and human beings are suspicious at best, the probable tools of an idea and its agents seeking dominance. To the postmodern mind it becomes almost obligatory, therefore, to transgress boundaries, whether physical, geographic, legal, cultural, or intellectual. Post-modernism finds its heroes not in the individual who embodies cultural values but in the one who challenges them, moving through barriers, breaking laws, violating taboos, even piercing the skin, which comes to represent all illusory but transgressible barriers between the so-called self (more on that in the next section) and the Other. Postmodernists style themselves as subversives.

Two postmodern critics help connect postmodernism's admiration of transgression to its preceding intellectual positions. Jameson connects it to the poststructuralists' understanding of language and its inability to represent the real, describing earlier "realistic epistemology" as viewing "representation as the reproduction, for subjectivity, of an objectivity that lies outside it" but arguing that postmodern thought has torn down the barrier between subjectivity and objectivity ("Foreword" viii). Wittenberg agrees, applying the point to Faulkner. She explains that earlier conceptions of language presumed a barrier between the "signifier and signified," one that becomes "highly tenuous" in Faulkner ("Race" 154). In other words, she argues that Faulkner anticipates postmodernism in probing that boundary between the words used by human beings (the "signifiers") and the world those words attempt to capture (the "signified"), making readers increasingly aware that the two do not exist apart but, rather, come together, all representations of the so-called objective world actually being subjective.

A logical, even predictable result of postmodernism's preference for transgression is its preference for instability. If neither the center (truth) nor the periphery (boundaries) can hold, all is up for grabs. McHale suggests the logic. When he describes a shift from modernism's interest in epistemology (our understanding of knowledge) to postmodernism's interest in ontology (our understanding of being), he assumes postmodernism's belief that humans live in separate, self-created, subjective worlds. "What happens," he then asks, "when different kinds of world are placed in confrontation, or when boundaries between worlds are violated" (*Postmodernist* 10)? The answer, he argues, is "ontological . . . instability" (11). Without stable boundaries, even the world the individual creates, lives in, and projects is subject to transgression, weakening, and collapse. Neither objective nor subjective "reality" can or should remain stable. Thus the frequently noted "anarchic impulse" in postmodernism (Fowler, "Revising" 104), its preference for "disruption" (Kreiswirth, "Intertextuality" 113), its admiration of subversion.

Edouard Glissant sees concern with transgressed boundaries and instability at the heart of Faulkner's portrayal of the South. He senses in that portrayal a South whose geographic and cultural boundaries were violated in the Civil War and whose racial boundaries are all the more rigid yet all the more doomed. He describes "Creolization" as the white South's perceived "menace," one bringing "unstoppable conjunction" despite all the "misery, oppression, and lynching" brought out to oppose it (30). Every crossing of racial boundaries is a reminder of "the unbearable idea that the world can invade the pure county and turn it inside out" (31). Charles Bon and Joe Christmas, both important in Glissant's work, lead readers of their novels to fuller consideration of these themes.

Postmodern interest in transgression and instability has most often led critics to *Absalom, Absalom!* Some have focused on narrative style. For instance, McHale says that Faulkner "crosses the boundary between modernist and postmodernist writing" in chapter 8 of *Absalom, Absalom!* when the narrators "reach the limit of their knowledge," only to transgress that boundary of knowledge as they "go on" to "project a world, apparently unanxiously" (*Postmodernist* 10). So alerted, readers might also note that as Quentin and Shreve do so, they also transgress two additional boundaries—those between past and present and between teller and tale. They are speaking in the Harvard residence hall in 1910, but they blend with the Bon and Henry galloping across Mississippi in 1861: "not two of them there and then either but four of them riding the two horses through the iron darkness" (237). All barriers disappear, geographic and temporal, and two worlds become one world, the fictional and the historical.

Following Glissant's lead, readers also profit from using transgression as a tool for examining character and plot in *Absalom, Absalom!* Transgression is the dominant characteristic of Charles Bon no matter which of the narrators projects him. Mr. Compson notes three major transgressive characteristics in Bon. He describes Bon as a cultural transgressor, who crossed the borders of New Orleans and its sophisticated world to enter the "puritan country" of North Mississippi [see also chapter 13] populated by "barbarian hordes" and "troglodytes" (74). He then makes Bon a gender transgressor, who dons "a flowered, almost feminised gown" as he almost languishes "in a sunny window in his chambers" and begins his seduction of Henry even before his seduction of Judith (76). Finally he introduces Quentin to the picture of Bon as racial transgressor, a white man from a Creole society who has entered a "morganatic" marriage with an octoroon, a woman whose body is itself a record of past racial transgression, a woman with whom Bon has produced a "sixteenth part negro son" in whose body the physical boundary between black and white utterly dissolves (80).

When all three of Bon's presumed transgressions show up in other characters, as well, the novel begins to reveal its attitude toward transgressions in general. Rosa Coldfield, for example, sees Sutpen as a cultural transgressor, a man with no gentility hiding himself among gentlemen, and as a racial transgressor too, entering the ring to wrestle his own slaves. She portrays Judith as a gender trans-gressor, Judith rather than her brother learning from the wrestling matches, Judith rather than her father inspiring the horses to race to the church. Mr. Compson, of course, accepts Bon's transgressions with equanimity, projecting his own presumed sophistication into Bon, and thus being quite ready to agree when his version of Bon treats the primitive taboos of North Mississippi with contempt. Rosa Coldfield, on the other hand, identifying with the fallen defend-ers of the Confederacy celebrated in her verses, finds the transgressions out-rageous. When Sutpen insults her with the suggestion of sexual transgression, she retreats to the impregnable walls and closed and shuttered windows of her Jefferson house, barriers she will defend from transgression.

Though Mr. Compson's and Miss Coldfield's reactions to transgression are poles apart, they both lead deathward. Rosa has made her impregnable home nothing less than a tomb for the living dead. It is dark, airless, dusty, and heav-ily scented, full of "coffin-smelling gloom sweet and oversweet" (4). In her out-rage at Sutpen's transgressive remark 43 years ago, Rosa stopped living in all but the body. Mr. Compson has started Quentin down the same path. Quentin picks up Mr. Compson's theme of racial transgression and makes it the key to his master narrative of the Sutpen saga, attributing Sutpen's rejection of Bon and Henry's murder of him to Bon's subversive racial status. Yet he cannot join Mr. Compson's acceptance of Bon as a fellow sophisticate. He becomes as outraged as Rosa. He leads Shreve gradually toward his picture of Bon's racial status as "the nigger that's going to sleep with your sister" (286) in order to maximize the outrage, his as well as Henry's, which results in Bon's death.

It will lead to his own, too. He spins this master narrative in a room repeatedly pictured as tomb-like, a reminder of the suicide readers already know lies ahead. By the time he arrives at the reason for the murder, he has made Henry not only the outraged upholder of subverted taboos but a self-annihilator as well. For nar-rative purposes, Henry Sutpen stopped living when he fired the shot that killed the racial transgressor. As far as his family and the community go, he disap-peared from life, a male Rosa Coldfield killed by his own outrage. Since Quentin has already identified himself with Henry as he has narrated the war experiences, when he looks on the shell of Henry lying in that bed back at Sut-pen's Hundred, he looks upon himself. The theme Quentin got from father—transgression—has led from subversion to anarchy to murder and suicide.

How could Mr. Compson's sophisticated acceptance of transgression inspire Quentin to join Rosa in puritan outrage and death? Perhaps Faulkner recognizes the value of transgression but does not celebrate it as a universal good as post-modernism does. Perhaps he sees how contradictory such a universalism is, since postmodernism celebrates transgression precisely because it rejects uni-versalisms. Perhaps then he sees transgression and stability as equal goods, both necessary for individual and social life. In that light, he may judge both sophis-tication and outrage to be equally ineffectual in the presence of transgression. Sophistication walks with transgression hand-in-hand, embracing instability, while outrage flees in horror into the stability of the tomb, but both leave transgression holding the field unengaged. Perhaps Faulkner looks for something different both from Quentin's and Rosa's outrage and from postmodernism's celebration of transgression and instability, something able to live in tense engagement with it, something that brings it into the temperate zone between the poles of outrage and admiration.

Light in August is a good place to explore this proposition, for it is as full of transgression as *Absalom, Absalom!* It sets up the theme by its multiple pictures of boundary crossing. Characters repeatedly violate boundaries as vast as geographic borders. The novel opens and closes with Lena Grove on the road, for example, crossing the state lines of Alabama, Mississippi, and Tennessee, with Byron beside her at the end. It has Joe Christmas even more footloose, apparently born in Arkansas, residing in a Memphis orphanage, adopted into Mississippi, running for 15 years on a street from Mexico to Detroit and back to Mississippi and into Jefferson, and running again at the end across county lines from Jefferson to Mottstown and back to Jefferson. Other major characters have violated Jefferson's borders as well, entering the town from elsewhere but remaining apart from it, abscessed within it—Lucas Burch/Joe Brown like Lena having arrived from Alabama and hightailing it out at the end; Gail Hightower in his dark house; Joanna Burden in hers (born in Jefferson but still a Yankee); and Byron Bunch, innocuous but still foreign, befriending only Hightower and worshipping at a church 30 miles away. And if characters violate vast geographic boundaries, they violate those as simple as walls, as well. They repeatedly come and go not through doors but through windows—Lena when she slipped out to meet Lucas Burch and then when she leaves home to search for him, Joe Christmas as he comes and goes from the McEacherns' to meet Bobbie and as he first enters Joanna Burden's house and even on the run from Grimm when he picks up a pistol, Hightower's wife as she commits suicide, Lucas Burch/Joe Brown as he flees from Lena and his baby. These crossings of state and county lines and these violations of walls are both positive and negative, for they sometimes set characters free to pursue new life but sometimes set them on paths of destruction.

These external transgressions express the characters' internal states. Like Charles Bon, all the major characters are destabilizing transgressors, and for good reason. They live in a world that has classified humans by gender and race and has erected strong boundaries between the classes of people in its determined groupings. The characters challenge those boundaries repeatedly. Even their names challenge gender categories, with androgyny suggested in names like "Gail" and "Bobbie" and even "Joe," which is shared among two males and one female, Joanna. Androgynous names predict the behavior of the gender-crossing characters. Despite all her earth-mother characteristics, for example, Lena has broken gender taboos even as the novel begins, having sex outside marriage and traveling alone, both behaviors culturally reserved for men but denied women. Joanna Burden joins her, conducting business and educational affairs with a "calm, coldfaced, almost manlike" behavior (258). Hightower has broken gender taboos in the opposite direction, the town suspecting that he failed to satisfy his wife as a man should and thus drove her to suicide. Byron

Bunch breaks the same taboos, though he hides it from Jefferson. He is a bachelor in his thirties, a choir director, and a friend of the suspiciously feminized Hightower, a ruined preacher and would-be art teacher. Finally, despite all the rampant heterosexuality attributed to him in the novel, even Joe Christmas becomes sexually suspect when he takes the young Lucas Burch/Joe Brown as his roommate and business partner and then slaps him around as an abusive husband would. The sheriff calls Christmas the "husband" of Brown (321). Suspicion of homosexual transgression culminates in Byron Bunch's request that Hightower claim a homosexual relationship with Christmas, and it partially explains his castration at the end, leaving him unmanned. Percy Grimm has already expressed his outrage that Christmas may have had sex with "every preacher" as well as every "old maid in Jefferson" (464).

Even more important in this novel, these characters are subversive racial transgressors. Hightower is rumored to have suspicious relations with African Americans, from his house servants to the neighbor whose stillborn baby he delivered. Joanna Burden has relationships only among African Americans, from neighbors who have worn paths to her door to the black colleges she supports and visits. Although her intentions seem benign or even beneficent, she finally reveals a distorted obsession with African Americans as "Other," describing them as the cross of her crucifixion yet crying "Negro! Negro!" in the midst of her sexual throes (260). Most important, of course, is Joe Christmas. Because of his grandfather's brutal enforcement of the world's obsessive racial boundaries, when he faces those strict boundaries between black and white he finds himself unable to live peacefully on either side of them and equally unable to ignore them. "You don't know what you are," the yardman tells him in the orphanage. "And more than that, you wont never know" (384). And sure enough, after his arrest in Mottstown, near the end of his life, one narrator complains that Joe "never acted like either a nigger or a white man," adding that that "was what made people so mad" (350).

Despite the destruction it sees transgression bringing, *Light in August* is largely on the side of these transgressors. After all, it sees much in need of destruction. The novel rejects the boundaries defining the world's gender roles, for example. It makes Lena a continually attractive character who elicits sympathy even from the disapproving Mrs. Armstid and who draws the love of Byron Bunch. It makes her transgressions the source of new life, not only of her child but also of Hightower and Byron Bunch. It approves of her continuing boundary breaking in its conclusion, sending her across another state line and making her utterly unconcerned that the world deems her in dire need of a wedding band and a cookstove. She is sufficient unto herself no matter what categories the world would cram her into (making her out to be an itinerant whore like Bobbie, perhaps?), as fully convinced at the end as at the beginning that she is what she makes herself, like "a lady travelling" (26). By contrast, Joanna Burden's outraged flight from her own transgression back into conformity, from sex on the grounds to prayer in her room, catapults her into death, just as Rosa Coldfield's flight does. Though Rosa's death is prolonged and Joanna's sudden, both deaths are accompanied by burning houses, as if to suggest the impermanence of the walls, the boundaries both retreated to so tragically. Lena's way is the way of life, Joanna's the way of death.

The novel rejects racial boundaries with even greater force. It presents Joe Christmas as an abused child, time and again in the hands of psychological and physical tormentors like Eupheus Hines, Miss Atkins the dietician, Simon McEachern, and even Bobbie and Max, who beat and "be-nigger" him at the very end of his youth. In doing so, it builds sympathy that stays with readers as they come to terms with Joe's violent adulthood. More important, it makes the gender and racial boundaries of his world, not Joe himself, the sources of his violence. That bounded world has no place for Joe. Lacking Lena's self-assurance, he alternately lives within the world's "white" and "black" boundaries, but some kind of internal integrity that insists he acknowledge his mix seems to subvert his attempts in every case. When he vomits at his vision of the cracked and leaking urns, their boundaries violated, he demonstrates his own agonized inability to keep either of his opposing identities locked within boundaries demanded by the world (189). He hopes in his subsequent relation with Bobbie, however, to have found a world comfortable with his lack of racial boundaries, yet his last, best chance to be simply himself disappears in Bobbie's racial accusation, so forcefully echoing those he heard at the orphanage: once again Christmas is "a nigger son of a bitch" (218). As in Quentin's depiction of Charles Bon, racial boundaries dissolve in Joe Christmas, and like Bon he finds no door open to him as an unclassified man. Even Joanna Burden insists that he be single rather than double. As a lover he is "Negro," and as a companion he is to become a black attorney. He lives his whole life as an orphan, perpetually crossing state lines and cultural boundaries, because no matter where he is he must tell himself, "*I don't belong here*" (258). As Wittenberg argues, *Light in August* shows "flight, death or perpetual apartness" as the price of transgression even as it "quite explicitly assails both the human tendency to categorize and the validity of the categories themselves" ("Race" 163). Like Quentin's Charles Bon, Joe Christmas's fate is death.

When Joe's death fulfills his role as a Christ figure, it suggests how strongly the novel supports his transgression. Throughout, the novel has shaped readers' response to this violent character in part by connecting him to Christ. His name incorporates Christ's, and his initials echo those of "Jesus Christ." His mother became pregnant without marriage. He effectively enters his world on Christmas Eve. He recognizes that "a stable floor, the stomping place of beasts, is the proper place for the word of God" (149). He rejects the pharisaical Simon McEachern and associates with thieves and whores. He leaves his home and becomes itinerate as Jesus did in his ministry, and then stays in Jefferson three years, the length of Jesus' ministry. Finally he dies, condemned by the mob because he challenges the order they cannot stand to have challenged. The point is that like his namesake, Christmas is a scapegoat. He bears the sins of many, in this case the world's demeaning and constricting racial boundaries. It is an ironic death, of course, for Christmas dies not so that the world may be free from such sins but rather so that it can once again believe that its categories are real and their boundaries safe. He dies, the world hopes, so that it can keep on sinning.

But the world has it wrong. Percy Grimm, speaking for that world, may condemn Christmas to Hell, where no doubt the Sanhedrin believed it had safely ensconced the blasphemer Jesus, but the novel predicts something else entirely. Its last picture of Joe Christmas is in a Christ-like ascension. He "seemed to rise soaring" into a realm both "serene" and "triumphant." There he will live "forever and ever," returning to the world's valleys and streams not to threaten but to witness, to speak the truth to young and old alike (465). The transgressor undergoes apotheosis. He is a god.

If Joe Christmas's story were the only story of *Light in August,* it would be on the side of Mr. Compson's sophistication: Jefferson is full of troglodytes whose oppressive boundaries need to be violated but whose barbarian outrage destroys the violator. But Joe's is not the only story, of course, and not the one with which the novel ends. Lena Grove's story trumps Joe's. It gives readers a character who achieves serenity not in death but in life. Why does Lena "get away with" transgression when Joe does not?

The answer may lie in what Joe lacks in his role as a Christ figure and what Lena, by contrast, possesses. Unlike the Christ, Joe Christmas lacks any sense of the fatherhood of God. Before he enters Joanna Burden's dark house for the last time, he stares at a road sign assuring passersby that *"God loves me too"* (105), but it has no meaning to this fatherless man whose grandfather and stepfather have been adversaries rather than fathers, accusers rather than lovers. His first stop after fleeing the Burden house is at a church where he stands "in the pulpit cursing God" (324). Lena, on the other hand, feels the presence of a Father God from the beginning of the novel. "I reckon the Lord will see to that" (21), she says when challenged on her plan to find Lucas Burch. The difference is key. If Joe is a transgressor the world has no place for and if he also lives without God, he must remain solely a transgressor. Lena, on the other hand, also a transgressor with no home in the world of the novel, still can claim a home beyond the world, one whose boundaries she can accept rather than transgress. The church may become a part of the world, erecting boundaries like ramparts and barricades, in Hightower's words (487), but Lena avoids the church and goes straight to the source, finding in her Lord a loving will that she does not wish to transgress, one that gives her what Hightower longs for, "that peace in which to sin [i.e., break boundaries, transgress] and be forgiven which is the life of man" (487). Access to an eternal realm and an eternal being, then, allows Lena to be both a transgressor and a member.

Not surprisingly, a marginal couple seems to confirm such a take on transgression. That would be the couple who discuss Lena and Byron in the final chapter. This couple, of course, is not marginal in Duvall's sense, for they are married and, with the husband a businessman, seemingly engaged in their community. They are marginal to the novel, however, individuals who have played an exceedingly minor role in the lives and actions of the major characters. They unfold their part of the novel's tale in a place and time readers must find both charming and significant. The episode is charming because they are lying in their marital bed where they have just made love and are flirting about doing so again: "*I just showed you once* [what Byron had in mind]," the husband says. "*You aint ready to be showed again, are you?*" "*I don't mind if you don't,*" the wife replies (499). A bit later, the husband, speaking of Lena waiting for Byron to make his move, teases his wife that "*she had a little more patience than you*" (500). The most important element in the charm this couple provides is that their sexuality is mutual, male and female desire of equal importance, unlike Faulkner's tragic pictures of "female sexuality under male control" (Duvall, *Marginal* 3). The episode is significant precisely because such happy, harmonious married couples are very rare in Faulkner's fiction. They almost never appear in the fiction preceding *Light in August.* Men and women are either unmarried—like Quentin and Jason and the cast-off Caddy or the Bundren children or Popeye and Temple—or they are unhappily married—Bayard and Narcissa Sartoris, for example, or Horace and Belle Benbow, or Jason and Caroline Compson, or the Bundrens. Dilsey and Roskus Gibson may be an exception, but readers get very little of their life together, nothing so intimate as this couple at the end of *Light in August.*

This couple fills the chapter with sexual energy and marital joy. With that, their presence powerfully suggests that lives inexorably separated by barriers of physiology (male and female) and of gender (the cultural roles imposed on males and females) possess the power to come together in a whole that, ironically, depends on their very difference. In their marriage and especially in its sexuality, this couple has become what Joe Christmas's namesake called "one flesh," yet to do so they have remained distinctly male and female. Marriage, as it so often does in literature, thus becomes a model for the novel's comic conclusion. We end with Rosalind and Orlando united, with Mr. Darcy and Elizabeth Bennett in their conjugal bed. Transgression—subversion and instability—will vanish, not at some point when all difference disappears, but when difference becomes attractive and the self partners with an Other that maintains its distinctiveness. In other words, Faulkner returns to his own universalism—heterodoxy.

Once again, then, Faulkner has anticipated postmodernism's position that transgression trumps oppression, and his work accords with that part of postmodern thought. But Faulkner's work does not suggest that transgression, subversion, instability, and anarchy are the universal goods that postmodernism, again contradictorily, seems to make them. Transgression is a means, not an end, an expedient, not a universal. Faulkner uses marriage to return readers to the heterodoxy that remains one of his chief universalisms. Heterodoxy, love of the other, surpasses both sophistication and outrage, for it makes transgression a partner of stability.

INDIVIDUAL SELFHOOD IS AN ILLUSION

In holding that individuals as such do not exist, postmodernism contradicts almost the entirety of Western thought. It repudiates the individualism at the heart of Western political and economic thought since the Enlightenment [see chapter 7]. It denies the sanctity of individual life central to the Judeo-Christian tradition [see chapters 1 and 13]. It is best understood, perhaps, as the orphan child of Marxism, which repudiates the Western belief that autonomous individuals form the best governments out of their freely entered social contracts and build the richest economies when left unhampered in free markets [see chapter 7]. Rather than free individuals forming political and economic systems, Marxism insists that humans are simple extrusions of the social and economic systems that determine their lives.

Postmodernism insists that there is no such thing as an individual, nor can there ever be. Psychologist Kenneth Gergen puts it this way in his exposition of postmodern identity: "In the postmodern world there is no individual essence," he writes (139), for "Selves as possessors of real and identifiable characteristics—such as rationality, emotion, inspiration, and will—are dismantled" (7). Literary critics have described the same point in similar language. Jameson, a Marxist critic, not surprisingly speaks of the "illusion of the coherent self or ego" ("Foreword" x), and Gerhard Hoffman refers to postmodernism's "deconstruction of identity" (278). Fowler describes the "distinctly postmodern and, more specifically, Lacanian, notion" that there is no "unified, coherent, autonomous self" ("Revising" 98) and that the "self" or "speaking subject" is thus merely another "fiction" (*Return* 3). The traditional Western view that every human is an autonomous individual is called **essentialism** because it rests on the notion that each human has an essential core distinct from others' and valuable in its own right. That essential core or essence, traditional thought holds, is the foundation, perhaps the steel skeleton, on which and around which individuals build full lives, including their characters, relationships, and careers. Postmodern rejection of the autonomous self rests on the reverse notion already cited in Gergen: Individual human beings do not possess essences. They have no cores.

In the place of essential cores, postmodernism offers relationships. Gergen explains it thus: "One's identity is continuously emergent, re-formed and redirected as one moves through the sea of everchanging relationships" (139). These relationships provide the only self a human possesses, Gergen says, for in postmodernism "the self vanishes fully into a stage of relatedness" (17). Gergen recognizes how radically anti-Enlightenment this notion is, for if so-called individuals are no more than "manifestations of relationships," then these relationships have come to occupy "the central position occupied by the individual self for the last several hundred years of Western history" (146–47). Literary criticism echoes Gergen's substitution of relationships for essences. In his study of the postmodern fascination with metaphor and mask, for instance, Lothar Hönnighausen describes the contemporary understanding of "identity as context-dependent" (*Faulkner: Masks* 137). Fowler agrees, explaining the Lacanian self as "socially constructed" ("Revising" 98). To speak metaphorically, one might say that postmodernism sees the individual as something like a collection of blue Wal-Mart sacks snagged on a barbed-wire fence. The collection has an apparently autonomous existence, a form and shape analogous to the skin that wraps the individual human being, but it has no essential identity, having been born and shaped by the winds of chance, which in a moment may rip a blue sack away and smack a yellow one in its place. In the postmodern vision of human life, those sacks are the genes and life experiences that create identity, and the fence and wind are the happenstances that link them up.

Postmodernism has a name for the living, breathing collection of Wal-Mart sacks, the so-called individual who is reading this essay. That coreless being is not an individual, not a self, not a subject but an "agent." Bertens makes the point precisely: "the autonomous and stable subject of modernity has been replaced by a postmodern agent whose identity is largely other-determined and always in process" (9). Agents, unlike subjects, act not on their own volition but on others', guided by forces they may not even recognize; they are the mere embodiments of cultural forces—like Marxism's masses produced by their roles in the system of production. "Roles," in fact, is an important term in the postmodern substitution of **agency** for identity, for postmodernism describes the actions of people conceived of as agents to be no more than "performances," like those given in a theater, with actors as the agents of the playwright and the director, and influenced by the remainder of the cast as they play their roles. Philip Weinstein, for instance, describes postmodern writer Donald Barthelme's "penchant for the performance of roles rather than genuine identity" ("Postmodern" 20). Coreless human beings with no essential identities are agents of circumstance; they go through life becoming whatever their relationships, their contexts, make them, playing roles in lifelong performances.

Hassan suggests that Faulkner saw this postmodern vision of human life as relativistic and rejected it as "ideological manipulation intended to justify what most human beings would find unjustifiable" ("Privations" 8). Hassan offers invasion of privacy as such an unjustified aim, and we might add other twentieth-century schemes to manipulate human beings into the perfect forms the schemers have determined they should possess—both Stalinism, for example, as well as its opposite, contemporary corporate-sponsored consumerism. So warned, readers might expect to find Faulkner such a thoroughgoing modernist that his fiction neatly divides between portraits of sound and healthy "essentialist" characters fully expressing their individual identities, and Iago-like postmodern manipulators, self-consciously "constructing" and using others to fit their hidden schemes. But, of course, it is not that simple. Faulkner created a number of characters whose lives are socially constructed, or context-dependent, and he learned a great deal from them. He seems to have anticipated this facet of postmodernism as he did others. Postmodernism helps readers see it in his work, and his engagement with it helps postmodernists see the shortcomings of their point of view.

Once again, *Absalom, Absalom!* is the critics' favorite entry into Faulkner's engagement with this facet of postmodernism. Focusing on the narrators, Gerhard Hoffman sees the novel going "part of the way" toward the full postmodern vision of a coreless, identity-less humanity when the characters' voices (their "identity") and their version of the Sutpen saga ("historic truth") undergo "dissolution," and "actuality" of identity and truth give way to "possibility" (285). In other words, "performance" takes the place of essence when Quentin and Shreve, for instance, simultaneously cast themselves as Henry and Bon, and Henry and Bon as themselves. If four can so easily become two, readers must wonder if the four ever possessed autonomous, whole human identities and may conclude that "establishing one's own identity" is finally an "impossibility" (Gerhard Hoffman 282). Apparently agreeing with Hoffman's point but looking primarily at Sutpen, Doreen Fowler moves on to describe what takes the place of the absent identity in the novel. Interpreting Sutpen's "innocence" to be his "naïve belief in the cultural fiction" that he might achieve "autonomous and complete" individual human identity like that of the patriarch in the big house, she argues that this fiction ironically leads to Sutpen's "induction into the social order that constructs him" ("Revising" 101). In other words, his design does not free him as he intends but rather shapes him to be just another agent of the social system, a clone of the patriarchy. Concurring while focusing on Charles Bon and the novel's treatment of race, Philip Weinstein describes the novel's insistence on "the outrageous constructedness of racial identity" (*What Else* 55). The social system that constructs Sutpen as a white patriarchal demigod constructs Bon as his opposite, a "nigger" who belongs in the mud with the rest of his animal-like brothers. The postmodern notion that identity may be socially constructed rather than essential opens up much of what *Absalom, Absalom!* is about.

The question remains, however, whether Faulkner understands social construction as postmodernists do. Does the power of society to construct identity necessarily rule out the existence of individual identity? Does accepting that power and our social constructedness free us? In Gerhard Hoffman's vision, recognizing and accepting social constructedness opens the door to "imaginative play" (285) and "what one might hesitantly call freedom" (284). Fowler and Weinstein agree, at least on the need to recognize social constructedness, suggesting that ignorance of society's power to construct humans can lead to enslavement and annihilation of both self and others. Recognizing society's power to construct identity would seem to be in order.

But perhaps Faulkner is on the side of recognition without acceptance. Such is the case if *Absalom, Absalom!* indeed produces Philip Weinstein's "outrage" at the socially constructed identities foisted on Sutpen and Bon. If these characters were born to be no more than socially constructed, why should the novel produce outrage that they take one shape rather than another? What difference does it make that a cyborg contains one program rather than another? What difference does it make that the Wal-Mart sacks take any particular shape along the fence? The novel would not produce outrage if it saw social construction as "all there is" and the recognition of social construction as freeing. Yet it does produce outrage, and that seems to be because it sees social construction as necessarily enslaving and annihilating whether recognized or not, the silent but ubiquitous enemy of the individual identity the novel values. Sutpen's boy at the door finds no freedom in recognizing that society constructs himself and his family as beasts—"as cattle, creatures heavy and without grace, brutely evacuated into a world without hope or purpose for them" (190). Nor does Bon in recognizing his construction as a "nigger." Nor, truly, does Quentin Compson. Though he and Shreve refer to their narration as "play" and excitedly move the story to the subject of "love," Quentin's final picture is one of annihilation, Henry's annihilation foreshadowing his own. And it is one of hatred, Quentin's hatred of the South explicitly and of himself as its socially constructed product. Quentin is hardly free.

Such a reading returns to Faulkner's central universal truth, human hetero-doxy. It suggests the major question Faulkner asks the orthodox postmodernist: Why are we to value the widest possible range of human life if no one human life is uniquely valuable in and of itself? By contrast, is one not to value every possible expression of Otherness as equal to oneself precisely because every human being has intrinsic individual value? If, as Hassan argues, "Faulkner defines the postmodern view without acceding to it" ("Privations" 8), in his con-sideration of individual identity and social construction, he seems to have found the latter to be destructive of the former, which he continues to uphold. To accept social construction as all there is would be to join what Bertens calls the "anti-humanist" side of postmodernism (17). Faulkner remains a humanist, challenging postmodernism to recognize that it has made individual identity and social construction into a false dichotomy.

Go Down, Moses offers a good test of such an understanding of Faulkner's take on postmodern identity. The novel focuses narrowly on one branch of soci-ety, the McCaslin family, examining its construction of race and of gender, par-ticularly of masculinity. In doing so, it becomes what Patrick O'Donnell calls a "postmodern revision/reversal" of *Absalom, Absalom!* ("Faulkner" 36), *re-*creating the Thomas Sutpen of Quentin's narration and then offering alternate versions of what Sutpen might have become, not just in Ike, as O'Donnell has it, but in various McCaslins. It extends the Sutpen saga, various McCaslins living out alternatives Sutpen rejected as they negotiate the path between essential identity and social construction.

The McCaslin patriarch, Lucius Quintus Carothers McCaslin, and his great-great-grandson Roth Edmonds re-create the Sutpen that Quentin narrated. Like Sutpen, both McCaslins are plantation owners. Sutpen's rigid, design-shaped identity leads him to turn away both his first, mixed-race wife, paying her off, and then his mixed-race son, Charles Bon. Old Carothers denies his mixed-race daughter Thomasina when he takes her as a lover, and Roth denies his mixed-race cousin and lover when he turns her away in "Delta Autumn," both McCaslins buying their way out of the relationships with a $1,000 legacy and a sheaf of banknotes. Just as Roth bears "the face of his ancestor" (321), both McCaslins bear the face of Sutpen.

The novel makes it clear that this Sutpen/McCaslin identity is socially con-structed rather than essential. It does so when it shows Roth acquiring the iden-tity as a child. When he excludes his mixed-race cousin Henry from his formerly shared bed, he feels descending upon him "the old curse of his fathers, the old haughty ancestral pride based . . . on an accident of geography" (107). That curse is an identity external to and different from his essential identity, family providing postmodernism's identity-forming "relationships" and "geography" its "context." As I have argued elsewhere, "Roth becomes a postmodern unit in the McCaslin line" (" 'I'm the Man' " 85). He bears not only the name and "the face of his ancestor too" (321), but his socially constructed identity as well. Like old Carothers before him and like Sutpen, he may believe himself to be an individual making his own decisions, but he has become an agent performing a role in the Southern drama.

As in *Absalom, Absalom!,* however, Roth's contextual identity does not bring happy freedom. Indeed, it brings a misery that suggests that Roth's change is something more than a switching of one mask for another. Even as he becomes a McCaslin-unit, Roth suffers a "grief he could not explain [and a] shame he would not admit" (109), for he experiences his postmodern McCaslin identity as a violation of something innate, as the ruination of a modernist essence still making its claims despite his denial of it. Neither Sutpen nor old Carothers reveals a division between social and essential identities so explicit as Roth's, but the similarity of all three characters suggests that Roth's shame and grief may have been old Carothers' when Eunice drowned herself and Sutpen's, perhaps, when he stopped before the grave of Charles Bon. Faulkner understands the social construction of identity, but he does not accept it. Indeed, he protests it vehemently as a violation of something that coexists with it, at the heart's core.

But what would Sutpen have been, *Go Down, Moses* seems to ask, if he had gone back to the mountains after his boy-at-the-door experience, abandoning the designs constructed by society in favor of the wilderness of mountain life? It asks this as it portrays another descendant of old Carothers, his grandson Ike McCaslin. The wilderness of Ike's big woods duplicates the wilderness of Sutpen's mountain origins. In both spots the land seems undivided and held in common: in *Absalom, Absalom!* "anybody and everybody" owns the mountain land, and anyone who would "fence off a piece of it and say 'This is mine' was crazy" (179), and in *Go Down, Moses* one would be "fatuous . . . to believe . . . to pretend that any fragment of it had been his" (183), because "the land belonged to no man [but rather] to all" (337). In both wildernesses, no one possesses a socially constructed identity that makes him any better or worse than anyone else, but rather all are as worthy as their personal attributes make them. In Sutpen's wilderness, individuals measure themselves "by lifting anvils or gouging eyes" (183), boasting that "*my arms and legs and blood and bones are superior to yours*" only because they could do more, certainly not because "*I own this rifle*" (185). In Ike's wilderness, Ike must relinquish that very rifle to look upon Old Ben, and hunters must learn to be humble and to accept "the communal anonymity of brotherhood" (246). Sutpen, of course, never returns to his wilderness, embracing his patriarchal design in its place, but Ike does embrace his wilderness, weds it even more than he weds his wife, and shuns the social identity of his patriarchal legacy.

The question, then, is whether Ike's retreat to the wilderness has freed him from his cousin Roth's fate, freed him from becoming another postmodern

McCaslin avatar, a unit in the patriarchy. At one point he thinks he has escaped: "I'm free," (285), he tells his cousin Cass; "Sam Fathers set me free" (286). But then he must hear his very words tumble from the very unfree lips of his cousin Fonsiba, fled like him into a wilderness: "I'm free" (268), she claims as she crouches in "an icy gloom where not even a fire for cooking burned" (265). And finally Ike comes to realize, according to the narrator, "that no man is ever free" (269). Ike does not seem to have escaped being shaped into an agent of the social order. Would he join Roth in sending away his mixed-race cousin if he had? As Diane Roberts argues, Roth and Ike are both representatives of the "masculine hegemony" (*Faulkner* 87). They are both postmodern agents.

Ike's repudiation of his inheritance and relinquishment to the wilderness seem like a heroic sacrifice aimed solely at breaking his family's claim on his identity, yet he ends up as much the product of the family as his cousin. So does Ike's defeat suggest that humans have no cores, no essences, no chance at individual identities? Perhaps the vision here is a bit more subtle than that. What if the narrator of "Race at Morning" is right that "the hunting and the farming wasn't two different things at all—they was jest the other side of each other" (Faulkner, *Uncollected* 309)? What if the wilderness is just a disguised patriarchy, visited only by men, inhabited by beasts who reincarnate lost fathers ("'Oleh, Chief,' Sam said. 'Grandfather'" [177]), presided over by a man whose name is "Fathers" and whose own father was known as "Doom" (from *du homme,* the man), and haunted by an old male bear who sounds a lot like old Carothers: "he's the head bear. He's the man" (190). Ike has fled from the plantation patriarchy but only to embrace the opposite-but-equal wilderness patriarchy. As I have argued in another essay, in trying to avoid becoming his grandfather's avatar, Ike becomes old Carothers's "anti-avatar, 180 degrees from sick and thus still sick" ("Tense" 197). Would Sutpen have been served, then, to flee back to the mountains? Not if he carried the patriarchy with him. Is there any alternative to postmodern agency? Hadn't these characters better accept their agency and begin enjoying their own performances?

Not if the novel's other major McCaslin and its third reconsideration of Sutpen is its fullest version of the man and its final word on identity. That McCaslin is Lucas Beauchamp, like Ike the grandson of old Carothers. He is the Sutpen who lets Charles Bon enter through the front door. In his case, Charles Bon comes in the form of his wife Molly.

Lucas Beauchamp barely escapes becoming a McCaslin-unit, an agent of the patriarchy like Sutpen. His near capture comes in "The Fire and the Hearth" when, briefly, he chooses gold over Molly. His hunt for gold reenacts the role of his grandfather as planter, both men attempting to make the land produce riches. His forcing Molly to resort to divorce reenacts his grandfather's treatment of Eunice and Thomasina and anticipates Roth's denial of his lover and son in "Delta Autumn." And, of course, Lucas's farming for gold and rejection of his wife reenact Sutpen's whole career—his determination to get rich by farming the land, his setting aside his first wife and son, whom he found to be hindrances to this design, and in Quentin's version, at least, his rejection of Charles Bon. Is it any wonder that Lucas's cousin Roth thinks "with something like horror: *He's more like old Carothers than all the rest of us put together, including old Carothers*" (114)? African American ancestry notwithstanding, Lucas Beauchamp seems to be an agent in the patriarchy, subjecting the land and other humans alike in his lust for wealth, subjecting the feminine to his patriarchal domination.

Unlike his cousins Roth and Ike, however, Lucas does become something else. He enters the courtroom and retracts his consent to the divorce, and he takes the offending metal detector to Roth's house and relinquishes it as surely as Ike once relinquished his rifle. In the latter act, he reveals how short Ike fell in his relinquishment. When Ike relinquishes his compass, watch, and rifle, he does so only to lay eyes on Old Ben, the patriarch of the wilderness, and Old Ben obligingly leads him right back to his equipment, which he keeps and uses the rest of his life. When Lucas relinquishes the metal detector, he does so utterly and finally. He even faces down the temptation offered by old Carothers's avatar Roth to keep it on the sly. He does so not to meet the wilderness's version of old Carothers but to return his wife to their home and the fire to their hearth. Rather than subjecting the feminine to his patriarchal will, he accepts the feminine as his equal and his mate.

In doing so, Lucas strengthens an individual identity beyond postmodern agency of Roth, Ike, old Carothers, and Sutpen. Their lack of individual identity, of self-realization, appears in their "sterility." Interestingly, all the postmodern family-units—Sutpen, Ike, and Roth—end up being culturally sterile clones, mass-produced units incapable of keeping their families going as such. It is as if their agency has destroyed the only quality worth passing on, the vital spark of individuality. Lucas, by contrast, has a functioning family. The famous fire on his hearth represents the vital spark he retains and passes on, the flame contained within a firebox suggesting the individual essence that can stay alive in the human heart whatever contexts one enters, constructions one meets, relationships one finds. Passing on the vital flame is no simple matter. The agents of the white patriarchy, the avatars of Pharaoh, destroy Lucas's grandson Butch in "Go Down, Moses," and they destroy Rider in "Pantaloon in Black" despite his lighting a fire like Lucas's in his own hearth. But the novel has shown Lucas with his son Henry, and it promises a reconciliation with his daughter Nat to accompany his reconciliation with Molly. By contrast, when Roth hardens his heart against the shame and regret he feels in his rejection of Henry, when Ike hardens his heart against his wife and chooses the wilderness patriarchy over her claims, when old Carothers scorns mates and children alike, when Quentin's Sutpen closes his door to Charles Bon, they extinguish the fire that Lucas Beauchamp keeps alive. They relinquish their individual identity.

These three McCaslin versions of Quentin's Sutpen, then, expand Faulkner's consideration of the outrageous social identities foisted on human beings. Some humans are like Roth; they accept them unreflectively. Quentin believes this was Sutpen's path. Some are like Ike; they recognize and flee from them only to embrace them in disguised form. Could this have been Henry Sutpen's path, since he and Ike both end up as desiccated old men sheltered in others' houses, with no wives or children at their sides? But others can be like Lucas; they can judge the identities the world lures them toward by consulting their heart's core, and they can follow its lead. Lucas is Sutpen having second thoughts and reclaiming his first wife and child, letting Charles into his home. He is old Carothers *"saying My son to a nigger"* (258). He is Ike giving up his rifle for good and restoring the feminine to the plantation, in the form of his wife. He is Roth as a child calling his black cousin back up into the bed and Roth as an adult restoring the feminine to the family and to his own identity by marrying the mother of his child. The heart's core is complex, and individual identity is myriad, as black as it is white, as feminine as it is masculine. No mask can match it. It is "of itself alone serene, of itself alone triumphant" (Faulkner, *Light* 456).

Faulkner once said Sutpen was "too big" to be captured by any of those telling his tale. So is Faulkner too big for postmodernism. Its particular insights do open up his fiction in new ways, but once they have done so, that same fiction challenges those postmodern insights. In this case, Faulkner agrees that many human beings end up like those blue Wal-Mart sacks snagged on the fence, nothing but what the happenstance of geography would have them be. But he argues, in turn, that such a condition by no means rules out the existence of a core, an essence, an individual identity, a fire on every human's hearth. In fact, he protests that such a condition violates and destroys that precious individual identity. He elicits outrage that it should do so, and he makes readers long for an authenticity beyond the reach of such evil.

FINAL THOUGHTS

André Bleikasten is right in part: "Faulkner was a modernist" ("Ideologues" 12). But he is also wrong, for Faulkner is also more than a modernist. His relationship to postmodernism tells us that. Faulkner's fiction and postmodern thought have a symbiotic relationship. Postmodernism has given life to themes that lay dormant in the fiction, little noticed before it arose—the fragility of language, the elusiveness of truth, the celebration of heterodoxy, the value of transgression, and the social misconstruction of identity. For its part, the fiction gives new life to some of postmodernism's highest values, leading them out of self-defeating contradiction, assuring postmodern readers that language can still connect despite its fragility, that truth may find humans if they cannot find truth, that the celebration of heterodoxy can rest on universal truth, that transgression is a means but not an end in itself, and that recognizing society's power to construct identity does not mean that individuals lack identity. Faulkner's ability to anticipate and engage these postmodern themes suggests his power to transgress the boundaries of modernism, to "resist, disrupt, or exceed" it, as O'Donnell puts it ("Faulkner" 31). It promises that his fiction will remain alive in decades and centuries to come, becoming a master narrative itself precisely because of its heterodoxy, its resistance to single, orthodox readings. Like the dust in *Absa-*

lom, Absalom! that will always "get there first accumulating ahead," Faulkner's fiction awaits readers in the future, abiding and serene, patient as readers live toward its vision.

NOTE

1. All quotations from Faulkner novels in this chapter are taken from the Vintage International editions.

7

Cultural-Studies Criticism

Peter Lurie

Faulkner's "career" within cultural studies began, within the history of the cultural-studies movement itself, comparatively late. This is not an especially remarkable point about Faulkner or any one particular writer; as a critical movement, cultural studies was never concerned more with any one figure than another, and was always concerned with an interdisciplinary and interdiscursive focus rather than a writer's singularity. It is a point worth noting, however, because of the specific ways in which Faulkner's work seems hospitable to cultural studies' concerns. From his earliest stages of writing, Faulkner was aware of his work's position within a field of cultural production, as well as within a series of interrelated cultural meanings and social structures. The fact that there is a strong body of work on Faulkner that bears several common elements of a culturalist approach is perhaps less striking than that it took Faulkner studies time to make use of them.

TOWARD DEFINITION

Before suggesting the reasons for this critical lag, as well as providing an account of the most effective examples of culturalist Faulkner criticism, it is useful to consider a brief history of the cultural-studies movement and an effort at an overall definition. (As we will see, and for reasons having to do with its aims, the movement is difficult to define in a straightforward, summary way.) One challenge in describing the study of culture more precisely as an academic field is the fact that the various approaches cultural studies takes each define culture differently. Traditional literary and cultural criticism defined culture as the rarefied products and refined expressions of trained, gifted, or visionary artists; the various modes of cultural studies depart markedly in their terms for approaching culture as both an entity and a term. Marxist modes of analysis stress the impact on culture's production by vested, economic interests (publishing houses, film studios, or magazine editors), as well as its depiction of class differences and struggle. Ethnographers study culture as the empirically observable rituals of a particular ethnic, religious, or national group. Sociology describes a culture's institutions and their regulation of culture from distant, centralized sites of production.[1] Cultural studies combines (and questions) all of these definitions, drawing from them what it finds useful in identifying what culture is, what it says, and—importantly—what culture may be said to *do*. For throughout its various incarnations, cultural studies seeks to intervene in the political, social, and material experience of those individuals and groups that it sees culture in all its modes affecting.

In its progressive orientation, cultural studies seeks to give voice to individuals and groups that are not in possession of the means of protest or social redress, to those "who have the least resources" (During 2). Unlike earlier forms of cultural analysis, cultural studies sees social reality and, most importantly, its inequities as central to understanding literature. As Simon During puts it, "Most individuals aspire and struggle the greater part of their lives and it is easier to forget this if one is just interpreting texts rather than thinking about [cultural activity] as a life-practice" (2). Social-scientific studies of culture, which sought objectivity or neutrality, or earlier forms of criticism that appreciated the unique or formal beauty of art (to the exclusion of its political content) are thus seen by cultural studies as distinctly limited. By contrast, cultural studies directly addresses the political dimensions of literature and culture.

An important aspect of this approach is the treatment of subjectivity. Cultural studies treats subjectivity as constructed by individuals' interactions with influences and agencies that exist independently of personal autonomy. Assumptions about social positioning or personal behavior, for instance, perpetrated in the form of dominant images, messages, or codes exert tremendous pressure on the formation of our sense of self. Sexuality, racial identity, class biases—all, according to cultural studies, are conditioned largely by our interactions with(in) the social and cultural field. In light of this recognition, culturalist work traces the interactions of the private self with public or "official" discourse. As Richard Johnson says, "It is because we know we are not in control of our own subjectivities, that we need so badly to identify their forms and trace their histories and future possibilities" (61). Referring to Marx's "preoccupation with those social forces through which human beings produce and reproduce their material life," Johnson declares: "*Our* project is to . . . describe and reconstitute in concrete studies the social forms through which human beings 'live,' become conscious, sustain themselves subjectively" (45).

Obviously the early New Critical readers of Faulkner had little interest in such deliberate "reconstituting" of the author or his work's "social forms." Admittedly, Faulkner's formal experiments and stylistic richness lend themselves well to the kind of formalist readings encouraged by the Vanderbilt group. And as we shall see, formalism remains an important aspect of much culturalist criticism. Yet for cultural studies this is only one component of an approach to writers that deliberately seeks to break down the divisions between a text and its surroundings in cultural and social life. More purely formalist readings like the New Critics' avoided that breakdown scrupulously, offering instead "pure," **aestheticist** appreciations and explications of Faulkner's complicated language and plot constructions. Even when informed by discourses outside of the texts themselves, such as Freudian psychoanalysis or considerations of Southern history, they used those considerations largely in the service of a well-wrought declamation of a text's internal or hermeneutic meaning, beautiful and forceful in its completeness. Surely, Faulkner's often misleading claim to being the "sole owner and proprietor" of Yoknapatawpha County—and straightforward readings of him as such—contributed to this view of the major fiction as a Balzacian chronicle or self-sufficient world.

Before turning to demonstrations of the ways in which Faulkner scholarship manifests various lines of culturalist analysis, it is helpful to see the roots of those approaches in the movement's history. Cultural studies in its earliest form grew out of a British literary study current in the 1950s named after the critic F. R. Leavis. "Leavisism" was committed to a cultural project that, in many ways, differs significantly from many common understandings of cultural studies today. Yet in its motives, Leavisism may be seen to also share an interest in the same equalizing or democratizing motives of contemporary culturalist work.

Leavis sought to unify English cultural life and sensibility through a common, traditional canon, propagated to a wide public through the educational system (During 2). Subverting what Leavis saw as the profound moral and intellectual value of readings from the Western tradition (which included figures such as Pope or Austen, but discarded early twentieth-century experimental writing) was the influence of then-contemporary mass culture. Leavisism stands in direct opposition to what would become cultural studies' later emphasis on the importance of mass art to considerations of cultural life. Yet Leavis's thinking also included a component that attracted two later English critics who were to have a profound impact on the development of cultural studies as it came to be practiced. Richard Hoggart and Raymond Williams, with *The Uses of Literacy* (1957) and *Culture and Society* (1958), respectively, took up Leavis's notion of culture as a way to both identify and unify members of a particular social group or "subculture" and define culture as a "whole way of life," one that included practices not ordinarily considered as culture, per se—such as work, family experience, social and racial identity, sexual orientation and experience, and gender roles.[2] In these early books, Hoggart and Williams pioneered studies that stressed the importance of reading "culture" alongside and as integrated with social life.

The Uses of Literacy offers this sense of engagement with the world that produced both culture *and* experience (or "life") in its celebration of older, industrial working-class communities in Britain. Related to this celebration was Hoggart's assault on then-contemporary mass culture. For like another system Hoggart opposed (state-run education), commercial art posed a threat to Hoggart's image of the traditional English working class. In this, Hoggart shared with Leavis a distrust of modern commercial culture. Unlike Leavis, however, he opposed a uniform educational system. Hoggart's affinities with Williams more clearly mark the direction cultural studies was to take. With Williams, Hoggart shared a broadened definition of culture, one that saw it not as a canonical set of "high cultural" texts but as a "way of life" that bound peoples together and that included its own modes, values, and terms for identity. (Both Hoggart and Williams drew from Leavis a focus on social groups' way of living as a vital definition of modern cultural experience.) This could include activities in a British working-class context like pub life or watching soccer, as well as club songs that reflected a sense of solidarity between a group's members. In its move away from high culture and its attention to culture defined more broadly, including, in its later versions, popular and commercial art, cultural studies (following Hoggart and Williams) began to acquire the position it takes today [see chapter 11].

One of the most significant developments historically for cultural studies was a shift in the way social classes identified themselves. Following the advent of mass-cultural means of addressing and, arguably, unifying national populations (such as television), members of distinct classes within those populations stopped seeing themselves as part of a discrete, self-sustaining culture with its own ways of life, connected to specific material and political interests. This shift contributed to the development of a phenomenon described by the Italian social theorist Antonio Gramsci as "hegemony." **Hegemony** describes the processes by which a disadvantaged segment of the population participates, apparently willingly, in its own oppression. Identifying with the existing purveyors of power, rather than with others within their social class, members of oppressed groups fail to see their complicity in their own domination. Gramsci's thinking is important to cultural studies because it stresses the way in which groups within a society often with opposed interests and positions—but without the ability to exercise power—maintain a shared view of the way social reality "should be." Members of an oppressed working class in England, for instance, or post–Civil War blacks suffering under the privations of Jim Crow laws, are encouraged to see their position as part of a natural (or naturalized) system, one that is not readily subject to intervention or change.[3]

Along this line, cultural studies notes the connection between a dominant ideology and the formation of identity. Louis Althusser defines ideology as "the imaginary relationship of individuals to their real conditions of existence."[4] Within this imaginary sense, individuals see themselves addressed (interpellated or "hailed," in Althusser's terminology) by the dominant ideology in ways they find flattering. Encouraging members of a society to see themselves as fully autonomous or self-determining agents, for instance, suppresses their awareness of the ways in which their lives are more frequently determined by forces—usually economic and political—that function beyond their control. "Dominant ideology turn[s] what [is] in fact political, partial, and open to change into something seemingly 'natural,' universal and eternal" (During 5).

A brief example of the kind of approach to Faulkner that illustrates Althusser's thinking is Thadious Davis's early work. Though she does not identify it as such, Davis's approach to *The Sound and the Fury,* for instance, suggests Althusserian notions of ideology formations. In her book *Faulkner's "Negro": Art and the Southern Context,* Davis focuses on a highly suggestive passage involving Quentin on his return home to Mississippi from the North and Harvard. She seizes on the account Quentin offers of an older, African American man he encounters sitting astride a mule outside Quentin's stalled train. Seeing the man outside his window, Quentin reveals a perspective that, Davis points out, is clearly marked by an ideological belief in the "naturalness" of black servitude. " . . . he sat straddle of the mule, his head wrapped in a piece of blanket, as if they had been built there with the fence and the road, or with the hill, carved out of the hill itself, like a sign put there saying [to Quentin] You are home again."[5] Davis does not invoke Althusser, but her analysis of this passage points to how Quentin demonstrates his understanding of the African American man (who addresses Quentin as "young marster" and who demonstrates a "shabby and timeless patience") as part of the natural scene, "carved out of the hill itself" (Davis 77).

Another main feature of cultural studies is its opening up of the whole category and field of what constitutes culture. The motive for this is the recognition that culture is not limited to "high" culture and its academic or elitist modes but is rather produced by several parties and at different levels of a society. Within an ethnographic practice, this latter aspect led to culturalist attention to ritual, primitive, or folk art. It has also led to impressions of cultural studies as being committed to readings of "low" forms of contemporary culture (television programming, advertising, newspaper copy, magazine articles, commercial film, gossip columns, pornography, cartoons) as being as serious or important as "high" culture (Shakespeare, Dante, or Monet). The relevance of such claims is that cultural studies does in fact avoid evaluative approaches to its material or objects of study. This is not to say, however, that it seeks a flattening of all value or that it tries to replace established cultural texts with others. Rather it asks questions about the *ways* in which the value of culture is determined. As an important part of the category "culture," then, popular, commercial, or mass art needs to be considered alongside—not necessarily in the place of—high culture.

The field of cultural studies promulgates a definition of culture at odds with not only traditional conceptions of art, but with approaches to individual artists or writers. As Richard Johnson sees it, culture should be "understood as a social product, [and] not a matter of individual creativity only" (53). In this respect, the notion of a Faulknerian cultural studies is, on its face, something of a misnomer or an impossibility. Culturalist approaches to Faulkner succeed to the extent that they take Faulkner or his text(s) as an orienting point, an object of study that shares prominence with other concerns such as the contexts for that work's production; its reception by its various readers—including critics, "the public," and later reworkings of Faulkner's work; and the experience of those individuals and groups his fiction endeavors to represent [see chapter 10].

A final, but key aspect of cultural studies is its urge to see itself as a spontaneous, loosely defined movement more than a codified methodology (Johnson 38–40). Allowing itself a sense of orthodoxy or program, cultural studies would become part of an academic life that it sets itself very much against, concerned as it is with questioning traditional hierarchies and structures of value. It follows from this resistance that cultural studies does not ally itself strictly with any one discourse or academic discipline. Used by several disciplines, including English and literary studies; sociology, ethnography, and anthropology; political science and history; media and film studies; studies of race, gender, and sexuality; as well as various Marxist currents, including Althusserian and Gramscian modes of thought, cultural studies is perhaps above all interdisciplinary—even antidisciplinary.

By its own account, then, cultural studies is a far messier affair than traditional approaches to literature and art. Most often this "dirt" is identified as the formerly less seriously considered realm of popular culture or as areas of experience not generally considered culture at all (dating; the way people drive; the Balinese cockfight). Inimical to cultural studies, though, is the impulse to question categories of cultural distinction in an effort to discover the effects of such distinctions and their implied hierarchy. As a paradigmatic modernist, Faulkner appeared to provide earlier critics with a model for the ways in which high art sought to separate itself from the consumer and mass culture that developed contemporaneously with it. Yet, as much of the work described below asserts, such a distinction about modernism, and about Faulkner in particular, overlooked his work's deep involvement in the practices and effects of contemporary life, including mass and commercial art.

Additionally, from its beginning Faulkner's work made clear its intention to make cultural conflicts, as well as those conflicts' often violent consequences, its central focus. This attention to the unresolved tensions of his period and region marks Faulkner's fiction as directly engaged with phenomena and events that existed beyond the boundaries of his texts and which his texts sought to change. For all their insistence on formal and narrative experimentation, Faulkner's stories and novels implicated themselves, and often their reader, in the dissonance of racial, gender, and class antagonisms, painful or ugly realties about contemporary social reality in which he saw his texts intervening. Furthermore, those texts often use formal properties to comment on themselves as a certain kind of cultural product—high or low—as well as on readers' experience of them. In these ways, Faulkner's work may be said to be tainted or "dirtied" with the problems of the social world around it.

Culturalist readings of Faulkner pay particular attention to those workings. Of primary interest to culturalist readings are moments in Faulkner's work that show Faulkner as inconsistent or divided about the concerns he addresses. Contradictory treatments of the often marginal subjects of his society or of troubled social relations reveal the pressures Faulkner experienced in his own position in the early twentieth century as a white male writer in the South. Later reworkings of his earlier material, as well, often bear the signs of

Faulkner's change in perspective about his work's cultural meanings. Finally, his work written especially for or with an eye toward the culture industry—film scripts, short stories, and particular novels—bear the marks of Faulkner's critical regard of that industry in general and, specifically, its treatment of Faulkner's "native" subjects: rural blacks, poor white farmers, Reconstruction and the New South, and the Civil War. As such, that work is of particular interest to cultural studies.

One thing helpful in identifying a Faulknerian cultural studies may be to show an example of what it is not. Several early critics avow to doing something like what cultural studies attempts: placing Faulkner in his social and cultural context and drawing interpretations from that positioning. Yet in their efforts, these readers perform the very detachment, "abstraction," and mystification of Faulkner and his world that cultural studies denies in its approaches to literature.

Well before the New Critics, and in the very midst of Faulkner's most forceful and prolific period of writing, George Marion O'Donnell attempted to situate Faulkner culturally. Referring to him as "a traditional man in a modern South" in an essay from 1939 ("Faulkner's Mythology" 23), O'Donnell treats Faulkner in some of the ways I have described above: as reflecting on a society defined by its conflicts and tensions. Yet O'Donnell does something very different with Faulkner's troubled historical context than does culturalist work. Rather than describe the reasons for the cultural changes Faulkner faced, or how his fiction elaborates the effects of these changes on his characters' interactions or understanding of their world, O'Donnell retreats from that world and its material reality. The Snopes/Sartoris interaction, for instance, O'Donnell sees simply "as a universal conflict" (24). The nature of this conflict is not the widespread and historically specific one between an owning and a managing (or bourgeois) class, or between a residual and an emergent social group, but, in O'Donnell's view, is rather between moral abstractions. "The Sartorises act traditionally. . . . They represent vital morality, humanism" (24). The Snopeses, on the other hand, are not even human—let alone part of a meaningful human history. "The Snopeses . . . acknowledge no ethical duty. Really, then, they are amoral; they represent naturalism or animalism" (24). Certainly O'Donnell is right in characterizing the Snopes as amoral, even evil. Yet he casts his argument in terms that are the antithesis of cultural studies' efforts at an active engagement with their subject, "abstracting" (27) Faulkner's characters to a mythical status or principle.

Granville Hicks, another contemporary reader of Faulkner, performs a similar disengagement with Faulkner's world. In describing Faulkner's approach to his culture's violence, for instance, Hicks sees only Faulkner's effort to shock readers throughout his work with a pervasive, uncritical vision of corruption, "horror," suffering, and disgust. This generalized quality, Hicks writes in *The Great Tradition,* prevents Faulkner from coming to terms with the causes for his characters' suffering—or even from trying to. To Hicks, Faulkner can show superficially the degradations of fallen families like the Compsons, Sartorises, or

Hightowers, or the abject squalor—moral as well as physical—of the Bundrens, Hineses, or Groveses (265). But he maintains that this is all Faulkner does. "Faulkner has . . . watched the people of the South carefully; he is one of them and he knows them from the inside. But he will not write realistically of southern life. He is not primarily interested in representative men and women; certainly he is not interested in the forces that have shaped them" (265–66). In pursuing his supposedly detached "bitterness" and unassimilated "hatred" towards his region (266), Faulkner produces merely an undifferentiated gloss or projection.[6] In doing so, Faulkner presents readers with a violence that he (or rather, as Hicks demonstrates, readers like himself) fails to analyze. "If he tried to see why life is horrible, he might be willing to give a more representative description of life, might be willing to occupy himself with . . . suffering. . . . As it is, he can only pile violence upon violence in order to convey a mood that he will not or cannot analyze" (266).

Culturalist readings of Faulkner reveal precisely Faulkner's willingness to "occupy himself with suffering" and to analyze the forces and moods that produced it. In a vastly different tenor from critics like O'Donnell and Hicks, culturalist readings of Faulkner show him strenuously and penetratingly analyzing the losses and suffering of his characters' world. Where the readings in this first wave of criticism were right in recognizing the harsh vision and even violent mood of his fiction, and later, second-generation schools like the New Critics recognized the beauty and force of Faulkner's formal experiment and psychological probing, it was a later group of scholars that combined an attention to formal complexity with Faulkner's deep, critical engagement with social and historical reality. In their use of such analytical strategies, several "newer" Faulknerians exemplify this mode.

A Faulknerian strand of cultural studies, it should be pointed out, is not exactly new. While there is not an exemplary single text of a cultural-studies approach to Faulkner, there have been several collections or editions of journals that offer a common, culturalist approach to his work. One of them, the special issue of the *Faulkner Journal* (volume 7) entitled "Faulkner and Cultural Studies," edited by John T. Matthews, is already 10 years old. Additionally, the Faulkner and Yoknapatawpha Conference at Oxford, Mississippi, annually publishes editions of the conference proceedings; these volumes offer a number of collections that are of a culturalist orientation. Among them are the volumes *Faulkner and Popular Culture* (1990), *Faulkner and Ideology* (1995), and most recently—and most thoroughly a version of cultural studies—*Faulkner in Cultural Context* (1997).[7] In the discussion of representative culturalist criticism of Faulkner that follows, I refer to several of the essays from these and Matthews's collections. Now an established way of reading Faulkner, if not an actual discipline (as we have seen, it manifests unease toward the very notion of disciplinarity), cultural studies has provided a supple and vigorous set of terms for interpreting Faulkner. If no longer new, it has moved Faulkner scholarship well beyond the terms offered by his first readers and has produced an area of study that was and continues to be highly versatile and productive.

THE SOCIAL AND CULTURAL POWER OF GENDER AND RACE

Cultural studies' interest in gender and its cultural construction is a pervasive element of the field, and it is taken up by several recent approaches to Faulkner, works, for instance, that make use of Judith Butler's work in cultural and gender theory, in particular her book *Gender Trouble*.[8] Accounts of Faulkner's challenge to or exploration of gender construction include scenarios of gender performance (and its undermining); instances of female "hysteria"; examples of the "containing" of female characters; the transcending of female victimization; and the "policing" of lines of gender identity.

More specifically, theories of sexuality, homosexuality, and gender crossing have flourished in recent years, and cultural studies has made lively use of them. Although Faulkner can hardly be said to foreground issues related to gay culture and thought, certain of his works—particularly *Mosquitoes* and "Divorce in Naples"—have elicited cultural studies' interest in queer identity and its potential for questioning heterosexual behavior and modes of socialization that present themselves as "natural." These readings have also seen gender transgression in the context of Faulkner's broader questionings of patriarchy.

Such topics invite, as Richard Johnson points up, cultural studies' emphasis on "critique in the fullest sense: not criticism merely, nor even polemic, but procedures by which other traditions are approached both for what they may yield and what they inhibit. Critique involves stealing away the more useful elements and rejecting the rest. From this point of view cultural studies is a process. . . . codify it and you might halt its reactions" (38). Anne Goodwyn Jones's essay "'Like a Virgin': Faulkner, Sexual Cultures, and the Romance of Resistance" offers an example of scholarship as "process" and as this kind of selective critique. As such, it is a useful place to begin a survey of what we may provisionally term Faulknerian cultural studies. Written fairly recently, it addresses a central culturalist concern (the cultural construction of sexuality) and it uses a culturalist method (referring to a popular text for an elucidation of its terms). It also reveals a self-consciousness about cultural studies' position and strategies. Resisting the dominance of the term "resistance," Jones seeks to avoid allowing an aspect of culturalist thought to rigidify into a form of orthodoxy. She also questions Faulkner's apparent social critique.

Suggesting that authors' well-intentioned critical strategies can mask their own reactionary motives, Jones examines Faulkner's negotiation in *Sanctuary* of traditional Southern, Victorian sexual mores with what she terms modern and "national" developments and attitudes. Challenging the notion of Temple Drake as a virgin, Jones endeavors to demonstrate that Faulkner challenges ("resists") Southern cultural hegemony through his depiction of her as sexually experienced. Ultimately, however, Jones argues that Faulkner's own cultural resistance is limited, that it itself falsely romanticizes the notion of resistance to more conservative ends. She makes use of contemporary Southern social discourse, such as behavior manuals, to suggest Faulkner's and the South's acceptance of a limited and unidirectional "crossing" of gender lines. Southern discourse about gender roles reveals the ways that men of the 1920s and 1930s could allow themselves to be "feminized" and otherwise modernized—for instance, by allowing their wives a more active sexual desire. (Jones analogizes this gesture of male feminizing to the Southern valuation of a heroic and "noble" acceptance of loss after the Civil War.) One such source that Jones cites, Judge Ben Lindsey's *Companionate Marriage,* offers an image of a modern, vital woman who embraces an active sexual identity. And it does so without casting such a woman as deviant or trangsressive.

For Jones, Faulkner's treatments of sexuality and gender in key texts like *Sanctuary* and the "Wild Palms" section of *If I Forget Thee, Jerusalem* may be said to partake of this newer, national model of behavior and thus resist earlier paternalistic sexual mores. Yet Jones argues this resistance is more apparent than real. Faulkner presents Temple's sexuality, especially when she is presumed to possess a history other than the traditional Southern status of virgin, as dissipated, problematic, or unhealthy (49, 66)—nothing like Judge Lindsey's liberated "flapper." And Jones reads Faulkner's depiction of a Southern "feminized" man as similarly resistant to accounts of modern male-female union. The values endorsed by Lindsey's image of the companionate marriage, and which the relationship of Harry and Charlotte Rittenmeyer resembles, end up being violently punished. Similarly, the idea of a different cross-gendered move—toward a "masculinized" woman—is consistently demonized in other Faulkner texts. Temple Drake, Caddy Compson, Joanna Burden, Drusilla Hawk—examples of a modern, potentially resistant female sexuality—are all reduced or "punished" by Faulkner's narratives, Jones claims.

An important fault line running through culturalist approaches to Faulkner separates two distinct positions. On one side are readings like Jones's that see Faulkner reproduce systems of power, belief, or cultural hierarchy, such as patriarchy. Another example of this perspective is Deborah Wilson's in "'A Shape to Fill a Lack': *Absalom, Absalom!* and the Pattern of History." Wilson sees *Absalom, Absalom!* as a means by which Faulkner reconstitutes a male narrative power and commensurate power over history. Describing her sense that Rosa Coldfield is silenced or her language appropriated by male narrators, Wilson sees Faulkner's novel as asserting the act of narrating history as a male prerogative. In doing so, she situates Faulkner as the last—and most definitively authoritarian—in the line of male "narrators" of the Sutpen story. In Wilson's terms, the novel's conclusion appears to offer an unsettling, and therefore progressive, stance. In failing to finish the story or show the succession of Sutpen's patriarchal design, the narrative fractures the vision of a "pure" Sutpen legacy (and a white South) because the mixed-race heir Jim Bond is still at large (76). Against this sense of disruptive openness to the end of the novel, however, Wilson asserts that Faulkner himself restores the patriarchal order lost to the Old South by virtue of his own form of ordering: the book's various narrators as versions of Faulkner's own "master" voice. In doing so, Faulkner "constructs a world even more patriarchal than the Old South he has lost" (78).

Though attentive to potential limits in Faulkner's political horizon, approaches like those of Jones and Wilson may neglect Faulkner's extranovelistic position. As a result, some critics read him in the same category and through the same terms as those they use to read the characters he's created. Thadious Davis, for instance, in the book cited earlier, collapses Faulkner's perspective on the "natural" state of the African American man on the mule with Quentin's, as though by describing him through Quentin's eyes, Faulkner shared his vision. Readings of moments like these might well consider the inherent separation between Faulkner and the fabricated Yoknapatawpha world, a distance that is a key element of Faulkner's strategy throughout his fiction. Faulkner's depictions of Quentin's (or Thomas Sutpen's or Horace Benbow's) ideologically tainted attitudes are deliberately set at a distance, one that allows readers to see their workings critically.

Some such awareness is needed if we are to approach the works as they deal with any topic but most especially as they deal with Faulkner's ongoing and varied treatment of race, arguably the broadest and deepest realm of Faulkner's work that commands culturalist thinking. So much of Faulkner's fiction suggests the complicated ways race is constructed culturally that it is difficult to limit readings of this central fact of his world to cultural-studies approaches. However, several works make use of theoretical terms or ways of configuring race and culture that are most specific to cultural-studies practice. Among those terms are the following: concerns with the way race informs the exercise of power, especially as that power informs other social relations (class- or gender-based); connections of race to definitions of sexuality; attention to Faulkner's awareness of conflict in racial identity that reflects on its broader social and cultural bases; events or developments in African American historical experience that affect white cultural expression and historical thought; treatments of racialized "categories" and cultural acts like ritual, performance, violence, and blood; and the control and definition of racial identity and race relations through the management of surveillance, mirroring, and the look.

A major tenet of culturalist Faulkner scholarship is Faulkner's critical awareness of the gender, class, and racial assumptions of his characters. Of course, this awareness does not always obtain; Faulkner certainly possessed biases that show up in his writing. Yet despite the very real presence of ideological blind spots in Faulkner's handling of his characters and narratives, culturalist readings evince Faulkner's much sharper critical capacity toward Southern social life than some readings allow.

Karen Andrews uses Gramsci's theory of hegemony to show this perspective in her essay "Toward a Culturalist Approach to Faulkner Studies: Making Connections in *Flags in the Dust*." In it, Andrews examines various reactions of African Americans in the novel to white domination, particularly Capsey's challenge to the Jim Crow systems of the South. Most important to Andrews is Caspey's objections to his and other blacks' treatment by whites after the First World War, in which many of them served to help defeat Germany only to return to an American caste system that refused to recognize their war contribution or their status as full citizens.

> I dont take nothin' f'um no white folks no mo' . . . War done changed all dat. If us colored folks is good enough to save France f'um de Germans, den us good enough to have de same rights de Germans has. French folks thinks so, anyhow, and if America dont, dey's ways of learnin' um. (*Flags in the Dust* 53; quoted in Andrews 20)

Caspey's thinly veiled threat to white power seems to evidence Faulkner's anti-hegemonic stance with the novel: Caspey (unlike other black characters) refuses to submit to the docile position expected of him. The fact that Caspey and his threat are forcibly recontained within a position of submission reveals, however, what Andrews claims to be Faulkner's mixed feelings about African American rebellion (Andrews 19).[9] Describing Caspey's statements as a "pseudo-rebellion," Andrews points to his reinscription by the novel into a position of subservience as well as his eventual return to a hegemonic stance, one in which he "is portrayed as an accommodating black servant" (21).

Ultimately, however, Andrews offers a more subtle analysis: she connects the miscegenist aspect of Caspey's other, more challenging threat (to "have" a white woman in the American South, as he has in France) to Faulkner's short story, "There Was a Queen." In *Flags,* there is only a hint of the actual occurrence of the racial admixing that Caspey threatens. In "There Was a Queen," Andrews points out, this fact is more clearly articulated (22). Violent white opposition to threats to its power emerges in a comparison of *Flags* and "Queen" as a manifestation of white Southern guilt over its own miscegenist past—that is, instances of white slave owners fathering mixed-race children. This fact of Southern history is made explicit in the later story, a perspective that explains the pattern of strident white opposition to black male sexual involvement with white women in the South. It also, as Andrews puts it, "circles back to Caspey's original criticism of the double standards of the dominant caste" (22). Her reading exposes the way that Caspey's punishment in *Flags* emerges through a reading of "There Was a Queen" as an effort to silence "the reality of miscegenation affecting black women while adamantly prohibiting the other form involving white women" (24).

In "Reading Faulkner Reading Cowley Reading Faulkner: Authority and Gender in the Compson Appendix," Susan Donaldson offers a similar reading of Faulkner's ability to question Southern male impulses toward control over white women, as well as black men. She uses the trope of watching, and she examines the connections between vision, narrative, and gender in *The Sound and the Fury,* locating in all three Compson brothers a longing to contain Caddy within their (narrative) vision. Although Donaldson contends that Faulkner reveals this to be a male purview in his own "masculine," totalizing perspective in the book's closing section, she suggests that Faulkner later revises his impulse toward mastery in his work on the Compson appendix. Here, Donaldson sees Faulkner resist his editor Malcolm Cowley and Cowley's editorial surveillance, what Donaldson calls a repeated gesture of male "domain building." Faulkner avoids the mantle of totalized authority, first in his and Cowley's correspondence, which includes Cowley's efforts to push Faulkner towards greater legibility about the Compson story. Donaldson points to Faulkner's reticence to engage in acts of narrative clarifying and control, especially through vision, in his approach to the appendix. These are evident in his refusal to allow Caddy's imagined photograph to be used to control her, as had her brothers' surveilling gaze(s) in the novel. In Faulkner's evasions of consistency with the appendix, as well as what Donaldson sees as his identifying with Caddy, he offers a (culturalist) corrective to Cowley's cultural-editorial suasions.[10]

These issues of gazing, gender construction, narration, and the male control of female sexuality pervade other Faulkner novels, particularly *Sanctuary* and the novel's criticism. *Sanctuary* offers a useful way to gather several discussions of Faulkner's treatment of sexuality and patriarchy, as well as of commercialism. Because of the novel's popular success (and its resemblance to and use of popular-culture models), *Sanctuary* holds particular interest for critics of a cultural-studies bent. Some of these essays, such as D. Matthew Ramsey's "'Lifting the Fog': Faulkners, Reputations, and *The Story of Temple Drake*" ask important questions about the definition of culture as it applies to our understanding of Faulkner's cultural positioning. Ramsey suggests a more fluid definition of the terms "low" and "high" culture in the 1920s and 1930s than we often allow in discourse about the period. As well, he examines the casting of Miriam Hopkins in the film's role of Temple Drake, a decision that, Ramsey suggests, reflected the studio's equating of Hopkins's supposed lesbianism with contemporary discourse about what was labeled as unnatural or perverse. Ramsey looks at the film's advertising as a way in which the studio sought to capitalize on interest in outré subject matter and to present Temple, like the presumably gay Hopkins, as an illicit pleasure while also appearing to judge women's "aberrant" sexual behavior.

Ramsey's essay shares certain concerns with a much earlier treatment of the novel, Leslie Fiedler's "Pop Goes the Faulkner: In Quest of *Sanctuary*." Like Ramsey, Fiedler traces the two "grounds" of the novel's success—commercial and critical—as well as the fact that Faulkner worked assiduously to manage both. Fiedler's "quest" in the essay is to prove that Faulkner was, in fact, no modernist, but rather an "entertainer" on the order of a Dickens or Twain, that his popular novel *Sanctuary* lay close to "the essence, the very center of his achievement" as a novelist (77). As such, for Fiedler *Sanctuary* more closely resembles Faulkner's work in a novel like *The Sound and the Fury*. Fiedler's reasoning has to do with what he sees as Faulkner's use in *The Sound and the Fury* of racial clichés, or what he elsewhere describes as Faulkner's melodramatic and bathetic war fictions (79).

Despite the provocative nature of such views, Fieldler foregoes examining the reasons for the success of the representations of history, gender, or race he attributes to Faulkner's various novels. Referring to the "stock of misogynist platitudes current in [Faulkner's] time and place" (81) that inform *The Sound and the Fury* as well as *Sanctuary*, Fiedler avoids analyzing what particular cultural work the use of such platitudes might have accomplished. He also neglects to consider what a writer's movement between the categories of high and low culture could afford.[11] Asserting that Temple is "responsible for all the deaths that occur in [*Sanctuary*'s] pages" (87), Fiedler fails to examine what sorts of attitudes (including his own) lie behind considering women "responsible" for the violence that surrounds them.

Fiedler's essay does, however, anticipate cultural analyses of *Sanctuary* when he refers to the generalized dread of sexualized women in Faulkner and in this novel in particular. One of those is Kevin Railey's "The Social Psychology of Paternalism: *Sanctuary*'s Cultural Context." Fiedler's attention to the "flipside" of Faulkner's sentimentalizing of women like Dilsey or Ruby Lamar, namely what Fiedler called his "misogynist . . . nauseated rage at" the "reality" of women (Fiedler 80) is strikingly similar to Railey's theorizing of *Sanctuary*'s paternalist ideology. In an essay that squarely addresses the two sides of paternalistic thought in the book (Horace's protective and idealizing, nonphysical approach to Southern women, and Popeye's violent, perverted sexual punishment of them), Railey points out the connections between intimately held sexual attitudes and social positioning. Drawing on Klaus Thewelit's studies of male fantasy, Railey finds in Horace a troubling connection to his inverse reflection in Popeye, as well as an aristocratic tendency towards sexual repression. To Railey, Horace shares with the German Friekorpsmen of post–World War I Germany (who, like Horace, saw themselves as the upholders of a threatened aristocratic and civilized tradition) an aversion to any suggestion of femininity or desire, as well as its manifestations in images of fluidity, movement, or social collectives.[12] Women like Temple, with their overtly unsettling sexuality and motion, arouse men's desire and their reaction to it: the impulse to fix women within rigid social categories of behavior.

What distinguishes Railey's essay as an example of cultural studies is its consistent efforts to avoid the kind of strict Freudianism that characterizes earlier readings of Horace and to connect private psychology (or subjectivity) to its manifestations in and projections onto bodies—social *and* physical. As he puts it, *Sanctuary* demonstrates the ways in which "neuroses . . . are never simply 'private'" (85), particularly when they belong to members of the ruling class who have a vested interest in making the effects of those neuroses felt in the broader public sphere. Thus Horace's treatment of women, in particular Temple (and that treatment's violence, manifested in inverted form in Popeye), shows this working out of a paternalistic mentality. In his reading of the end of the novel, Railey offers a way out of the usual manner of implicating Faulkner in the novel's effort at containing women. Noting that Temple's forced stasis at *Sanctuary*'s close occurs in Europe and in "the season of death," Railey sees Faulkner here marking Horace and his ideology's need for control of women as impossible in the changing world of the twentieth-century South, colored as it was by changes that allowed for the more mobile, fully realized female subjectivity that we'd seen in Temple in the novel earlier.

Running through considerations of Faulkner's treatment of women in *Sanctuary* is the awareness of Faulkner's conflict over the cultural meaning of femininity, expressed generally as a split between emulation and horror. Railey, for instance, sees a strict division between, on the one hand, the novel's depictions of Temple and Narcissa Benbow, images of women as virginal, pure idealizations, and on the other Miss Reba or Ruby Lamar, lamentably fallen and therefore "dirtied" prostitutes. But Anne Goodwyn Jones sees Faulkner find a way out of his depiction of female duality in *If I Forget Thee, Jerusalem*. With Charlotte Rittenmeyer, Jones claims that Faulkner finds a third position, one that "he uses to explore and contest the ontological certainty of the gender dichotomy itself" ("The Kotex Age" 143). Part of that exploration involves a variation on the negative association of women with popular culture and commercial success. In Jones's view, *Jerusalem* is atypical in showing a woman in Charlotte with an avowedly sexual activity and lively intelligence, as well as in the novel's unapologetic use of popular-culture materials and strategies.

Jones refers to the "masculine fears" that underscore the interests and needs of a patriarchal ideology and that find expression in *Jerusalem*. Here Jones uses Janice Radway's study *Reading the Romance: Women, Patriarchy, and Popular Literature* to describe Faulkner's novel as a "male romance." As a study of the culture or "whole way of life" of middle-class, married women, Radway's book identifies the reasons for the romance's immense popularity. Radway points to the romance as a model for women's freedom from cultural constraints: in it, the heroine is loved "for herself," not for her conformity to a cultural construction. Their reading of romances also provides women at least temporary relief in their role as wives and mothers from the work of caring, largely, for others. Due to the fact that this relief is only temporary, however, women reread the plots of these novels continuously in different books, consuming them as "as [they] might any other drug" (Jones, "The Kotex Age" 151). Jones offers "Wild Palms" as a kind of "male romance," one that cautions male readers of the threat of engulfment in sexuality, liquidity, and a collateral loss of self. In "Old Man" she finds a case of another "hooked" reader. Like Radway's readers of female romance, the Tall Convict, due to his naïve and overly literal reading, fails to find his way to real freedom though his acceptance of his dime novels as well as his increased sentence (both of which Faulkner reveals to be transparently constructed fictions [160]).

Jones posits, though, that Faulkner ultimately questions the gender-biased, male fantasy of self-protection and the disavowal of the feminine, present in both "Wild Palms" and "Old Man." In the novel's modernist, contrapuntal form, *If I Forget Thee* critiques modernist and masculinist assertions of autonomy from the feminine, figured as the popular, the bodily, and the collective. For Jones the novel's form belies the capacity for "isolation"—that of the book's discrete narratives and the male characters in them. As such, *If I Forget Thee, Jerusalem* "presents an alternative to the loneliness and anxieties of the men in it who fear not only women but, more importantly, their own deepest feelings" (161).

FAULKNER AND POPULAR LITERATURE

Faulkner's work has been read by critics as both remote from and, conversely, deeply engaged with modernism's supposed "Other": contemporary commer-

cial and popular art. The latter view obviously reflects a cultural-studies perspective, and Faulknerians who pursue it have produced imaginative and animated work, as well as a strong argument for Faulkner's contextualizing within
cultural history. Areas of Faulkner's own cultural production, such as stories or
screenplays written ostensibly as a source of needed income, are shown in several essays to reveal a sharply critical and self-reflexive eye toward both themselves and the cultural market. From the opposite side, as well, are culturalist
readings that see Faulkner's "high-art" works as both influenced by and critical
of mass-cultural modes. Faulkner's use of indigenous, popular, or folk genres as
well take on substantive or political meanings in culturalist work.

At first glance, Faulkner appears an unlikely candidate for analyses of his
work's intersection with "low" or mass art and a commensurate questioning, on
critics' part, of the construction of categories like "high" or refined literature
[see chapter 11]. Yet recent work in Faulkner studies aggressively pursues these
very intersections, seeking to show the extent not only of Faulkner's awareness
of popular-culture strategies, formulas, and techniques, but his critical use of
them in his writing. These approaches identify mass-market consumption and
tastes as the (oblique) subject of a portion of Faulkner's mature writing. According to several studies, Faulkner incorporated into the thematics [see chapter 13]
and formal strategies of his work the subject matter of popular novels, stories,
journalism, and film. Above all, his own short stories—written specifically for
the mass audience of magazines like *Scribner's* and, more invidiously, the *Saturday Evening Post*—reveal Faulkner's critical awareness and foregrounding of
the ways in which short stories fashioned themselves in order to conform to
market formulas and imperatives.

In "Dismantling the *Saturday Evening Post* Reader: *The Unvanquished* and
'Changing Horizons of Expectations,'" Susan Donaldson takes up the notion of
Faulkner's address to a mass readership. In her reading of Faulkner's revisions of
The Unvanquished, Donaldson sees Faulkner producing a critical distance in
Bayard Sartoris and in the *Post*'s readers (where the *Unvanquished* stories originally appeared) from what had become a formulaic and commodified "horizon
of expectations." Refusing to avenge the death of his father, a Civil War hero, at
the end of "An Odor of Verbena," as his family and the "audience" of Jefferson
onlookers expect him to, Bayard offers an alternative ending to those that
Faulkner's reading audience expected of popular Civil War fiction. Because of
what was considered the "peculiar" ending of "An Odor of Verbena," one noted
by both defenders and detractors of the book, *The Unvanquished* becomes in
Donaldson's analysis a much more provocative, unsettling novel than other
mass-market fare, and than the novel itself has often been considered to be.

She also describes the position of the *Unvanquished* stories as they appeared
in the *Post.* Donaldson points to the magazine's advertisements of dutiful black
servants and whites in blackface, images that suggest the *Post*'s aversion to story
material like Faulkner's that would force readers to question assumptions about
race associated with the Civil War South. In directing readers toward an examination of the values that informed and undergirded their consumption of earlier

Southern fiction and of magazines like the *Post,* Donaldson avers, Faulkner took "vengeance" on a periodical that more often than not refused his stories, and one that had forced him to conform to the magazine's formulas. In doing so, however, Faulkner included his own, ultimately more disquieting revisions. As a result, he ultimately rewrote not only the stories themselves, but "the magazine's readers as well" (194).

In two essays on Faulkner's short stories, John T. Matthews examines the intersection of Faulkner's writing for the cultural market and his literary or "art" fiction. "Faulkner and the Culture Industry" shows Faulkner using short stories and screenplays written ostensibly as a source of quick, easy money to comment on the conventions and formulas of commercial fare. The story "Turnabout," which he reworked into a screenplay for *Today We Live,* shows evidence of Faulkner's awareness of the story as potential fodder for Hollywood, addressing as it does the popular themes of honor and male companionship during wartime that were popular in the period. Matthews points out, however, that this awareness included a sharply critical edge, evident in both the story's antiwar rhetoric (in a period of jingoistic militarism), its questioning of technology,[13] and its homoerotic or, as he describes it, using Eve Sedgewick's term, "homosocial" undertones (63). He also shows Faulkner working with the changes imposed on him by the studio when the story became a movie—such as creating a role for Joan Crawford in a story without a female character to complicate its wartime and "buddy" themes. Matthews's approach is important in that it discovers an alertness on the part of the stories toward themselves as (potential) products, one that comments on the nature of mass-market inclinations and tastes.[14]

Matthews's essay "Shortened Stories: Faulkner and the Market" makes an even stronger claim for the singularity of the short fiction as revealing Faulkner's culturally critical eye. Describing Faulkner's "segregating" of his novel and short-story work, Matthews claims that the shorter form allowed Faulkner access to a more direct, immediate engagement with his historical and cultural situations than did the novels, in which various critical impulses were collapsed into these works' larger engagement with Southern mythology (5–6). Matthews also suggests that the form of the short story may be seen as manifesting objectively the conditions of the characters it depicts, particularly those marginalized members of Southern society. "The broken, brief form of the short story," he posits, "accommodates the heterogeneity of the lives of the underclasses" (14). Isom and Elnora in "There Was a Queen"; the customers at the Texan's horse auction in "Spotted Horses"; Henry Armstid, as well as his audience of hill folk who watch him dig for gold on the Old Frenchmen's place in "Lizards in Jamshyd's Courtyard"—all of these characters represent classes and social groups that, Matthews claims, are well represented in the short story's stunted, distended form.

Matthews here also sees Faulkner use the stories to comment on the circumstances of their production. Like Susan Donaldson, he finds several traces, for instance, of resistance to the demands of the very market the stories sought to satisfy. Stories such as "There Was a Queen," "Dry September," and "Spotted

Horses" directly or indirectly present scenarios of commodification, consumption, or the production of acquisitive desire through modern practices like advertising and "the mystifying power of group desire" (18). In "Spotted Horses," Matthews sees the intense longing of the auction's farmer customers and the empty "promise [of] gratification" held forth by the "spirited, almost otherworldly" ponies the Texan sells (18). Elsewhere, in an analysis of "Red Leaves," Matthews finds potential representatives of popular-magazine readers (and of magazines themselves, "fat" with their advertising and its attendant revenue) in the story's depiction of its obese, slave-breeding Indians. The image of the story's condemned and starving slave gorging himself on his last meal, only to then arrest and deny his insatiable appetite, becomes self-reflexive; it evokes the "marginal man in a senselessly acquisitive society" (21). Like a Marxist version of Kafka's Hunger Artist, Faulkner's slave in this story rejects his modern, sensationalist, and acquisitive culture, reflected in the aggressive marketing and advertising of the magazines.

In addition to these gestures, Matthews points to an important dimension of Faulkner's depiction of Southern rural life: his willingness to "retail" it, like the sewing-machine salesman Surrat in the comical anecdotes he tells to prospective customers. This example of Faulkner's self-criticism is key. Pointing to Faulkner's own complicity in the market he critiques, Matthews does not present Faulkner as superior and aloof to it. At such moments, Matthews avoids remystifying Faulkner's modernist position as transcending the cultural market that he resisted—but which he also needed and used.

CLASS, HISTORY, AND IDENTITY

Another strong intersection of Faulkner scholarship and cultural studies includes attention to class, both class struggle and economic forces as a determinant aspect of identity. In a similar mode are perspectives that recognize the intervention of other Marxist-defined, "superstructure" factors such as the state and public institutions in areas of personal, private experience. As with many examples of cultural studies, the field of inquiry in these works often overlaps with others: concerns with gender, race, sexuality, or the body arise in the context of considerations of labor, employment, wage systems, or politics. Of particular interest to Faulkner critics concerned with class are instances in his work that reflect on aspects of American cultural life such as 1930s debates about socialism, class solidarity, and collectives.

One fascinating tendency among culturalist readings of Faulkner is the attention to specifically modernist aspects of his work that have been used to criticize modernism as ahistorical. Those aspects include modernism's "excessive" formalism, its insistence on its originality or historical presentness, or its focus on individual psychology and social isolation. Though this strategy of "redeeming" modernism's historicity shares much with the New Historicism, it also pursues specifically culturalist goals.

High on the culturalist agenda is attention to culture defined as not only aesthetic production and encounters with works of art, but as part of everyday, quotidian life. Particularly as that experience may be seen to express personal agency or, conversely, the ways that agency is "seized," placed within culturally defined constraints or impinged upon from sources of power (such as institutional or state agencies), it compels cultural studies' attention. Faulkner's treatment of these intersections informs many of his narratives. As with other categories, this branch of Faulknerian cultural studies shares concerns with related phenomena: gender, health care, the separation of public and private spheres, and cross-cultural encounters and education.

The attention in the following group of essays to formal and stylistic matters, as well as their treatment of questions of state and economic power, mark them forcefully as versions of cultural studies.

Charles Hannon demonstrates this approach convincingly in "Signification, Stimulation, and Containment in *If I Forget Thee, Jerusalem.*" He opens his essay with an elaboration of Faulkner's "freeing" himself from modernist assumptions—namely its "programmatic distancing of art from political, economic, and social concerns" (137). "Dismantling" the analogy between the Tall Convict ("captive" to a nineteenth-century faith in realism) and himself (theretofore "imprisoned" in modernist ideas about writing), Faulkner shows himself in this novel to be deeply engaged with historical processes, especially as they intersected with the individual exercise of independence and freedom.

One way Hannon shows Faulkner doing this is to suggest that Faulkner makes use of changes in the South's penal system during the 1930s. Declaring his "concern with modern and modernist modes of producing and containing the subject" (134), Hannon uses Foucaultian analyses of discipline to analyze the Tall Convict's treatment by Parchman and the state. He points out that the use of prison chain gangs, for instance, was nearly obsolete by the late 1930s (when *Jerusalem* was published) and was already in decline in the period of the novel's events (140). Formerly, chain gangs had been used as an instance of what Foucault calls the "political investment of the body," an exercise of state power that visits itself on the condemned man's physical self. As with other archaic forms of punishment (such as public execution or dismemberment), the use of chain gangs had diminished due to the "degrading" nature of such spectacles—for both prisoners and those who observe them. In moments of natural and political crises, however, like the flood (when it loses its "natural" markers of power at the Parchman plantation), the state reverts to external markings on prisoners' bodies and their physical, corporeal management such as the chain gang and the Convict's "prison billboards." At the same time, the Tall Convict elsewhere demonstrates the state's modern exercise of power on a prisoner's interiority or "soul." Here Hannon connects his analysis of discipline to his reading of the novel as "a commentary on crisis conditions within the modern capitalist State" (134). He points to episodes of the Tall Convict alligator hunting, for in this section the convict perceives—as modern penal systems have taught him to—his imprisonment as a denial of what is rightfully his "freedom": his own marketable capital, the ability to labor and wage earn.[15]

Another way Hannon sees Faulkner's modernism as engaged with history is Faulkner's departure, in the "Wild Palms" section, from modernist modes of signification. This part of the novel shows Faulkner's strategy resembling a postmodern culture in that it relies on simulation and a willful "emptying" of signifying structures and strategies. Harry and Charlotte's narrative resembles a Hollywood film, Hannon asserts, in its simulation of marriage, as well as in its reliance on terms peculiar to photographic and cinematic technology. He points out that their relationship refers not to an elemental truth but offers only a postmodern structure of referring to other signs. In this respect their story effects an alteration in the relationship between the object (their simulated "marriage") and the viewer (the reader, say, or the doctor of the novel's frame)—an alteration similar to that of film from earlier, static art forms such as painting.[16] Thus the novel opens with filmic "effects" such as the doctor descending the stairwell and his flashlight that resembles a film projector, or the anachronic "flashbacks" in the early sections or "frames" of "Wild Palms." This emulation of modern mass media combines with the influence of market economics on Charlotte's art in "Wild Palms" to instigate another disavowal of modernist assumptions: the "separation of aesthetics from the lived experience of everyday life" (143). Hannon links Walter Benjamin's concept of *aura* to modernist aesthetics, and he points to the eventual use of Charlotte's objects as the source for magazine and advertising photos as evidence of their shift from a position of modernist significance and **auratic** self-presence to a postmodern assimilation of a "depthless," purely commercial functioning.

Hannon uses the concept of simulation to describe a range of functions within the novel as well as their implications for its depiction of state power. Harry and Charlotte's simulated marriage, for example, seeks to overturn cultural containments and legal definitions of women like mother and wife, as well as husband and wage earner. Hannon claims that Charlotte's powerful negation of the role of wife and mother, as well as the "domesticating bonds of [the birth metaphor] of female creativity" in her decision to abort her and Harry's child frees her to maintain an autonomy that such metaphoric and socialized meanings deny her (146). It also resists the state mandates towards family life and unfettered reproduction as a source for capitalism's labor pool (147).[17]

In many ways, Hannon sees the novel operate pessimistically. For he sees it repeat the binary opposition and dependence that initially it seeks to overcome. Modernism, he points out, usually manifests a limited form of historical autonomy precisely because of its reliance on discursive and textual practices from earlier literary history, against which it defines itself (most specifically, nineteenth-century realism). Charlotte's death appears as a reiteration of a similar dilemma. For it, too, is the result of an effort to deny the containing system of marriage through a sustained simulation of that very system: marital life. Hannon reads the novel's two conclusions as showing a similarly painful end to different acts of cultural and ideological transgression. Both Charlotte's and the

Tall Convict's efforts at transgression, however—analogous to efforts to escape cultural containment, such as modernism—initiate the state's reassertion of power and control, evident in the convict's and Harry's incarceration.

In a mode similar to Hannon's, but more optimistically, John T. Matthews rigorously treats Faulkner's 1930s novels and their oblique historicity and engagement with class. In two essays—"*As I Lay Dying* and the Machine Age" and "Faulkner and Proletarian Literature"—Matthews initiates a traditional realist-leftist critique of modernism. He points to Faulkner's formal abstractions and focus on characters' interiority as indications of a difference from a more materialist and Marxist depiction of social reality and class conflict. Although he admits the relevance of accounts of modernism as apolitical, Matthews reveals how Faulkner's novels of the 1930s actively engage the very issue of class antagonism central to the decade's chief political debate: "the widespread effort of artists and intellectuals to imagine and instigate a class revolution" ("Faulkner and Proletarian" 167). Strikingly, Matthews reveals how in Faulkner's case that enterprise is tied to his novels' formal complexities—precisely those elements of literary modernism that drew the attack of varied leftists like Georg Lúkacs and Mike Gold (Matthews 168–69).[18] "Wash," for instance, appears to be a relatively realistic narrative; however it possesses a "modest wrinkle in narrative temporality" that allows Matthews to connect the story to *Absalom, Absalom!*'s more full-blown experimentation and Faulkner's "multivariant analysis of the South's system of exploitation" (172). Although "Wash" appears to omit a recognition of class solidarity or the connections of the South's various disempowered groups, moments like Milly's cry of protest at Wash's murder suggest her connection to women like Addie Bundren and Rosa Coldfield who, though not oppressed as violently, also protest Southern patriarchal prerogatives through sustained voices or "cries."

Matthews uses a decidedly Adornian approach to *Absalom, Absalom!* in the "Faulkner and Proletarian Literature" essay. Describing that "a kind of violence governs [the] process" in which consumer goods are "converted into some common measure in order to be exchanged" and in which "ideas distill essences and eliminate particularity," Matthews traces the connections of brutality and genocide to "the project of rational enlightenment" (183).[19] Matthews connects Faulkner's critique of instrumental reason in nineteenth-century American capitalist development, evident in Sutpen's failed "logic" about his design, to proletarian literature of resistance and revolution. He finds the unsettling power of Guy Endore's 1934 historical novel *Babouk,* about black uprisings in Haiti, in the novel's account of the "obdurateness" of bodies—black bodies, specifically, that rupture the abstract logic of capitalist equivalency *and* the white superiority it subsidizes. *Absalom, Absalom!* becomes in Matthews's analysis a novel that similarly shows itself as marked bodily: tics, folds, and "scars" abound in Faulkner's stylistic and formal excess. This strategy, ultimately, is where Matthews finds Faulkner's greatest capacity for a "modernist social critique." In its insistence on its bodily presence and materiality—its "particularity"—*Absalom, Absalom!* eschews the process of abstraction whereby whites like Sutpen and, more damagingly, the capitalist system of equivalence abstracts out the presence and physical suffering of others.

With his discussion of *As I Lay Dying,* Matthews similarly demonstrates how modernist formal abstraction, rather than denying history and social reality, in fact compellingly mediates and thus reveals it. No less than other realist or socially oriented 1930s novels, Faulkner's particular modernism in *As I Lay Dying* shows his capacity to allow social experience and conflict into his work as a vital part of its organizing. One of those historical realities is the process of **reification** accompanying modernity, examples of which abound in the novel's depictions of labor, personal relations, and the money economy. The novel's signs of the empirical reality surrounding it also include examples of the commodification of social and economic life, mass-market goods (evident in the family's longing for consumer products), as well as the increased role in the Bundrens' consciousness of mechanization and technology.[20]

Matthews's interest in the novel is with Faulkner's capacity to maintain and express an active and dialectical ambivalence toward the various strands of modernization it depicts. Women's, blacks', and poor whites' emancipation through modern developments in the post-Reconstruction era (including wage as opposed to slave labor; suffrage; and crop rotation and agricultural cooperatives) provided causes for optimism as well as the spur to the displacements and alienation attendant on capitalist social and economic organizing. The processes of social disintegration and relocation that the novel incorporates emerge obliquely, Matthews suggests, in the novel's formal complexity—notably, its manifestation of disembodiment and disintegration. Matthews describes *As I Lay Dying*'s means of resisting the corrupting forces of modernism such as the commodification of experience or labor, as well as of cultural products (like novels), by maintaining a disintegrative, noncoherent form. In its radical insistence on its own de-composition, its simultaneous critique and celebration of modernity, and its "exorcism" of its own "effete" formal and stylistic lavishness (figured by Darl's lyrical voice and meditations) (93), *As I Lay Dying* remains a book that retains a powerful emotional and analytic edge.

Patrick O'Donnell also notes Faulkner's treatment of Darl as a self-conscious departure from his own modernism in his compelling essay "Between the Family and the State: Nomadism and Authority in *As I Lay Dying.*" Conceived generally as a novel about the private longings or secret bonds of individuals and between family members, and as such a novel that typifies Faulkner's meditations on the family romance, *As I Lay Dying* also "publicizes the inadequacies of 'romance' . . . to [an] understand[ing of] the cultural contexts of family dynamics" (83–84). O'Donnell presents those contexts specifically as the state's public mediation and control of desire, here as an ironic consequence of the Bundren's effort to fulfill Addie's private wish to be buried in Jefferson. Fulfilling a private "contract" with Addie, Anse and the Bundren children move from their isolation at home to the public realm as consumers and participants in the public spaces of town, marketplace, and road. Drawing Addie's putrefying body through the streets of Jefferson and defying orders of the police, the Bundrens appear as unlawful, alien nomads, arriving in the public sphere from outside its purview. As such, they force a recognition of the way that the state and its manifestations of power seek to maintain what Gilles Deleuze and Félix Guattari see as the essential function of state authority: its act of "striating " the masses.[21] Allowed to fulfill their "contract" with Addie, the Bundrens are also successfully integrated into the public and state-authorized functions of consumer culture and lawful, capitalist exchange.

That integration, however, comes at a price. In Darl's institutionalization at the novel's end, he appears as a kind of sacrifice on the family's part, made to ensure its "continuance within the bounds of state authority" (84). Positioned "within" the society and the law's power at Jackson, Darl is at the same time marginalized, placed outside its terms of normalcy and social belonging. As a representative of the psychological depth we are accustomed to seeing in modernism, Darl's removal from the space of the novel allows for a recognition of historically determined realities that determine the life of the Bundren family. Rather grimly, but forcefully, O'Donnell summarizes those realities as the fact that "the expression of desire necessarily leads to its commodification and confinement under the law" (93).[22]

A similar approach to that of Hannon and Matthews, and one that draws together several culturalist strands, is Michael Grimwood's treatment of *If I Forget Thee, Jerusalem* in *Heart in Conflict: Faulkner's Struggles with Vocation*. Grimwood asserts that both the novel's stories take up subject matter and motifs that were popular in the period in which Faulkner wrote it, specifically in order to question the reasons for their appeal. Imagery such as floods, chain gangs, and lovers escaping society were appealing to Faulkner precisely because they had proven to be readily consumable in commercial cultural fare. Images of flooding themselves were significant for their suggestions both of the overwhelming cataclysm of the Depression itself, as well as the suggestion of a purifying wiping out of the decade's economic hardship. Grimwood also sees Faulkner coin a new kind of "symbolic documentary" method, offering in images of a devastated rural scene in Mississippi a figure for a national "Depression-scape" (121).[23] Grounding Faulkner in his social and historical reality, Grimwood sees him conflate chain gangs and sharecroppers. This emerges in Grimwood's sense that the 1930s realities of tenant farming produced situations in which sharecropping farmers were—like incarcerated prisoners—bound to the land.

Grimwood also shows Faulkner's novel reflecting on cultural as well as economic history. He cites several examples of popular disaster narratives, in both literature and film, as inspirations for Faulkner's depiction of the flooded Mississippi and Parchman prison in "Old Man." Here he shows Faulkner taking on popular genres in order to reveal to readers their own expectations—and stubbornly refusing to satisfy them. In particular he refers to two very different 1937 film depictions of flooding: Pare Lorentz's documentary *The River,* produced by the Farm Security Administration to document projects of the New Deal, and John Ford's commercial release *The Hurricane,* based on the novel by the same name by Charles Nordhoff and James Hall (1935). Though Faulkner's novel indeed shares several elements with its possible sources, Grimwood shows Faulkner avoiding the kinds of positive and sentimental endings associated with early documentary and commercial film models. Contrary to the romantic close of Ford's movie, and the political rhetoric about the New Deal of Lortenz's film, Faulkner offers a deliberately downbeat ending of reincarceration. His motives, Grimwood claims, were culturally critical: "fretful attunement to the American public's taste for artful, and thus safe, disasters" (119).

Grimwood takes up two final examples of generic narrative in fiction and film from the 1930s that, he claims, Faulkner "burlesques" in *Jerusalem* for specific ends. He points to a wide range of travel works from the period, all of which manifest an awareness of the Depression. The interest of Grimwood's analysis is his attention to the difference between other forms of travel literature and what he calls "Depression Picaresque," which the lovers' peripatetic wanderings in "Wild Palms" exemplifies. "Wild Palms" is a significant example of the genre, he claims, for its protagonists' disavowal of conspicuous consumption. Like the characters and writers of other 1930s road books, they do not seek pleasure in landscape, architecture, or a return to nature. Grimwood points out, however, a significant variation in Faulkner's version of this genre: Harry and Charlotte's strict avoidance of security and work, an anomaly during the Depression. Grimwood provocatively ends his discussion of Faulkner's perhaps most complex novel about class, economics, and labor by suggesting that it stands as a kind of anti- or inverted proletarian novel. He points out that Harry and Charlotte, for instance, diffuse the Utah miners' rage at their exploitation, an aspect of "Wild Palms" that makes Faulkner appear conservative. But Grimwood suggests that there is a powerful, negative charge in Faulkner's inversions of generic expectations. As he puts it, "A 'sharecropper' documentary [in "Old Man"] that is not ameliorative, a travel book that subordinates economics to romance, and a strike novel that is defeatist" all suggest Faulkner's nonleftist politics. They also, however, perform an important gesture of resistance toward what, by the end of the decade, had become to Grimwood a form of artistic orthodoxy in political and class-based literature.

FAULKNER AND FILM

Faulkner and his work's contact with the visual and film culture of Hollywood offers a final grouping of culturalist scholarship on Faulkner. Several readings of this type take up the complex relationship between Faulkner's novels and film adaptations of them; more recently, they point to Faulkner's incorporating of the methods of film representation in his novels. Read as moving in either "direction," the novel/film connection has allowed Faulknerians to raise provocative questions about how cinema both responded to and shaped Faulkner's modernism.

Charles Hannon's essay "Race Fantasies: The Filming of *Intruder in the Dust*" shows the way Faulkner's novel and the filming of it play out cultural attitudes

and their ideological securing in the South's national and self-image. As such, he
refers to the film as the third in a sequence of cinematic, "consumable" images
of the South (after *Gone With the Wind* and *Birth of a Nation*) that perform a
strenuous act of cultural work. He favors the novel, as it includes details the film
suppresses in maintaining its ideological coherence. Hannon nevertheless uses
the film to question Faulkner's book, as he traces several acts of social and historical "erasure" enacted by various cultural apparatuses. At the heart of both
Faulkner's novel and the film of it, he claims, are efforts to deny a black presence
at the protected "white center" of Oxford. These efforts include refusing Lucas
Beauchamp a mixed-race identity and the construction, within the film and the
novel, of a Jefferson that is emptied of its black presence due to fears produced
by the lynching. This unified, homogenized social space, the "object of desire"
for the novel, is reproduced in the film's spatial and visual field—which offers
its idealized viewer a sense of mastery over its perspectival positioning and constructions.[24] As well, it offers a deferred, future moment of fulfillment: the
screening of the movie in Oxford's (and the country's) segregated cinemas.

Hannon further points to journalistic and historiographic accounts of Southern life that similarly desubjectivize blacks. He cites the Oxford *Eagle*'s 1908
account of the Nelse Patton murder and lynching—notably ambiguous and
without detail, particularly concerning Patton himself—to suggest this process
of denial; he also refers to a body of historiography that ignores blacks' historical experience and role in the region. From his discussion of real and fictional-
ized blacks like Patton and Beauchamp, Hannon points out other subgroups of
the South that Faulkner's novel and the film "erase" and marginalize. Politically
mobilized Southern white women, working for Progressive causes like anti-
lynching laws, as well as poor white farmers and laborers, are smoothed over
into stereotypes like the spinster and, more generally, a white middle and professional class in the imagined Oxford. Particularly in the case of the film and
its reception, the distancing of Oxford's rising middle class from what were
often its own roots in the labor classes allowed it to scapegoat poor whites for
much of their own racism.

In a similar mode, Stephanie Li reads the novel version of *Intruder* as more
reflective—and critical—of the ways white Southern men construct their sense
of self through a reliance on conceptions of black subservience. In "*Intruder in
the Dust* from Novel to Movie: The Development of Chick Mallison," Li sees
Lucas offering a clear challenge to Chick's process of individuation and maturity—but only, she claims, in the novel. As such, Faulkner's own version of the
story possesses a far more powerful and culturally critical charge than the film,
which simply presents again the very codes of blackness and racial stereotype
that the novel examines. One crucial difference Li sees is in the novel's attributing to both Chick and Lucas an "understanding [of social codes] derived from
an experience outside of adult social conventions and a white dominated space"
(112). The film replaces the novel's emphasis on this type of awareness by positing Gavin Stevens as its central consciousness. Li points out that in the novel,
episodes such as the decision to exhume the Gowrie grave demonstrate Chick's

ambivalence over his sense of self and the dim, but powerful recognition that he needs Aleck Sander's help.[25] She closes the article on a note similar to Hannon's by pointing to the novel's and the film's shared "abstraction" of blacks in the "maintenance of white identity" (117).

Other critics have seen Faulkner's relationship to film move in the other direction: not in adaptations of his work for the film industry, but as an influencing factor in his supposedly more rarefied literary high modernism. As indicated in my recent article, "'Some Trashy Myth of Reality's Escape': Romance, History, and Film Viewing in *Absalom, Absalom!*," the novel's repeated references to characters' "watching" the Sutpen narrative, as well as the romanticizing and visualizing tendencies of Rosa's section, suggest the novel's awareness of historical film. *Birth of a Nation* figures specifically in my analysis of Faulkner's effort in the novel to depict the damaging consequences, personally and culturally, of a morbid and romantic vision of the Old South, one effected by both Griffith's film and the novel's characters in their treatment of Sutpen's narrative.

The earliest and most sustained analysis of this kind is Bruce Kawin's. No account of the symbiotic relationship of Faulkner's screenplay and novelistic work would be complete without reference to Kawin's extensive studies in this area, particularly his book *Faulkner and Film*. Though not strictly speaking an example of cultural studies, Kawin's work took seriously Faulkner's own writing for Hollywood and showed strong evidence of Faulkner's influence by cinematic technique. The montage techniques of the Russian formalist Sergei Eisenstein figure especially, Kawin shows, as a way of understanding Faulkner's modernism. In his innovative approach, Kawin made possible later considerations of Faulkner's Hollywood work, as well as the use of film theory to talk about his fiction. Several later commentators who pursue culturalist readings of Faulkner have followed Kawin's lead in this respect, including Lurie ("'Some Trashy Myth'") and Miranda J. Burgess in her "Watching Jefferson Watching: *Light in August* and the Aestheticization of Gender."

The most recent volume of work on Faulkner that seeks to relate his work to the cinema is the special edition of the *Faulkner Journal,* "Faulkner and Film" (volume 16). Edited by Edwin T. Arnold, the issue collects a range of essays that show Faulkner's awareness of and potential involvement with the film culture that developed around him, particularly as he experienced it as a screenwriter in Hollywood in the 1930s. Most often, the articles in this issue tend toward a fairly straightforward textual and formal analysis of the cinematic aspect of Faulkner's narrative experiment. Doug Baldwin's essay "Putting Images Into Words: Elements of the 'Cinematic' in William Faulkner's Prose," for example, reveals several effects of Faulkner's verbal inventiveness that show a striking resemblance to the visual language of film. Despite Baldwin's subtle observations about these affinities, though, he offers little by way of analysis of their possible cultural meanings. There are also discussions of the shifts in emphasis in Faulkner's screen adaptations of his story material, such as Dallas Hulsey's, "'I don't seem to remember a girl in the story': Hollywood's Disruption of Faulkner's All-Male Narrative in *Today We Live*."[26] Even where Hulsey comments on the shift in emphasis in the film versions of stories, however, he declines to analyze what such a revision would suggest about the effects of Hollywood on either Faulkner's anticipated readers or viewers.

More productively, Robert Hamblin moves to a consideration of Faulkner and film in a contemporary European context. In "The Curious Case of Faulkner's 'The De Gaulle Story,'" his essay on a long-deferred Faulkner script for Warner Brothers, Hamblin demonstrates thematic similarities between "The De Gaulle Story" and later Faulkner projects such as the screenplay for *To Have and Have Not* and the novel *A Fable*. (He notes the recasting of Hemingway's novel as an episode of the French resistance in World War II, and the use of a Christ allegory and allusion in *A Fable* and "The De Gaulle Story," respectively). He also traces the political reasons for the various deferrals of the project as well as its eventual production by French television.

CULTURAL CRITICISM AT WORK

A number of works and critics deserve mention for their specific use of culturalist approaches to Faulkner that have not, otherwise, been represented in this discussion. Richard Godden's recent book *Fictions of Labor: William Faulkner and the South's Long Revolution* is more New Historicist in its treatment of the shift in the South from slavery to a wage economy. Godden's extraordinarily subtle reading of this move and the way it produced occlusive tendencies in the ways the South's planter class thought about itself and labor, tendencies reproduced in Faulkner's prose, extends from a consideration of *The Sound and the Fury* and *Absalom, Absalom!* to what Godden calls Quentin and Henry Sutpen's revenant, Harry Wilbourne in *If I Forget Thee, Jerusalem*. In Godden's final chapter, he reprises work from "Degraded Culture, Devalued Texts," an essay he coauthored with Pamela Rhodes Knight [see chapter 10] in which they identify Hollywood as Faulkner's "Babylon," the setting where Faulkner feared he would "forget" his real writing while pandering to a "degraded" consumer culture. Citing the shared prison-cell endings of *Jerusalem* with earlier noir novels like James Cain's *The Postman Always Rings Twice* and Horace McCoy's *They Shoot Horses, Don't They?*, Godden suggests that the prison genre's confessional format encourages readers' empathy and "absorption" into the imagined world of the text. Such absorption, Godden goes on to show, implicates Faulkner's own readers but also reveals to them their pleasure in generic fare.

In a very different mode, but demonstrating cultural studies' interest in social scientific discourse like anthropology, Carey Wall in "*Go Down, Moses:* The Collective Action of Redress," offers an example of a (literally) "culturalist" reading. Drawing on the cultural anthropology of Victor Turner and Clifford Geertz, she calls for a radical rereading of Ike McCaslin's efforts toward a shift in cultural assumptions—specifically the history of white racial domination. She draws heavily on concepts such as "communitas" and "liminality" to argue that Ike participates in a "pacific," nonrational act of resistance at the novel's end in denying his patrimony. Disagreeing with critics who see Ike's act as a failure in efficacy, Wall argues that Ike's action holds meaning in its participation in a collective, "effervescent" affirmation of systems of thought that run contrary to his culture's own. Ike occupies a key position in the novel because, socially, he is located between the privileged, white, members of the owning class (the adult hunters of "The Bear") and the not overly rational and nonhierarchical consciousness of Sam Fathers.

As a Faulknerian with a particularly culturalist bent, Jay Watson deserves mention. His position at the close of this essay belies the imaginative and significant work he has offered in several essays that defy easy categorization but that bear the marks of a keen eye toward different cultural problems and concerns. For example, his fascinating article "Writing Blood: The Art of the Literal in *Light in August*" orients its argument about the novel's "decisive" moments of bloodletting (such as Christmas's mutilation) from an analysis of San Francisco's gay S&M culture. Using theories of racial ideology, Watson seeks to restore the "literal" meanings of blood (and blood sports) to metaphorical, cultural definitions of race. In his essay about Southern male identity, "Overdoing Masculinity in *Light in August;* or, Joe Christmas and the Gender Guard," Watson uses Judith Butler's *Gender Trouble* to describe Joe Christmas's troubling evasions of Jefferson's "policing" of cultural dictates about race, gender, marriage, and incest.

Finally, several collections exhibit methods and concerns of culturalist studies. There are first the Faulkner and Yoknapatawpha Conference anthologies: *Faulkner and Popular Culture, Faulkner and Ideology, Faulkner in Cultural Context,* and, most notably, *Faulkner and the Natural World: Faulkner and Yoknapatawpha, 1996.*[27] Several of the essays here take the conference topic as a way to treat the cultural construction of race and gender as part of what are understood as "natural" categories. In doing so, they attribute to Faulkner's project a resistance to noncorporeal (i.e., cultural) definitions of the "natural." They point to Faulkner's traditional associations of women with the natural world and its "silence," for instance, but see him offer as well powerful alternatives to that association. They also treat Joe Christmas's racializing as a function of his culture's punitive treatment of female (or "natural") sexual activity.

Also, a number of anthologies offer useful gatherings of culturalist perspectives and concerns, most notably *The Cambridge Companion to William Faulkner,* edited by Philip Weinstein. The essays in this collection generally seek to relate Faulkner to his work's theoretical, cultural, and ideological contexts, with emphases on definitions of modernism and postmodernism, popular culture, postcolonialism, Southern patriarchy, and the cultural construction of race.

Finally, there are comparative studies, prominently *Unflinching Gaze: Morrison and Faulkner Re-Envisioned,* edited by Carol A. Kolmerten, Stephen M. Ross, and Judith Bryant Wittenberg, that show a culturalist bent.

As an interdisciplinary practice, cultural studies finds particular interest in Faulkner's relationship to other forms of culture. We have seen the extensive ways that culturalist critics have decentered Faulkner in the cultural field and have brought other discourses and texts to bear on his work. *Unflinching Gaze* is important among intertextual studies of Faulkner (such as *Intertextuality in Faulkner*[28]). For unlike earlier collections that stress Faulkner's own use of other writers and (largely) his connection to a traditional or European canon, *Unflinching Gaze* shows Faulkner's capacity for reworking by a writer positioned nearly opposite him culturally (as an African American woman writing in the postmodern period), but one who is also, arguably, his most important literary reinterpreter and heir.

One issue that the volume takes up is the questioning of evaluative terms for social identity, especially since the categories of cultural, ethnic, and gender difference are so extensive in Faulkner and Morrison's work. Other essays pose questions that are central to cultural studies, such as the ways that academic discourse uses writers differently, and at different times, to define cultural value. They also examine the various cultural issues embedded in influence and "fathering"—both within the texts, and as a way of considering Faulkner's and Morrison's relationship. Finally, the critics here use Faulkner's and Morrison's placement within the categories "modernist" and "postmodernist" to uncover the function within both categories of historical remembrance, but also, particularly in modernism, of historical erasure and forgetting.

RANGES OF CULTURAL MEANING

As we have seen, cultural studies has made its presence felt in Faulkner scholarship. Though calling the body of work that I have described in this essay a "Faulknerian" branch of the cultural studies movement is, for reasons having to do with the methodology's sense of itself, problematic, nevertheless readers of Faulkner have used a culturalist approach to produce new, provocative readings of his fiction. If the vitality of cultural studies lies in large part in its very lack of disciplinary method or definition, it is also the case that its flexibility has allowed it to add to original thinking about twentieth-century American literature's most analyzed figure. If there is an American writer whose readers would stand to benefit from a still-emerging critical methodology, particularly one that allows for ways to return to material that has been read carefully, meticulously, and scrupulously by several generations of critics, that writer is Faulkner.

One of the benefits of culturalist work in general, and on Faulkner in particular, seems to me its opening up a critical discourse that is imposing in its breadth and weight. In particular, work of a culturalist bent is exciting in that it draws its energy from the very places that earlier criticism of Faulkner, or of modernism generally, overlooked or closed off from the possibility of bearing meaning. Several voices and currents—and not all of them as sensitive to Faulkner's linguistic and structural genius as the New Critics—have prevented considering some of Faulkner's most trenchant social and cultural critique. Modernism's detractors in the social realist movement of the 1930s; first-generation readers who saw in Faulkner's work a detached violence or purified myth; feminist readers who targeted Faulkner's (not solely) disdainful treatment of women; critics who viewed Faulkner as an apologist for his region or as a largely unreconstructed nostalgist of the Old South—cultural studies has found ways of not only responding sensitively to these laments, but often of using the very texts, even the same passages that would seem to betray Faulkner's misogyny, race bias, or political conservatism. In doing so, they have suggested those works' progressive, at times opposite meanings. Critics like Charles Hannon, Susan Donaldson, Michael Grimwood, Richard Godden, John T. Matthews, and Anne Goodwyn Jones all have looked closely at key moments in Faulkner's work that provide pivotal or revisionist readings of it. Seeing Faulkner's formalism as in fact part of a deep engagement with his social and historical reality, Matthews, Godden, and Hannon manage to do more than turn the tables on leftist critics who saw formalist practices as signs of indifference to the hard realities existing outside of texts. They have changed the way that formal considerations of a text's meaning can be thought of generally, and beyond specific examples in Faulkner. Readings of the critical dialectic of Faulkner and popular culture, like Donaldson's, Grimwood's, and Jones's, add to both the interest of Faulkner's "culture industry" material and another dimension of Faulkner's historicity: his work's inflection by cultural as well as social history.

As a writer who confronted cultural definitions of masculinity within the South and who was born and lived in a period that witnessed the vestigial effects of Reconstruction, the development of the New South, Jim Crow, the Depression, national foment over two world wars, and a period of both radical literary experimentation and a rapidly increasing consumer culture, Faulkner poured an enormous range of cultural "meanings" (and meanings of culture) into his writing. Faulkner's definitions of culture—that which he lived as well as that which he made, thought about, and saw—reflected its position within the incredible period of transformation he observed, a result of which is that cultural studies has reinterpreted it in the light of what those definitions allow us to say about his work. This adds new shape and dimension to our understanding of Faulkner's writing. As the work discussed here suggests, Faulkner's fiction offers an encompassing vision of high-literary and mass culture, and of culture as lived and felt—most often painfully. Cultural studies, finally, sees Yoknapatawpha County as a still-evolving, variegated social world, one that manifests issues and extremes that are part of both Southern and national life and in which Faulkner expresses its inhabitants' conflicting perspectives and needs. It also sees Faulkner and Yoknapatawpha as incredibly open to discourses that are neither specifically traditional nor Southern. If Faulkner is that imaginative country's "sole owner and proprietor," cultural studies shows him to be generous in his depiction of it—welcoming to visitors, that is, but often critical, and even willing to give parts of it away.

NOTES

1. This overview draws largely from the accounts of cultural studies offered by Simon During in his comprehensive introduction to *The Cultural Studies Reader* (New York: Routledge,

1999) and Richard Johnson's narrative essay about the movement's development, "What Is Cultural Studies, Anyway?" (*Social Text* 16 [1987]: 38–80). Subsequent references are to these editions and will appear parenthetically in the text.

2. Richard Hoggart, *The Uses of Literacy* (London: Chatto and Windus, 1957); Raymond Williams, *Culture and Society, 1780–1950* (New York: Columbia University Press, 1958).

3. For an example of this kind of thinking in the context of educational theory, see Paolo Freire, *Pedagogy of the Oppressed* (New York: Continuum, 1986), and especially the chapter "The 'Banking' Concept of Education."

4. "Ideology and Ideological State Apparatus" (*Lenin and Philosophy and Other Essays*. Trans. Ben Brewster. New York: New Left Books, 1971. 18).

5. William Faulkner, *The Sound and the Fury* (2nd Critical ed. New York: W. W. Norton, 1994. 55).

6. This sense of Faulkner's own violent impulse informed some contemporary discussion of his writing. Henry Seidel Canby, reviewing *Sanctuary*, referred to Faulkner's "sadism" that, in this novel, "reached its American peak" (*Saturday Review of Literature* 7 [May 21, 1931]; qtd. in Joseph Blotner, *Faulkner: A Biography*, 1-vol. ed. New York: Random House, 1974. 275).

7. These references are to the anthologies' publication dates. The years for the conferences themselves, which appear in the title of each of the collections, are 1988, 1992, and 1995.

8. Judith Butler, *Gender Trouble* (New York: Routledge, 1990).

9. We might say, somewhat differently than Andrews, that Caspey's recontainment represents Faulkner's sense that, historically, post–World War I rebellion was recontained *socially* by Jim Crow and did not re-emerge as a political force until the Civil Rights movement.

10. Donaldson's critique would also engage Leslie Fiedler's claim that the appendix traffics in sentimentality and cliché. See Fiedler's "Pop Goes the Faulkner: In Quest of *Sanctuary*" (*Faulkner and Popular Culture: Faulkner and Yoknapatawpha, 1988*. Ed. Doreen Fowler and Ann J. Abadie. Jackson: University Press of Mississippi, 1990. 75–92).

11. He points out, for instance, that Faulkner likely saw the irony in the way another modern, but immensely popular, writer like S. S. Van Dine could scorn the masses in his critical study *The Creative Will* while profiting from them in his commercial writing. Yet Fiedler comes short of suggesting how or why a writer, Faulkner or Van Dine, may have sought to use such commentary to position himself within the cultural field—as both of them did.

12. Andreas Huyssen traces the connection in the modernist imagination between women's role in modern political and economic life such as suffrage and, more pervasively, women as early consumers of mass-market fiction. In their capacity as consumers, women became for male writers a figure for the fears of "the wrong kind of [literary] success"—commercial success, as opposed to the supposedly modernist imperatives of difficulty and indifference to the market (*After the Great Divide: Modernism, Mass Culture, Postmodernism*. Bloomington: Indiana University Press, 1986. 53).

13. Like Matthews's other readings of Faulkner's culturally critical bent, this essay uses Theodor Adorno to suggest Faulkner's critique of instrumental reason as it is manifest in capitalism and technology, such as modern weaponry. It also rigorously grounds itself in Adorno and Max Horkheimer's thinking about Enlightenment values and modern, commercial entertainment in their essay "The Culture Industry: Enlightenment as Mass Deception" (*Dialectic of Enlightenment*. Trans. John Cumming. New York: Verso, 1987). (See Matthews, "Faulkner and the Culture Industry," 51–57; 62; 64).

14. One ready analysis that Matthews avoids would be the suggestion that Faulkner uses these aspects of the stories as a way to wholly subvert their potential for consumption. He does partly make this claim, but Matthews also points out that Faulkner was not naïve about the cultural market or his own dependence on it, and he suggests that the self-critical parts of the stories reveal Faulkner's savvy toward his position as a writer in a particular cultural climate and period. Rather than a dilettantism or quietude towards the market (only available if he chose not to make money on his writing at all), Matthews suggests, Faulkner demonstrates a hard-nosed professionalism in

his commercial writing while including elements in it that took critical stock of its positioning and financial value.

15. Hannon relies for these readings on Foucault's influential book *Discipline and Punish: The Birth of the Prison* (Trans. Alan Sheridan. New York: Vintage, 1979). A range of culturalist readings have used Foucault's work in this text, particularly its elaborate analysis of the development of different modes of coercion and subject formation.

16. Hannon refers to Walter Benjamin's seminal essay "The Work of Art in the Age of Mechanical Reproduction" (see *Illuminations,* ed. Hannah Arendt [New York: Shocken Books, 1968], 217–52) in making these points about the different relationship between viewer and object in modern, technological media.

17. Hannon draws on the key text of women's history that asserts this aspect of debate about reproductive rights, Linda Gordon's *Women's Body, Women's Right: A Social History of Birth Control in America* (New York: Grossman, 1976).

18. In this regard, Matthews cites Georg Lúkacs's book *The Meaning of Contemporary Realism* (Trans. John Mander and Necke Mander. London: Merlin Press, 1963).

19. Matthews makes his essay's connection to Adorno's *The Dialectic of Enlightenment* explicit when he states, "Horkheimer and Adorno want to trace the inner dynamic of brutality within the project of rational enlightenment, ultimately to explain how Western culture could have produced the barbarity of the Holocaust. In the case of another genocide, New World slavery, Faulkner helps us see that 'the peculiar institution' did not prove a helpful instrument to Southern plantation agriculture. Rather, the brutal mastery of humans grotesquely magnifies a logic that depends on commodification" (183).

20. See also Charles Peek's essay on *As I Lay Dying* in *Faulkner and America,* ed. Urgo and Abadie, for a similar reading of the Bundrens' melancholy longings for modern commodities.

21. O'Donnell uses Deleuze and Guatarri's book *A Thousand Plateaus: Capitalism and Schizophrenia* (Trans. Brian Massumi. Minneapolis: University of Minnesota Press, 1987) to point to "culture" as "a series of 'flows' and circulations." Against this disorderly flow "there must be a regulation of . . . nomadic forces and energies: [in response to which] the state organizes itself as a network of 'striations' . . . that channels these energies" (O'Donnell 85). Here, O'Donnell deepens his account of the Bundrens as representatives of what lies "outside" the order of public space by way of Julia Kristeva's conception of the "abject": "something that threatens the public" realm with that "which [the social body] recognizes as other than itself" (88).

22. Here, modernism's acute preoccupation with interiority, though undeniably an aspect of *As I Lay Dying,* becomes part of an ironic strategy on Faulkner's part of addressing directly that private, subjective realm's opposite: the control by or intervention in private life of public or state authority. Like Matthews, O'Donnell sees Faulkner perform a kind of "exorcism" of one of modernism's (and Faulkner's own) preferred modes—the privileging of the individual and troubled psyche—in the interests of engaging social or historical considerations. This occurs through his treatment of Darl.

23. Grimwood here shows Faulkner pointing to his readers' vicarious pleasure in scenarios of suffering and abjection (similar to Matthews's discussion of the onlookers in "Lizards in Jamshyd's Courtyard"). Grimwood reads the appeal of disaster stories in two directions, as stories that both reflected economic and social cataclysms of the decade and offered distraction and escape from those very circumstances.

24. Hannon relies here on Slavoj Zizek and his cultural theory in *Looking Awry: An Introduction to Jacques Lacan through Popular Culture* (Cambridge, MA: MIT Press, 1991) and *The Sublime Object of Ideology* (London: Verso, 1989).

25. This image corresponded to whites' need to countenance images of black weakness, one that Li points out black viewers of the film noted and protested. She cites contemporary issues of *Ebony* magazine to point up blacks' rejection of the movie's distortions of Aleck's character (115).

26. In "Faulkner and Film" (Spec. issue of *Faulkner Journal* 16 [Fall 2000/Spring 2001]: 65–77).

27. *Faulkner and Popular Culture: Faulkner and Yoknapatawpha, 1988* (published 1990) is edited by Doreen Fowler and Ann J. Abadie. *Faulkner and Ideology: Faulkner and Yoknapatawpha, 1992* (published 1995), *Faulkner in Cultural Context: Faulkner and Yoknapatawpha, 1995* (published 1997), and *Faulkner and the Natural World: Faulkner and Yoknapatawpha, 1996* (published 1999) are edited by Donald M. Kartiganer and Ann J. Abadie.

28. Ed. Michel Gresset and Noel Polk (Jackson: University Press of Mississippi, 1985).

8

Psychological Criticism

Doreen Fowler

With his model of the unconscious mind, Freud laid the groundwork for all psychoanalytic literary criticism. According to Freud, the mind is a dynamic operation between conscious mental processes and unconscious ones. The **unconscious** is constituted by **repression,** the refusal or denial of guilty desires, instincts, thoughts, or impulses. For Freud, repression is "the cornerstone on which the whole structure of psychoanalysis rests" (*Standard Edition* 14:16). His famous essay "Repression" (1915) sets forth his theory that repressed material always returns—"repression itself produces substitute formations and symptoms, . . . indications of a return of the repressed" (14:154)—but it returns in disguised forms so as to elude conscious censors. Scrambled and transformed, repressed material surfaces in dreams ("the royal road to the unconscious" [5:608]), in parapraxes (Freudian slips), in jokes, and in art. Just as the psychoanalyst decodes hidden, outlawed meanings in the analysand's dreams, images, or narrations, so psychoanalytic criticism deciphers veiled, returned meanings in literary texts. For Freud, art enacts the reality of the unconscious mind, if we can only learn to read its submerged or latent content; and, in his classic work "The Interpretation of Dreams," he instructs us in the methods (or "**dream-work**") by which dreams subvert and distort a meaning that cannot be accepted by the conscious mind. In each of these methods, shifts and substitutions take place usually by means of a chain of associations.

For Freud, whatever the specific content of repressed material, repression always invokes **primary repression,** the original psychic trauma that opens up the unconscious and introduces identity formation, particularly male identity. (Freud admits that, "our insight into these developmental processes in girls is unsatisfactory, incomplete, and vague" [19:179]). To develop a sense of a separate self, Freud theorizes, the child must overcome an early dependence on and identification with the nurturing mother, and this occurs when the child represses a guilty desire to take the place of the seemingly all-powerful father, who possesses sexually the mother. This desire Freud calls Oedipal desire, and, at the moment of primary or primal repression, the child achieves a sexual identity by driving it underground. Freud further hypothesizes that the repression of Oedipal desire is motivated by a fear of castration; more specifically, the child imagines that the father will punish Oedipal desire with castration, a threat that is made real for the child by the sight of female genitalia. Seeing that the mother lacks a penis, the child imagines that she is castrated, and, to avoid being similarly castrated, the child performs a symbolic self-castration; that is, to preserve the genital organ, the child "has paralysed it—has removed its function" (19:177). Proper sexual identity and socialization is assumed when the castration complex represses the Oedipal complex. Juliet Mitchell writes: "Together with the Oedipal complex . . . the castration complex . . . embodies the law that founds the human order itself" (14). Because identity is constructed on an unforgettable psychic trauma, the **Oedipal complex** and the **castration complex** are ceaselessly recurring paradigms in psychoanalysis and in art. According to Elizabeth Wright, these two complexes are the "*raison d'être* of the psychoanalytic process" (15). In his essays on art and literature, Freud goes so far as to argue that the object of the creative enterprise is "to allay ungratified wishes" (13:187) suppressed in the moment of ego formation.

The application of psychoanalytic principles to literary studies has undergone a number of significant developments in the past decades. Early psychoanalytic literary criticism tended to psychoanalyze the author. A famous example is Marie Bonaparte's book-length study of Edgar Allen Poe, published in 1933, which reads Poe's fiction as an expression of the author's pathology, an unresolved passion for his dead mother. Such studies were followed by psychoanalyses of fictional characters, like Frederick Crews's book, *The Sins of the Father: Hawthorne's Psychological Themes* (1966), which argues that Hawthorne's characters are driven by Oedipal desire. Both such approaches have been subject to the charge of reductivism; that is, they seem to reduce the meaning of a text to a set of pathological symptoms, and the single-minded focus on either the author or the characters prevents the literary critic from considering textual figurizations of psychological meanings. Another controversial psychoanalytical critical practice, sometimes termed **vulgar Freudianism,** applies an oversimplified version of Freudianism (particularly Freud's notion that sexuality structures the psyche) directly to the text and identifies sexual symbology, usually phallic or yonic (concave/female) symbols. An important critical development, **archetypal criticism,** derives from the theories of Carl G. Jung. According to Jung, dreams and fantasies are not only the representations of the desires of an individual, they are the product of a collective unconscious, the storehouse of the cumulative knowledge, experiences, and images of the whole human race. This **collective unconscious** "is detached from anything personal and is common to all men" (Jung 66), and it explains why "certain motifs from myths and legends repeat themselves the world over in identical forms" (65). These repeated motifs Jung calls archetypes, and archetypal literary criticism purports to open up the meaning of a text by identifying and explicating archetypes. Objections to this approach have centered on the ungrounded nature of Jung's archetypes, which derive neither from a particular body nor from a specific historical context.

Whereas the focus of Freud's work is on internal psychic processes, **object-relations theory,** another important offshoot of Freudian thought, examines the reciprocal interaction between the self and the world. This development in psychology, most often associated with a major proponent, Melanie Klein, is part of a larger movement in current thought to consider the organism in relation to its surroundings, including other people. (As it is used here, the word "object" does not have a pejorative meaning when it is applied to people.) Klein argues that, to negotiate the world, the child makes use of **projection** and **introjection.** Projection refers to the practice of expelling onto another unwanted wishes or feelings. Introjection occurs when the child unconsciously regards as belonging to the self qualities that belong to another. Object-relations aesthetics have had an impact on art criticism as followers of Klein, like D. W. Winnicott, have used the premises of this theory to study the interaction between the artist and the art-object and between the art-critic and art-object.

The theories of Jacques Lacan, particularly Lacan's now-famous dictum that language is structured like the unconscious, reinvigorated psychoanalytic literary criticism. If language, like the unconscious, is constituted of a ceaseless interplay of meanings and is the site of repression and a **return of repressed** material, then the literary text reflects the psyche, and the language of the text is the proper subject of the psychoanalytic critic. The major achievement of Lacan's psychoanalytic project, which rewrites Freudian theory in terms of contemporary language theory, is to focus attention on the constitutive power of language. In Lacan's view, there is no essential human nature or objective truth; rather, we exist as creatures in language, and "the world of words . . . creates the world of things" (*Écrits* 65); that is, meaning is constructed through language. For Lacan, words do not designate already-existing meanings; instead, words arbitrarily assign a meaning to a thing. What this means is that all identity, including gender identity and racial identity, is arbitrarily assigned through language. The word or **signifier** dominates the **signified,** and this arbitrary and subordinating relationship Lacan designates with the formula S/s, with the uppercase *S* standing for the signifier and the lowercase *s* representing the signified.

For Lacan, there is a fundamental similarity between the structure of language and the constitution of subjectivity. In the formula S/s, the bar represents repression; every word indicates the absence of what it stands for. Language is based on alienation, and, in Lacan's schema, so also is **subjectivity.** Lacan rewrites Freud's castration complex, which instigates the subject into subjectivity, as **alienation.** For Lacan, as for Freud, primary repression ushers the child into the cultural order, the world of signs or **symbolic order.** Before the moment of primary repression, the child exists in the **imaginary,** in one continuous totality of being, one with the mother's body, with no awareness of self or of an other. The disruption of the imaginary gives rise to language and conceptualization. For there to be meaning, there has to be difference. Identity and meaning come about only by exclusion, since, as Ferdinand de Saussure pointed out, a sign's meaning depends solely on its difference from other signs. The **paternal metaphor,** usually represented by the biological father, ordains difference by decreeing the separation of the child from the maternal body. Under the threat of castration, the child renounces the maternal connection and a gap, the distance between subject and object, opens up. This absence, an absence identified with the renounced mother, makes identity and meaning possible. However, all is not well with the newly created subject, since subjectivity is constituted by repression. "Repressed, it reappears" (*Écrits* 311), Lacan writes; and the desire repressed by the father's prohibition ceaselessly returns, disguised, in dreams, fantasies, and art.

Lacan's understanding that man-made symbols take precedence over any primal Real situates psychoanalysis in the domain of cultural history and makes of it an instrument of social change in a world of power relations. For example, Lacan's poststructural revision of Freudian principles has made psychoanalysis a useful tool for feminists who seek to expose and redress cultural biases against women. As feminists have observed, Freudian theory reflects a cultural assumption of a biological male superiority. For Freud, biology dictates that "women [are] castrated" (*SE* 19:176), and the recognition of "female castration" drives the child to separate from the mother and to identify with the father. In Lacan's revision, men and women alike experience privation (symbolic castration) as the price of human subjectivity, and the possession of a penis is not enabling: "What in reality [the male] may have that corresponds to the phallus . . . is worth no more than what he does not" (*Écrits* 289). At the same time, however, Lacan notes that *within culture* gender roles are assigned on the basis of the presence or absence of a penis and that culture identifies the penis with authority and superiority. That is to say, women are not castrated, but they are inscribed within culture as castrated so as to invent a phallic distinction. Woman, Jacqueline Rose writes, "is defined purely against the man (she is the negative of that definition—'man is not woman')" (49). Thus Lacan's theory uncovers a vast unconscious cultural connivance to subordinate women that originates at the very constitution of subjectivity because the original repression that makes difference and meaning possible is identified with the mother's absence; it uncovers, in other words, that the symbolic order, the order of language and culture, is built on a psychic repression of the feminine that is enforced by cultural practices. Armed with an understanding of this theory and practice, feminist critics can attempt to expose a cultural derogation of women, to free women from bondage to cultural stereotypes, and to refuse and subvert masculine constructions of female identity.

The psychoanalytic critical method has proven to be particularly applicable to the works of William Faulkner. As a reader familiar with Faulkner's texts intuitively apprehends, his novels are boundary phenomena; deeply subversive, they reflect the uneasy frontier between consciousness and the unconscious. Repression, the "cornerstone" of psychoanalysis, appears to be the foundation of Faulkner's art. He writes of the South, a region walled off for decades from the rest of the country, a defeated nation committed to denying defeat. If contemporary psychoanalysis posits a fractured self and an unstable identity, a character like Faulkner's Quentin Compson seems to be a textbook illustration. In fact, Faulkner's novels, rife with fratricide, incest, miscegenation, rape, castrations, paternal rejection, even necrophilia, read like Freudian case histories. The psychoanalytic narrative proposes an origin in loss, and a sense of loss obsessively haunts characters like *The Sound and the Fury's* Benjy Compson, who inconsolably grieves for his lost sister. In a move suggestive of Faulkner's psychic investment in his art, twice in the course of his literary career, for both *Light in August* (1932) and *Absalom, Absalom!* (1936), Faulkner began a fiction with the working title, "Dark House"; and, while he ultimately rejected (or displaced) it, the title denotes the psychic symbology of his art. According to Freud, in dreams, fantasies, and in art, the house is a recurring symbol for the self; Faulkner's working title, "Dark House," suggests that his art seeks to explore the dark, hidden, inner recesses of the self.

Faulkner was characteristically unforthcoming when asked to discuss his aesthetic theory or practice; but his few, sparing remarks hint at the psychic origins of his art. Perhaps his most revealing comment on this subject was uttered in conversation with his editor, Malcolm Cowley: "I listen to the voices, and when I put down what the voices say, it's right. Sometimes I don't like what they say, but I don't change it" (114). With these words, Faulkner very nearly admits that unconscious meanings return in his texts. The "voices" that Faulkner heard may well be the voice of the unconscious mind. Indeed, much of what we know about the Faulkner's composition process—he appears to have rarely used notes or outlines and sometimes began writing a novel, as in the cases of both *The Sound and the Fury* and *Light in August,* guided only by an image—suggests that he was an artist whose narrations, like Freud's case histories, map the interplay between the conscious and the unconscious mind.

An account of psychoanalytic interpretations of Faulkner's luminous texts in many key respects is reflective of Faulkner scholarship irrespective of particular approach. For example, like criticism of a more general nature, psychoanalytic studies have tended to gravitate toward his novels—as opposed to his short fiction, poetry, or nonfiction prose—and, in particular, to the novels written during "the major phase," that is, between 1929 and 1942. Of these novels, the ones that have been most frequently read through psychoanalytic frames are *The Sound and the Fury* (1929), *As I Lay Dying* (1930), *Sanctuary* (1931), *Light in August* (1932), and *Absalom, Absalom!* (1936). Psychoanalytic literary criticism, like other critical approaches to Faulkner, increased seemingly exponentially in the 1980s and 1990s, and in the twenty-first century, the sheer volume of scholarship on Faulkner is daunting. Regretfully, much of this criticism is repetitive; that is, with disturbing regularity, scholars produce and publish familiar readings of the texts. Taking a long view of this body of scholarship, we can detect certain trends. Not surprisingly, early studies applied Freudian principles; since the 1980s, Lacan has replaced Freud as the theorist of choice. Some early studies tended to analyze Faulkner, while more recent interpretations focus on his linguistic strategies. In a trend that began in the 1980s and continues into the present, psychoanalytic methods have been effectively adopted to consider issues of gender and sexuality [see chapter 9] and ethnicity and race [see chapters 2, 7, and 13] in Faulkner's works. In particular, feminist studies have productively used psychoanalytic models to identify subversions or disruptions of the patriarchal or symbolic order. In the opinion of this critic, the most successful studies do not merely apply psychoanalytical principles; rather they pose an intertextual reading of theory and practice and avoid what Shoshana Felman calls the subordination of the literary text to "the higher authority" of theory.

What follows is a historical survey of the essays, chapters, and books that read Faulkner's body of work through a psychoanalytic lens. Because so much has been written on Faulkner from this perspective, I can cite here only those essays that, in my estimation, represent significant developments in the field.

Sanctuary (1931), the first of Faulkner's novels to achieve popular, if not critical, recognition, was also the first to prompt a psychoanalytic commentary. As early as 1934, Lawrence S. Kubie, a neurologist and psychiatrist, reviewed *Sanctuary* for the *Saturday Review of Literature.* In his twice-reprinted and frequently cited essay, Kubie astutely observes that a fear of instinctual helplessness or castration anxiety drives men in the novel to rape or fantasize rape. The next application of Freudian principles to Faulkner arrived more than 20 years later in the form of Carvel Collins's well-known essay, "The Pairing of *The Sound and the Fury* and *As I Lay Dying*" (1957). Collins aligns Faulkner and Freud by posing the provocative thesis that the 3 Compson brothers, Benjy, Quentin, and Jason embody, respectively, the Freudian concepts of id, ego, and superego.

Critical interrogation of Faulkner's texts began in earnest in the 1970s, and during that decade a number of critics applied Freudian and Jungian principles to Faulkner to good purpose. In 1972, Faulkner's short fiction, "A Rose for Emily" (1930), the account of a Southern lady who apparently poisons her lover, Homer Barron, and sleeps each night beside his decaying corpse, attracted the attention of a major psychoanalytic critic, Norman Holland. According to Holland, Emily's perverse behavior expresses Oedipal desire: on Homer, Emily projects her repressed desire to kill her father and to be her father's lover. As well, Emily, who is fiercely possessive of both her father's and lover's bodies, exhibits an anal retentive fixation. To date, Holland's findings must be reckoned with by anyone who aspires to interpret "A Rose for Emily." Another early Freudian study, John T. Irwin's *Doubling and Incest/Repetition and Revenge* (1975), revolutionized the way we read Faulkner. While Irwin applies his thesis to many of Faulkner's novels, he focuses principally on the relationship between *The Sound and the Fury* and *Absalom, Absalom!,* and reads the latter novel as the reflection of the repressed desires of Quentin Compson of the former novel.

Irwin interprets both the double and the revenge theme in terms of the Oedipus complex. Female doubles, like Caddy or Judith, are figurizations of a repressed desire for the mother of the pre-Oedipal stage; and revenge enacts a ceaselessly returning desire to supplant father surrogates. An early Jungian study, David Williams's *Faulkner's Women: The Myth and the Muse,* sees incarnations of the Jungian archetype of the Magna Mater or Great Goddess in four of Faulkner's novels, *The Sound and the Fury* (1929), *As I Lay Dying* (1930), *Sanctuary* (1931), and *Light in August* (1932). The archetype of the Great Mother, like all archetypes, "is two-faced, ambivalent, and has a 'good' and a 'bad' side according to the attitude the conscious mind adopts toward it" (Neumann 7). For Williams, the correspondence between Faulkner's female characters and this archetype explains the benevolent/malevolent aspects of these women and answers the charge of misogyny that was sometimes leveled against Faulkner in the 1970s.

In 1974, Joseph Blotner published the first biography of Faulkner; five years later, Judith Bryant Wittenberg attempted to write Faulkner's psychobiography; that is, she sought to uncover the psychic wounds that drive Faulkner's art. In *The Transfiguration of Biography,* Wittenberg posits, for example, that the recurrence of incestuous feelings in Faulkner's works can be traced to his courtship of and marriage to Estelle Oldham, his childhood playmate and "twin sister" (23). Similarly, according to Wittenberg, fratricidal impulses in Faulkner's fiction derive from Faulkner's deep resentment and jealousy of his youngest brother, Dean.

In the early 1980s two distinguished Lacanian approaches were published that set a standard of excellence for all future forays into the field. The essays, by Lacanian theorist Robert Con Davis and French Faulkner scholar André Bleikasten, seem like companion pieces; both address Faulkner's representations of Lacan's Symbolic Father. In "The Symbolic Father in Yoknapatawpha County" (1980), Davis maintains that in *Absalom, Absalom!* "the father refuses to die and, thereby, to become a symbol" (54); in a somewhat similar vein, in "Fathers in Faulkner" (1981), Bleikasten writes that Sutpen "stands for . . . the quintessential *phallacy:* the omnipotence of infantile desire as projected onto the father" (143).

After Davis's and Bleikasten's groundbreaking Lacanian contributions, there appeared several critical works that marked a return to Freud as well as an application of object-relations theory to Faulknerian motifs. In "Gerald Bland's Shadow" (1981), psychiatrist Richard Feldstein psychoanalyzes Quentin Compson of *The Sound and the Fury* and argues that Quentin's obsession with men like Gerald Bland, Dalton Ames, and Spoade is evidence of a homoerotic fixation. While Feldstein psychoanalyzes one of Faulkner's characters, Jay Martin, in a continuation of the project begun by Judith Bryant Wittenberg, psychoanalyzes Faulkner. According to Martin's "'The Whole Burden of Man's History of His Impossible Heart's Desire': The Early Life of William Faulkner" (1982), Faulkner's aesthetics display oral ambivalence and retentiveness, and these psychic defenses can be traced to a number of disappointments but ultimately to his mother's nurturing of him in infancy, which lacked "the warm glow of mutuality in feeding and playing that . . . seems necessary to nourish the psyche at its source" (612). Focusing not on Faulkner's life, but on a search for stability in his fiction, Gail Mortimer's book-length study, *Faulkner's Rhetoric of Loss: A Study in Perception and Meaning* (1983), uses object-relations theory [see chapter 9] "to explicate the quality of the consciousness that informs Faulkner's fiction" (9). In "'The Dungeon Was Mother Herself': William Faulkner: 1927–1931" (1984), Noel Polk, like Jay Martin before him, interrogates Faulknerian maternity, but, unlike Martin, Polk's field of inquiry is the fictional mother, specifically those in the novels and short stories written between 1927–1931. Polk finds that the mothers of this period "are, almost invariably, horrible people" (66), and he turns to Freud for an explanation. Citing transpositions and inversions of the Oedipal complex and the primal scene, Polk concludes that these maternal figures are the avatars of "*something* connected with sex and aggression and death and disgust and his mother" (75). Another critical application of Freudian principles is Peter Brooks's chapter on *Absalom, Absalom!* in *Reading for the Plot: Design and Intention in Narrative* (1984). Using Freudian theory as a "masterplot" or dynamic model of psychic processes, Brooks explores correspondences between textual and psychic dynamics, and, in *Absalom, Absalom!* he locates a dialogic narration and a transgression of accepted structures or "designs" comparable to the interplay between consciousness and the unconscious mind. Still another study that makes use of Freudian principles is Judith L. Sensibar's *The Origins of Faulkner's Art* (1984). While the thrust of Sensibar's work is textual and developmental—she argues that Faulkner's early poetry made possible his later fictional achievements—she often invokes Freudian theory to interpret themes of incest, narcissism, and fragmentation.

   With some notable exceptions, in the latter half of the decade and beyond, Faulkner's body of work fell under a Lacanian gaze. For example, Lacanian theorist James M. Mellard makes a significant contribution to Faulkner scholarship with his essay "Lacan and Faulkner: A Post-Freudian Analysis of Humor in the Fiction" (1986). Applying Lacan's revision of Freud's interpretation of jokes to Faulkner's comic practice, Mellard finds that all humor exists because of the primal debarring of the signifier from the signified, consciousness from unconsciousness, desire from attainment. Strictly speaking, James A. Snead's *Figures of Division: William Faulkner's Major Novel* (1986) is a deconstructionist, not a Lacanian interpretation; however, because Snead's book frequently cites Lacan's theory of language as it explores the construction of racial meanings in Faulkner's fiction, it merits consideration here. In Snead's incisive reading, black/white distinctions in Faulkner's texts are imposed by language—rhetorical figures of division—and close inspection reveals that these alleged opposites inhere within one another. Homer Pettey's Lacanian interpretation "Reading and Raping in *Sanctuary*" (1987) essentially updates Lawrence Kubie's early Freudian analysis of the novel. According to Pettey, the dominance of the signifier over the signified in Lacan's theory corresponds to "dual systems at play within *Sanctuary*'s language, between the phallogocentric and the feminine, between self and other, between reader and narrative" (74). Invoking both Freudian and Lacanian insights, Michel Gresset's book, *Fascination: Faulkner's Fiction, 1919–1936* (1989), traces Faulkner's artistic development from his earliest poetry and essays to *The Reivers,* with special attention to the novels written before 1936. Gresset's work is notable for its application of Lacan's notion of the **gaze** to Faulkner's works. Another work that frequently has recourse to Lacan is Wesley and Barbara Alverson Morris's *Reading Faulkner* (1989). This wide-ranging study is remarkable for its attempt to uncover the social and political dimensions of discursive practice. For example, in the Morrises' reading, Faulkner's *Intruder in the Dust* is a revisionary narrative that attempts to differentiate without discrimination, that is, to find a way to articulate the difference necessary for meaning without marginalizing a community of "outsiders" (235). Faulknerian maternity, analyzed earlier in Freudian studies by Polk and Martin, is the subject of Philip Weinstein's Lacanian reading "'If I Could Say Mother': Construing the Unsayable about Faulknerian Maternity" (1989). According to Weinstein, Mrs. Compson, in *The Sound and the Fury,* is trapped between two defective male symbolic scripts, a virginal and an adulterate script.

This spate of Lacanian interpretations was interrupted by two essays informed by, respectively, Freudian and Jungian principles. In "Some Remarks on Negation and Denegation in William Faulkner's *Absalom, Absalom!*" (1989), François Pitavy decodes unconscious meanings in Faulkner's arguably most difficult novel by applying Freud's theory that negation allows repressed material to appear. Continuing the Jungian project begun by David Williams, Terrell L. Tebbetts [see chapter 6] focuses, in particular, on the development of an integrated personality in "Shadows of Jung: A Psychological Approach to *Light in August*" (1989).

In the 1990s, scholars often turned to psychoanalytic theories of subject formation in language to read issues of gender, race, and power relations. For example, in *The Feminine and Faulkner* (1990), Minrose Gwin draws primarily on the theories of Hélène Cixous and Julia Kristeva to identify feminine disruptions of a patriarchal narrative in *The Sound and the Fury, Absalom, Absalom!,* and *The Wild Palms.* As the title suggests, subjectivity, particularly the plight of the beleaguered male subject, is the focus of Philip M. Weinstein's *Faulkner's Subject: A Cosmos No One Owns* (1992). Weinstein contemplates Faulkner's narratization of the dilemma of the subject created by lack in *The Sound and the Fury, Light in August, Absalom, Absalom!, Go Down, Moses,* and *Intruder in the Dust.* In another aptly titled study, *Forensic Fictions: The Lawyer Figure in Faulkner* (1993), Jay Watson applies Lacan's concept of the **Law-of-the-Father,** a symbolic status that denotes an authority that is lacking in all subjects as a condition of subjectivity. Breaking with the standard practice of analyzing Faulkner's major novels, Michael Zeitlin's "The Passion of Margaret Powers: A Psychoanalytic Reading of *Soldiers' Pay*" (1993) argues that Faulkner's first novel exhibits both an impulse to objectify women and a contrary wish to construct a female subject "more or less resistant (if not wholly immune) to the pressures of male desire" (352). Faulkner's first novel and *The Sound and the*

Fury provide the verbal slips, omissions, puns, and Latin misquotations that Thomas L. McHaney analyzes with the help of Freud in "At Play in the Fields of Freud: Faulkner and Misquotation" (1993).

A banner year for psychoanalytic criticism of Faulkner, 1994 marks the publication of *Faulkner and Psychology,* a collection of essays delivered at the 1991 Faulkner and Yoknapatawpha Conference held in Oxford, Mississippi. The volume opens with a group of (mostly) Lacanian interpretations. The first essay, my "'Little Sister Death': *The Sound and the Fury* and the Denied Unconscious" argues that the Compson brothers project onto Caddy their own sense of lack as subjects in language. Caddy, thus, becomes the reflection of what they deny. In a comparable essay, "Of Mothers, Robbery, and Language: Faulkner and *The Sound and the Fury,*" Deborah Clarke contends that, while the Compson men fail to control women's bodies, Caddy and Mrs. Compson subvert patriarchal structures. Male failure also figures importantly in Anne Goodwyn Jones's intriguing essay, "Male Fantasies?: Faulkner's War Stories and the Construction of Gender." Using a feminist Lacanian approach, Jones investigates the relationship between the development of masculinity as laid out in the psychoanalytic narrative and the structures of the traditional war narrative. Like Jones, Carolyn Porter successfully applies Lacanian theory to pursue a feminist agenda in her contribution to the conference, "Symbolic Fathers and Dead Mothers: A Feminist Approach to Faulkner." Looking specifically at *As I Lay Dying* (1930) and *Absalom, Absalom!* (1936), Porter identifies feminine disruptions of the masculine symbolic order. Another application of Lacanian principles, Jay Watson's "Faulkner's Forensic Fiction and the Question of Authorial Neurosis" explores the passage into language and alienation as it is negotiated by various lawyer figures, which, Watson proposes, represent authorial surrogates. Last in this group, David Wyatt's "Faulkner and the Reading Self" is a kind of anti-Lacanian essay. Wyatt challenges Lacan's assertion that we come into consciousness through language. Examining scenes of reading in *The Bear* (1942) and "An Odor of Verbena" (1938), Wyatt argues that, for Faulkner, the self comes into being through reading.

Four of the essays in *Faulkner and Psychology* practice some form of Freudian literary criticism. Lee Jenkins, for example, categorizes the major characters in *Light in August* according to various Freudian disorders in "Psychoanalytic Conceptualizations of Characterization, Or Nobody Laughs in *Light in August.*" In "Faulkner and Psychoanalysis: The *Elmer* Case," Michael Zeitlin examines the Freudian concept of fetishism as it plays out in the early unfinished work, *Elmer.* John T. Irwin reads *Sanctuary* in terms of primary narcissism, an excessive self-love that is rooted in an incestuous love for the mother, in "Horace Benbow and the Myth of Narcissa." And, in perhaps the most complex essay of the group, "'What I Chose to Be': Freud, Faulkner, Joe Christmas, and the Abandonment of Design," Donald M. Kartiganer compares Freud's abandonment of his seduction theory as the origin of a patient's neurosis to Faulkner's choice of an indeterminate racial origin for Joe Christmas of *Light in August.* Both developments lead away from determinacy and express a courageous openness to endless possibilities. Finally, in a turn to psychobiography and in accordance with a model of identity formation advanced by proponents of men's studies, Jay Martin's "Faulkner's 'Male Commedia': The Triumph of Manly Grief" describes Faulkner's own development in terms of a conflict between maternal attachment and paternal identification.

In 1994, in addition to *Faulkner and Psychology,* there appeared two ventures into psychobiography, a critical study informed by French feminist theory, and no less than three psychoanalytic interpretations of *As I Lay Dying.* In *The Life of William Faulkner* (1994), Richard Gray successfully integrates two methodologies. He reads Faulkner in terms of Southern history and culture at the same time as he also speculates about the relationship between typical fictional preoccupations and unresolved psychic conflicts, as, for example, Faulkner's lifelong attachment to his mother. In "Faulkner's Muse: Speculations about the Genesis of *The Sound and the Fury,*" Thomas C. Moser proposes that Faulkner's relationship to his wife, Estelle Oldham, was the inspiration for an elusive female presence in his fiction. An important reading that draws on French feminist psychoanalytical theory, Deborah Clarke's *Robbing the Mother: Women in Faulkner* (1994) argues persuasively that Faulkner's creativity is based in matricide, that is, a repression of the feminine that can be traced back to the development of subjectivity in the Oedipal moment. Complementing Clarke's work, there also appeared in this same year two studies of the Kristevan concept of abjection in *As I Lay Dying*—Diana York Blaine's "The Abjection of Addie and Other Myths of the Maternal in *As I Lay Dying*" and Bonnie Woodbery's "The Abject in Faulkner's *As I Lay Dying*"—and a Lacanian analysis of Darl Bundren's use of language to cope with his mother's death—Michel Delville's "Alienating Language and Darl's Narrative Consciousness in Faulkner's *As I Lay Dying.*"

In 1994, a special issue of the *Faulkner Journal* was devoted to the topic of "Faulkner and Sexuality," and many of the essays in the volume are informed by psychoanalytical accounts of the construction of sexuality. In one of three essays on Faulkner's apprentice novel, *Mosquitoes* (1927), "'A Perversion that Builds Chartres and Invents Lear Is a Pretty Good Thing': *Mosquitoes* and Faulkner's Androgynous Imagination," Lisa Rado finds in the novel a cultural construction of sexuality that is consistent with French feminist psychoanalytic theory; in "The Bug That Dare Not Speak Its Name: Sex, Art, Faulkner's Worst Novel, and the Critics," Meryl Altman contends that, like Freud, Faulkner's critics identify any form of nonconformist sexual behavior with homosexuality; and, in "*Mosquitoes'* Missing Bite: The Four Deletions," Minrose C. Gwin argues persuasively that the four homoerotic passages, which were editorially deleted from the published text, functioned to normalize homosexuality. Applying Irigaray's concept of **mimicry** to Addie Bundren's monologue, Amy Louise Wood's "Feminine Rebellion and Mimicry in Faulkner's *As I Lay Dying*" traces Addie's subversions of patriarchal scripts. Taking up *Sanctuary,* Amy Lovell Strong argues that Temple Drake refuses to accept the erotic self that Popeye constructs for her in "Machines and Machinations: Controlling Desires in Faulkner's *Sanctuary.*"

Leading off another trio of essays, Cathy Peppers's "What Does Faulkner Want? *Light in August* as a Hysterical Male Text" applies Freud's definition of female hysteria to *Light in August.* Masculinity and hypermasculinity are the subjects of Jay Watson's "Overdoing Masculinity in *Light in August;* or Joe Christmas and the Gender Guard," which maintains that Joe's sexual transgressiveness inspires homosexual panic in the people of Jefferson. In a more explicitly Lacanian approach, my essay "'I am dying': Faulkner's Hightower and the Oedipal Moment" interprets Hightower as an incomplete subject outside of the social order who only achieves subjectivity in the final pages of the novel. Focusing on *Go Down, Moses,* Neil Watson identifies a homosexual subtext, which he analyzes in terms of the theories of Luce Irigaray and Eve Kosofsky Sedgwick, in "'The Incredibly Loud . . . Miss-fire': A Sexual Reading of *Go Down, Moses.*" Finally, Evelyn Jaffe Schreiber's "What's Love Got to Do with It? Desire and Subjectivity in Faulkner's Snopes Trilogy," turns to Slajov Zizek's reading of Lacan to interpret female acts of empowerment in the Snopes trilogy.

Several essays published in 1995 merit attention. Continuing her Lacanian project with "*Absalom, Absalom!:* (Un)Making the Father," Carolyn Porter investigates Faulkner's representation of the Symbolic Father and reasons that the failure of Sutpen's design "reveals the symbolic function on which [the cultural] order depends" (192). Turning from psychobiography to Lacan, Judith Bryant Wittenberg contributes two essays: she examines race as a linguistic function in "Race in *Light in August:* Word-symbols and Obverse Reflections," and she reads *Requiem for a Nun* in terms of Lacan's "Function and Field of Speech and Language in Psychoanalysis" in "Temple Drake and *La parole pleine.*" As well, Terrell Tebbetts weighs in with another Jungian reading of Faulkner, "Dilsey and the Compsons: A Jungian Reading of Faith and Fragmentation," which argues that Dilsey's ego, animus, and shadow are perfectly harmonized.

Because in the latter half of the decade of the 1990s and into the twenty-first century, critical practice is largely informed by postmodernist thought [see chapter 6], which, in turn, is supported by psychoanalytical descriptions of the construction of identity and meaning, most of the scholarship produced, particularly investigations of gender, sexuality, and race, come under the rubric of psychoanalytic literary criticism. For this reason, my account must be ever more selective and identify only explicitly psychoanalytic works of criticism. Mention should be made, however, of Noel Polk's collection of previously published essays, *Children of the Dark House: Text and Context in Faulkner* (1996), which often alludes to Freudian paradigms to interpret Faulknerian meanings. Also noteworthy is Philip M. Weinstein's *What Else but Love? The Ordeal of Race in Faulkner and Morrison* (1996), which examines the construction of identity in language in Faulkner and Morrison. Identity formation is also Susan V. Donaldson's subject in "Cracked Urns: Faulkner, Gender, and Art in the South" (1996), which argues, with French feminist psychoanalytic theory lurking in the background, that male identity is bought by female containment. Also focusing on the female body, Candace Waid identifies woman's body as the generative source of language in "The Signifying Eye: Faulkner's Artists and the Engendering of Art" (1996).

In 1996, the essays presented at the 1994 Faulkner and Yoknapatawpha Conference were published in the volume *Faulkner and Gender*. Almost all of these essays are informed by the feminist psychoanalytic argument that gender is constructed by culture's dominant discourse of binary thought (that is, to establish male difference and superiority, woman is culturally and linguistically contained and subordinated); and several of them argue persuasively that Faulkner's texts both expose the cultural production of gender and reveal the instability of cultural polarizations. See, for example, Minrose Gwin's "Did Ernest Like Gordon?: Faulkner's *Mosquitoes* and the Bite of 'Gender Trouble,'" which examines the disruptive performance of the "queer" abject; John N. Duvall's "Faulkner's Crying Game: Male Homosexual Panic," which looks for the feminine constitutive component in masculinity; Robert Dale Parker's "Sex and Gender, Feminine and Masculine: Faulkner and the Polymorpohous Exchange of Cultural Binaries," which identifies a dizzying proliferation of gender possibilities in Faulkner's fiction; Deborah Clarke's "Gender, War, and Cross-Dressing in *The Unvanquished*," which holds that Faulkner uses war as a context to challenge fixed gender roles; and David Rogers's "Maternalizing the Epicene: Faulkner's Paradox of Form and Gender," which finds that Faulkner's recurring deployment of the epicene figure in his fiction denotes a blurring of the cultural order's boundaries. In addition to these essays, two other studies in the collection should be noted: James Polchin's "Selling a Novel: Faulkner's *Sanctuary* as Psychosexual Text," which contends that Faulkner wrote *Sanctuary* to appeal to the popularity in the 1920s of the new Freudian psychology; and my "'I want to go home': Faulkner, Gender, and Death," which draws on two key Freudian texts, "The Uncanny" and *Beyond the Pleasure Principle,* to interpret a recurring desire to return in Faulkner's fiction and in his life.

The year 1996 also saw the publication of *Approaches to Teaching Faulkner's* The Sound and the Fury, and two of the essays in the collection provide practical applications of psychoanalytic methods to the classroom situation. In "Teaching *The Sound and the Fury* with Freud," Judith Bryant Wittenberg suggests that Freudian models, particularly Freud's Oedipus complex, can help students to come to terms with the Compson brothers' obsessions. Similarly, Terrell L. Tebbetts's "Giving Jung a Crack at the Compsons" proposes that Jung's theory of individuation, the process of achieving full human wholeness, can offer students a model for interpreting the fragmentation that characterizes the novel. Finally, in 1996 as well there appeared my Lacanian reading of Lena Grove as a figure of the pre-Oedipal mother, "'You cant beat a woman': The Preoedipal Mother in *Light in August*"; Judith L. Sensibar's study of the instability of racial representations in *Go Down, Moses,* "Who Wears the Mask? Memory, Desire and Race in *Go Down, Moses*"; and an essay influenced by French feminist thought, Linda Dunleavy's "*Sanctuary,* Sexual Difference, and the Problem of Rape," which argues that Faulkner's narrative locates sexual difference not in biology but in social configurations of power.

One Freudian and three Lacanian readings of Faulkner's texts were produced and published in 1997. Leading the trio of Lacanian attempts is my *Faulkner: The Return of the Repressed.* Beginning with Faulkner's contention that he was "telling the same story over and over again which is myself and the world" (Cowley, *Faulkner-Cowley File* 14) and focusing on the major novels, I interrogate the dilemma of subjectivity when identity, difference, and meaning are contingent upon fragmentation, and the subsequent subject is forever haunted by a repressed desire for a presubjective completeness. Such a project leads me to various interpretations. To suggest only two: I read the funeral journey in *As I Lay Dying* as Addie Bundren's revenge on a male symbolic order that survives by denying her existence; and I interpret Charles Bon in *Absalom, Absalom!* as a disguised evocation of a forbidden desire for a fusion that must be excluded, and, for this reason, not only is he killed by Henry but his meaning is also repressed by the character-narrators at the level of narration. The second in this Lacanian series, "Reading for the 'Other Side': *Beloved* and *Requiem for a Nun,*" also my work, is an intertextual reading of Faulkner and Morrison. A Lacanian framework of subjectivity, I propose, can help us to interpret the focal paradox of both novels, namely that both Sethe and Nancy, a mother and a mother surrogate, kill a child to save a child. Briefly, Nancy and Sethe, avatars of the pre-Oedipal mother, refuse to allow a child to pass into subjectivity in a life-destructive, "unlivable" cultural order and choose for the child instead the dissolution of the "I" in the presymbolic. A paradox is also the focus of Evelyn Jaffe Schreiber's Lacanian reading, "Imagined Edens and Lacan's Lost Object: The Wilderness and Subjectivity in Faulkner's *Go Down, Moses.*" Alluding to foundational American-studies scholarship, Schreiber observes that in mandating that all are equal, paradoxically, democracy robs citizens of their individuality. Ike's answer to this paradox is to retreat into the wilderness where democracy becomes Lacan's **lost object.** Last, the Freudian interpretation in this group, Denise Tanyol's "The Two-Way Snake Bite: The Dead Doctor Wounds His Son in William Faulkner's *The Wild Palms,*" reads Harry Wilbourne as an Oedipal son with a number of fathers, including Rat and McCord. In performing the abortion, Harry is killing his son; and, like Oedipus, he seeks to punish himself for his crime.

Psychoanalytic frames figure significantly in several essays published in 1998. Michael Zeitlin's "Returning to Freud and *The Sound and the Fury*" argues that the novel reuses and transforms certain Freudian concepts such as splitting, excess, and unconscious power. Just as Faulkner returns to Freud, Faulkner scholars repeatedly return to Kristeva's concept of abjection and apply it to Addie Bundren: the latest instance is Paul Luís Calkins's "Be Careful What You Wish For: *As I Lay Dying* and the Shaming of Abjection." *Sanctuary* once again invites psychoanalytic speculation as Kathryn M. Scheel, in "Incest, Repression and Repetition Compulsion: The Case of Faulkner's Temple Drake," hypothesizes that Temple has repressed an earlier trauma, her brothers' rape of her, and this repressed memory, in various guises, returns throughout the novel. *Sanctuary's* sequel, *Requiem for a Nun,* and, more particularly, female discourse in the novel, is the subject of Kelly Lynch Reames's investigation in "'All That Matters Is That I Wrote the Letters': Discourse, Discipline, and Difference in *Requiem for a Nun*." For Reames, the novel undertakes a feminist project: it asks how women can maintain their subjectivities despite public narratives that constrain their identities.

The Sound and the Fury, As I Lay Dying, Sanctuary, and *Absalom, Absalom!* were the subjects of psychoanalytical speculation in 1999. Tackling representations of race, Patricia McKee's "Self-Division as Racial Divide: *The Sound and the Fury*" finds that the Compson men seem to embody Lacan's fractured, self-alienated subject, while the black men and women of the novel are capable of merging individual with group identity. As his title suggests, Michael Hardin applies Freud's theory of the death drive to Faulkner's 1930 novel in "Freud's Family: The Journey to Bury the Death Drive in Faulkner's *As I Lay Dying*." In "The Policing and Proliferation of Desire: Gender and the Homosocial in Faulkner's *Sanctuary*," Charmaine Eddy draws on the theories of Luce Irigaray to argue that the sexual violence against Lee Goodwin functions "as a fantasy of sexual aggression against the feminine enacted through homosexual practice" (37). And George B. Handley's comparative essay "Oedipal and Prodigal Returns in Alejo Carpentier and William Faulkner," which reads the drive for autonomy in postcolonial nations in terms of the Oedipal complex, reminds us of the political dimensions of psychoanalytic practice.

In the twenty-first century, the psychoanalytic method was deployed effectively to consider fatherhood, mother fixations, race, and masculinity in Faulkner's works. In "Faulkner's Grim Sires," Carolyn Porter draws on Freud and Lacan to interrogate fatherhood "as the enigmatic source and vehicle of social identity and political sovereignty" (121) in *Absalom, Absalom!* In the aptly titled "Jason Compson and the Mother Complex," Kathleen Moore contends that Jason of *The Sound and the Fury* manifests the signs of a mother fixation as outlined in Freud's clinical case histories. My essay "Reading the Absences: Race and Narration in Faulkner's *Absalom, Absalom!*" traces the return of repressed racial meanings in the novel; that is, I propose that the character-narrators, without conscious awareness, refuse to speak a fusion of black and white and that this repressed meaning returns disguised. More specifically, the character-narrators unconsciously censor Charles Bon's identity as both Sutpen and black Other, and, repressed, it returns. Another essay that uses theories of the unconscious mind to interpret racial repression is Beth Widmaier's, "Black Female Absence and the Construction of White Womanhood in Faulkner's *Light in August*." Examining identity construction in the novel, Widmaier concludes that Joe Christmas "shares with the absent black females of the text the abject, fluid Otherness that threatens the social structure of Jefferson" (36). Three twenty-first-century essays draw on psychoanalytic theory to ponder Faulknerian masculinity. By applying to Faulkner's texts Freud's theory that jokes preempt criticism, Harriet Hustis, in her essay "Masculinity As/In Comic Performance in *As I Lay Dying* and *The Sound and the Fury*," finds that Jason Compson's and Anse Bundren's humor assists them in their performance of masculinity. In "Love of Masculinity," Thomas Loebel speaks of masculinity as a design or process that originates in the psychic trauma of the self's constitution and is enabled by subsequent constituent repressions of women, slaves, and homoeroticism. Finally, I conclude this overview of psychoanalytic Faulkner scholarship with Noel Polk's "Testing Masculinity in the Snopes Trilogy." Citing Judith Butler's definition of gender as a signifying practice, Polk begins by stating that "our culture works to rob men and women both of an *instinctual* sexual life, by forcing them to conform to a performative sexual role" (6) and then applies this insight to the men of the Snopes trilogy.

The explanatory power of the psychoanalytic literary project as applied to Faulkner's work perhaps has been amply demonstrated by the preceding review of scholarship; however, in closing, I would like to address a closely related and frequently misunderstood topic—the cultural relevance of psychoanalytic criticism. For too long, the psychoanalytic method has been assumed to be ahistorical and apolitical. Nothing could be further from the truth. The psychoanalytic critique, which overlaps with feminist, deconstructive, and poststructuralist agendas, teaches that there are no essential or intrinsic meanings, that meanings are culturally produced, and that repression, psychological and social, plays a crucial role in the cultural construction of meaning. According to the psychoanalytic narrative, the natural world, including our own bodies, is unknown to us, and all our meanings are our own invention. We know a thing by its name— black, white, male, female—and culture assigns names (i.e., meanings) to all materiality, but the relationship between the object and its meaning is fictional and arbitrary. Even more important, in order to assign a meaning to a thing, we must repress other meanings. In this way, through repression, culture, historically shaped and informed by politics (i.e., power relations), constructs our identity and all identity and exerts a terrible power over our lives since, whether true or not, definitions define and have real consequences in the world.

It is precisely this process of making meaning that fictions—in particular, Faulkner's fictions—can help us to question and critique. Because fictional meanings are constituted in the same way that culture constructs "real" meanings—by repressing meanings so as to isolate and identify one—fiction, like language and the unconscious, is the site of an endless play of meaning. In other words, because, as Freud and Lacan teach, the other meaning that is displaced can never be totally erased, but always returns disguised, to be re-erased and return again in a different form, the text is the site of a negotiation between what has been displaced, the body in the world, and the social structure that appropriates it. It is important to understand what is at stake in this exchange. Absent governing social structures, materiality is without meaning, or, more precisely, we are left with a dizzying omnipresence of meaning. Repression, the singling out of one meaning at the expense of others, confers identity on material existence but leaves always in its wake a desire for what has been lost. The site of this incessant struggle in a text we call the textual unconscious, and the psychoanalytic method provides the roadmap to read this interface of the body and culture, the place where consciousness and the unconscious meet. Using psychoanalytic frames, we can ask: who gets to make meaning and who or what has paid the price of marginalization? We can read the text as a site of rebellion against the tyranny of culturally enforced meanings; we can read for cultural interdictions and for subliminal subversions of the social order.

This approach is most useful when applied to an author like Faulkner. In the words of Toni Morrison, Faulkner was a writer who never looked away: "He had a gaze that was different. It appeared . . . to be . . . a sort of staring, a refusal-to-look-away approach in his writing that I found admirable" (297). As I interpret Morrison's remark, she suggests that Faulkner's texts refuse to accept uncritically any meaning—that they ceaselessly search for the authority behind any governing social structure. In this critical mode, Faulkner's body of work is analogous to the theories of psychoanalytic thinkers; and, as analogous texts, they should not only be read through psychoanalytic frames, but psychoanalytic speculation should be interpreted through Faulknerian paradigms. Read intertextually, we may find that Faulkner's texts modify the psychoanalytic narrative or even that they propose less repressive ways of constructing meaning. Ultimately, such an intertextual reading may lead us to better negotiate the relation between language and the world body.

9

Feminist and Gender Criticism

Caroline Carvill

"Unlike the natural women of Hemingway, Faulkner's dewiest dells turn out to be destroyers rather than redeemers, quicksands disguised as sacred groves."
—Fiedler, *Love and Death in the American Novel* (321)

"Faulkner writes woman, but she writes him too."
—Gwin, *The Feminine and Faulkner* (152)

Since the 1970s, feminist critics have analyzed Faulkner's work: his women characters, his male characters' reactions to them, his paradigms of "masculine" and "feminine" in his society. The South's (both Old and New) view of women as both central and marginal, both paragons of virtue and inferior beings, both powerful and ineffectual, permeates Faulkner's fictional world. A world that simultaneously puts (white) women on a pedestal *and* subjugates them creates tensions both real and fictional. In addition, the intersections of gender and race come into play, as both women and blacks are the "Other." Faulkner's portrayals of women and men, and "feminine" and "masculine" are as varied as his fiction. However, throughout his work, his society's paradoxical view of women helps to shape his artistic vision.

Feminist criticism has reshaped the map of Faulkner critical studies. After a brief overview of the map of feminist criticism, this chapter will look at the beginnings against which feminist critics of Faulkner were working, how feminist scholarship has redrawn the map, the case of one novel, *Absalom, Absalom!,* and a personal reflection on the future.

THE MAP OF FEMINIST CRITICISM

> "What's a radical feminist doing with a canonical male text anyway?" (Gwin, "Feminism" 55)

Using a variety of theories—and overlapping with psychoanalytical [see chapter 8], Marxist [see chapter 7], poststructuralist, and other critical schools—feminist critics approach Faulkner texts to examine the portrayal of the characters, how they operate in the text, how their gender defines them for the author and other characters, and how society's expectations define their lives. These representations exist on several levels: biological, the facts of the female body and how others' perceive it; societal, the paradigms of "masculine" and "feminine" as they operate in people's expectations; and mythic or symbolic, the associations of the female with larger patterns. Because women often operate as the "Other," investigating their roles requires both analyzing the characters' themselves and analyzing the patterns of male representation and reaction to them. No single critical approach or set of conclusions constitutes feminist interpretations of Faulkner (invoking the term "feminisms" instead).

In "Feminist Criticism," in *Redrawing the Boundaries: The Transformation of English and American Literary Studies,* Catherine Stimpson succinctly summarizes the five ways that feminist critics proceed:

> (1) by charting the course of women as writers, who they are, how and why they write, their reception and reputations—a job that Elaine Showalter has named "gynocritics"; (2) by charting the cultural representations of gender, patterns of masculinity and femininity, a complementary task that Alice A. Jardine calls "gynesis"; (3) by showing the complex relations among these representations and patterns of masculine dominance and then asking for the erasure of such patterns (feminist critics are like cartographers of the vanishing rain forest who both *see* and *stop* the damage); (4) by establishing the unreliability of other maps because they overlook or misconstrue women and the issue of gender; (5) by so doing, stimulating vigilance about the processes of map making themselves. (251)

Within these major areas, a great number of theoretical strategies or "maps" emerge. The theoretical underpinnings offer a variety of interpretations, often complementary, often contradictory. Many of these theories begin with the concepts of psychoanalytic and structural criticism to build on, vary from, or contradict. How one's sexual identity is formed, whether gender is socially or biologically constructed, how language constructs our realities—these are among the myriad issues feminist critics analyze. Several threads are worth noting before turning to the work of feminist critics on Faulkner.

Feminist critics set out to break with traditional readings of literature. Breaking with the New Critical prohibition against extrinsic criticism, they began to examine the women characters and authors in terms of social, economic, and cultural terms. They often took issue with the ways other critical approaches dealt with women authors and the worlds of fiction by both men and women. Judith Fetterley, in *The Resisting Reader,* offered strategies for rereading and rethinking

texts and analyzed several male authors, including Faulkner. Building on Fetterley's work, Patrocinio P. Schweickart calls for "reading the text as it was *not*
meant to be read, in fact, reading it against itself" (50). While some concentrated
on studying women writers within a feminist framework (Showalter's "gynocritics"), others advocated widening the scope, such as Myra Jehlen's strategy of
"radical comparativism" between gynocritics and the dominant traditions.

One major feminist critical undertaking has been in psychoanalysis. In
response to phallogocentrism, Freud's use of male development as the norm
against which females are measured, numerous critics have set out to redefine
sexual development and gender-identity formation. Object-relations theory, in
the work of Melanie Klein, Margaret Mahler, D. W. Winnicott, and others,
rethinks the Freudian Oedipal crisis for both men and women, focusing on the
mother-child bond and its phases of attachment and separation. Nancy
Chodorow's work *The Reproduction of Mothering: Psychoanalysis and the
Sociology of Gender* argues that rejecting the mother is unnecessary and recasts
gender formation. Julia Kristeva argues that we make meaning and achieve
identity through the dialectic between the semiotic (prediscursive, pre-Oedipal)
domain and the symbolic domain. Many theorists believe that the feminine disrupts symbolic, patriarchal order, and this pre-Oedipal relationship to the
mother uncovers female language. Shoshana Felman's work focuses on the "performative" (rhetorical acts) and the "constative" (the meaning created) and how
their interactions form the basis of our doing and knowing.

A related vein of theory focuses on patriarchal discourse. Theorists confront
the issues of phallogocentrism and logocentrism (Derrida's term for opposi-
tional systems relying on mastery and unified principles). Hélène Cixous
pointed out that the hierarchies set up in patriarchy repress the feminine in a sexual economy, and she reaches the repressed feminine through her theory of
bisexuality. Luce Irigaray sought ways to change the language that inscribes the
patriarchal system to disrupt it. Monique Wittig proposed to change language in
ways that depart from categories of gender, what she calls a lesbianization of
language. [See also chapter 8.]

Feminist critics of Faulkner have employed all these, and many more, theoretical stances. For William Faulkner, a writer long held to uphold the patriarchal,
authoritative, binary (male/female, black/white) system of the South, reading
against the text has unearthed various new, often conflicting, interpretations.
Map making is a particularly apt metaphor for Faulkner's work; created within
the boundaries of his literal map of Yoknapatawpha County, we find shifting
maps of gender, race, class, and expectations that often conflict, often conflate,
and often undermine themselves.

THE BEGINNINGS

In short, the interpretive community of Faulkner critics, on matters of sexual politics, frequently sound very much like the good people of Jefferson. (Duvall,
"Faulkner's Critics" 42)

Critics have variously argued that Faulkner presents a misogynistic view of women, that he negatively presents women who move outside their "proper role," that he uses the traditional views of the Old South and Southern women to uphold the system. Early feminist criticism of Faulkner questions the prevailing critical perceptions. For instance, in *Love and Death in the American Novel,* Leslie Fiedler concludes that Faulkner is misogynist:

> In the work of William Faulkner, the fear of the castrating woman and the dis-ease with sexuality present in the novels of his contemporaries, Fitzgerald and Hemingway, attain their fullest and shrillest expression. Not content with merely projecting images of the anti-virgin, he insists upon editorializing against the woman he travesties in character and situation. No Jiggs and Maggie cliché of popular anti-feminism is too banal for him to use; he reminds us (again and again!) that men are helpless in the hands of their mothers, wives, and sisters; that females do not think but proceed from evidence to conclusions by paths too devious for males to follow; that they possess neither morality nor honor; that they are capable, therefore, of betrayal without qualm or quiver of guilt but also of inexplicable loyalty; that they enjoy an occasional beating at the hands of their men; that they are unforgiving and without charity to other members of their own sex; that they lose keys and other small useful articles with maddening regularity but are quite capable of finding things invisible to men; that they use their sexuality with cold calculation to achieve their inscrutable ends, etc., etc. (320)

Younger women, Fiedler says, fall into two categories: "great, sluggish, mindless daughters of peasants, whose fertility and allure are scarcely indistinguishable from those of a beast in heat; and the febrile, almost fleshless but sexually insatiable daughters of the aristocracy" (321). Throughout most of Faulkner's career, Fiedler says, only older women, postmenopausal, are "exempt from travesty and contempt" (321). Late in his career, Faulkner "seems to have repented of his many blasphemies against women and to have committed himself to redeeming one by one all his anti-virgins; but his attempts at redemption somehow do not touch the level of acceptance reached by his original travesties" (324).

This strain of criticism, while not always so vehement, has a well-established history. Irving Howe agrees that ladies "conspicuously past the age of sexual distraction" receive admiring treatment, while "there is hardly a young woman in his books who does not provoke quantities of bitterness and bile, and so persistent is his distaste for the doings of 'womanflesh' that it cannot be dismissed merely as a vagary of the characters who convey it. Few writers have trained such ferocity on the young American bitch" (97). While finding positive portrayals in his work, Cleanth Brooks, in his introduction to Sally Page's book on Faulkner's women, sees Faulkner as defending the "proper" order of things: "In fact, as one explores Faulkner's fiction, it becomes plain that he believes it a mistake for either sex to try to adopt the special values of the other. (Obviously they share basic human values.) The sexes must maintain their roles" (xvi). To borrow a phrase from Fiedler above, "etc., etc."

The 1970s produced two book-length works on women in Faulkner. Sally R. Page's *Faulkner's Women: Characterization and Meaning* looks at Faulkner's women characters in two broad categories, creative or destructive, based on their fulfilling or defying their "proper" feminine roles. Deviation from this role—whether a result of choice or thwarting—takes women from their "proper" sphere and results in perversity, death, and decay. Page also makes the point that their repressive societies often thwart the women's desires—a point made loudly by later feminist critics—but Page takes as a given that women's desires are always the same: love, marriage, and motherhood. "In *The Sound and The Fury* and *Sanctuary* Faulkner makes it clear that in the face of familial and social decay, the only source of moral order and endurance is woman's ability to fulfill the creative and sustaining role of motherhood" (93). If she can't, characters like Minnie Cooper and Emily Grierson "reiterate Faulkner's theme that if woman is prevented from achieving the normal fulfillment of her sexual drives, she will become engaged in a denial of reality in which she clings to an illusory view of life in order to overcome her sense of the inadequacy and abnormality of her real existence" (102). Page counteracts the vehement misogynist label, yet ends up reinscribing the patriarchal view of women.

David Williams, in *Faulkner's Women: The Myth and the Muse,* approaches the women characters as Jungian archetypes, focusing on their symbolic functions: "Faulkner's lasting concern throughout the works we have been exploring is with the fateful importance for man of the emergent mother archetype" (242–43). The male reaction to these characters is as much a concern for Williams as the female characters themselves: "All of Faulkner's tortured, agonized men are resistant one way or another to the creative forces of life" (243). Williams sees Faulkner using variations of the mythic archetype throughout his work: "From the story of Caddy Compson through to the story of Lena Grove, the archetype of the feminine is communicated by symbols possessing all the dynamism and the spontaneity of the daemon itself" (245). In *The Hamlet,* however, Williams finds "the literary record of the usurpation of the mother goddess by the patriarchate. In narrative terms, it means the overturning of a mythos (the defeat, mythically, of Eula Varner) and an attendant demystification of the symbols (the adoption of the art of allusion)." In his work thereafter, Faulkner turns away from these concerns to new ones. "Some of these new concerns are just as mythic in degree as the myth of woman; but when Faulkner returns to the content of the myth again in the latter part of the Snopes trilogy, he returns to very limited, human women and to formally inferior art" (246).

Other critics saw Faulkner refusing to categorize women. Ilse Dusoir Lind points out that *"Faulkner is the only major American fiction writer of the twenties and thirties who incorporates into his depiction of women the functioning of the organs of reproduction"* ("Faulkner's" 92, Lind's italics). She discusses medical writers of Faulkner's time and his apparent familiarity with their work. To Lind, "generalizing about Faulkner's women seems . . . as fruitless as generalizing about Faulkner's men, or about women in general, or about the human race" (90–91). She asserts that, "in the Divine Comedy of Faulkner's creation, women appear in every part—in his Paradiso, in his Inferno, and in his Purgatorio. Nor can it be gainsaid that the eyes which perceive imaginative reality in

Faulkner's work are masculine eyes, belonging to a man of epical ambition, one who strives for Homer's gift of narration" (104). Other critics point out women's inability to overcome the repressive society around them. A variety of works give a variety of explanations, roles, and functions of the women characters.

Judith Bryant Wittenberg, in "William Faulkner: A Feminist Consideration" in 1982, builds on earlier critics to work toward a different interpretation of Faulkner than the critics discussed previously. For those critics who see Faulkner as a misogynist, Wittenberg asserts that "such willful misreadings are as often projective as inept, revealing the persistence of such visions in the critics' own psyches" (326). Like Lind and others, she sees Faulkner's women as much more varied: "Faulkner was obviously aware of the effects of a rigidly patriarchal social structure upon its female members. Even though his own status as a product of that structure sometimes led him to imply that it was more admirable to accept than to rebel, his awareness of its oppressiveness was responsible for a number of memorable portraits of women" (328). Calling Faulkner "an embryonic psychoanalyst" (330), she traces his use of psychoanalytical insights: "the idea that any individual has the potential to contain traits of both sexes, the belief that a person's character is largely formed by his or her own early experiences and family relationships, and the concept of projection, of one's 'reality' as created out of one's own desires and fears" (330).

She also discusses some of the female characters' "lack of language, Logos, the Word—predominantly a male possession" (334) and concludes that "Faulkner presents women who make effective use of language, figures that contrast with and serve to offset the portrayals of those who are voiceless and consequently identified only in and through masculine discourse" (335). For Wittenberg, female characters in Faulkner fail to fall into neat categories, just as his male characters do. "The only real 'villains' in the Faulknerian world are a restrictive society that is inadequately responsive to the needs and desires of its individual members and a nuclear family that fails its children by offering poor examples or providing inadequate affection—and their victims are both men and women" (335).

Minrose C. Gwin questioned feminist inquiry into Faulkner in her article "Feminism and Faulkner: Second Thoughts or, What's a radical feminist doing with a canonical male text anyway?" She recounts her first reading of Faulkner, "A Rose for Emily:"

> And although I didn't know it when I first met Emily Grierson, I know now that most women live out their lives with several male corpses in their attics. We are all, in some sense, I believe, "madwomen in the attic," in that the closed back rooms of our houses and our psyches are often those very places where it is possible to exert power over men in ways that are unthinkable in the real world. I think that Faulkner knew this when he wrote "A Rose for Emily." I think he liked her too. (55)

Gwin addresses the questions of whether feminist scholarship can contribute to Faulkner studies, whether feminist readers learn from canonical male writers, and what the effects of those readings are. She notes that the Faulkner scholarly community is male dominant, using male discourse that positions the feminist critic outside, "in somewhat the same sense, I think, that Rosa Coldfield and her hysterical voice remain outside the margins of the male discourse of southern patriarchy" (57), leaving the question "what *is* a feminist critic's position *vis-à-vis* this male community, and (how) do we speak within a male-dominated system about male texts?" (57–58). Just as Rosa provides the difference in the male text, the hysteric's voice that disrupts the patriarchal system, feminist critics "are the voices of difference in male scholarly communities; we serve a narrative function in that we create tension" (61). While stating that finding "authentic female subjectivity" will be achieved reading female authors, Gwin does stake out work for feminist critics in Faulkner: "Some male writers create fascinating female characters that they allow to disrupt the texts they inhabit. Faulkner is one of those. Some male writers have intimate knowledge of hegemonic structures which oppress women and people of color and a particular talent for revealing their workings. Faulkner is sometimes one of those as well" (64).

Faulkner criticism has never been uniform. While influential early critics labeled him a misogynist, others argued that his women characters escaped stereotypes, with both positive and negative portrayals. Various critics questioned the binary roles of male/female in Faulkner's texts, along with his portrayals of "masculine" and "feminine." Building on these shifts, a number of writers have produced new readings of Faulkner.

REDRAWING THE MAP

> Seldom has a writer examined so thoroughly and so obsessively the concept of woman as other. Yet ultimately the boundaries of that "otherness" break down, and women become uncannily and paradoxically the emblems of his fictional vision.
> (Clarke, *Robbing the Mother* 6)

One of the ways Catherine Stimpson lists for feminist critics to proceed is "by establishing the unreliability of other maps because they overlook or misconstrue women and the issue of gender" (251). Much of the feminist criticism of Faulkner begins by pointing out where earlier critics have, in their view, overlooked, misconstrued, or relied overmuch on the opinions of Faulkner's male characters. Elisabeth Muhlenfeld says of Leslie Fiedler's judgments, "it is difficult to see how the critic could have been more wrong" (290). Jenny Jenning Foerst claims that taking Mr. Compson's and Quentin's story in *Absalom, Absalom!* as true while ignoring Rosa Coldfield's "belies a prevalent critical prejudice" (38). About *Sanctuary,* Abby H. P. Werlock says, "The general critical approach seems to be this: 'Of course these men are bad, and no one questions that rape is a terrible thing. That concluded, let us proceed to examine Temple Drake's depravity'" (11). [See also chapter 6.]

Against these readings, many feminist critics create new maps of meaning in Faulkner's fiction. Feminist critics have produced a large enough, and different enough, body of work that summarizing it briefly proves impossible. Two collections provide a good starting point for readers wishing to familiarize themselves with the criticism: the proceedings of the 1985 Faulkner and Yoknapatawpha Conference devoted to his portrayal of women (*Faulkner and Women: Yoknapatawpha, 1985,* edited by Doreen Fowler [see chapter 8] and Ann J. Abadie) and a special edition of the *Faulkner Journal* devoted to "Faulkner and Feminisms" (4.1–2 [Fall 1988/Spring 1989]). The introduction to *Faulkner and Women* points out, "while the subject of Faulkner in relation to women has elicited a welcome outpouring of critical enthusiasm, so complex and problematic is this field of inquiry that as yet there has been little consensus on the most fundamental questions" (vii). While there may be little consensus, these two volumes illustrate several major directions for feminist inquiry.

Several articles set out to establish the unreliability of other critical maps. To point out the links between "Faulkner Studies and Women's Studies," Ilse Dusoir Lind argues that feminist criticism has much to offer the study of Faulkner: working "with the determination to include women's experience and outlook, rather than to exclude it, it is more self-consciously ideological and hence more able to bring what it examines into sharper focus. This is why, when the insights provided by such outstanding feminist studies as these are brought to bear upon unresolved problems in the Faulkner field, they manifest so surprising a capacity to correct" ("Mutual" 38–39). John N. Duvall discusses various previous interpretations, making the point that "the interpretative community of Faulkner critics, on matters of sexual politics, frequently sound like the good people of Jefferson." He advocates approaching the texts with "radical suspicion, particularly of those ways of describing character relations that seem more secure" ("Faulkner's Critics" 55).

Several articles offer new critical assumptions about the portrayal of women. Sergei Chakovsky claims that "from his outset as a novelist Faulkner's inner tendency in the depiction of women has been from stereotype to individuality, from superficial to mythologizing to the realistic comprehension of their full-fledged humanity" (71). Phillip Weinstein, in "Meditations on the Other: Faulkner's Rendering of Women," discusses the different way women are approached in the narratives. Male characters are seen in community, interacting with each other, while female characters are isolated, seen only from the outside, leaving them "considerably handicapped, from a narrative perspective, when compared with his men" (97). Myriam Díaz-Diocaretz, in "Woman as Bounded Text," points out the constraints placed on women, arguing that "underneath Faulkner's aesthetic questioning and the arrangement of his argument centered on women, we must also acknowledge the makings of an alternative vision implying that perhaps women are not what they are said to be; the transcendence of such a rendering reveals Faulkner's testing of his own presuppositional design for women" (259). Diane Roberts looks at the character of Temple Drake, noting that she "has a powerful story, an *empowering* story to tell; in examining the assaults on her body and her mind, we can recover the feminine in Faulkner in a way that honors and enriches it" ("Ravished" 22, italics in original).

Critics also address what Stimpson summarizes as "charting the cultural representations of gender, patterns of masculinity and femininity" and "showing the complex relation among these representations and patterns of masculine dominance" (251) Doreen Fowler addresses Joe Christmas's antipathy to the "womanshenegro," pointing out that women and blacks are both victimized in *Light in August.* Joe, refusing to be identified with the weak, treats them with contempt. She concludes that, "with Joe Christmas, Faulkner implies that male/female, black/white distinctions are not irreconcilable opposites, but rather only the opposing ends of one continuum" ("Joe" 159). Marsha Warren uses Kristeva to analyze Quentin Compson in "Time, Space, and Semiotic Discourse in the Feminization/Disintegration of Quentin Compson." She concludes that, "by denying time and ultimately language through the silence of death and the fragmentation of order, Quentin denies the very organizing principle of gendered identity—male or female. And it is this genuine threat of subversion that must be disguised as somehow reinscriptive of the symbolic" (110); the symbolic order—male, linear, patriarchal—is challenged but ultimately reinforced, inscribed again upon the struggle.

Michel Frann discusses Faulkner's "preoccupation with male feminization" (5), using the term "lesbian author." "Faulkner's 'lesbianism' consists in a **doubling** of a version or versions of the feminine generated by a masculine ideology characterized by gynophobia, misogyny, and male gender anxiety" (11). Gail Mortimer looks at cognitive mindset: "The decisive separateness between self and other, the cautious attitude toward the unknown, and the dichotomized thinking so characteristic of Faulkner's protagonists are part of a mindset seen by Bardo, Chodorow, and Gilligan as essentially masculine" ("Masculinity" 79), and Faulkner's "particular genius is that he should have expressed so candidly and powerfully the implications of such a cognitive style" (80).

Feminist psychoanalytical theories offer new ways to interpret the texts. Karen Sass uses Chodorow to look at male-female relationships in *The Hamlet,* concluding that the polarization of the genders (for instance, Houston and Lucy, Ab and Mink Snopes and their wives) results in the males "disempowering the women who become their wives and often holding them in contempt. This relationship between men and women sets the stage for these mistreated wives to become an abjected maternal image for their children, ensuring the continuation of the rural patriarchy" ("Rejection" 137). Doreen Fowler discusses *As I Lay Dying,* concluding that it's about "matricide and a mother's revenge" ("Matricide" 113). Drawing on Irigaray and Chodorow, Fowler argues that the Bundrens can enter the symbolic order only with Addie's death, which they each desire; Addie seeks revenge against "a patriarchal order that mandates the mother's death" (115). Other articles in these two collections point out the directions of much later scholarship on Faulkner—the representations of gender, the psychological implications of the characters, and the language of "masculinity" and "femininity."

Several book-length feminist studies of Faulkner offer insights into the ways different readings affect the interpretation of his works. In *The Feminine and Faulkner: Reading (Beyond) Sexual Difference,* Minrose Gwin builds on the works of Luce Irigaray, Julie Kristeva, Alice Jardine, and Hélène Cixous to show that Faulkner, "becomes in his greatest works the creator of female subjects who, in powerful and creative ways, disrupt and sometimes even destroy patriarchal structures" (4).

She seeks out "those in-between spaces where the codes constituting character intersect cultural codes and create the relationship of character to cultural matrix, out of which both character and authorial voice(s) emerge" (5). These in-between spaces rely "on a willingness to accept uncertainty and decentering" (7). She points out the places, like Rosa's interruptions in *Absalom, Absalom!* or Caddy's refusal to be silenced in *The Sound and the Fury,* where feminine voices disrupt the text and undermine the patriarchal or male story being told. Gwin draws on Cixous's theories of pre-Oedipal "bisexuality" in writing, claiming "it denotes an *exacerbation* of both male and female elements in the self and in writing. Bisexual writing is in a permanent state of tension" (10, italics in original). In the creation of some of his characters, "this area of 'in-between' affirms rather than denies difference but *at the same time* dissolves binary constructions of gender" (11, italics in original). The female in Faulkner serves as "a group of superimposed codes, which serves as a matrix of semiotic, psychoanalytic, and cultural interaction" (16).

In *The Sound and The Fury,* according to Gwin, Caddy Compson's simultaneous presence and absence confounds our abilities to see her clearly. To Benjy, she is the maternal who communicates with him in semiotic language. Quentin and Jason both try to construct order out of symbolic language to silence her, but both fail. She disrupts their narratives again and again. Gwin argues that even though Caddy "disappears" from the text after the third section, her voice lingers on in the "in-between space . . . the difference that deconstructs phallic authority" (55). In the midst of the male narratives about her, Caddy resists others' efforts to control and silence her.

In *The Wild Palms,* Charlotte's "feminine 'flooding' leads us into the bisexual spaces, the fluid fluctuations in Faulkner's writing which allow us a way of reading and thinking outside binary opposition" (30). Gwin sees the parallel stories connected by feminine desire. The two texts operate like the bends in a river, where new channels are formed: "a new channel *between* stories out of the flooding of female sexuality" (140, italics in original). (Gwin's treatment of *Absalom! Absalom!* is discussed later.)

Gwin sets out to let the female characters speak to her instead of accepting the narrative interpretation. In *The Feminine and Faulkner,* Gwin constructs meaning out of the silences, the filters through which we see the characters, and their own voices, which even though usually told through another narrator, refuse to be silenced even with great effort. The in-between space proves an apt metaphor for Faulkner, with his multiple narrations, conflicting and missing facts, and intertextuality. All readers must fill in the gaps, and Gwin sets out her own process of hearing what is not said.

Deborah Clarke, in *Robbing the Mother: Women in Faulkner,* analyzes women characters in relation to the maternal. She uses a variety of theoretical approaches, including Nancy Chodorow's object-relations theory in mothers who recreate themselves in their daughters and identify "permeable ego boundaries"; Julia Kristeva's contention that poetic language arises from the dialectic between semiotic (the communication between mother and child that precedes language) and symbolic (language) discourse; and Jacobus and Sprengnether's location of identity at birth and its corresponding loss, not in the Oedipal, the realm of the Father of Freud and Lacan. Clarke claims she sets out to examine how "Faulkner's texts reflect, challenge, and undermine established cultural paradigms," since an author, however, influenced by society, "questions the beliefs which underlie his or her culture and analyzes both the power and limitations of such paradigms" (17).

Beginning with Faulkner's assertion that good writing "is worth any number of old ladies," Clarke sees "a movement from body to language, literal to figurative, semiotic to symbolic, feminine to masculine" (7). Her chapters analyze *The Sound and the Fury* and *As I Lay Dying* ("Erasing and Inventing Motherhood"), *Sanctuary* and *The Hamlet* ("Sexuality, Inhumanity, and Violation"), *Light in August* and *The Wild Palms* ("Bodies and Language"), and *Absalom, Absalom!* ("Fantastic Women and Notmothers"). She pairs *The Sound and The Fury* and *As I Lay Dying* because, in her terms: "both books reverberate with the paradoxical power of women's bodily absence and presence, of women's silence and language. Both examine men's desperate attempts to deal with maternal absence, to use language is a replacement for the mother" (19). The very facts of their bodies fascinate and repel the other characters.

In *Sanctuary* and *The Hamlet,* Clarke looks at the threatening nature of female sexuality to the worlds of the novels. For instance, Eula Varner "uncovers that Frenchman's Bend is a figure of speech, highlights the fictionality of masculinity, and challenges the barter system on which the social discourse is grounded" (89). Eula and Temple provide "the excess which jams the machinery of patriarchal society" (91).

In *Light in August* and *The Wild Palms,* Clarke finds "considerable similarity in their multi-plot structures, their pairing of a procreating and a murdered woman, and their evocation of the language gap as central to the problems between men and women" (108). (Clarke's treatment of *Absalom, Absalom!* is discussed later in this chapter.)

Diane Roberts's *Faulkner and Southern Womanhood* traces Southern stereotypes of women through Faulkner's novels: the Confederate Woman, the Mammy, the Tragic Mulatta, the New Belle, the Night Sisters, and Mothers. She first grounds each type in Southern culture and literature and then discusses its appearance in Faulkner's work.

> Women, along with blacks, are the objects of the South's most careful defining and categorizing. Yet women in Faulkner can dissolve the boundaries. Women can slip toward black. Women are Other precisely because they imperil this symbolic order. Faulkner's fictions often show a culture determined to reassert boundaries and failing, as the class, race, and gender roles on which the South sustains itself collapse. (xiv)

She discusses the social, cultural, and historical contexts of those stereotypes and concludes that, "while political and social forces were trying to reinscribe the binary and tear it apart, Faulkner makes fiction out of the struggle" (xv).

Roberts offers numerous examples of the types in Faulkner's work and how he uses those types. For the Confederate Women, she discusses Granny Millard, Drusilla Hawk, and the women of *Absalom, Absalom!* For the Mammy, she discusses *Soldiers' Pay, The Reivers, The Unvanquished, Go Down, Moses, The Sound and The Fury,* and several short stories. The Night Sister discusses unmarried women in a variety of works. Throughout this study, Roberts shows how Faulkner was influenced by his culture—its mores, its traditions, its literature—and how he used those influences in creative and sometimes startling ways. Looking at these types and "reading them against the Souths that created them for different social purposes, or reinvented them at crucial moments in history, can provide insight into the anxieties and aspirations of a culture. Looking for how Faulkner responds to them, remaining, revising, recovering, helps us to understand Faulkner as a writer making fiction out of a time and place" (xii). For a useful analysis of the books by Gwin, Clarke, and Roberts, see Anne Goodwyn Jones's essay-review, "Female, Feminine, Feminist, Femme, Faulkner."[1]

If we view Faulkner criticism as a continuum, from Fielder's misogyny to Gwin's bisexual spaces, myriad voices fill in the spaces between.

THE CASE OF *ABSALOM, ABSALOM!*

Absalom, Absalom! provides an illustration of the various positions that feminist critics stake out. While much of the earlier critical focus on *Absalom, Absalom!* concerns Sutpen and his patriarchal design, Susan V. Donaldson asks the following:

> What happens, though, if we consciously resist the stories told by and about Thomas Sutpen, if we direct our attention not to Sutpen, the center of those stories, but to their margins and shadows? In short, what happens if we read as feminist readers and refuse to accept the making of history in *Absalom, Absalom!* as inevitable or "natural"? . . . We might discover, in fact, not one but two stories, one about the making of historical narrative and patriarchy and one about their unmaking. ("Subverting" 19–20)

Numerous critics have focused on the unmaking of the story, with various conclusions. According to Gwin, in *Absalom! Absalom!* male characters attempt to shut Rosa Coldfield up. Mr. Compson, Quentin, and Shreve all collaborate to create the symbolic language of Sutpen's design; they share the story by speaking. However, "this Rosa Coldfield, won't stay in *or* stay out of the Father's House; she won't shut up and she won't stay put" (*Feminine* 114). Rosa is the hysteric who confronts those around her with their own madness. In a novel with numerous abrupt shifts, gaps in the narrative, narrative lines stopping and starting, the "in between space" says much: " . . . while Quentin allows himself to be encoded by one master narrative of culture, while he denies bisexuality, difference, madness, women, *his own text speaks against him. . . .* But what he also says is the cost of writing the narrative of mastery." That cost requires the negation of Rosa. The interplay of the two narratives "writes the gaps and ruptures within patriarchal culture. This tension in turn creates a bisexual space in the novel, which, like the hysteric, emerges to write its own mad text of **alterity**," that "curls around upon us in a mysterious yet highly political way, to affirm its own madness by affirming the difference it configures as feminine" (121, italics in original).

Jenny Jennings Foerst looking, like Gwin, at the "bisexual spaces" of the text, finds that, "by replacing female performative agency with static tropes that, paradoxically, *represent* female agency, Mr. Compson creates a mad, deconstructing rhetorical text without, of course, realizing that it is such" (38, italics in original). The bisexual tension exists "between male inscription and the silencing of its subsumed voices, between male presence and female absence" (39). One central issue of Foerst's discussion concerns the myth of Psyche and the quest for psychic wholeness, where one can emerge as an individual. Ellen the butterfly and Rosa the chrysalis, as Mr. Compson calls them, refuse to stay in their cocoons shut away from the world.

The male narrators fail, ultimately, at their goal:

> Performatively, Rosa, though silenced, *is* center: her rhetorical enactments of male myth and male madness, if recognized, restore Rosa's status as the female subject both authorially originating *Absalom, Absalom!* and authoritatively blocking its, and therefore her, status as a literary product finished by men. Paradoxically, *because we do not* receive her story as a finished object, we must continually refer the failure of it to emerge as a coherent "whole" among the male texts to the persistence of that "hole," that silent center, because vortex, of all the collectively incoherent male superscriptions." (50, italics in original)

Thus, the narration undermines the performative goal of its male tellers. By continually attempting to reduce the female characters to fixed images, Mr. Compson, Quentin, and Shreve undermine their own attempts to create a patriarchal story.

Other interpretations focus on the women characters, both in terms of characterization and narrative function. Donaldson focuses on "characters who seem to live in the breaks and empty spaces of the narrative, who threaten to disrupt and even destroy the continuities of history woven by the narrators" ("Subverting" 20–21): Ellen, Judith, Sutpen's first wife, and Clytie. While the male narrators and characters attempt to tell the story, "they re-enact the line of succession that Sutpen himself yearns to establish—the passing of grand design from father to son" (23). The four characters listed above, while perhaps marginal to the story told, persist in subverting and disrupting the main story, telling the "muted" or "untold" story instead. As contradictory characters, they resist the male narrators' attempts to classify them. In narrative terms, they also disrupt the story itself; Donaldson points out numerous examples of the presence of these characters creating breaks in the sequence, transporting the narrative back and forth in time (28). And Clytie, Donaldson points out, brings the whole tale to an end by burning down the house. These female characters are "the empty space providing not just the tools for making patriarchy and narrative but also the breaks, discontinuities and precipitous endings bringing that effort to a close" (30).

In her discussion of the Confederate Woman, Roberts looks at the female characters as the ghosts of the narrative. While readers might first see them as subordinate to the story, "this would be a mistake. Rosa Coldfield, Clytemnestra Sutpen, Eulalia Bon, Ellen Coldfield, the Octoroon, Judith, Milly: these are the specters, living or dead; inhabiting, frustrating, held hostage to, Sutpen's 'design.' They are the ghosts worth listening to as they conjure the past" (*Faulkner* 27–28). Their role is "like poltergeists disguising, shifting things around, creating diversions" (29). Judith Sutpen, a character created by the narrators' voices in the text, also faces the male narrators' attempts to contain her, but according to Roberts, they fail: "She is freed to express herself, if not in language, in the very disruption she occasions" (39). Clytie, an example of the Tragic Mulatto, also disrupts the story. She blurs the lines between black and white, between slaves and masters and "offers a glimpse into a world on the brink of racial and sexual collapse" (100).

Heloísa Toller Gomes also discusses women characters wanting to assert their identity. Discussing Faulkner and José Lins do Rego, she says, "woman submits herself—socially, economically, morally—to the demands of a society in which masculine values prevail. However, as she is not directly involved in issues of class and competition whose resolution is delegated to man, woman allows herself to think," and she is "capable of thinking and of questioning and demystifying the values she had been taught to honour" (57). The male characters in the novel see the women as inferior, as existing only in terms of the sexual economy. The women, in turn, criticize their treatment, as Rosa Coldfield does in describing her childhood and her treatment by Sutpen. Because the women must "sublimate her repressed instincts," they in turn "replace them by a rigid sense of morality" (61) and often respond with cruelty to those around them who also appear inferior, relying on their own privileged social position. These social realities bring negative consequences to the women characters, and Gomes claims that Faulkner criticizes that world: "The literary discourse, by means of fictive plots, characterizations, descriptions, weaves a sombre feminine landscape, which it criticizes with lucidity. Submission . . . materializes itself at the cost of one's own identity" (66).

Deborah Clarke argues that while women in Faulkner often appear contradictory, with dual natures, in *Absalom, Absalom!* they go beyond conventional reality to the fantastic, where the limits of real and unreal come into question. Mothers are mostly absent in the novel, yet "maternal power is eerily transformed into a far more pervasive force, reaching beyond mothers and, for the first time in Faulkner's work, beyond white women as well" (*Robbing the Mother* 126). The women seem fantastic, in part, due to the male characters' descriptions and explanations of them. The male characters, who see female bodies as incidental to patrilineal descent, transform them into something else—ghosts, butterflies, vampires. However, the women defy male attempts to turn them into the supernatural.

For Clarke, Rosa doesn't move between semiotic and symbolic discourse, but uses both at once. Her emphasis on what she didn't witness and her love for Charles Bon, whom she has never seen, point out her creation of the stories. Rosa's power is "explicitly feminine yet separated from maternity" (140); she is the "not-mother." As such, "she functions as a source both of negation, in her refusal to bear Sutpen sons, and productivity, in her originating the tale itself" (140).

Judith also confounds their descriptions "becoming not mother nor love nor empty vessel of imaginative fantasy, as Henry and Charles are forced to break through the illusions and confront each other as they truly are: similarly descended but racially different" (144). She confounds Quentin's and Shreve's descriptions as well. Rosa, Judith, and other aunts in the novel overshadow mothers, with the "notmothers" (including Quentin) taking over her role: the unleashed maternal power "usurps even the paternal function, taking maternal duality beyond a merging of sameness and difference, self and other, to a collapse of feminine and masculine" (148).

Clytie also refuses to be categorized, taking her place in the family despite all of society's strictures. Clytie represents miscegenation in her very body; her "existence and position uncover the lack of logic at the core of southern notions of segregation and racial purity and denies them universal status" (149). For Clarke, "Clytie is what Dilsey is not: a powerful black mother" (150). With its collection of notmothers, aunts, and African Americans, *Absalom, Absalom!* presents "a powerful maternal challenge" (152) that goes beyond language, race, and gender.

Critics have also seen Sutpen's own contributions to the unmaking of his history. Joseph A. Boone analyzes Sutpen's father-centered plot to show how it undermines itself. Once the story finally gets told, it "ends up being less a demonstration of the ubiquity of the father than of the threats to paternal ubiquity that make the father's story an impossibility from its very inception." Sutpen's authority is "founded on a profound anxiety about the meaning of masculinity itself" (211). This anxiety stems from all the repressed elements in the novel, the "visible signifiers of otherness, of nonmaleness" (212). Boone concludes that despite all the efforts of repression, Sutpen's story is doomed by those very elements. "Escaping the shapers of dynastic and narrative designs by their very exclusion, these transgressive elements remain, then, to unravel the ends whereby the father would explain his origins and to return the reader to the obsessions that remain in play, despite the paternal effort to repress difference, in the midst of a story doomed by its very premises never to end" (232). [See also chapter 6.]

John N. Duvall discusses the novel, along with *Uncle Tom's Cabin* and *Beloved,* as ghost stories, or stories that explore the "ghostly space." Duvall sees *Uncle Tom's Cabin* as upholding a patriarchal order, unlike Faulkner's, which "through the character of Thomas Sutpen, scrutinizes the epistemic base of logocentrism," making it "available for feminist analysis" ("Authentic" 89). Sutpen adheres to the values of Derrida's definition of logocentrism: belief in an external, fixed truth beyond challenge. Hélène Cixous adds that logocentrism causes binary thought—male/female, culture/nature, and so forth—in which the male is always privileged. Duvall discusses how Sutpen's whole world operates in terms of binaries. Ghosts emerge in the novel in the moment of nonrecognition—his first wife, Rosa, Milly, and Charles Bon. "An economy is created in the novel by which each act of repudiation is a repetition of the social repressed—namely, the mutually constitutive play of the terms comprising the binary oppositions that undergird patriarchy" (90). Sutpen actively denies the feminine in all of its forms, ultimately causing his downfall.

Duvall discusses the primal scene in the barn, where Henry is forced to watch his father fight his slaves, with Judith and Clytie watching in the hayloft. By "attempting a purely masculine transmission, he [Sutpen] insures that the son is positioned passively in the role of the cultural feminine" (91). Henry's "femininity" makes him an unsuitable heir, just as Charles Bon's blackness does. The scene in the colonel's tent, when Sutpen acknowledges Henry as his son, both enacts Sutpen's design and dooms it. "Henry kills the brother he loves to earn the love of his father; as a result, both of Sutpen's 'tainted' sons are removed: the 'feminine' son's removal of the 'black' son simultaneously removes the 'feminine' son" (93).

By focusing on the unmaking of the story, critics have paid attention to the margins, the ruptures, the silences. In the midst of a story that stops, starts, doubles back on itself, the gaps in the novel can tell us much. The male narrators continually try to marginalize the women (and the feminine and the maternal), and sometimes, they succeed. Yet, what they reject and trivialize disrupts Sutpen's design and the male narrators' story, and the feminist criticism points out a number of possible explanations for the undoing.

THE FUTURE AND ITS QUESTIONS

> In discussing Faulkner's women characters I shall not attach labels to Faulkner's attitudes toward women nor to the women he created: simple classifications are inadequate for either the author's attitudes or for the characters he created, men or women alike. (Kerr, "The Women" 83)

Discussing *The Sound and The Fury* in a graduate class, I clearly remember my professor saying, "Caddy doesn't speak in the novel because Faulkner couldn't write a woman's voice. Faulkner only gives us male perspectives." She summed up the portrayal of women in Faulkner with one word: sexist. At that moment, I became both a resisting reader and a resisting student. Like Minrose Gwin, I could "hear" Caddy. I could also hear Mr. Compson's and Jason's sexist views of her. Yet, the very things that drew me to Faulkner's fiction in the first place, the multivalence of truth, the numerous perspectives, the variety of writing, made me resist any simple categorization of what Faulkner did or did not do. For the same reason, I'll admit, I'm often a resisting reader of Faulkner criticism, believing that Faulkner's works defy encapsulating in theory just as much as Sutpen's story defies the telling. Nevertheless, feminist criticism has proffered illuminating psychological, sociological, and linguistic insights into Faulkner that have deepened my understanding of his work.

In the very complexity of his fiction, Faulkner offers fertile ground to feminist critics. His fictional renderings of his culture's view toward women—both the stereotypes and bounded conditions, and his critiques of the same—underscore the shifting grounds of gender representation and expectations. Mr. Compson's proclamations on what women are like, his sons' reactions to their sister, Horace Benbow's reaction to Temple Drake, Joe Christmas's revulsion of the "woman-shenegro," and Byron Snopes's romantic yearnings all contribute to Faulkner's depiction of his society's views of women, its definitions of masculinity and femininity, and the great anxiety produced as a result. And for every man with a patriarchal design or an attempt to uphold the system—Sutpen, Jason Compson, Doc Hines—we can find a corresponding woman protesting—Rosa, Caddy, Mrs. Hines.

The paradoxical position of women in the South (both on the pedestal and inferior) creates similarly paradoxical patterns of representation in Faulkner's fiction. For instance, before we see Emily Grierson's and Minnie Cooper's horrific acts, we see how their communities have written them off, how they're bound by others' expectations. Female sexuality runs the gamut from Dewey Dell's full-sack logic to Caddy Compson's teenage defiance, to Joanna Burden's "phases," to Rosa Coldfield's virginity. Women in Faulkner are both stereotypical and varied, both ineffectual and threatening, both victim and perpetrator, both "masculine" and "feminine." Faulkner offers no "truth" about women, or men, or their relationships to each other: not one stereotype, but many. Feminist critics have broadened our understandings of what those shifting paradigms mean.

With *Absalom, Absalom!*, Faulkner creates male narrators who attempt to tell a patriarchal story patriarchally, while women (and Sutpen himself) continually disrupt both Sutpen's and those narrators' plans. It's a story made for considerations of gender representation, male-female relationships, "masculine" and "feminine" discourse, and the undermining of patriarchal authority. It's also a story made to be read "against." While Rosa Coldfield's story may be "muted," she is not silenced. Whether Rosa is subdued, subsumed, shut up, or successful, one thing is clear: she emerges as a far more complicated character than Mr. Compson, Quentin, Shreve, and Sutpen perceive her. While Sutpen reacts to the binary of black and white, Clytie and Charles Bon stand in his way. For all Mr. Compson's attempts to turn Ellen into a butterfly, she remains a woman.

I still wrestle with the same questions about Faulkner and his characters that arose in that graduate class, and I know that Faulkner was there before me, asking the same questions himself. Feminist analysis has answered some questions for me, left some unanswered, and created new ones, including the following: Can feminist criticism contribute further to Faulkner studies? Can even those of us who find ourselves "resisting readers" of feminist theory learn from its conclusions? In other words, in those times when we find the theory "performative," can we still draw "constative" conclusions from its insights? Does feminist criticism subvert binary readings of the text, or set up new binaries all its own? Does Caddy Compson betray her brothers or do they betray her? Does Addie Bundren produce the outrage or react to it? Do his male characters speak for Faulkner on this subject or is the truth in the "in-between space" of the text? Does Joe Christmas's "womanshenegro" define women and blacks in Faulkner or define Christmas's own limitations? Does Faulkner reify his society's ideas about gender or does he undermine them? Does Faulkner uphold the patriarchal order or deconstruct it?

Yes, yes, yes, yes, yes, yes.

NOTE

1. *Mississippi Quarterly* 47.3 (Summer 1994): 521–45.

10

Rhetorical and Reader-Response Criticism

Pamela Knights

Q. . . . [I]n *Absalom, Absalom!* does any one of the people who talks about Sutpen have the right view, or is it more or less a case of thirteen ways of looking at a blackbird with none of them right? A. . . . [E]xactly. . . . when the reader has read all . . . thirteen different ways of looking at the blackbird, the reader has his own fourteenth image of that blackbird which I would like to think is the truth.[1]

INTRODUCTION

Being told that our response holds the "truth" of a text might come as a surprise to many readers—writers and literary critics seldom credit us with such importance. Faulkner himself, in other interviews, emphasized the supremacy of the writing—"I myself am too busy to care about the public. I have no time to wonder who is reading me."[2] Traditional literary appreciation, too, kept the spotlight upon the author and the work, guiding the audience in how to value, to interpret, and to understand. Contemporary critical theory has shown less ambition to illuminate literature; much of it aims, rather, to make readers question what they are seeing, to dismantle certainties about the centrality of authorship or the stability of meaning. Readers even feature from time to time in its arguments—for example, in this *Companion,* we meet them as gendered [see chapter 9] or historical subjects [see chapter 2], as case studies in psychological investigations [see chapter 8], or as celebrants in postmodern textual play [see chapter 6]. Nevertheless, the texts and their interpretation remain at the center of attention. The approaches in this chapter, however, place the reader (or us) in the foreground. Rather than suggesting yet further "readings" of Faulkner's (or any author's) work, these approaches take us back into the experience of reading itself, and in so doing, offer us new roles and relationships. Some versions of this criticism give more emphasis to Faulkner's rhetoric—his power to influence us through his language—and to the ways his texts control, define, or even create us as a new kind of audience; others highlight our responses more vigorously—the ways we react to, engage with, or even, in turn, create the texts. But, whether casting us as sensitive recipients or active coauthors, reader-oriented approaches assign us a significant part in the literary process and in the critical enterprise.

In Anglo-American criticism, such approaches emerged as an influential constellation only during the 1970s, well after William Faulkner's death; they remained visible throughout the 1980s, but by the early 1990s had been eclipsed by other theoretical interests. However, we can glimpse some of their tendencies in reactions to Faulkner as early as the 1930s, and they continue to register in the reception of his work today. Many of the perspectives in this chapter shade into those discussed elsewhere in this volume, and readers will find that this category brings together critics who might otherwise seem theoretically and temperamentally far apart, from formalists to feminists, psychological critics to poststructuralists. Precise definition, however, is impossible. "Rhetorical and Reader-Response Criticism" is a deceptively tidy classification, embracing numerous groups and individuals, who worked with a wide variety of critical practices, rooted in very different intellectual traditions; and even at the height of their influence, only a few identified themselves as part of a distinct movement.

It is little wonder, then, that most general introductions to this topic sound cautionary notes. In 1980, at the start of *The Reader in the Text,* a landmark collection of original essays on reader-response theory, Susan Suleiman memorably warned that those setting out into this terrain are faced with "a multiplicity of divergent tracks . . . whose complexity dismays the brave and confounds the faint of heart."[3] If identifying an approach brings problems, so too does defining "the reader" whose "response" the general label evokes. Like the unitary "we" I conventionally address in this chapter, this is a simplifying shortcut, disguising differences. In almost every instance, the reader's specific "character" underwent often-radical variations and revisions as an individual critic's approach evolved, and new branches of the species multiplied like Snopeses.

Many of these will lie beyond the scope of this chapter. A thorough survey would need a lengthy book. At one end of the spectrum, for example, we find analyses drawing on the traditional schema of classical and Renaissance rhetoric (from the neo-Aristotelian work of R. S. Crane and the Chicago group in the 1950s to James A. Snead's Faulknerian "figures of division" in the 1980s) and at the other, empirical studies of real readers, or the pedagogic projects described in *College English,* where many of the most animated reader debates of the 1970s were aired. (The special issue entitled "'The' Reader, and Real Readers" in 1975 offers a particularly lively cross section.) We might include, too, statistical accounts of stylistic or linguistic data that strike some literature students as more akin to the discourses of science. (In the 1970s, the Faulkner chapter in the annual review, *American Literary Scholarship,* reserved a special section for these relatively neglected topics, but eventually broadened the category to include more-familiar matters of technical form.) Or we might look at speech-act theory—the contention that literary texts, too, like vows, curses, or prom-ises, can be "performative utterances," of the same order as everyday discourse. (So Mary Louise Pratt suggests that even Benjy Compson's poetically charged fragments arise along the same language continuum as ordinary speech.[4]) Again, we might spend time on the assorted post-Romantic schools of aesthetic philosophy that energized much reader-oriented theory in continental Europe: phenomenology, hermeneutics, and reception theory *(Rezeptionsästhetik)*—the studies of Hans Robert Jauss and the "school of Konstanz," which place our readings of any individual text within the light of the ever changing "horizon of expectation" shed by our experience of previous works. Any one of these labels would open up many subgroupings—phenomenology, alone, ranges from Roman Ingarden's explorations of the structure of the literary work of art and its "concretization" in the mind and imagination of the reader to the work of the "Geneva school," associated with Georges Poulet among others, who saw in the act of reading the encounter of the reader's innermost self with a work's essence, its expressive consciousness. (This group influenced the early work of the American critic J. Hillis Miller, and the shade of the reader continues to haunt his later deconstructive criticism.) We might then turn to the scrutinies of read-ing conventions—embedded in analysis of the minutiae of textual codes and reading strategies—that draw semioticians, narratologists, and structuralists into the reader camp. (Umberto Eco, Michael Riffaterre, Gerald Prince, Gérard Genette, Jonathan Culler, Seymour Chatman, and Robert Scholes all made dis-tinctive contributions to new reader interests.)[5] Beyond these would come the subjective appraisals of texts, written in a personal register, and seeming per-haps classified more fittingly as independent writings, detached from the work of art that stimulated them. And at the furthest limits, perhaps, we would find readers' own creative tributes: the intertexts and the influences, the translations, or even the parodies, that distill "response" into new art forms.

It seems appropriate, then, to add my own warning here and, like Mark Twain, issue an "ordinance" to this book's readers, whoever you are. Hopeful seekers of motives, morals, and plots will not be shot, but anyone seeking instructions on how to apply "Rhetorical and Reader-Response Criticism" to William Faulkner will find no single line of inquiry, distinctive methodology, or central theoretical position. Instead, this chapter will attempt to present something of the history, rationale, and critical life of these approaches by retracing some of the dialogue between Faulkner's texts and their readers. Unlike some of the approaches else-where in this *Companion,* reader theories emerged dynamically from uniquely literary engagements—particularly with startling or strenuous texts for which existing approaches seemed inadequate. In the United States, Faulkner's work was a significant presence in many of the pioneering and most influential explo-rations into reader-response territory, and this suggests that, at times, we are see-ing a two-way process. It was not merely that certain critics began to apply to Faulkner analytical tools developed in relation to other texts or (as with psychoanalytical theories) within another discipline, but that the experience of reading Faulkner's texts themselves helped to produce new approaches more closely attuned to the excitement and the energies of his writing.

Accordingly, I shall enter the field through the responses of some of Faulkner's early readers. Next, within a sketch of some wider contexts for these approaches, I shall look at some of the most significant figures for North American reader-based criticism—Wayne C. Booth, Wolfgang Iser, Stanley Fish, David Bleich, and Norman Holland—and highlight the way these, and others, engaged with Faulkner's writings in establishing their theoretical ground. Then, drawing examples from throughout Faulkner's work, I shall try to outline some of the features that come into particular relief if we take "the reader" as a viewpoint and try to indicate, too, some of the ways Faulknerians have adopted and adapted these perspectives. As the standpoints are so various, I have found no way to organize the survey tidily. To minimize complications, however, I shall avoid rigid demarcation between rhetorical and response approaches, but throughout shall concentrate upon ideas which have given new inflections to our understanding of the reader/text dynamic in Faulkner, and signal (if highly selectively) some of the various forms this interest has taken. In the spirit of these approaches, I have tried, too, to leave space simply to gesture to some possible routes into Faulkner, which you, the reader, are free to ignore, to pursue, or to adapt, as you wish.

EARLY RESPONSES TO FAULKNER

> INTERVIEWER: Some people say they can't understand your writing, even after they read it two or three times. What approach would you suggest for them?
> FAULKNER: Read it four times.[6]

Faulkner's work might seem to be stony ground for approaches that emphasize the reader. His advice to his struggling public was often uncompromising or enigmatic; for many, his texts remained unyielding, even inaccessible—as William Styron observed: "Faulkner doesn't give enough help to the reader."[7] This indifference seemed to emanate from an artistic program that elevated the work at its center. With Flaubert, Symbolist poetry, and T. S. Eliot among his early literary influences, Faulkner often spoke as a natural-born modernist, endorsing an aesthetic of impersonality. Throughout his life, in published prefaces, letters, or conversations with students, he would characteristically refer to his own works as autonomous entities. In many of his most-quoted pronouncements, he muses on the text as a precious artifact (a vase, an urn) or as something not made, but overheard, a product of careful attentiveness, careful listening to "the voices." He would talk, too, of his own characters as if they somehow lived an independent life: at a particular point in the work, he suggested, it is they, not the writer, who "rise up and take charge and finish the job."[8] Yet we might read in such statements a double story—that, in writing as he did, Faulkner was also bringing into being a new kind of reader, one who would put aside preconceptions and work with the dynamics of his ever startling texts.

Faulkner marked his own turning point as an artist (as a writer and a reader) as the day the door clapped silently shut on the outer world and he began to compose *The Sound and the Fury*. For many first-time readers then, as now, his text seemed to defy access: "The deliberate obscurity of the opening pages repels rather than invites; and when the reader perseveres, he struggles out at the other end of Benjy's maunderings with no clearer idea of what has happened, or may be expected to happen, than he had when he entered."[9] In its very excess and extremity, however, *The Sound and the Fury* changed the terms of reading. Percipient reviewers—as we shall see, like theorists subsequently—recognized that its rewards were inseparable from its difficulties and attempted to convey its impact [see chapter 13]. Readers could try to bypass the more refractory passages, extract the Compson history, impose interpretations, or reshape the text according to expectations; but even the most disoriented often communicated some sense of the actual reading process. While Dudley Fitts, the bemused reader above, recommended beginning at page 93 and returning to Benjy's section last, even he declared, "It is the study of Mr. Faulkner's style, the consideration of the book as a rhetorical exercise, as a declamation, that repays the reader."[10] Whether feeling confused, exhilarated, or somewhat resentful, many other readers, too, realized early on that they were being faced with something intensely challenging that asked for new forms of understanding. Viewed with hindsight, their responses seem to bring into the foreground many of the issues and textual experiences that later reader-theorists would attempt to articulate and define.

Faulkner's fellow writer and influence, the poet Conrad Aiken, in an essay appraising the extraordinary decade that had followed *The Sound and the Fury,* gave one of the clearest signposts in 1939. Having read Faulkner's then-most-recent novel, *The Wild Palms,* Aiken had found himself reeling again from the impact of Faulkner's style and was reminded how even "the most passionate" of Faulkner's admirers "must find, with each new novel that the first fifty pages are always the hardest, that each time one must learn all over again *how* to read this strangely fluid and slippery and heavily mannered prose" (243–44).[11] Pursuing Faulkner's stylistic and syntactical idiosyncrasies in an attempt to describe the experience, Aiken kept his eye on the effects. He highlighted the frustration of waiting for the completion of a sentence, of the gaps between subject and object, of the "Chinese eggs" of parentheses, of trailing clauses "shadowily in apposition, or perhaps not even with so much connection as that"; and he described the compulsion—the way Faulkner works on, draws in, the reader through "a process of *immersion,*" hypnotism, fluidity, a sense of a "*continuum*" (245–46, italics in original). Seen from the vantage point of later reader-response approaches, two observations seem especially astute. In the first, Aiken drew an analogy between the micro-units of the sentences and the novel as a whole:

> They parallel . . . the whole elaborate method of *deliberately withheld meaning,* of progressive and partial and delayed disclosure. . . . It is a persistent offering of obstacles, a calculated system of screens and obtrusions, of confusions and

ambiguous interpolations and delays, with one express purpose; and that purpose is simply to keep the form—and the idea—fluid and unfinished, still in motion, as it were, and unknown, until the dropping into place of the very last syllable. (246, italics in original.)

In the second, he confronted the "difficulties for the reader." Admitting that Faulkner does "little or nothing" to clarify matters for us, he suggests that we take up a more active role: "The reader must simply make up his mind to go to work, and in a sense to cooperate" (246). These two poles—the play of Faulkner's rhetorical and narrative devices, and the participatory kind of reader we learn (or they teach us) to become—marked out the main territory for the reader-centered critics who would follow.

THE RISE OF READER THEORIES

When reader perspectives began to enter mainstream discussions at the turn into the 1970s, they confronted an established formalism—literary models (New Criticism in particular) that valued "objectivity" in both the aesthetic work and in criticism. The critic's responsibility was to approach a literary work with a judgment purged (in Wimsatt and Beardsley's famous formulation) of the "intentional" and the "affective" fallacies: that is, leaving both author's purposes or reader's reactions out of any aesthetic assessment. This doctrine of impersonality privileged certain kinds of text (notably, the "verbal icon" of the modernist poem) and downgraded others (especially any with designs on its audience). The heterogeneous discourses of the novel were harder to accommodate; such intrusive elements as authorial intervention or sociological detail adulterated the pure work of art. Where criticism upheld Archibald McLeish's dictum, "A poem should not mean but be," rhetoric seemed a prime offender. Associated, even in popular usage, with excrescence and redundancy ("empty rhetoric"), it signified above all other-directed instrumentality.[12] As Debrah Raschke's chapter [see chapter 5] makes clear, many of Faulkner's novels could be treated, to a degree, as modernist poems. Critics highlighted their unity, their "spatial form"—the patterns and tensions apprehended when the reader had finished reading and could, somehow, hold in mind for aesthetic contemplation the work in its entirety. Others, *A Fable,* for instance, remained less appreciated: doubly tainted with propaganda and allegory, it seemed "an extended piece of rhetoric, rather than a novel."[13]

However, even in the 1930s, some critics and educators (most notably D. W. Harding and Louise Rosenblatt) had questioned New Criticism's confident distinction between the subject and the object of reading. Throughout the heyday of formalism, some voices continued to protest that this dualist paradigm ignored the most important dimensions of any reading: the temporal and the interactive nature of literature. Texts are linear; we engage with words as they unfold in time; we wait in suspense, make predictions, change our minds. When we read, we do not encounter a static, self-contained set of words that we analyze only in retrospect, but we enter an experience, an event—a dynamic happening within the "text-continuum" (the place where author, text, and reader interact). As readers, we "get into" texts, as they get into us.

Of these challenges to formalist limits, Wayne C. Booth's *The Rhetoric of Fiction* (1961) remains a landmark.[14] Among the array of voices in Booth's protracted conversation with the Western novel, Faulkner was an animating presence. For Booth, fiction did not have to be justified by being frozen or spatialized, but was valuable for its own form, its art of communicating with readers. Declaring with Henry James, in his epigraph, "The author makes his readers, just as he makes his characters," Booth sought to make his own audience into nondogmatic participants willing to explore new paths into fiction. Perfection, he pronounced, was impossible in art and "degrees of purity are useless as general criteria" (99). Criticism's major task was to rehabilitate the importance of rhetoric and to defend on aesthetic grounds the techniques through which writers control, move, and influence their audiences. "If the most admired literature is in fact radically contaminated with rhetoric, we must surely be led to ask whether the rhetoric itself may not have had something to do with our admiration" (98–99). Art, in short, cannot simply *"be"* but must always *"mean"*; and readers must work for that meaning. To demonstrate the complex activities that his rhetorical model entailed, Booth, like Aiken, attended to the subtleties of narration, the fine-spun threads through which fiction draws readers into a particular world. For Booth, the "real" author (in his example, the Faulkner who prepares his Stockholm address) was distinct from the "implied author"—the "second self" of the author as he manifests himself to us in every fiber of the literary text (137–38). This implied author creates for us the entire scheme of values of the fictional universe, expressed in every element of the work. Even the seemingly most impartial art, then, seeks to compel our interest through whatever technical means the (implied) author can command: intellectually (through mysteries and problems), qualitatively (through setting up and satisfying various kinds of expectation and patterning), and practically (through sheer concern about the characters).

Booth offered the reader a crucial part in this creative process. Our once-derided "affective" responses, are, he suggested, built into "the very structure of fiction" (133). Like the real author, we too leave behind our actual self to enter the work as an implied, or "postulated," reader. In this role, we become the reader the text creates. If we actively submerge our own beliefs and practices, in a successful reading, we become a kind of mirror image of the implied author, sharing his judgments; we learn the pleasures of the "communion, and even . . . deep collusion" we share with Faulkner behind Jason Compson's back (307). This delight generates a kind of creative energy that assists the author. Where Faulkner saw the characters as finishing the job, Booth gave this role to readers: "In dealing with Jason, we must help Faulkner write his work by rising to our best, most perceptive level"; indeed, "when we have seen all that Faulkner has packed into [a sentence], we feel almost as if we had written it ourselves, so effectively has he demanded of us our best creative effort" (307–8). Booth sought to restore the novel to a central place in a humane value system; for him, one of the deepest rewards of reading is to reach "a mature moral judgment" (307). An approach that values Jason as much as Benjy or Quentin encourages us to enter into dialogue with a novel's voices, each with its own origin, design, compulsion to tell.

Other critics, too, had begun to look more closely at the effects of an author's rhetoric on the reader at the receiving end—and, as with Aiken, reading Faulkner seemed to stimulate such inquiry. Impressionistic criticism had produced ever more extreme metaphors to describe the experience. With Milton Rugoff, we view "as through the windows of a bathysphere, distorted creatures moving through a weird twilight world, performing before our eyes, casually, grotesquely, shamelessly most astonishing acts";[15] and images of readers gasping or drowning in the waves of rhetoric abound elsewhere. Others attempted a more rigorous analysis. Of these, Walter J. Slatoff offered the fullest account. In his view, too, the rhetoric left readers in difficulties, but mainly, he suggested, because Faulkner did not intend the pieces to fall into place.[16] This is a rhetoric of "failure"; Faulkner's stylistic and formal devices express his deepest uncertainties about the nature and meaning of life. To move beyond merely asserting moral and technical parallels, Slatoff tried to describe the moment-by-moment reading experience of encountering Faulkner's fictional "world," from *Sartoris* to *The Town:* the effects on us of the persistent patterns of antitheses, "motion and immobility, sound and silence, and quiescence and turbulence."[17] These extremes of Faulkner's "polar imagination" are concentrated above all in the rhetorical figure of oxymoron ("soundless yelling," "Will Varner is 'both active and lazy'").[18] Creating tension and refusing release, this construction disturbs and prevents our usual desire for logical resolution.

At the start of the 1960s, Slatoff was interested in what such organizing categories revealed about Faulkner's work, his vision, and ultimately his temperament. But he also made interesting speculations about the reader, which pointed forward to other branches of reader-oriented criticism. He suggested, for instance, that Faulkner's writings produce "empathy" in us, because of their "dance"-like dynamic, a mesmeric pattern of tension and release, which stimulates "kinesthetic and motor responses," possibly even "emotional trance."[19] Like the Reverend Shegog, Faulkner works on his audience to suspend intellectual activity—to write to the "heart." This rhetoric produces a different kind of reader, responding through what we might now see as an alternative (emotional, noncognitive, even somatic) form of intelligence. Although Slatoff did not pursue that reader in this early book, it seems as if the experience of reading Faulkner in this way helped to (re)form Slatoff himself as a critic. Here he was already beginning to turn from description to expression, from rhetoric to response, dramatizing in layperson's language the unease he felt at the gap between the reading experience and conventional literary analysis. It was not a long step from reading with the heart to his own polemical contribution 10 years later to the reader debate: *With Respect to Readers: Dimensions of Literary Response.* Here, he urged critics to acknowledge their own biases and to risk themselves in their writing. Each reader needed to tell, not about "the work itself nor the effect of the work on him but his experience of the work," of the text's "own moment-to-moment rhythms and contours"; critics should, above all, express passion, awe, engagement, and admit that after all, "human responses always matter."[20]

In the late 1960s, such alternative models at last began seriously to challenge the dominant New Criticism, and the following decade saw the rise of the "Age of Reading," in M. H. Abrams's term. Coinciding with the stirring of libertarian movements in Europe and North America, this focus on the audience seemed, to traditionalists like Abrams, less a rational literary enterprise than a political demonstration—a pluralistic free-for-all over the explosive issue of correct interpretation.[21] Although Roland Barthes denied a program of "reader's rights," "The Death of the Author" remains a milestone for reader-oriented approaches, as it does for poststructuralist critics. Published in 1968, a year of widespread unrest on campuses, its ending might serve as a rallying cry for a democratic literary practice: "Classic criticism has never paid any attention to the reader; for it, the writer is the only person in literature. . . . we know that to give writing its future, it is necessary to overthrow the myth: the birth of the reader must be at the cost of the death of the Author."[22]

Barthes made clear that his "reader" was a theoretical construction, the place where textual "meanings" came together, not a biographical or historical audience; but many critics moved vocally into the space the Author had vacated. Throughout the 1970s and early 1980s, "Newreaders" (as M. H. Abrams styled them) positioned and repositioned themselves in fierce internal debates about the distribution of energies in the "text-continuum." Should more weight be placed on the rhetoric or on the response? Is meaning "in" the text? Or do we create it? Stanley Fish, primarily a Renaissance scholar, was one of the most colorfully argumentative Newreaders, and attacks on Fish, and his retaliations and recantations, occupied center stage of reader-response theory in the United States throughout the period—"Fish Baits Audience" announced a Kenyon College newspaper editorial after a week of especially exciting combat.[23] In his self-declared manifesto, "Literature in the Reader: Affective Stylistics," written in 1970, Fish spelled out his practice (less a "method," than "a language-sensitizing device"), opposing Wimsatt and Beardsley from the title onwards, to denounce "The Affective Fallacy Fallacy."[24] For Fish, individual interpretations of a text were a second-order event; what the critic needed to describe were the "primary effects," the perceptual responses shared by every reader in the initial encounter with the text: "whether the reader likes or dislikes the experience of Faulkner's delays, he will, in common with every other reader, experience them."[25] Fish's early descriptions of how texts lured him into hypotheses, then jumped out and surprised him were highly influential, but also attracted criticism. As Jonathan Culler summed up, these seemed artificial reconstructions, remote from any intelligent individual's actual responses; and Fish's "informed reader" (the one who has become sensitized to every textual ploy) emerges, in the end, rather, as a poor learner, continually ambushed at every twist of a sentence, and a mere puppet of the rhetoric.[26]

Wolfgang Iser sought to present a less passive model, defining the "implied reader" as a co-creator of the text. Translated from German soon after their first publication in the 1970s, Iser's books stirred up both enthusiasm and violent disagreement in reader-centered circles. (Fish was a strong antagonist.) Like Roman Ingarden and other European theorists of "reception aesthetics," Iser concentrated on how readers "actualize" or "concretize" the work of art.[27] That is, a book remains inert and lifeless until we interact with it, sentence by sentence, sequence by sequence; our expectations, reversals and memories of our initial reactions become part of our reading, transforming the text. We make meanings from the text and feed our responses back through them. The reader, then, is a product of the rhetoric (we are "implied" by the text's prestructuring of its own potential meanings), but also a real agent who brings the text into meaning, through completing its "blanks" or indeterminacies—or as Faulkner might have said, through supplying a final blackbird. Iser took *The Sound and the Fury* as a key example. Faulkner's divided narrative offered a pattern (possibly an inspiration) for his reading model: it is "a sort of no-man's-land of unformulated connections . . . that involve the reader directly in the novel."[28] Iser's metaphor echoes and explains the paradoxical responses of many Faulkner readers: the sense that the text both excludes and engages us, and that, at every reading, it seems to become a different book. Analyzing the means by which its structure "evokes" these different appearances, Iser makes many familiar observations— the estranging effect of Benjy's impressions; the lack of coherence between individual sentences, which promise and then frustrate the reader's sense that there is a plot. Other critical approaches in this *Companion* find an anchor for that plot elsewhere—perhaps in history, in theories of the unconscious, in myth or in intertextuality. Iser located the narrative dynamics in the interaction between the textual signals and the "counter-force" they prompt in the reader. Benjy is a passive register, a "deintellectualized perception"[29] (a view held by many critics before and since), whose seemingly plotless impressions provoke different reactions in different readers as they negotiate the gaps. Iser finds common ground for their responses in a chain of tension, which runs—to be schematic—(1) the expectation of relief: that after Benjy, the narrative will supply "an active consciousness" that will "provide all the missing links" (educators will recognize this as the role a class will often project onto the teacher); (2) the frustration of expectation; and (3) increased tension.[30] The narrative trains the reader to be detached, to live with frustration. Filtered through this sequence, the reader at last apprehends what each section enacts—the senselessness suggested in the novel's title. We do not so much understand the novel, then, as *experience* it—as a fragmented and broken subjectivity trying to process and grasp the world, obliquely emerging at last from the sound and fury into a gesture at meaning.

Other critics, most notably David Bleich, centered the debate on issues of authority or academic expression, or both. They asked questions about who had the right to legislate meanings; or, like Slatoff, they urged fellow critics to use a personal voice, to cast off the deadening discourse of professional journals like the *PMLA*—"one of the world's chief repositories of the passive impersonal voice."[31] Bleich enjoined critics to open up the power relations of the classroom and (as Slatoff had) to include students' responses alongside their own magisterial interpretations.[32] Taking criticism into the domain of actual readers, Bleich explored "subjective criticism." Where Iser's "implied reader" remained strangely invisible, for Bleich readers always come to texts with histories that criticism should recognize and acknowledge. He disagreed with Booth's idea that our response should somehow reflect the author's own creative vision; rather, we create the vision and fill the "blanks" from our memories and (socially regulated) experiences. Journals such as *College English* offer rich testimony to the way such reader-response approaches appealed to many teachers as supporting a student-centered pedagogy. Garrison, for example, wrote of his attempts to allow students "free play" in imagining narrative alternatives in Faulkner's "The Brooch" before closing down response by subjecting them to the story as a whole: "Our students have resources. We must find out what they are and learn how to use them."[33] Bleich himself sought to dissolve the authority of "objective" literary language through examining gendered differences in his male and female students' constructions of literary texts. Bleich's findings suggested the kind of divisions feminist thinkers were concurrently exploring. For women, Faulkner's "Barn Burning" was a story about extended family relations, poverty, Abner's emotional and mental instability, and revenge; they approached the story through inference, concern for Sarty's feelings, "human situations . . . motives, allegiances, and conflicts." Male students, in contrast, kept their distance and hid their feelings. They avoided speculation and tried either to keep to literal retellings of facts and events or to dissolve human relationships into abstractions—a boy's division between "lying and telling the truth," rather than, as the women viewed it, between "what he knows is right and his ties with his father."[34]

Where Bleich's argument points us towards larger social formations, Norman Holland's studies, with which Bleich conducted a running debate, take us into the individual psyche. Just as Holland's work offered a high-profile, if eccentric, contribution to psychological criticism, so *5 Readers Reading* (1975) stirred up a storm of rejoinders from "Newreaders" too (and confirmed Faulkner's "A Rose for Emily" as a ubiquitous critical test piece).[35] Dissatisfied with explanations (by Fish and others) that our literary responses are conditioned by the text, Holland began to look for motives within the individual personality, and particularly within that individual's way of dealing with reality. Holland agreed with Iser that a text was an "interactive" event, but contended that in reading we construct our own vision of the text that both deflects and reveals our own anxieties (our "defenses"). Meaning resides in the mind of the reader, and the rhetoric has little bearing on our response. It would be impossible to predict from a text alone how any individual might react (an argument supported by the often bizarre readings supplied by Holland's five subjects), but Holland stopped short of saying the text could take any meaning we threw at it. He ruled certain responses as self-evidently illegitimate, providing as an example a hypothetical view of the "tableau" of Miss Emily and her father, in the second section of the story, that became probably the most quoted proposition in all the reader debates: "One would not say . . . that a reader . . . who thought the 'tableau' described an Eskimo was really responding to the story at all—only pursuing some mysterious inner explanation" (12). Looked at now, Holland's experiments underplayed or ignored much—most conspicuously, the power relations inherent in his own relationship with the students (whom he interviewed individually, week by week) and the possibility that he had merely projected his own "identity-themes" onto their readings. Describing subjective responses is fraught with difficulties, and Bleich's work, too, seems subject to similar criticisms. How far did the exercise itself determine the answers? Were these critics themselves unintentionally teaching their students the kind of responses they wanted to hear? Can anyone ever capture a "response"? Or would Holland's book, as Jeremy Hawthorn suggests, "more accurately have been entitled *5 Readers Remembering What They Read*"?[36]

For many, to show any interest at all in subjective elements seemed to invite interpretive license, from students rejecting grading, to literature classes abdicating any effort to reach consensual judgments on a text—"Is There a Text in This Class?" asked Fish in the most famous of his typically provocative titles. Some strove to temper the threat by seeking to refine the descriptions of response (along similar lines to those tested by Fish and Iser) and to emphasize the need for constant check mechanisms, anchoring vague response in specific rhetorical device. Menakhem Perry's intensive blow-by-blow account of "A Rose for Emily"[37] focused on how readers processed the "primary effects" within the text-continuum. Calibrating how the rhetoric manipulates our perspectives and keeps interpretive possibilities open at each stage of the reading, Perry took critics to task for merely advancing their individual visions of Emily. Instead, we need to examine the status of our hypotheses—why do we opt for one view rather than another? Which rhetorical devices make us go back and revise? How does the text trap and surprise us? Dillon adapted the approach to a stylistic analysis of "language processing," inviting his own readers to work through what he claimed were randomly chosen extracts from difficult texts, from Edmund Spenser to *The Portable Faulkner.* Referring to Aiken, he tried to link response to syntactical features—the unspecific referents, delayed objects, and main verb, through which Faulkner strings out his reader's suspense to "almost intolerable" limits.[38]

Fish himself reviewed his own earlier methods. He ceased to attend to the "affective" experiences of an individual figure (with all their threat of relativist anarchy), and posited instead the power of the "interpretive community," within which the reader learns and acts through a negotiated critical language, built on shared values. To argue this, Fish returned, for his main example, to Holland's "Eskimo" Emily. He agreed that within the current consensus of literary discourse such a claim would not command serious attention. Then, with the élan of somebody proving he was his own grandfather, he went on to suggest a possible "Eskimo 'A Rose for Emily'" scenario.[39] Involving the discovery of a hitherto unknown letter, Faulkner's confession to a lifelong conviction that he was "an Eskimo changeling," and the mass conversion of Faulknerians to tracing "Eskimo meanings" throughout his canon—this fiction, he suggested, was no less plausible than other recent transformations. (His example was James Miller's queer reading, a reading before its time, of T. S. Eliot's *The Waste Land.*) Given institutional agreement, this new reading could credibly stand beside the current array of other Emilies—the Freudian, mythological, regional, sociological and other versions; in short, the metamorphosing text as unfolded chapter by chapter in a critical *Companion* such as this one. Crosman and Dillon both followed a similar route, each surveying various readings of—again—"A Rose for Emily." Crosman compared his own responses with those of one of his students;[40] Dillon focused on the different ways various readers saw its chronology, its "event chain," and looked at the questions they asked about it. Faced with such inquiries as to what Miss Emily thought of men scattering lime about her house, or why she allowed so much dust, how do we determine whether some are more relevant than others?[41] For Dillon, although nothing about a story could be objectively described (not even plot), response was never entirely subjective: we can see patterns in "reading styles," originating not (as in Holland's theory) in the individual unconscious, but in publicly sanctioned approaches. Crosman, too, saw private readings as always caught up in larger public meaning and value systems. Such radical models take reading beyond the individual; they admit a broader horizon of intersubjectivity within our individual responses (which will be culturally and historically variable) and dispel any lingering formalist insistence on the primacy (or even sacredness) of the text.

"THE READER" AND FAULKNER STUDIES

In 1983, André Bleikasten took "Reading Faulkner" for his keynote address at the annual Faulkner and Yoknapatawpha Conference, where the theme that year was "New Directions in Faulkner Studies."[42] Bleikasten celebrated Faulkner as a mesmeric, seductive, challenging writer, whom (as Aiken realized) we must not only learn to read but learn to experience. Yet the main wave of the "reading" movement retreated relatively soon after. Indicatively, for example, in *Approaches to Teaching Faulkner's* The Sound and the Fury (1996), there is no specific essay about reader theory, as there was in the equivalent volume on Kate Chopin's *The Awakening* less than 10 years before; and only Charles Peek [see chapter 13] and John Matthews significantly register the impact of the text on the reader—the former draws on Rosenblatt to engage student responses and the latter declares, "I begin with the premise that Faulkner sets out to devastate the reader."[43] Facing the circularity of many reader-text arguments, problems of methodology, doubts about how to record "response," and the logistical difficulties of empirical research, many critics opted instead for the safe high ground (and high academic status) of neoformalism—the purer cognitive procedures of deconstruction or other entirely text-based theories. Nevertheless, reader-oriented theories had a far-reaching influence—in large measure because they proved adaptable and could be assimilated to more familiar approaches. As Steven Mailloux comments, the majority of literary critics in the United States avoided the more radical ground, but found, particularly in the reading models of Iser and the rhetorical studies of the early Fish, ways of keeping in touch with the text and the author. Such models helped to embed more impressionistic criticism in theory and opened up further dimensions in formalism—they offered "just enough of the reader but not too much."[44]

Faulkner's work invites and rewards reader perspectives—as much for us today, perhaps, as for critics influenced (even indirectly) by reader-oriented theories. For the rest of this chapter, I shall point to some of the ways these elements entered Faulkner studies, and, as importantly, suggest how we might try out such readings for ourselves. Among critics, the works that first excited Aiken stimulated most attention, but Faulkner's entire body of work yields richly to such approaches. When we take the routes these critics opened, we find ourselves asking the kind of questions many literature students once learned, early on, to suppress: What is reading? Who is "the reader" or "the Faulkner reader"? How does the text work on us, and why? What does it signify if we feel baffled, frustrated, moved, dazzled by a work of fiction? What do we *do* while reading? What is the difference between our first reading and any subsequent ones? Are our responses somehow part of the text? How much do we contribute to its meanings? If our blackbird is the true blackbird, can any text mean anything we like? Any single question opens up multiple dimensions of almost any of his texts and plunges us into the central issues that occupied reader-oriented criticism. Simply asking, "Who is the 'reader'?" can take us off down wildly divergent tracks according to which critic we are following. As Elizabeth Freund reminds us:

> [The reader] may be anything from an idealized construct to an actual historical idiosyncratic personage, including the author. Personifications—the mock reader (Gibson), the implied reader (Booth, Iser), the model reader (Eco), the super-reader (Riffaterre), the inscribed or encoded reader (Brooke-Rose), the narratee (Prince), the ideal reader (Culler), the literent (Holland), the actual reader (Jauss), the informed reader or the interpretive community (Fish)—proliferate.[45]

To take the "actual" (or "real") reader might launch us into exciting new field studies, as Warwick Wadlington encourages, "outside the academic setting, covering fairly long-term histories of individual or group reading and, in the context of particular cultural and social systems, focusing on person-shaping habits of performing and evaluating works."[46] It might lead into a historical study of Faulkner's reviewers, critics, or changing reputation, as in O. B. Emerson;[47] or of the intended audiences and occasions of the pieces collected in *Essays, Speeches and Public Letters;* or of the books' dedicatees. Like James Watson, we might examine the relationship between Faulkner's rhetoric and his intended addressee, even in his private correspondence. We might also want to look at Faulkner's impact on other writers whose creative (re)appropriations also register their responses as readers—from Graham Swift's *Last Orders,* a British *As I*

Lay Dying published in 1997, to the works of the Japanese Nobel laureate, Kenzaburo Ohe; from the doubled vision of Faulkner and Morrison traced by Philip Weinstein,[48] to the readers, writers, and translators analyzed in Fayen's Jaussian "reception" study of the "Latin American Faulkner." (For Fayen, "the translator may be regarded as a sort of superreader whose job it is to understand the foreign work before the reader does.")[49] If we follow the author himself as reader, we might find ourselves caught up in a panoramic critical investigation of Faulkner's career, encompassing (among other elements) his own encounters with books and influences [see chapters 1 and 13], the postmodern [see chapter 6] play of intertexts with his own and other authors' writings, and textual analyses [see chapter 12] of his own responses and revisions to his work in progress. We might move in more closely, as Michel Gresset or Warwick Wadlington do, to thinking about Faulkner's own voice, speaking and reading aloud, and to ponder those inflections in our own readings of the fiction. Or, we might want to speculate, as Gary Lee Stonum, Judith Sensibar, Michael Millgate, Martin Kreisworth, Richard Moreland, and many others have, about Faulkner's lifelong creative process, as he became his own reader, revisiting his earlier visions, in ever widening and elaborated responses in new fictions, maps, prefaces, appendices, story collections, or (in later years especially) interviews.[50]

We might, too, want to take this a step further, and, like Dirk Kuyk Jr., study our own or other "Readers' Designs" as a revelation of our own process of pattern making, or to explore how we impose our own culturally and historically specific sense of coherence on a set of miscellaneous writings.[51] From here we might move into the area of Bleich's "subjective reader," redistributing authority from critic (or teacher) to reader (or student), and legitimating our own consciousness—including our emotions, associations, and memories—as topics centrally important to our literary knowledge and sense of "the work." So Arthur Kinney remembers "the absorbing, even electrifying experience of reading Faulkner for the first time, from cover to cover, cramped in one corner of our family's old gray mohair sofa: lunch came and went, and dinner, dusk came and night"; his own book, he suggests, is a way of "trying to explain that experience."[52] Philip Weinstein, too, reflecting on Faulkner's created cosmos, acknowledges his own construction, over a quarter of a century, as "Faulkner's subject"—as reader, teacher, critic, and devotee. Tracing his journey from his first (New Critical) love affair with *The Sound and the Fury* and his own white, masculinist struggles to master the text, he recognizes that "in this book—the subjectivity under scrutiny—bears my name as much as Faulkner's."[53] In a later book, he takes autobiographical process further, reflecting back on his own Southern childhood, his devotion to his mother and to the black woman she employed. Such personal memories, he confesses, have always been part of his reading: "I think of Vannie every time I encounter *The Sound and the Fury's* Dilsey." This knowledge, he realizes now, is inseparable from larger political readings—it is what "shapes [his] optic not just upon Dilsey but upon Faulkner's work more generally and indeed upon the realities of race itself during the middle of the twentieth century in the South."[54]

Equally, we might decide, however, to pursue the reader as a "construct"—
that is, the characteristics of the hypothetical reader to whom the text seems to
be addressed and whose character we can try to deduce through examining the
rhetoric (the textual codes and strategies). This reader is unlikely to resemble
many actual readers, but we may step into this position for the duration of a
reading. It is also unlikely to be identical with the narratee (the immediate audience of the narrator, inside or just outside the text).[55] Jason Compson's (unde-
fined) narratee may or may not be the same as Quentin's or Benjy's, but the
assumed reader, at a further remove, surveys all four narrational circuits and can
speculate about the nature of each transaction. (Similarly, we may be invited to
distance ourselves from both narrator and narratee, say through irony or superior judgment.) We might begin, like Walker Gibson, simply by extending a
familiar formalist category—the distinction between the actual, living author
and the fictitious *speaker* of a text—to examine the gap between ourselves as an
actual person and the role of the "mock reader" the text assigns us (the social
sophisticate, perhaps, the conservative, or the sage); if that gap is too great, we
can even refuse to play the part, and instead of revering the text, ask questions
about the value systems, knowledge, and attitude it assumes.[56] Or exercising
scholarly effort, we might bridge that gap; we set aside our less adequate and
partial selves, our naïve readings, to turn ourselves into Stanley Fish's
"informed reader"—"neither an abstraction, nor an actual living reader, but a
hybrid—a real reader (me) who does everything within his power to make himself informed."[57] Umberto Eco points to the text itself as contributing to such
competence: in becoming a "model reader," we look to outside sources, but we
also improve our reading strategies as we grow acquainted with the communicative patterns and rhetoric of the text.[58] (As Aiken said, we learn the rules
afresh with each of Faulkner's works.)

So, entering Faulkner's apprentice work via his constructed reader, we might
find ourselves looking again at his literary sources and allusions, at their tone
and timbre, at what we are expected to have read, and at *how,* in short, Faulkner's
verse, drama, prose sketches, even drawings invite us to respond. Are we
assumed to be fellow initiates, model or even "ideal" (or "optimal") readers who
are uniquely sensitive to every subtlety of the poet's imagination? Or is this a
"showy and self-conscious display" (as Polk says of *The Marionettes*[59])—an
elaborate rhetorical performance aimed at impressing the (albeit small) real
public whose admiration or bewilderment Faulkner needed in order to define his
own vocation. (In this case, the "mock reader" would merge with the actual college audience of "Count No 'Count," against whose provincial philistinism the
dandy poet deliberately created his distinct poetic identity.[60]) Or, where we can
identify an intended real-life addressee, as in the sonnet cycle to Helen Baird,
how might we differentiate the real and the "mock" reader? And what is our
position when we intervene, through reading in a published version, in what
might have been conceived solely as a private transaction? Are we eaves-
droppers, intimates, or surrogates? Do we identify ourselves with Helen, or with
the poet, or does the verse offer us a further position somewhere in between?

Are we, at this point, talking about literary biography or ethics, and can reading keep these separate?

However, we might also wonder whether this writing, heavily influenced by fin de siècle poetics, postulates any reader at all. Although Faulkner distributed handcrafted works to those close to him, many of these earliest poetic writings seem to turn their back on an audience, looking inward to spaces far from the loud world: Marietta's garden in *The Marionettes* (ca. 1920), Orpheus's enclosing gray walls in the verse sequence *Vision in Spring* (1921). These writings, with their repeated tropes of mirrors, echoes, and reflections, encourage a sense that perhaps, in this phase, it was Faulkner who was his own work's projected ideal reader; that in trying on a range of literary masks, he was writing himself into the role of poet. (Significantly, many remained long unpublished). As John McClure observed in a perceptive review of *The Marble Faun* in 1925, "Nobody but the poet himself ever understands all the overtones and implications in a piece of imaginative verse."[61] As we ask about shades of reading, we find ourselves also looking carefully at shades of language. Within these hermetic spaces, language seems designed less to communicate than to decorate, to entrance: in *The Marionettes,* Pierrot is his own audience (the Shade of Pierrot dreams, while the other acts), the gray and lilac Figures' speeches double and redouble back on themselves. In Faulkner's Symbolist aesthetics, writing seems to draw attention to itself, to signal that the purest work perhaps is the one that remains unread—like an unplayed play, like unheard music—at the opposite pole from rhetoric or dialogue. Opaque, solipsistic even, these works may be asking us, as readers, only to take up the role of distant worshipper—a passive subject, receiving through the melting, insubstantial words impressions of the ideal.

Alternatively, we might argue that, from his earliest writings, Faulkner implied a highly active reader; that long before *The Sound and the Fury,* he was building in the "screens and obtrusions" that together compose a complex rhetoric of gaps, delays, and indeterminacies, which, as Aiken saw, ask us to cooperate. In looking at symbolist paintings, we are told, we are frequently "expected to piece together from the evidence available some not entirely obvious narrative."[62] Similarly, the very vagueness of Faulkner's early poetic scenes invites us to fill the spaces for ourselves, inserting our own plots, emotions, meanings, glosses. From the opening of *The Marionettes* to the enigmatic little endplate, where Pierrot stares at himself in the mirror, the body of the dead girl between, the play is all gaps and guesses. Stories such as "The Hill," "Nympholepsy," or many of the pieces collected in *New Orleans Sketches* hint at experiences untold and revelations just beyond reach. After this, Faulkner's first novels seem perhaps more obviously accessible. Many reviewers in the 1920s commented positively on the way they reached out to and directly engaged the postwar audience, *Soldiers' Pay* for striking "a note of deepfelt distress that is more akin to us all," and *Mosquitoes* for its humor and dialogue. (Aiken even suggested that it could easily transfer to the stage as a "farce-comedy."[63]) But even these texts disconcerted some readers, disrupting narrative progression and interjecting realism with poetic passages. *Soldiers' Pay* transmutes Georgia in 1919 into a world of nymphs, fauns, and satyrs, where even cigarette smoke curls, stylistically, in art nouveau tendrils, decelerating the action; the war seems strangely bracketed and displaced, and its returned hero, Donald Mahon, acquires his significance from the subtexts of myth and allusion rather than from any social critique of the fighting. *Mosquitoes* never names the insects that give it its title, and in its collage-like structure, strange shifts of register, and, as we now know, editorial deletions prompt its readers into making cross-connections and drawing out implications to construct a narrative out of seeming stasis. Faulkner's publisher, Horace Liveright, found *Flags in the Dust* disappointingly "diffuse and non-integral,"[64] and reviewers suggested the same even of Ben Wasson's tidied up and more compact *Sartoris.* Some readers attributed such elements to inexperience, or self-indulgence. Others sensed something more willful and responded in ways that anticipated the shock of *The Sound and the Fury.* Arnold Bennett, the British novelist and elder statesman of realism, noted Faulkner's promise, at the same time exclaiming over the "heavy work" *Soldiers' Pay* demanded of its reader. He saw this as modish perversity, part of a trend to tell the audience: "We will not smooth your path. Indeed we intend to make your path as hard as we know how."[65]

However, as Aiken would suggest, through such obstructions, Faulkner was tutoring us in new practices—it was not up to the novelist to smooth our path, but for the reader to enter the new ones his text was trying to open. The reader who is willing to work with the stylistic disjunctions, narrative spaces, and mythic materials of the early fiction is well on the way to negotiating the even stronger challenges of the cubistic monologues in *As I Lay Dying,* the circling movements and startling juxtapositions of *Light in August,* the counterpointed stories of *The Wild Palms,* or the frames and play scenes of *Requiem for a Nun.* But attuning ourselves to how readers respond and to what they do also productively opens up features of texts written in a seemingly more mimetic register. In "Dry September," for example, the five short sections (and the gaps between them), each ending with a question, a teasing negation, or a resonant image, invite us to speculate—to test different readings of Minnie Cooper, Will Mayes, McLendon; to view the action with Hawkshaw; to see through, around, and beyond the eyes of the town or of Southern culture; to discover or to project into the story a rape, a lynching, hysteria, sexual exhibitionism—narrative possibilities the text neither confirms nor denies.

The concept of the "inscribed reader" offers a further guide to this often-difficult process. At the center of the fictions are numerous characters whom Faulkner presents directly in scenes of reading, talking, or puzzling over all manner of texts—and whose presence foregrounds debate about the kind of roles required of us. The coterie discussion of the poems in *Mosquitoes,* for example, involves us in questions about aesthetics, pertinent to reading the novel itself, filtered through a complicated layering of readers, inscribed, hypothetical, and actual. The reading experience itself will vary according to its cultural moment— here, one very different, presumably, for Faulkner's public in 1927 than for an audience who had also come across extracts from Eva Wiseman's *Satyricon in*

Starlight in William Faulkner's later *A Green Bough* (1933) and different, again, perhaps for today's "gendered reader" (hyperaware of the gender-specific cross-currents in the dialogue) or "queer reader" interested in the positioning, in relation to Mrs. Wiseman, of the audiences inside and outside the text and in a heterosexual male author's attribution of his own (then unpublished) verse to a lesbian poet. The end of *Pylon,* again, offers a multilayered scene of reading. Faulkner does not simply refer to the reporter's obituary of Roger Shumann, but first sets before us the copyboy's excited salvage of the fragments and his exulted response to his reading (which inspires him to turn writer), then the scene of the joint reading at the desk with Hagood (the response to which, this time, we are left to infer). In so doing, he gives us the actual texts of both the romantic first and prosaic second copy, and, finally, introduced with only six words of narratorial linking, the savage personal postscript. All these take us into the process of composition, revision, and reaction, and so encourage us to go back over the preceding narrative, to puzzle over the status of the much-debated interpolation. (Is it the Reporter's imaginings, or has it, as Hugh Ruppersburg suggests, independent authority?[66]) They underline, too, the prominence of reading and writing throughout the novel in repeated allusions, from newspaper headlines to airport runways described as capital *F*s, from Morse code to dollar bills, from the crowd's efforts to decipher what the movements of the airplanes write against the sky to Dr. Shumann's attempts to read little Jack's paternity. In a narrative organized around mechanized consumer spectacle, such reading inscriptions jolt us into a more critical position by highlighting textuality, the need to make meanings, the partiality and provisionality of any conclusion, and the potential always to rewrite "reality."[67]

Inscribed readers play a crucial role in engaging the audience in what continues to be, for many, the most astonishing and demanding of all Faulkner's fictions. Much reader criticism has, not unexpectedly, centered on *Absalom, Absalom!* to focus on the story-making and interpretive strategies of the audiences who both share in and shape the inner narratives. Here, reader-response approaches merge both with a general formalist interest in ambiguity and with versions of postmodern criticism to question the stability of any form of wider narrative that presents itself as an authoritative truth—history, time, religion, concepts of the self, the certainties of racial or gender identity. Many critics have seen Shreve as a surrogate for the reader, but *Absalom, Absalom!* presents us with numerous others, as they struggle to make meanings from a cracked gravestone or a faded letter of doubtful source, or as they listen to and try to make sense of stories—efforts that reflect back our own activities as we pore over the book in front us. As David Krause warns, we cannot just accept any of these depictions of reading as transparent. None of the inscribed readers is the "ideal" reader who can take from the text every possible shade of meaning (for Krause, this role is reserved for the author); but their responses prompt us to examine what we take from Faulkner's text and how we go about it. For Krause, for instance, Sutpen's literal reception of his teacher's words, as he reads aloud, clearly models an undesirable extreme in its passive relation to what is said in books.[68] Whereas, if we attend closely to all the different perspectives on Bon's letter (Krause identifies at least six of these) and to the wording of the letter itself, we gain access to a set of instructions as to how to read William Faulkner.[69] We should be prepared to reread patiently, to revise our expectations and hypotheses, in a constant weighing of nuance and possibility. As Krause comments, this book expects "exhausting, exhaustive" (238) work; or in other words, to repeat Faulkner, we need to "read it four times."

Similar reading events demand our attention throughout Faulkner's texts, whether Minnie's response to the silver dream of the picture show in "Dry September," or Howard Boyd's obsession with *Green Mansions* in "The Brooch," or the agonizing shock of encounter with the ledger items in "The Bear."[70] We read outward from these scenes, even the most intricate, to reorient ourselves in the yet infinitely more-complex fictions in which they are embedded. We might also expand the inscribed-reader category to include all the inscribed speakers and listeners, or narrators and narratees, who channel so many of Faulkner's narrative energies and draw us into the highly charged act of telling. We might examine, with Stephen Ross in *Fiction's Inexhaustible Voice*, the complex layerings of rhetoric, the acts of oratory; or examine, with Jay Watson, the lawyer figure as surrogate author and decipherer. Beyond the verbal signs or encoded narratives (the gossip or the movie, say, in "Dry September"), we might move on, too, to viewing an entire text as an extended piece of rhetoric that enjoins us to participate in elaborated acts of reading. The Freudian transactions of the narrative—a form of transference, so Peter Brooks argues in his compelling account—collapse the "distance between telling and listening, between writing and reading . . . ; the reader has been freed to speak in the text, towards the creation of the text."[71] For readers as well as for Quentin and Shreve, Karen Ramsay Johnson agrees, "the encounter with narrative is a marriage, an embrace"; and Karen McPherson affirms that "we do not write about *Absalom, Absalom!* merely because, like Miss Rosa, 'we want it told.' We are more deeply implicated than that: we want *in on the telling*."[72] For Carolyn Porter, the novel leaves us little choice—it is as much about the relationship "between the reader and the novel" as about that between Quentin and Thomas Sutpen, and it forces us into participation.[73]

Many of the most turbulent and exciting dynamics of experiencing Faulkner's writing take place along this continuum of involvement. Sometimes we are positioned in a similar location to readers in (or just outside) the text, listening to V. K. Ratliff's anecdotes or Dawson Fairchild's tall tales. Many of Faulkner's first-person fictions are addressed to an unnamed and (usually) silent interlocutor, who offers us a space to occupy in role—perhaps, like Charles Mallison in *The Town* as a sort of generalized "cousin" and member of a communal "we," or as one of Grandfather's auditors in *The Reivers,* or as the narratee to whom "Uncle Willy's" young narrator makes his desperate self-justifying appeal. Sometimes, as in "The Courthouse" pages of *Requiem for a Nun,* we find ourselves in an impossibly privileged coign of vantage, overseeing the entire panorama of evolutionary history. (This fine-tuned relationship between narratorial point of view and the reader is Ruppersburg's particular focus.[74]) Structurally, Faulkner integrates our responses with the spectrum of reactions and judgments that swirl round his enigmatic, blank, or even "unreadable" central characters: Caddy, Joe Christmas or Addie Bundren; Thomas Sutpen; the Unknown Soldier; Donald Mahon or Margaret Powers in *Soldiers' Pay;* Marietta in *The Marionettes,* caught between the competing similes of the gray and lilac watchers. Or he engages us in historical reconstruction or detection, not only as in *Intruder in the Dust* or *Knight's Gambit* but, as Robert Dale Parker emphasizes, in a move that he takes back to Aiken, throughout all the texts it is the power of *withheld* information that draws us into the action.[75]

THE PARTICIPATORY READER

However we define *the reader,* negotiating Faulkner's texts from this standpoint keeps us in touch with the text as an event and complicates for us (the real readers) the very activities with which we are engaged. Perhaps the most striking effect of all reader-oriented theories has been to reinvigorate our sense that, in reading, we become active, creative participants in the text. The heightened energies of these reading models are evident in such widely diverse analyses as those by Wesley Morris and Barbara Alverson Morris on the one hand and Richard Gray on the other, and rhetoric is at the center of other significant studies. Gail Mortimer, like Walter Slatoff, traces the implications of the characters' (and narrators') perceptual style to illuminate the absences—Faulkner's "rhetoric of loss," the psychological trauma at the heart of so much of the fiction. For James Snead, like Wayne Booth, rhetorical devices reveal social and ethical perceptions. Faulkner's fictions illustrate how linguistic "figures of division" embed and perpetuate racist hierarchies. Encoding patterns of opposition, separation, and differentiation in the minutiae of rhetorical forms, Faulkner challenges "large-scale ideological concepts encoded in the form of rhetorical narratives."[76] Positioning us with Benjy, "a castrated white whom a younger black servant completely dominates," he engages us in "attempts to rewrite large-scale social rhetoric" (19). Davies, too, reads "The Bear" in terms of Boothian ethics; here, the poetics of form open up the emotional dynamics of how we respond to Ike's troubled value system, how we transform our own attitudes.[77]

Much of the most memorable criticism, from Aiken on, has testified to our sense of involvement; and the reader movement sharpened and refocused analysis. Arnold L. Weinstein explores how Faulkner and other writers "tap the affective potential" of "forms of ellipsis, mystery and disorder."[78] We enter *The Sound and the Fury* through emotional immersion; we reach any "knowledge" in *Absalom, Absalom!* not through intellectual inquiry but through "feeling." Arthur Kinney, too, represents at book length how, while Faulkner's characters may (or may not) bring all the fragments of consciousness together, the reader seeks to grasp the text as a whole. This wholeness is not, as in earlier modernist criticism, a pre-given quality of the text; it is the reader whose *"constitutive consciousness"* drives toward integration, our perception and response shapes what we see.[79] For Carolyn Porter, in contrast, the Faulkner reader can never assemble a coherent narrative; yet she, too, describes the intensity of involvement: "Faulkner implicates the reader in the stream of event, then, by forcing him to share the burden of narrative construction."[80] Cathy Waegner draws on Iser to develop a taxonomy for Faulkner's "rhetoric of character." Through a rhetoric of "revision," "negation," "displacement," or other strategy, according to the specific text in question, Faulkner invites us to actualize the characters, as we do in conversation, through revising and reconstituting our perceptions.[81]

Warwick Wadlington takes up our role most fully. In his richly intricate, reader-informed study of Faulkner's works from *The Marionettes* onward, he argues for a radical change in reading practices. We should cease to approach literary texts as intellectual puzzles, but see interpretation as only one aspect of reading. Texts are more analogous to musical scores or dramatic scripts that the reader "performs." Faulkner's rhetoric gives actual readers hints on how to enter and "voice" his texts, even through physical reading aloud. We actualize the breathtaking style quite literally, in our bodies as well as in our emotions. As for Faulkner, novels were part of saying "no" to death, so as readers we share the "ritual defiance of death" that, for Wadlington, depends in tragedy on the participation of the audience. At the same time, Wadlington turns reader criticism back to look afresh at itself, alerting us to its own rhetoric about rhetoric. He dislikes such phrases as "Faulkner *forces* the reader,"[82] preferring to view Faulkner's rhetoric as coaxing a response, as persuasive rather than coercive.

Nevertheless, such critical metaphors are revealing, emphasizing the energies stirred up in our encounters with texts. Some of the most active (and exhausting) verbs indicate the turmoil of reading and witness especially to moments where we feel least comfortable. Some of the most uneasy moments in reading Faulkner are those where we recognize in our involvement not merely acts of witnessing, judgment, or emotion, but a kind of complicity. Being a participatory reader can entangle us in horrors—regional, racial, sexual, or others—from which we would prefer to remain detached. Just as in "Dry September," the trope of voyeurism seems to pass, structurally, from characters to the reader, so we might frequently find ourselves caught up in the very social or psychological formations the story could be read as exposing. Where our imaginations supply a rape or a lynching, how far do we share the guilt of a culture? Such reading experiences might even seem, disturbingly, to echo the outraged responses of some of Faulkner's first audiences. Rather than dismissing the uncomfortable elements in an apology for the author, many critics have suggested that such complicity is inseparable from the aesthetic process. Many of Faulkner's texts bring this process into close-up, but for many critics, none more so than *Sanctuary* (as John Matthews presents it, a text marked by ellipses[83]). So, within a psychoanalytic frame, Homer Pettey argues that all reading reproduces the "fetishistic allurements" of a text—any interpretation enacts a desire for control, and is, in short, a form of rape: "Faulkner implicates his reader in Temple's rape by seducing his reader, enticing a series of meanings, and creating an object to be fetishized. As readers, we are inculcated into a culture of rape—social, psychological, textual—from which we cannot escape any more than Temple could."[84] For Laura Tanner, too, the gaps in *Sanctuary* maneuver us into some of our darkest reading actions: "*Sanctuary*

pressures the reader not only to perceive the rape from the perspective of the violator, but to assume the position of that violator, to anticipate, to plan, and to exe-
cute—in the arena of the imagination—the crime of rape." The novel "shifts the
burden of creation away from Faulkner and toward the reader."[85]

Similar violently controlling movements strike other critics in *Light in August.*
Meir Sternberg describes how it lures the reader into "a trap deliberately baited
with stereotypes"; once swallowed, "the sequel bursts upon him like an unexpected slap in the face." The novel leaves "little to choose between us and the mob
of lynchers who are out for Joe Christmas's blood."[86] John Duvall's "reader" is
himself, both as a subjective individual (introduced to us in the preface) and as a
member of the "interpretive community" (acting within a generally recognizable
critical discourse). Teasing out the assumptions embedded within the standard
account that Joe Christmas *murders* Joanna, Duvall traces the way the text invei-
gles us into sharing Jefferson's misogynist and racist ideology: "When we call her
death 'murder,' we tacitly affirm that woman is victim—and we unknowingly participate in the crowd's hope that she has been raped. . . . We take, it seems, a perverse pleasure, disguised as moral outrage, in the violent death of a woman."[87]

Such criticism takes its cue from feminist theory; it recognizes that such textual and reading tendencies need articulating and require a tactical counter-
response. As Patrocinio Schweickart asks: "Does the text manipulate the reader,
or does the reader manipulate the text to produce the meaning that suits her own
interests?" She argues that the woman reader should choose the latter.[88] For
Judith Fetterley, recording real readers' reactions to canonical American classroom favorites ("A Rose for Emily" among them), the masculinist imperatives
of the narrative vision seemed overwhelming: "In such fictions the female
reader is co-opted into participating in an experience from which she is explicitly excluded."[89] Where a story turns on playing with stereotypes (Miss Emily
Grierson's spinsterly repression, for instance), it can also come dangerously
close to endorsing them. (Even Menakhem Perry's exhaustive analysis of the
story leaves unglossed some of its own universalizing remarks—Emily's "feminine naivety," for instance—and, though assuming that the narrator is a fellow
"townsman," never suggests any misogynistic shading in that vision.[90]) In "Dry
September," Miss Minnie is represented through the male gaze, and speculation
about her as a hysteric and sexual fantasist relies on the reader's adoption of the
masculinist mindset that casts her as "Other." By laying bare the process, we
turn ourselves into Fetterley's "resisting reader"—who keeps it in view that
books (stories) are political, powerful, always part of wider cultural dialogues.
For Porter, as "the reified reader," we struggle, like Quentin Compson, to resist
the entrapments of history, as Faulkner's narrative strategies undercut our more
comfortable position of detachment. Porter suggests that, unlike Quentin, we
can resist to a degree, as for us the book remains a "spatial object"; we can
"reread or walk away from it."[91] Out of these entanglements, we might, also
retrieve control in a stronger, more ethical position. As Leona Toker discovers,
as a rereader we may open ourselves to a different set of rhetorical effects as narrative gaps and reticences cancel and resolve themselves; on our first journey

through *The Sound and the Fury,* our experience parallels that of the characters, on the second, we transcend it.[92]

Why should we be interested in approaches that, as many have discovered, lead up theoretical blind allies—to contradictions, circular arguments, endless revisions, and a sense of failure in even the attempt at a survey? For Faulknerians, "failure" has a splendid resonance; it is the badge of ambition and defiance and, like *The Sound and the Fury,* the "failed" work may have a more dazzling impact than the finished one. Reader-oriented approaches challenged many of the governing critical orthodoxies of the mid–twentieth century in often-provocative textual engagements. If they produced neither a consistent methodology nor a lasting knowledge, they generated lively debate, opened up new arenas for literary study, and stimulated fresh energies in readers. For the reader-oriented critic, of any persuasion, at the center of reading is dialogue—between ourselves and the text, between ourselves and our own reactions, between ourselves and the voices of our culture; we need to keep asking what we are reading, what we are experiencing. Though the first critical debates soon faded, this dialogue has continued. In pedagogy, especially, connections between writing and reading, literature and audience, and models of collaborative learning owe a large debt to this period, and contributions to journals such as *Teaching Faulkner* and *College English* attest to its long-term impact. Many of the practices these critics encouraged have become almost second nature to many students and teachers of literature, and to critics of widely varying theoretical dispositions. Many of us now feel free to write in a more direct, personal way, should we choose; to reflect on our own assumptions; to admit to the stir, the excitement, the driving suspense of reading; to acknowledge our responses; to speak of what we see in the evasions, absences, and silences of a text; to question literary authorities; even, if we see fit, to raise questions about Faulkner and his creations; and to accept that to redefine is not to destroy the value of the work or the pleasures of the text.

Perhaps, above all, these approaches give us a role in literature. In some aesthetic theories, the work of art can exist alone, with no need for an audience. Although Faulkner himself often suggested such a vision, at other times, however, he seemed less certain, expressing worries that in locking himself behind impenetrable barriers, he might put an end to his career: "Maybe I will end up in some kind of self-communion—a silence—faced with the certainty that I can no longer be understood."[93] Terrifying as this vision is, it contains its saving opposite. As rhetorical and reader-response criticism attests, even the most inward-looking writing—the manuscript left in a drawer, the notoriously "unreadable" text—always gestures towards its audience and needs the audience to complete its meaning. It is the reader (each of us) whose understanding will keep Faulkner's writing alive.

NOTES

1. Frederick L. Gwynn and Joseph Blotner, *Faulkner in the University: Class Conferences at the University of Virginia, 1957–1958* (1959) (Charlottesville: University Press of Virginia, 1995), 273.

2. Malcolm Cowley, ed., *Writers at Work: The Paris Review Interviews* (New York: The Viking Press, 1958), 128.

3. Susan R. Suleiman and Inge Crosman, eds., *The Reader in the Text: Essays on Audience and Interpretation* (Princeton, NJ: Princeton University Press, 1980), 6. Other key overviews of this movement offer similar warnings: Elizabeth Freund, *The Return of the Reader: Reader-Response Criticism* (London: Methuen, 1987) and Peter Rabinowitz, "Other Reader-Oriented Theories," in *The Cambridge History of Literary Criticism,* vol. 8, *From Formalism to Poststructuralism,* ed. Raman Selden (Cambridge: Cambridge University Press), 375–403.

4. Mary Louise Pratt, *Toward a Speech Act Theory of Literary Discourse* (Bloomington: Indiana University Press, 1977), 182–91.

5. For a helpful introduction to many of the theories in this paragraph, see the essays collected in the section, "Reader-Oriented Theories of Interpretation," in *From Formalism to Poststructuralism,* 255–403.

6. Cowley, ed., *Writers at Work,* 134.

7. Cowley, ed., *Writers at Work,* 275.

8. Cowley, ed., *Writers at Work,* 129.

9. Dudley Fitts, "Two Aspects of Telemachus" (1930), in *William Faulkner: The Critical Heritage,* ed., John Bassett (London: Routledge and Kegan Paul, 1975), 88.

10. Fitts, in *William Faulkner: The Critical Heritage,* 88–89.

11. Conrad Aiken, "William Faulkner: The Novel as Form" (1939), in *William Faulkner: The Critical Heritage,* 243–50.

12. McLeish is quoted approvingly in W. K.Wimsatt, with Monroe C. Beardsley, *The Verbal Icon: Studies in the Meaning of Poetry* (1954) (London: Methuen, 1970), 4. Faulkner himself suggested that when style went dead, it became mere "rhetoric." *Faulkner in the University,* 84.

13. William Van O'Connor, cited in Henry Claridge, ed., *William Faulkner: Critical Assessments,* vol. 1, *General Perspectives: Memories, Recollections and Interviews: Contemporary Critical Opinion,* Critical Assessments of Writers in English series (Mountfield, East Sussex: Helm Information, 1999), 77.

14. All quotations drawn from Wayne C. Booth, *The Rhetoric of Fiction,* 2d ed. (1983) (Harmondsworth, Middlesex: Penguin Books, 1987). This edition is recommended for Booth's useful afterword, which reflects back on the two decades of reader-oriented theories that followed the first publication of his book.

15. Milton Rugoff, "Out of Faulkner's Bog," *New York Herald Tribune Books,* 31 March 1940, ctd. in O. B. Emerson, *Faulkner's Early Literary Reputation in America* (Ann Arbor, MI: UMI Research Press, 1984), 153.

16. Slatoff pioneered his ideas in an essay, "The Edge of Order: The Pattern of Faulkner's Rhetoric" (*Twentieth Century Literature* 3 [1957]: 107–27), developing them more fully in *Quest for Failure: A Study of William Faulkner* (Ithaca: Cornell University Press, 1960).

17. Slatoff, *Quest,* 83.

18. Slatoff, *Quest,* 35, 85. Slatoff offers many more examples.

19. Slatoff, *Quest,* 25, 240.

20. Walter J. Slatoff, *With Respect to Readers: Dimensions of Literary Response* (Ithaca: Cornell University Press, 1970), 171, 7, 5.

21. M. H. Abrams, "How to Do Things with Texts," *Partisan Review* 46 (1979): 566–88.

22. Roland Barthes, "The Death of the Author" (1968), in *Image-Music-Text,* ed. and trans. Stephen Heath (London: Fontana, 1979), 148.

23. Stanley Fish, *Is There a Text in This Class?: The Authority of Interpretive Communities* (Cambridge, MA: Harvard University Press, 1980), 304. The publication of this book, along with the closely associated anthologies, Jane Tompkins, ed., *Reader-Response Criticism: From Formalism to Post-Structuralism* (Baltimore: Johns Hopkins University Press, 1980) and Suleiman and Crosman, ed., *The Reader in the Text* (1980) is usually seen as marking the era's critical peak.

24. Fish, 67, 42. The essay was included as the first chapter of *Is There a Text in This Class?*

25. Fish, 5.

26. Jonathan Culler. *On Deconstruction: Theory and Criticism after Structuralism* (1982) (London: Routledge, 1987), 65–66.

27. See particularly, Wolfgang Iser, *The Act of Reading: A Theory of Aesthetic Response* (1976) (Baltimore: Johns Hopkins University Press, 1978).

28. Wolfgang Iser, *The Implied Reader: Patterns of Communication in Prose Fiction from Bunyan to Beckett* (1974; reprint Baltimore: Johns Hopkins University Press, 1987), 136.

29. Iser, *Implied,* 140.

30. Iser, *Implied,* 141.

31. Slatoff, *With Respect to Readers,* 173. See too Robert Crosman, "Do Readers Make Meaning?" in *The Reader in the Text,* 149–64.

32. See particularly David Bleich, *Subjective Criticism* (Baltimore: Johns Hopkins University Press, 1978) and Slatoff, *With Respect to Readers,* 191–207.

33. Joseph M. Garrison, "Faulkner's 'The Brooch': A Story for Teaching," *College English* 36, no. 1 (September 1974): 57.

34. David Bleich, *The Double Perspective: Language, Literacy, and Social Relations* (New York: Oxford University Press, 1988), 149.

35. For a strong attack on Holland's general theory, see, for example, Jonathan Culler, "Prolegomena to a Theory of Reading," in *The Reader in the Text,* 46–66; and Wayne A. Tefs, "Norman N. Holland and 'A Rose for Emily'—Some Questions Concerning Psychoanalytic Criticism," *The Sphinx: A Magazine of Literature and Society* 2 (1974): 50–57.

36. Jeremy Hawthorn, *A Concise Glossary of Contemporary Literary Theory* (London: Edward Arnold, 1992), 147.

37. Menakhem Perry, "Literary Dynamics: How the Order of a Text Creates Its Meanings [With an Analysis of Faulkner's 'A Rose for Emily']," *Poetics Today* 1, nos. 1–2 (Autumn 1979): 35–64, 311–61.

38. George L. Dillon, *Language Processing and the Reading of Literature: Toward a Model of Comprehension* (Bloomington: Indiana University Press, 1978), 32.

39. Fish, *Is There a Text in This Class?,* 345–47.

40. Robert Crosman, "How Readers Make Meaning," *College Literature* 9 (1982): 207–15.

41. George L. Dillon, "Styles of Reading," *Poetics Today* 3, no. 2 (1982): 77–88.

42. André Bleikasten, "Reading Faulkner," in *New Directions in Faulkner Studies: Faulkner and Yoknapatawpha, 1983,* ed. Doreen Fowler and Ann J. Abadie (Jackson: University Press of Mississippi, 1984), 1–17.

43. In Stephen Hahn and Arthur F. Kinney, *Approaches to Teaching Faulkner's* The Sound and the Fury (New York: Modern Language Association of America, 1996), 122.

44. Steven Mailloux, *Interpretive Conventions: The Reader in the Study of American Fiction* (Ithaca: Cornell University Press, 1982), 56–57.

45. Elizabeth Freund, *The Return of the Reader: Reader-Response Criticism* (London: Methuen, 1987), 7. Andrew Bennett usefully extends the list in *Readers and Reading* (London: Longman, 1995).

46. Warwick Wadlington, *Reading Faulknerian Tragedy* (Ithaca: Cornell University Press, 1987), 225.

47. Emerson, *Faulkner's Early Literary Reputation in America* (1984). This is a revised version of a 1962 thesis, written before the main interest in reader-oriented criticism, but published at its height.

48. Philip Weinstein, *What Else but Love? The Ordeal of Race in Faulkner and Morrison* (New York: Columbia University Press, 1996).

49. Tanya T. Fayen, *In Search of the Latin American Faulkner* (Lanham, MD: University Press of America, 1995), 177; and the wide-ranging influences charted in *Faulkner: International Perspectives, Faulkner and Yoknapatawpha, 1982,* ed. Doreen Fowler and Ann J. Abadie (Jackson: University Press of Mississippi, 1984).

50. Michel Gresset, "Faulkner's Voice," in *Faulkner's Discourse: An International Symposium,* ed. Lothar Hönnighausen (Tübingen: Max Niemeyer Verlag, 1989), 184–94; Wadlington,

Reading Faulknerian Tragedy; Gary Lee Stonum, *Faulkner's Career: An Internal Literary History* (Ithaca: Cornell University Press, 1979); Judith L. Sensibar, *The Origins of Faulkner's Art* (Austin: University of Texas Press, 1984); Michael Millgate, *Faulkner's Place* (Athens: University of Georgia Press, 1997); Martin Kreiswirth, *William Faulkner: The Making of a Novelist* (Athens: University of Georgia Press, 1983); Richard C. Moreland, *Faulkner and Modernism: Rereading and Rewriting* (Madison: University of Wisconsin Press, 1990).

51. Dirk Kuyk Jr., *Sutpen's Design: Interpreting Faulkner's* Absalom, Absalom! (Charlottesville: University Press of Virginia, 1990), 98–137.

52. Arthur F. Kinney, *Faulkner's Narrative Poetics: Style as Vision* (Amherst: University of Massachusetts Press, 1978), 264.

53. Philip Weinstein, *Faulkner's Subject: A Cosmos No One Owns* (Cambridge: Cambridge University Press, 1992), 3.

54. Philip Weinstein, *What Else but Love?,* 5. Any number of guest writers addressing the Faulkner and Yoknapatawpha Conference have shared their reading experience of Faulkner and how it affected their own writing, Houston Baker, Clyde Edgerton, and Albert Murray figure among them.

55. Gerald Prince, "Introduction to the Study of the Narratee" (1973), in *Reader-Response Criticism,* 7–25.

56. Walker Gibson, "Authors, Speakers, Readers, and Mock Readers" (1950), in *Reader-Response Criticism,* 1–6. Tompkins placed Gibson's essay at the start of her landmark anthology, because: "in retrospect, it constitutes the first step in a series that gradually breaks through the boundaries that separate the text from its producers and consumers and reconstitutes it as a web whose threads have no beginning and no end" (xi).

57. Fish, *Is There a Text in This Class?,* 49.

58. Umberto Eco, *The Role of the Reader: Explorations in the Semiotics of Texts* (1979) (London: Hutchinson, 1981). See especially 3–11.

59. Noel Polk, introduction to *The Marionettes: A Play in One Act* by William Faulkner ([Charlottesville]: Bibliographical Society of the University of Virginia and the University Press of Virginia, 1977), x.

60. See especially Sensibar, *The Origins of Faulkner's Art,* and Lothar Hönnighausen, *William Faulkner: The Art of Stylization in His Early Graphic and Literary Work* (Cambridge, England: Cambridge University Press, 1987).

61. John McClure, review, New Orleans *Times-Picayune,* 25 January 1925, ctd. in *William Faulkner: The Critical Heritage,* 50.

62. Maly and Dietfried Gerhardus, *Symbolism and Art Nouveau* (Oxford, England: Phaidon, 1979), 25.

63. Unsigned review, *New York Times Book Review,* 11 April 1926, ctd. in *William Faulkner: The Critical Heritage,* 54; Conrad Aiken, review, *New York Evening Post,* 11 June 1927, ctd. in *Critical Heritage,* 64.

64. Blotner cites Liveright's letter of rejection (1974 *Faulkner*), 560.

65. In *William Faulkner: The Critical Heritage,* 62.

66. Hugh M. Ruppersburg, *Voice and Eye in Faulkner's Fiction* (Athens: University of Georgia Press, 1983), 76–80.

67. See Michael Zeitlin, "Faulkner's *Pylon:* The City in the Age of Mechanical Reproduction," *Canadian Review of American Studies* 22 (1991): 229–40 and "*Pylon,* Joyce, and Faulkner's Imagination," in *Faulkner and the Artist: Faulkner and Yoknapatawpha, 1993,* ed. Donald M. Kartiganer and Ann J. Abadie (Jackson: University Press of Mississippi, 1996), 181–207.

68. Or one might see the convict's reading in *If I Forget Thee, Jerusalem.* Similarly, Karl Zender's comments on Gavin Stevens, reading to Linda Snopes, depicts a "seeming dependence of reader on writer." See his *The Crossing of the Ways: William Faulkner, the South, and the Modern World* (New Brunswick: Rutgers University Press, 1989), 40–41.

69. David Krause, "Reading Bon's Letter and Faulkner's *Absalom, Absalom!*" *PMLA* 99 (March 1984): 225–39. In other articles, Krause submits other letters (Shreve's and Mr. Compson's)

to similar scrutiny: see "Reading Shreve's Letters and Faulkner's *Absalom, Absalom!*" *Studies in American Fiction* 11 (Autumn 1983): 153–69, and "Opening Pandora's Box: Re-reading Compson's Letter and Faulkner's *Absalom, Absalom!*" *Centennial Review* 30 (Summer 1986): 358–82.

70. See, for example, Karl F. Zender, "Reading in 'The Bear,'" *Faulkner Studies* 1 (1980): 91–99.

71. Peter Brooks, "Incredulous Narration: *Absalom, Absalom!*" *Comparative Literature* 34, no. 3 (Summer 1982): 263. This influential essay became part of Brooks's book *Reading for the Plot: Design and Intention in Narrative* (Oxford: Clarendon, 1984).

72. Karen Ramsay Johnson, "Gender, Sexuality, and the Artist in Faulkner's Novels," *American Literature* 61 (March 1989): 14; Karen McPherson, "*Absalom, Absalom!: Telling Scratches*," *Modern Fiction Studies* 33, no. 3 (Autumn 1987): 432.

73. Carolyn Porter, *Seeing and Being: The Plight of the Participant Observer in Emerson, James, Adams, and Faulkner* (Middletown, CT: Wesleyan University Press, 1981), 260.

74. Ruppersburg, *Voice and Eye.*

75. Robert Dale Parker, *Faulkner and the Novelistic Imagination* (Urbana: University of Illinois Press, 1985).

76. James A. Snead, *Figures of Division: William Faulkner's Major Novels* (New York: Methuen, 1986), xi.

77. Walter A. Davis, *The Act of Interpretation: A Critique of Literary Reason* (Chicago: University of Chicago Press, 1978), 1–62.

78. Arnold L. Weinstein, *Vision and Response in Modern Fiction* (Ithaca, NY: Cornell University Press, 1974), 16.

79. Kinney, *Narrative Poetics,* 9.

80. Porter, *Seeing and Being,* 254.

81. Cathy Waegner, *Recollection and Discovery: The Rhetoric of Character in William Faulkner's Novels* (Frankfurt am Main: Peter Lang, 1983).

82. Wadlington, *Reading Faulknerian Tragedy,* 131, 61.

83. John T. Matthews, "The Elliptical Nature of *Sanctuary*," *Novel: A Forum on Fiction* 17 (1984): 246–265.

84. Homer B. Pettey, "Reading and Raping in *Sanctuary*," *Faulkner Journal* 3 (Fall 1987): 72.

85. Laura E. Tanner, "Reading Rape: *Sanctuary* and *The Women of Brewster Place*," *American Literature* 62, no. 4 (December 1990): 560, 561. For an essay similarly influenced by Wolfgang Iser, see, too, Terry Heller, "Terror and Empathy in Faulkner's *Sanctuary*," *American Quarterly* 40 (1984): 344–64.

86. Meir Sternberg, "Temporal Ordering, Modes of Expositional Distribution, and Three Models of Rhetorical Control in the Narrative Text: Faulkner, Balzac and Austen," *PTL: A Journal for Descriptive Poetics and Theory of Literature* 1 (1976): 305.

87. John Duvall, *Faulkner's Marginal Couple: Invisible, Outlaw, and Unspeakable Communities* (Austin: University of Texas Press, 1990), 24, 25.

88. Patrocinio P. Schweickart, "Reading Ourselves: Toward a Feminist Theory of Reading," *Gender and Reading: Essays on Readers, Texts, and Contexts,* ed. Elizabeth A. Flynn and Patrocinio P. Schweickart (Baltimore: Johns Hopkins University Press, 1986), 48.

89. Judith Fetterley, *The Resisting Reader: A Feminist Approach to American Fiction* (Bloomington: Indiana University Press, 1978), xii.

90. Perry, "Literary Dynamics," 318.

91. Porter, *Seeing and Being,* 276.

92. For Toker, the role of the knight redeemer in "*The Waste Land*" of the novel is played by the reader—"to integrate the Compson tragedy into a broader perspective, yet without losing the aftershine of the emotional response that it has elicited on the first reading." Leona Toker, *Eloquent Reticence: Withholding Information in Fictional Narrative* (Lexington: University of Kentucky Press, 1993), 41.

93. Reported by Loic Bouvard, "Conversation with William Faulkner," trans. Henry Dan Piper, *Modern Fiction Studies* 5 (Winter 1959–1960): 363.

11

Popular-Culture Criticism

M. Thomas Inge

To put the subject of popular-culture criticism in perspective, some history may be in order. In 1982, I submitted to Evans Harrington and Ann Abadie (then charged with the conduct of the Faulkner and Yoknapatawpha Conference) the following suggestions for research in the area of popular culture as it touched on William Faulkner:

The Popular Performing and Visual Arts

Faulkner on the Screen: Adaptations of the fiction to film and television. Topics might consider the adaptations of specific works or the general history of making movies about the books with a focus on what they have contributed to the popular image of Faulkner.

Faulkner in Hollywood: His motion picture scripts. How serious was he about his writing for the movies? (I suspect more serious that we have been led to believe. A reading of *The De Gaulle Story* shows he was a conscious film craftsman, and Hollywood is not in the habit of hiring writers who don't produce good scripts.) The whole subject requires reevaluation.

Faulkner on Stage: It would be interesting to examine Faulkner's attitudes toward drama, his writing and the production of *Requiem for a Nun,* plays based on his works, impersonations (such as John Maxwell's *Oh, Mr. Faulkner, Do You Write?*), and plays using Faulkner's life and times (such as Heather McDonald's *Faulkner's Bicycle*).

Faulkner and the Fine Arts: Musical adaptations, opera, and ballet. I'm not sure exactly how many of these have been done, but a few over the years. It would be informative to have them evaluated by music and dance critics.

Faulkner and Photography: J. R. Cofield, Martin J. Dain, and others. What were Faulkner's attitudes toward photography? How did the work of Cofield and others contribute to his public image, and did he consciously participate in shaping it through intentional poses?

The Illustrated Faulkner: Who were the artists who designed the dust jackets and title pages and did drawings for the fiction in books and magazines? How did they interpret Faulkner and influence our understanding of the works?

The Print Media

Faulkner and Journalism: His criticism of journalism is most strongly expressed through the nameless reporter in *Pylon.* What were his opinions of the press? How did he use the press himself, through letters to the editor and contributions to the *Oxford Eagle,* to create an image?

Faulkner and the Popular Magazine: What were his intentions (aside from money) in placing stories with certain popular magazines? Were his aesthetic intentions different when writing for a large audience of magazine readers? How did his appearances there influence his general reputation as a writer?

Faulkner and Detective Fiction: What detective novelists did Faulkner read and how did they influence his work, not only his own detective stories but his general fiction as well? What kind of case can be made out for him as a detective-story writer, and where does he fit in the tradition of such writing in America?

Faulkner Satirized: From time to time, certain writers and journalists have set out to burlesque and lampoon the famous Faulkner style. How effectively do they work as critiques, and what do they tell us about popular attitudes toward the man and the work?

Faulkner in Paperback: How much have paperback sales contributed to his success? Did he hope or aim for a large reading audience? How has he fared as a popular writer? Who reads the numerous Vintage paperback reprints? Some reader-response criticism would be useful here.

Promotion and the Public Myth

Faulkner as a Public Figure: How did his image in the public eye evolve? Were his efforts to discourage cover stories by *Life* and *Time* mere ploys in creating an intentional image? What eventually led him to travel for the U.S. State Department, make public pronouncements, and lecture at the University of Virginia? Was he finally as conscious of image as F. Scott Fitzgerald or Ernest Hemingway? Was his public persona one of his fictional creations?

Faulknerian Folklore: Private jokes, public fictions, and outright lies. Faulkner was given to creating, encouraging, or simply refusing to deny all sorts of outrageous stories about himself. Many of them have become often-repeated bits of folklore about the man and a part of the traditions in American and Southern folklore.

The Promotion of a Genius: Faulkner and his publishers. How did his publishers promote and advertise his books? Were their approaches suitable for a writer of

Faulkner's talent and complexity? Did they understand what they were promoting? To what degree were they responsible for public perceptions of Faulkner?

In the twenty intervening years, critics have pursued many of these lines of inquiry. Their work firmly establishes that any assessment of the work of a great writer of the twentieth century must necessarily entail an examination of the cultural contexts in which the writer worked and lived. Writers do not create in a vacuum, and a work of literature relates to and is influenced by everything the writer reads, sees, and experiences. As Faulkner indicated, "Anyone who wants to write must read everything, trash, the best, the worst, everything, because he will never know when he will find something he can need and he will use" (Meriwether and Millgate 181). Since the twentieth century especially witnessed the complex development of a massive media environment and several new forms of popular culture that reached people at all social and economic levels in all regions of the United States, it is necessary to examine not only the classic and so-called "high" culture of the century but the popular and mass culture as well. Those who study such questions of late have begun to believe that the distinctions between high and low culture are blurred or are figments of the academic imagination altogether. In any case, the total culture of a society provides the hothouse in which talent blooms and matures.

For this reason, any definition of popular culture is problematic (and the list of my 1982 suggestions offered at the beginning of this chapter may form as good an outline as any). The common assumption is that the term applies to all the various forms of entertainment distributed to the largest part of the population through the mass media, which have come into being as a consequence of the technology and science of the industrial revolution. Some critics have argued that popular culture reflects the values and experiences of the majority through rituals, lifestyles, myths, and establishments that involved people in pursuit of pleasure, beauty, fulfillment, and understanding. I have argued elsewhere that "popular culture is what we do by choice to engage our minds and our bodies when we are not working or sleeping. This can be active—playing baseball, driving an automobile, dancing—or passive—watching television, sunbathing, or reading a book. It can be creative—painting a portrait, writing a poem, cooking a meal—or simply responsive—playing a game, watching a circus, or listening to music" (Inge, Introduction xxvi). For my purposes, here, however, I will apply a more practical approach and consider William Faulkner in relation to such specific forms of popular culture as film, the print media, popular literature, and music.

Following the examples of Walt Whitman and Mark Twain in the nineteenth century, many twentieth-century American writers attempted to establish a presence in the popular culture of their time. Ernest Hemingway and F. Scott Fitzgerald most prominently succeeded, to the point that the grinning, bushy face of the great white hunter and the sophisticated, handsome image of the jazz-age philosopher seem permanently embedded in the American imagination. John Steinbeck has possibly outdone both of these by having a National

Steinbeck Center created in his honor, developed by the city of Salinas and supported by a daily flood of tourists (see http://www.steinbeck.org). Thomas Wolfe, Norman Mailer, and Truman Capote are others who seemed to thrive in the public eye, such efforts no doubt calculated to encourage book sales, as well as feed the ego. Notable exceptions include J. D. Salinger, Thomas Pynchon, Cormac McCarthy, and William Faulkner, the first two extreme examples of writers avoiding public scrutiny altogether.

For the most part, Faulkner saw the media as a mixed blessing, wanting to promote and sell his books so as to support his family and his patrician way of life in Oxford but also resisting the intrusiveness of interviewers and promoters into his private life. Basically a shy man, he developed rude strategies for dealing with intruders, turning them away from his doorstep, no matter how far they may have come to meet him, resisting offers of prominent magazines to feature his life story in their pages, or pretending to be a farmer or country rustic who knew nothing about literature or the world at large. Yet the occasional student, reporter, young writer, or professor was allowed in, courteously received, and generously treated, for reasons only Faulkner knew. Provoked by some controversy, especially Civil Rights, he would write letters to newspapers and magazines to let his views be known. Because he saw it as his patriotic duty, he allowed the State Department to send him off on diplomatic cultural missions to Europe, Japan, and South America and involve him in the People-to-People program. In his later years, he settled into Charlottesville as writer-in-residence at the University of Virginia, where he answered the most pedantic questions about his fiction and personal beliefs, even though he thought that a trip to Washington at the invitation of President John Kennedy to have dinner with Nobel Laureates was too far to travel "to eat with strangers" (Blotner, 1984 *Faulkner* 703).

Faulkner expressed himself most explicitly on the subject in his 1955 essay for *Harper's* magazine, "On Privacy," where he explained, "that only a writer's works were in the public domain, to be discussed and investigated and written about, the writer himself having put them there by submitting them for publication and accepting money for them. . . . But that, until the writer committed a crime or ran for public office, his private life was his own" (Meriwether 66). But a more revealing statement may be something he said in response to a student's question at the University of Virginia in 1958 about success: "Success is peculiar. If you beg and plead she scorns you. If you show her the back of your hand, she will cling to your knees" (Inge, *Conversations* 166).

Ironically enough, Faulkner's contradictory attitudes and actions served only to generate even more interest. If a reporter is denied access, he or she will try even harder to get the story, usually turning to secondary information or less-reliable sources, which is why the Faulkner public print record is filled with errors and misinformation. Refusing a presidential invitation to dinner will create more publicity than accepting it would. Sometimes one has the suspicion that Faulkner knew exactly what he was doing and was using the media to his own calculated ends.

Given these attitudes, along with the complexity of his fiction, which created difficulties for all of his readers, as well as his reputation for drinking to excess,

Faulkner emerged in the popular perception as a rude, drunken, backwoods genius with pretensions to social status that he didn't deserve but a reputation for literary greatness that he did. In the satiric literary history *American Lit Relit,* Richard Armour notes that when *The Marble Faun* failed, Faulkner "began to write stories and novels peopled with idiots, drunkards, thieves, murderers, prostitutes, and perverts, and won a devoted following among readers who wished to learn how things were going in the South" (155). When David Levine caricatured him for the *New York Review of Books* in 1963, Faulkner was dressed like Huckleberry Finn (15). In a 1996 comic strip sequence of *Zippy,* artist Bill Griffith satirizes the Nobel Prize speech, particularly the phrase "last ding-dong of doom," Hostess Ding Dongs being Zippy's favorite junk food.

While William Faulkner seldom addressed himself directly to the subject of popular culture—aside from his own efforts in writing film and television scripts and detective fiction—he was fully aware of its all-pervasive presence in the social and cultural milieu of the twentieth-century world in which he lived and worked. Although the development of a modern mass culture began with the invention of the printing press and the technology necessary to wide dissemination of multiple reproductions of pictures and texts, it was not until the twentieth century that the means became available for reaching millions of people through improvements in linotype machines, photography, film, color printing, and airwave communications—so much so that no small corner of the continent was left untouched, even the remote, rural areas of the South, or a place like Oxford, Mississippi. Thus, Faulkner's fictional world is filled with the various forms and ways we have entertained and informed ourselves in this century.

As we move through his fiction, Faulkner unobtrusively mentions and displays the popular culture of the time in which the novel is set. In *Sartoris,* Dr. Peabody is always reading what Faulkner calls "lurid, paper-covered nickel novels" (95); the women are frequently found leafing through the pages of magazines, while Miss Jenny prefers the salacious tabloid newspapers filled with "accounts of arson and murder and violent dissolutions and adultery" (48). In addition to mentions of the circus, Coca-Cola, Babe Ruth, and baseball, *The Sound and the Fury* (together with the Compson "Appendix") includes among its minor characters the Yoknapatawpha County librarian who attempts to keep high school students from reading copies of *Forever Amber* by Kathleen Winsor, *Jurgen* by James Branch Cabell, and the *Topper* novels of Thorne Smith—some of the most titillating and sexually suggestive popular fiction of the period (Vintage ed. 413–14). A member of the same high-school class as Caddy, she is the one who confronts Jason and Dilsey with the photograph clipped from a magazine of Caddy with a German officer in a European setting; thus it is a medium of popular culture that gives us our last glimpse of the fate of Caddy Compson.

Light in August contains that haunting scene in which Joe Christmas compulsively reads a men's magazine from cover to cover before heading for town to wander the streets and end up in Joanna Burden's bedroom with a razor in his hand. The magazine, Faulkner says, "was of that type whose covers bear either pictures of young women in underclothes or pictures of men in the act of shooting one another with pistols" (Vintage ed. 102–3), in other words, of the police detective or murder variety, with an emphasis on masochism and bondage. In any case, Christmas was receiving suitable visual and emotional reinforcement for the horrible mutilation he was about to enact.

The boxer John L. Sullivan, motion pictures, and the stage version of *Ben Hur* are sources of comparison and metaphor in *Absalom, Absalom!;* college football is central to the plot of *The Hamlet;* and, in addition to horse racing, one of the themes of *The Reivers* has to do with the impact of the automobile on Southern life—after the first one arrives, the manners, mores, and morals of the isolated rural community are never to be the same again. The automobile becomes the instrument of man's final fall in the Garden of Eden—once Memphis is put within the easy distance of Jefferson. The automobile was also the conveyance by which Temple Drake was delivered to her disgrace and corruption in *Sanctuary,* a novel that refers to the fashions of the 1920s, popular slick magazines, the mail-order catalog (used as it was in the outhouse), and the film actor John Gilbert (compared in ironic counterpoint with the unromantic, ungentlemanly, debased *Popeye*). *Sanctuary* also draws on the comic strips when the author gives the villain the name Popeye, and as I have pointed out elsewhere, Faulkner used names from and allusions to comic-strip characters in much of his fiction (Inge, "Faulkner Reads" 78–99). What is clear from these selected references is that Faulkner used elements of popular culture as ways to reflect on the characters of the people who populate his fiction and to reveal indirectly important things about their symbolic functions.

Since he was a man who professed to scorn public attention, it is interesting to note that Faulkner has also entered popular culture, whatever his own wishes might have been. His presence is not as extensive as that of Fitzgerald or Hemingway perhaps, the first an inevitable figure included in all illustrations and commercial paintings of the jazz age on book covers, in magazines, and in advertisements, and the second so popular among clothing, food, fishing rod, and gun vendors that the Hemingway family has registered the name as a trademark for all commercial uses. For example, I have seen at least one greeting card featuring Faulkner. The outside reads, "I know what you are thinking. . . . If William Faulkner could write 23 novels, 72 short stories, 109 essays, and 6 plays [those figures, of course, are purely fictional] . . . the least I could do is write one lousy letter. Well, I just want you to know . . . ," and the inside concludes, " . . . I ain't no Faulkner!" Faulkner does appear in advertisements from time to time— a want-ad promotion notes that "William Faulkner Wrote Want Ads, Too!" and quotes one he published in the *Oxford Eagle,* and the Davey Company promoted its book binding service through a full page ad, in which, beside a photograph of Faulkner in his hunting outfit, the text describes him as a guide to life in the South, leading readers to assume that, like the Davey product, his opinions could be counted on to be strong and enduring. The U.S. Post Office once used Faulkner on a poster to promote careers in the postal service, apparently overlooking his having been officially reprimanded for his own poor performance as postmaster in Oxford and hardly, therefore, a proper model for beginners. Perhaps all has been forgiven, though, as witnessed by the special stamp issued with his portrait in August of 1987 (Beard, "Footnotes"). Faulkner, who didn't want to be at the beck and call of every son of a bitch with the price of a two-cent stamp, could then be licked by anyone with the price of a twenty-two-cent stamp, thanks to inflation.

One book reviewer created a scheme for rating books according to how many little old ladies they are worth, with reference to Faulkner's famous statement that Keats's "Ode on a Grecian Urn" is, in the larger scheme of things, worth any number of old ladies, including his own mother, whom he would rob for the sake of art. The maximum rating on the Old Lady Scale is four, I might note (Fiore). In 1985, off-Broadway theater was treated to a play by Heather McDonald called *Faulkner's Bicycle* in which Faulkner, played by Addison Powell, whizzes through Oxford at midnight on a bicycle whistling "Toot, Toot, Tootsie, Good-bye," and having had too much bourbon, repeatedly crashes into a pond. There is nothing biographical or factual in the play, but Faulkner's eccentricity is used as a symbolic touchstone for the three eccentric women on which the play is centered (Gussow; Sommers). An oddity in the category of drama is a one-act play by Joseph Robinette based on "A Rose for Emily" but designed for juvenile audiences from the sixth- to eighth-grade school levels. It takes liberties with the chronology, adds some unlikely details (Emily Grierson throws corn from an upstairs window to feed the chickens), and provides some names for several characters that would sound Southern only to a non-Southern ear (Dewey Nix, Elda Tate, Eulola Holcomb, and Reavis Quinton). The play remains faithful to the horrific gothic conclusion, however, presumably to the delight of adolescent participants and viewers. One of the most mysterious and engaging presences of Faulkner in popular culture, or rather of his creation Quentin Compson, is found on a brass plaque on the Anderson Bridge over the Charles River at Harvard University, which originally read "Quentin Compson III. June 10, 1910. Drowned in the fading of honeysuckle." Students who admired Faulkner and identified with Quentin's sense of displacement and tragic idealism placed it there anonymously in 1965. Although accidentally destroyed in 1983, and replaced by another plaque, it has been for over two decades secretly visited by ardent readers on the anniversary of Quentin's suicide from the bridge (Russakoff). Few literary characters are paid such a tribute in the minds and imaginations of his admirers.

Faulkner has often proven to be eminently quotable in the media. Ann Landers once resorted to Faulkner for one of her "Gems of the Day," when she credited him with "Man isn't really evil—he just doesn't have any common sense." In the comic strip *Kudzu,* about a Southern adolescent who aspires to be a writer in the tradition of Thomas Wolfe, creator Doug Marlette has Kudzu quote Faulkner to the Reverend Will D. Dunn, "Y'know, a preacher and a novelist have a lot in common. . . . They both need to have a feel for what Faulkner called 'the contradictions of the human heart.'" At that moment, the only contradiction that seemed to be worrying the reverend, however, was how junk food can taste great but be less filling. A thorough knowledge of Faulkner's life and work were necessary to complete successfully a crossword puzzle and a quiz in a collection devoted to *Fifty American Authors* (Maloska and Burnanelli 161–64). A sign of his continued presence in the popular mind is the fact that the staff of *Who Wants to be a Millionaire* called the present writer during the 2002 season to verify a question about Faulkner that was to be put to a contestant on the popular television show (it had to do with the change in the spelling of his name).

An almost altogether unexplored area of Faulkner criticism is the illustration of his fiction, particularly odd since Faulkner himself contributed cartoon drawings for his unpublished high-school yearbook (now available in volume 5 of Brodsky and Hamblin's *Faulkner: A Comprehensive Guide to the Brodsky Collection*) and drawings for the Ole Miss yearbook (published in Collins, *William Faulkner: Early Prose and Poetry*). This would include the drawings that accompanied magazine stories, the several books that were illustrated on first publication (Edward Shenton illustrated both *The Unvanquished* and *Big Woods;* see Blotner, 1984 *Faulkner* 595–96 on Faulkner's participation), and the cover art that appeared on all his works. Matters for discussion would include how well the art reflected the fiction, the extent to which each illustration itself was an interpretation of the work, and what the visual representation conveyed to the reader about the meaning of the book or story. Who were the artists and what were their contributions to our understanding and appreciation of Faulkner and his reputation in the eye of the public?

One figure especially worth investigation is New Jersey native James Sante Avati (1912–), the prolific and popular cover artist for over 200 novels published in the Signet edition series from New American Library in the 1950s. Avati also worked for Avon, Ballantine, Bantam, and Pocket Books among others and during his career helped sell millions of copies of paperback editions of the novels of such writers as Erskine Caldwell, James T. Farrell, Richard Wright, Tennessee Williams, John O'Hara, D. H. Lawrence, Theodore Dreiser, J. D. Salinger, Kathleen Winsor, Truman Capote, Robert Penn Warren, Gore Vidal, and Mickey Spillane among the best known. He was especially recognizable for his sultry and sexually charged covers, usually depicting a provocative female figure or a couple at some moment of passion or disturbed transgression. It is arguable that the 50-some painted covers Avati did for Erskine Caldwell novels did as much to sell the books for New American Library as did the steamy prose inside, which nearly always dealt with near-pornographic tales of lust and perversion down South. The cover for *God's Little Acre,* for example, with a toothless Ty Ty Walden protectively standing before the three sensual women in his household, but provocatively reaching out to touch them, powerfully conveyed the perverse personality of the old rogue who viewed his own daughters with a combined sense of lust and exaltation. Occasionally, however, even Caldwell's prose failed to live up to the promise of the seductive sexuality of the cover art.

Avati painted the covers for seven Faulkner volumes published in the Signet series between 1949 and 1954 (*The Wild Palms* twice, *Intruder in the Dust, Soldiers' Pay,* a combined edition of *Sanctuary* and *Requiem for a Nun, The Unvanquished,* and *Sartoris*). He claimed to read every book before he designed the cover and to select a central point of crisis for portrayal. He told Piet Schreuders, "I try to make my covers have a certain amount of shock in them so they will be interesting. I like a dramatic emotional conflict" (Schreuders 23). Thus his cover for *Intruder in the Dust* shows Lucas Beauchamp being carried into jail by the sheriff as a threatening crowd looks on. But a sexually intense situation interested him more, and the majority of his covers portray a man and a woman in some such arrangement. "One of the universals, after all, is man and woman," Avati has said. "And everybody's interested" (23). The combined volume of *Sanctuary* and *Requiem for a Nun* portrays Temple Drake posed on a wrinkled-sheeted bed while Miss Reba looks on and Gavin Stevens appears to be reasoning with her. Her fallen state seems clear. These and other cover paintings, no doubt, gave Faulkner a higher cachet on the newsstand than they might have had otherwise. It is possible too that the association of Avati with the enormously popular Erskine Caldwell gave Faulkner a boost among many readers who ordinarily would not have selected one of his novels from the rack. A study of Avati in terms of his influence on the reputation of Faulkner, and all the other writers mentioned, would tell a lot about reader response [see chapter 10] and the appreciation of American literature during the 1950s.

While many classics of American literature have been adapted to the graphic novel and its progenitor, the comic book, as in the frequently revived *Classics Illustrated* series, none of Faulkner's works has been so treated. The complexity of his major novels would offer interesting but difficult challenges to any visual interpretation, but a step in this direction was taken in 1991 in Paris with the publication of a special edition of *Tandis que j'agonise,* or *As I Lay Dying,* jointly sponsored by Faulkner's French publisher, Gallimard, and Futuropolis, a major press devoted to anthologies of classic comic strips and graphic novels. It was one of a series of such editions in which a major comic-book artist was asked to select his favorite author and work to illustrate. Volumes devoted to Proust, Dostoyevski, Dos Passos, and Céline preceded Faulkner.

This edition incorporates the Maurice Coindreau translation of *As I Lay Dying* with 150 black-and-white drawings by comic-book artist André Juillard. Juillard's first comic-book works were tales of chivalry and romance in the style of Harold Foster's Sunday feature *Prince Valiant,* and much of his subsequent work was historically based, especially his popular series *Les sept vies de l'epervier* (1983–1991) and *Arno* (1984–1987). When invited to illustrate any author of his choice, as a longtime admirer of his fiction, Juillard chose Faulkner. Among his favorite novels, he thought *Light in August* was too long, *The Sound and the Fury* too complicated, and *Sanctuary* insufficiently graphic, so he settled on *As I Lay Dying* because of its engaging story line and the deeply felt Freudian themes, which touched him personally.

Not having visited the American South, Juillard relied on Depression-era photographs by such people as Dorothea Lange and Arthur Rothstein, as well as more recent photographs of Oxford and Mississippi by Alain Desvergues. While faithful to his visual sources in background and detail, he focuses more fully on the faces of characters in an effort to invest them with the psychological complexity of the originals in Faulkner's novel. The traditional design of the separate drawings, combined with a strong sense of physical reality and his ability to capture the truth of human nature, make the book a striking and admirable collaboration. It remains a work of which Juillard is especially proud and suggests that a full-scale comic-book adaptation of a novel by Faulkner is possible, if not inevitable.

At least one major graphic novel has been inspired by a passage in one of Faulkner's novels. The British-born artist Martin Vaughn-James was raised in Australia and lived in London, Montreal, Toronto, and Paris before settling in Brussels, Belgium. In the 1970s, before devoting himself exclusively to painting, he published four graphic novels in Canada: *Elephant* (1970), *The Projector* (1971), *The Park* (1972), and *The Cage* (1975). All of them are provocative combinations of words and pictures, produced under the influence of the French *nouveau roman* and designed not to respond to any "externally imposed system or logic or reasoning" but rather to "answer to its own demands, those made from within, following its own chronology, its reason for being, and its own reality on many levels simultaneously." More specifically of *The Cage* he has said that he intended "to develop a story without any character. A story where the reader (the spectator) replaces the character(s)" (quoted in Groensteen 16–17).

Vaughn-James kept a set of notebooks in which he recorded the genesis of *The Cage* and which are on deposit in the *Musée de la bande dessinée* in Angoulême, France. On the very first page of the first notebook, he recorded the source of the title and the work. It is a quotation from *Light in August:* " . . . though he did not then know that, like the eagle, his own flesh as well as space was still a cage" (reproduced in Groensteen 18).

The quotation is from chapter 7 of the novel in which the young Joe Christmas is struggling with the stern discipline and punishment of his puritanical adoptive father Simon McEachern. Following such an altercation, Joe thinks:

> When he went to bed that night his mind was made up to run away. He felt like an eagle: hard, sufficient, potent, remorseless, strong. But that passed, though he did not then know that, like the eagle, his own flesh as well as all space was still a cage. (150–51)

As the remainder of the novel indicates, Joe is totally trapped in a nexus of cultural, political, racial, religious, and social institutions that will deprive him of any freedom to act. He is trapped in a cage not of his own making, and his efforts to resist will lead to murder, emasculation, and death.

In *The Cage,* Vaughn-James leads the reader visually by way of 177 images through a desolate landscape and cityscape entirely empty of human beings, with only remnants to testify to their existence—vacant buildings, broken furniture, torn clothing and bedsheets, and abandoned possessions, with evidence of violence scattered throughout. It is as if some sudden and violent eruption or, to quote the text, "inevitable flood of mute destruction" has wiped out life in some pitiless Armageddon. The whole novel is framed visually by a wire cage through which the reader is led into and out of the book like a continuing moving camera shot in a film (suggestive of some of the camera shots in the 1961 Alain

Resnais film version of Alain Robbe-Grillet's *nouveau roman, Last Year at Marienbad*).

In a sense, *The Cage* is an extrapolation of Faulkner's meditation on the inescapability of certain forces in life—psychological, theological, and institutional—that trap humans and render them impotent. While the fight is over, the remnants of their struggle testify to the power of their challenge to the forces of destruction—one scene contains abandoned tape recorders, cameras, tapes, records, books, and a typewriter, all evidence of efforts to make sense and art out of a confused and brief existence.

There is another connection as well. Vaughn-James has provided prose that runs above and below the illustrations throughout the book, reportedly written later and with no necessary connection to the pictures. It is distinctly Faulknerian prose, echoing no specific passages but imitating the master's endless apocalyptic style, as in the opening line. It begins, " . . . the cage stands as before . . . unfinished and already decayed as if its construction had been abruptly and inexplicably arrested . . . ," a sentence which does not come to rest for 24 pages. Faulkner was famous for his lengthy sentences that went on for pages. Vaughn-James uses such breathless phrases and sentences in an effort to capture some sense of the entrapment and destruction so vividly rendered in his merciless visual holocaust. One may view *The Cage* as a tribute to Faulkner, who tried to capture the mean nature of man's existence in a style finally incapable of distilling the whole of its tragic circumstance. The nobility lies in the attempt. Faulkner would have found *The Cage* admirable.

Unlike Hemingway and Fitzgerald, no feature-length film of a biographical or fictional nature has ever been based on Faulkner's life (excluding the several documentaries made for television, the best of which is *William Faulkner: A Life on Paper,* scripted by Faulkner's friend and fellow Hollywood scriptwriter, Albert I. Bezzerides, directed by Robert Squier, narrated by Raymond Burr, and first shown on PBS in December 1979). He has made noteworthy appearances in at least two, however. The 1994 film *Foreign Student* was based on an autobiographical best-selling French novel by journalist and filmmaker Philippe Labro, who spent a year as an exchange student at a Virginia college. He seems to have heard Faulkner speak at one of his appearances as writer-in-residence at the University of Virginia in 1957 or 1958. In the motion-picture version, filmed on the campuses of Washington and Lee University, Hampden-Sydney College, Randolph-Macon College, and Virginia State University, the older narrator recalls the occasion in a voiceover. Faulkner, played by actor John Habberton, shuffles onto the stage in the Washington and Lee chapel and takes a seat in front of the recumbent mausoleum statue of Robert E. Lee located there. While Faulkner reads and comments in an inaudible background, the narrator presents a portrait that combines personal impressions with a general view of how the public perceived the novelist:

> Everything about him breathed distance, or perhaps he was crushed by a kind of boredom, or embarrassed, as if he was wondering what in the world he was doing in front of all these strangers. He exuded the kind of suave patience that only some

people from the Deep South possess. . . . I'll never forget that handsome face, ravaged by whiskey and sleepless nights, his mouth moving like a sinner in his deathbed confession.

A young woman attending the reading with the French student weeps, touched by an elegant beauty she finds in the weathered author.

Actor John Mahoney, as the character named W. P. Mayhew, plays the most intriguing appearance by Faulkner, in the Coen brothers' 1991 surrealistic fable about a writer in Hollywood, *Barton Fink.* Based loosely on events in the life of proletarian playwright Clifford Odetts, Barton Fink ends up in Hollywood in 1941 assigned to write a script for a low-budget wrestling film with Wallace Beery, as had Faulkner when he arrived in California. Macabre events in a strange hotel where he is staying exacerbate Fink's writer's block, and he seeks the help of veteran writer W. P. Mayhew, whom he meets in a restaurant men's room. The similarities between Bill Mayhew and Faulkner quickly fall into place. Both are heavy drinkers, if not complete alcoholics; both have wives back home named Estelle; and both have Hollywood girlfriends, although Meta Carpenter never wrote scripts or ghosted prose for Faulkner, as does her counterpart, Audrey Taylor, played by Judy Davis in the film. Mayhew is working on a script for a film called *Slave Ship,* which is a project on which Faulkner actually worked, and he presents Fink with a signed copy of his novel, *Nebuchadnezzar,* obviously a counterpart to *Absalom, Absalom!* The film parts ways with reality, however, in several respects. Faulkner had the reputation of turning out work in record time and never let the alcohol stand in the way of meeting his deadlines, as happens to Mayhew, always lost in an alcoholic haze. And neither Faulkner nor Meta met the brutal and shocking end of Mayhew and Audrey in *Barton Fink.*

Marie-José Lavie reads the use of these parallels as a "grand burlesque" in "a spirit both caustic and respectful" of Faulkner (104). I regard the entire film as a satiric fable and send-up of the classic myth of how American writers were used and abused in Hollywood. The Coen brothers have never explained their intentions, but they have admitted that Faulkner is one of the writers they greatly admire. When asked to name their favorite novel, Joel Coen confided:

> *Light in August,* but don't ask me why. The other one I like a lot is *The Wild Palms.* We steal many names from Faulkner, but we haven't attempted to steal a whole book, yet [laughing]. *O Brother, Where Art Thou,* for instance, has a character named Vernon T. Waldrip, and we got that from *The Wild Palms.* (McKenna 73).

What are some of the ways Faulkner's work has been influenced by the pervasive presence of popular culture? Sometimes he appears to have been sensitively attuned to and reshaped for his own artistic purposes elements of the popular culture of his own time. This is especially true, for example, of the culture of African Americans, which Faulkner partly learned by paying careful attention to their music. As David Krause once noted, "William Faulkner listened compulsively to the music of the Afro-American experience, recording its rhythms and voices in his prose, trying to find new ways to make us listen. . . . Throughout his fiction, Faulkner takes and remakes the black man's words and music. 'That

Evening Sun,' for example swells with the submerged passion of Bessie Smith crooning (wordlessly and far away) her 'St. Louis Blues.' . . . 'Go Down Moses,' of course, revoices the rituals, histories, and myths of a familiar spiritual" (80–81). Moreover, "That Evening Sun" cites in its title not only the opening line of W. C. Handy's familiar "St. Louis Blues," but the language, events, and themes of the story reflect a full range of phrases borrowed from gospel music, spirituals, and the blues having to do with promiscuity, sin, death, judgment, and redemption (Bennett; Gartner). The indigenous music, words, and emotions of the African Americans were appropriated and made new in the crucible of the powerful rhetorical sweep of Faulkner's prose style (see Charles A. Peek, "'Handy' Ways to Teach 'That Evening Sun'").

Likewise, Faulkner seems to have absorbed and profited from all the kinds of popular writing that was being published around him as he learned to write for the paying market, so as to earn a living, as well as to satisfy his own artistic sensibilities. Thomas McHaney, who has demonstrated a remarkable facility for probing into little-explored and unexpected corners of areas of influence, has examined most of the magazines and publications that probably passed through Faulkner's hands when he served as postmaster at the University of Mississippi between 1922 and 1924. He was notorious for holding onto patrons' periodicals until he had read them. These would have included such literary publications as *The Dial* and *The Little Review,* as well as such larger circulation magazines as *Time, American Mercury, Nation, New Republic,* and *North American Review.* McHaney convincingly speculates that the novice writer was "reading in both the popular and literary press, and thereby discovering through essays, reviews, anecdotes, and conversations not only what books to read but why he should be reading them. . . . The postmaster who read his patrons' or the university's magazines, experiencing what art critic Robert Hughes has called 'the shock of the new,' also read the novels by writers who were repeatedly featured, reviewed, explicated, and recommended in those magazines" ("What Faulkner Read" 180, 186). More of this kind of difficult but often rewarding and enlightening contextual research is needed to appreciate fully the extent to which Faulkner's cultural milieu influenced his writing.

A more fully explored area of influence is the reading Faulkner did in the popular pulp fiction of his day, where he probably learned how to write for a wide reading audience so as to make his work turn a profit in the literary marketplace. It was Leslie Fiedler who first suggested, in explaining why *Sanctuary* remained his favorite Faulkner novel, that it included "a potpourri of almost *all* the popular genres of the late 1920s" ("Pop" 88), which would have included detective, mystery, horror, and gangster or crime novels. Furthermore, "the novel which Albert Camus believed to be the greatest of Faulkner's fictions belongs to the most disreputable and unredeemable pop genre of all, being pornography," especially "sadomasochistic porn in the tradition of the divine Marquis's *Justine* and *Juliette,* ambiguously and disturbingly blurring the distinction between murder and desire, violence and passion, *thanatos* and eros" (90). Finally, like all true pornography, *Sanctuary* "is essentially voyeuristic in its appeal. When reading it, that is to say, we do not typically identify with its erotically active characters, rapist or raped; but with the Peeping Tom author, who compels us to keep our eye glued to the keyhole, ashamed but unable to withdraw" (90–91). It is the association, then, with disreputable forms of popular fiction that may have led Faulkner later to dismiss the novel as cheaply conceived only to make money.

Walter Wenska, however, has found it revealing to study what Faulkner learned from such writers as Dashiell Hammett, Max Brand, Ring Lardner, Dorothy Sayers, Agatha Christie, Rex Stout, Raymond Chandler, S. S. Van Dine, W. R. Burnett, and other "lords of popular culture" in the days he was trying to break into the commercial short-story market in the years before *Sanctuary:* "A case could be made that these efforts did not deflect him from the major novels he had not yet written so much as enable him to write them. Without what he learned from writing for the slicks, that is, there might not have been a revised *Sanctuary* and the sensation it was designed to arouse" (35–36).

Wenska documents numerous parallels in plots, characterization, character names, themes, and even phraseology between the short stories and *Sanctuary* and the best-selling pulp crime fiction of the 1920s. "Even more appealing to Faulkner, however," Wenska notes, "would be the way detective stories unfold (while telling one tale the detective story uncovers another) and necessarily involve those displacements of chronological time made familiar to us by the Russian formalists. . . . Temporal displacements and dislocations, as well as digressions, generate suspense (and pleasure) by impeding the story and delaying its resolution" (41). Faulkner learned his lessons so well that he would go on to write his own detective fiction such as *Intruder in the Dust* and the stories collected in *Knight's Gambit.*

Vincent Allan King shifts the focus of this discussion to another novel that deeply absorbed the ethos and many of the characteristics of pulp fiction: *The Wild Palms,* a work that alternates chapters of two distinct stories, one featuring a convict who has been misled into a life of crime by his literal reading of dime novels, and the other a couple, Charlotte and Harry, misled by reading cheap romances to pursue some ideal state where only true love can flourish and remain permanent (Harry even makes a living for a while writing stories for confessional magazines). Thus one unifying concern of the novel's two parts is the matter of the authority of pulp or any other kind of fiction. King concludes:

> *The Wild Palms* allows Faulkner to distance himself as far as possible from the pulp fictions that figure so prominently in the novel. Faulkner attempts to liberate his readers from the illusion that fiction is to be received passively, that it is a kind of pill that makes one sick or well, good or bad. Not coincidentally, he simultaneously seeks to free himself from the accusation that he is dispensing bad medicine. (525)

Both Wenska and King brilliantly demonstrate how much is to be learned by placing Faulkner into conjunction with the lowbrow culture of his time and place (as similarly, though not Wenska's and King's point, the novel itself places its characters in conjunction with the lowbrow culture of their times, as in, for example, Charlotte's and Harry's "artistic" endeavors).

If Faulkner absorbed and turned to his own use much of the world of popular literature, this is even more true of film. Early on, critics began to detect, in his impressive stylistics and innovative narratives, elements of the ways film tells stories visually. In 1971, in an intelligent and insightful explication of *Absalom, Absalom!*, J. R. Raper took note of methods in the novel Faulkner may have acquired while writing for the movies in the 1930s: "Using the alogical structure created through technical maneuvers similar to those employed by skilled cinematographers, Faulkner represents the major theme of the novel (the thwarted life) in key images (especially those of closed doors), and, rather than stating the theme statically on the page, calls it to life in the reader" (9). Writing at about the same time, and apparently without reference to Raper's essay, in *The Cinematic Imagination: Writers and the Motion Pictures,* Edward Murray observed Faulkner's filmic imagination and detailed his discovery of filmic qualities, especially in the stream-of-consciousness techniques found in *The Sound and the Fury* and *Light in August.*

In the wake of these suggestions, there would follow a veritable flood of critical essays down to the present building on the rudimentary observations by Raper and Murray. D. M. Murray turned to silent comedies and animated films in a study of Faulkner's humor and argued that Faulkner was at the end line of a series of comic conventions (frantic action, pinwheel imagery, the sudden appearance, delayed gravity, etc.) that came down to him from the humorists of the Old Southwest through silent film comedy and animated cartoons. In a broad study of the visual richness of modern literature, *Fiction and the Camera Eye: Visual Consciousness in Film and the Modern Novel,* Alan Spiegel began with Flaubert and moved through all the major world writers from Zola and Lawrence to Joyce and Woolf discussing their use of cinematic visualization. Faulkner, he found, "is perhaps the most elaborate and prodigious exponent of the cinematized narrative" in that "retinal imagery, camera angles, and montage sequences are to be found everywhere in his novels and stories" (117). Jeffrey J. Folks argued not only that the silent film informed his humor, but also that all of Faulkner's work is saturated by scenes, characters, themes, and sensibilities fostered by the silent movies he probably saw early in his life at the Lyric Theatre in Oxford.

"*The Wild Palms:* Faulkner's Hollywood Novel" by Pamela Rhodes [now Knights] and Richard Godden provided an exhaustively detailed and highly theoretical reading out of the Frankfurt school of criticism and predictably found that, like T. W. Adorno, Georg Lukács, and others, Faulkner found the capitalistic culture industry negative and totalitarian in impulse [see chapter 7]. Miranda J. Burgess found filmic metaphors and ways of seeing to be central to an understanding of gender issues [see chapter 9] in *Light in August.* Joseph R. Urgo and Peter Lurie [see chapter 7] (respectively) published two brilliant essays focusing on the same novel, in light of its cinematic qualities and reflections of the romantic culture in which it was written, "*Absalom, Absalom!:* The Movie" and "'Some Trashy Myth of Reality's Escape': Romance, History, and Film Viewing in *Absalom, Absalom!*" These are astute, articulate, and informative essays. In what is by no means the final word on the topic, Doug Baldwin usefully summarized much of this criticism in "Putting Images into Words: Elements of the 'Cinematic' in William Faulkner's Prose" while advancing his own arguments in behalf of Faulkner's sophisticated use of cinematic aesthetics. He concludes that not only has Faulkner absorbed cinematic imagery but he has in turn suggested "to filmmakers ways in which they can extend the narrational potentials of movies" (60). To return to the full phrase from which the title of the first story of Faulkner's to be adapted to the screen was taken, "turnabout is fair play."

Faulkner's personal relationship with Hollywood, the film scripts he wrote there and to which he contributed, as well as the various adaptations of his novels and stories to the screen have been extensively explored by a great number of critics in book-length works and collections of essays. They cover the essential facts of his work for Warner Brothers in the 1940s, work often turned to the purposes of Hollywood's massive propaganda effort on behalf of the U.S. war effort, including Faulkner's work on Hemingway's story, *To Have and Have Not,* the only time a novel by a Nobel Prize winner was reworked as a script by another Nobel Prize winner, this in an attempt to reprise *Casablanca* (see Hamblin, "The Curious Case of Faulkner's 'The De Gaulle Story'").

Aside from the biographical work of Joseph Blotner and Tom Dardis, the first full-scale assessment of Faulkner's place in film history was Bruce Kawin's *Faulkner and Film* in 1977. While Kawin focused on selected scripts and adaptations and broke essential new ground, Gene D. Phillips undertook a more expansive, leisurely, and detailed study 10 years later in *Fiction, Film, and Faulkner: The Art of Adaptation.* The studies are equally useful and complementary, although not always in agreement. Kawin brings to bear more theory from the field of film criticism, while Phillips is more sensitive to the aesthetics of literature and the art of adaptation. Both confirm Faulkner's importance as a part of the history of filmmaking in America as both a contributor of scripts and a source of scripts by others. Valuable collections of essays include *Man and the Movies,* edited by W. R. Robinson; *Faulkner, Modernism, and Film,* edited by Evans Harrington and Ann Abadie; and the special issue of the *Faulkner Journal* (volume 16) devoted to "Faulkner and Film" under the editorship of Edwin T. Arnold. Two thorough studies of specific adaptations are Regina Fadiman's *Faulkner's* Intruder in the Dust: *Novel into Film* and *Tomorrow and Tomorrow and Tomorrow,* edited by David G. Yellin and Marie Connors. The majority of Faulkner's Warner Brothers screenplays have been brought into print in volumes edited by Louis Daniel Brodsky and Robert W. Hamblin, with the MGM screenplays collected and edited by Bruce Kawin.

There are, unfortunately, no book-length general studies of Faulkner and popular culture, at least not yet, although such works are inevitable. For a beginning, and for topics not mentioned in the present essay, one can turn to the studies gathered in *Faulkner and Popular Culture,* edited by Doreen Fowler and Ann J. Abadie. These are the proceedings of the 1988 Faulkner and Yoknapatawpha Conference held at the University of Mississippi. Because I had taught Faulkner at Moscow State University on a Fulbright lectureship in 1979, I was invited to take part in the 1982 conference on "Faulkner: International Perspectives." Subsequent to that conference, I proposed and outlined for the organizers three topics I thought worth pursuing in the future: Faulkner and humor, Faulkner and popular culture, and Faulkner and folklore. The first two were adopted and mounted in 1984 and 1988, but the last suggestion was never used. Besides *Faulkner and Popular Culture,* at least one essay worth mentioning is "Faulkner and the Culture Industry" by John Matthews. While Matthews attempts to break free of the "myth of the artist corrupted by newly dominant commercial media like movies and magazines" (51) so often applied to Faulkner, he turns to the Frankfurt school of criticism and looks for evidence of resistance, individuality, and subversion in his film work. While this may seem to save Faulkner from the charge of selling out and pandering to commercial expectations, it finally serves to imprison Faulkner in one more theoretical cage. Because Faulkner served few masters in his life as an individual or an artist, however, the way is open for any number of theoretical approaches that will explain and elucidate the unlimited range and complexity of the body of work bequeathed to us by the twentieth-century's major American and world-class author.

NOTE

This chapter incorporates some information first published in "Faulknerian Folklore: Public Fictions, Private Jokes, and Outright Lies," in *Faulkner and Popular Culture: Faulkner and Yoknapatawpha, 1988,* ed. Doreen Fowler and Ann J. Abadie (Jackson: University Press of Mississippi, 1990), 22–33.

12

Textual Criticism

Amy E. C. Linnemann and Philip Cohen

We begin not with *The Sound and the Fury* or *Absalom, Absalom!* or some other Faulkner work but with *Pale Fire,* that difficult and delightful triumph of post-modernist fiction by quite a different sort of author, Vladimir Nabokov. Published in 1962, this dazzlingly original collection of puzzles and parodies masquerading as a novel is both a side-splittingly funny and painfully moving meditation on the parallels and differences between art and lunacy, artists and madmen, and artistic creation and schizophrenic projection. Conceiving of both art and delusion as apparently similar but ultimately quite different forms of thievery and transformation, *Pale Fire* is a tour-de-force self-reflexive entertainment about the necessities and dangers that attend our compulsive need to create fictions to live by.

A narrative disguised as a **scholarly edition** of the last poem by John Shade, a recently murdered American poet, with notes and commentary by his self-proclaimed intimate friend and literary adviser Charles Kinbote, a professor of Zemblan language and literature at Wordsmith University, *Pale Fire* is also a savage parody of academic literary criticism. Through a series of increasingly comic dramatic ironies, the reader gradually learns that Kinbote is a loveless and unloved paranoid schizophrenic, a failure constantly ridiculed by those around him. To keep his demons at bay, moreover, he has manufactured a wildly romantic fantasy world in which he is actually Charles the Beloved, the adored, dispossessed king of a Central European kingdom named Zembla. Kinbote's mad ramblings are ultimately delusions of grandeur designed to minister to the insecurities and fears generated by his miserable existence. And his edition of Shade's poem, also entitled "Pale Fire," is less a celebration of his alleged friend and his art than his revenge on the man who spurned his friendship, his homo-sexual advances, and his hope that his own "story" and not that of Shade's much-loved wife and dead daughter would be the subject of Shade's last poem. This revenge seeps into every line of Kinbote's annotations, transforming Shade's "Pale Fire" into the poem that Kinbote so wanted him to write.

Nabokov's novel thus posits a parasitical relationship between authors and critics, proposing that the latter consciously or unconsciously hijack the former's creative efforts by disguising as an act of interpretation their importation of their own obsessions into the literary work at hand. And its parody of editorial work may hit a little too close to home for those academic critics, like ourselves, who are interested in **textual scholarship,** the discipline of literary study traditionally concerned with the genesis, transmission, and editing of texts and the physical documents that contain them. After all, Kinbote is a comic disaster as Shade's utterly obtuse and misguided editor. His annotations, usually more about himself than Shade, are almost always grandly irrelevant, betraying a thoroughly sweep-ing ignorance of Shade's aesthetic program, his poetry, and this particular poem. Every editorial comment exhibits a powerful self-aggrandizement at the expense of Shade and his poetry. Under the guise of equanimity and disinterested analy-sis, Kinbote maintains a proprietorial attitude toward Shade, defending his own reputation and settling old scores with rivals. Just as importantly, he often pres-ents as fact speculations that lack any supporting evidence whatsoever. He rarely remembers the exact literary or critical passage he wishes to cite or where it may be found. As a scholarly editor, however, Kinbote's worst crime is that he writes variant readings in broken meter and then palms them off as Shade's. At every turn then, Kinbote drives out Shade and his poem, even rewriting it at cer-tain points to fit his mad fantasies. Yet he insists that "Pale Fire" is incompre-hensible without his commentary: "Let me state that without my notes Shade's text simply has no human reality" and "for better or worse, it is the commenta-tor who has the last word."[1]

What, one may ask, does Nabokov's deluded editor have to do with Faulkner and his fiction? Perhaps Faulkner's reactions to his own editors regarding *The Sound and the Fury* ("And don't make any more additions to the script, bud. I know you mean well, but so do I") and *Go Down, Moses* ("Print as is without caps and stops unless put there by me") may remind us that he was often con-cerned with the details attending the publication of his work.[2] As a group whose projects are often grounded in such details, we want to inoculate readers against the charge that contemporary textual scholars like ourselves have anything in common with Kinbote's appropriation of Shade's poetic labors because we are interested in the relevance of contemporary textual scholarship and editorial theory to literary study in general and to Faulkner studies in particular. And while we would hesitate to go so far as Jerome J. McGann in identifying textual critics as a "small band of angels," we would argue that the project of attending to a work in its manifold stages of development is integral to the rigorous study of literature.[3] Simply put, our thesis is that the entire textual process of a literary work is an important if often neglected body of evidence for critics, regardless of their theoretical orientation and the arguments they wish to make about that work, because literary works often manifest themselves in different versions that contain significantly different and differently ordered stanzas, passages, and chapters. The interpretive significance of such substantive variation goes well beyond earlier editorial stress on the importance of the numerous but essentially minor variants in the different published texts of literary works.[4]

The inherent value of encountering a work with deference to the process of its creation and production has developed at the center of textual scholarship even as the discipline of literary study on the whole has evolved around it. The nature of this evolution can be illustrated in an apocryphal story from art history's rich, folkloric oral tradition. Overwhelmed by the almost Platonic perfection of the swan a sculptor was completing in preparation for display, an onlooker supposedly asked, "How is it, amidst so many who struggle to create a swan's approximate likeness, that you have fashioned from a mere stone the perfect swan?"[5] The sculptor's alleged response exemplifies the tenet that dominated Anglo-American textual criticism for the better part of the twentieth century: "I simply carve away everything that is not the swan." When W. W. Greg argued in "The Rationale of Copy-Text," the essay that soon became a widely acclaimed treatise for textual scholarship in literary study, for the supremacy of the earliest available manifestation of a work as the most viable **copy-text** because of its alleged proximity to the author's intentions, he was, in effect, offering a distorted echo of the sculptor's aesthetic call to arms: "I simply edit away everything that is not the author's."[6] Appropriating a term coined by R. B. McKerrow, Greg addresses the textual critic's search for the most authentic and authoritative version of a particular work by positing the theory of copy-text, a theory largely reliant upon a pragmatic but problematic distinction drawn between substantive and accidental variations in different stages of a work's development and publication. According to Greg, those variations that manifestly alter the meaning of an author's work are regarded as **substantive** readings while **accidental** variations affect such formal elements as punctuation and spelling. Greg's copy-text theory does not mark the inception of textual criticism as a practice or a discipline. On the contrary, studying the transmission of texts and editing them are among the oldest pursuits in literary study and indeed in academia as a whole. From the millennia spent ordering and reordering the manuscripts, scrolls, and transcriptions of sacred texts to the centuries spent excavating the elusive intentions of Shakespeare, the activities of **bibliography,** linguistics, **textual genealogy,** analytical editing, sociology, and historical research have long distinguished the efforts of textual scholars. In Anglo-American literary study, however, Greg's work does mark a turning point in both theory and methodology.

The conception of textual criticism propounded by Greg and those textual scholars who subsequently elaborated his copy-text theory exhibits an insistent preoccupation with authorial intention and editorial reconstruction. In his essay "The Ideal of Textual Criticism," James Thorpe claims unequivocally that the "ideal of textual criticism is to present the text which the author intended."[7] Echoing this ideology, Fredson Bowers asserts in "Textual Criticism" that the "recovery of the initial purity of an author's text and of its revision (insofar as this is possible from the preserved documents), and the preservation of this purity despite the usual corrupting process of reprint transmission, is the aim of textual criticism."[8] In their pursuit of this purified single text, these earlier textual scholars found their project repeatedly complicated by the intricacies of unearthing authorial intention from the layers of development that comprise a book. While clearly working within the tradition of Greg, Fredson Bowers and Matthew J. Bruccoli have both identified the pragmatic and ideological problems with distinguishing accidental and substantive variants, blurring the line between the mistakes of form and deliberate attempts by authors to amend or subvert that form.[9] And later, in his explication of textual theory since Greg, G. Thomas Tanselle discusses the problematic nature of the pursuit of an authentic text even as he locates authorial intention at the heart of textual criticism's historical heritage.[10]

Over the last two decades, textual scholarship has increasingly focused on the reality of textual instability. Whereas earlier Anglo-American textual scholars and editors sought to constitute texts and editions according to single-text and authorial-intentionalist premises, recent textual scholars as diverse as George Bornstein, Jerome McGann, Peter Shillingsburg, D. C. Greetham, and Hans Walter Gabler have argued that competing theoretical assumptions lead editors to constitute different texts for the same literary work.[11] Contemporary textual scholarship now seeks less to stabilize texts than to draw our attention to textual instability, to the fact that most writers collaborate, delegate, and cooperate with friends, lovers, colleagues, editors, and publishers and that they continue to rewrite the texts of literary works for different reasons, for different audiences, and under different circumstances.[12] But one does not have to be an editor to observe that our modern critical emphasis on a single authorial-textual manifestation of a much more complex textual process derives from the romantic-modernist notion of the literary work as a physical object best represented by a single stabilized text. And this textual conception has its origins in both the development of print technology from Gutenberg on with its ability to produce a series of texts that closely resemble each other and in the Romantic emphasis on authorial consciousness as the ultimate source and ground of the constitution and unity of a text.

Although a complex dialectical relationship exists between literary theory and criticism (with its current emphasis on reception) and textual scholarship (with its emphasis on production), many contemporary critics continue to overlook the contribution that textual scholarship can make to the study of texts and textuality. Despite their various cutting-edge critical methodologies with their stress on multiple, overlapping interpretive contexts, for example, many of the contributors to David McWhirter's recent collection *Henry James's New York Edition: The Construction of Authorship* display little interest in employing textual scholarship for interpretive and theoretical purposes.[13] While they scrutinize various aspects of the edition's physical format, photographs, and order and omission of selections, many of the contributors frequently treat the edition as a fixed, stable textual product even when discussing James's theories of writing and revision. In particular, few of the essays bring James's composition of the prefaces, his substantive revision of earlier work, and his authorial intertextuality—that is, the other works he wrote while he worked on the edition—to bear on their arguments. Indeed, most of the contributors expatiate at length on James's published and unpublished comments on composition and revision but curiously avoid exploring in any substantive way what he actually did to his earlier fiction as he prepared the edition.[14] George Bornstein's excellent collection *Representing Modernist Texts: Editing as Interpretation,* on the other hand, seeks to remedy this neglect by exploring in a series of pieces on modernist writers by different hands "the implications for literary critics and theorists of the recent revolution in editorial theory."[15] These implications are at the crux of the paradox in American literary studies of massive authorial, single-text editions produced by substantial investments of time, money, and labor being used, if at all, by poststructuralists quoting Foucault, Derrida, Barthes, Kristeva, and Fish, who seem to have accepted without cavil that an authoritative text has been produced.

This is still the case in Faulkner studies, where many critics have a postmodern critical orientation but a traditional if unacknowledged and unexamined romantic-modernist textual orientation.[16] Postmodernist Faulkner scholars, for example, have generally drawn on Noel Polk's 1980s corrected Random House editions of the novels for their quotations with little or no comment on the eclectic editorial assumptions and policies used to constitute them. Even more telling, they have often simply replaced some novel titles that may have been imposed on Faulkner with titles that evidence shows he preferred. In "The Guns of *Light in August:* War and Peace in the Second Thirty Years War," for example, Warwick Wadlington thoughtfully examines Faulkner's fiction produced during the period bounded by World War I and World War II as a "peculiarly intense hybrid of war and peace,"[17] but frequently refers to Douglas Day's edition of *Flags in the Dust*[18] without ever alluding to Harcourt, Brace's initial 1929 publication of the novel in a truncated form as *Sartoris.*[19] Similarly, Neil Schmitz's "Faulkner and the Post-Confederate" explores the historical, social, and literary contexts of *Intruder in the Dust*'s reworking of the narrative and linguistic practices of postbellum Southern writing, cites Faulkner's treatment of race in passages from *Flags,* but never mentions its earlier incarnation as *Sartoris.*[20] And Pamela Rhodes's discussion in "Who Killed Simon Strother, and Why?" of Faulkner's abrupt racist termination of his development of a realistic African American character in *Flags* makes no mention of *Sartoris* either.[21] The actual novel and title that Faulkner originally published, which has just as much historical and social and literary significance as the novel and title he preferred, has simply disappeared.

In a similar situation, editors of Faulkner's 1939 book, *The Wild Palms,* replaced his original title, "If I Forget Thee, Jerusalem," with its subtitle. Thomas L. McHaney's critical text *William Faulkner's* The Wild Palms: *A Study,* rather than ignoring the revision, places the significance of the changed title and the textual process as a whole at the center of his study of Faulkner's work.[22] "This substitution," McHaney suggests, "perceptibly altered the immediate effect of the novel." Citing the integral thematic significance of the 137th psalm, from which the original title was paraphrased, to the novel's thematic development of freedom and history, he explains that "although it was not the only factor that delayed understanding of one of Faulkner's most important books, the retitling was the first of a series of arbitrary and unnecessary changes that affected the book's reception and directed attention away from Faulkner's artistry."[23] Extending this textual analysis of the title to the development of the novel as a whole, McHaney deftly grounds philosophical and literary issues in arguments that seamlessly incorporate the textual process, a process often ignored in more recent critical discussions.

This lack of interest in the relevance of contemporary textual scholarship to critical work on Faulkner may be seen in Stephen Hahn and Arthur F. Kinney's excellent collection *Approaches to Teaching Faulkner's* The Sound and the Fury, which features a number of essays by scholars representing diverse critical approaches and interpretations of the novel, from traditional to poststructuralist.[24] Regardless of their theoretical orientation, however, the various contributors share a common tendency: in a collection devoted, among other things, to ways of teaching Faulkner's brilliant modernist poeticizing of prose in the novel through a variety of linguistic, stylistic, and typographical innovations, few of them comment on the difficulty of establishing which of the book's many variants were introduced by Faulkner and which were introduced by his editors during the publication process.[25]

Twentieth-century formalist critics typically focused on a single authorial-textual manifestation of a Faulkner work rather than its entire textual process because their **textual ontology** was primarily spatial rather than temporal in nature. Their emphasis on a solitary textual manifestation of a work frequently led them to ignore the much larger textual process that often lies behind a published Faulkner text. Thus Cleanth Brooks's influential 1963 New Critical study *William Faulkner: The Yoknapatawpha Country* rarely draws on the composition, revision, and publication of Faulkner's fiction to support its critical judgments. For example, his description of *Sanctuary* as "Faulkner's bitterest novel" in which Horace Benbow realizes "that women have a secret rapport with evil which men do not have, that they are able to adjust to evil without being shattered by it" applies questionable gender assumptions only to the 1931 published version of the novel and not to the earlier version that Faulkner tried to publish in 1929.[26]

But formalist premises alone cannot explain the widespread critical refusal to consider the entire textual situation of a work. Indeed, formalism in no way provides an a priori guarantee that its adherents will emphasize only the published version of a textual process. David Madden's entertaining, semiautobiographical, but ultimately formalist discussion of "Photographs in the 1929 Version of *Sanctuary*," for example, contends that Faulkner's excision of many of these images for the 1931 version of the novel radically disrupted and altered a good deal of its meaning.[27] Madden is particularly concerned with how Faulkner's revisions made certain portions of the earlier version that survive in the published version problematic to the point of incomprehensibility. Thus Horace's repeated contemplation of the increasingly ambiguous appearance of Little Belle's photograph, a sequence in the original version that was radically truncated in the revised version, was clearly intended to prepare for and to help explain his climactic shattering bout of hallucinatory nausea in his bathroom after his interview with Temple at Miss Reba's brothel. In this argument and throughout his discussion, Madden's formalist approach to the work relies heavily upon the textual process.

Conversely, when mythic and psychoanalytic [see chapters 1 and 8] critic Leslie Fiedler discusses Faulkner's commercial manipulation of popular literary genres in *Sanctuary,* he examines only the published version of the novel. Fiedler merely refers to the earlier version as "inchoate" because "Faulkner had not disentangled the Popeye-Temple story from the Sartoris saga."[28] And earlier critics who paid close attention to Faulkner's manuscripts, typescripts, galleys, and proofs, critics such as Michael Millgate in his seminal *The Achievement of William Faulkner,* frequently did so in order to explicate better the published version of the work.[29] Unlike Millgate's, however, the work of some of these scholars was often vitiated by a formalist New Critical conception of Faulkner as an ahistorical, abstract entity whose revisions allegedly brought texts closer to the unified ideal work he originally intended regardless of the passage of time. Indeed, most Faulkner critics have shared a common albeit unrealistic view of how and why a professional author writes and revises his or her work and assumed that the best text of a work is usually the published one or the last one that an author revised.[30]

But why should contemporary Faulkner scholars focus on a single, stable textual product, rather than delimit it, when their own **poststructuralist** theories often decenter and disperse interpretation by means of multiple contexts? Why should they accept without cavil stabilized Faulkner texts that reflect a textual ontology ratified by capitalism, individualism, and romantic-modernist ideology, critical dispensations now so out of favor in the academy? Why should they bring postmodern critical practice to bear on such texts while ignoring the available evidence about their genesis and transmission, especially when they have often severed the act of interpreting them from Faulkner's intentions? True, assembling a work's entire textual history through collation can often be a tedious, time-consuming, and labor-intensive process. But numerous scholarly resources that contain such collations and facsimiles of many of the texts of Faulkner's works are available. Among these inestimably useful tools are Gerald Langford's collations of various stages in the textual process for works such as *Absalom, Absalom!* and *Sanctuary.*[31] Additionally, books like Douglas Day's edition of *Flags in the Dust*[32] and Noel Polk's edition of *Sanctuary*'s original text[33] pair a significant stage in each work's publication with a valuable commentary on its textual history. In Faulkner's *Soldiers' Pay: A Bibliographic Study,* Francis J. Bosha makes a rigorous account of the textual evolution of Faulkner's novel through both his discussion of the book's development and his historical collation of available published and unpublished materials,[34] and Judith L. Sensibar's bibliographical guide to Faulkner's poetry also offers further opportunity for research into both published and unpublished work through its textual analysis of many lesser-known pieces.[35] Along with Joseph Blotner's edition of *Faulkner's Uncollected Stories,*[36] James B. Meriwether's bibliographical study of Faulkner's literary career[37] and the collection of essays in *A Faulkner Miscellany,*[38] which Meri-wether edits, also serve as resources for critics interested in addressing the various manifestations of a work and its different stages of development. Finally, the capacious 40-volume set of manuscripts, typescripts, and commentaries published by Garland offers a broad range of perspectives into a number of Faulkner's works and their textual processes.[39] With this substantial litany of textual resources accessible to readers, the lack of deference to textual development in more-recent discussions of Faulkner's books is, at least, notable. The academy's emphasis on reception and its general ignorance about the relevance of contemporary textual scholarship to English studies along with the authorial orientation and positivistic tendencies of earlier textual scholars may be to blame for the current critical disposition that tends to brush aside this rich and readily available textual information on Faulkner's work.

Poststructuralist scholars often seem unconcerned with the origins of physical documents and the texts contained therein, and they frequently underestimate how relevant the entire textual process of a work may be to their projects. We are simply proposing that scholars may be able to answer some sorts of critical questions better by looking at a work's entire textual process. In arguing that scholars need not confine themselves uncritically to a single text or version of a work, whether produced by a commercial publisher or a scholarly editor, we are not trying to argue that scholarly editors ought to produce only certain sorts of editions or edited texts. Although novels are indeed written for readers, different sorts of general and academic readers may wish to read different parts of a work's textual process or as much of that process as possible for different reasons. Indeed, consulting only published versions of a work may be entirely appropriate for some kinds of critical activity. Thus text constitution and selection ought to be a function of the various needs that different readers have.

If individual Faulkner works often cannot be adequately represented by a single text, his lifelong habit of retelling earlier stories in later works further complicates the nature of Faulknerian textuality by blurring the borders between what are sometimes only nominally discreet textual processes. One thinks immediately of the episodes that are retold in varying ways throughout the Snopes stories, *The Hamlet* (1940), *The Town* (1957), and *The Mansion* (1959). But Faulkner also routinely imported characters from previous works into later narratives. Thus Quentin Compson from *The Sound and the Fury* (1929) reappears in *Absalom, Absalom!* (1936); Horace Benbow from *Sartoris* and *Flags in the Dust* is a central character in *Sanctuary* (1931); *Sanctuary's* Temple Drake appears again in *Requiem for a Nun* (1951). Indeed, a venerable if often controversial tradition in Faulkner criticism has been to discuss such characters in terms of their previous incarnations in earlier works.[40] Such a critical practice generally has the merit of emphasizing qualification, development, and conflict in Faulknerian textuality. Yet all too frequently, traditional and poststructuralist critics have assumed unproblematic relationships between recurring characters and narratives in different works. They have also tended to attribute such continuity to authorial intention even though a glance at *Faulkner in the University* suggests that Faulkner's memory of the specifics of his earlier novels was often hazy. Exemplary though they may be in other ways, such readings may seem ahistorical when they treat Faulkner's retellings as conscious and deliberate revisions of earlier work.[41]

Even one of the most sophisticated postmodern discussions of Faulknerian **authorial intertextuality** we have yet encountered, Martin Kreiswirth's "'Paradoxical and Outrageous Discrepancy': Transgression, Auto-Intertextuality, and Faulkner's Yoknapatawpha," limits the textual embodiment of Faulkner's works to their published versions, ruling out any consideration of the larger textual processes behind those texts. Kreiswirth takes as his subject the "transformations, absorptions, and 'operative repetitions'" of elements from one Faulkner text to another.[42] He quite rightly observes that many previous studies of Yoknapatawphan intertextuality have stressed comprehensiveness, totality, unity, and monologism, thus marginalizing those other equally important "semiotic, rhetorical, and narrative maneuvers that leave fissures, gaps, and discrepancies, and point toward instability, indeterminacy, and otherness" (165). Uninterested in questions of intentionality, Kreiswirth deliberately avoids any discussion of "Faulkner's exchanges with his editors and the minutia of textual revisions, balks, reversals, [and] rerevisions" (171). But attending to the complete textual process of a Faulkner work in no way entails an allegiance to the authorial orientation. Indeed, the consideration of a work's many manifestations throughout its development can easily have the opposite effect of rejecting authorial and editorial claims to limit that textual process to one of several texts.

Poststructuralist critics like Kreiswirth who resist attempts to stabilize textual boundaries and meanings and delight in "irresolvable base-level contradictions" and "textual instabilities" are unnecessarily limiting the number of these contradictions and instabilities by restricting their critical attention to a single manifestation of an entire textual process (177). But why should scholars uninterested in questions of intentionality limit themselves to a single text constituted by an author and his various commercial and scholarly editors? Attending to a work's entire authorial and nonauthorial textual process instead frequently adds even more contradictions and instabilities to those already present in Faulknerian auto-intertextuality of the sort that Kreiswirth explores so ably.[43]

If meaning is indeed the product of the dialectical relationship between textual production and textual reception, moreover, postmodern criticism of Faulkner might be better served by relating the process by which different hands constructed different stages of an entire textual situation to the process by which its individual products have been received. This actual web of inextricably interconnected documents, texts, and textual processes, both published and unpublished, suggests a notion of collaborative intertextuality that is the material counterpart of postmodernist notions of intertextuality, which focus on the discursive relationships between works by different authors. Instead of the stable, fixed texts produced by modern Anglo-American editors for formalist critics, this notion of collaborative intertextuality assumes that it is only in the context of particular theoretical frameworks or of particular commercial and scholarly publishing arrangements that we can think of published works as discrete entities.

In this light, the process of textual criticism can be understood as a recasting of the conception of intertextuality altogether. Decentering the physical document of a text and regarding as critically significant the various stages in which the textual process is manifest initiates a new intertextual tension between a work and itself. In "The Textual Event," Joseph Grigely codifies this tension by distinguishing a literary work from the act and representative aspects of its production.[44] Grounded firmly in Derridean theory, Grigely's formulation of a work as a continuously evolving composite of the equally significant texts, or a "polytext," goes a long way toward re-envisioning the phenomenology of text production and redefining the role of textual criticism in the theoretical discourse of literature.[45] Similarly, Gary Taylor touches upon the inexhaustible possibilities that a theory of manifold texts within the process of a single work opens up by exploring the ramifications of the assertion that every "theory of editing must therefore be a theory of intertextuality."[46] Indeed, the complex production histories of Faulkner's works demonstrate how substantially the instability of a published text implicitly adjusts the status of drafts and production stages to texts in themselves, rendering increasingly slight the gap between the postmodern preoccupation with intertextuality and fragmentation and the concerns of contemporary textual scholarship.

The advantages that can accrue to applying postmodernist interpretive strategies to an entire Faulknerian textual process rather than to a single textual manifestation of that process may be seen, for example, in Minrose Gwin's deft application of gender and queer theory in "Did Ernest Like Gordon?" to the cuts that Faulkner's editors at Boni and Liveright made in his second published novel, *Mosquitoes* (1927).[47] In exploring uneasy "disruptive performances of the 'queer' **abject**" in several textual spaces in the novel, Gwin makes a persuasive case that male homoeroticism in the text works with masturbatory, incestuous, and lesbian sexual activity in cut and uncut material to reveal the compulsory nature of normative heterosexuality.[48] Her nuanced attention to how the homoerotic material in the cut passages originally worked in tandem thematically and structurally with similar passages in uncut material to destabilize heterosexual activity and bodies ultimately persuades one that the excisions reduced the amount of gender trouble in the novel. With the recent publication of the facsimile edition of the **holograph manuscript** draft of about one-third of *Mosquitoes,* Gwin and other scholars may be able to test her argument about gender trouble in the novel against this newly available portion of the novel's textual process.[49]

Compared to the composition and publication processes of the work of other modern authors, Faulkner's textual situations are representatively rather than exceptionally unstable, and much of the documentary evidence for this instability survives in various library special collections such as those at the Harry Ransom Center at the University of Tennessee in Austin, the Center for Faulkner Studies at Southeast Missouri State University in Cape Girardeau, the University of Virginia in Charlottesville, and the University of Mississippi in Oxford. Multiple versions of his works abound with substantive differences between manuscripts, typescripts, galleys, proofs, and published versions that reflect the conflicts, agreements, and compromises that Faulkner struck with others and with himself. For example, he was not personally involved in cutting his third novel, *Flags in the Dust,* by 15 percent, which Harcourt, Brace then published as *Sartoris* in 1929.[50] An earlier allegiance to individual authorship and to single authorial texts once led one Faulknerian textual scholar to privilege *Flags* in an intermediate version of the novel that appeared posthumously in 1973 over *Sartoris.*[51] But it is the entire textual process of *Flags/Sartoris,* a process that is not limited either to the text validated by the act of publication or to the text that Faulkner preferred, that enables us to understand better his exploration of the early twentieth-century crisis of traditional masculinity at the beginning of a crucial period in his artistic development.[52] Much of what was cut in *Flags* was material dealing with failed Prufrockian lawyer Horace Benbow and sexually frustrated Sartoris bank teller and eventual bank robber Byron Snopes, characters that were originally juxtaposed with the more aggressive but equally frustrated and doomed young Bayard Sartoris. This crisis of masculinity connects Faulkner to other early twentieth-century American male writers like Hemingway and Fitzgerald for whom the destabilization of traditional gender roles had turned the world upside down as much as had World War I.

Faulkner, however, was the primary agent in the peculiar revision process during the fall of 1930 that transformed the galleys of the original version of *Sanctuary* into a best-seller: in order to save money, he reordered chapters, cut whole chapters and beginnings and endings of chapters, and did very little rewriting or new writing.[53] The extant evidence suggests that Faulkner did not, as he claimed in his notorious introduction to the Modern Library edition of the novel, originally write a potboiler and then revise it with an eye toward improving it aesthetically so that it would not shame *The Sound and the Fury* and *As I Lay Dying.*[54] Rather, he may have deliberately abandoned his initial attempt at a serious, experimental successor to *The Sound and the Fury* in order to create a more commercial work. Thus his revisions, it may be argued, were not improvements on his original plan for *Sanctuary* but rather efforts to subvert it. Moreover, the published novel bears the stamp of Faulkner's attempt to alter the original version drastically with a minimum of rewriting or writing of new material in order to keep his share of the costs of publishing *Sanctuary* down.

As with *Flags* and *Sartoris,* the complete textual process of *Sanctuary* rather than either the 1929 or the 1931 version alone may help feminist scholars [see chapter 9] better understand how central the failure of traditional masculinity actually was to the young Faulkner and his work. Much of what Faulkner cut in *Sanctuary* was again material dealing with Horace Benbow, whose passivity and idealism were originally juxtaposed with Popeye's aggressive misogyny. Feminists and New Historicists [see chapter 7] might be interested in how the complex editorial processes that produced both of these print novels were, in part, ideologically inflected collaborative acts involving Faulkner and other agents such as friends and publishers that resulted in downplaying and obscuring his earlier depictions of this crisis. Rather than argue for the superiority of one version over another, Faulkner critics might do better to attend to the work's entire textual history. Noel Polk makes a similar point when he writes that "taken together, in their inter- and intratextual relationships with each other and with the other novels and stories in the space between, the two versions form a single literary text that is far more significant than either of the versions taken singly" and that we cannot "understand either *Sanctuary* without also coming to terms with the other."[55]

Nevertheless, contemporary scholars frequently discuss Faulkner's most controversial novel by appealing only to the originally published version of *Sanctuary*. In a densely argued Freudian essay, for example, Gregory Forter interprets the novel's pervasive incidents of vomiting, spitting, oozing, and bleeding as signaling "the novel's tendency to 'say' things that it also does not say."[56] Although he does cite one alteration to the original version that supports his thesis (545 n. 13), Forter seems unaware of the extensive nature of Faulkner's rewriting and reordering of the novel and of any relevance to his argument that this process might have. Believing that the novel's deliberate confusion between subjectivity and objectivity creates "insoluble interpretive difficulties" that can result in "proportionally impoverished" readings, he neither inquires whether Faulkner's revisions provide evidentiary support for this claim nor asks if one version is more confused than the other (543). Similarly, James Polchin maintains that Faulkner courted commercial success with *Sanctuary* by drawing on popular interest in Freudian psychology with its emphasis on "psychosexual behavior and the importance of proper childhood mental development."[57] But he fails to recognize that Faulkner's numerous alterations in the novel's galleys, especially his late addition of Popeye's childhood biography, could help him confirm or qualify his arguments. And Michael Lahey's insightful discussion of Faulkner's corpus as a provocative critique of the law's complicity in constructing terrible social norms and realities focuses on Horace's utter failure before the district attorney during the novel's climactic trial scene, but Lahey seems unaware that Faulkner cut lengthy passages dealing with Horace's relations with women from the original version of *Sanctuary,* wrote some new material, and rearranged large chunks of already-composed material.[58] Thus Lahey cannot say whether any part of this process confirms, revises, or refutes his arguments or explore how the trial, which remained relatively unaltered, functions differently in each version of the novel because different and differently ordered material led up to it.[59]

In marked contrast, Kevin Railey's plea in "The Social Psychology of Paternalism: *Sanctuary*'s Cultural Context" for an ideological, Althusserian rather than humanistic, Freudian interpretation of *Sanctuary* gains from his interest in the novel's entire textual process. Railey explores how "the dynamics of Horace Benbow's world set the conditions for Temple Drake's story" and how the novel's narrative perspective emphasizes the "upper-class, aristocratic paternal-ist male mentality" that constitutes their world.[60] His treatment of the original and the published versions of *Sanctuary* as a single extended text is a useful strategy because Faulkner excised so much material dealing with Horace, espe-cially his waking and sleeping dreams about the women in his life.

Faulkner also occasionally wrote introductory pieces for his novels not only to make some money but also to shape his readers' expectations and responses. For example, he insisted on placing the influential Compson Appendix, initially written for Malcolm Cowley's *The Portable Faulkner,* 16 years after the publica-tion of *The Sound and the Fury,* at the front of what became the most important reissue of any of his works: Random House's Modern Library double edition of *The Sound and the Fury* and *As I Lay Dying* (1946). As a result of Faulkner's steadily increasing popularity, this edition was reprinted and reissued frequently from 1954 to 1961 under the inexpensive paperback Modern Library and Vin-tage imprints.[61] During the 1960s, the appendix appeared at the back of several reissues of the novel, and some omitted it entirely.[62] The wheel came full circle when Noel Polk omitted the appendix from his Random House corrected text of *The Sound and the Fury* in 1984, his Vintage paperback of the same text in 1987, and a facsimile reprint of the 1984 text in a different format in a 1990 Vin-tage International volume. Polk did indeed include the appendix along with a brief explanatory note at the rear of another facsimile reprint, the 1992 Modern Library volume.[63]

In attempting to explain his favorite novel once again to readers who had rejected it earlier by framing rather than rewriting it, Faulkner created a kind of authorially sanctioned fifth section of the novel that shaped the readings of a generation of critics in the 1950s and the 1960s.[64] If earlier critics tended to view the appendix ahistorically as a faithful guide to the 1929 novel, more-recent commentaries have instead stressed the many conflicts between the 1929 novel and the appendix.[65] Indeed, Faulkner's inclusion of the piece in later editions of *The Sound and the Fury* recontextualizes the work and thus may be said to reon-tologize it as well, to recast it in a way that alters the scope and character of even the most fundamental elements in the book's form and content. Regardless of the many clashes between the novel and the appendix, its addition arguably cre-ates either a new version of the work or a new and separate work.[66] Skeptical scrutiny of the appendix constitutes a marked improvement over earlier critical practice, which often read it as a gospel guide to the novel rather than to the fic-tion Faulkner had written in the years since the publication of *The Sound and the Fury.* Still, contemporary discussion over whether the appendix is or is not part of *The Sound and the Fury* becomes a false choice if one accepts the reality of textual instability and the existence of multiple versions of a work. The appen-dix *is* part of the 1946 version of the work known as *The Sound and the Fury* and a number of subsequent versions as well, even though it is not part of the 1929 version of that same work.

Yet another feature of Faulknerian textual instability is that he substantially reworked in varying degrees a number of published and unpublished short stories and sketches into novels such as *The Unvanquished* (1938) and *Go Down, Moses* (1942). Exploring this relationship, many of the papers in Hans H. Skei's recent collection *William Faulkner's Short Fiction: An International Symposium* provide a welcome counter to the current critical tendency to ignore the larger textual process behind a particular Faulkner text.[67] In his incorporation of shorter pieces, Faulkner made changes that reflect the different purposes, needs, and audiences of the longer works.[68] He produced *The Unvanquished* by making substantive additions to the five Civil War and Reconstruction stories that the *Saturday Evening Post* had published earlier and by writing the concluding story, "An Odor of Verbena," three years after the publication of those stories. Noel Polk notes that Faulkner's revision of these five stories in 1937 for book publication reflects "the same sort of commercial haste that had gone into their writing," and other readers have also found them too romantic, uncomplicated, and superficial.[69]

While scholars have often neglected the entire textual process of *The Unvanquished,* those critics whose work incorporates the various stages of the book's evolution present ideas that are enriched by their textual roots. Susan Donaldson's "Dismantling the *Saturday Evening Post* Reader" demonstrates the value of combining textual scholarship with a postmodern interest in disruption and contradiction.[70] Employing Jaussian reception aesthetic [see chapter 10], she shows how Faulkner's "An Odor of Verbena" and his revisions of the earlier pieces first arouse and then undermine the expectations of conservative white middle-class readers of the sort who read the formulaic Civil War stories the *Post* ran in the 1930s. Attentive to the book's larger textual process, Donaldson concludes that Faulkner's additions support "An Odor of Verbena" in cautioning readers that "expectations attuned to tales of adventure and glory can be misleading and even dangerously blind to the rigid codification of storybook legends."[71] John Pilkington also draws upon the *Saturday Evening Post* publications in his discussion of *The Unvanquished.*[72] His claim that "*The Unvanquished,* dealing, as it does, with the Civil War and Reconstruction, represents one of the poles of history from which Faulkner measured motion to his own time" is sharply backlit by an analysis of the thematic and artistic commercialism surrounding the book's publication history.[73] Likewise, Peter Nicolaisen makes productive use in "'Because we were forever free': Slavery and Emancipation in *The Unvanquished*" of Faulkner's revisions in a close reading that draws attention to Faulkner's vacillations and contradictory attitudes concerning race, slavery, and freedom by focusing on "the often abrupt transitions from one mode of writing to another," transitions that seem deliberate given the details of Faulkner's revision of the earlier stories.[74]

As with *The Unvanquished,* Faulknerians have often produced readings of *Go Down, Moses* that stress the narrative, imagistic, or thematic unity and coherence of its very different constituent stories or that comment on the difficulty of doing so.[75] The unusual structure of *Go Down, Moses* may have resulted, in part, from

Faulkner's creation of the novel by combining new material with rewritten unpublished pieces and six previously published short stories.[76] In fact, the novel's complicated textual history provides a wealth of evidence that would seem relevant to any discussion of whether *Go Down, Moses* is a novel, a collection of stories, or some sort of hybrid genre. In his attempt to unravel of the problematic ambiguities of form that entangle Faulkner's genre-defying work, James Early addresses the book's various stages of textual development. Early's *The Making of* Go Down, Moses offers an in-depth examination of the book's conglomeration of characters and stories, steeped in an analysis of both authorial intertextuality and publication history.[77] Ultimately, Early's approach to Faulkner's work is so colored by the lens of textual criticism that its assertion of the book's importance in both the Faulkner canon and a broader literary discourse depends upon the accounts of development and revision supporting his argument.

Nevertheless, contemporary critics frequently overlook the intricate aggregate of vision and revision that comprises the textual process of *Go Down, Moses*. Even Susan Donaldson's ambitious "Contending Narratives: *Go Down, Moses* and the Short Story Cycle" could have benefited, as did her piece on *The Unvanquished,* from yoking the available textual evidence to her poststructuralist interpretive moves. Reading the book as a postmodern short-story cycle within which "individual stories of resistance and discontinuity" contend with the McCaslins' patriarchal narrative of brutal appropriation, domination, and exploitation of blacks, women, and Native Americans, Donaldson emphasizes how these stories formally and thematically counteract this inflexible system of power and authority.[78] It is a deft and instructive performance. At the same time, she might have ascertained whether the substantive textual variations among versions of individual stories reflect an increase in either unity or disruption.[79]

With its overlapping interests in subject formation, subjectivity, and the complexity of Faulkner's textual situations, Philip Weinstein's "'He Come and Spoke for Me': Scripting Lucas Beauchamp's Three Lives," on the other hand, demonstrates how postmodernist scholarship can effectively draw upon textual scholarship. Weinstein's argument that the character of Lucas Beauchamp's identity depends on the signifying economy and textual situation within which he is situated rests on the fact that Faulkner produced Lucas three different times: first, in the group of short stories that appeared in 1940; then in the revised stories for *Go Down, Moses;* and finally in *Intruder in the Dust* (1948). The differences behind these several versions of Lucas chart, for Weinstein, shifts in Faulkner's own racial identity as he repeatedly tried and failed to imagine a black consciousness. If Lucas is first a racial stereotype of the wily Negro, he becomes in *Go Down, Moses* a character whose "heroic status is conditional upon his being figuratively removed from his own black heritage" and finally more a "congealed icon" than an "imagined subjectivity" in *Intruder.*[80] True, Weinstein does not try to corroborate this shift in representations of Lucas by comparing passages dealing with him in the magazine stories with their revised counterparts in *Go Down, Moses.* Nor is he much concerned with exploring conflicts in Lucas's character that may result from Faulkner's side-by-side placement of new and old material and of revised and unrevised material in *Go Down, Moses*. In place of the racist aspects of Lucas's depiction in the magazine stories, for example, Faulkner occasionally presents the readers of his novel with a more-complex character that may appear somewhat inconsistent with the comic Uncle Remus figure Lucas cuts in earlier-inscribed but unrevised material. Moreover, the omniscient narrator of *Go Down, Moses* occasionally seems ambivalent on the issue of race perhaps because he is the product of different periods of composition and revision. Nevertheless, Weinstein's discussion of the linguistic entity known as Lucas Beauchamp as it manifests itself in several compositionally related Faulkner texts demonstrates that poststructuralist analysis and textual scholarship need not be at odds with each other.

Of course, determining the boundaries between the textual process of one work and that of another is a notoriously difficult, perhaps impossible interpretive task. Most writers, professional and amateur, repeatedly employ the same material in more than one context, often developing new material out of old material. As James McLaverty notes, these issues of textual identity and ontology recall the often-debated philosophical problem of Theseus's ship: "Theseus sets sail with a new ship, but before long it has got to go in for repair: old planks, nails, and sails are taken out and replaced by new ones. Over a long period of time, through numerous repairs, all the old material is replaced by new, and the problem is raised: Is this the same ship that Theseus started out with?"[81] Like his beloved twilight, that time when day merges indistinguishably but inevitably into night, Faulkner's texts and textual processes, seemingly so distinct, often blend into one another because he frequently used the same characters and events in different works and mined different works from the same quarry of imaginative materials.

Faulkner's work in Hollywood is also intimately connected to the textual processes of his fiction. While many of Faulkner's screenplays are far from being first-rate scripts, they are proof, as Bruce Kawin argues in his edition of Faulkner's MGM screenplays, that his derogatory comments and subsequent disdainful critical comments about his years in Hollywood's salt mines need to be qualified somewhat.[82] True, screenwriting kept Faulkner from Oxford and drained him of time and energy needed for his fiction, but it also exerted some influence, for good or bad, over that fiction. In their textual explication of "The De Gaulle Story," editors Robert W. Hamblin and Louis Daniel Brodsky point out that among the "most impressive features of 'The De Gaulle Story' is the manner in which it anticipates content and themes treated in later Faulkner works."[83] Although fiction would always remain his primary medium, the products of his efforts in Hollywood suggest that Faulkner genuinely cared about some of them. In fact, as Hamblin and Brodsky attest in their introduction to *Stallion Road*, Faulkner's forays into the venue of screenplay often demonstrated "his skillful mastery of the conventions of scriptwriting while at the same time [manifesting] his compulsion to incorporate, at least to a degree, the subject matter, characterization, and language of realistic fiction."[84] More importantly, his screenplays frequently show him transforming and revising earlier and current work in fiction, which then plays into his later works even as these screenplays probably reflect Faulkner's already-established narrative techniques. In *Country Lawyer and Other Stories for the Screen,* Hamblin and Brodsky elaborate on such intersection, noting "readers versed in Faulkner's fiction and biography will find themselves traveling over familiar territory in 'Country Lawyer,'" a story that they suggest "represents one of the few instances in which Faulkner sought to adapt and extend his Yoknapatawpha material to the purposes of Hollywood."[85] Many of the essays in the collection *Faulkner, Modernism, and Film* expound upon similar overlaps between the world of Faulkner's fiction and the worlds of his Hollywood scripts.[86] Even if Faulkner as screenwriter began by cynically cutting creative corners by recycling his work into script, his imagination frequently kicked in, and soon he was rewriting rather than hacking, driven by obsession to revisit issues and themes.

A daunting number of novels, stories, film treatments, screenplays, and speeches, some worthy, some less worthy but all related to each other, were constantly overlapping and jostling each other for his attention. Thus Faulkner wrote the original text of *Sanctuary,* wrote *As I Lay Dying,* and then reordered and rewrote the *Sanctuary* galleys. Or consider how the writing of *Pylon* (1935) interrupted the composition of *Absalom, Absalom!* (1936) and how 11 years passed between the initial conception of *A Fable* in 1943 and its eventual publication in 1954. Or consider how Faulkner wrote *Father Abraham* in the mid-1920s, used some of this material in the Snopes stories of the 1930s, but did not complete the Snopes trilogy until the publication of *The Mansion* in 1959. Faulkner's constant revisiting of his own texts exemplifies Gabler's observation that the "act of publication does not bar continuation of the act(s) of writing."[87] Like the mythologized curator who allegedly banned Picasso from an art museum for repeatedly altering his own paintings, the textual critic may be tempted to arrest Faulkner's canon in a single stage of its development for the sake of brevity, convenience, or accessibility. But because his texts often elaborate on, influence, and argue with each other, the study of what he was working on at a given time may help elucidate another work from the same period.

Faulkner scholars can only benefit from mining the rich vein of authorial and nonauthorial intertextuality constituted by the entire textual process of his works.[88] Noel Polk's interpretive work often demonstrates both an interest in the relation between authorial intertextuality and biography and an awareness of the limits involved in making such connections, especially through psychoanalysis. His essays routinely make intriguing connections between the primary work under discussion and whatever else Faulkner was writing at the time, whether published or unpublished.[89] Along the same lines, the introduction to *William Faulkner: Early Prose and Poetry* by the work's editor, Carvel Collins, also draws heavily upon the self-reflexive development of Faulkner's poetry, prose, and artwork. In his biographically rooted analysis of Faulkner's early work, Collins attends to ways in which issues of authorship, creation, and publication influenced and informed both Faulkner's evolution as an author and the textual processes linking various sketches, stories, and books.[90]

Although such revisions and intersections provide key evidence for those crit-ics interested in authorial intention, attending to the entire textual process of a work, to the changes made by various hands over time in its texts, does not pre-suppose a critical practice founded on authorial intention. As we have seen, the entire textual process of a work can be an important, if neglected, body of evi-dence for confirming, revising, or refuting arguments that nonauthorial critics wish to make about a particular Faulkner text or work. Moreover, postmodern textual scholarship encourages us to see that both the complete textual process of a work and even a single textual embodiment of that work are frequently the site of conflicts rather than resolutions, conflicts between authors and publishers and editors and collaborators. Such conflicts in textual production are often the norm rather than the exception and make formalist assumptions about unity and coherence as a priori aesthetic criteria seem mistaken. Indeed, many textual scholars have become as suspicious as any poststructuralist **hermeneut** con-cerned with the underpinning theoretical assumptions and methodological moves of literary interpretation about the formal unity of literary works. Recog-nizing that Faulkner, like most writers, routinely revised and recycled his work for various reasons and that many other agents routinely joined him in altering these texts can only help postmodernist scholars explore textual contradiction, disruption, and discontinuity in his novels rather than search for hitherto unrec-ognized unifying figures in the carpet.

Up to this point, we have concentrated on the linguistic dimension of Faulkner's texts. Postmodern textual scholars such as Jerome McGann and George Bornstein, however, have also expanded our notion of what constitutes a text or a work by attending carefully to the interpretive significance of the "bibliographical" codes governing the physical documents that contain linguis-tic texts.[91] That the physical features of a document containing a linguistic text may also be constitutive of meaning is itself, of course, a postmodern social conception of text construction and textuality.[92] Now Faulkner scholars have often commented on those features of his visual codes that are clearly authorial in origin like the image of an eye in *The Sound and the Fury,* the image of the coffin in *As I Lay Dying,* and the map of Yoknapatawpha County in *Absalom, Absalom!*[93] But the nonauthorial bibliographical features of his books such as layout, typeface, ornamentation, and dust-jacket art and copy may also be important insofar as they helped shape the responses of readers to his work. Thus scholars interested in Faulkner's critical and commercial reception ought to examine the physical documents that contain the linguistic texts of his works.

Panthea Reid's analysis of how Faulkner's nonrepresentational modernist aes-thetic evolved in "The Scene of Writing and the Shape of Language for Faulkner when 'Matisse and Picasso Yet Painted'" provides a fascinating example of how to make critical use of the materiality or physicality of textual production.[94] Reid observes that extant manuscript evidence reveals that Faulkner's composition process for prose, unlike that of his poetry, involved interlineations, marginal insertions, and the reordering of passages and blocks of fictional material. Faulkner's "spatial sense of arrangement" led him to create the literary equivalent of a postimpressionist collage and involve the reader in making connections and thus in constructing meaning by juxtaposing materials with disparate characters, events, linguistic styles, and narrative techniques.[95]

Attempting to factor such material features into considerations of Faulkner's critical reception seems an important if difficult critical task. Indeed, aspects of his reception may have been shaped by whether or not readers were holding in their hands a first edition of a particular novel, a New American Library or Signet paperback from the late 1940s and the 1950s with its lurid cover art and breathless, suggestive blurbs, or one of the glossy, upscale Library of America trade editions of the late 1980s and the 1990s. Such comparisons suggest that a work's different physical texts may indeed help regulate the expectations and responses of different audiences. Of course, gauging whether or not these bibliographical differences are actually substantive enough to have had an impact on readers is no easy task. A sociology of Faulkner's readers might enable us to measure, if even roughly, the efficacy of the cultural and ideological work, such as constructing and supervising subjects, that poststructuralist critics often see the writing, publishing, and reading of his novels performing. A major obstacle to developing such a sociology, however, is that detailed responses to fiction other than the published record of reviews and academic criticism are notoriously difficult to document. Moreover, a causal connection would have to be established between the responses of Faulkner's readers to his fiction and their actual choices and actions. Such considerations may also lead us to attend more to how the linguistic and bibliographical codes of a particular work may conflict as well as work in tandem with each other.

Textual and documentary instability and intertextuality in Faulkner's fiction are fundamental realities of his and indeed any writer's corpus, but an awareness of such instability has no necessary connection with a biographical orientation that stresses authorial intention. Poststructuralist practices that value social discursive formations over individual consciousness and collaboration and circulation over self-sufficiency and autonomy also stand to benefit from thinking of Faulkner's fictions as textual processes that involve negotiations among an author and other individuals and that produce a variety of textual products. Charles Kinbote's lesser light may pale, like that of the moon to the sun, in comparison with John Shade's poetic genius. But attending to the entire textual process of Faulkner's work is no mad attempt to supplant the man from Mississippi. A postmodern theorist of historiography commented recently that when faced with several variants in a text, he is increasingly prone to say that they are all valid. Precisely. And much contemporary Faulkner scholarship has yet to make use of this recognition.

NOTES

1. Vladimir Nabokov, *Pale Fire* (1962; reprint New York: Random House, Vintage International, 1989), 28, 29.

2. See Peter Shillingsburg, *Scholarly Editing in the Computer Age,* 3rd ed. (Ann Arbor: University of Michigan Press, 1996), 11. The remarks from Faulkner are quoted from Michael Mill-

gate, *The Literary Achievement of William Faulkner* (New York: Random House, 1996), 94 and an oral account by James B. Meriwether respectively.

3. Jerome J. McGann, *A Critique of Modern Textual Criticism* (Chicago: University of Chicago Press, 1983), 9.

4. Bruce Harkness's "Bibliography and the Novelistic Fallacy" (*Studies in Bibliography* 12 [1959]: 59–73), for example, reflects this earlier emphasis.

5. Quoted from memory of an oral account by Maxwell McQueen.

6. W. W. Greg, "The Rationale of Copy-Text," *Bibliography and Textual Criticism: English and American Literature 1700 to Present,* ed. O. M. Brack Jr. and Warner Barnes (1949; reprint Chicago: University of Chicago Press, 1969), 41–58.

7. In *The Task of the Editor* (Los Angeles: William Andrews Clark Memorial Library, 1969), 3.

8. In *The Aims and Methods of Scholarship in Modern Languages and Literatures,* ed. James Thorpe (New York: Modern Language Association of America, 1963), 23–42 (30).

9. See Bowers's "Some Principles for Scholarly Editions of Nineteenth-Century American Authors" (1962), 194–201, and Bruccoli's "Some Transatlantic Texts: West to East" (1968), 244–25, in *Bibliography and Textual Criticism.*

10. *Textual Criticism Since Greg: A Chronicle 1950–1985* (Charlottesville: University Press of Virginia, 1987).

11. Readers may consult essays by these scholars in Philip Cohen's collection *Devils and Angels: Textual Editing and Literary Theory* (Charlottesville: University Press of Virginia, 1991). Also helpful are D. C. Greetham's "Editorial and Critical Theory: From Modernism to Postmodernism," in *Palimpsest: Editorial Theory in the Humanities,* ed. George Bornstein (Ann Arbor: University of Michigan Press, 1993), 9–28, and "Literary and Textual Theory: Redrawing the Matrix" in *Studies in Bibliography* 42 (1989): 1–24; and Michael Groden's "Contemporary Textual and Literary Theory," in *Palimpsest,* 259–86. Contributors to Cohen's collection *Texts and Textuality: Textual Instability, Theory, and Interpretation* (New York: Garland, 1997) attempt to bring different theoretical orientations to bear upon different textual situations or histories in order to explore how different textual situations and their material means of production help generate different theories of textuality and how different conceptions of textuality help generate an understanding of different textual situations and their material means of production. Thus the contributors take as their collective subject the dialectical relationship between texts and textuality.

12. For a useful critique of the myth of individual authorship, see Jack Stillinger's *Multiple Authorship and the Myth of Solitary Genius* (Oxford: Oxford University Press, 1991).

13. Palo Alto, CA: Stanford University Press, 1995.

14. For an extended review of this collection, see Philip Cohen's "The Lesson of the Master," *Studies in the Novel* 31 (Spring 1999): 98–115.

15. Bornstein, *Representing Modernist Texts* (Ann Arbor: University of Michigan Press, 1991), 5. Readers interested in how critics may make use of a work's entire textual process may also consult James West's collection *Dreiser's "Jennie Gerhardt": New Essays on the Restored Text* (Philadelphia: University of Pennsylvania Press, 1995), with its essays on West's 1992 University of Pennsylvania edition of an earlier version of the novel that Dreiser sought to publish before the editorial staff at Harpers cut and revised the work for its 1911 publication. In placing the novel in a host of autobiographical, biographical, literary, and historical contexts, many of the volume's contributors refer not only to the restored text but also to the numerous substantive differences between the two versions.

16. For a delightful discussion of the relevance of the entire textual histories of Faulkner's works to criticism and scholarship and of the principles behind his new Random House editions, see Polk's "Where the Comma Goes: Editing William Faulkner," in Bornstein, *Representing Modernist Texts,* 241–58.

17. In *Faulkner in Cultural Context: Faulkner and Yoknapatawpha 1995,* ed. Donald M. Kartiganer and Ann J. Abadie (Jackson: University Press of Mississippi, 1997), 131.

18. New York: Random House, 1973.

19. See also Wadlington in *Faulkner in Cultural Context,* 128, 129, 139, 143.

20. In *Faulkner in Cultural Context,* 248.

21. In *Faulkner and Race: Faulkner and Yoknapatawpha 1988,* eds. Doreen Fowler and Ann J. Abadie (Jackson: University Press of Mississippi, 1987), 93–110.

22. *William Faulkner's* The Wild Palms: *A Study* (Jackson: University Press of Mississippi, 1975).

23. *William Faulkner's* The Wild Palms: *A Study,* xiii.

24. *Approaches to Teaching Faulkner's* The Sound and the Fury, eds. Stephen Hahn and Arthur Kinney (New York: Modern Language Association, 1996).

25. Although the manuscript and carbon typescript for the first edition of *The Sound and the Fury* (New York: Cape & Smith, 1929) survive, the setting copy and galleys that would help document the extensive copyediting of the novel do not. Noel Polk discusses the various issues involved in editing the novel and Faulkner's repudiation of some of the editorial changes in the introduction to his *Editorial Handbook for William Faulkner's* The Sound and the Fury (New York: Garland, 1985), 1–22.

26. Cleanth Brooks, *William Faulkner: The Yoknapatawpha Country* (1963; reprint New Haven, CT: Yale University Press, 1966), 127, 128. Brooks is aware of *Sanctuary's* unusual composition history, but he accepts Faulkner's assertion in his notorious introduction to the Modern Library edition of the novel that he originally conceived of the novel as a "cheap idea" but then "thoroughly . . . reworked the original galleys" in order to improve the book (396, 397). He never attempts to support his arguments by looking at the original version of the novel that Faulkner sought to publish.

27. In *Faulkner and Popular Culture: Faulkner and Yoknapatawpha 1988,* ed. Doreen Fowler and Ann J. Abadie (Jackson: University Press of Mississippi, 1990), 93–109.

28. Leslie Fiedler, "Pop Goes the Faulkner: In Quest of *Sanctuary*" in *Faulkner and Popular Culture,* 83.

29. See Michael Millgate's *The Achievement of William Faulkner* (1966; reprint Lincoln: University of Nebraska Press, Bison Books, 1978). Regina Fadiman's excellent Light in August: *A Description and Interpretation of the Revisions* (Charlottesville: University Press of Virginia, 1975) uses bibliographical and linguistic evidence derived from a close examination of the methods and stages of Faulkner's revision of the novel to support her interpretation of the published work. Similarly, James Early's *The Making of* Go Down, Moses concerns itself with "the gradual development of [Faulkner's] themes, his verbal and narrative techniques, and his conception of his characters" from the hunting stories of 1934 and 1935 to the published novel in order to better understand *Go Down, Moses* (Dallas: Southern Methodist University Press, 1972. ix).

30. Wordsworth editor Stephen Parrish has dissented from this approach, which he humorously but accurately refers to as "Whig interpretations of a literary text, with their notions of an inner logic of inexorable growth toward what could have been foreseen from the start as the author's final intention." See his "The Whig Interpretation of Literature," *TEXT* 4 (1988): 349. He notes that for such critics "rejected drafts, discarded variants, abandoned versions, while sometimes dutifully catalogued, are looked upon as false starts, misjudgments, or lapses of taste on the part of the poet, all happily rectified as the work, by obedience to some inner logic, reaches final form" (344–45).

31. *Faulkner's Revision of* Absalom, Absalom!: *A Collation of the Manuscript and the Published Book* (Austin: University of Texas Press, 1971); *Faulkner's Revision of* Sanctuary: *A Collation of the Unrevised Galleys and the Published Book* (Austin: University of Texas Press, 1972).

32. New York: Random House, 1973.

33. New York: Random House, 1981.

34. *Faulkner's* Soldiers' Pay: *A Bibliographic Study* (Troy, NY: Whitston Publishing Company, 1982).

35. *Faulkner's Poetry: A Bibliographical Guide to Texts and Criticism* (Ann Arbor: University of Michigan Research Press, 1988).

36. *Uncollected Stories of William Faulkner* (New York: Random House, 1979).

37. *The Literary Career of William Faulkner: A Bibliographical Study* (Princeton, NJ: Princeton University Library, 1961).

38. *A Faulkner Miscellany,* ed. James B. Meriwether (Jackson: University Press of Mississippi, 1974).

39. For facsimiles and commentary on a number of works and their textual processes, see the William Faulkner Manuscripts series (New York: Garland Publishing, 1987).

40. One of the most influential attempts at this approach is John T. Irwin's *Doubling and Incest/Repetition and Revenge: A Speculative Reading of Faulkner* (1975; reprint, expanded ed., Baltimore: Johns Hopkins University Press, 1996). Irwin psychoanalytically reads *The Sound and the Fury* and *Absalom* as a sort of metatext in which Quentin Compson's tortured relations in the earlier novel with his parents and siblings, especially his father and Caddy, are crucial for understanding his situation in the later one. Similarly, Estella Schoenberg, in *Old Tales and Talking: Quentin Compson in William Faulkner's* Absalom, Absalom! *and Related Works* (Jackson: University Press of Mississippi, 1977), argues that *Absalom* is "Faulkner's means of retelling Quentin's story and explaining Quentin's suicide," drawing on published fiction and unpublished stories and fragments by Faulkner to make the case that Quentin's "dejection and psychic withdrawal throughout the last half of [*Absalom*]" is inexplicable to readers unless they are aware of his suicide in *The Sound and the Fury* (4).

41. See Frederick L. Gwynn and Joseph L. Blotner, eds., *Faulkner in the University: Class Conferences at the University of Virginia 1957–1958* (1959; reprint, New York: Random House, Vintage, 1965). For example, Judith Bryant Wittenberg's penetrating "Temple Drake and *La parole pleine*" (*Mississippi Quarterly* 48 [1995]: 421–41), an intertextual, dialectical reading of *Requiem* and an important paper by Lacan from the early 1950s, argues that Temple undergoes a Faulknerian "talking cure," moving toward self-understanding, subjectivity, and a fully individualized speech. This movement is constrained by the linguistic codes and conventions available to her, however, and by Gavin Stevens's patriarchal inadequacies, which take their toll on Temple's rhetorical versatility and ability to narrate lucidly. Citing *Requiem*'s numerous explicit references to *Sanctuary,* Wittenberg then examines how the failures of Horace Benbow, Temple's failed interlocutor-analyst in the earlier novel, compound her "relative lack of individualized speech" and her inability "to arrive at a state of integrated psycho-linguistic selfhood" (428). As insightful as it is, the essay's assumption that *Sanctuary* played such a key role in the genesis of *Requiem* has perhaps a whiff of the totalizing impulse behind it. We know that Faulkner rarely reread earlier work and frequently remembered it incorrectly in details both small and large. Moreover, he had also written a great deal of fiction in the intervening years, and his current projects may have had more relevance to the writing of *Requiem* than *Sanctuary.* If Wittenberg had pointed out and accounted for the many differences between the two novels, one might object less to her so intimately connecting aesthetically, intellectually, and biographically works separated by over 20 years.

In the same vein, Michael E. Lahey's "Narcissa's Love Letters: Illicit Space and the Writing of Female Identity in 'There Was a Queen'" discusses how the negotiations between Narcissa Benbow and an FBI agent over Byron Snopes's love letters play "with available notions of feminine identity, as they are privately and publicly imagined" to demonstrate how "female identity in the world of the story is imagined and written by men, with women serving as screens onto which identity is projected." In *Faulkner and the Artist: Faulkner and Yoknapatawpha, 1993,* ed. Donald M. Kartiganer and Ann J. Abadie (Jackson: University Press of Mississippi, 1996), 161. Much more so than Wittenberg, Lahey assumes an unproblematic, seamless intertextual relationship between Narcissa's character and actions in "There Was a Queen" and the earlier *Flags in the Dust* (see especially 164–5, 172–3).

42. "'Paradoxical and Outrageous Discrepancy': Transgression, Auto-Intertextuality, and Faulkner's Yoknapatawpha," in *Faulkner and the Artist,* 162.

43. Thus Barbara L. Pittman argues persuasively in "Faulkner's Big Woods and the Historical Necessity of Revision" that when Faulkner transformed parts of *Go Down, Moses* into *Big Woods* (1955), he excised, perhaps for commercial reasons, from the material he would use in *Big Woods* much of the earlier work's insistent emphasis on racial injustice, miscegenation, and incest. Unlike the obsessive historical investigation of these issues in *Go Down, Moses,* the truncated *Big Woods* becomes a dehistoricized allegory that "preserve[s] the past in a static myth" and its ele-

giac tone becomes "a lament for the loss of white domination" and "the sense of the white man's increasing insignificance in the face of the newly decreed sharing of his power." In *Mississippi Quarterly* 49 (1996): 478, 477, 492.

44. In *Devils and Angels,* 167–194.

45. In *Scholarly Editing in the Computer Age,* Shillingsburg disagrees with the fundamental significance of this premise, stating, "It has been argued that a thoroughly revised work is a new work, not a new version of the same work. This argument is not one of substance but of terminology" (103). In a critical and theoretical model of textual production, however, there can be no overlooking the essential substance of terminology and its impact upon the reception and interpretation of literature.

46. Taylor's discussion of this internal intertextuality and its relevance to postmodern theory occurs in his essay "The Renaissance and the End of Editing," in *Palimpsest,* 121–50, 125.

47. Gwin's "*Mosquitoes*' Missing Bite: The Four Deletions" (*Faulkner Journal* 9 [Fall 1993/Spring 1994]: 31–41) helpfully prints for the first time the complete text of the four excised passages.

48. "Did Ernest Like Gordon?: Faulkner's *Mosquitoes* and the Bite of 'Gender Trouble'" in *Faulkner and Gender,* ed. Donald M. Kartiganer and Ann J. Abadie (Jackson: University Press of Mississippi, 1996), 121.

49. With the help of David Vander Meulen, Thomas L. McHaney has edited *William Faulkner: Mosquitoes: A Facsimile and Transcription of the University of Virginia Holograph Manuscript* (Charlottesville: Bibliographical Society of the University of Virginia and the University of Virginia Library, 1997). Another example of how postmodern criticism and textual scholarship may be fruitfully combined in Faulkner studies may be found in Joseph R. Urgo's "Faulkner Unplugged: Abortopoesis and *The Wild Palms,*" which maintains that printing "Old Man" and "Wild Palms" separately, as some editions in the 1950s did, destroys Faulkner's poetics and thematics of abortion in the novel's twinned alternating narratives that interrogate "the discordant sexual bases of male and female social and cultural autonomy" (in *Faulkner and Gender,* 256).

50. George Hayhoe's "William Faulkner's *Flags in the Dust*" contains a concise biographical account of the composition of the novel, Ben Wasson's editorial surgery, and its publication as *Sartoris.* See his article in *Mississippi Quarterly* 28 (1975): 370–86; reprinted in *Critical Essays on William Faulkner: The Sartoris Family,* ed. Arthur P. Kinney (Boston: G. K. Hall, 1985), 233–45. See also Joseph L. Blotner's *Faulkner: A Biography,* Vol. 1 (New York: Random House, 1974), 527–611. In 1987, Garland published Blotner's edition of the manuscript and typescript of *Flags in the Dust* in two volumes as *William Faulkner Manuscripts 5.*

51. See "The Last Sartoris: Benbow Sartoris' Birth in *Flags in the Dust*" (*Southern Literary Journal* 18 [1985]: 30–39), for example, in which Philip Cohen argued that the excision of *Flags* material dealing with Horace and Narcissa Benbow for *Sartoris* unintentionally turned an ironic closed ending in which the future holds little promise for the young Sartoris whether paternal or maternal genes come to dominate his character into a more ambiguous open-ended conclusion even though the endings remain substantially the same in both versions.

52. See "William Faulkner, the Crisis of Masculinity, and Textual Instability" (in *Textual Studies and the Common Reader: Essays on Editing Novels and Novelists,* ed. Alexander Pettit [Athens: University of Georgia Press, 2000], 64–80), where Philip Cohen contends that the entire textual process of *Flags/Sartoris* anticipates Faulkner's work to come on the psychological, social, and cultural perils of masculinity.

53. For concise accounts of *Sanctuary*'s composition, revision, and publication, see Noel Polk's introduction to his edition of the 1987 two-volume Garland facsimile of the *Sanctuary* manuscript and typescript (Vol. 1, vii–ix) and the afterword to his edition of the original version of the novel that Faulkner sought to publish in 1929 (in *Sanctuary: The Original Text* [New York: Random House, 1981], 293–306).

54. See Faulkner's introduction to the 1932 Modern Library edition of the novel, reprinted in *Sanctuary: The Corrected Text,* ed. Noel Polk (New York: Random House, Vintage, 1987), 339. See also Philip Cohen's "'A Cheap Idea . . . Deliberately Conceived to Make Money': The Bio-

graphical Context of William Faulkner's Introduction to *Sanctuary*," *Faulkner Journal* 3 (Spring 1988): 54–66 and Noel Polk's afterword to *Sanctuary: The Original Text,* 295.

55. "The Space Between *Sanctuary*," in *Intertexuality in Faulkner,* ed. Michel Gresset and Noel Polk (Jackson: University Press of Mississippi, 1985), 34.

56. "Faulkner's Black Holes: Visions and Vomit in *Sanctuary*," *Mississippi Quarterly* 49 (1996): 553.

57. "Selling a Novel: Faulkner's *Sanctuary* as a Psychosexual Text," in *Faulkner and Gender,* 145.

58. See Michael Lahey's "The Complex Art of Justice: Lawyers and Lawmakers as Faulkner's Dubious Artist Figures," in *Faulkner and the Artist,* 250–68.

59. In like fashion, Kathryn M. Scheel contends in "Incest, Repression, and Repetition Compulsion: The Case of Faulkner's Temple Drake" (*Mosaic* 30 [1997]: 39–55) that the real mystery of *Sanctuary* is not Temple's rape at the Old Frenchman's Place but her very real earlier incestuous rape by her brothers. Scheel's provocative psychoanalytic reading suggests that Temple has repressed any awareness of this previous rape but that the repressed trauma nevertheless manifests itself in her complex and apparently contradictory speech and behavior. Given the controversial nature of her argument and her assignation of agency to Faulkner, Scheel might have consulted the original version of *Sanctuary* to see if Faulkner's drastic revisions provide any confirmation or qualification of her thesis.

60. In *Faulkner in Cultural Context,* 75.

61. The text of the 1946 Modern Library edition was first reprinted as a Modern Library paperback in 1954 and first published as a Vintage paperback in 1961. The 1946 Modern Library text forms the basis for the text in Random House's *Faulkner Reader* (1954) and for the 1959 New American Library Signet edition of the novel. The appendix appears at the end of the novel in both the 1954 *Reader* and its reprint in the Modern Library, but is located at the front of the 1959 New American Library Signet edition. Most of the relevant bibliographical information on *The Sound and the Fury* may be found in James B. Meriwether's "Notes on the Textual History of *The Sound and the Fury*," *Publications of the Bibliographical Society of America* 56 (Third Quarter 1962): 285–316; his "The Books of William Faulkner," *Mississippi Quarterly* 35 (Summer 1982): 268–69; and his "The Books of William Faulkner: A Guide for Students and Scholars," *Mississippi Quarterly* 30 (Summer 1977): 419.

62. In 1962, Vintage reissued the novel's 1929 text in paper with "Appendix: Compson: 1699–1945" at the back of the volume (Polk, *Editorial Handbook,* 18). In 1966, a Modern Library reissue of the 1946 text also positioned the appendix at the novel's rear, while Random House reissued the 1929 text of *The Sound and the Fury* without it. The next year saw the 1929 text reissued as a "Modern Library College Edition" in paperback with the appendix once again at the rear.

63. When David Minter reprinted Polk's text in his 1987 and 1994 Norton Critical Editions of *The Sound and the Fury,* however, he included the appendix in the "Backgrounds and Contexts" sections.

64. On this subject, see Philip Cohen's "'The Key to the Whole Book': Faulkner's *The Sound and the Fury,* the Compson Appendix, and Textual Instability," in Cohen, *Texts and Textuality,* especially 246–47 and 250–52.

65. For example, Dawn Trouard finds in the "discrepancies and ruptures" in the 1929 novel's representation of Caddy and the other Compson women a progressive rewriting of the novel in terms of gender, arguing that the appendix continues to present in the persons of Melissa Meek and Caddy "a [feminist] model of the caring possibilities yet to be realized." See her "Faulkner's Text which Is Not One," *New Essays on* The Sound and the Fury, ed. Noel Polk (Cambridge: Cambridge University Press, 1993), 25, 57. Similarly, Susan Donaldson has contended that the Compson Appendix is Faulkner's self-reflexive critique of "the [patriarchal] structures of narrative, authority, and gender defining" in the 1929 *Sound and the Fury.* See her "Reading Faulkner Reading Cowley Reading Faulkner: Authority and Gender in the Compson Appendix," *Faulkner and Cultural Studies.* Spec. issue of *Faulkner Journal* 7.1–2 (Fall 1991/Spring 1992): 27–28. Alternatively, Thadious M. Davis describes the piece as a conservative revision that emphasizes the Compson patriarchal line at the expense of women and blacks, whose roles are diminished, thus presaging Faulkner's work in the 1950s with its "ridiculing of women . . . the complicated

immersions in historical narratives of war, the dismissal of blacks from all but the most visually benign texts." See "Reading Faulkner's Compson Appendix: Writing History From the Margins," *Faulkner and Ideology*, 251.

Several essays in Hahn and Kinney's *Approaches to Teaching Faulkner's* The Sound and the Fury recapitulate the historical diversity of critical opinion on the appendix's relationship to the novel by differing widely over whether the appendix is part of the novel, is a separate work, or is part of the novel's ongoing textual process. Whereas Walter Taylor writes, in "The Compson Appendix as an Aid to Teaching *The Sound and the Fury*," that "the appendix may create [for first-time readers] as many problems as it solves" (64), Charles Peek, in "Order and Flight: Teaching *The Sound and the Fury* Using the Appendix," sees no insurmountable discrepancies between the 1929 novel and the appendix, which he claims enables readers to "engage issues of race and gender without being so influenced by Dilsey's indomitability or distracted by the Compson brothers' obsession with their sister, Caddy" (68). If Jun Liu suggests, in "Nihilists and Their Relations: A Nietzchean Approach to Teaching *The Sound and the Fury*," that teachers draw students' attention to Faulkner's comments on Jason in the appendix as a means of understanding him better (93), John T. Matthews, in "Text and Context: *The Sound and the Fury* after Deconstruction," advises them to concentrate instead "on what the novel itself looks at (and what it does not)" (123).

For examples of earlier ahistorical readings of *The Sound and the Fury* in terms of the appendix, see Cohen, "'The Key to the Whole Book,'" 250–52. In "Jason's Role-Slippage: The Dynamics of Alcoholism in *The Sound and the Fury*," Gary Storhoff continues this tradition of uncritical intertextual readings when he notes that Jason has in the novel amassed a small fortune over the years from stealing Caddy's money and working in Earl's store; "Yet we discover [in the appendix] that he has accumulated less than $7,000" (*Mississippi Quarterly* 49 [1996]: 530). Storhoff then analyzes how Jason has thrown his money away in the novel, in effect reading the novel through the lens of the appendix with little awareness that it represents Faulkner's rewriting of the novel many years later. Similarly, Rick Wallach argues, in "The Compson Family Finances and the Economics of Tragic Farce," that Jason's ultimate failure in the cotton market proceeds "according to principles of exchange which reflect and elaborate the [novel's] themes of emotional dissolution and loss" but uncritically uses the Compson family's long history of financial decline in the appendix to interpret Jason's motives in the 1929 novel (*South Atlantic Review* 62 [1997]: 80).

66. For extensive discussion of some of these clashes, see Cohen, "'The Key to the Whole Book,'" especially 237–38 and 242–49.

67. Oslo: Solum Forlag, 1997. Many of the papers by well-known Faulkner scholars at this 1995 conference concentrate on the relationship between various published and unpublished stories and sketches and the novels. See especially the volume's fourth section, "From Short Story to Fiction."

68. Faulkner's revisions for *The Unvanquished* of stories that had earlier appeared in the *Saturday Evening Post* are discussed in Joseph L. Blotner's notes in *Uncollected Stories of William Faulkner* (New York: Random House, Vintage Books, 1979), 681–84; James B. Carothers's *William Faulkner's Short Stories* (Ann Arbor: University of Michigan Research Press, 1985), 84–87; and Joanne V. Creighton's *William Faulkner's Craft of Revision: The Snopes Trilogy,* The Unvanquished, *and* Go Down, Moses (Detroit: Wayne State University Press, 1977), 73–84. For discussions of Faulkner's composition of short stories for various magazines and his subsequent revision of them for *Go Down, Moses,* see Carothers, 88–89, 91, and Blotner, *Faulkner: A Biography,* Vol. 2, 1077–78, 1087–88, 1089, and 1093.

69. In *Faulkner: Novels 1936–1940* (New York: Library of America, 1990), 1110. In "Diving into the Wreck: Faulknerian Practice and the Imagination of Slavery," Philip Weinstein calls *The Unvanquished* "for the most part (and despite a good deal of current critical attention), a racially retrograde text," citing the prior publication of much of the novel in the *Post* as "one explanation for its conventional thinking" (*Faulkner Journal* 10 [1995]: 29).

70. Neither Deborah Clarke nor Patricia Yaeger evince much interest in Faulkner's revision of the stories that constitute the book. Emphasizing the social construction of gender, in "Gender, War, and Cross-Dressing in *The Unvanquished*," Clarke claims that Drusilla Hawk presents a radical challenge to the South's race and gender hierarchies by dressing and fighting like a man "in

order to preserve the man's world against which she rebels" (in *Faulkner and Gender,* 242). When the war ends and she is returned to dresses, marriage, and an antebellum gender position, Drusilla "uncovers the power of the feminine in language" by using her femininity and sexuality with a vengeance to urge men, including Bayard, to violence (246). For Yaeger, in "Faulkner's 'Greek Amphora Priestess': Verbena and Violence in *The Unvanquished,*" Drusilla's white woman's body, especially in "An Odor of Verbena," "becomes a screen or symbol for the text's [and the region's] unresolved political issues," a screen on which Faulkner maps "the grotesque trivialization of African-American's [sic] rights and humanity" (in *Faulkner and Gender,* 207, 219). Although neither Clarke nor Yaeger discuss the genesis of *The Unvanquished,* the textual relationship of the first five stories to the last-written "Odor of Verbena"—the stories were written at different times for different audiences—seems relevant to arguments about characters like Drusilla that recur throughout the collection.

71. "Dismantling the *Saturday Evening Post* Reader: *The Unvanquished* and Changing 'Horizons of Expectations,'" in *Faulkner and Popular Culture,* 180.

72. *The Heart of Yoknapatawpha* (Jackson: University Press of Mississippi, 1981).

73. *The Heart of Yoknapatawpha,* 189, 190–216.

74. *Faulkner Journal* 10 (1995): 82.

75. In one such recent attempt to unify the various stories, Glen Meeter displaces Cass Edmonds's and Isaac McCaslin's competing visions in the novel with the competing visions of Isaac and Molly Beauchamp. Reading the book's biblical allusions typologically, Meeter sees Molly as a prophetic visionary who envisions the South as Canaan, a land promised to the inheritors of both races, while Ike's repudiation of his inheritance reflects the story of the Fall and the original sin of "trying to own and tame the land." See his "Molly's Vision: Lost Cause Ideology and Genesis in Faulkner's *Go Down, Moses,*" in *Faulkner and Ideology,* 288. The novel's meaning thus arises from the dialectical relationship between these two visions, which ultimately gives primacy to Molly. To counter the objection that Molly does not receive as much time, space, or dialogue as Ike, Meeter might have looked for textual evidence, especially in Faulkner's revision of the magazine stories, that supports his claim.

Those critics who have attended to the entire textual process of *Go Down, Moses* have often viewed Faulkner's revisions of previous published and unpublished work as authorially intended improvements that serve the different purposes of the novel and create a more-unified work. Thus Jane Millgate's detailed examination of Faulkner's revision of his *Atlantic Monthly* story "Gold is not Always" concludes that he "deliberately reworked his material in such a way as to fit it into the framework of an overall thematic pattern." See her "Short Story into Novel: Faulkner's Reworking of 'Gold is not Always,'" *English Studies* 45 (1964): 315. Millgate is not much interested in the issue of how these revisions may have created new problems at the same time that they solved others. Joanne Creighton's *William Faulkner's Craft of Revision,* one of the earliest studies of Faulkner's incorporation of preexistent short stories into longer works, also exhibits a similar lack of interest in the conflicts or problems created by Faulkner's revisions. Creighton emphasizes Faulkner's "skillful revision" and "the control that [he] exercises over the diffuseness of his Yoknapatawpha material" as he refashioned in *Go Down, Moses* "comparatively simple and one-dimensional stories into an integrated whole" (149, 154). A refreshing if extreme exception to this tendency is Marvin Klotz, who contends that Faulkner jammed "great chunks of unassimilated, mostly expository, prose" into his "tightly structured and lucid magazine stories," material which blurred thematic focus and destroyed established characterization. See his "Procrustean Revision in Faulkner's *Go Down, Moses,*" *American Literature* 37 (March 1965): 16.

76. Faulkner also produced a heavily revised and abridged version of "The Bear," a new story he had already written for the novel, and sold it to the *Saturday Evening Post* for publication in early 1942.

77. *The Making of* Go Down, Moses (Dallas: Southern Methodist University Press, 1972).

78. "Contending Narratives: *Go Down, Moses* and the Short Story Cycle," in *Faulkner and the Short Story,* ed. Evans Harrington and Ann J. Abadie (Jackson: University Press of Mississippi, 1992), 147.

79. Similarly, John Carlos Rowe has argued in "The African-American Voice in Faulkner's *Go Down, Moses*" that because Faulkner was unable to grant his African American characters the independent voices he knew they deserved, the book contains two narratives contending with each other for dominance: Ike McCaslin's myth and the stories of African Americans seeking freedom. In *The Modern Short Story Sequence: Composite Fictions and Fictive Communities,* ed. J. Gerald Kennedy (Cambridge: Cambridge University Press, 1995), 76–97. Rowe's contention that the volume's short-story sequence defends the integrity of its threatened cohesion might have profited from an examination of the variants in the work's textual history. On the other hand, Arthur F. Kinney's account of the centrality of the issues of racism and miscegenation to its themes, characters and families, and narrative and metaphoric structures in Go Down, Moses: *The Miscegenation of Time* (New York: Twayne, 1996) is notable for its frequent attempts to relate what we know about Faulkner's composition and revision of the novel and related texts to his developing plan for the novel and to how we might best collaborate in producing its meanings. Nevertheless, some may disagree with how tightly integrated he feels the individual chapters of *Go Down, Moses* are.

80. Philip Weinstein, "'He Come and Spoke for Me': Scripting Lucas Beauchamp's Three Lives," in *Faulkner and the Short Story,* 237, 244. Weinstein here parallels, in part, Michael Grimwood's argument in *Heart in Conflict: Faulkner's Struggles with Vocation* (Athens: University of Georgia Press, 1987) that as Faulkner revised the short stories, he repudiated the formulaic Anglo-American depictions of comic "darkies" inherited from plantation literature that characterized the stories in their original appearance in national magazines such as *Harper's,* the *Atlantic Monthly,* and *Collier's* (275–77).

81. James McLaverty, "Issues of Identity and Utterance: An Intentionalist Response to 'Textual Instability,'" in Cohen, *Devils and Angels,* 136.

82. *Faulkner's MGM Screenplays* (Knoxville: University of Tennessee Press, 1982), xxxvii–xxxix. See also Bruce Kawin's *Faulkner and Film* (New York: Frederick Ungar Publishing Company, 1977).

83. *Faulkner: A Comprehensive Guide to the Brodsky Collection,* Vol. III: *The De Gaulle Story* (Jackson: University Press of Mississippi, 1984), xxxi.

84. *Stallion Road: A Screenplay,* ed. Louis Daniel Brodsky and Robert W. Hamblin (Jackson: University Press of Mississippi, 1989), xvi.

85. *Country Lawyer and Other Stories for the Screen* (Jackson: University Press of Mississippi, 1987).

86. *Faulkner, Modernism, and Film: Faulkner and Yoknapatawpha, 1978,* ed. Evans Harrington and Ann J. Abadie. (Jackson: University Press of Mississippi, 1979).

87. *Contemporary German Editorial Theory,* ed. Hans Walter Gabler, George Bornstein, and Gillian Borland Pierce (Ann Arbor: University of Michigan Press, 1995), 6.

88. For example, contemporary reviewers frequently praised *Sanctuary* at the expense of *The Sound and the Fury* and *As I Lay Dying* in part because Cape and Smith included the following copy on the front inside flap of the first five printings: "This new novel shows the further simplification of an amazing style which, while it could not hide the greatness of Faulkner's work, made both *The Sound and the Fury* and *As I Lay Dying* difficult for many readers" (in *Sanctuary* [New York: Cape and Smith, Fifth Printing, July, 1931], Linton Massey Faulkner Collection, Alderman Library, University of Virginia). Reviews of *Sanctuary* with their slighting of his two earlier novels, both tour de forces, may have been one of several factors that inspired Faulkner to write his notorious introduction for the 1932 Modern Library edition of the novel, in which he contemptuously dismissed both the book and its readers and profoundly shaped criticism of *Sanctuary* for several decades. For an extensive discussion of this issue, see Cohen, "'A Cheap Idea . . . Deliberately Conceived to Make Money.'"

89. See, for example, his "'The Dungeon was Mother Herself': William Faulkner: 1927–1931," in *New Directions in Faulkner Studies: Faulkner and Yoknapatawpha, 1983,* ed. Doreen Fowler and Ann J. Abadie (Jackson: University Press of Mississippi, 1984), 61–93; "The Space Between Sanctuary," in *Intertextuality in Faulkner,* ed. Michel Gresset and Noel Polk (Jackson: University Press of Mississippi, 1985), 16–35; and "'Polysyllabic and Verbless Patriotic Nonsense': Faulkner at Mid-

century—His and Ours," in *Faulkner and Ideology: Faulkner and Yoknapatawpha, 1992.,* ed. Donald M. Kartiganer and Ann J. Abadie (Jackson: University Press of Mississippi), 297–328.

90. *William Faulkner: Early Prose and Poetry* (Boston: Little, Brown, 1962).

91. See Jerome J. McGann's "How to Read a Book," in *The Textual Condition* (Princeton, NJ: Princeton University Press, 1991) and *Black Riders: The Visible Language of Modernism* (Princeton, NJ: Princeton University Press, 1993), and Bornstein's "What is the Text of a Poem by Yeats?" in *Palimpsest,* 167–93. For instructive examples of criticism that makes use of the bibliographical or material features of a work, see Marta Werner's *Emily Dickinson's Open Folios: Scenes of Reading, Surfaces of Writing* (Ann Arbor: University of Michigan Press, 1995) and Cathy N. Davidson's "The Life and Times of *Charlotte Temple:* The Biography of a Book" in *Reading in America: Literature and Social History* (Baltimore: Johns Hopkins University Press, 1989), 157–79.

92. In *Making the Team: The Cultural Work of Baseball Fiction* (Urbana: University of Illinois Press, 1997), Tim Morris has astutely observed that the journey of Patrick O'Brien's Aubrey/Maturin novels from genre fiction to Literature with a capital *L* is materially manifested in the contrast between the "kitschy cover art and pulpy pages" of Lippincott's editions of his novels in the early 1970s and Norton's repackaging of them in the 1990s as "a uniform set of exquisitely produced trade paperbacks" (150).

93. For further discussion of such images, see Barry R. McCann's "Faulkner's *As I Lay Dying:* The Coffin Pictogram and the Function of Form," *University of Mississippi Studies in English* 11–12 (1993–1995): 272–81, and Robert W. Hamblin's " 'Longer than Anything': Faulkner's Grand Design in *Absalom, Absalom!*" in *Faulkner and the Artist,* 269–93.

94. In *Faulkner and the Artist,* 82–109. Reid thus provides textual evidence to support arguments about Faulkner and postimpressionist painting that she earlier advanced in "The Cubist Novel: Toward Defining the Genre," in *"A Cosmos of My Own": Faulkner and Yoknapatawpha 1980,* ed. Doreen Fowler and Ann J. Abadie (Jackson: University Press of Mississippi, 1981), 36–58; "Faulkner's Cubist Novels," in *"A Cosmos of My Own,"* 59–94; and "The Economy of Desire: Faulkner's Poetics from Eroticism to Post-Impressionism," *Faulkner Journal* 4 (1988–1989): 159–77.

95. *Faulkner and the Artist,* 100.

13

Thematic Criticism

Charles A. Peek

FAULKNER (flatly): There isn't any theme in my work.[1]

As we arrive at the final chapter of this book, it might be argued that there is no category remaining to be called "thematic" criticism, that all the work to be included under such a catchall title has already appeared under the separate categories of the other chapters of this book. And, indeed, other contributors have already treated many of the themes ("race," for example) that could be named. However, despite this and despite Faulkner's own denial, there are four justifications for this concluding chapter. First, it is one thing to treat a theme like race as a part of a timely critical trend and quite another to treat it as a persistent theme running across critical periods, thereby calling on us to explore what it means to call something (race, in this instance) a "theme." Second, "thematics" is the most appropriate category under which to consider the vexed question of "genetic" or "source" critics: how much Oxford and Mississippi Faulkner used and didn't use. Third, since a writer's themes are not hers alone but have their own history, such a chapter is the appropriate place to consider what his themes say about Faulkner's place in both literary history and the history of ideas. And fourth, by whatever name, there must be a place for the critical miscellany omitted in the other chapters.

The rationale for such a chapter, therefore, suggests that within it we will be examining a broad variety of topics including conventions of genre; Faulkner's reflections of specific literary traditions; the religious, moral, and political contexts of the themes he most consistently addresses; and the manner of his address. The specific themes that inform Faulkner's work, though numerous, are not difficult to enumerate. Give or take a theme or two, the list is much the same as almost any reader or critic would compile and would consist of the following:

Abnormality: Faulkner's exploration, following Anderson's notion of "grotesques," of insanity, imbecility, paranoia, sadism, the sinister, the perverted, horror, degeneracy, brutality, obsession, the thwarted life, including here the dynamic between Puritanism and "the exotic."

Art: the role of the artist, sensibility and sensitivity and their treatment in the world, articulateness and inarticulateness, the figurative and the literal, story-telling, humor, consciousness, how civilizations and peoples represent themselves.

Grief and loss: war, violence, crisis, dismemberment, abandonment, neglect, good and bad fortune, suffering, flight and pursuit, haves and have-nots, disorders and dislocations.

Maturation: childhood, innocence, growth, striving and seeking, choice, initiation, the primitive and the social, mentors (or the lack or corruption thereof), freedom and restraint.

Nature: evolution, motion, flux, Bergson's *élan vital,* wilderness/isolation, causes and effects of the machine age, nature receding before human advance, the mystery of existence, the physicality of soil, air, light, heat, sound and their emotional resonance.

Nurture: including family relationships (husband/wife, parents and children, siblings), incest, lineage and dynasty, collapse of social structures related to the family, Oedipal (and other) complexes, roles and contentions of male and female, home, community, place, sacred space, church and faith, small town/village life.

Race and caste: miscegenation, invisibility, blood, color, white/black relations, arts and culture, jazz and blues, poor whites, the aristocracy, planters and sharecroppers, social rise and fall, cursed inheritances, the plantation legend and legends of reconstruction.

Time: history, the past, pastoral, tragedy, the Old South, the death struggle of an old order, the South as region and as tradition, tradition versus modernity, decay and progress, the loss of order, alienation, the American Dream, time-lessness, universality.

And of course, *the human heart in conflict with itself:* that is, flesh versus spirit; the moral psychologies of revenge, lust, greed, despair, delusion; savage tyranny of evil; abolition of human values; reality of evil; waste *versus* love; self-sacrifice; pity; courage; respect; vision; the heroic age and humane tradition; the dignity of freedom, endurance, prevailing; humanism versus materialism.

From the critical literature, two things are easily established. First, and most obviously, these categories are not mutually exclusive but blend with one another, support and challenge one another, and provide a thematic dynamic as focus shifts from one to the other. Second, by the time of the first major, full-length critical work in 1951, all of these themes had been identified and had received critical response.[2]

It will be convenient to divide our overview of thematic criticism into three *overlapping* eras, each with a period of transition at the end of one and the beginning of another. Very roughly these would be (a) from the beginning to the end of the world wars—1924–1946, (b) a transition period from Cowley's *Portable* through the Nobel Prize—1946–1952, (c) the next two decades roughly through the withdrawal of U.S. troops from Viet Nam and the foundation of the Faulkner and Yoknapatawpha Conference[3]—1952–1976, (d) a transition through the post-Nixon/pre-Reagan era—1976–1981, and then (e) from that time to a transition beginning fin de siècle—1981–present. Clearly I mean to suggest here that criticism is an interface between intellectual and political history and hence serves to dramatize an author's place in both.

In turn, each critical era serves as the occasion for a particular discussion. The earliest period raises the question of what we mean by theme and how theme is related to content and style. The second era demonstrates how thematic criticism can problematize our reading. In the final period, the question of sources comes to the fore. How much did his locale serve as the origin of Faulkner's fiction, or much the same thing, how much is Yoknapatawpha the fictional center? Or, alternatively, how much are we to see the fiction born of more distant sources that emerge in literary history, especially traditions of psychological realism and of those genres most readily associated with psychology (e.g., bildungsroman)? Here, too, we may encounter critical questions regarding the relationship of Faulkner's fiction and nonfiction.

1924–1946

In the first of our time periods, the earliest evidence must come from reviews (including book notes and prefaces) since for over a decade they constituted virtually the whole critical story. Earlier I indicated that critics soon called attention to nearly all of the major themes later to be explored. What is not so evident from the earliest responses is a critical awareness that in Faulkner hardly ever is one of these themes treated in the absence of the others.

For an example we might take a 1930 review of *The Sound and the Fury* in which Clifton Fadiman readily notes the theme of "mental and physical disintegration" but finds the effort to get to that theme tedious and irritating ("Hardly Worth While" 74–75). In his argument he presumes that the layers to be penetrated constitute only gratuitous experimentation rather than thematic depths. To Fadiman, the characters are not "sufficiently interesting" because he reads them as only examples of disintegration. Thus, while a Faulkner publication was the occasion for reviews in significant journals of opinion *(Nation, New Republic, Kenyon Review),* the reviews generally treated themes in isolation. They had not yet discerned that the collocation of themes was itself a theme, the interdependence of all things, and that it was this collocated theme that necessitated the linguistic experiments.

Fadiman's review is significant to thematic considerations in still another way: his idea that Faulkner's subject matter lacks "Joycean proportions" suggests that he was unaware of the political, moral, and historic issues Faulkner encompassed in the story of one family and its servants of a different race. This must strike the modern reader as odd until we remember that a world war and a depression put on hold the volatile subject of race as a major theme in the American conversation until circa 1940, when it was again put on hold by another world war until the late 1940s when, just on the verge of emerging, a police action of major proportions held it at bay until the Eisenhower era.

In 1930, to a large portion of America's literary elite, race was not yet a significant question even in the context of American history, let alone as an archetype of worldwide colonialism. Criticism, too, can be color-blind or color-conscious, racist or open to diversity, and national trends in these matters particularly affect reviews, the above-water portion of the critical iceberg. Meanwhile, more than has perhaps been recognized, America's relationship to the world and to history was becoming a theme of Faulkner's from the earliest work. Whatever, then, may be made of them critically, Faulkner's work on *A Fable* or his film work for *Land of the Pharaohs* are far from anomalous and represent his continued interest in those connections that belied the parochialism not only of the South but also of America itself. That this interest is surfacing as early as *The Sound and the Fury* is evident from the novel itself as well as from the appendix and various prefaces Faulkner would later want appended to it. It would be some time before first reviewers and then critics came to acknowledge this.

Criticism is, in a sense, the effort to articulate the qualities that have garnered or might garner an audience for a writer's work. Reviews take the measure of audiences with regard to currently published work. Over a period of time, reviews track how an author is attracting readers whose concerns are moving or shifting to parallel his own. In our specific case, if race is a theme of Joycean proportion for Faulkner, even if cultural blinders cause early reviews to miss this, later reviews will register it by being attuned to the kind of cultural awareness that Faulkner, among others, helped bring about. And so it seems to have been.

In this light, without implying a simplistic direct line of development, it is nevertheless instructive to see the shift in the area of thematic criticism between Fadiman's 1930, early Great Depression review and Lionel Trilling's 1942, era-of-growing-international-focus review of *Go Down, Moses, and Other Stories.* As Fadiman saw that *The Sound and the Fury* dealt with the theme of a white Southern family and the Negroes associated with it, so Trilling begins with the recognition that, apart from "Pantaloon in Black," *Go Down, Moses* deals with "a single theme, the relation of the Mississippi McCaslins to the Negroes about them" ("The McCaslins" 632–33).[4] However, in contrast, Trilling sees that this relationship convincingly explores "the complex tragedy of the South's racial dilemma." Moreover, although he has a modernist [see chapter 5] understanding of the race question as hinging on "the spiritual condition of the white men who have . . . at their disposal" the fate of both races, Trilling can give the theme a postmodernist twist [see chapter 6] by noting that the novel revolves around a "failure of love which *Edmonds's tradition imposed upon him*" (my emphasis). Because, therefore, the novel exposes the deep entrenchment of tradition,

Trilling understands that Ike McCaslin's merely individual response to the novel's central conflict cannot serve as a "'solution' to the racial problem."

In short, although both reviews identify the theme of race, the latter review sees it as a theme of epic proportions, whereas the earlier review did not.[5] Because of this, Trilling can also see Faulkner's story as tragic rather than merely horrific, its tragic dimension one frequently denied in the earliest reviews. Hence, what is meant by the "theme" of race has changed considerably. It has changed in keeping with the development through the Great Depression of an awareness of the very complex interrelationship between personal views and social realities, the very interrelationship Trilling's review notes in the novel itself.

The Trilling review introduces a second expansion of our conception of thematic criticism. Although Trilling refers to a "single theme," his review is well aware that this theme appears in the context of other themes. Set in counterpoint to the McCaslins' possession of blacks often "related . . . through more lines than one" is the theme of the "unpossessable wilderness." Moreover these issues, as "the Southern problem," are seen here as cultural issues "to be found crystallized" in the expectations of sexual roles in the South. What then should we say is *the* theme? Race? Wilderness? Gender? Surely theme, here, is meant to suggest something larger, to suggest that race, wilderness, and gender are merely particulars of that ageless desire to possess what cannot be possessed, a theme recognizable from Homer and Sophocles alike, making most likely their epic and tragic proportions. Or we might put it this way: In the early criticism there was a tendency to see many themes. As later critics perceived relations among them, these individual themes came to be seen less as themes in their own right and more as instances of more comprehensive themes, themes by their very nature of greater profundity than was first understood.

This phenomenon of well-identified themes but only partially grasped significance accounts for the overwhelmingly prevailing tone of these reviews. In almost all of them, there is some acknowledgment of a kind of genius in Faulkner coupled with dismay over his failures or dismissal of his achievement. The virtue ascribed (sometimes begrudgingly) ranges from his creation of an original cosmos (Fadiman, Kronenberg) to his rendering of the abnormal or decaying (Lovett, Basso). The vice that vitiates Faulkner's achievement is almost always seen to lie in his approach, his eccentricity, his belabored stylistics, his medium never quite appropriate to his message. The problem with Faulkner's gift, Louis Kronenberg suggests, is in its "handling." Malcolm Cowley's view sums up the sentiments of the times: "I have always felt . . . that theme and treatment were somehow disharmonious" ("Faulkner by Daylight" 510).

Today, however, we might ask to what extent a limited or even skewed view of theme was responsible for this sense of disharmony. Is "Dry September," in any but the most superficial sense, the "story of a lynching" (Cantwell), or does "Pantaloon in Black" merely evince the typical sentimentality associated with telling about lynching (Trilling)? Is it true that Faulkner truly "accepts the tradition" of the plantation legend (Cowley)? Do we find trivial the Compson family dynamic? Or the Compson relationship to Dilsey and her family? Or the racial implications of both? Our acceptance of any of these "readings" would at best be guarded and, consequently, it is easier for us to see that limitations in the identification of theme are directly related to underestimations of the "handling" of style and structure, subject and character.[6]

The earliest reviews, then, indicate a tendency toward a sympathetic thematic criticism whose limitations created an anomalously unsympathetic stylistic criticism. This, however, is not to suggest that future thematic criticism gained nothing from these early endeavors. Indeed, critics of no mean reputation filed several claims on mines where rich deposits would later be discovered. Four of these discoveries, representative of others, are worth a moment here.

As early as in his 1931 review of *Sanctuary,* Clifton Fadiman had noted a singularly important force in Faulkner's writing. Examining the relation of Temple Drake's story to Horace Benbow's, Fadiman suggested, "they revolve about one another like the components of a binary star system, connected by lines of force but none the less separated" ("The World of William Faulkner" 423). In this insight, Fadiman hit upon a major device in Faulkner's telling of stories, indeed a major device in the narrative structures of American modernism. Much of the more important later thematic criticism (e.g., McHaney's treatment of *If I Forget Thee, Jerusalem*) would rely on the substance within the force holding two stories together, foundations for which had been laid earlier by Michael Millgate, William Van O'Connor, and Hyatt H. Waggoner.

Similarly, that same year, in an early insight into "That Evening Sun," Robert Cantwell suggested, "The real story is not the written one of Nancy's foreboding, but the unexplained, unanalyzed condition of strain within the white family" (271). Cantwell's notion here applies to Faulkner something similar to the "silence . . . always at the edge of Hammett's style,"[7] the thing made more lastingly famous by both Cather and Hemingway: the thing not said, the iceberg, the importance of the untold story to the story told. And, in turn, thematic criticism would later see the importance of this in Faulkner's stories, for instance, those ostensibly about war(s).

If Fadiman's and Cantwell's insights prepared for the second wave (1952–1976) of thematic criticism, Giorgio Lovati prepared the way for the more ideological criticism of 1976 and after. In particular, Lovati saw that, "without the colorless desolation of the Middle West, without its immense, uniform metropolises, without America's chill, rigorous Puritanical morality, together with the cruelty of a capitalistic system which recognizes only money, Faulkner could never have written" (72). Although Lovati is here referring specifically to *Sanctuary* and *Light in August,* he is also commenting more generally on Faulkner's "non-dogmatic but profoundly felt accent of revolt whose excesses tend to reduce the human element if not to abolish it altogether" (72). We should note, here, too, that Lovati sees Faulkner as responding to more broadly American, not simply peculiarly Southern material. Though preceding Faulkner's post-Nobel public remarks and essays by two decades, Lovati's understanding prepares us to incorporate the nonfiction into our critical purview and alerts us to the fact that, even early on, thematic criticism is not so much to be viewed as connected with formalism as with interpretive schools seeking the relation of literature and the social issues that form its context.[8]

Finally, we would be remiss to ignore Cowley's incisive remark that the fiction is "dealing with a community where Faulkner seems to have known every single inhabitant from birth to deathbed" ("Faulkner by Daylight" 510). However we evaluate Cowley's contribution to Faulkner, whatever may have been his biases, this remark is both palpably true and seldom brought to bear. It is, however, prophetic of the bent of criticism today, as we are emerging from its last period and its next period begins to take shape. Already, however, thematic criticism at the turn of the century seems to be looking more at the strange and knowing relations of author and characters, and I will return to this at the close of this piece.

The seminal piece of criticism, the first to explore Faulkner's themes at greater length than a review or book note, was George Marion O'Donnell's "Faulkner's Mythology" [see chapter 1]. It is an interesting piece both for the way it breaks from earlier misunderstandings and for the way it remains in their grip. For O'Donnell, Faulkner's major theme was "the Southern social-economic-ethical tradition which [he] possesses naturally, as part of his sensibility" (285). In the development of this theme, according to O'Donnell, Faulkner emerges not as a purveyor of "a cultural psychosis" (à la Maxwell Geismar) but, to the contrary, "really as a traditional moralist" exploring "two worlds: the Sartoris world and the Snopes world," or as he later says, "humanism and naturalism," and dramatizing them "convincingly in the terms of particular history and of actual life" (286). O'Donnell is not suggesting that Faulkner was unaware of the "fatal defects" in the old tradition. Far from it. Rather, Faulkner's attraction to the world of tradition was that, in it, "action is of heroic proportions," that is, that it was the stuff of which epic and tragedy could be made. O'Donnell draws for support on a passage that was to echo in the criticism of the next decade: "victims of a different circumstance, simpler . . . more heroic . . . loving once or dying once instead of being diffused and scattered" (*Absalom* 89).

O'Donnell, too, focuses readers on the significance of genre to Faulkner's work. "All his work," O'Donnell writes, "is really a striving toward the condition of tragedy" (299). Occasionally, "it has the quality of gusty humor . . . the outrageously grotesque heroic." Moreover, the work "is definitely romantic" (298). While later critics would quarrel with these designations, they would remain those most often considered in determining the sorts of sources that informed Faulkner's work. Notwithstanding, the quirkiness of his exploration (O'Donnell oddly finds humor "rare in Mr. Faulkner's work") leads O'Donnell to echo early reviews by suggesting that Faulkner's failures are owing to several "difficulties of form," here seen as his lapsing from legend and myth into allegory and satire. Clearly, even with a seminal work, theme has not yet found a comprehensive enough articulation to justify method.

Still, for over a decade, most serious critics agreed with O'Donnell; and his critique set the terms of debate for a great deal of Faulkner criticism for the following three decades. (See for example Dayton Kohler's piece for *College English* and Richard Chase's for the *Kenyon Review.*) Certainly, the line of thought begun with O'Donnell is picked up and furthered by Malcolm Cowley in his creation of *The Portable Faulkner* and reinforced by no less a literary light than Robert Penn Warren in his immediate review of Cowley's accomplishment in which Warren wrote, "Cowley's interpretation of the legend . . . is indebted, no doubt, to that of George Marion O'Donnell (the first and still an indispensable study of Faulkner's theme)" (177). For Warren and Cowley, too, far from being an apologist for the Old South, Faulkner was seen as depicting a "plight and problem" of the Old South, New South, and modern world in general. This plight is precisely that, though the old order "allowed the traditional man to define himself as human," it nevertheless "did not satisfy human needs" because it was "accursed" by its injustice. Indeed, what was human in that order survives it "among the despised and rejected" (Warren 177). A story, then, of what Warren called "contamination" and "redemption" becomes "the central theme of Faulkner" and the principle for selection and organization of Cowley's materials for the *Portable.*

Even in pushing O'Donnell's premises further, however, Cowley also distances himself from one of their consequences. Whatever traditional moralist Faulkner might be, as an artist he was dealing in legend and myth, not in sociology or even history. Thus Cowley: Yoknapatawpha "is obviously no more intended as a historical account of the country south of the Ohio than *The Scarlet Letter* was intended as a history of Massachusetts" (*Portable* 13).

As the early period of Faulkner criticism worked its way from the earliest notice of Faulkner as a rising writer to a more comprehensive sense of the themes with which he was working, reviewers and authors of book notes were helping readers to see a major thematic pattern. Beginning with a critical revolt from the Southern traditions that had coalesced in the post–Civil War South (see Basso), Faulkner had set out to explore the forces at work dehumanizing the twentieth century, forces at once peculiarly American (Puritanism and capitalism) and more universal (collectivism, totalitarianism). As a result of his perceptive understanding of these forces, Faulkner explored a myriad of essentially "prison-formed" personalities and the "major themes of flight and refuge" (Lovett 153) necessitated by the violation of their integrity and dignity, discovering, to his and our dismay, how often we are each accomplices in our own oppression.[9] Sixty years and a critical industry later, we haven't come upon a much better synopsis than that.

1946–1952

Criticism was propelled into its future by a matched pair of events during the transition from the earliest "reviews of" phase to the "books about" phase: the 1946 publication of Cowley's *Portable* and the subsequent 1950 award of the 1949 Nobel Prize. The seven categories into which Cowley organized the stories and excerpts also announce the themes Cowley found in the work: the old people who once inhabited the land, the unvanquished who carried on, the wilderness dwindling away, and the peasants—all representing an old order passing in its confrontation with the new world and New South and modern times in general . . . many of these themes being recapitulated in section 6, where Cowley included "Old Man" under the heading "Mississippi Flood." What Cowley was after was the "interconnected pattern . . . which almost all his critics have overlooked," a pattern that became for Cowley a set of symbols "of commerce and machinery destroying the standards of the past" (*Portable* 1). It is this pattern, according to Cowley, that forms in each work "a subject bigger than itself" (8). In other words, Cowley had "discovered" a sort of American agrarian Marxist sensibility that was turning into legend his vision of characters who, in Cowley's phrase, "dig for gold frenziedly after they have lost their hope of finding it" (17). No wonder, then, that Cowley preferred stories like "The Bear" and "Old Man," where the writer can be seen battling against modernity, rather than stories where the writer seems the quintessential modernist;[10] and no wonder the stylistic and structural qualities of the work continue, in Cowley's *Portable,* to be considered weaknesses in the work. To be sure, for Cowley, they are forgivable, even endearing weaknesses—but it is this thematic pattern, seemingly lived rather than observed, that is the greatness of the work.

Since criticism has long since given up the effort to make the real William Faulkner please stand up, who would say that Cowley's Faulkner is not a real Faulkner? He is certainly not the only real Faulkner. He is not, for instance, the Faulkner of the French critics enamored with his psychological depths and experimental style. He is not the many other Faulkners that later critics would interpose over biographical skeletons like clear plastic overlays of nerves and arteries in a college textbook. But, although assessment of the precise role Cowley played is a legitimate scholarly enterprise, it seems at best ungenerous not to acknowledge the extraordinary role Cowley played in advancing Faulkner's fortunes by focusing readers at least for a few years on the Faulkner of a particular theme that struck the literate imagination of a post–World War II world as meriting a Nobel Prize.[11] In any event, although Cowley's *Portable* clearly raises the question of sources, critics didn't meet this question head on until later. At this point, it seemed that the question of sources was seen as so straightforward as to be almost merely a rhetorical question.

As a final comment on the period, it is instructive to note how thematic criticism was advanced by insights such as those written by Ray B. West Jr. Addressing "A Rose for Emily," West reminded critics that "a theme may be emotive as well as intellectual and logical" (72). Indeed, since this is so, "the extraction of theme . . . is dangerous and never wholly satisfactory" (72). Though West alludes to themes (e.g., coming to "terms with both the past and the present" [72]; or, "heroism in an attempt to rise above" our human plight [73]), these extracts can never quite do justice to our "tragic efforts to conform both to the will of the gods and to the demands of [our] own . . . society" (72). Theme, here, is at best a shorthand for a complex relationship among a work's mode, perspective, and action (65). Criticism, then, had come to see that by theme we often mean the connection between a physical aspect, such as landscape, and its emotional concomitants, the actual setting being the key to the symbolic world that provides its meaning.[12]

1952–1976

Harry Modean Campbell and Ruel E. Foster initiated something more than a cottage industry when they published their *William Faulkner: A Critical Appraisal* in 1951. Like much of the scholarship of the ensuing years, their approach is New Critical to the extent that they focus largely on technique, including examinations of Faulknerian symbols and images, and provide a good deal of insight into how Faulkner's themes are achieved, linking thematic and structural achievement. It may well be that the distinctive difference between criticism of this and of the preceding period is the newfound appreciation for Faulkner's aesthetic achievement. This difference, however, is rooted in shifts in the understanding of his themes.

Campbell and Foster credit their list of major themes (the Southern tradition, the contemporary chaos, and man's future) to Cowley (12). Of these themes, they write that, although "there is nothing ultimately more hopeful than self-respect" (115), still, "people who follow the simple, primal drive of primitive societal life are more likely to survive than those people who have been cor-rupted by the false debilitating stimuli of modern society" (143). Despite this, they maintain that "the primitivism that runs through much of Faulkner's work is not magnolia blossom nostalgia for the ante-bellum South" (163); and they are clear that Faulkner was never under "any illusion about any kind of tradi-tional order" (165). As a matter of fact, drawn from the emphases of their study, they really seem more interested in more original approaches to theme, such as the thematic formulation of the "nature as norm thesis" (11), which they credit to Donald Davidson; thematic summation, "the primacy of the will and the unconscious in man's behavior" (42); or the thematic statement, "the world is a great sanitarium where Everyman is a patient" (44).

There emerges here a tension between kinds of traditional moralism and less-traditional exploration. This tension is a good indicator of one of the liabilities of thematic criticism: it lends itself to unnecessarily problematizing our reading. This can be illustrated by a brief look at the dominant criticism of what Cowley considered Faulkner's most problematic novel, *As I Lay Dying*. What is it, we might ask, that the Bundrens represent? Are we meant to see their journey as a vehicle for observing a family caught in the absurdity of their world, seeing enough of their dysfunctional antics that we finally agree that Darl is, indeed, better off in the asylum, better off anywhere, than with this ragtag parade and its carnivalesque inversion of values? Or is their journey, however macabre or even burlesque, a moral struggle to fulfill a promise, a mission within which they come to a shared life, a kind of communion, from which Darl, the only member who can't share, must be excommunicated?

Today these questions might not seem the most fruitful or promising critical approaches to pursue, but the rhetoric of such questions is conducive to critical debate and, hence, came to dominate a period of critical inquiry. Critics joined in vigorous defense of one or the other of these propositions, or, of course, staked out territory in between but whose parameters were still defined by these positions. And, weren't there many details of the novel to support each thematic take?

On one hand, Addie's father's nihilism prompts her misbegotten attempts to escape her lonely isolation; her dissatisfaction with her marriage leads her to her ill-conceived affair; and its aftermath propels her toward exacting the promise to be buried in Jefferson, a promise through which she exacts her revenge. Her revenge, however, is thwarted by the selfishness of each member of the family, each undertaking to fulfill the promise out of ulterior motives, all of them banal. Thus we have a promise exacted in hate and fulfilled in self-indulgence. The deception necessary to perpetrate this travesty makes a mockery of the burial ritual, a "monstrous burlesque of all bereavement," as Darl puts it (74). Dr. Peabody gives wry commentary to all the neighbors' observations of this battle between vengeance and hypocrisy; however, as the journey continues, the stakes get higher: Gillespie loses his barn and Darl is thrown down in the street and carted away. His laughter is a testimony to how much more insane is the world he is leaving than the asylum to which he is being taken. The total triumph of materialism is one of Faulkner's "victories without hope."

From such a scenario, critics drew their sense of Faulkner's themes. To Campbell and Foster, the novel makes Faulkner a spokesperson for cosmic pessimism (55), a term Inge would also call "preponderant."[13] Carvel Collins, linking the novel to *The Sound and the Fury,* would infer from its portrait of the "lack of love in a family" ("The Pairing" 115) that the novel is an inversion of the Demeter myth, whereas to Elizabeth Kerr, it was inverted romantic quest (*Yoknapatawpha* 17). The novel showed the "ultimate futility of . . . wasted lives" (Dickerson 130), or "the incapacity of man" (Goellner 47), or the failure to come to grips with reality (Olga Vickery). Championing Darl alone, James Roberts saw the novel as "a criticism and condemnation of the backward hill people who, through their ignorance, deny any value to life" (38).[14]

On the other hand, there was an opposite scenario. Driven to escape the futility of her father's nihilism, Addie never stops pursuing possibilities that would make life meaningful. The promise she exacts is drawn from this same enterprise. Addie is not fooled by her family but knows that they can be saved by action, an action for which Cash and Jewel will be the catalysts. While the members of the family have ulterior motives for the trip, each is understandable and none of them, even collectively, would be worth the sacrifice the journey demands. Thus, they may sully the purity of the journey but never overshadow its primary motive. Particularly in the river scene, their sacrifices begin to manifest real concerns for each other. Before they are through, the journey will have cost them time, humiliation, pain, and possessions. Darl alone seems unable to enter this common quest. Fueled by earlier resentments, his refusal to assist eventually becomes overt action against the family welfare. His antagonism is the ultimate threat to the fragile thread on which the family enterprise hangs, and both Jewel, representing action, and Cash, representing words, have to rise to the threat Darl poses. We may start out laughing at their hill-country ways, but before the novel finishes we recognize their heroic fulfillment of a moral obligation.

Here then was another critical bandwagon. Backman could extol the "victorious love of mother and son" (66), the "sense of community" (51) found in the novel. Cleanth Brooks could argue that we aren't concerned with the traditional custom being observed (burial) but with the traditional qualities that allow the family to act (*Yoknapatawpha Country* 141–66). For Irving Howe the novel demonstrated "the capacity for suffering and dignity which human beings have" (189). Pointing to the "heroism possible among them," George Marion O'Donnell saw the progress of the burial journey as being "not unlike that of the medieval soul toward redemption" (291). The novel was, thus, "an affirmation of life" (Brylowski 86), a "triumph for . . . the human spirit" (Millgate, *William Faulkner* 38), an assertion of the "validity of Biblical and Christian symbolism" (Waggoner 85), and an illustration of "compassion, sacrifice, endurance" (Ora Williams 100). Robert Penn Warren could suggest that *As I Lay Dying* "indicates . . . that even such a fellow as Anse Bundren . . . in the grip of an idea . . . is capable of rising out of his ordinary level" ("Cowley's Faulkner" 234).

There are, of course, problems with all this, to be addressed shortly. But two things are remarkable here in their own right. First, major critical figures (Brooks, Millgate, Warren *versus* Collins, Kerr, Vickery in the gunfight at the Bundrens are OK or not OK Corral) could be engaged in finding almost diametrically opposite themes in the same works. Second, there is now an assumption that Faulkner is in control of his materials and addressing issues with moral seriousness; no longer is he seen as a writer with unfortunate stylistic traits or a young Turk out simply to horrify—that is, whatever he has to say about it, his theme is the moral nature of our kind and how it is to be grasped. So, for example, Percy Adams found the humor in the Snopes trilogy to be a structural device meant to propound the theme of "the self-destruction inherent in evil" (210). Similarly, though mindful that "Faulkner, in actual practice, is highly distrustful of such an artificial dichotomy [as] good and evil," this is the larger context in which P. P. Sharma sees the chief thematic concern of the trilogy to be "the power of evil and an inadequate effort to contain it" (34, 39).[15] Leslie Angell would see "inherent themes," at once more specific and more inclusive: "relationships between Negro and white, aristocrat and slave, man and man, father and son, brother and brother, and, on the more conceptual level, past and present, good and evil, reality and illusion" (110). (For a commentary on *Absalom, Absalom!*, Angell's omission of parent and daughter, sister and sister today seems glaring [see chapter 9]). Commenting on "A Rose for Emily," William Davis would spell out a moral theme: "To covet life too highly, thereby attempting to stop time, to freeze the flux of life, is to make of something 'dear' a perversity" (38).[16] These three examples were chosen somewhat at random except for the thing they share: each occurs within a study whose title makes explicit the linkage between the theme and the craft that supports it. Hence, the juncture of "theme and structure" (or "structure and theme" or "theme and pattern") represents one of the trademarks of this period, setting it apart from earlier criticism.

Yet, if Faulkner was a moralist, what morality was he propagating? This prob-lematizing mode, perhaps owing something to the times in which it began, car-ried within it the seeds of its own dissolution. Try as the critics might to conform their criticism to the prevailing debates, their own insights often verified how porous were the walls containing it.[17] Where others saw virtuous or vicious Bun-drens, Robert Hemenway saw "Enigmas of Being" regarding whether we were reading a "promise to the past" (therefore "ultimately absurd") or a "commitment to the present" (therefore "justified") (144). Tucked away in the debate were questions confounding simplistic categorizations. Does being nonheroic equal being "wholly despicable" (Kerr, *Yoknapatawpha* 17)? If the Bundrens' disor-dered lives are emblematic of the universe they occupy, then aren't some of their "postures . . . in a limited way, heroic"?[18] At what edge of what order do we find ourselves when we realize that the ending of *As I Lay Dying* both "suggests that the story we have been told is highly significant and worthy of serious contem-plation and emotion and that it signifies nothing and deserves primarily a bitter laugh" (Slatoff 120)? Suppose we grant the follies and vices of the Bundrens; what then are we to make of Faulkner's "superb sympathy" for them (Howe 189)? Suppose the Bundrens are distracted by self-interest; are they more or less so than "members of more self-conscious classes of society" (Arthos 29)?

In other words, even under the constraints of academic debate and publisha-bility, critical attention was acknowledging once again, but more strongly and deeply now, that Faulkner's themes were complex, interrelated counterpoints rather than simple, isolated advocacies. For example, in pointing to the theme of maturation, Walter Brylowski could note how a Chick Mallison, initiated into action, differed from an Ike McCaslin, initiated into repudiation, and how that difference might shift our attention from the initiate to the mentor and from adjustment to transcendence (173, 176). Or, in an almost Pauline diction, Philip Rule could suggest of the theme of "man's struggle" that it was not against any readily identifiable opposition but rather to be seen as the necessity to "face the mystery of life" from a position of being "caught up in an enigmatic existence" (123, 128).[19] Hence, in keeping with the times, thematic criticism took its own existential turn.

Such twists in the search for Faulkner's themes were paralleled by efforts to ascertain the genres he chose as vehicles for his themes.[20] Cowley had suggested in the *Portable* that Faulkner's works were the stuff of legend, that he was con-structing a "tragic fable of Southern history" (xx). Campbell and Foster would note, in addition, the "pastoral idyll" (51) and the story of the "cheater cheated" (47), noting that genre was often a "comic inversion" produced through "per-spective by incongruity" (56). James Justus would add the "ghost" story (150). Sometimes such forays into genre would lead to opposite readings, as for exam-ple when Campbell and Foster point to how hopeless we are rendered by intro-spection while Justus saw in Faulkner an exploration of the Socratic theme: the tragic absence of self-knowledge.[21]

More often than not, generic and thematic criticism home in on the Olympian feel of the Yoknapatawpha world. Faulkner's novels and stories (no one much attended to the poetry then, or to the nonfiction prose), it was felt, were the stuff of ancient literature, of myth and epic, of Homer and Ovid [see chapter 1]. We could discover in Faulkner tragedy "in the high sense," could see in the wilderness hunt the annual ritual at the time of "the year's death" (Lydenberg 92, 88). We could read a work as "a parable of mutation" (Gold 81). And, in keeping with such classic genres, the themes were seen as classic as well: Man versus Nature, or the "saving virtues of pride and humility," or how what we must do is wrong to do (Lydenberg 90, 92): man "unable to regain innocence" (Gold 82).[22] Much of this followed from Cowley's own echo of Gide's observation about Faulkner's principal characters: "not one . . . exercises the faculty of conscious choice . . . something takes possession of them" (*Portable* 16).

Of course, the principal advantage critics of this last period had was that they had most of Faulkner already before them, as a body of work, not unfolding before them piece by piece with the end not yet in sight. The criticism naturally became more holistic with several still-major volumes (and any number now forgotten) treating all the works as some sort of unity and measuring, in Millgate's terms, the "achievement" of their author. It should be noted that, as a consequence, this was an era of criticism in which critics looked for the similarities that bore out the assumption of a Faulkner "signature." They could ask, of a technique seen in an early work, what had happened to it by the time of a later one? They could assume development. They could imagine Faulkner as having set out with the end, however dimly, in view. And because they could do these things, these are the things they did. And since their own ends—to show what constituted Faulkner, indeed usually what constituted Yoknapatawpha, indeed even more narrowly the Yoknapatawpha of what Melvin Backman termed "the major years" —were most easily expressed as themes, this era lent itself to thematic criticism. Faulkner was to be found, somewhere, in "the fundamental human themes with which he is always primarily concerned" (Millgate, *Achievement* 292). Moreover, these fundamental concerns "were ultimately moral" (287).

Looking today at the contents of major book-length critical efforts, one can see that critics regarded their approaches as "natural" (how else would you do it?) although now we would say no approach is natural. In retrospect, the similarity in their approaches can be taken as evidence of a kind of trope that was driving the critical enterprise in a particular direction and that unintentionally revealed itself in the critics' tables of contents. Basically, these are of a type with only minor variations: First, the type itself is the simple listing of the novels; then, often prefixed to the listing is some concern for Faulkner's "apprenticeship" (O'Connor, Vickery, Waggoner; "career" in Millgate and Thompson; "background" in Howe); this listing of titles is then connected to theme, sometimes by means of an appended section of thematic topics—for example, Brooks *(Yoknapatawpha Country)* offers a chapter on "The Plain People: Yeoman Farmers, Sharecroppers, and White Trash." Howe gives us "Classes and Clans," "The Southern Tradition," and "Faulkner and the Negroes," these contents reading like caveats of the sort, "don't look here for the corncob pipe"; or, often, the themes are tied to the novels, as for instance in Waggoner: "Past as Present: *Absalom, Absalom!*" or Vickery: "The Dimensions of Consciousness: *As I Lay Dying*" or Brooks: "The Community in Action (*Intruder in the Dust*)," this latter a case of theme almost taking precedence over the work, the work relegated to the parenthesis. Sometimes these themes seem less specific than might be helpful, more driven to find the universal theme whose presence might rescue the author from the misunderstandings of previous critics. A case in point might be Brooks's treatment of *The Sound and the Fury,* almost comically entitled "Man, Time, and Eternity."

It is the force of the trope driving the criticism that allows us, reading in O'Connor's table of contents simply "Two Types of Love," with no chapter title but listed as the eighth chapter, to guess that this might refer to the two stories in what was then known as *The Wild Palms.* The guess would be right. And although isolated critics, for example Millgate, essayed the poetry and short fiction as well, one would also be right in guessing that the search for themes focused largely on the novels, on Faulkner as novelist, on the novel as a site for unified vision, of moral vision, such phrases often the titles of final chapters in the major critical works on Faulkner of this period (see Howe, Thompson).[23]

1976–1981

It should not be assumed that the criticism of the second major period is in any way laughable except only in this: its practitioners would have largely assumed they wrote from an almost Olympian objectivity, one arrived at through both their method and subject. While we would no longer grant them their own terms, the fact still remains that, far from merely rescuing Faulkner from critical oblivion, they catapulted him into a critical world heretofore known only to Shakespearean studies. Towering figures, for instance, Cleanth Brooks, not only produced absorbing work, but these same figures (Carvel Collins, Joseph Blotner, James Meriwether, Michael Millgate, Elizabeth Kerr, Olga Vickery, John Pilkington, just to name a few of the more prominent) were busy in their respective universities preparing future generations of scholars, some of whose work began to appear at the end of this period and to forge the transition to the whole new scholarship then about to emerge.[24]

The growing industry turned up new materials, such as Faulkner's own comments on war, circa 1924 (see Millgate, "Faulkner"). Such materials, in turn, allowed more complex investigations of theme and often raised new avenues of pursuing sources and influences outside the usual suspects.

Moreover, the thematic criticism that ended the era was not the same as the thematic criticism with which it began. The effect of critic weighing in upon critic was not only a lively debate but also a refinement of thinking. By the end of the era, the simplest themes were seen as in great need of both adumbration and qualification; and the inherited dichotomy of substance and style was gone for good. For instance, Robert Hamblin [see chapter 1] would point to how "Faulkner develops the theme of initiation in 'That Evening Sun' by ironically juxtaposing the adult world of sex . . . and of death . . . with the ignorance and innocence of children" (86), noting how, "Faulkner's interest in the children" could be both thematic and technical at the same time.[25]

Because Weldon Thornton's "Structure and Theme in Faulkner's *Go Down, Moses*" is illustrative of both, reference to that article alone aptly suggests the tenor of others.[26] Thornton begins from the premise, common then, that "the basis of the structure of Faulkner's novels is always primarily thematic" (75). But, drawing on Lawrance Thompson and Millgate's discussions, he notes how theme is impossible apart from structure. Referring (as had Robert Hamblin) to Faulkner's use of "latent juxtaposition," Thornton notes how "this technique . . . calls on the reader to make a close comparison and contrast of certain scenes, situations, events, and characters in the novel, for the purpose of realizing thematically important similarities and differences" (76). Based on his study in this mode, Thornton certainly finds, as had Brooks, that a dominant theme of *Go Down, Moses* is "what freedom means to man, how he achieves and preserves it, and perhaps more important, how he loses it" (79). But, for Thornton, the novel accentuates "the most dangerous threats to a person's freedom . . . baseless moral notions, adherence to ideas which have lost their content, lack of courage and self-confidence and baneful traits of personality" (80). In other words, stating freedom as a theme of the novel is useless apart from understanding the kind of indictment in which the novel is engaged, an indictment of a series of culturally embedded historical oversimplifications, for the remedy of which the novel raises the ambiguities of "adversity in building character, the heinous sin of disregard of one's descendants . . . [the substitution of] something tangible for our failure to fulfill our obligations to others; and the importance of ritual both as enhancer and threat to man's freedom" (89).

One might say, here, that increasingly thematic criticism was being affected by rhetorical concerns [see chapter 10] for discourse analysis (as might have been likely, given the new and growing emphasis on composition and rhetoric in English departments). We could see more clearly how the aim of the work would color our interpretation of its theme. So, for example, the theme might well be race, but would it be race as seen by a critic defending the gradualism of a Gavin Stevens? Or would it be race as seen by a critic exposing the stereotypes embedded in some of Faulkner's early portraits of black characters?[27] Or, if place is the theme, is place written as a way in which a locale and its natural surroundings ennoble us, nature providing the very metaphor, "roots," for the ennoblement, or is place rather a witness to a locus for a profane desecration of the sacred duty to be inclusive of others?[28] Is point of view a structural device, a theme, or both? That is, once structure and theme are linked, how does the linkage work? Such questions were necessitated by, for example, more sophisticated studies of genre, as in Ira Levin's "The Four Narrative Perspectives in *Absalom, Absalom!*" where the handling of spatial detail, in its turn the key to the theme, alters "depending on who is narrating," so that "there is not *one* 'space' . . . but . . . *four* 'spaces' conjured up" (38).[29] Or, finally, if themes are developed through O'Donnell's Sartoris/ Snopes (aristocrats/rednecks) scheme of opposition, what happens to our idea of theme if we now see that seesaw tilting in favor of the rednecks and not the Sartoris (Falkner!) clan?[30] Such rich questions were a salutary part of the beginnings, during this period, of the challenge of ideological criticism [see chapter 7].

In time, critics came to recognize more-complex themes, but to leave it simply at that would be to miss the context in which this recognition developed. Faulkner critics of the transition were not writing in a vacuum. Most American certainties were being shaken to the foundations by Civil Rights and war protests, by increasing despair in the nation's inner cities, by a generation gap of monumental proportions. Born from a collation of the Civil War and First World War, achieving prominence by themes congenial to the values surviving World War II, how could Faulkner's fiction survive the tectonic shifts in the earth's plates occasioned by Viet Nam? Would it survive? How did its grand design look from the steps of the Lincoln Memorial to eyes that had seen a naked Asian girl fleeing a napalm bombing in the company of countless dispossessed? Could Yoknapatawpha encounter, if not the wretched of the earth, at least the hearts and minds of a revolutionary age no longer content to ignore the wretched or defend the fact of their wretchedness?

1981-PRESENT

There is no doubt that literary criticism is an academically driven enterprise. It may crop up in public journals of opinion, but its principal venues are academic journals, presses, and conferences. For this reason, sea changes in academia mean watersheds in critical approach. For the most part, academia here means not the common run of general courses taught unsuspecting undergraduates but the core of academic disciplines found in doctoral programs; for the subject of interest to us, that means graduate programs in English. Somewhere in the 1970s, fully recognizable before the decade was over, graduate education changed in two distinct ways that eventually would drive Faulkner criticism in new directions.

For some time previous, the New Criticism had held sway over much of English graduate education. In practice, its major tenet was often reduced to this: that criticism, to determine the meaning of a work of literature, need not look outside the work itself, say to history or biography, but could find the work's meaning by looking within it, principally at its own ambiguities. Good critical works were those that resolved the ambiguities of a particular work. If you were looking for ambiguities to resolve, then no doubt in Faulkner you had hit the mother lode! While this may only caricature the critical mode itself,[31] it isn't so far from an accurate description of how the mode was often practiced; and if this mode didn't have every professor and every department in its grip, it is still safe to say it was the dominant (and dominating) critical mode of a generation or two of American literary scholars, scholars such as Cleanth Brooks, long the "dean" of Faulkner studies.

In the growing social unrest of America in the late 1960s and 1970s, in the widening generation gap that began with rock and roll and continued in sit-ins, protests, and civil strife over racial injustice and Viet Nam, this critical posture began to seem merely academic, academic in the most pejorative sense of an ivory tower isolated against the pressing issues of society. In the wake of large-scale protests, academia gave way to pressures for more relevant studies, studies, say, in "Black Literature," where the critical issues were rhetorical: how did the literature show its readership their circumstances, and how did it move them to alter their world? And, seeing literature in relation to its world swept through not only new courses of study but also the old as well, the standard graduate courses in American letters. To see the critical difference, one could ask, what is the greatest work of the nineteenth century in America? New Critics would have been likely to hold up a work by Hawthorne or Melville or Dickinson. But growingly, academia would point to works such as *Uncle Tom's Cabin* or authors such as Whitman. And whatever had become of Louisa May Alcott, anyway? That this new posture would accrue to good effect is not hard to see. For example, the century would end yielding a study of Emerson's mother and her influence. But where would Faulkner fit into these new interests?

In academia, of course, new interests have to find theoretical underpinnings, and the shift from New Criticism found its philosophical bearings in a complex of theoretical sources, many of them French, including the works of Foucault, Ricoeur, Derrida, and Saussure, as well as the feminist/Lacanian works of Cixous and Irigaray. In their turn, these theories, essentially theories of how language worked (or failed to work) and how power played out, began to question if literary ambiguities were resolvable, if they were not instead symptoms of a work's complicity with the power advantages existing in society. How were we to see texts' relations to the world? Or was there a world outside the texts? Were texts referential only of other texts? [See chapters 6–9.] The earliest critics had condemned Faulkner's "assault" on language, and critics of the middle period had resurrected him in great part for his mastery of manipulating language to articulate theme, but here was a new challenge: if the tension of inner ambiguities had made Faulkner a darling of critics, how would his work survive the new questions of a work's significance in term of its reflection of power relations through the suspect medium of language, suspect in part for the ways it was being manipulated by the writer?

The campus as a center of protest did not go unnoticed in the corridors of power. President Nixon was not unaware that the majority of those protesting Viet Nam came from the arts and humanities, the humanities offering in those halcyon days the default majors for almost all students who weren't ready to specify some preprofessional or vocational field and for many who were. It was not, then, accidental that federal education initiatives would begin to lead away from the former emphasis in the humanities to the vocational education more dominant in today's universities. One of the significant results of this was a change in metaphors for measuring educational institutions. They now had a "product" to sell, and those who "bought" that product were their "customers." Within this business model, it soon became clear that the "market share" for English Ph.D. graduates had dwindled. With large numbers of English graduate

students and few jobs awaiting them, graduate education became a highly com-
petitive enterprise, often pitting students against one another for a dwindling
food supply. The demands of "publish or perish" moved down the academy into
the ranks of students. If their work couldn't be relevant, if it wasn't cutting edge,
how would it get an audience? What resulted is by now well known as the "culture wars" of English Departments in the 1980s and 1990s. From the vantage
point of this little history, it isn't hard to see why these wars were being fought
so vehemently. Jobs, promotion and tenure, security all depended on one's
stance and prowess. Could the study of Faulkner's works qualify one for laurels
in these new academic Olympics?

   What effect would these shifts have on thematic criticism? On the one hand,
conference papers devoted principally to theories drawn largely from psychology and linguistics could not be expected to leave much room for explorations
of theme. Indeed, on occasion, one wondered if they left room for explorations
of Faulkner at all. On the other hand, if what mattered were relevance to social
reality, including the play of power and privilege across the whole social spectrum, then who had examined these in more depth and breadth than Faulkner?
Of course, his perspective might be skewed as a white, male Southerner, but that
could only make his treatments of African Americans and poor whites and
women all the more significant. And if, for example, the presence of women in
his stories gained new attention, what about their absence? What of the way in
which they were often narrated by others but given no voice of their own? [See
chapters 6–9.]

   And what of the sources of Faulkner's fiction in his family, his Mississippi, his
South? Were these to be considered stable entities or were they, too, constructed
by their "sole owner and proprietor"? Earlier critics had assumed the objectivity
of the world from which Faulkner drew his fiction, labeling them in some fashion similar to that adopted by Ward Miner, "Actuality" and "Legend."[32] Later
critics would challenge this view. James G. Watson, granting that in his youthful periods away "Faulkner was thinking of home almost continuously," nevertheless sees that "'home,' as it emerges [in his letters], is represented not only as
an actual place but as a sustaining idea" ("My Father's" 749). For Watson,
Faulkner was "writing" home not only in the sense of addressing letters to an
actual place and people, but "reconstituting them in . . . ways that met his immediate emotional needs" (749). Recently, Bart H. Welling speculated that this
constructed home and family served a therapeutic role, giving him "a language"
that would "bridge the distance between his feelings" for his black mother,
Mammy Callie Barr, and his birth mother, Maud, thus expressing the "inextricable but warring strands of his own hybrid cultural makeup" (540, 541).[33] Taking the relation of language and reality as a theme in itself, Mark Edelman
Boren would argue that, despite the constructedness of both, "language has the
power to disrupt its own stream of endlessly deferring metaphorical motion
and . . . this energy can intervene in the 'real'" (35).

   Of course, autobiography and family and local history were major sources of
Faulkner's fiction; that in itself is not the subject of the critical debate [see chapter

2]. From the first Faulkner and Yoknapatawpha Conference in 1974, scholars have turned their attention to the ways and extent to which in some way the mythical Yoknapatawpha County and its county seat, Jefferson, mirror Oxford, Mississippi (and other nearby towns such as New Albany and Ripley), and Lafayette County. Elizabeth M. Kerr's *Yoknapatawpha: Faulkner's Little Postage Stamp of Native Soil* establishes several direct links, and David Sansing set the first and future conferences to thinking of how Faulkner reflected not only the state—the "political and geographic subdivision designated Mississippi" (5)—but also the state of mind.[34] Faulkner's use of such materials has been driven home more recently by the 2001 publication of Don H. Doyle's *Faulkner's County: The Historical Roots of Yoknapatawpha* [see chapter 2]. There, Doyle documents how Faulkner used as "raw materials" the events, people, and attitudes that surrounded his own growing up and that of his family for some generations and finds Faulkner authoritative "not as a historian dealing with facts and evidence but as an intuitive interpreter of the past and an astute observer of his contemporary social environment" (5, 7).[35] Thomas Hines extends the scope of materials used by Faulkner in his "William Faulkner and the Meaning of Architecture: The Greek Revival of Yoknapatawpha" (*Faulkner and the Artist* 110–40). [See chapters 1 and 2 for the tension between Faulkner's making of myth and use of history.]

More important than any actual representation of the past, it now seems clearer that the family history was not so much imposed on the past as a template, but instead derived from readings and rereadings of history, Southern history helping Faulkner see his family as much as his family history helping him see the South.[36] In other words, as Carvel Collins had written in 1975, he "wrote through that regional reality to something larger" (141).[37]

It is easy to see that certain themes from the earlier criticism found renewed critical prominence during this third and to date final period of Faulkner criticism. For example, in the post–Civil Rights era, it was inevitable that critics would reexamine the whole issue of race-related themes in Faulkner. Indeed, of the themes listed at the beginning of this chapter, not one would fail to yield at least some aspect, some question that would play out well in the new critical climate. Nor is it hard to imagine how each of these resurrections of theme challenged some critical orthodoxy established during the long middle period of critical effort, the period dominated by the New Critics. And finally—to use again the example of race—since Faulkner, upon the award of the Nobel Prize, had sometimes taken on the role of public spokesperson on topics of public interest, it is easy to see how attention to race-related themes would call on critics to examine not only Faulkner's fiction but his public speeches and letters as well and how, in the light of the views and interests of this period, any discrepancies between the personal and literary views would take on heightened importance, most notably when Oxford itself became a world arena for racial tragedy with the attempt of James Meredith to register at Ole Miss.[38] (The prominence of Faulkner's voice in the racial conflicts of his time is evidenced by the cover story and picture in *Time* magazine for July 17, 1964, which looks at Faulkner in the context of Civil Rights debates.)

To illustrate these developments for thematic criticism, we will revisit an issue raised early in this chapter and connect it to the yet-unexamined theme of the role Faulkner's own life and background played in his development of themes. Earlier I noted how Lionel Trilling had suggested the tragedy and complexity of race as a theme in Faulkner's work. This is not the place to examine the sufficiency or insufficiency, felicity or infelicity of Faulkner's treatment of race itself [see chapter 2]. Clearly, race as a theme plays a major role in most all Faulkner's work. However, in this period we can chronicle two dramatic changes in our understanding of this theme in his work. If during the 1950s through 1970s Faulkner was generally read as considerably liberal on issues of race, he was so read in the light of the country's views as a whole. Left and right are, if nothing else, relative terms. In many ways, the country's views took a dramatic turn, and by the 1980s Faulkner's portraits no longer seemed so liberal. Moreover, even when the liberalism of the literary portrait was granted, it was seen at odds with his public statements, which included what seemed an only halfhearted condemnation of lynching and the infamous comment at the time of Meredith's enrollment of what action he was prepared to take in the streets of Oxford.[39]

Once, the treatment of the theme of race emphasized how it bore witness to a viewpoint: the curse of slavery, seen in *Go Down, Moses;* the humanity of Negroes, represented in *Intruder in the Dust;* the absurdity of color, in *Light in August;* the moral discrepancy between corrupt and declining aristocracy and virtuous and enduring servants, in *The Sound and the Fury.*[40] Now the treatment shifted. The treatment of race-related issues did not so much show a theme as it showed how the author was implicated in the racism he supposedly repudiated. If, at best, it showed Faulkner's willingness to see in the lives of African Americans fit matter for fictional portraiture, at the same time it showed both his inability to see black lives from the inside and to see the effect of race on blacks as more important than its effect on whites. In other words, still granting that the presence of race in the works made an interesting study, the focus on race became less that of a theme and more that of a problem, a problem of interpretation for the reader and a problem of identity for the writer. One could say that, in a sense, postmodernism rendered the search for themes extraneous [see chapter 6].

We are involved here, however, in a dialectic. The idea of the author's own implication in his themes, while it initially abolished theme in favor of psychobiography, would yield a portrait of the artist that allowed new insight into his themes. What, for instance, was happening in Faulkner's apparent shift from the Sartoris family to the McCaslin/Edmonds family, the former of which launches the Yoknapatawpha saga (*Flags in the Dust*) and the latter of which ends it (*The Reivers*)? Might not the shift portend a difference in the author's own understanding of his implication in the racism in which he was raised? If in some way Faulkner's story is an apocrypha [see chapter 1], that apocrypha begins with what all the major works of the middle period acknowledged as the use of the mostly fictional Sartorises to mirror the mostly actual Falkners. Among the analogs are duels, derrings-do, railroads and banks, and seemingly similar family trees. If the analogy holds true, both Sartorises and Falkners saw Negroes somewhat at a distance, through unusual representatives of the race, and in a paternalistic manner. By the close of the decade of the 1930s, as he was preparing the publication of *Go Down, Moses,* Faulkner had found it necessary to refictionalize his family as the McCaslins. Here, though the family tree is far more complex and in some ways does not so neatly parallel the Falkners, it did allow a parallel of which most readers were unaware until the publication of Joel Williamson's *William Faulkner and Southern History.* The Falkners themselves had been participants in the fact of miscegenation and in the milieu that provided both its occasion and justification.

To accomplish this shift, Faulkner not only had to create a new family but focus not on the hill country known to the Falkners but to the Delta where he himself had found release in a counterculture of blues, blacks, and bootlegging. Delta history, especially the symbolic place in its landscape of the plantation commissary, would play a large role in Faulkner's refiguration of his family.[41] This should be enough to suggest to us that Ike's learning how to read his own history in poring through the commissary ledgers paralleled a new attempt of Faulkner's to reread his own and his people's history. In this attempt, he saw more clearly how corrupt was the paternalistic view in which he had been raised, how truly kin to blacks he himself was.[42]

If the McCaslins in fact replace the Sartorises in the design of Yoknapatawpha, what then of the formerly supposed opposition of Sartoris and Snopes that so dominated earlier critical assumptions? Already questioned by Faulkner's growing appreciation for the heroic struggles of many of the sharecropper class, the displacement of the Sartorises might even presage some thought that Sartoris and Snopes were less divided by their differences than critics had thought. This in turn sheds new light on treatments of the themes of family and Southern history [see chapter 2] in Faulkner's work and might suggest, too, a cause for Faulkner's identification with his characters, the fellow feeling Cowley had noted years before in "Faulkner by Daylight." It would certainly account for the reworking of materials suggesting his revisiting the earlier portrait of Dilsey, focusing on the dignity of her responsibility for the Compson family in *The Sound and the Fury* but omitting any delineation of the cost of that to her and her family, the reworking seen in the tragedy of Nancy Mannigoe, cast in a role of similar responsibility for the Gowan Stevens family in *Requiem for a Nun.* Possibly, as characters, they were, as Faulkner described: "people I invent and after that I just run along and put down what they say and do" (Gwynn and Blotner 141). That said, they were also the many facets of Faulkner himself; he and his legion of alter egos were implicated up to their eyeballs in peasant and aristocrat, townsman and country folk, men and women, white and black, the sheep and the goats.

From this reciprocal relationship, it is again possible to see race as a theme. Now, however insightful or flawed his portrait of individual characters across the color lines may have been, the theme annunciates not only a liberal but a radical view of race, such a radical view that it is possible to see Faulkner, in the final chapter of *Go Down, Moses,* extending the pen that writes race to those most able to write it, authors of color in America. In any case, it becomes clear that what was once seen as Faulkner's theme of race must come to be seen as Faulkner's theme of the complexity of race and the necessity of our understanding of race to be multiracially constructed. The name of the theme may have remained or re-emerged the same; its meaning, as I've argued elsewhere, has been radically altered.[43] Although the critics' treatment of race as a theme crosses many critical periods, they have only attended to this complexity in the theme of race compar-atively recently. This latter-day treatment of the theme was initiated by Noel Polk (*Children of the Dark House*) in 1996 and has reached its most insightful treat-ment to date in Theresa Towner's *Faulkner on the Color Line.*[44] Towner suggests that the Faulkner canon "reflects his increasing interest in how racial identity is formed and maintained," an interest that emerges in characters who "race to gather information . . . against what the community 'knows'" (8, 52).

Along with old themes such as race, critics investigated new themes, promi-nent among them the related themes of law and justice in what Jay Watson would call Faulkner's "forensic" fiction. In his *Forensic Fictions: The Lawyer Figure in Faulkner* Watson explores, through a great number of avenues (e.g., the etymology of legal terms, the connection of law and rhetoric), the way in which legal figures represent a negotiation of the path from private to public, personal to ideological. Examining many features of Faulkner's legal landscape, including its both positive and negative roles in producing social stability, Wat-son focuses on how Faulkner found "in the figure of the lawyer . . . his most habitual, and in many ways most rewarding, authorial surrogate" and at the same time "an abundantly suggestive set of resources for cross-examining his own vocation" (5).[45] Michael Lahey also couples a discussion of forensic figures with Faulkner's representation of the artist in his "The Complex Art of Justice: Lawyers and Lawmakers as Faulkner's Dubious Artist-Figures" (*Faulkner and the Artist* 250–68).

These alterations were each instances of the general critique Frederick Crews leveled at the post-Cowley school, namely that their criticism, in which "com-munity" becomes the principal Faulkner concern and error is seen as whatever draws down misfortune, "occluded Faulkner's improvisation and interior debate, reduced his often daring characterizations to illustrated moral lessons and sub-tly adulterated and softened his anguish over southern history" ("The Strange Fate" 48). What Crews portends was the shift in critical focus in the 1990s to a pre-Cowley, larger-than-Yoknapatawpha Faulkner, the shift that rescued him from the increasingly harsh ideological critiques of the 1980s. Freudian and Lacanian critics, often seeing flaws in Faulkner's portraits, especially of women [see chapters 6 and 9], nevertheless reminded readers of that earlier appreciation of Faulkner as psychologist, a quality not absent from the earliest poetry and fic-tion nor from the "major" works. Hence, Martin Bidney could explore how Faulkner, the one-time poet, could employ allusions to Romantic writers, to adumbrate in a "defamiliarizing, tragic-comic perspective," the theme of that "extreme difficulty nearly all the . . . characters have in extricating themselves

from their self-tortures" (277, 285).[46] Similarly, Thomas Nordenberg's 1983 thesis could explore how Faulkner dealt so little with historical categories and so
much with psychological categories in his war stories—not that Faulkner doesn't
attend carefully to the actual conditions of World War I warfare, but rather that
all this serves the focus of "the psychological effect of war almost without mentioning the cause proper" (20). Nordenberg applies this to both the immediate
psychology of how it is young people who become "victims of the moral fallacies of their society" (91), and to how, by extension, "it is in the end left with the
younger persons to deal with the heritage of the Lost Cause" (84). The numerous incidences of stories of youth or young adults suffering from the lack of nurturing guidance in the generations that should have been their teachers and
mentors prompted David Vanderwerken to see Faulkner working out this theme
in an "antibildungsroman," or what I would term a continuation of the World
War I poets' "tell them that our fathers lied" theme.[47]

In this regard, too, there was a similar resurrection of Faulkner, the daring
experimentalist, the stylist, whose reworkings of the language saved literature
from its own fossil forms. If his Bergsonian vision was of "man in motion," his
craft was in motion as well.[48] One could call Faulkner's works "time and
motion" studies, attempts to work out the complex relationship of space and
time, in this case as that applies not to physics but to art. Indeed, it became possible to suggest that, in very real ways, no matter what the ostensible theme (nor
what the ostensible structure that conveyed it), Faulkner's principal interest was
in literature itself, art itself, and how art posed possibilities denied by history.
Thus Ursula Brumm could suggest of Faulkner's "Old Man" that, "literature and
its functions in human life are the dominant" theme of the story.[49] Art as a theme
could be tied to more postmodern treatments of ideological themes, as Susan V.
Donaldson does in her "Cracked Urns: Faulkner, Gender, and Art in the South."
And Hamblin could develop Faulkner's role in the modernist religion of art in
"'Longer than Anything': Faulkner's 'Grand Design' in *Absalom, Absalom!*," a
theme to which I will return in the conclusion of this chapter.[50]

Before looking at the religion of art, however, it should be noted that religion
itself is a theme in Faulkner's works, a theme often obscured by focus on him as
a moralist and psychologist alike. Although Cowley disparaged the idea of
Faulkner as a religious man, Cleanth Brooks would maintain that he was "a profoundly religious writer," by which he meant that "his characters come out of a
Christian environment, and represent, whatever their shortcomings and whatever their theological heresies, Christian concerns; and that they are finally to be
understood only by reference to Christian premises" (in Barth 57).[51] As Faulkner
develops his themes from this perspective, he uses it to critique the hypocrisy of
established, mainline religion, to expose the psychological damage done by the
Puritan tradition, and to show how what was admirable in religion could sustain
people surrounded both by distorted religion and empty secularism. The development of these themes is readily seen in the fiction so, for the purposes of thematic criticism, whether or not Faulkner was himself religious is beside the
point.[52]

If, as Harold J. Douglas and Robert Daniel point out, "the cruelly warping effect that Calvinism may have constitutes a significant part of the characterization in such novels as *The Wild Palms, Absalom, Absalom!,* and *As I Lay Dying,* and forms the very core . . . in *Light in August,*" so, too, Brooks could maintain that the discovery "that evil is rooted in the very nature of things" informed works such as *Sanctuary* and *The Sound and the Fury* (in Barth 40, 59). The two are not as antithetical as they might at first seem, both joining to form, in John W. Hunt's words, Faulkner's "full rendering of a world at once fallen and redeemed" (in Barth 81). Critics have seen his frequent use of Christ's Passion story [see chapter 1] as both a tool for challenging the theology of substitutionary atonement (as in Dinnah Pladott's "Faulkner's *A Fable:* A Heresy or a Declaration of Faith") and as a vehicle for describing a faith that, once having freed us "from the trap of the ego, from the limits of need and fear and denial," allows us to achieve "psychological wholeness" (as in Tebbetts's "Dilsey and the Compsons," 78–98) [see chapters 6 and 8]. Hunt has argued that, in the "total structure of his individual fictions" the reader finds what "is best described as a tension between Stoic and Christian visions" and that "he has given lyrical validity to both alternatives" (in Barth 82–83). It should be clear that the role of literature is not dogma, nor is it the role of the writer to preach; rather, whatever the theme, it is his task to render it, if it can be so rendered, in just such lyrical validity. Within that "validity," Faulkner's emphasis on the Christmas story, the Moses saga, and the Passion seem to identify him less with either the Protestantism in which he was raised or the Catholicism he encountered in New Orleans and Paris than with the stories stressed in the southern black religious heritage, stresses that paralleled biblical story with the lived experiences and hopes of the race.[53]

Faulkner's uses of religious themes could be seen as more or less precise. Glenn Meeter, arguing for seeing a biblical design in Faulkner's works, suggests that biblical allusions are replete and that following them "changes our reading of the South" (287) and of the fiction.[54] In this vein, Virginia V. James Hlavsa has argued that *Light in August* is patterned after the Gospel of John, seeing each of John's chapters (and related figures from *The Golden Bough*) as providing motifs for each of the novel's chapters. Even emptied of specific reference, or even of dogma, most readers would find, as Doreen Fowler found, that "the power of human belief" is a consistent theme in his fiction, a theme that, to give a specific example, "relates all the diverse episodes and disparate characters in *Light in August*" (Fowler, "Faith" 50). The thematic dimension of others of his stories would also seem to demonstrate "the awesome power of faith to coerce empirical reality into conformity with the image of reality held unshakably by conviction" (Fowler 56).[55]

CONCLUSION

In the titles of the articles in and volumes of the now nearly 30 volumes of the proceedings of the annual Faulkner and Yoknapatawpha Conference, all of which come from this last critical period or the transition to and from it, one can readily identify Faulkner's principal themes. Art, race, the land, the South—they form brief summaries of the thematic threads identified over a half century ago.

In a sense, in terms of surface labels, it would seem little has changed from the very beginning. Later lists might merely seem to verify earlier lists already available by the end of the first period of thematic criticism. And yet, in a sense everything had changed except the labels, a fact that might have amused Faulkner, or at least would have amused Addie Bundren. The Faulkner who was once held to have begun as a gifted amateur, throwing away his talents on attempts to shock and horrify, had become, in turn, not only gifted stylist, depth psychologist, and traditional moralist, but even, if oxymoron must suffice, secular theologian, chronicling a spiritual current running from the Creation to later creative efforts depicting the radical wisdom that is in the province of suffering and art. Faulkner's themes show him to be a writer who could capture and convey the "mysterious pattern of fateful ironies which the characters themselves never see, or do not see until it is too late" (Merton 35).[56]

Throughout most of the major critical years, the sense of Faulkner as an American modernist has prevailed over other views [see chapter 5]. However, the implications of seeing Faulkner as a modernist have for some time raised troubling questions regarding the Faulkner canon as a whole. What vision of reality was this where Caddy Compson, despite being his "heart's darling," had no voice of her own? If Faulkner had been taken to be, for instance, a naturalist, then we would read Caddy's lack of her own voice as both an indication and an indictment of a reality: the absence of voice for women of that time. But if we take him to be a modernist, for whom reality is as much our mental perception as a factual existence, then how are we to see Caddy having no role in telling her own story? It is with such questions as this, among others, that criticism is now wrestling.[57]

Nevertheless, the identification of Faulkner and modernism [see chapter 5], although not comprehensive enough, is in essence correct, and it may give us a clue to the theme that presides over his fiction like a monarch who is seldom to be seen but whose emissaries are never to be missed. Modernism rested not so much on a belief that the old gods were no longer viable as that the old religion was bankrupt.[58] The way in which we had institutionalized the cosmic wisdom had ultimately failed us. The only way forward was to jettison completely the institutionalized tradition and recover whatever original truths it had once conveyed.

No other vehicle for reconstruction was available but art. Reconstruction required acts of the imagination. For that, of course, as Frazer indicated, the old myths could provide suitable symbols, and for this purpose the older the better.[59] This did not mean, of course, that individuals couldn't dress themselves in the institutionally approved words, formulas, and trappings. They could, would, and did; Woodrow Wilson indeed had.[60] But it would no longer mean the same thing. The words no longer represented a connection to wisdom, the rhetoric all the more flawed for seeming to carry on a tradition that, at heart, it violated. This is the meaning of D. H. Lawrence's enigmatic phrase, "it isn't religious to be religious."

"I don't like ghosts," Faulkner told Howard Hawks, explaining why he disliked a movie Hawks had taken him to see. Yet, he would later hand him a script saying, "This is my idea of a ghost story" (Blotner, 1984 *Faulkner* 313). Faulkner, who always wanted to name some novel "the dark house," knew only too well how ghosts could confuse our minds and contaminate our world.[61] It was George Marion O'Donnell who had noted of Quentin that "his world is peopled with 'baffled, outraged ghosts'; and although Quentin himself is 'still too young to deserve to be a ghost,' he is one of them" (288–89). Moreover, O'Donnell is clear, Quentin is one of them precisely "because his moral code is no longer vital" (289). One could call those who appear in trappings from which the religious reality has long since ceased to be present "phantoms" after the manner of medical descriptions of lost limbs, or more simply "ghosts." How could they be exorcized? Modernist writers, where they differed, differed mostly in terms of how thoroughgoing the jettisoning needed to be to exorcise the ghosts, how much shock it would take for people to see the need to exorcise them. Such is the difference, for instance, between Hemingway's *A Farewell to Arms* and Faulkner's *If I Forget Thee, Jerusalem,* to read which is as though to observe duplicate bridge and watch a finesse capture a trump card the previous table had lost. That *Jerusalem* displays the more "cosmic pessimism" in no way mitigates the attempt of modernism to find a way home; whether the self-imposed exile of the Lost Generation, the existential alienation of modern "man," or the more classic struggle of the soul for paradise, the longing seems always to have been for home. One thinks of Huck Finn's ambiguous statement: "We said there warn't no home like a raft, after all" (end of chapter 18).[62]

Clearly, whether Moby Dick had or had not read Freud, the search for home is fraught with Freudian overtones. The struggle, as Faulkner well knew, had been foregrounded by Nietzsche, Schopenhauer, Joyce, and Freud. The coordinates they provide are suggestive of most of the themes critics have examined in Faulkner, and suggestive as well of the genres in which he chose to unfold his tale and the purposes by which he shaped his use of his family and locale. We might include in such genres the maps he drew and included, almost as hints that the texts were to be seen as maps themselves, maps of a spiritual territory, directions toward home.

Faulkner, of course, always disclaimed being an intellectual, by which he apparently meant that his stories were shaped not by how they might affix themselves to the academic concerns of his day but how they might engage the imagination of Everyman and Everywoman.[63] In that light—call it reader response, discourse analysis, or simply fellow feeling [see chapter 10]—it may well be that no theme so arches over all of Faulkner's work as does what James Watson calls the "sustaining idea" of home. That he could, in Watson's pun, "write" home was the creative grounding for a faith of sorts and one perhaps not so unorthodox as has been thought. As Watson puts it, commenting on the letters home during Faulkner's absence between 1918 and 1925, "'home,' as it emerges here, is represented not only as an actual place but as a sustaining idea" ("My Father's" 749). This may well have been the central theme all along. And perhaps what that theme meant to Faulkner may be seen best in the last words Blotner records him saying at Rowan Oak: "I want to go home" (1984 *Faulkner* 712). Could such a desire have, all along, been the overarching theme his life and work address?

NOTES

1. James B. Meriwether, and Michael Millgate, *Lion in the Garden: Interviews with William Faulkner 1926–1962,* Lincoln: University of Nebraska Press, 1968, 221.

2. McHaney's *William Faulkner: A Reference Guide* (Boston: G. K. Hall, 1976) lists Harry M. Campbell and Ruel Foster's *William Faulkner: A Critical Appraisal* (Norman: University of Oklahoma Press, 1951) as the first book-length study.

3. Completely coincidental but an interesting juxtaposition whose "dynamics of possibility" should be explored.

4. Trilling's piece was republished as "Race as a Theme in *Go Down, Moses*" in *Readings on William Faulkner,* San Diego: Greenhaven Press, 1998, 168–71.

5. It is conceivable, of course, that the difference noted has a different explanation, that being the clear superiority of the latter novel over the former. While many readers prefer one or the other, I doubt there is a credible critical case to be made for a clear superiority, at least not in the particulars here in question: characterizations of individuals in their interrelationship.

6. See Hamilton Basso, "Letters in the South," *New Republic,* 19 June 1935: 161–63; Robert Cantwell, "Faulkner's Thirteen Stories," *New Republic,* 21 October 1931: 271; Louis Kronenberger, "The World of William Faulkner," *Nation,* 13 April 1940: 481–82; Robert Morss Lovett, "Ferocious Faulkner," *Nation,* 4 February 1939: 153.

7. Claudia Roth Pierpont, "Tough Guy: The Mystery of Dashiell Hammett," *New Yorker,* 11 February 2002: 66–75, 75.

8. Thus, while the New Critics would contribute to thematic criticism, thematic criticism and New Criticism are not the same thing, just as New Criticism is not to be equated with modernism [see chapter 5].

9. For kinds of prisons as metaphors for modern life, see for example Richard Chase's "the forbidding orphanage (a true symbol of the condition of modern life)" from his "The Stone and the Crucifixion: Faulkner's *Light in August*," *Kenyon Review* 10.4 (Autumn 1948): 539–551.

10. See my "An Interview with Malcolm Cowley," *Faulkner Journal* 5.1 (Fall 1989): 51–59, here especially 55.

11. See also Frederick Crews, "The Strange Fate of William Faulkner," *New York Review of Books* 38.5 (7 March 1991): 47–52. Crews's article, critical of Cowley "worship," cites as the theme Cowley promoted: "a formalist-Agrarian Faulkner—formalist, because his works were assumed to possess a unifying 'moral vision,' and Agrarian because the alleged content of that vision flattered southern traditionalism without counting its cost in misery" (48). The fact that the first Faulkner and Yoknapatawpha Conference advertised Cowley as its featured speaker would indicate the general importance assigned him in the Faulkner critical enterprise. His remarks on that occasion are available in *Studies in English* 14 (1974): 79–97, 119–61. Campbell and Foster assert, after Cowley, that "it is Yoknapatawpha County that gave Faulkner the Nobel Prize" (*William Faulkner: A Critical Appraisal* 6).

12. True, as well, of other modernist writers [see chapter 5] such as Cather and Hemingway.

13. They seem to have brought this term, drawn I suspect from Chesterton, to some prominence.

14. Mary Jane Dickerson, "*As I Lay Dying* and *The Wasteland:* Some Relationships," *Mississippi Quarterly* 17 (Summer 1964): 129–35; Jack Gordon Goellner, "A Closer Look at *As I Lay*

Dying," Perspective 7 (1954): 42–54; James L. Roberts, "The Individual and the Family," *Arizona Quarterly* 16 (1960): 26–38.

15. Percy G. Adams, "Humor as Structure and Theme in Faulkner's Trilogy," *Wisconsin Studies in Contemporary Literature* 5 (1964): 205–12; P. P. Sharma, "The Snopes Theme in Faulkner's Larger Context," *Indian Journal of American Studies* 1.4 (1971): 33–41.

16. Leslie E. Angell, "The Umbilical Cord Symbol as Unifying Theme and Pattern in *Absalom, Absalom!*," *Massachusetts Studies in English* 1 (1968): 106–10; William V. Davis, "Another Flower for Faulkner's Bouquet: Theme and Structure in 'A Rose for Emily,'" *Notes on Mississippi Writers* 7 (1974): 34–38.

17. As quantum mechanics, almost simultaneously, was doing to the walls of Newtonian physics.

18. William Rossky, "*As I Lay Dying:* The Insane World," *William Faulkner's* As I Lay Dying: *A Critical Casebook,* ed. Dianne L. Cox (New York: Garland, 1985), 185.

19. Walter Brylowski, "The Theme of Maturation in *Intruder in the Dust,*" excerpted from his *Faulkner's Olympian Laugh,* Detroit: Wayne State University Press, 1968, 172–76; Philip C. Rule, "The Old Testament Themes in *As I Lay Dying,*" excerpted from his "The Old Testament Vision in *As I Lay Dying,*" *Religious Perspectives in Faulkner's Fiction: Yoknapatawpha and Beyond,* ed. J. Robert Barth, 1972, 120–128. Both reprinted in Clarice Swisher, ed., *Readings on William Faulkner.*

20. Although he clearly invested a good deal of reading and writing in the genre, very little attention was paid to Faulkner's extensive use of the genre of detection/confession and even its especially American "hard-boiled" detective figure. Faulkner repeatedly skewered the false "notion that popular forms of entertainment were somehow beneath the notice of serious art and artists" (Towner, *Faulkner* 48 ff.)

21. An excerpt from Campbell and Foster's *Critical Appraisal* appeared as "Humor in Faulkner's Works" in *Readings on William Faulkner,* edited by Clarice Swisher. Page numbers here are to that excerpt; for James H. Justus, see also *Readings,* 49–58, an excerpt from "The Epic Design of *Absalom, Absalom!*" *Texas Studies in Literature and Language* 4 (Summer 1962), 157–76.

22. Joseph Gold, "'The Bear' as Allegory and Essay," *Readings on William Faulkner,* 78–83 (an excerpt from his *William Faulkner: A Study in Humanism from Metaphor to Discourse,* Norman: University of Oklahoma Press, 1966); Joseph Lydenberg, " 'The Bear' as a Nature Myth," *Readings,* 84–93 (excerpted from his "Nature Myth in Faulkner's 'The Bear,' " *American Literature* 24.1 [March 1952]: 62–72).

23. Meriwether and Millgate's *Lion in the Garden* was published in 1968. Though its index is not much given to thematics, they do list "blood-relationship"/father and son/initiation, nature and time, injustice and "Man will prevail"; and they add, of his themes, "their consistency" (296). One of the major differences between earlier and later critics is that, for the former, Faulkner's words meant his literary works, while, for the latter, Faulkner's words included his public utterances.

24. Noel Polk had begun publishing on Faulkner by 1970, warning about the then-current trend to identify Oxford and Jefferson, Lafayette County and Yoknapatawpha. By 1969, David Minter had already collected criticism on *Light in August.* Even in 1964, Arthur Kinney had raised critical questions about how to relate the later Ike of "Delta Autumn" to the early Ike of "the Bear" based on the then-heretical view that it was not the supposed unity but the actual disunity of *Go Down, Moses* that was most important. Thomas McHaney was already connecting Faulkner to local lore. Richard Godden, Robert Hamblin, and Jim Carothers were just in the offing.

25. Hamblin's "Before the Fall: The Theme of Innocence in Faulkner's 'That Evening Sun,'" *Notes on Mississippi Writers* 11 (1979): 86–94, is a prime example of the growing sophistication of thematic criticism even while at the same time being still in the grip of this middle critical period's moralism. Does, for instance, Jesus "personify" the evil that hangs over the characters (as this period would largely assume) or is he (as the coming critical period would be more likely to ask) the scapegoat for it?

26. The article appeared in *Costerus* 3 (1975): 73–113.

27. See, for example, Terry L. Heller, "Intruders in the Dust: The Representation of Racial Problems in Faulkner's Novel and in the MGM Film Adaptation," *Coe Review* 8 (1977): 79–90 (insightful on race as involved in the film's adaptation of the novel but a patent willingness to excuse Stevens because what he gives Chick is better than what Chick would have otherwise had). Thadious Davis would show how, coming out of a period of "reverse acculturation" that "positioned blacks as referential structures for white," Faulkner's early portraits of blacks exhibited "a primarily nameless collectivity, or a lack of individuation, and an implicitly comic portraiture." However, partly through the influence of the blues, he would come in his portrait of Rider in "Pantaloon in Black" to a "genuine 'type'" whose portrait is "powerful with meaning that is both personal and communal" (71, 81, 90). See her "From Jazz Syncopation to Blues Elegy: Faulkner's Development of Black Characterization," *Faulkner and Race: Faulkner and Yoknapatawpha, 1986,* ed. Doreen Fowler and Ann J. Abadie, Jackson: University of Mississippi Press, 1987, 70–92. For more particulars on Davis's thesis, see my "Handy Ways to Teach 'That Evening Sun,'" *Teaching Faulkner,* ed. Stephen Hahn and Robert W. Hamblin. Westport, CT: Greenwood Press, 2001, 52–57.

28. See the fine study of P. S. Walters, "Hallowed Ground: Group Areas in the Structure and Theme of *Absalom, Absalom!*" *Theoria* 47 (1976): 35–55. Note here, once again, the conjoining of theme and mechanics.

29. Levin's article appears in *PMLA* 85 (January 1970): 35–47; see also John B. Rosenman, "A Matter of Choice: The Locked Door Theme in Faulkner," *South Atlantic Bulletin* 41.2 (1976): 8–12. This brief but persuasive study should also be put with other hints of Faulkner's use of thresholds to form the basis of a major study on the theme(s) developed by this device. For instance, each section of *The Sound and the Fury* opens with a focus on a particular threshold; these in turn serve as the loci for issues of tradition and transgression. See Hamblin, "Before the Fall," and also Campbell and Foster.

30. See my "Adjusting the Apocrypha: The Thirties and Faulkner's Radical Critique of 'The Old Plantation,'" *Arkansas Review* 31.1 (April 2000): 16–20.

31. While Cleanth Brooks is often thought of as a leading exemplar of the New Criticism, one look at the anthology of American literature he edited will indicate how heavily he believed in the critical value of biographical and historical contexts.

32. Ward L. Miner, *The World of William Faulkner,* New York: Grove Press, 1952, 85.

33. Bart H. Welling, "In Praise of the Black Mother: An Unpublished Faulkner Letter on 'Mammy' Caroline Barr," *Georgia Review* 55.3 (Fall 2001): 536–542. This issue also publishes the Faulkner letter referenced in the article, 529–35.

34. David Sansing, "History of Northern Mississippi," *Studies in English* 14 (1976): 5–21. See Theresa Towner's comments on this article in chapter 2 of this *Companion.*

35. Don H. Doyle, *Faulkner's County: The Historical Roots of Yoknapatawpha,* Chapel Hill: University of North Carolina Press, 2001.

36. Gabriele Gutting expands on Faulkner's relationship to history and how that is marked in his fiction in *Yoknapatawpha: The Function of Geographical and Historical Facts in William Faulkner's Fictional Picture of the Deep South,* New York: Peter Lang, 1992. Gutting makes central use of Faulkner's map making, not "as a mere reproduction of Lafayette County's geographical features or a simplified sketch map of reality" but as sites of "the complex creative process which produced the literary terrain" (34).

37. Carvel Collins, "Faulkner and Mississippi," *Studies in English* 15 (1975): 139–59.

38. If it seemed at the time that Faulkner returned from Europe that he had chosen a backwater in comparison to, say, Hemingway's choice of Paris, that would change by the end of their lives, Hemingway dying in rural Idaho, Faulkner in a town that held the focus of the world.

39. He was echoing a formal statement: "I'd fight for Mississippi . . . even if it meant going out into the street and shooting Negroes." See Meriwether and Millgate, *Lion in the Garden,* 261. Later, however, he would say these "are statements which no sober man would make, nor, it seems to me, any sane man believe" (*Lion* 265). Faulkner also disclaimed that he would shoot Mississippians, either black or white, asserting that "Ninety percent of the Negroes are on one side with the whites, against a handful like me who believe that equality is important" (*Lion*

261). These disclaimers are surely sufficient to suggest racist comments did not coincide with what Faulkner had really learned to think; they just as clearly indicate the residues of racism within us even if we have come to a new mind. For a full, and so far the most cogent discussion, see Towner, *Faulkner.*

40. The author's statements on the folly of school segregation could match this emphasis; see his letter to the editor of the Memphis *Commercial Appeal* in *Essays, Speeches, and Public Letters,* 215–16.

41. The idea of symbolic landscape expands the notion of nature, especially of nature as norm, as a theme; it is also a good reminder that in many ways Faulkner was not a novelist but a poet who daringly adapted the novel form to poetic purpose. This, of course, would mean he was not a failed poet turned novelist but a poet who discovered a new medium. This becomes all the more interesting in the light of Edward Said's concept of the interrelationship between the novel form and the imperialist project, but my point here is not its impact on ideological criticism [see chapter 7] but its role in resurrecting to critical attention both Faulkner's own poetry and his relationship to the other arts. See, for example, Judith Sensibar and the conference volume *Faulkner and the Artist,* edited by Donald M. Kartiganer and Ann J. Abadie.

42. How well Ike reads the ledgers is the subject of Richard Godden's and Noel Polk's recent article, where they argue that Ike's attachment to the ledger's possible suggestions of miscegenation really mask his avoidance of their stronger suggestion of homosexual rape. See Richard Godden and Noel Polk, "Reading the Ledgers," *Mississippi Quarterly* 55.3 (Summer 2002 [2003]), 301–359.

43. "Adjusting the Apocrypha: the Thirties and Faulkner's Radical Critique of 'The Old Plantation.'"

44. See particularly her discussion of "That Evening Sun" and of the McCaslins and *Go Down, Moses.*

45. Though many of Faulkner's forensic figures are of necessity peripheral to Watson's focus on Benbow and Stevens, the whole rich panoply of legal "space" is suggested and much of it accounted for in Watson's adept and insightful presentation.

46. It becomes increasingly clear that modernism often owed at least as much to the Romantic movement as it did to the realism that was its immediate precursor, as Faulkner's uses of Blake and fondness for Keats's "Ode on a Grecian Urn" would already indicate. See Martin Bidney, "Faulkner's Variations on Romantic Themes: Blake, Wordsworth, Byron, and Shelley in *Light in August,*" *Mississippi Quarterly* 38.3 (1985 Summer): 277–86.

47. David L. Vanderwerken, "Faulkner's Anti-Bildungsromane," *Journal of American Studies Association of Texas* 25 (1994 October): 50–58; the phrase is Kipling's "Common Form" from his "Epitaphs of the War 1914–1918." See *Norton Anthology of Poetry,* 3rd ed., Ed. Alexander W. Allison, et al. New York: Norton, 1983, 873. Or one could cite Eliot's East Coker, "Do not let me hear / Of the wisdom of old men, but rather of their folly" (*Collected Poems* 185).

48. *Man in Motion* was the title of Warren Beck's study of the Snopes trilogy. In his later remarks and interviews, Faulkner repeatedly stressed this "motion" and its momentary arrest in art.

49. Ursula Brumm, "Theme and Narrative Voice in Faulkner's 'Old Man,'" *Faulkner's Discourse: An International Symposium,* ed. Lothar Hönnighausen. The convict's earlier reading, "instead of liberating, imprisons him"; however, "the great river . . . releases him from the prison, teaches him to fulfill his tasks, and in the end, even educates him to narrate his experience" (243).

50. Susan V. Donaldson, "Cracked Urns: Faulkner, Gender, and Art in the South," 51–81, Robert Hamblin, "'Longer than Anything': Faulkner's 'Grand Design' in *Absalom, Absalom!,*" 269–93, and Panthea Reid, "The Scene of Writing and Shape of Language for Faulkner when 'Matisse and Picasso Yet Painted,'" 82–109, all in *Faulkner and the Artist: Faulkner and Yoknapatawpha, 1993,* ed. Donald Kartiganer and Ann J. Abadie. Jackson: University of Mississippi Press, 1996.

51. J. Robert Barth, *Religious Perspectives in Faulkner's Fiction,* Notre Dame: University of Notre Dame Press, 1972; Dinnah Pladott, "Faulkner's *A Fable:* A Heresy or a Declaration of Faith?" *Journal of Narrative Technique* 12.2 (1982 Spring): 73–94; my "An Interview with Malcolm Cowley," *Faulkner Journal* 5.1 (Fall 1989): 51–59.

52. Some deny his religious leanings because he remained a skeptical and ironic observer. Being a skeptic, however, doesn't deny one's religious leanings but only verifies one's intellectual caution and rules out evangelical single vision. Blotner's biography shows Faulkner attending church, if infrequently nonetheless with interest, and the two books he took with him to Byhalia were Jeremy Taylor's *The Art of Holy Living* and *The Art of Holy Dying.* One doesn't have to be either fanatical or orthodox to believe in some kind of holiness.

53. Faulkner's affinity with black religious expression was the substance of extended remarks made by Sister Thea Bowman at the 1989 Faulkner and Yoknapatawpha Conference: Faulkner and Religion. His awareness of Southern religious culture, including the "religion" of the Lost Cause, is well attested by Charles Reagan Wilson. See, e.g., his "William Faulkner and the Southern Religious Culture," *Faulkner and Religion: Faulkner and Yoknapatawpha, 1989,* ed. Doreen Fowler and Ann J. Abadie. Jackson: University Press of Mississippi, 1991, 21–43. Faulkner's loose affiliation with St. Peter's Episcopal Church suggests that, if he was anything, he was Anglican in the most broad-church sense.

54. In "Mollie's Vision: Lost Cause Ideology and Genesis in Faulkner's *Go Down, Moses,*" *Faulkner and Ideology,* 277–296; see also "Beyond Lexicon: Biblical 'Allusion' in Faulkner, *Mississippi Quarterly* 49.3 (Summer 1996): 595–602.

55. Doreen F. Fowler, "Faith as a Unifying Principle in Faulkner's *Light in August,*" *Tennessee Studies in Literature* 21 (1976): 49–57.

56. Thomas Merton, "'Baptism in the Forest': Wisdom and Initiation in William Faulkner," *Mansions of the Spirit: Essays in Literature and Religion,* ed. George A. Panichas, New York: Hawthorne, 1967, 19–44. Merton's discussions of the themes in two novels, *Go Down, Moses* and *The Wild Palms,* is profound, not only in its general insights about Faulkner but also in its understanding of the levels at which theme operates in literature.

57. I have to confess to no little amusement over the image of critics wrestling; it seems a forced metaphor at best, a dangerous trope at worst. Leave wrestling, I say, to our nation's governors!

58. In this view, modernism was fighting just as much—unsuccessfully it turns out—against the replacement of the old consciousness with a new consciousness in which there was no room for God, for the cosmic. It would take postmodernism not only to throw out the inadequate expressions of the divine but also to throw out the gods altogether. See Merton 34–35.

59. Frazer has never been very far in the background of Faulkner criticism, and yet never quite treated enough either. A fuller study of the contribution of themes in *The Golden Bough* to themes in Faulkner would find no end of material to work with, reminding us of how much the whole realm of cultural anthropology had captured the imagination of youngsters born in the late-nineteenth and early twentieth centuries. For significant studies that attend to Frazer, see chapter 1 in this *Companion.* Hamblin there points to titles whose wording alone indicates the influence of ancient materials. Thomas Merton characterizes the appropriation of old symbols outside their theological context as "the creative effort to penetrate the meaning of man's suffering and aspirations in symbols that are imaginatively authentic" (41). One needn't believe in Zeus (what would that even mean among us?) to be moved by Greek tragedy.

60. See the "Body of an American" at the close of *Nineteen Nineteen* in Dos Passos's *USA* or Frederic Henry's suspicion of abstract words (*A Farewell to Arms,* chapter 27), both of which allude to Wilsonian rhetoric.

61. Donald Philip Duclos looks at the idea of Faulkner's work as a ghost story in *Son of Sorrow: The Life, Works and Influence of Colonel William C. Falkner 1825–1889,* Bethesda: International Scholars Publications, 1998, 269–70.

62. Both *Jerusalem* and *A Farewell to Arms* make use of an image developed by Henry James, the hotel (or its like) as signifying transience, as opposed to the home.

63. I have drawn my use of the language of mapping, coordinates, and Everyman from Campbell and Foster.

Glossary

These definitions, supplied by the contributors to this volume, are, like most definitions, somewhat arbitrary and subject to developments in literary theory and practice. Several widely used literary handbooks might also provide useful guides to critical usage of specific terms. These would include but are not limited to *The Bedford Glossary of Critical and Literary Terms, A Dictionary of Literary Terms and Literary Theory, A Handbook of Critical Approaches to Literature, The Johns Hopkins Guide to Literary Theory and Criticism, A Handbook to Literature, The Penguin Dictionary of Critical Theory, Key Concepts in Communication and Cultural Studies,* and *New Vocabularies in Film Semiotics: Structuralism, Post-Structuralism and Beyond.*

Accidentals In Greg's copy-text theory, those variants in different stages of a work's development and publication that affect such formal elements as punctuation and spelling.

Aestheticism A movement in the nineteenth century that was based on the concept of "art for art's sake."

Agency The concept of agency within Marxist theory and criticism stems from a now-famous letter Frederich Engels wrote to Ernest Bloch in which he stated, "We make our history ourselves, but, in the first place, under very definite assumptions and conditions." As a theory diametrically opposed to abstractions of all sorts, Marxism asserts that people's actions and decisions occur within a specific environment, a specific time and place that influences actions and thoughts. Nonetheless, Marxism includes this notion of agency—the human capacity to exercise will and will power in the face of influences and social forces. People's actions and decisions are not independent, not separate from the social environment and its influences, but these forces do not control them either. There is an interaction, a dialectic, between the individual subject and its environment, the environment exerting pressures and the human subject exercising agency in the face of these pressures. As a term used by postmodern critics, it describes the roles of characters in fiction and drama. Its use suggests that characters (and thus the humans they represent) are not so much self-willed and self-determining as they are determined by the social settings they inhabit, with economic, political, and cultural forces forming them so fully that they become agents of those historical forces.

Alienation For Lacan, alienation is an essential constitutive feature of the subject. The subject is fundamentally split, that is, alienated from him/herself. Subjectivity itself arises out of division. In other words, alterity inhabits the inmost core of the subject.

Alterity Otherness; excluded; placed outside the norm.

Archetypal criticism According to Jung, certain motifs from myths and legends repeat themselves the world over in identical form and appear in dreams, fantasies, and art. Jung theorizes that these images, or archetypes, are produced by a collective unconscious, and archetypal criticism attempts to identify and explicate archetypes.

Archetype Literally, an original model or pattern, but, according to Karl Jung, the "primordial images" that have accumulated in the "collective unconscious" or "racial memory" from the experiences of the entire human race. These archetypes, Jung argues, provide the ever-recurring character types, situations, symbols, and themes that appear in narratives. In general critical usage, the term is used to refer to any older, well-known narrative or poetic pattern that is reemployed by later writers.

Aura/auratic A term used by the modernist theorist and Marxist Walter Benjamin to describe the quality or feelings associated with art in a premodern period and in its sacral, religious function (as in an object of a ritual). He also uses it to raise questions about the nature of art in modern experience and whether or how its "auratic" quality can be maintained and, if so, what uses that aura is put to.

Auteurism A term used most often in film theory, defined by André Bazin in "La Politique des Auteurs" (1957) as the analytical process of "choosing the personal factor in artistic creation as a standard of reference, and then assuming that it continues and even progresses from one film to the next" (255). Romantic in nature, auteurist critics emphasize the notion of individual authorship and creative "genius," usually with regard to the director of the films. Despite its flaws, and its waning popularity in the face of poststructuralism's "death of the author," it introduced into film studies a system designed to recognize and analyze particular artistic traits. While it has been critiqued and problematized throughout the history of film studies, auteurism has never really gone away and has proven a useful concept in the analysis of film texts.

Authorial intertextuality Intersections of plot, character, or concept within two or more works written by a single author or the self-referential quality that accompanies such an intersection.

Bibliography A specialized use of the term to mean the study of books as physical objects.

Carnivalesque A term introduced by Mikhail Bakhtin to describe a spirit of carnival in literature, marked by fun, attention to the body, defiance of authority, variety, heteroglossia, and play. Out of the primordial roots of the carnival tradition in folk culture, Bakhtin argues, arises the many-voiced novel of the twentieth century. His great example is Dostoyevsky, who writes out of a rich tradition of seriocomic, dialogic, satiric literature that may be traced through Socratic dialogue and Menippian satire, Apuleius, Boethius, medieval mystery plays, Boccaccio, Rabelais, Shakespeare, Cervantes, Voltaire, Balzac, and Hugo. In the modern world, this carnivalized antitradition appears most significantly in the novel. Just as the public ritual of carnival inverts values in order to question them, so may the novel call closed meanings into question. Through carnivalization in the novel, opposites may come to know and understand one another in a way not otherwise possible.

Castration complex Freud argues that when the child discovers the anatomical difference between the sexes (the presence or absence of a penis), he/she concludes that females are castrated. To avoid being similarly castrated, the boy ceases to identify with the mother. For Lacan, all subjects—male or female—experience privation or symbolic castration as a function of the primal or primary repression that makes possible subjectivity.

Cavalier Emphasizes themes of love, chivalry, bravery, and loyalty. The term was initially used to describe the lighthearted, melodious, and frequently courtly verse of a group of poets in the seventeenth century. Daniel Singal uses this term to designate codes of honor in the Victorian period.

Collective unconscious Jung theorizes that there exists a collective unconscious, that is, a common store of primordial images perceived across cultures. These images or archetypes, as Jung terms them, are the "inherited possibilities of human imagination as it was from time immemorial " (65).

Commodification A term used to describe the phenomenon in which an object—but also an action (such as physical labor), an image (either a reproduction like a photograph or an actual body), or the end result of an imaginary or creative process (a story, novel, or poem)—becomes subject to the imperatives and demands of the capitalist market. It often refers to experiences and things that are not immediately considered "saleable" and to what the effects of this transformation are—on consumers, as well as on those who produce or offer different kinds of commodities.

Contingency The state of all truths to the postmodern mind. Since postmodernism considers all truths to be human constructions, they remain arbitrary and historical, "contingent" upon affirmation by the particular cultures that produce and propagate them.

Copy-text The most authoritative state of a text, according to some criteria, that a scholarly editor takes as her starting point in editing that text.

Cubism In painting, cubism fragments an image or a representation in order to create a new synthesis. In poetry, it is the application of these painterly techniques. For example, Gertrude Stein applied these methods in some of her poetry.

Cultural Studies A loosely collective, interdisciplinary term for scholarly work done based on the general assumption that works of art do not exist independent of the culture surrounding the artist. Critics who study literature in this way, for example, might examine the legal, political, or historical circumstances of the time in which the writer worked in order to cast light on the behavior of certain characters and the writer's development of certain themes. Stephen Greenblatt explains that studying the cultures surrounding art can help us "recover a sense of the stakes that once gave readers pleasure and pain" ("Culture" 226).

Culture Webster's *New Collegiate Dictionary* defines culture as "1. CULTIVATION, TILLAGE, 2. the act of developing the intellectual and moral faculties esp. by education, 3. expert care and training, 4. enlightenment and excellence of taste acquired by intellectual and aesthetic training, 5. acquaintance with and taste in fine arts, humanities, and broad aspects of science as distinguished from vocational and technical skills." Immediately we may see the problems such standard definitions pose for understanding the term in the context of cultural studies. As Raymond Williams has noted, "Culture is one of the two or three most complicated words in the English language" (*Keywords: A Vocabulary of Culture and Society* [New York: Oxford University Press, 1985], 87). As the cornerstone of the field of cultural studies, the definition of "culture" is hugely important. Yet as Williams's own attempt at a definition shows in *Keywords,* as well as in his foundational text for cultural studies, *Culture and Society, 1790–1950* (New York: Anchor Books, 1960), culture proves an enormously elusive term. Offering several variations on its root in the Latin *cultura,* many of which spring from notions of cultivation, nurturance, or the sustaining of life, Williams's several-page gloss on the word is testimony to its multivalence. Ultimately, however, he emphasizes its meaning as an organizing or energizing force in sustaining social as well as natural life. This definition, as well as those suggested by Webster's *New Collegiate Dictionary*—but especially as they are subjected to scrutiny for what they imply—may be the most useful in approaching "culture" as a critical term.

Deconstruction A form of textual analysis and a principal strand within poststructuralism, associated mainly with French philosopher Jacques Derrida, and more specifically within literary studies with figures such as Paul de Man, Harold Bloom, Geoffrey Hartman, and J. Hillis Miller (collectively known as the "Yale Deconstructionists"). Precursors include Ernst Cassirer, phenomenological philosophers Edmund Husserl and Martin Heidegger, and Ferdinand de Saussure, whose conclusion that "in language there are only differences" proved key to Derrida's notion of *différance,* which suggests that words are only the deferred presences of the things they "mean" and that the meaning of a word is grounded in its difference from other words. Other key principles of deconstructive practice include reading closely, refraining from the use of external evaluative criteria, and recognizing little distinction between genres. Unlike structuralism, deconstruction concentrates on the rhetorical rather than the grammatical.

Dialogism A feature of certain literature, identified most extensively by Valentin Volosinov and Mikhail Bakhtin, that permits the polyphonic interplay of many different voices rather than allowing a single monologic voice to dominate. Volosinov coined the term in order to stress the continuous, interactive, generative process of language, as opposed to the Saussurian emphasis on its abstract, structural form. All language is expressive of social relations, and hence every individual utterance is structured as dialogue. That is, the way an utterance is organized by a speaker/writer is oriented towards an anticipated response in the hearer/reader.

Diegetic Pertaining to the narrated events in a fictional world.

Discipline/disciplinarity A discipline is an academic or intellectual field of study. It requires a set of skills, basis of knowledge, or methodological practice associated with being a professional or demonstrating "expertise" in that field. Cultural studies is suspicious of "disciplinarity" as such because of the ways it may encourage a narrowly defined vision of how to think about literature and culture in general, or a certain writer in specific, and at the same time fail to recognize perspectives from outside of culturally sanctioned functions or institutions.

Discourse A term used for a way of speaking or writing about a subject that openly (as well as covertly) serves a rhetorical as opposed to strictly descriptive end. It generally follows certain guidelines or interests established by a community of users; it often addresses that community, implicitly or explicitly, as its appropriate audience. Discourse analysis can serve critical or conservative purposes.

Doubling From the German *doppelgänger,* using two characters to represent a character's divided mind.

Dream-work A word that Freud coined to describe the methods by which dreams subvert and distort a meaning that cannot be accepted by the conscious mind. In each of these methods, shifts and substitutions take place usually by means of a chain of associations.

Epistemological loss The metaphysical uncertainty that marked the turn of the twentieth century.

Essentialism A postmodern descriptor of earlier, rejected concepts of the individual human being, both religious and secular concepts that described the individual as an autonomous self with a particular "essence" or "nature" and a free will governing the self. Those who maintain belief in the autonomous self often join postmodernists in denying that gender and race play significant roles in determining one's essence, rejecting such essentialist concepts as "female nature." (See also "agency.")

Ethnicity The relationship between individuals in a group that contrasts them with another, larger group that would in some sense exclude them (see Sollors). Skin color, religious preference, and national origin are a few of the most recurrent and powerful sources of ethnic difference.

"Faulkner and Yoknapatawpha" The annual conference on Faulkner held at the University of Mississippi, which began in 1974 and takes up a different theme in Faulkner studies each year. Since 1976, the phrase has provided the subtitle for the published proceedings of this conference.

Feminist In the most narrow sense, the political movement that emerged in the United States in the 1970s on behalf of women. The movement sought equal pay for equal work and more equitable social and educational opportunities such as admission to historically male strongholds. From this political position emerged a new way of reading history, literature, and art from the point of view of the women involved in such productions, be they creators or subjects.

Form The organization of elementary parts, or internal relationships of a work of art in relation to its total effect, usually referring either to its general type or the unique structure. Some approaches distinguish form from content (or form from substance), form being the pattern that gives expression to content or substance. Form is accounted for by close analysis of the "internal logic" of words, phrases, metaphors, images, symbols, chapter breaks and smaller and larger units, and so on. Form is also sometimes loosely used for the common attributes used to distinguish genres.

The gaze For Jean Paul Sartre, the gaze, or act of looking at another, makes it possible for the subject to realize that another is also a subject. Whereas Sartre conflates the eye and the gaze, in his revision, Lacan separates the eye and the gaze; that is, while the eye that looks is the subject's, the gaze, which reflects the object, belongs to the object. This disjunction between eye and gaze reflects the nature of subjectivity itself, which is constituted by a radical split.

Gender Studies An interdisciplinary term for the study of how gender affects society and art. Gender is not the same as the biological sex of any given subject; one may be born male, for example, yet what it means to be "a man" differs from one part of the world to the next and from time to time. As Myra Jehlen puts it, "Culture, society, history define gender, not nature" ("Gender" 263).

Hegemony The term the Italian Marxist and social theorist Antonio Gramsci uses to describe a culture's manner of compelling all its members, even those the culture may ignore or oppress, to adopt its priorities, politics, and worldview. It describes the way in which a powerful society or part of one may silently but effectively impose its sense of its own centrality or importance on individuals or groups who live in very different circumstances or under different terms of privilege, subsistence, education, employment, or power. See also discussions of Gramsci's theory of hegemony in Raymond Williams's *Marxism and Literature* (Oxford: Oxford University Press, 1977, 108–14) and Joseph V. Femia's *Gramsci's Political Thought: Hegemony, Consciousness, and the Revolutionary Process* (Oxford: Oxford University Press, 1981).

Hermeneut/Hermeneutic Although the methods vary, hermeneutics refers to the attempt to recover the inherent meaning of a text. In the eighteenth century, J. A. Ernesti, in his hermeneutical manual, claims that the only criteria in interpretation is words.

Heteroglossia Term used by Bakhtin to designate the presence of more than one voice in a given narrative or other work, distinguishing between the language used to represent the attitudes and opinions of the author and that used by individual characters in fiction and epic. Heteroglossia suggests that careful analysis can recognize within a narrative a multiplicity of social voices and a wide variety of their links and interrelationships (always more or less dialogized).

Holograph manuscript A manuscript in the author's own hand.

Ideology In its use in cultural studies, ideology refers to a way of thinking or imagining one's world and one's place in it relative to others, especially as that idea differs from the actual, material reality of those positions and relations. See also Louis Althusser's discussion of ideology, "Ideology and Ideological State Apparatuses" in *Lenin and Philosophy and other Essays* (London: New Left, 1971).

The imaginary The imaginary is one of the three orders of being (the imaginary, the symbolic, and the Real) that constitute the center of Lacanian thought. According to Lacan, the imaginary is the pre-Oedipal, prelinguistic stage in the development of subjectivity. In this early, identificatory stage, the infant exists in an amorphous state, in one continuous totality of being, one with the mother's body and the world. It is the disruption of the imaginary relation with the mother that gives rise to language and conceptualization.

Imagism A poetic movement that flourished in England and America during the early part of the twentieth century. Associated with poets such as Amy Lowell, Ezra Pound, H. D., and William Carlos Williams, imagism emphasized the use of the concrete image, the use of everyday language, the avoidance of clichés, a freedom in subject matter, and the paring away of all unnecessary words.

Impressionism Literary impressionism derives from its counterpart movement in painting, which attempted to capture fleeting moments (particularly shifts in light) on canvas. In a similar spirit, literary impressionism attempts to capture fleeting emotions, thoughts, and observations. The emphasis falls not on realistic or photographic representation, but on what is seen or felt in the passing moment. Impressionism shares affinities with imagism in poetry and with the camera eye in fiction. The "Time Passes" section of Virginia Woolf's *To the Lighthouse* is a well-known example of the camera eye.

Inscribed Written upon with societal or cultural expectations, assumptions, or beliefs.

Interior Monologue A form of stream of consciousness that presents the interior feelings, impressions, images, as they emerge in a consciousness of a character, particularly at a prelinguistic level. Interior monologues can be both indirect and direct, the latter creating the effect that the author does not exist, for example, Molly Bloom's section at the end of Joyce's *Ulysses*.

Introjection In Kleinian theory, introjection refers to a child's fantasy that the qualities of an external object or another person belong to the self.

Law-of-the-Father The cultural laws and codes that enforce hierarchy and patriarchy.

Logocentric/logocentrism An important concept in deconstruction, logocentrism refers to the central role of rational thought and meaning in the Western tradition, critiquing its logical constructs as merely linguistic and thus human and temporal rather than ultimate or eternal. (See "contingency.")

Lost object According to Lacan, loss or lack constitutes subjectivity; that is, to attain a sense of a separate self, we must repress others, beginning first with the mother. The subject created in this way is haunted by a sense of a lost object.

Marginal/marginality The condition of being outside the prevailing patterns of a culture. One's race, religion, ideology, or sexuality might render one "marginal," as may one's pattern of behavior. Postmodernism tends to examine "marginal" literary characters as a way of exposing the fissures and contradictions within the presumed "whole" produced by the dominant culture inhabited by major characters.

Master narrative Any myth, sacred text, historical tale, or literary work that has such stature within a culture that it has the power to shape the lives and works of human beings within that culture.

Metafiction Fiction that concerns itself with fictionality itself in addition to the story it tells and the characters it creates. It invites readers to consider the nature and role of fiction in its broadest sense, examining such topics as the differences, if any, among fiction, experience, and memory.

Mimicry Luce Irigaray uses this term to describe a form of female rebellion against masculine constructions of feminine identity. More specifically, a woman who engages in mimicry reclaims and redefines her identity by deliberately adopting a cultural role and then manipulating and distorting it.

Montage A technique used in impressionism and film to create a scene, atmosphere, or mood through a series of brief pictures. Effects are produced through juxtaposition. T. S. Eliot uses this technique in *The Waste Land*.

Myth Ancient stories, generally understood to be part factual and part fictional, that come to be accepted by a given community as explaining its origins and embodying its most significant historical, psychological, and spiritual values. For inhabitants of the Western world, the principal myths are Greek, Roman, and biblical. Mythic critics tend to view the essences of these old stories as universal truths that are repeated generation after generation (see, for example, Joseph Campbell's *The Hero with a Thousand Faces*), whereas more recent critics—deconstructionists, for example—argue that mythic structures of belief are always provincial and relative.

Mythical method As defined by T. S. Eliot in his influential 1923 review of James Joyce's *Ulysses,* a writer's juxtaposition of a contemporary story with an ancient myth in order to give added weight and significance to the narrative. This technique, whether employed literally or ironically, represents a hallmark of modernist technique.

Narratology According to Gerald Prince's definition, narratology is "a theory of narrative. It examines what all narratives, and only narratives, have in common as well as what enables them to differ from one another qua narratives, and it aims to describe the narrative-specific system of rules presiding over narrative production and processing" (in Groden and Kreiswirth 524). Important figures within the field include Gérard Genette, Tzvetan Todorov, Seymour Chatman, and Mieke Bal, along with Prince himself. While its emphasis lies within linguistic and rhetorical formations, narratology focuses on many of the same questions of textual meaning found in New Criticism, structuralism, and poststructuralism. Broadly speaking, narratology is the analysis of the structural components of a narrative, the way in which those components interrelate, and the relationship between this complex of elements and the narrative's basic story line. Narratologists treat narratives as explicit, intentionally and meticulously constructed systems rather than as simple or natural vehicles for an author's representation of "reality." They seek to explain how an author transforms (or how authors in general transform) a story line into a literary plot by analyzing the "rules" that generate plot from story. They pay attention to such elements as point of view; the relations among story, teller, and audience; and the levels and types of discourse used in narratives.

New Criticism In its strictest sense, a movement in American literary criticism begun in the 1940s and dominating literary criticism through the 1970s. Largely a reaction to the pervasiveness of philology (or historical linguistics) and antiquarianism (the exclusive study of ancient texts) in American universities at that time, New Criticism privileges close reading of a text and views the aesthetics of the work as self-sufficient and self-contained, discounting the need for biographical, sociological, psychological, and historical context. Its focus is thus on the analysis of a text's symbols, images, metaphors, repetitions, juxtaposition, syntax, word choice, and structure.

The name derives from John Crowe Ransom's 1941 book, *The New Criticism.* Featured practitioners include Ransom, Allen Tate, Cleanth Brooks, Robert Penn Warren, and R. P. Blackmur. The majority of the New Criticism was directed at the interpretation of poetry, but attempts to apply New Critical theories to the novel and story were made more frequently as the movement progressed. More generally, the term refers to the body of "objective" criticism that concentrates on the work of art as an object in itself, which relies on "close reading" to detect patterns, structures, paradoxes and, ultimately, value and integrity within the literary artifact. This school emerged alongside and in turn promoted works in the movement we now call modernism.

New Historicism A term coined by Stephen Greenblatt in 1982 to describe the process of questioning certain scholarly assumptions made by scholars of the English Renaissance. In seeking reassessments of the relationships between writing and other forces operating in any given culture, New Historicism is a variety of cultural studies.

Object-relations theory In contrast to ego psychology, which focuses on psychic drives, object-relations theory takes account of the reciprocal relationship between external objects (including other people, particularly, the mother) and the psyche.

Oedipal complex Freud found himself unable satisfactorily to apply the Oedipal complex to girls. His theory with regard to boys argues that the boy desires his mother and sees his father as a rival. Fearing the harshest punishment—castration—for his forbidden desires, the boy renounces his desire for the mother and identifies with the father, and proper sexual identity ensues. For Lacan, the Oedipal complex and the castration complex initiate the child into the cultural order. Prior to the Oedipal moment, the child exists in a dyadic relation with the mother, unaware of self or other. The child's awareness of loss, the loss of the mother or, more specifically, the loss of the always mythical phallus with which the child imagines he/she might satisfy the desire of the mother, introduces the child into a world of difference and cultural meanings.

Overdetermination A difficult concept to convey in English, its intended meaning in German is determination by multiple factors. Determination refers to the way in which a given social formation exerts pressures on individuals to behave and act in particular ways—for Marxist theory, ways that help support the class system as it exists at the time. Through the theory of ideology, Marxism has systematically refined the understanding of the ways in which a dominant class works to maintain its dominance. Ideology, and the ways in which people come to accept it almost unknowingly, allow a class to maintain its dominance without violence and repression. Overdetermination refers to the ways in which a dominant class's ideology becomes manifest simultaneously in many institutions—courts, schools, religion, media, politics, and cultural productions—and thus exerts pressure on human beings in many ways and in multiple sites. At any given moment and place in history, there will be accepted and dominant definitions of what it means to be a man or woman, white or black, successful or not (to use examples relevant to Faulkner study). These definitions will exert pressures on people and determine the boundaries that people with different ideas and values encounter. The more any individual human subject identifies with the values of the dominant class, the more that person will share in the rewards of that class. The more one pushes against those boundaries, the more risks one takes.

Paternal metaphor Whereas for Freud the father is a referent, for Lacan, the father is a function, and thus he coins the term paternal metaphor for the function that defines fatherhood, that is, the induction of the child into the symbolic order (the world of signs or language) by substituting a signifier or metaphor (the mythical phallus) for the lost mother.

Polysemous The multiplicity of meaning in words, signs, and texts.

Postmodernism A term first applied to architecture in the late 1940s, it has since expanded into areas of music, film, art, media, and sexuality, as well as into studies in ideology and commodification. It engages a cultural politics and practice that breaks down boundaries (including the boundary between high and low culture). It emphasizes heterogeneity and a multiplication of voices and perspectives.

Poststructuralism As opposed to postmodernism, poststructuralism is primarily focused on language praxis. Its concern is the instability of language and the interrelation of texts. It emerged as critique of structuralism, emphasizing an impossibility of origin, a decenteredness, and a collapse of binary oppositions so important to structuralism. Jacques Derrida's work contributed significantly to poststructuralism, as did that of Ferdinand de Saussure.

For many, poststructuralism and deconstruction are virtually synonymous, but the former term carries more critical and cultural cachet than the latter, which is more often attacked as an ahistorical and sterile methodology. As an attempt to contest and subvert structuralism and to formulate new theories regarding interpretation and meaning, it was initiated in part by deconstruction but also associated with aspects of psychoanalytic, Marxist, cultural, reader-response, New Historicist, feminist, and gender criticism. As most critics suggest, there is no unified poststructuralist theory or methodology. Other theorists typically considered poststructuralist include Julia Kristeva, Michel Foucault, Roland Barthes, and Jacques Lacan. Poststructuralists have radically revised the traditional concept of theory even as they have elevated it to a position of prime importance. In the view of poststructuralists, theory has more than literature to account for, since everything from the unconscious to social and cultural practices is seen as functioning like a language; thus the goal of poststructuralist theorists is to understand what controls interpretation and meaning in all possible systems of signification. One of the most definitive qualities of poststructuralism is the questioning of the distinction between language and metalanguage, which renders problematic the idea of a science of literature or of culture. For poststructuralists, the language in which analysis is conducted is to be regarded as continuous with, rather than distinct from, the phenomena being analyzed.

Primary repression For Freud, primary repression occurs when the child represses Oedipal desire. For Lacan, as for Freud, primary repression is the original psychic trauma that introduces subject formation, and it occurs when the child renounces the maternal connection and substitutes for it a signifier, the paternal metaphor.

Primitivism The idea that civilization corrupts and that those who are closest to nature are the most enlightened. Much of D. H. Lawrence's work invokes this principle.

Projection In Kleinian theory, projection is a defense mechanism and refers to a psychic process whereby a child fantasizes the expulsion onto another of an unwanted feeling, thought, or quality.

Reification Marx used this expression to describe the process in which the actual, physical labor involved in making a product as well as its specific, material use-value get transformed into an idea or conception of that object's value. It emphasizes an object's extrinsic, as opposed to intrinsic value, and it describes a number of ways in which the idea, feeling, or "charge" (conceptual, ideological, or erotic) provided by an object becomes more important than what the object offers in itself. To reify, then, means to abstract or transform physical work into a concept, monetary value, or idea.

Repression A psychic mode of defense. It is a universal mental process and lies at the root of the unconscious mind as a domain separate from the rest of the psyche. Simply put, repression refers to the process whereby the conscious mind refuses to accept material (thoughts, feelings, desires, images, memories) that would provoke displeasure.

Resistance A common term in culturalist criticism, it refers to efforts, generally by writers or artists, but also by individuals and members of various social subgroups, to question, subvert, or oppose expectations forced on them by dominant forces. Those forces may be political, as in legal or state authorities and institutions; familial, as in the proscribed roles of the biological, nuclear structure; social, as in the range of social expectations for attitudes, thought, and behavior; or cultural, as in the dictates of cultural authorities like editors, publishers, schools, or more broadly defined, public attitudes and tastes.

The return of the repressed Freud always insisted on the indestructibility of the contents of the unconscious. Repressed material not only escapes destruction, it also re-emerges into consciousness and succeeds in doing so by shifts and distortions in the repressed material.

Scholarly edition A text assembled and edited with deference to critical issues surrounding the textual process. According to the thorough explication of scholarly editions by William Proctor Williams and Craig S. Abbott (*An Introduction to Bibliographical and Textual Studies* [New York: Modern Language Association, 1985], 72), the "apparatus should allow a user to reconstruct any form of the text, and thus it should record the history of the variants."

The signified Lacan takes the term "signified" from the work of Swiss linguist, Ferdinand de Saussure. The signified is the conceptual element of the sign; that is, it is not the real object denoted by a sign (the referent) but a psychological entity corresponding to such an object.

The signifier Signifiers refer to words, but they also refer to units of language smaller than words (morphemes and phonemes, for example) and to acts. For Lacan, the signifier is a material element in a closed differential system, which takes its meaning purely by virtue of its difference from the other elements in the system.

Simulation Refers to a pattern of behavior or mode of representation that self-consciously makes use of imitative, deliberately false strategies. It is used in opposition to, and often to comment on, traditional aesthetic practices like realism or the illusion of presence, fullness, or depth.

Stream of consciousness A literary technique that depicts thoughts, feelings, and impressions of character. Its methods of psychological association permit the yoking of past, present, and future experience. William James coined the term.

Structuralism A movement that emerged in France in the 1950s and 1960s and later in the United State in the 1960s and 1970s. Structuralism was heavily influenced by linguist Ferdinand de Saussure and anthropologist Claude Lévi-Strauss and then picked up by Jacques Lacan, Roland Barthes, Michel Foucault, and Louis Althusser, among others. As an intellectual movement utilizing the methods of structural linguistics and structural anthropology, it holds that the structure of a work or body of work (its codes, its conventions, and its ordering) is the key to analysis. Structuralism shares affinities with formalism and with contemporary practices of narratology.

Its heyday is sometimes identified as the years 1945 to 1970, although critics continue to use structuralist methods and principles, both broadly as an attempt to unify the human sciences and as a critical theory, where it is concerned with the elaboration of broad typologies of narratives or narrative grammars that seek to explore and classify the working of literature. It tends to evoke individual texts as examples of broader categories rather than to be studied in their own right.

There are two main types of structuralism. One concentrates on the patterns formed by linguistic elements in a work in order to find which ones unify the text and throw certain elements in relief. The more common type, which has close affinities to semiotics, sees literary conventions as a system of codes that contribute to and convey meaning. Its main exponents include Tzvetan Todorov, Gérard Genette, and Algirdas Julien Greimas, and in this regard structuralism has close ties with narratology. Like the New Criticism, structuralism tends to locate value inside a text instead of in some realm outside a text and has been attacked on the same grounds as being too assured of the objective reliability of the supposed text.

Subjectivity A term used by Lacan to avoid connotations of selfhood and personhood. For Lacan, subjectivity is an illusion constituted by a fundamental split that makes possible an entrance into the symbolic order, the order of language.

Substantive In Greg's copy-text theory, an adjective for those variants in different stages of a work's development and publication that manifestly alter the meaning of the author's work.

Symbolic A term coined by Jacques Lacan to designate that which is governed by language and culture as opposed to the imaginary, a prelanguage state.

The symbolic order According to Lacan, the symbolic order is one of three essential orders of existence—the imaginary, the symbolic, and the Real. The symbolic order refers to the world of language and cultural meanings, a system of human-made differential meanings, into which the human being is inserted and in accordance with which he/she will have to structure him/herself.

Textual genealogy The lineage or stemma of a specific work, including its draft, revision, production, and publication history.

Textual ontology The study of the nature of a text's existence.

Textual scholarship The discipline of literary study traditionally concerned with the genesis, transmission, and editing of texts and the physical documents that contain them.

The unconscious Constituted by repression, the unconscious mind refers to material (events, thoughts, desires, feelings, images, fears, traumas, etc.) that have been radically separated from consciousness by repression and cannot enter the conscious mind without distortion. When Lacan writes that "the unconscious is structured like a language" (*Seminar 3* 167), he means that, like language, the laws of the unconscious are repetition and desire.

Vulgar Freudianism A name given to a literary practice that prioritizes Freudian symbology over the literary text and reduces the text to a series of Freudian motifs.

Selected Bibliography

GENERAL BIBLIOGRAPHIES

American Literary Scholarship: An Annual. Durham, NC: Duke University Press, 1963–2000.

Bassett, John E. *Faulkner: An Annotated Checklist of Recent Criticism.* Kent, OH: Kent State University Press, 1983.

———. *Faulkner in the Eighties: An Annotated Critical Bibliography.* Metuchen, NJ: Scarecrow Press, 1991.

———. *William Faulkner: An Annotated Checklist of Criticism.* New York: David Lewis, 1972.

McHaney, Thomas L. *William Faulkner: A Reference Guide.* Boston: G. K. Hall, 1976.

Ricks, Beatrice. *William Faulkner: A Bibliography of Secondary Sources.* Metuchen, NJ: Scarecrow, 1981.

FILMS CITED

Barton Fink. Dir. Joel Coen. Prod. Ethan Coen. Perf. John Turturro, John Goodman, and Judy Davis. 116 min. Twentieth Century Fox, 1991. ISBN 8616-21905.

Foreign Student. Dir. Eva Sereny. Perf. Robin Givens and Marco Hofschneider. 96 min. Gramercy Pictures, 1994. ISBN 9689-81725-3.

William Faulkner. Dir. Marc Jampolsky. Prod. Anne-Francoise de Buzareingos. Wr. Michel Abescat. Nar. Nick Calderbank. 45 min. Gédéon/France 3, Films for the Humanities, Kultur Video, 1995. ISBN 0-7697-2183-5. (Documentary.)

William Faulkner: A Life on Paper. Dir. Robert Squier. Prod. Walter Towe. Wr. Albert I. Bezzerides. Nar. Raymond Burr. 120 min. Mississippi Center for Educational Television and Films, 1979. (Documentary.)

William Faulkner: American Writer, 1897–1962. Dir., Prod., and Wr. Malcolm Hossick. 30 min. White Star Video, Skan Productions, and Kultur International Films, 1993. ISBN 1-56127-818-1. (Documentary.)

HANDBOOKS

Abrams, M. H. *A Glossary of Literary Terms.* 4th ed. New York: Holt, 1981.

Cuddon, J. A., ed. *A Dictionary of Literary Terms and Literary Theory.* 3rd ed. Cambridge, MA: Doubleday, 1991.

Guerin, Wilfred L., Earle Labor, Lee Morgan, Jeanne C. Reesman, and John R. Willingham, eds. *A Handbook of Critical Approaches to Literature.* 4th ed. New York: Oxford University Press, 1999.

Harmon, William, and C. Hugh Holman, eds. *A Handbook to Literature.* 7th ed. Upper Saddle River, NJ: Prentice Hall, 1996.

Inge, M. Thomas. Introduction. *Handbook of American Popular Culture.* Ed. M. Thomas Inge. 2nd ed. 3 vols. Westport, CT: Greenwood Press, 1989. xxi–xxxiii.

Lentricchia, Frank, and Thomas McLaughlin, eds. *Critical Terms for Literary Study.* Chicago: University of Chicago Press, 1990.

Macey, David. *The Penguin Dictionary of Critical Theory.* New York: Penguin, 2000.

Murfin, Ross, and Supryia M. Ray. *The Bedford Glossary of Critical and Literary Terms.* Boston: Bedford Books, 1997.

SELECTED WORKS CITED

Abel, Marco. "One Goal Is Still Lacking: The Influence of Friedrich Nietzsche's Philosophy on William Faulkner's *The Sound and the Fury*." *South Atlantic Review* 60.4 (1995): 35–52.

Adamowski, T. H. "Faulkner's Popeye: The 'Other' As Self." *Canadian Review of American Studies* 8 (1977): 36–51. Rpt. in *Twentieth Century Interpretations of Sanctuary.* Ed. J. Douglas Canfield. Englewood Cliffs, NJ: Prentice-Hall. 32–48.

———. "'Meet Mrs. Bundren': *As I Lay Dying*—Gentility, Tact, and Psychoanalysis." *University of Toronto Quarterly* 49 (Spring 1980): 205–27.

Adams, Richard P. *Faulkner: Myth and Motion.* Princeton, NJ: Princeton University Press, 1968.

Adams, Robert M. "Poetry in the Novel: or Faulkner's Esemplastic." *Virginia Quarterly* 29 (1953): 419–34.

Aiken, Conrad. "William Faulkner: The Novel as Form." *Atlantic Monthly* 164 (November 1939): 650–54.

Alldredge, Betty. "Spatial Form in Faulkner's *As I Lay Dying*." *Southern Literary Journal* 11.1 (1978): 3–19.

Allen, William Rodney. "The Imagist and Symbolist Views of the Function of Language: Addie and Darl Bundren in *As I Lay Dying*." *Studies in American Fiction* 10 (1982): 185–96.

Altman, Meryl. "The Bug That Dare Not Speak Its Name: Sex, Art, Faulkner's Worst Novel, and the Critics." *Faulkner Journal* 9.2 (1993): 42–68.

Andrews, Carol M. "Faulkner and the Symbolist Novel." *Modern American Fiction: Form and Function.* Ed. T. D. Young. Baton Rouge: Louisiana State Press, 1989. 118–35.

Andrews, Karen M. "Toward a 'Culturalist' Approach to Faulkner Studies: Making Connections in *Flags in the Dust.*" *Faulkner Journal* 7.1–2 (Fall 1991/Spring 1992): 13–26.

Armour, Richard. *American Lit Relit.* New York: McGraw-Hill, 1964.

Arnold, Edwin T., ed. *Faulkner and Film.* Spec. issue of *Faulkner Journal* 16.1–2 (Fall 2000/Spring 2001): 1–221.

Arthos, John. "Ritual and Humor in Faulkner." *Accent* 9 (Autumn 1948): 23–30.

Backman, Melvin. *Faulkner: The Major Years: A Critical Study.* Bloomington: Indiana University Press, 1966.

Baldwin, Doug. "Putting Images into Words: Elements of the 'Cinematic' in William Faulkner's Prose." *Faulkner and Film.* Spec. issue of *Faulkner Journal* 16.1–2 (Fall 2000/Spring 2001): 35–64.

Banta, Martha. "The Razor, the Pistol, and the Ideology of Race Etiquette." *Faulkner and Ideology: Faulkner and Yoknapatawpha, 1992.* Ed. Donald M. Kartiganer and Ann J. Abadie. Jackson: University Press of Mississippi, 1995. 172–216.

Barker, Stephen. "From Old Gold to I. O. U's: Ike McCaslin's Debased Genealogical Coin." *Faulkner Journal* 3.1 (1987): 2–25.

Barrett, William. "Backward toward the Earth." *In Time of Need: Forms of Imagination in the Twentieth Century.* New York: Harper & Row, 1972. 96–142.

Barth, J. Robert, ed. *Religious Perspectives in Faulkner's Fiction.* Notre Dame: University of Notre Dame Press, 1972.

Basic, Sonja. "Faulkner's Narrative: Between Involvement and Distancing." *Faulkner's Discourse: An International Symposium.* Ed. Lothar Hönnighausen. Tübingen: Max Niemeyer Verlag, 1989. 141–48.

———. "Faulkner's Narrative Discourse: Mediation and Mimesis." *New Directions in Faulkner Studies: Faulkner and Yoknapatawpha, 1983.* Ed. Doreen Fowler and Ann J. Abadie. Jackson: University Press of Mississippi, 1984. 302–21.

———. "Parody and Metafiction: *Ulysses* and *The Hamlet.*" *Faulkner, His Contemporaries, and His Posterity.* Ed. Waldemar Zacharasiewicz. Tübingen: Francke, 1993. 41–55.

Bassett, John E. "*Absalom, Absalom!:* The Limits of Narrative Form." *Modern Language Quarterly* 46 (1985): 276–92.

———. *Visions and Revisions: Essays on Faulkner.* West Cornall, CT: Locus Hill Press, 1989.

Basso, Hamilton. "Letters in the South." *New Republic,* 19 June 1935: 161–63.

Bazin, André. "On the Politique des Auteurs." *Cahiers du Cinema: The 1950s–Neo-Realism, Hollywood, New Wave.* Ed. Jim Hillier. Cambridge, MA: Harvard University Press, 1985. 248–59.

Beard, David. "The Stamp of Faulkner." *Washington Post,* 11 February 1987: C6.

Beck, Warren. *Man in Motion: Faulkner's Trilogy.* Madison: University of Wisconsin Press, 1961.

Beja, Morris. *Epiphany in the Modern Novel.* Seattle: University of Washington Press, 1971.

Bell, Michael. "The Metaphysics of Modernism." *The Cambridge Companion to Modernism.* Ed. Michael Levenson. Cambridge: Cambridge University Press, 1999. 9–32.

Bennett, Ken. "The Language of the Blues in Faulkner's 'That Evening Sun.'" *Mississippi Quarterly* 38.3 (Summer 1985): 339–42.

Benson, Jackson J. "Quentin Compson: Self-Portrait of a Young Artist's Emotions." *Twentieth Century Literature* 17 (July 1971): 143–59.

Bergson, Henri. *Matter and Memory.* New York: Zone Books, 1991.

Berman, Jill, "'this was the answer to it': Sexuality and Maternity in *As I Lay Dying.*" *Mississippi Quarterly* 49 (Summer 1996): 393–407.

Bertens, Hans. *The Idea of the Postmodern: A History.* New York: Routledge, 1995.

Bezzerides, Albert I. *William Faulkner: A Life On Paper.* Ed. Ann J. Abadie. Jackson: University Press of Mississippi, 1980.

Bidney, Martin. "Faulkner's Kinship with Schopenhauer: The Sabbath of the Ixion Wheel." *Neophilologus* 71 (1987): 447–59.

Blaine, Diana York. "The Abjection of Addie and Other Myths of the Maternal in *As I Lay Dying.*" *Mississippi Quarterly* 47 (1994): 419–39.

Bleikasten, André. "Fathers in Faulkner." *The Fictional Father: Lacanian Readings of the Text.* Ed. Robert Con Davis. Amherst: University of Massachusetts Press, 1981. 115–46.

———. "Faulkner and the New Ideologues." *Faulkner and Ideology: Faulkner and Yoknapatawpha, 1992.* Ed. Donald M. Kartiganer and Ann J. Abadie. Jackson: University of Mississippi Press, 1995. 3–21.

———. "Faulkner and the Paradoxes of Description." *Faulkner's Discourse: An International Symposium.* Ed. Lothar Hönnighausen. Tübingen: Max Niemeyer Verlag, 1989. 170–83.

———. *Faulkner's As I Lay Dying.* Trans. Roger Little. Bloomington: Indiana University Press, 1973.

———. "For/Against an Ideological Reading of Faulkner's Novels." *Faulkner and Idealism: Perspectives from Paris.* Ed. Michel Gresset and Patrick Samway. Jackson: University Press of Mississippi, 1983. 27–50.

———. "'A Furious Beating of Hollow Drums Toward Nowhere': Faulkner, Time and History." *Faulkner and History.* Ed. Javier Coy and Michel Gresset. Salamanca: Edicions Universidad de Salamanca, 1986. 77–95.

———. *The Ink of Melancholy: Faulkner's Novels from* The Sound and the Fury *to* Light in August. Bloomington: Indiana University Press, 1990.

———. "*Light in August:* The Closed Society and Its Subjects." *New Essays on* Light in August. Ed. Michael Millgate. New York: Cambridge University Press. 81–102.

———. *The Most Splendid Failure: Faulkner's* The Sound and the Fury. Bloomington: Indiana University Press, 1976.

———. "The Novelist as Historian in *Requiem for a Nun.*" *Rewriting the South: History and Fiction.* Ed. Lothar Hönnighausen and Valeria Gennaro Lerda. Tübingen: Francke, 1993. 344–56.

Bloom, Harold. *The Anxiety of Influence.* New York: Oxford University Press, 1973.

Blotner, Joseph. "Did You See Him Plain?" *Fifty Years of Yoknapatawpha: Faulkner and Yoknapatawpha, 1979.* Ed. Doreen Fowler and Ann J. Abadie. Jackson: University Press of Mississippi, 1980. 3–22.

———. "The Falkners and the Fictional Families." *Georgia Review* 30 (1976): 572–92.

———. *Faulkner: A Biography.* 2 vols. New York: Random House, 1974. 1 vol. rev. ed., 1984.

———. "Faulkner and Popular Culture." *Faulkner and Popular Culture: Faulkner and Yoknapatawpha, 1988.* Ed. Doreen Fowler and Ann J. Abadie. Jackson: University Press of Mississippi, 1990. 3–21.

———. "The Sources of Faulkner's Genius." *Fifty Years of Yoknapatawpha: Faulkner and Yoknapatawpha, 1979.* Ed. Doreen Fowler and Ann J. Abadie. Jackson: University Press of Mississippi, 1980. 248–70.

———. "William Faulkner and Robert Penn Warren as Literary Artists." *Faulkner and the Artist: Faulkner and Yoknapatawpha, 1993.* Ed. Donald M. Kartiganer and Ann J. Abadie. Jackson: University Press of Mississippi, 1996. 22–40.

———. "William Faulkner: Life and Art." *Faulkner and Women: Faulkner and Yoknapatawpha, 1985.* Ed. Doreen Fowler and Ann J. Abadie. Jackson: University Press of Mississippi, 1986. 3–20.

———, ed. *Selected Letters of William Faulkner.* New York: Vintage Books, 1978.

Bockting, Ineke. "Whiteness and the Love of Color: The Development of a Theme in Faulkner's *Go Down, Moses.*" *William Faulkner's Short Fiction: An International Symposium.* Ed. Hans H. Skei. Proc. of the 1995 International Faulkner Symposium. Oslo, Norway: Solum, 1997. 197–211.

Bodkin, Maud. *Archetypal Patterns in Poetry: Psychological Studies of Imagination.* 1934. New York: Vintage Books, 1958.

Bogel, Frederic V. "Fables of Knowing: Melodrama and Related Forms." *Genre* 11 (1978): 83–108.

Boone, Joseph A. "Creation by the Father's Fiat: Paternal Narrative, Sexual Anxiety, and the Deauthorizing Designs of *Absalom, Absalom!*" *Refiguring the Father: New Feminist Readings of Patriarchy.* Ed. Patricia Yeager and Beth Kowaleski-Wallace. Carbondale: Southern Illinois University Press, 1989. 209–37.

Boren, Mark Edelman. "The Southern Super Collider: William Faulkner Smashes Language into Reality in *As I Lay Dying,*" *Southern Quarterly* 40.4 (Summer 2002): 21–38.

Bowling, Lawrence E. "Faulkner and the Theme of Innocence." *Kenyon Review* 20 (Summer 1958): 466–87.

———. "Faulkner and the Theme of Isolation." *Georgia Review* 18 (1964): 50–66.

Bradley, David. *The Chaneysville Incident.* New York: Harper and Row, 1981; Perennial ed., 1990.

Braidotti, Rosi. *Patterns of Dissonance: A Study of Women in Contemporary Philosophy.* Trans. Elizabeth Guild. New York: Routledge, 1991.

Brodhead, Richard, ed. *Faulkner: New Perspectives.* Englewood Cliffs, NJ: Prentice-Hall, 1983.

Brodsky, Louis Daniel. "'Elder Watson in Heaven': Poet Faulkner as Satirist." *Faulkner Journal* 1.1 (Fall 1985): 2–8.

———. "Faulkner and the Racial Crisis." *Southern Review* 24 (Autumn 1988): 791–807.

———. "Faulkner's Life Masks." *Southern Review* 22 (Autumn 1986): 738–65.

Brodsky, Louis Daniel, and Robert W. Hamblin, eds. *Country Lawyer and Other Stories for the Screen.* By William Faulkner. Jackson: University Press of Mississippi, 1987.

———, eds. *Faulkner: A Comprehensive Guide to the Brodsky Collection.* Vol. 1: *The Biobibliography.* Vol. 2: *The Letters.* Vol. 3: *The De Gaulle Story.* Vol. 4: *Battle Cry.* Vol. 5: *The Documents.* Jackson: University Press of Mississippi, 1982–1988.

———, eds. *Stallion Road: A Screenplay by William Faulkner.* Jackson: University Press of Mississippi, 1989.

Brooks, Cleanth. *The Hidden God: Studies in Hemingway, Faulkner, Yeats, Eliot, and Warren.* New Haven, CT: Yale University Press, 1963.

———. Introduction. *Faulkner's Women: Characterization and Meaning*. By Sally R. Page. Deland, FL: Everett/Edwards, 1972. xi–xx.

———. "The Narrative Structure of *Absalom, Absalom!*" *Georgia Review* 29 (1975): 366–94.

———. *On the Prejudices, Predilections, and Firm Beliefs of William Faulkner*. Baton Rouge: Louisiana State University Press, 1987.

———. *The Well-Wrought Urn*. New York: Harcourt, 1947.

———. *William Faulkner: First Encounters*. New Haven, CT: Yale University Press, 1983.

———. *William Faulkner: Toward Yoknapatawpha and Beyond*. New Haven, CT: Yale University Press, 1978.

———. *William Faulkner: The Yoknapatawpha Country*. New Haven, CT: Yale University Press, 1963. Baton Rouge: Louisiana State University Press, 1991.

Brooks, Peter. "Incredulous Narration: *Absalom, Absalom!*" *William Faulkner's* Absalom, Absalom! Ed. Harold Bloom. New York: Chelsea House Publishers, 1987. 105–27.

———. "The Narrative Structure of *Absalom, Absalom!*" *Georgia Review* 29 (1975): 366–94.

———. *Reading for the Plot*. New York: Knopf, 1984.

Broughton, Panthea Reid. "Faulkner's Cubist Novels." *"A Cosmos of My Own": Faulkner and Yoknapatawpha, 1980*. Ed. Doreen Fowler and Ann J. Abadie. Jackson: University Press of Mississippi, 1981. 59–94. [See also Reid, Panthea]

Brown, Calvin S. *A Glossary of Faulkner's South*. New Haven, CT: Yale University Press, 1976.

———. "*Sanctuary:* From Confrontation to Peaceful Void." *Mosaic* 7 (1973): 75–95.

Bryant, Cedric Gael. "Mirroring the Racial 'Other': The Deacon and Quentin Compson in William Faulkner's *The Sound and the Fury*." *Southern Review* 29.1 (Winter 1993): 30–40.

Brylowski, Walter. *Faulkner's Olympian Laugh: Myth in the Novels*. Detroit: Wayne State University Press, 1968.

Budd, Louis J. "Playing Hide and Seek with William Faulkner: The Publicly Private Artist." *Faulkner and Popular Culture: Faulkner and Yoknapatawpha, 1988*. Ed. Doreen Fowler and Ann J. Abadie. Jackson: University Press of Mississippi, 1990. 34–58.

Burgess, Miranda J. "Watching Jefferson Watching: *Light in August* and the Aestheticization of Gender." *Faulkner and Cultural Studies*. Spec. issue of *Faulkner Journal* 7.1–2 (Fall 1991/Spring 1992): 95–114.

Burrows, David J., and others, eds. *Myths and Motifs in Literature*. New York: Free Press, 1973.

Bush, Laura L. "A Very American Power Struggle: The Color of Rape in *Light in August*." *Mississippi Quaterly* 51 (Summer 1998): 483–501.

Butterworth, Keen. *A Critical and Textual Study of Faulkner's* A Fable. Ann Arbor: University of Michigan Research Press, 1983.

Calkin, Paul Luís. "Be Careful What You Wish For: *As I Lay Dying* and the Shaming of Abjection." *Faulkner Journal* 12.1 (1996): 90–109.

Campbell, Harry Modean, and Ruel E. Foster. *William Faulkner: A Critical Appraisal*. Norman: University of Oklahoma Press, 1951.

Campbell, Joseph. *The Hero with a Thousand Faces*. Rev. ed. Princeton, NJ: Princeton University Press, 1968.

————. *The Masks of God.* 4 vols. 1972. New York: Viking Penguin, 1976.

Canfield, J. Douglas, ed. *Twentieth Century Interpretations of* Sanctuary. Englewood Cliffs, NJ: Prentice-Hall, 1982.

Cantwell, Robert. "Faulkner's Thirteen Stories." *New Republic* 21, October 1931: 271.

Capps, Jack L., ed. Editor's Preface. *William Faulkner and the Military.* Spec. issue of *Faulkner Journal* 2.2 (Spring 1987): 2–3.

Carothers, James B., and John T. Matthews. Editors' Introduction. *Faulkner Journal* 1.1 (Fall 1985): back of front cover.

Cather, Willa. Prefatory Note. *Note Under Forty.* Lincoln: University of Nebraska Press, 1988. v.

Chakovsky, Sergei. "Women in Faulkner's Novels: Author's Attitude and Artistic Function." *Faulkner and Women: Faulkner and Yoknapatawpha, 1985.* Ed. Doreen Fowler and Ann J. Abadie. Jackson: University Press of Mississippi, 1986. 58–80.

————. "Word and Idea in *The Sound and the Fury.*" *New Directions in Faulkner Studies: Faulkner and Yoknapatawpha, 1983.* Ed. Doreen Fowler and Ann J. Abadie. Jackson: University Press of Mississippi, 1984. 283–301.

Chase, Richard. "The Stone and the Crucifixion: Faulkner's *Light in August.*" *Kenyon Review* 10 (Autumn 1948): 539–551.

Chodorow, Nancy. *The Reproduction of Mothering: Psychoanalysis and the Sociology of Gender.* Berkeley: University of California Press, 1978.

Christ, Carol. *Victorian and Modern Poetics.* Chicago: University of Chicago Press, 1984.

Cixous, Helene. *The Helene Cixous Reader.* Ed. Susan Sellers. London: Routledge, 1994.

Clarke, Deborah. "Gender, War, and Cross-Dressing in *The Unvanquished.*" *Faulkner and Gender: Faulkner and Yoknapatawpha, 1994.* Ed. Donald M. Kartiganer and Ann J. Abadie. Jackson: University Press of Mississippi, 1996. 228–51.

————. "Of Mothers, Robbery, and Language: Faulkner and *The Sound and the Fury.*" *Faulkner and Psychology: Faulkner and Yoknapatawpha, 1991.* Ed. Donald M. Kartiganer and Ann J. Abadie. Jackson: University Press of Mississippi, 1994. 56–77.

————. *Robbing the Mother: Women in Faulkner.* Jackson: University of Mississippi Press, 1994.

Cohen, Philip. "Faulkner by the Light of a Pale Fire: Postmodern Textual Scholarship and Faulkner Studies at the End of the Twentieth Century." *Faulkner and Postmodernism: Faulkner and Yoknapatawpha, 1999.* Ed. John N. Duvall and Ann J. Abadie. Jackson: University Press of Mississippi, 2002. 167–91.

Cohn, Deborah N. *History and Memory in the Two Souths: Recent Southern and Spanish American Fiction.* Nashville, TN: Vanderbilt University Press, 1999.

Coindreau, Maurice. Préface. *Les palmiers sauvages.* Paris: Gallimard, 1952.

————. "Preface to *The Sound and the Fury.*" Trans. George M. Reeves. *Mississippi Quarterly* 19 (1966): 107–15.

Collins, Carvel. "'Ad Astra' through New Haven: Some Biographical Sources of Faulkner's War Fiction." *Faulkner and the Short Story.* Ed. Evans Harrington and Ann J. Abadie. Jackson: University Press of Mississippi, 1992. 108–27.

————. "Are These Mandalas?" *Literature and Psychology* 3 (November 1953): 3–6.

————. "Biographical Background for Faulkner's Helen." *Helen: A Courtship and Mississippi Poems.* Ed. Carvel Collins and Joseph Blotner. Oxford, MS: Yoknapatawpha Press; New Orleans: Tulane University Press, 1981. 9–105.

———. "A Conscious Literary Use of Freud?" *Literature and Psychology* 3 (June 1953): 2–4.

———. "The Interior Monologues of *The Sound and the Fury.*" *English Institute Essays 1952.* New York: Columbia University Press, 1954. 29–56. Also in *The Merrill Studies in* The Sound and Fury. Columbus: Ohio State University Press, 1970. 59–79.

———. Introduction. *Mayday.* By William Faulkner. Notre Dame: University of Notre Dame Press, 1976. 3–41.

———. Introduction. *William Faulkner: Early Prose and Poetry.* Ed. Carvel Collins. Boston: Little, Brown, 1962. 3–33.

———. Introduction. *William Faulkner: New Orleans Sketches.* Ed. Carvel Collins. New York: Random House, 1958. xi–xxxiv.

———. "The Pairing of *The Sound and the Fury* and *As I Lay Dying.*" *Princeton University Library Chronicle* 18 (Spring 1957): 114–23.

Cominos, Peter T. "Innocent Femina Sensualis in Unconscious Conflict." *Suffer and Be Still: Women in the Victorian Age.* Ed. Martha Vicinus. Bloomington: Indiana University Press, 1972. 155–72.

Connolly, Thomas E. "Point of View in Faulkner's *Absalom, Absalom!*" *Modern Fiction Studies* 27 (Summer 1981): 255–72.

Connor, Steven. *Postmodernist Culture: An Introduction to Theories of the Contemporary.* Oxford, England: Blackwell, 1989.

Conrad, Joseph. *Heart of Darkness.* 1902. New York: Oxford University Press, 1998.

Cottrell, Beekman W. "Christian Symbols in *Light in August.*" *Modern Fiction Studies* 2 (Winter 1956–1957): 207–13.

Coughlan, Robert. *The Private World of William Faulkner.* New York: Avon Book Division, 1953.

Cowan, Michael H., ed. *Twentieth Century Interpretations of* The Sound and the Fury. Englewood Cliffs, NJ: Prentice-Hall, 1968.

Cowley, Malcolm. "Faulkner by Daylight." *New Republic,* 15 April 1940: 510.

———. *The Faulkner-Cowley File: Letters and Memories 1944–1962.* New York: Viking, 1966.

———. Introduction. *The Portable Faulkner.* Ed. Malcolm Cowley. New York: Viking, 1946, 1949; Penguin, 1977. vii–xxxiii.

———. "Magic in Faulkner." *Faulkner, Modernism, and Film: Faulkner and Yoknapatawpha, 1978.* Ed. Evans Harrington and Ann J. Abadie. Jackson: University Press of Mississippi, 1979. 3–19.

———, ed. *The Portable Faulkner.* New York: Viking Press, 1946; Penguin, 1977.

———, ed. *Writers at Work: The Paris Review Interviews.* New York: Viking Press, 1958.

Crews, Frederick, and John N. Duvall. "Faulkner's Strange Fate." *New York Review of Books,* 24 Oct. 1991: 73.

Culler, Jonathan. *Structuralist Poetics: Structuralism, Linguistics, and the Study of Literature.* Ithaca: Cornell University Press, 1975.

Dabney, Lewis P. *The Indians of Yoknapatawpha: A Study in Literature and History.* Baton Rouge: Louisiana State University Press, 1974.

Dalgarno, Emily. "*Soldiers' Pay* and Virginia Woolf." *Mississippi Quarterly* 29 (1976): 330–46.

Dardis, Tom. *Some Time in the Sun.* New York: Scribner's, 1976.

Daufenbach, Claus. "A Portrait of the Modernist as a Young Aesthete: Faulkner's *Mosquitoes*." *Amerikastudien* 42 (1997): 547–58.

Dauner, Louise. "Quentin and the Walking Shadow." *Arizona Quarterly* 18 (1965): 159–71. Reprinted in Michael H. Cowan, ed. *Twentieth Century Interpretations of* The Sound and the Fury. Englewood Cliffs, NJ: Prentice-Hall, 1968. 75–80.

Davey Company. "Bound to Last." Advertisement. *Publishers Weekly,* 11 April 1980: 61.

Davis, Robert Con, ed. *The Fictional Father: Lacanian Readings of the Text.* Amherst: University of Massachusetts Press, 1982.

———. "The Symbolic Father in Yoknapatawpha County." *Journal of Narrative Technique* 10 (1980): 39–55.

Davis, Thadious. *Faulkner's "Negro": Art and the Southern Context.* Baton Rouge: Louisiana State University Press, 1983.

DeKoven, Marianne. *Rich and Strange: Gender, History, and Modernism.* Princeton, NJ: Princeton University Press, 1991.

Delville, Michel. "Alienating Language and Darl's Narrative Consciousness in Faulkner's *As I Lay Dying*." *Southern Literary Journal* 27.1 (1994): 61–72.

de Man, Paul. *Blindness and Insight: Essays in the Rhetoric of Contemporary Criticism.* New York: Oxford University Press, 1971.

Díaz-Diocaretz, Myriam. "Woman as Bounded Text." *Faulkner and Women: Faulkner and Yoknapatawpha, 1985.* Ed. Doreen Fowler and Ann J. Abadie. Jackson: University Press of Mississippi, 1986. 235–69.

Dickerson, Mary Jane. "*As I Lay Dying* and *The Waste Land*—Some Relationships." *Mississippi Quarterly* 17 (Summer 1964): 129–35.

Donaldson, Susan V. "Cracked Urns: Faulkner, Gender, and Art in the South." *Faulkner and the Artist: Faulkner and Yoknapatawpha, 1993.* Ed. Donald M. Kartiganer and Ann J. Abadie. Jackson: University Press Mississippi, 1996. 51–81.

———. "Dismantling the *Saturday Evening Post* Reader: *The Unvanquished* and Changing 'Horizons of Expectations.'" *Faulkner and Popular Culture: Faulkner and Yoknapatawpha, 1988.* Ed. Doreen Fowler and Ann J. Abadie. Jackson: University Press of Mississippi, 1990. 179–95.

———. "Making a Spectacle: Welty, Faulkner, and Southern Gothic." *Mississippi Quarterly* 50 (1997): 567–84.

———. "Reading Faulkner Reading Cowley Reading Faulkner: Authority and Gender in the Compson Appendix." *Faulkner and Cultural Studies.* Spec. issue of *Faulkner Journal* 7.1–2 (Fall 1991/Spring 1992): 27–41.

———. "Subverting History: Women, Narrative and Patriarchy in *Absalom, Absalom!*" *Southern Quarterly* 26.4 (Summer 1988): 19–32.

Dondlinger, Mary Joanne. "Getting around the Body: The Matter of Race and Gender in *Light in August*." *Faulkner and the Natural World: Faulkner and Yoknapatawpha, 1996.* Ed. Donald M. Kartiganer and Ann J. Abadie. Jackson: University Press of Mississippi, 1999. 98–125.

Douglass, Paul. *Bergson, Eliot, and American Literature.* Lexington: University Press of Kentucky, 1986.

Dowling, David. *William Faulkner.* New York: St. Martin's Press, 1989.

Doyle, Don H. *Faulkner's County: The Historical Roots of Yoknapatawpha.* Chapel Hill: University of North Carolina Press, 2001.

Duclos, Donald P. "Damned Sartorises! Damned Falkners!" *Critical Essays on William Faulkner: The Sartoris Family.* Ed. Arthur Kinney. Boston: Hall, 1985. 249–64.

———. *Son of Sorrow: The Life, Works and Influence of Colonel William C. Falkner 1825–1889.* Bethesda: International Scholars Publications, 1998.

Dunleavy, Linda. "*Sanctuary,* Sexual Difference, and the Problem of Rape." *Studies in American Fiction* 24 (1996): 171–91.

Duvall, John N. "Authentic Ghost Stories: *Uncle Tom's Cabin, Absalom, Absalom!,* and *Beloved.*" *Faulkner Journal* 4.1–2 (Fall 1988/Spring 1989): 83–97.

———. "Contextualizing *The Sound and the Fury:* Sex, Gender, and Community in Modern American Fiction." *Approaches to Teaching Faulkner's* The Sound and the Fury. Ed. Stephen Hahn and Arthur Kinney. New York: Modern Language Association of America, 1996. 101–107.

———. "Faulkner's Critics and Women: The Voice of the Community." *Faulkner and Women: Faulkner and Yoknapatawpha, 1985.* Ed. Doreen Fowler and Ann J. Abadie. Jackson: University Press of Mississippi, 1986. 41–57.

———. "Faulkner's Crying Game: Male Homosexual Panic." *Faulkner and Gender: Faulkner and Yoknapatawpha, 1994.* Ed. Donald M. Kartiganer and Ann J. Abadie. Jackson: University Press of Mississippi, 1996. 48–72.

———. *Faulkner's Marginal Couple: Invisible, Outlaw, and Unspeakable Communities.* Austin: University of Texas Press, 1990.

———. "Postmodern Yoknapatawpha: William Faulkner as Usable Past." *Faulkner and Postmodernism: Faulkner and Yoknapatawpha, 1999.* Ed. John N. Duvall and Ann J. Abadie. Jackson: University Press of Mississippi, 2002. 39–56.

———. "Using Greimas' Narrative Semiotics: Signification in Faulkner's 'The Old People.'" *College Literature* 9.3 (1982): 192–206.

Duvert, Elizabeth. "Faulkner's Map of Time." *Faulkner Journal* 2:1 (Fall 1986): 14–28.

Eagleton, Terry. *Literary Theory: An Introduction.* 2nd ed. Minneapolis: University of Minnesota Press, 1996.

Eby, Cecil D., Jr. "Ichabod Crane in Yoknapatawpha." *Georgia Review* 16 (Winter 1962): 465–69.

Eddy, Charmaine. "The Policing and Proliferation of Desire: Gender and the Homosexual in Faulkner's *Sanctuary.*" *Faulkner Journal* 14.2 (1999): 21–39.

Eliot, T. S. *Collected Poems 1909–1962.* San Diego: Harcourt, 1963.

———. "Ulysses, Order and Myth." *Dial* 75 (November 1923): 480–83.

———. The Waste Land *and Other Poems.* New York: Harcourt, Brace and World, 1963.

Elmore, A. E. "Faulkner on the Agrarian South: Waste Land or Promised Land?" *The Vanderbilt Tradition.* Baton Rouge: Louisiana State University Press, 1991. 175–88.

Epstein, William H. "(Post)Modern Lives: Abducting the Biographical Subject." *Contesting the Subject: Essays in the Postmodern Theory and Practice of Biography and Biographical Criticism.* Ed. William H. Epstein. West Lafayette, IN: Purdue University Press, 1991. 217–36.

Eysteinsson, Astradur. *The Concept of Modernism.* Ithaca: Cornell University Press, 1990.

Fadiman, Clifton. "Hardly Worth While." *Nation,* 15 January 1930: 74–75.

———. "The World of William Faulkner." *Nation,* 15 April 1931: 422–23.

Fadiman, Regina. *Faulkner's* Intruder in the Dust: *Novel into Film.* Knoxville: University of Tennessee Press, 1978.

Fant, Joseph L., III, and Robert Ashley, eds. *Faulkner at West Point.* New York: Random House, 1964; reprint Jackson: University Press of Mississippi, 2002.

Fasal, Ida. "A 'Conversation' Between Faulkner and Eliot." *Mississippi Quarterly* 20 (Fall 1967): 195–206.

———. "Spatial Form and Spatial Time." *Western Humanities Review* 16 (1962): 223–34.

Faulkner, William. *Absalom, Absalom!: The Corrected Text.* New York: Random House, 1986.

———. *As I Lay Dying.* 1930. New York: Vintage, 1964; New York: Random House, 1986; New York: Vintage International, 1990.

———. *Battle Cry.* Ed. Louis Daniel Brodsky and Robert W. Hamblin. Jackson: University Press of Mississippi, 1985.

———. *Big Woods.* New York: Random House, 1955.

———. *Collected Stories.* New York: Random House, 1950.

———. *Country Lawyer and Other Stories for the Screen.* Ed. Louis Daniel Brodsky and Robert W. Hamblin. Jackson: University Press of Mississippi, 1987.

———. *The De Gaulle Story.* Ed. Louis Daniel Brodsky and Robert W. Hamblin. Jackson: University Press of Mississippi, 1984.

———. *Doctor Martino and Other Stories.* New York: Harrison Smith and Robert Haas, 1934.

———. *A Fable.* New York: Random House, 1954; *Novels 1942–1954.* New York: Library of America, 1994. 665–1072.

———. *Flags in the Dust.* Ed. Douglas Day. New York: Random House, 1973; New York: Vintage, 1974.

———. *Go Down, Moses.* 1942. New York: Vintage Books, 1973; New York: Vintage International, 1991.

———. *A Green Bough.* New York: Harrison Smith and Robert Haas, 1933.

———. *The Hamlet.* 1960. New York: Vintage, 1972.

———. *Helen: A Courtship.* New Orleans: Tulane University Press; Oxford, MS: Yoknapatawpha Press, 1981.

———. *Idyll in the Desert.* New York: Random House, 1931.

———. *If I Forget Thee, Jerusalem* [*The Wild Palms*]. New York: Vintage International, 1995.

———. *Intruder in the Dust.* New York: Random House, 1948.

———. *Knight's Gambit.* New York: Random House, 1948.

———. *Light in August.* New York: Random House, 1932; New York: Vintage, 1972; New York: Vintage International, 2002.

———. *The Mansion.* New York: Random House, 1959.

———. *The Marble Faun* and *A Green Bough.* New York: Random House, 1965.

———. *The Marionettes: A Play in One Act.* Ed. Noel Polk. [Charlottesville]: Bibliographical Society of the University of Virginia and the University Press of Virginia, 1975.

———. *Mayday.* [Notre Dame]: University of Notre Dame Press, 1977.

———. *Mississippi Poems.* Oxford, MS: Yoknapatawpha Press, 1979.

———. *Miss Zilphia Gant.* [Dallas]: Book Club of Texas, 1932.

———. *Mosquitoes.* New York: Boni & Liveright, 1927; New York: Liveright, 1965; New York: Pocket Books, 1985.

———. *New Orleans Sketches.* Ed. Carvel Collins. New York: Random House, 1968; reprint Jackson: University Press of Mississippi, 2002.

———. *Notes on a Horsethief.* Greenville, MS: Levee Press, 1951.

———. *The Portable Faulkner.* Ed. Malcolm Cowley. New York: Viking Press, 1946.

———. *Pylon.* New York: Harrison Smith and Robert Haas, 1935; New York: Random House, 1965.

———. *The Reivers.* New York: Random House, 1962.

———. *Requiem for a Nun.* 1951. *Novels 1942–1954.* New York: Library of America, 1994. 471–664.

———. *Sanctuary.* New York: Jonathan Cape and Harrison Smith, 1931.

———. *Sanctuary: The Original Text.* Ed. Noel Polk. New York: Random House, 1981.

———. *Sartoris.* New York: Harcourt, Brace, and Company, 1929; New York: Signet/ New American Library, 1964.

———. *Soldiers' Pay.* New York: Boni and Liveright, 1926; New York: Liveright, 1951.

———. *The Sound and the Fury.* New York: Jonathan Cape and Harrison Smith, 1929; New York: Random House, 1946; New York: Vintage, 1954; New York: Vintage International, 1990. 2nd Norton Critical ed. Ed. David Minter. New York: W. W. Norton and Company, 1994.

———. *Stallion Road.* Ed. Louis Daniel Brodsky and Robert W. Hamblin. Jackson: University Press of Mississippi, 1989.

———. *These Thirteen.* New York: Jonathan Cape and Harrison Smith, 1931.

———. *The Town.* New York: Random House, 1957.

———. *Uncollected Stories.* Ed. Joseph L. Blotner. New York: Random House, 1979; New York: Vintage, 1997.

———. *The Unvanquished.* New York: Random House, 1938; New York: Vintage International, 1991.

———. *The Wild Palms.* New York: Random House, 1939.

———. *William Faulkner: Early Prose and Poetry.* Ed. Carvel Collins. Boston: Little, Brown, 1962.

———. *The Wishing Tree.* New York: Random House, 1967.

Feaster, John. "Faulkner's *Old Man:* A Psychoanalytic Approach." *Modern Fiction Studies* 13.1 (1967): 89–94.

Feldstein, Richard. "Gerald Bland's Shadow." *Literature and Psychology* 31 (1981): 4–12.

Felman, Shoshana. "To Open a Question." *Literature and Psychoanalysis: The Question of Reading Otherwise.* Ed. Shoshana Felman. Baltimore: Johns Hopkins University Press, 1980. 5–10.

Ferrer, Daniel. "*In Omnis Iam Vocabuli Mortem:* Representation of Absence: The Subject of Representation and Absence in William Faulkner's *As I Lay Dying.*" *Oxford Literary Review* 5 (1982): 21–36.

Fetterley, Judith. *The Resisting Reader: A Feminist Approach to American Fiction.* Bloomington: Indiana University Press, 1978.

Feuerlicht, Ignace. "Christ Figures in Literature." *Person* 48 (October 1967): 461–72.

Fiedler, Leslie. *Love and Death in the American Novel.* Rev. ed. New York: Stein and Day, 1966.

———. "Pop Goes the Faulkner: In Quest of *Sanctuary.*" *Faulkner and Popular Culture: Faulkner and Yoknapatawpha, 1988.* Ed. Doreen Fowler and Ann J. Abadie. Jackson: University Press of Mississippi, 1990. 75–92.

Fiore, R. "Funnybook Roulette." *Comics Journal* 107 (April 1986): 41.

Fisher, Marvin. "The World of Faulkner's Children." *University of Kansas City Review* 27 (October 1960): 13–18.

Flores, Ralph. *The Rhetoric of Doubtful Authority.* Ithaca: Cornell University Press, 1984.

Foerst, Jenny Jennings. "The Psychic Wholeness and Corrupt Text of Rosa Coldfield, 'Author and Victim Too' of *Absalom, Absalom!*" *Faulkner Journal.* 4.1–2 (Fall 1988/Spring 1989): 37–53.

Folks, Jeffrey J. "William Faulkner and the Silent Film." *Southern Quarterly* 19 (1981): 171–82.

"Footnotes." *Chronicle of Higher Education,* 15 July 1987: 4.

Forrer, Richard. "*Absalom, Absalom:* Story-telling as a Mode of Transcendence." *Southern Literary Journal* 9.1 (1976): 22–46.

Fowler, Doreen. "Faith as a Unifying Principle in Faulkner's *Light in August.*" *Tennessee Studies in Literature* 21 (1976): 49–57.

———. *Faulkner: The Return of the Repressed.* Charlottesville: University Press of Virginia, 1997.

———. "'I am dying': Faulkner's Hightower and the Oedipal Moment." *Faulkner Journal* 9 (1994): 139–48.

———. "'I want to go home': Faulkner, Gender, and Death." *Faulkner and Gender: Faulkner and Yoknapatawpha, 1994.* Ed. Donald M. Kartiganer and Ann J. Abadie. Jackson: University Press of Mississippi, 1996. 3–19.

———. "Joe Christmas and 'Womanshenegro.'" *Faulkner and Women: Faulkner and Yoknapatawpha, 1985.* Ed. Doreen Fowler and Ann J. Abadie. Jackson: University Press of Mississippi, 1986. 144–161.

———. "'Little Sister Death': *The Sound and the Fury* and the Denied Unconscious." *Faulkner and Psychology: Faulkner and Yoknapatawpha, 1991.* Ed. Donald M. Kartiganer and Ann J. Abadie. Jackson: University Press of Mississippi, 1994. 3–20.

———. "Matricide and the Mother's Revenge: *As I Lay Dying.*" *Faulkner Journal* 4.1–2 (Fall 1988/Spring 1989): 113–25.

———. "The Nameless Women of *Go Down, Moses.*" *Women's Studies* 18 (1993): 525–32.

———. "The Ravished Daughter: Eleusinian Mysteries in *The Sound and the Fury.*" *Faulkner and Religion: Faulkner and Yoknapatawpha, 1989.* Ed. Doreen Fowler and Ann J. Abadie. Jackson: University Press of Mississippi, 1991. 140–56.

———. "Reading for the 'Other Side': *Beloved* and *Requiem for a Nun.*" *Unflinching Gaze: Morrison and Faulkner Re-envisioned.* Ed. Carol A. Kolmerten, Stephen M. Ross, and Judith Bryant Wittenberg. Jackson: University Press of Mississippi, 1997. 139–51.

———. "Reading the Absences: Race and Narration in Faulkner's *Absalom, Absalom!*" *Faulkner at One Hundred: Retrospect and Prospect: Faulkner and Yoknapatawpha, 1997.* Ed. Donald Kartiganer and Ann J. Abadie. Jackson: University Press of Mississippi, 2000. 132–39.

———. "Revising *The Sound and the Fury: Absalom, Absalom!* and Faulkner's Postmodern Turn." *Faulkner and Postmodernism: Faulkner and Yoknapatawpha, 1999.* Ed. John N. Duvall and Ann J. Abadie. Jackson: University Press of Mississippi, 2002. 95–108.

———. "'You can't beat a woman': The Preoedipal Mother in *Light in August.*" *Faulkner Journal* 10.2 (Spring 1995): 55–64.

Fowler, Doreen, and Ann J. Abadie, eds. *Faulkner and Humor: Faulkner and Yoknapatawpha, 1984.* Jackson: University Press of Mississippi, 1986.

———, eds. *Faulkner and Popular Culture: Faulkner and Yoknapatawpha, 1988.* Jackson: University Press of Mississippi, 1990.

————, eds. *Faulkner and Race: Faulkner and Yoknapatawpha, 1986.* Jackson: University Press of Mississippi, 1987.

————, eds. *Faulkner and Religion: Faulkner and Yoknapatawpha, 1989.* Jackson: University Press of Mississippi, 1991.

————, eds. *Faulkner and Women: Faulkner and Yoknapatawpha, 1985.* Jackson: University Press of Mississippi, 1986.

————, eds. *Faulkner: International Perspectives: Faulkner and Yoknapatawpha, 1982.* Jackson: University Press of Mississippi, 1984.

————, eds. *Fifty Years of Yoknapatawpha: Faulkner and Yoknapatawpha, 1979.* Jackson: University Press of Mississippi, 1980.

————, eds. *New Directions in Faulkner Studies: Faulkner and Yoknapatawpha, 1983.* Jackson: University Press of Mississippi, 1984.

Frann, Michel. "Faulkner as a Lesbian Author." *Faulkner Journal* 4.1–2 (Fall 1988/Spring 1989): 5–19.

Frazer, Sir James George. *The Golden Bough.* Abridged ed. New York: Macmillan, 1963.

Freedman, William A. "The Technique of Isolation in *The Sound and the Fury.*" *Mississippi Quarterly* 15 (1962): 21–26.

Freud, Sigmund. *The Standard Edition of the Complete Psychological Works of Freud.* Ed. and trans. James Strachey. 24 vols. London: Hogarth Press, 1961. 1953–74.

Friedman, Susan Stanford. "Definitional Excursions: The Meanings of *Modern Modernity/Modernism.*" *Modernism/Modernity* 8 (2001): 493–513.

Froehlich, Peter. "Faulkner and the Frontier Grotesque: *The Hamlet* as Southwestern Humor." *Faulkner in Cultural Context: Faulkner and Yoknapatawpha, 1995.* Ed. Donald M. Kartiganer and Ann J. Abadie. Jackson: University Press of Mississippi, 1997. 218–40.

Froula, Christina. *Modernism Body: Sex, Culture, and Joyce.* New York: Columbia University Press, 1996.

Frye, Northrop. *Anatomy of Criticism.* Princeton, NJ: Princeton University Press, 1957.

————. *Fables of Identity: Studies in Poetic Mythology.* New York: Harcourt, Brace and World, 1963.

Galanos, Iorgos. "The Metaphoricity of Memory in Faulkner's *As I Lay Dying.*" *Faulkner Journal* 5.2 (1990): 3–13.

Gantt, Patricia M. "'This Guerilla Warfare of Everyday Life': The Politics of Clothing in Faulkner's Fiction." *Mississippi Quarterly* 49 (Summer 1996): 409–23.

Garlick, H. F. "Three Patterns of Imagery in Benjy's Section of *The Sound and the Fury.*" *Journal of the Australian Modern Language Association* 52 (1979): 274–87.

Gartner, Carol B. "Faulkner in Context: Seeing 'That Evening Sun' through the Blues." *Southern Quarterly* 34.2 (Winter 1996): 50–58.

Gelfant, Blanche H. "Faulkner and Keats: The Ideality of Art in 'The Bear.'" *Southern Literary Journal* 2 (Fall 1969): 43–65.

Gergen, Kenneth. *The Saturated Self: Dilemmas of Identity in Contemporary Life.* New York: Basic Books, 1991.

Gibbons, Kathryn G. "Quentin's Shadow." *Literature and Psychology* 12 (Winter 1962): 16–24.

Gidley, Mick. "The Later Faulkner, Bergson, and God." *Mississippi Quarterly* 37 (1984): 377–83.

Gilbert, Sandra M., and Susan Gubar. *No Man's Land.* Vol 1: *The War of Words.* New Haven, CT: Yale University Press, 1988.

Glissant, Edouard. *Faulkner, Mississippi.* New York: Farrar, 1999.

Godden, Richard. "*Absalom, Absalom!* and Faulkner's Erroneous Dating of the Haitian Revolution." *Mississippi Quarterly* 47.3 (Summer 1994): 489–95.

———. "*Absalom, Absalom!,* Haiti and Labor History: Reading Unreadable Revolutions." *English Literary History* 61.3 (Fall 1994): 685–720.

———. "Call Me Nigger: Race and Speech in Faulkner's *Light in August.*" *American Studies* 14.2 (1980): 235–48.

———. "Earthing *The Hamlet,* an Anti-Ratliffian Reading." *Faulkner Journal* 14.2 (Spring 1999): 75–116.

———. "*A Fable:* Whispering about the Wars." *Faulkner Journal* 17.2 (Spring 2002): 25–88.

———. *Fictions of Labor: William Faulkner and the South's Long Revolution.* Cambridge: Cambridge University Press, 1997.

———. "Lips by 'Laus Veneris,' Breasts by 'Anactoria,'" Anecdote by William Faulkner." *Essays in Poetics* 14.1 (1989): 1–27.

Godden, Richard, and Noel Polk. "Reading the Ledgers." *Mississippi Quarterly* 55.3 (Summer 2002): 301–59.

Godden, Richard, and Pamela Rhodes. "Degraded Culture, Devalued Texts." *Faulkner and Intertextuality* Ed. Michel Gresset and Noel Polk. Jackson: University Press of Mississippi, 1985. 87–113.

Gomes, Heloísa Toller. "The Presence of Cassandra: Women in Faulkner's *Absalom, Absalom!* and José Lins do Rego's *Fogo Morto.*" *Brazilian Feminisms.* Ed. Solange Ribeiro de Oliveira and Judith Still. Nottingham, England: University of Nottingham Monographs in the Humanities, 1999. 57–67.

Gramsci, Antonio. *A Gramschi Reader: Selected Writings 1916–1935.* Ed. David Forgacs. London: Lawrence and Wishart, 2000.

Gray, Richard. *The Life of William Faulkner.* Oxford, England: Blackwell, 1994.

———. "On Privacy: William Faulkner and the Human Subject." *Faulkner and Ideology: Faulkner and Yoknapatawpha, 1992.* Ed. Donald Kartiganer and Ann J. Abadie. Jackson: University Press of Mississippi, 1995. 45–69.

Greenblatt, Stephen. "Culture." *Critical Terms for Literary Study.* Ed. Frank Lentricchia and Thomas McLaughlin. Chicago: University of Chicago Press, 1990. 225–32.

Gresset, Michel. *Fascination: Faulkner's Fiction, 1919–1936.* Durham, NC: Duke University Press, 1989.

———. "Faulkner's Self-Portraits." *Faulkner Journal* 2.1 (Fall 1986): 2–13.

———. "Faulkner's Voice." *Faulkner's Discourse: An International Symposium.* Ed. Lothar Hönnighausen. Tübingen: Max Niemeyer Verlag, 1989. 184–94.

———. "A Public Man's Private Voice: Faulkner's Letters to Else Jonsson." *Faulkner after the Nobel Prize.* Ed. Michel Gresset and Kenzaburo Ohashi. Tokyo: Yamaguchi, 1987. 61–73.

Griffith, Bill. *Zippy.* Comic strip. *Washington Post,* 30 October 1985.

Grimwood, Michael. *Heart in Conflict: Faulkner's Struggles with Vocation.* Athens: University of Georgia Press, 1987.

Groden, Michael. "Criticism in New Composition: *Ulysses* and *The Sound and the Fury.*" *Twentieth Century Literature* 21 (1975): 265–77.

Groden, Michael, and Martin Kreiswirth, eds. *The Johns Hopkins Guide to Literary Theory and Criticism.* Baltimore: Johns Hopkins University Press, 1994.

Groensteen, Thierry. *La construction de La Cage: Autopsie d'un roman visuel.* Paris: Les Impressiones Nouvelles, 2002.

Guerard, Albert J. "*Absalom, Absalom!:* The Novel as Impressionist Art." *The Triumph of the Novel: Dickens, Dostoevsky, Faulkner.* New York: Oxford University Press, 1976. 302–39.

———. "Faulkner: Problems of Technique." *The Triumph of the Novel: Dickens, Dostoevsky, Faulkner.* New York: Oxford University Press, 1976. 204–34.

Guetti, James. *The Limits of Metaphor: A Study of Melville, Conrad, and Faulkner.* Ithaca: Cornell University Press, 1967.

Gussow, Mel. "Evoking the Quirky Genius of Faulkner." *New York Times,* 16 June 1985: H3, H10.

Gutting, Gabrielle. "The Mysteries of the Map-Maker: Faulkner, *If I Forget Thee, Jerusalem,* and the Secret of a Map." *Faulkner Journal* 8.2 (Spring 1993): 86–93.

———. *Yoknapatawpha: The Function of Geographical and Historical Facts in William Faulkner's Fictional Picture of the Deep South.* New York: Peter Lang, 1992.

Gwin, Minrose C. *Black and White Women of the Old South: The Peculiar Sisterhood in American Literature.* Knoxville: University of Tennessee Press, 1985.

———. "Did Ernest Like Gordon? Faulkner's *Mosquitoes* and the Bite of 'Gender Trouble.'" *Faulkner and Gender: Faulkner and Yoknapatawpha, 1994.* Ed. Donald M. Kartiganer and Ann J. Abadie. Jackson: University Press of Mississippi, 1996. 120–44.

———. *The Feminine and Faulkner: Reading (Beyond) Sexual Difference.* Knoxville: University of Tennessee Press, 1990.

———. "Feminism and Faulkner: Second Thoughts or, What's a radical feminist doing with a canonical male text anyway?" *Faulkner Journal* 4.1–2 (Fall 1988/Spring 1989): 55–65.

———. "*Mosquitoes'* Missing Bite: The Four Deletions." *Faulkner Journal* 9.2 (Spring 1994): 31–42.

Gwynn, Frederick L., and Joseph L. Blotner, eds. *Faulkner in the University: Class Conferences at the University of Virginia 1957–1958.* Charlottesville: University of Virginia Press, 1959.

Hahn, Stephen, and Arthur Kinney, ed. *Approaches to Teaching Faulkner's* The Sound and the Fury. New York: Modern Language Association of America, 1996.

Hale, Dorothy. "*As I Lay Dying*'s Heterogeneous Discourse." *Novel* 23 (1989): 5–23.

Hamblin, Robert W. "Carcassonne in Mississippi: Faulkner's Geography of the Imagination." *Faulkner and the Craft of Fiction: Faulkner and Yoknapatawpha, 1987.* Ed. Doreen Fowler and Ann J. Abadie. University Press of Mississippi, 1989. 148–71.

———. "The Curious Case of Faulkner's 'The De Gaulle Story.'" *Faulkner and Film.* Spec. issue of *Faulkner Journal* 16.1–2 (Fall 2000/Spring 2001): 79–86.

———. "'Like a Big Soft Fading Wheel': The Triumph of Faulkner's Art." *Faulkner at One Hundred: Retrospect and Prospect: Faulkner and Yoknapatawpha, 1997.* Ed. Donald Kartiganer and Ann J. Abadie. Jackson: University Press of Mississippi, 2000. 272–84.

———. "'Saying No to Death': Toward William Faulkner's Theory of Fiction." *"A Cosmos of My Own": Faulkner and Yoknapatawpha, 1980.* Ed. Doreen Fowler and Ann J. Abadie. Jackson, MS: University Press of Mississippi, 1981. 3–35.

Hamblin, Robert W., and Louis Daniel Brodsky, comps. *Selections from the William Faulkner Collection of Louis Daniel Brodsky: A Descriptive Catalogue.* Charlottesville: University of Virginia Press, 1979.

Hamblin, Robert W., and Charles A. Peek, eds. *A William Faulkner Encyclopedia.* Westport, CT: Greenwood, 1999.

Handley, George B. "Oedipal and Prodigal Returns in Alejo Carpentier and William Faulkner." *Mississippi Quarterly* 52 (1999): 421–58.

Hannon, Charles. "Race Fantasies: The Filming of *Intruder in the Dust.*" *Faulkner in Cultural Context: Faulkner and Yoknapatawpha, 1995.* Ed. Donald M. Kartiganer and Ann J. Abadie. Jackson: University Press of Mississippi, 1997. 263–83.

———. "Signification, Simulation, and Containment in *If I Forget Thee, Jerusalem.*" *Faulkner and Cultural Studies.* Spec. issue of *Faulkner Journal* 7.1–2 (Fall 1991/Spring 1992): 133–50.

Hardin, Michael. "Freud's Family: The Journey to Bury the Death Drive in Faulkner's *As I Lay Dying.*" *Southern Studies* 5 (1994): 95–103.

Harrington, Evans, and Ann J. Abadie, eds. *Faulkner, Modernism, and Film: Faulkner and Yoknapatawpha, 1978.* Jackson: University Press of Mississippi, 1979.

———, eds. *The Maker and the Myth: Faulkner and Yoknapatawpha, 1977.* Jackson: University Press of Mississippi, 1978.

———, eds. *The South and Faulkner's Yoknapatawpha: The Actual and the Apocryphal: Faulkner and Yoknapatawpha, 1976.* Jackson: University Press of Mississippi, 1977.

Hassan, Ihab. *The Dismemberment of Orpheus: Toward a Postmodern Literature.* New York: Oxford University Press, 1982.

———. "The Privations of Postmodernism: Faulkner as Exemplar (A Meditation in Ten Parts)." *Faulkner and Postmodernism: Faulkner and Yoknapatawpha, 1999.* Ed. John N. Duvall and Ann J. Abadie. Jackson: University Press of Mississippi, 2002. 1–18.

Healy, Jack J. "Structuralism Applied: American Literature and its Subordination to Structure." *ARIEL* 14.2 (1983): 35–51.

Hemenway, Robert. "Enigmas of Being in *As I Lay Dying.*" *Modern Fiction Studies* 16 (1970): 133–46.

Henninger, Katherine. "'It's a outrage': Pregancy and Abortion in Faulkner's Fiction of the Thirties." *Faulkner Journal* 12.1 (1996): 23–41.

Hepburn, Kenneth W. "Faulkner's *Mosquitoes:* A Poetic Turning Point." *Twentieth Century Literature* 17 (1971): 19–28.

Herget, Winfred. "The Poetics of Negation in Faulkner's *Absalom, Absalom!*" *Faulkner's Discourse: An International Symposium.* Ed. Lothar Hönnighausen. Tübingen: Max Niemeyer Verlag, 1989. 33–37.

Heywood, Leslie. "The Shattered Glass: The Blank Space of Being in *Absalom, Absalom!*" *Faulkner Journal* 3.2 (1988): 12–23.

Hicks, Gina. "Reterritorializing Desire: The Failure of Ceremony in *Absalom, Absalom!*" *Faulkner Journal* 12.2 (Spring 1997): 23–39.

Hicks, Granville. *The Great Tradition: An Interpretation of American Literature since the Civil War.* New York: Macmillan, 1935.

Hill, Robert, Jr. *Tennyson's Poetry: A Norton Critical Edition.* 2nd ed. New York: Norton, 1971.

Hite, Molly. "Modernist Design, Postmodernist Paranoia: Reading *Absalom, Absalom!* with *Gravity's Rainbow.*" *Faulkner and Postmodernism: Faulkner and Yoknapatawpha, 1999.* Ed. John N. Duvall and Ann J. Abadie. Jackson: University Press of Mississippi, 2002. 57–80.

Hlavsa, Virginia V. James. *Faulkner and the Thoroughly Modern Novel.* Charlottesville: University Press of Virginia, 1991.

Hoag, Ronald Wesley. "Ends and Loose Ends: The Triptych Conclusion in *Light in August.*" *Modern Fiction Studies* 31 (1985): 675–90.

Hoffman, Frederick J. *The Twenties: American Writing in the Postwar Decade.* New York: Free Press, 1962. 246–49.

———. *William Faulkner.* New York: Twayne, 1966.

Hoffman, Frederick J., and Olga W. Vickery, eds. *William Faulkner: Three Decades of Criticism.* New York: Harcourt, Brace, 1963.

Hoffman, Gerhard. "*Absalom, Absalom!:* A Postmodernist Approach." *Faulkner's Discourse: An International Symposium.* Ed. Lothar Hönnighausen. Tübingen: Max Niemeyer Verlag, 1989. 276–92.

Holditch, W. Kenneth. "The Brooding Air of the Past." *Literary New Orleans: Essays and Meditations.* Ed. Richard S. Kennedy. Baton Rouge: Louisiana State University Press, 1992.

———. "William Spratling, William Faulkner, and Other Famous Creoles." *Mississippi Quarterly* 51.3 (Summer 1998): 423–34.

Holland, Norman N. "Fantasy and Defense in Faulkner's 'A Rose for Emily.'" *Hartford Studies in Literature* 4 (1972): 1–35.

———. *Five Readers Reading.* New Haven, CT: Yale University Press, 1975.

Holman, C. Hugh. "Faulkner's August Avatars." *Windows on the World: Essays on American Social Fiction.* Knoxville: University of Tennessee Press, 1979. 129–43.

Hönnighausen, Lothar. *Faulkner: Masks and Metaphors.* Jackson: University Press of Mississippi, 1997.

———. "Faulkner Rewriting the Indian Removal." *Rewriting the South: History and Fiction.* Ed. Lothar Hönnighausen and Valeria Gennaro Lerda. Tubingen: Francke, 1993. 335–43.

———, ed. *Faulkner's Discourse: An International Symposium.* Tübingen: Max Niemeyer Verlag, 1989.

———. "Faulkner, the Role-Player." *Faulkner at One Hundred: Retrospect and Prospect: Faulkner and Yoknapatawpha, 1997.* Ed. Donald M. Kartiganer and Ann J. Abadie. Jackson: University Press of Mississippi, 2000. 12–17.

———. *William Faulkner: The Art of Stylization in his Early Graphic and Literary Work.* Cambridge: Cambridge University Press, 1987.

Hönnighausen, Lothar, and Valeria Gennaro Lerda, eds. *Rewriting the South: History and Fiction.* Tubingen: Francke, 1993.

Hopper, Vincent F. "Faulkner's Paradise Lost." *Virginia Quarterly Review* 23 (Summer 1947): 405–20.

Horsford, Howard. "Faulkner's (Mostly) Unreal Indians in Early Mississippi History." *American Literature* 64.2 (1992): 311–30.

Howe, Irving. *William Faulkner: A Critical Study.* Chicago: University of Chicago Press, 1951; New York: Vintage, 1951; 2nd ed. New York: Vintage Books, 1962.

Howell, Elmo. "William Faulkner and the Mississippi Indians." *Georgia Review* 21 (Fall 1967): 386–87.

Howell, John M. "Faulkner's Prufrock, and Agamemnon: Horses, Hell, and High Water." *Faulkner and the Unappeased Imagination: A Collection of Critical Essays.* Ed. Glenn O. Carey. Albany: Whitson Publishing, 1980. 213–29.

Humphrey, Robert. *Stream of Consciousness in the Modern Novel.* Berkeley: University of California Press, 1955.

Hustis, Harriet. "Masculinity As/In Comic Performance in *As I Lay Dying* and *The Sound and the Fury.*" *Faulkner Journal* 15.1–2 (Fall 1999/Spring 2000): 107–23.

Hutcheon, Linda. *The Poetics of Postmodernism: History, Theory, Fiction.* New York: Routledge, 1988.

"I Know What You Are Thinking." Greeting card. Kingman, KS: Happy Time Greetings, [c. 1974].

Inge, M. Thomas, ed. *Conversations with William Faulkner.* Jackson: University Press of Mississippi, 1999.

———. "Faulkner Reads the Funny Papers." *Comics as Culture.* Jackson: University Press of Mississippi, 1990. 78–99.

———. Introduction. *Handbook of American Popular Culture.* Ed. M. Thomas Inge. 2nd ed. 3 vols. Westport, CT: Greenwood Press, 1989. xxi–xxxiii.

Irigaray, Luce. *The Irigaray Reader.* Ed. Margaret Whitford. Oxford, England: Blackwell, 1991.

Irwin, John T. *Doubling and Incest/Repetition and Revenge: A Speculative Reading of Faulkner.* Baltimore: Johns Hopkins University Press, 1975.

———. "Horace Benbow and the Myth of Narcissa." *Faulkner and Psychology: Faulkner and Yoknapatawpha, 1991.* Ed. Donald M. Kartiganer and Ann J. Abadie. Jackson: University Press of Mississippi, 1994. 242–71.

———. "Not the Having but the Wanting: Faulkner's Lost Loves." *Faulkner at One Hundred: Retropsect and Prospect: Faulkner and Yoknapatawpha, 1997.* Ed. Donald M. Kartiganer and Ann J. Abadie. Jackson: University Press of Mississippi, 2000. 154–63.

Jameson, Fredric. Foreword. *The Postmodern Condition: A Report on Knowledge.* By Jean-François Lyotard. Minneapolis: University of Minneapolis Press, 1984. vii–xxi.

———. *Postmodernism, or, The Cultural Logic of Late Capitalism.* Durham, NC: Duke University Press, 1991.

Jehlen, Myra. *Class and Character in Faulkner's South.* New York: Columbia University Press, 1976.

———. "Gender." *Critical Terms for Literary Study.* Ed. Frank Lentricchia and Thomas McLaughlin. Chicago: University of Chicago Press, 1990. 263–73.

Jenkins, Lee. *Faulkner and Black-White Relations: A Psychoanalytic Approach.* New York: Columbia University Press, 1981.

———. "Psychoanalytic Conceptualizations of Characterization, Or Nobody Laughs in *Light in August.*" *Faulkner and Psychology: Faulkner and Yoknapatawpha, 1991.* Ed. Donald M. Kartiganer and Ann J. Abadie. Jackson: University Press of Mississippi, 1994. 189–218.

Johnson, Julie M. "The Theory of Relativity in Modern Literature: An Overview and *The Sound and the Fury.*" *Journal of Modern Literature* 10 (1983): 217–30.

Jones, Ann Goodwyn. "'The Kotex Age': Women, Popular Culture, and *The Wild Palms.*" *Faulkner and Popular Culture: Faulkner and Yoknapatawpha, 1988.* Ed. Doreen Fowler and Ann J. Abadie. Jackson: University Press of Mississippi, 1990. 142–62.

———. "'Like a Virgin': Faulkner, Sexual Cultures, and the Romance of Resistance." *Faulkner in Cultural Context: Faulkner and Yoknapatawpha, 1995.* Ed. Donald M. Kartiganer and Ann J. Abadie. Jackson: University Press of Mississippi, 1997. 39–74.

———. "Male Fantasies?: Faulkner's War Stories and the Construction of Gender." *Faulkner and Psychology: Faulkner and Yoknapatawpha, 1991.* Ed. Donald M. Kartiganer and Ann J. Abadie. Jackson: University Press of Mississippi, 1994. 21–55.

———. "Penetrating Faulkner: Masculinity and Discourse in Selected Short Fictions." *William Faulkner's Short Fiction: An International Symposium.* Ed. Hans H.

Skei. Proceedings from the 1995 International Faulkner Symposium. Oslo, Norway: Solum, 1997. 38–48.

Joyce, James. *Finnegans Wake.* 1939. New York: Penguin, 1976.

———. *A Portrait of the Artist as a Young Man.* 1916. New York: Vintage, 1970.

———. *Ulysses.* 1922. New York: Random House, 1961.

Juillard, André. *Tandis que j'agonise de William Faulkner.* Paris: Futuropolis/Gallimard, 1991.

Jung, Carl Gustav. *The Archetypes and the Collective Unconscious.* 2nd ed. Princeton, NJ: Princeton University Press, 1968.

———. *Two Essays on Analytical Psychology.* Princeton, NJ: Princeton University Press, 1972.

Karaganis, Joe. "Negotiating the National Voice in Faulkner's Late Work." *Arizona Quarterly* 54.4 (Winter 1998): 53–81.

Karl, Frederick. *William Faulkner: American Writer.* New York: Weidenfeld and Nicolson, 1989.

Kartiganer, Donald M. "Faulkner's Art of Repetition." *Faulkner and the Craft of Fiction: Faulkner and Yoknapatawpha, 1987.* Ed. Doreen Fowler and Ann J. Abadie. University Press of Mississippi, 1989. 21–47.

———. *The Fragile Thread: The Meaning of Form in Faulkner's Novels.* Amherst: University of Massachusetts Press, 1979.

———. "Process and Product: A Study of Modern Literary Form." *Massachusetts Review* 12 (1971): 801–16.

———. "The Role of Myth in *Absalom, Absalom!*" *Modern Fiction Studies* 9 (Winter 1964): 357–69.

———. "*The Sound and the Fury* and Faulkner's Quest for Form." *English Literary History* 37 (1970): 613–39.

———. "'What I Chose to Be': Freud, Faulkner, Joe Christmas, and the Abandonment of Design." *Faulkner and Psychology: Faulkner and Yoknapatawpha, 1991.* Ed. Donald M. Kartiganer and Ann J. Abadie. Jackson: University Press of Mississippi, 1994. 299–314.

Kartiganer, Donald M., and Ann J. Abadie, eds. *Faulkner and the Artist: Faulkner and Yoknapatawpha, 1993.* Jackson: University Press of Mississippi, 1996.

———, eds. *Faulkner and Gender: Faulkner and Yoknapatawpha, 1994.* Jackson: University Press of Mississippi, 1996.

———, eds. *Faulkner and Ideology: Faulkner and Yoknapatawpha, 1992.* Jackson: University Press of Mississippi, 1995.

———, eds. *Faulkner and the Natural World: Faulkner and Yoknapatawpha, 1996.* Jackson: University Press of Mississippi, 1999.

———, eds. *Faulkner and Psychology: Faulkner and Yoknapatawpha, 1991.* Jackson: University Press of Mississippi, 1994.

———, eds. *Faulkner at One Hundred: Retrospect and Prospect: Faulkner and Yoknapatawpha, 1997.* Jackson: University Press of Mississippi, 2000.

———, eds. *Faulkner in Cultural Context: Faulkner and Yoknapatawpha, 1995.* Jackson: University Press of Mississippi, 1997.

Kawin, Bruce F. *Faulkner and Film.* New York: Frederick Ungar, 1977.

———. *The Mind of the Novel: Reflexive Fiction and the Ineffable.* Princeton, NJ: Princeton University Press, 1982. 251–72.

———. "The Montage Element in Faulkner's Fiction." *Faulkner, Modernism, and Film: Faulkner and Yoknapatawpha, 1978.* Ed. Evans Harrington and Ann J. Abadie. University Press of Mississippi, 1979. 103–26.

———, ed. *To Have and Have Not.* Madison: University of Wisconsin Press, 1980.

Kenner, Hugh. "Faulkner and Joyce." *Faulkner, Modernism, and Film: Faulkner and Yoknapatawpha, 1978.* Ed. Evans Harrington and Ann J. Abadie. Jackson: University Press of Mississippi, 1979. 20–33.

———. "Faulkner and the Avant-Garde." *Faulkner, Modernism, and Film: Faulkner and Yoknapatawpha, 1978.* Ed. Evans Harrington and Ann J. Abadie. Jackson: University Press of Mississippi, 1979. 182–96.

———. "The Last Novelist." *A Homemade World: The American Modernist Writers.* New York: Knopf, 1975. 194–221.

Kerr, Elizabeth M. "The Women of Yoknapatawpha." *University of Mississippi Studies in English* 15 (1978): 83–100.

———. *Yoknapatawpha: Faulkner's Little Postage Stamp of Native Soil.* New York: Fordham, 1969.

Kidd, Millie M. "The Dialogic Perspective in William Faulkner's *The Hamlet.*" *Mississippi Quarterly* 44.3 (1991): 309–20.

King, Richard H. "Memory and Tradition." *Faulkner and the Southern Renaissance: Faulkner and Yoknapatawpha 1981.* Ed. Doreen Fowler and Ann J. Abadie. Jackson: University Press of Mississippi, 1982. 138–57.

King, Vincent Allan. "The Wages of Pulp: The Use and Abuse of Fiction in Faulkner's *The Wild Palms.*" *Mississippi Quarterly* 51 (Summer 1998): 503–25.

Kinney, Arthur F. "Faulkner and Racism." *Connotations* 3.3 (1993/1994): 265–78.

———. *Faulkner's Narrative Poetics: Style as Vision.* Amherst: University of Massachusetts Press, 1978.

———. "Faulkner's Other Others." *Faulkner at One Hundred: Retrospect and Prospect: Faulkner and Yoknapatawpha, 1997.* Ed. Donald Kartiganer and Ann J. Abadie. Jackson: University Press of Mississippi, 2000. 195–203.

Kloss, Robert J. "Faulkner's *As I Lay Dying.*" *American Imago* 38 (1981): 429–44.

Knonagel, Axel. "Modernity and Mechanization: *Pylon* and the Novels of John Passos." *Amerikastudien* 42 (1997): 591–600.

Kodat, Catherine Gunther. "Pulp Fictions: Reading Faulkner for the Twenty-first Century." *Faulkner Journal* 12.2 (Spring 1997): 69–86.

———. "Writing *A Fable* for America." *Faulkner in America: Faulkner and Yoknapatawpha, 1998.* Ed. Joseph R. Urgo and Ann J. Abadie. Jackson: University Press of Mississippi, 2001. 82–97.

Kohler, Dayton. "*A Fable:* The Novel as Myth." *College English* 16 (May 1955): 471–78.

Kolmerten, Carol A., Stephen M. Ross, and Judith Bryant Wittenberg, eds. *Unflinching Gaze: Faulkner and Morrison Re-envisioned.* Jackson: University Press of Mississippi, 1997.

Krause, David. "Faulkner's Blues." *Studies in the Novel* 17.1 (Spring 1985): 80–94.

Kreiswirth, Martin. "Intertextuality, Transference, and Postmodernism in *Absalom, Absalom!:* The Production and Reception of Faulkner's Fictional World." *Faulkner and Postmodernism: Faulkner and Yoknapatawpha, 1999.* Ed. John N. Duvall and Ann J. Abadie. Jackson: University Press of Mississippi, 2002. 109–23.

————. "'Paradoxical and Outrageous Discrepancy': Transgression, Auto-Intertextuality, and Faulkner's Yoknapatawpha." *Faulkner and the Artist: Faulkner and Yoknapatawpha, 1993.* Ed. Donald M. Kartiganer and Ann J. Abadie. Jackson: University Press of Mississippi, 1996. 161–80.

————. *William Faulkner: The Making of a Novelist.* Athens: University of Georgia Press, 1983.

Kreyling, Michael. *Inventing Southern Literature.* Jackson: University Press of Mississippi, 1998.

Kristeva, Julia. *The Kristeva Reader.* Ed. Toril Moi. New York: Columbia University Press, 1986.

Kronenberger, Louis. "The World of William Faulkner." *Nation,* 13 April 1940: 481–82.

Kubie, Lawrence S. "William Faulkner's *Sanctuary:* An Analysis." *Saturday Review of Literature* 11 (Oct. 20, 1934): 218–25. Reprinted in J. Douglas Canfield, ed. *Twentieth Century Interpretations of* Sanctuary. Englewood Cliffs, NJ: Prentice-Hall. 25–31.

Kunkel, Francis L. "Christ Symbolism in Faulkner: Prevalence of the Human." *Renascence* 17 (Spring 1965): 148–56.

Kuyk, Dirk, Jr., *Sutpen's Design: Interpreting Faulkner's* Absalom, Absalom! Charlottesville: University Press of Virginia, 1990.

Labro, Philippe. *The Foreign Student.* New York: Available Press, 1988.

Lacan, Jacques. *Écrits: A Selection.* Trans. Alan Sheridan. 1966. New York: Norton, 1977.

————. *Feminine Sexuality: Jacques Lacan and the "École Freudienne."* Ed. Juliet Mitchell. Trans. Jacqueline Rose. New York: Norton, 1982.

Ladd, Barbara, "'Philosophers and Other Gynecologists': Women and the Polity in *Requiem for a Nun.*" *Mississippi Quarterly* 52 (Summer 1999): 483–501.

Landers, Ann. "Ann Landers." *Washington Post,* 31 January 2001: C11.

Larsen, Eric E. "The Barrier of Language: The Irony of Language in Faulkner." *Modern Fiction Studies* 12 (1967): 19–31.

Lasater, Alice E. "The Breakdown in Communication in the Twentieth-Century Novel." *Southern Quarterly* 12 (1973): 1–14.

Lavie, Marie-José. "Barton Fink and William Faulkner." *Joel and Ethan Coen: Blood Siblings.* Ed. Paul A. Woods. London: Plexus, 2000. 104–7.

Layman, Lewis. "The Influence of the Cyclops Episode of *Ulysses* on the Jason Section of *The Sound and the Fury.*" *Canadian Journal of Irish Studies* 13 (1987): 61–74.

Leary, Lewis. *William Faulkner of Yoknapatawpha County.* New York: Thomas Y. Crowell, 1973.

Leavis, F. R. "Dostoevsky or Dickens?" *Scrutiny* 2 (June 1933): 91–93.

Lecercle-Sweet, Ann. "The Chip and the Chink: The Dying of the 'I' in *As I Lay Dying.*" *Faulkner Journal* 2 (1986): 46–61.

Lester, Cheryl. "*If I Forget Thee, Jerusalem* and the Great Migration: History in Black and White." *Faulkner in Cultural Context: Faulkner and Yoknapatawpha, 1995.* Ed. Donald M. Kartiganer and Ann J. Abadie. Jackson: University Press of Mississippi, 1997. 191–217.

————. "Racial Awareness and Arrested Development: *The Sound and the Fury* and the Great Migration." *The Cambridge Companion to William Faulkner.* Ed. Philip Weinstein. Cambridge: Cambridge University Press, 1995. 123–45.

————. "To Market, To Market: *The Portable Faulkner.*" *Criticism* 29 (1987): 371–89.

Levenson, Michael. *A Genealogy of Modernism: A Study of English Literary Doctrine 1908–1922.* Cambridge: Cambridge University Press, 1984.

Levine, David. *Pens and Needles: Literary Caricatures.* Boston: Gambit, 1969.

Levins, Lynn Gartrell. *Faulkner's Heroic Design: The Yoknapatawpha Novels.* Athens: University of Georgia Press, 1976.

Lévi-Strauss, Claude. *Structural Anthropology.* Trans. Claire Jacobson and Brooke Grundfest Schoepf. Garden City, NY: Doubleday Anchor, 1967.; Trans. Monique Layton. New York: Peguin, 1978.

Lewis, R.W.B. *The American Adam: Innocence, Tragedy, and Tradition in the Nineteenth Century.* Chicago: University of Chicago Press, 1955.

———. "The Hero in the New World: William Faulkner's 'The Bear.'" *Kenyon Review* 13 (Autumn 1951): 641–60.

Li, Stephanie. "*Intruder in the Dust* from Novel to Movie: The Development of Chick Mallison." *Faulkner and Film.* Spec. issue of *Faulkner Journal* 16.1–2 (Fall 2000/Spring 2001): 105–18.

Libby, Anthony. "Conceptual Space: The Politics of Modernism." *Chicago Review* 34.2 (1984): 11–26.

Liles, Don Merrick. "William Faulkner's *Absalom, Absalom!:* An Exegesis of the Homoerotic Configurations in the Novel." *Journal of Homosexuality* 8 (1983): 99–111.

Lilly, Paul R., Jr. "Caddy and Addie: Speakers of Faulkner's Impeccable Language." *Journal of Narrative Technique* 3 (1973): 170–83.

Lind, Ilse Dusoir. "The Design and Meaning of *Absalom, Absalom!*" *PMLA* 70 (December 1955): 887–912.

———. "The Effect of Painting on Faulkner's Poetic Form." *Faulkner, Modernism, and Film: Faulkner and Yoknapatawpha, 1978.* Ed. Evans Harrington and Ann J. Abadie. Jackson: University Press of Mississippi, 1979. 127–48.

———. "Faulkner's Women." *The Maker and the Myth: Faulkner and Yoknapatawpha, 1977.* Ed. Evans Harrington and Ann J. Abadie. Jackson: University Press of Mississippi, 1978. 89–104.

———. "The Mutual Relevance of Faulkner Studies and Women's Studies: An Interdisciplinary Inquiry." *Faulkner and Women: Faulkner and Yoknapatawpha, 1985.* Ed. Doreen Fowler and Ann J. Abadie. Jackson: University Press of Mississippi, 1986. 21–40.

Litz, Walton. "William Faulkner's Moral Vision." *Southwest Review* 37 (Summer 1952): 200–9.

Liu, Jun. "Nihilists and Their Relations: A Nietzschean Approach to Teaching *The Sound and the Fury.*" *Approaches to Teaching Faulkner's* The Sound and the Fury. Ed. Stephen Hahn and Arthur F. Kinney. New York: Modern Language Association of America, 1996. 89–95.

Llewellyn, Dara. "Waves of Time in Faulkner's *Go Down, Moses.*" *Studies in Short Fiction* 33 (1996): 497–513.

Lockyer, Judith. *Ordered by Words: Language and Narration in the Novels of William Faulkner.* Carbondale: Southern Illinois University Press, 1991.

Loebel, Thomas. "Love of Masculinity." *Faulkner Journal* 15 (1999/2000): 83–106.

London, Bette. *The Appropriated Voice: Narrative Authority in Conrad, Forster, and Woolf.* Ann Arbor: University of Michigan Press, 1990.

Lovati, Giorgio. "Faulkner, Soldati and America." *Living Age,* September 1936: 71–72.

Lovett, Robert Morss. "Ferocious Faulkner." *Nation,* 4 February 1939: 153.

Lurie, Peter. "'Some Trashy Myth of Reality's Escape': Romance, History, and Film Viewing in *Absalom, Absalom!*" *American Literature* 73.3 (September 2001): 563–97.

Lynch, Jacquelyn Scott. "Postwar Play: Gender Performatives in Faulkner's *Soldiers' Pay.*" *Faulkner Journal* 14.1 (Fall 1998): 3–20.

Lyotard, Jean-François. *The Postmodern Explained: Correspondence 1982–1984.* Trans. Julian Pefanis and Morgan Thomas. Minneapolis: University of Minnesota Press, 1993.

Mahaffey, Vicki. "Heirs of Yeats: Eire as Female Poets Revise Her." *The Future of Modernism.* Ed. Hugh Witemeyer. Ann Arbor: University of Michigan Press, 1997. 101–17.

———. "Modernist Theory and Modernist Criticism." *The Johns Hopkins Guide to Literary Theory and Criticism.* Baltimore: Johns Hopkins Press, 1994. 512–15.

Maloska, Eugene T., and Albert Buranelli. *Fifty American Authors: The Educational Crossword Puzzle Series.* Vol. 1. New York: Pocket Books, 1963.

Malraux, André. "Préface." *Sanctuaire.* Paris: Gallimard, 1933.

Marlette, Doug. *Kudzu.* Comic strip. W*ashington Post,* 12 April 1997.

Marshall, Alexander J., III. "The Dream Deferred: William Faulkner's Metaphysics of Absence." *Faulkner and Religion: Faulkner and Yoknapatawpha, 1989.* Ed. Doreen Fowler and Ann J. Abadie. Jackson: University Press of Mississippi, 1991. 177–92.

Martin, Jay. "Faulkner's 'Male Commedia': The Triumph of Manly Grief." *Faulkner and Psychology: Faulkner and Yoknapatawpha, 1991.* Ed. Donald M. Kartiganer and Ann J. Abadie. Jackson: University Press of Mississippi, 1994. 123–64.

———. "'The Whole Burden of Man's History and His Impossible Heart's Desire': The Early Life of William Faulkner." *American Literature* 53 (January 1982): 123–64.

Martin, Reginald. "Faulkner's Conflicting Views of the Equality of Color." *Obsidian II* 4.2 (1989): 1–11.

Marx, Karl. "Money and Alienated Man" and "Free Human Production." *The Writings of the Young Marx on Philosophy and Society.* Ed. and trans. Loyd D. Easton and Kurt H. Guddat. New York: Doubleday, 1967. 265–82.

Matthews, John T. "*As I Lay Dying* and the Machine Age." *boundary 2* 19.1 (Spring 1992): 69–94.

———. "The Autograph of Violence in Faulkner's *Pylon.*" *Southern Literature and Literary Theory.* Ed. Jefferson Humphries. Athens: University of Georgia Press, 1990. 247–69.

———. "Faulkner and the Culture Industry." *The Cambridge Companion to William Faulkner.* Ed. Philip M. Weinstein. Cambridge: Cambridge University Press, 1995: 51–74.

———. "Faulkner and Proletarian Literature." *Faulkner in Cultural Context: Faulkner and Yoknapatawpha, 1995.* Ed. Donald M. Kartiganer and Ann J. Abadie. Jackson: University Press of Mississippi, 1997. 166–90.

———. "Faulkner's Stories and New Deal Interference." *William Faulkner's Short Fiction: An International Symposium.* Ed. Hans H. Skei. Proceedings from the 1995 International Faulkner Symposium. Oslo, Norway: Solum, 1997. 222–29.

———. "The Marriage of Speaking and Hearing in *Absalom, Absalom!*" *English Literary History* 47 (1980): 575–94.

———. *The Play of Faulkner's Language.* Ithaca: Cornell University Press, 1982.

———. "The Rhetoric of Commitment in Faulkner." *Faulkner's Discourse: An International Symposium.* Ed. Lothar Hönnighausen. Tübingen: Max Niemeyer Verlag, 1989. 55–67.

——— "The Sacrifice of History in the New Criticism of Cleanth Brooks." *Rewriting the South: History and Fiction.* Ed. Lothar Hönnighausen and Valeria Gennaro Lerda. Tubingen: Francke, 1993. 210–18.

———. "Shortened Stories: Faulkner and the Market." *Faulkner and the Short Story* Ed. Evans Harrington and Ann J. Abadie. Jackson: University Press of Mississippi, 1992. 3–37.

———. "Whose America? Faulkner, Modernism, and National Identity." *Faulkner at One Hundred: Retrospect and Prospect: Faulkner and Yoknapatawpha, 1997.* Ed. Donald M. Kartiganer and Ann J. Abadie. Jackson: University Press of Mississippi, 2000. 70–92.

McDonald, Heather. *Faulkner's Bicycle.* 1985. New York: Samuel French, 1994.

McGee, Patrick. "Gender and Generation in Faulkner's 'The Bear.'" *Faulkner Journal* 1 (1985): 46–54.

McHale, Brian. "Modernist Reading, Post-Modern Text: The Case of *Gravity's Rainbow.*" *Poetics Today* 1 (1979): 85–110.

———. *Postmodernist Fiction.* New York: Methuen, 1987.

McHaney, Thomas L. "At Play in the Fields of Freud: Faulkner and Misquotation." *Faulkner: His Contemporaries, and His Posterity.* Ed. Waldemar Zacharasiewicz. Tübingen, Germany: Francke, 1993. 64–76.

———. "Faulkner and Modernism: Why Does It Matter?" *New Directions in Faulkner Studies: Faulkner and Yoknapatawpha, 1983.* Ed. Doreen Fowler and Ann J. Abadie. Jackson: University Press of Mississippi, 1984. 37–60.

———. "The Modernism of *Soldiers' Pay.*" *William Faulkner: Materials, Studies, and Criticism* 3.1 (1980): 16–30.

———. "Oversexing the Natural World: *Mosquitoes* and *If I Forget Thee, Jerusalem* [*The Wild Palms*]." *Faulkner and the Natural World: Faulkner and Yoknapatawpha, 1996.* Ed. Donald Kartiganer and Ann J. Abadie. Jackson: University Press of Mississippi, 1999. 19–44.

———. "Robinson Jeffers' 'Tamar' and *The Sound and the Fury.*" *Mississippi Quarterly* 22 (Summer 1969): 261–63.

———. "What Faulkner Read at the P.O." *Faulkner at One Hundred: Retrospect and Prospect: Faulkner and Yoknapatawpha, 1997.* Ed. Donald A. Kartiganer and Ann J. Abadie. Jackson: University Press of Mississippi, 2000. 180–87.

———. *William Faulkner's* The Wild Palms*: A Study.* Jackson: University Press of Mississippi, 1975.

McHugh, Patrick. "The Birth of Tragedy from the Spirit of the Blues: Philosophy and History in *If I Forget Thee, Jerusalem.*" *Faulkner Journal* 14 (1999): 57–74.

McKee, Patricia. "Playing White Men in *Light in August.*" *Producing American Races: Henry James, William Faulkner, Toni Morrison.* Ed. Patricia McKee. Durham, NC: Duke University Press, 1999. 123–45.

———. "Self-Division as Racial Divide: *The Sound and the Fury.*" *Producing American Races: Henry James, William Faulkner, and Toni Morrison.* Ed. Patricia McKee. Durham: Duke University Press, 1999. 99–122.

McKenna, Kristine. "Playboy Interview: Joel and Ethan Coen." *Playboy* 48.11 (November 2001): 63–74, 168–69.

McKinley, Gena. "*Light in August:* A Novel of Passing?" *Faulkner in Cultural Context: Faulkner and Yoknapatawpha, 1995.* Ed. Donald M. Kartiganer and Ann J. Abadie. Jackson: University Press of Mississippi, 1997. 148–66.

McMillen, Neil R., and Noel Polk. "Faulkner and Lynching." *Faulkner Journal* 8.1 (Fall 1992): 3–14.

McPherson, Karen. "*Absalom, Absalom!:* Telling Scratches." *Modern Fiction Studies* 33 (1987): 431–50.

Meindl, Deiter. "Some Epistemological and Esthetic Implications of William Faulkner's Discourse." *Faulkner's Discourse: An International Symposium.* Ed. Lothar Hönnighausen. Tübingen: Max Niemeyer Verlag, 1989. 149–58.

Meisel, Perry. *The Myth of the Modern: A Study in British Literature and Criticism after 1850.* New Haven, CT: Yale University Press, 1987.

Mellard, James M. "The Biblical Rhythm of *Go Down, Moses.*" *Mississippi Quarterly* 20 (Summer 1967): 135–47.

———. "Lacan and Faulkner: A Post-Freudian Analysis of Humor in the Fiction." *Faulkner and Humor: Faulkner and Yoknapatawpha, 1984.* Ed. Doreen Fowler and Ann J. Abadie. Jackson: University Press of Mississippi, 1986. 195–215.

———. "Realism, Naturalism, Modernism: Residual, Dominant, and Emergent Ideologies in *As I Lay Dying.*" *Faulkner and Ideology: Faulkner and Yoknapatawpha, 1992.* Ed. Donald M. Kartiganer and Ann J. Abadie. Jackson: University Press Mississippi, 1995. 217–37.

———. "Something New and Hard and Bright: Faulkner, Ideology, and the Construction of Modernism." *Mississippi Quarterly* 48.3 (Summer 1995): 459–79.

Menakhem, Perry. "Literary Dynamics: How the Order of a Text Creates Its Meaning." *Poetics Today* 1 (1979): 35–64, 311–61.

Meriwether, James B., ed. *Essays, Speeches and Public Letters by William Faulkner.* New York: Random House, 1965.

Meriwether, James B., and Michael Millgate, eds. *Lion in the Garden: Interviews with William Faulkner 1926–1962.* New York: Random House, 1968.

Michel, Frann. "William Faulkner as a Lesbian Author." *Men Writing the Feminine: Literature, Theory, and the Question of Genders.* Ed. Thaïs E. Morgan. Albany: State University of New York, 1994. 139–54.

Miller, James E., Jr. "William Faulkner: Descent into the Vortex." *Quests Surd and Absurd: Essays in American Literature.* Chicago: University of Chicago Press, 1967. 41–65.

Miller, J. Hillis. "Ideology and Typology in Faulkner's *Absalom, Absalom!*" *Faulkner and Ideology: Faulkner and Yoknapatawpha, 1992.* Ed. Donald M. Kartiganer and Ann J. Abadie. Jackson: University Press of Mississippi, 1995. 253–76.

———. "The Two Relativisms: Point of View and Indeterminancy in the Novel *Absalom, Absalom!*" *Relativism in the Arts.* Ed. Betty Jean Craige. Athens: University of Georgia Press, 1983. 148–70.

Millgate, Michael. *The Achievement of William Faulkner.* 1963. Lincoln: University of Nebraska Press; Bison Books, 1978.

———. "Faulkner on the Literature of the First World War." *Mississippi Quarterly* 26 (1973): 387–93.

———. *William Faulkner.* New York: Grove Press, 1961.

———, ed. *New Essays on* Light in August. New York: Cambridge University Press, 1987.

Miner, Ward L. *The World of William Faulkner.* New York: Grove Press, 1952.

Minnick, Cheryl. "Faulkner and Gender: An Annotated Select Bibliography (1982–1994)." *Mississippi Quarterly* 48.3 (Summer 1995): 524–53.

Minter, David. "Faulkner, Childhood, and the Making of *The Sound and the Fury.*" *American Literature* 51 (November 1979): 376–93.

———. *William Faulkner: His Life and His Work.* Baltimore: Johns Hopkins University Press, 1980.

Moore, Kathleen. "Jason Compson and the Mother Complex." *Mississippi Quarterly* 53.4 (2000): 533–50.

Moreland, Richard C. "Faulkner and Modernism." *The Cambridge Companion to William Faulkner.* Ed. Philip M. Weinstein. Cambridge: Cambridge University Press, 1995. 17–30.

———. *Faulkner and Modernism: Rereading and Rewriting.* Madison: University of Wisconsin Press, 1990.

Morris, Wesley. *Friday's Footprint: Structuralism and the Articulated Text.* Columbus: Ohio State University Press, 1979.

Morris, Wesley, and Barbara Alverson Morris. *Reading Faulkner.* Madison: University of Wisconsin Press, 1989.

Morrison, Toni. "Faulkner and Women." *Faulkner and Women: Faulkner and Yoknapatawpha, 1985.* Ed. Doreen Fowler and Ann J. Abadie. Jackson: University Press of Mississippi, 1986. 295–302.

Mortimer, Gail L. *Faulkner's Rhetoric of Loss: A Study in Perception and Meaning.* Austin: University of Texas Press, 1983.

———. "The 'Masculinity' of Faulkner's Thought." *Faulkner Journal* 4.1–2 (Fall 1988/Spring 1989): 67–81.

Moser, Thomas C. "Faulkner's Muse: Speculations on the Genesis of *The Sound and the Fury.*" *Critical Reconstructions: The Relationship of Fiction to Life.* Ed. Robert M. Polhemus and Roger Henkle. Stanford: Stanford University Press, 1994. 187–212.

Muhlenfeld, Elisabeth. "Shadows with Substance and Ghosts Exhumed: The Women in *Absalom, Absalom!*" *Mississippi Quarterly* 25 (1972): 289–304.

Murray, D. M. "Faulkner, the Silent Comedies, and the Animated Cartoon." *Southern Humanities Review* 9 (Summer 1975): 241–57.

Murray, Edward. *The Cinematic Imagination: Writers and the Motion Pictures.* New York: Frederick Ungar, 1972.

Neumann, Erich. *The Archetypal World of Henry Moore.* Trans. R.F.C. Hull. New York: Pantheon Books, 1959.

Newman, David. "'the vehicle itself is unaware': New Criticism on the Limits of Reading Faulkner." *Mississippi Quarterly* 48.3 (Summer 1995): 481–99.

Nicolaisen, Peter. "Public Life and Private Experience in *The Hamlet.*" *Amerikastudien* 42 (1997): 649–60.

———. "William Faulkner's Dialogue with Thomas Jefferson." *Faulkner in America: Faulkner and Yoknapatawpha, 1998.* Ed. Joseph R. Urgo and Ann J. Abadie. Jackson: University Press of Mississippi, 2001. 64–81.

Noble, David. *The Eternal Adam and the New World Garden: The Central Myth in the American Novel Since 1830.* New York: George Braziller, 1968.

Oates, Stephen. *William Faulkner, the Man and the Artist: A Biography.* New York: Harper and Row, 1987.

O'Connor, William Van. *The Tangled Fire of William Faulkner.* Minneapolis: University of Minnesota Press, 1954.

O'Donnell, George Marion. "Faulkner's Mythology." *Kenyon Review* (Summer 1939): 285–99; reprinted *William Faulkner: Three Decades of Criticism.* Ed. Frederick J. Hoffman and Olga W. Vickery. New York: Harcourt, Brace, 1963. 82–93.

O'Donnell, Patrick. "Between the Family and the State: Nomadism and Authority in *As I Lay Dying.*" *Faulkner and Cultural Studies.* Spec. issue of *Faulkner Journal* 7.1–2 (Fall 1991/Spring 1992): 83–94.

———. "Faulkner and Postmodernism." *The Cambridge Companion to William Faulkner.* Ed. Philip M. Weinstein. Cambridge: Cambridge University Press, 1995. 31–50.

———. "The Spectral Road: Metaphors of Transference in Faulkner's *As I Lay Dying.*" *Papers on Language and Literature* 20 (1984): 60–79.

Orr, John. *The Making of the Twentieth-Century Novel: Lawrence, Joyce, Faulkner and Beyond.* New York: St. Martin's, 1987.

O'Sullivan, Tim, John Hartley, Danny Saunders, Martin Montgomery, and John Fiske, eds. *Key Concepts in Communication and Cultural Studies.* 2nd ed. New York: Routledge, 1994.

Ownby, Ted, "The Snopes Trilogy and the Emergence of Consumer Culture." *Faulkner and Ideology: Faulkner and Yoknapatawpha, 1992.* Ed. Donald M. Kartiganer and Ann J. Abadie. Jackson: University Press of Mississippi, 1995. 95–128.

Page, Sally R. *Faulkner's Women: Characterization and Meaning.* Deland, FL: Everett/Edwards, 1972.

Parker, Robert Dale. *Absalom, Absalom!: The Questioning of Fictions.* Boston: Twayne, 1991.

———. *Faulkner and the Novelistic Imagination.* Urbana: University of Illinois Press, 1985.

———. "Sex and Gender, Feminine and Masculine: Faulkner and the Polymorphous Exchange of Cultural Binaries." *Faulkner and Gender: Faulkner and Yoknapatawpha, 1994.* Ed. Donald M. Kartiganer and Ann J. Abadie. Jackson: University Press of Mississippi, 1996. 73–96.

Pater, Walter. *The Renaissance: Studies in Art and Poetry.* New York: Macmillan, 1905.

Peake, C. H. "The Irreconcilable Dimensions of Faulkner's *As I Lay Dying.*" *Essays and Studies 1985.* Ed. G. Harlow. London: John Murray, 1985. 98–110.

Pearce, Richard. *The Novel in Motion: An Approach to Modern Fiction.* Columbus: Ohio State University Press, 1983.

———. "The Politics of Narration: Can a Woman Tell Her Story in Yoknapatawpha County—Even with All Those Yarns?" *Narrative Poetics: Innovations, Limits, Challenges.* Ed. James Phelan. Columbus: Ohio State University Press, 1987. 39–53.

———. *The Politics of Narration: James Joyce, William Faulkner, and Virginia Woolf.* New Brunswick, NJ: Rutgers University Press, 1991.

Peavy, Charles D. *Go Slow Now: Faulkner and the Race Question.* Eugene: University of Oregon Books, 1971.

Peek, Charles A. "Adjusting the Apocrypha: The Thirties and Faulkner's Radical Critique of 'The Old Plantation.'" *Arkansas Review* 31.1 (April 2000): 16–20.

———. "'A-laying there, right up to my door': As American *As I Lay Dying.*" *Faulkner in America: Faulkner and Yoknapatawpha, 1998.* Ed. Joseph R. Urgo and Ann J. Abadie. Jackson: University Press of Mississippi, 2001. 116–35.

———. "'Handy' Ways to Teach 'That Evening Sun.'" *Teaching Faulkner: Approaches and Methods.* Ed. Stephen Hahn and Robert W. Hamblin. Westport, CT: Greenwood Press, 2001. 53–58.

———. "An Interview with Malcom Cowley." *Faulkner Journal* 5.1 (Fall 1999): 51–60.

Peppers, Cathy. "What Does Faulkner Want? *Light in August* as Hysterical Male Text." *Faulkner Journal* 9 (1994): 125–138.

Peternel, Joan. "The Double in *Light in August:* Narcissus or Janus?" *Notes on Mississippi Writers* 15 (1983): 19–37.

Peters, Erskine. *William Faulkner: The Yoknapatawpha World and Black Being.* Darby, PA: Norwood Editions, 1983.

Petrie, Dennis W. "Monument of the Famous Writer." *Ultimately Fiction: Design in Modern American Literary Biography.* West Lafayette, IN: Purdue University Press, 1981. 59–110.

Pettey, Homer B. "Reading and Raping in *Sanctuary.*" *Faulkner Journal* 3 (1987): 71–84.

Phillips, Gene D. *Fiction, Film, and Faulkner: The Art of Adaptation.* Knoxville: University of Tennessee Press, 1988.

Pierce, Constance. "Being, Knowing, and Saying in the 'Addie' Section of Faulkner's *As I Lay Dying.*" *Twentieth Century Literature* 26 (Fall 1980): 294–305.

Pikoulis, John. *The Art of William Faulkner.* London: Macmillan, 1982.

Pilkington, John. *The Heart of Yoknapatawpha.* Jackson: University Press of Mississippi, 1981.

Pitavy, François. *Faulkner's* Light in August. Trans. Gillian E. Cook. Bloomington: Indiana University Press, 1973.

———. "Narrative Voice and Function of Voice and the Function of Shreve: Remarks on the Production of Meaning in *Absalom, Absalom!*" *William Faulkner's* Absalom, Absalom!: *A Critical Casebook.* Ed. Elisabeth Muhlenfeld. New York: Garland, 1984. 189–205.

———. "Some Remarks on Negation and Denegation in William Faulkner's *Absalom, Absalom!*" *Faulkner's Discourse: An International Symposium.* Ed. Lothar Hönnighausen. Tübingen: Max Niemeyer Verlag, 1989. 25–32.

———. "Through Darl's Eyes Darkly: The Vision of the Poet in *As I Lay Dying.*" *William Faulkner: Materials, Studies, and Criticism* 4.2 (1982): 37–62.

Podhoretz, Norman. "William Faulkner and the Problem of War: His Fable of Faith." *Faulkner: A Collection of Critical Essays.* Ed. Robert Penn Warren. Englewood Cliffs, NJ: Prentice-Hall, 1966. 243–50.

Polchin, James. "Selling a Novel: Faulkner's *Sanctuary* as Psychosexual Text." *Faulkner and Gender.* Ed. Donald M. Kartiganer and Ann J. Abadie. Jackson: University Press of Mississippi, 1996. 145–59.

Polhemus, Robert M., and Roger B. Henkle, ed. *Critical Reconstructions: The Relationship of Fiction and Life.* Stanford: Stanford University Press, 1994.

Polk, Noel. Afterword. *Sanctuary: The Original Text.* New York: Random House, 1981. 293–306.

———. "The Artist as Cuckold." *Faulkner and Gender: Faulkner and Yoknapatawpha, 1994.* Ed. Donald M. Kartiganer and Ann J. Abadie. Jackson: University Press of Mississippi, 1996. 20–47.

———. *Children of the Dark House: Text and Context in Faulkner.* Jackson: University Press of Mississippi, 1996.

———. "'The Dungeon Was Mother Herself': William Faulkner: 1927–1931." *New Directions in Faulkner Studies: Faulkner and Yoknapatawpha, 1983.* Ed. Doreen Fowler and Ann J. Abadie. Jackson: University Press of Mississippi, 1984. 61–93.

———. "Enduring *A Fable* and Prevailing." *Faulkner: After the Nobel Prize.* Ed. Michel Gresset and Kenzaburo Ohashi. Kyoto: Yamaguchi, 1987. 110–26.

———. "'The Force That through the Green Fuse Drives': Faulkner and the Greening of American History." *Faulkner in America: Faulkner and Yoknapatawpha, 1998.* Ed. Joseph R. Urgo and Ann J. Abadie. Jackson: University Press of Mississippi, 2001. 45–63.

———. Introduction. *New Essays on* The Sound and the Fury. Ed. Noel Polk. Cambridge: Cambridge University Press, 1993. 1–21.

———. "Man in the Middle: Faulkner and the Southern White Moderate." In *Faulkner and Race: Faulkner and Yoknapatawpha, 1986.* Ed. Doreen Fowler and Ann J. Abadie. Jackson: University Press of Mississippi, 1987. 130–51.

———. "'Polysyllabic and Verbless Patriotic Nonsense': Faulkner at Midcentury—His and Ours." *Faulkner and Ideology: Faulkner and Yoknapatawpha, 1992.* Ed. Donald Kartiganer and Ann J. Abadie. Jackson: University Press of Mississippi, 1995. 297–328.

———. "Roland Barthes Reads *A Fable.*" *Faulkner's Discourse: An International Symposium.* Ed. Lothar Hönnighausen. Tübingen: Max Niemeyer Verlag, 1989. 109–16.

———. Series preface. *Reading Faulkner: The Unvanquished.* Jackson: University Press of Mississippi, 1995.

———. "The Space Between *Sanctuary.*" *Intertexuality in Faulkner.* Ed. Michel Gresset and Noel Polk. Jackson: University Press of Mississippi, 1985. 16–35.

———. "Testing Masculinity in the Snopes Triology." *Faulkner Journal* 16.3 (2000/2001): 3–22.

———. "Was Not Was Not Who Since Philoprogenitive." *Faulkner at One Hundred: Retrospect and Prospect: Faulkner and Yoknapatawpha, 1997.* Ed. Donald M. Kartiganer and Ann J. Abadie Jackson: University Press of Mississippi, 2000. 18–25.

Porter, Carolyn. "*Absalom, Absalom!:* (Un)Making the Father." *The Cambridge Companion to Faulkner Studies.* Ed. Philip Weinstein. Cambridge: Cambridge University Press, 1995. 168–96.

———. "Faulkner's Grim Sires." *Faulkner at One Hundred: Retrospect and Prospect: Faulkner and Yoknapatawpha, 1997.* Ed. Donald Kartiganer and Ann J. Abadie. Jackson: University Press of Mississippi, 2000. 120–31.

———. *Seeing and Being: The Plight of the Participant Observer in Emerson, James, Adams, and Faulkner.* Middleton, CT: Wesleyan University Press, 1981.

———. "Symbolic Fathers and Dead Mothers: A Feminist Approach to Faulkner." *Faulkner and Psychology: Faulkner and Yoknapatawpha, 1991.* Ed. Donald M. Kartiganer and Ann J. Abadie. Jackson: University Press of Mississippi, 1994. 78–122.

Pozetta, George E. "Ethnic Life." *Encyclopedia of Southern Culture.* Ed. Charles Reagan Wilson and William Ferris. Chapel Hill: University of North Carolina Press, 1989. 401–4.

Pruvot, Monique. "Faulkner and the Voices of Orphism." *Faulkner and Idealism: Perspectives from Paris.* Ed. Michel Gresset and Patrick Samway. Jackson: University Press of Mississippi, 1983. 127–43.

Pui-ling, Linda. "Landscape of the Heart: The City and the Feminine in William Faulkner's 'Artist at Home' and 'Idyll in the Desert.'" *William Faulkner: Achievement and Endurance.* Ed. Jie Tao. Proceedings of the International

Faulkner Symposium at Bejing University. Bejing: Bejing Univeristy Press, 1998. 246–65.

Putzel, Max. *Genius of Place: William Faulkner's Triumphant Beginnings.* Baton Rouge: Louisiana State University Press, 1985.

Radloff, Bernhard. "Time and Time-Field: The Structure of Anticipation and Recollection in the Quentin Section of *The Sound and the Fury.*" *Dalhousie Review* 65 (1985): 29–42.

Rado, Lisa. "'A Perversion That Builds Chartres and Invents Lear Is a Pretty Good Thing': *Mosquitoes* and Faulkner's Androgynous Imagination." *The Modern Androgyne Imagination: A Failed Sublime.* Charlottesville: University of Virginia Press, 2000. Also in *Faulkner Journal* 9 (1994): 13–30.

Railey, Kevin. *Natural Aristocracy: History, Ideology, and the Production of William Faulkner.* Tuscaloosa: University of Alabama Press, 1999.

———. "Paternalism and Liberalism: Contending Ideologies in *Absalom, Absalom!*" *Faulkner and Cultural Studies.* Spec. issue of *Faulkner Journal* 7.1–2 (Fall 1991/Spring 1992): 115–32.

———. "The Social Psychology of Paternalism: *Sanctuary*'s Cultural Context." *Faulkner in Cultural Context: Faulkner and Yoknapatawpha, 1995.* Ed. Donald M. Kartiganer and Ann J. Abadie. Jackson: University Press of Mississippi, 1997. 75–98.

Ramsey, D. Matthew. "'Lifting the Fog': Faulkners, Reputations, and *The Story of Temple Drake.*" *Faulkner and Film.* Spec. issue of *Faulkner Journal* 16.1–2 (Fall 2000/Spring 2001): 7–34.

———. "'Turnabout' is Fair(y) Play: Faulkner's Queer War Story." *Faulkner Journal* 15.1–2 (Fall 1999/Spring 2000): 61–82.

Raper, J. R. "Meaning Called to Life: Alogical Structure in *Absalom, Absalom!*" *Southern Humanities Review* 5 (1971): 9–23.

Reames, Kelly Lynch. "'All That Matters Is That I Wrote the Letters': Discourse, Discipline, and Difference in *Requiem for a Nun.*" *Faulkner Journal* 14.1 (1998): 31–52.

Reed, Joseph W., Jr. *Faulkner's Narrative.* New Haven, CT: Yale University Press, 1973.

Reid, Panthea. "Teaching *The Sound and the Fury* as a Postimpressionist Novel." *Approaches to Teaching Faulkner's* The Sound and the Fury. Ed. Stephen Hahn and Arthur Kinney. New York: Modern Language Association of America, 1996. 114–21. [See also Broughton, Panthea Reid]

———. "The Scene of Writing and the Shape of Language for Faulkner When 'Matisse and Picasso Yet Painted.'" *Faulkner and the Artist: Faulkner and Yoknapatawpha, 1993.* Jackson: University Press Mississippi, 1996. 82–109. [See also Broughton, Panthea Reid]

Rhodes, Pamela, and Richard Godden. "*The Wild Palms:* Faulkner's Hollywood Novel." *Essays in Poetics* 10 (1985): 1–49.

Richardson, H. Edward. *William Faulkner: The Journey to Self-Discovery.* Columbia: University of Missouri Press, 1969.

Rilke, Rainer Maire. *The Duino Elegies.* Trans. J. B. Lieshman and Stephen Spender. New York: Norton, 1963.

Roberts, Diane. *Faulkner and Southern Womanhood.* Athens: University of Georgia Press, 1994.

———. "Ravished Belles: Stories of Rape and Resistance in *Flags in the Dust* and *Sanctuary.*" *Faulkner Journal* 4.1–2 (Fall 1988/Spring 1989): 21–35.

Robinette, Joseph. *A Rose for Emily: A One-Act Play.* Woodstock, IL: Dramatic Publishing Company, 1983.

Robinson, W. R., ed. *Man and the Movies.* Baton Rouge: Louisiana State University Press, 1967.

Rogers, David. "Maternalizing the Epicene: Faulkner's Paradox of Form and Gender." *Faulkner and Gender: Faulkner and Yoknapatawpha, 1994.* Ed. Donald M. Kartiganer and Ann J. Abadie. Jackson: University Press of Mississippi, 1996. 97–119.

Rollyson, Carl E., Jr. "'Counterpull': Estelle and William Faulkner." *South Atlantic Quarterly* 85.3 (Summer 1986): 215–27.

Rose, Jacqueline. Introduction II. *Feminine Sexuality: Jacques Lacan and the "École Freudienne."* By Jacques Lacan. Ed. Juliet Mitchell. Trans. Jacqueline Rose. New York: Norton, 1982. 27–57.

Ross, Stephen M. "Conrad's Influence on Faulkner's *Absalom, Absalom!*" *Studies in American Fiction* 2 (1974): 199–209.

———. "Evocation of Voice in *Absalom, Absalom!*" *Essays in Literature* 8 (1981): 135–49.

———. *Fiction's Inexhaustible Voice: Speech and Writing in Faulkner.* Athens: University of Georgia Press, 1989.

———. "Shapes of Time and Consciousness in *As I Lay Dying.*" *Texas Studies in Literature and Language* 16 (1974): 723–37.

Ross, Valerie. "Too Close to Home: Repressing Biography, Instituting Authority." *Contesting the Subject: Essays in the Postmodern Theory and Practice of Biography and Biographical Criticism.* Ed. William H. Epstein. West Lafayette, IN: Purdue University Press, 1991. 135–66.

Rossky, William. "*As I Lay Dying:* The Insane World." *William Faulkner's* As I Lay Dying: *A Critical Casebook.* Ed. Dianne L. Cox. New York: Garland, 1985. 179–88.

Rubin, Louis D. "William Faulkner: Discovery of a Man's Vocation." *Faulkner: Fifty Years after* The Marble Faun. Ed. George H. Wolfe. Tuscaloosa: University of Alabama Press, 1976. 43–68.

Ruland, Richard, and Malcolm Bradbury. *From Puritanism to Modernism: A History of American Literature.* New York: Viking, 1991.

Ruppersburg, Hugh M. *Voice and Eye in Faulkner's Fiction.* Athens: University of Georgia Press, 1983.

Russakoff, Dale. "Faulkner and the Bridge to the South." *Washington Post,* 21 July 1985: B1, B7–B8.

Ryan, Marjorie. "The Shakespearean Symbolism in *The Sound and the Fury.*" *Faulkner Studies* 2 (Autumn 1953): 40–44.

Samway, Patrick. "Narration and Naming in *The Reivers.*" *Faulkner's Discourse: An International Symposium.* Ed. Lothar Hönnighausen. Tübingen: Max Niemeyer Verlag, 1989. 245–62.

Sansing, David. "History of Northern Mississippi." *University of Mississippi Studies in English* 14 (1976): 5–21.

Sass, Karen R. "At a Loss for Words: Addie and Language in *As I Lay Dying.*" *Faulkner Journal* 6 (1991): 9–21.

———. "Rejection of the Maternal and the Polarization of Gender in *The Hamlet.*" *Faulkner Journal* 4.1–2 (Fall 1988/Spring 1989): 127–37.

Saussure, Ferdinand de. *Course in General Linguistics.* Trans. Wade Baskin. 1916; reprint New York: McGraw-Hill, 1966.

Scheel, Kathryn M. "Incest, Repression, and Repetition Compulsion: The Case of Faulkner's Temple Drake." *Mosaic* 30.4 (1997): 39–55.

Scherer, Olga. "A Dialogic Hereafter: *The Sound and the Fury* and *Absalom, Absalom!*" *Southern Literature and Literary Theory.* Ed. Jefferson Humphries. Athens: University of Georgia Press, 1990. 300–17.

Schreiber, Evelyn Jaffe. "Imagined Edens and Lacan's Lost Object: The Wilderness and Subjectivity in Faulkner's *Go Down, Moses.*" *Mississippi Quarterly* 50 (1997): 477–92.

———. *Subversive Voices: Eroticizing the Other in William Faulkner and Toni Morrison.* Knoxville: University of Tennessee Press, 2002.

———. "What's Love Got to Do with It? Desire and Subjectivity in Faulkner's Snopes Trilogy." *Faulkner Journal* 9 (1994): 83–98.

Schreuders, Piet. "The Paperback Art of James Avati." *Illustration* 1.1 (October 2001): 16–33.

Schwartz, Delmore. "The Fiction of William Faulkner." *Southern Review* 7 (Summer 1941): 145–60.

Schwartz, Lawrence H. *Creating Faulkner's Reputation: The Politics of Modern Literary Criticism.* Knoxville: University of Tennessee Press, 1988.

Schweickart, Patrocinio P. "Reading Ourselves: Toward a Feminist Theory of Reading." *Gender and Reading: Essays on Readers, Texts, and Contexts.* Ed. Elizabeth A. Flynn and Patrocinio P. Schweickart. Baltimore: Johns Hopkins University Press, 1986. 31–62.

Scott, Arthur L. "The Myriad Perspectives of *Absalom, Absalom!*" *American Quarterly* 6 (1954): 210–20.

Scott, Bonnie Kime. *Refiguring Modernism.* 2 vols. Bloomington: Indiana University Press, 1995.

Scott, Evelyn. *On William Faulkner's* The Sound and the Fury. New York: Jonathan Cape and Harrison Smith, 1929.

Sensibar, Judith L. "'Drowsing Maidenhead Symbol's Self': Faulkner and the Fictions of Love." *Faulkner and the Craft of Fiction: Faulkner and Yoknapatawpha, 1987.* Ed. Doreen Fowler and Ann J. Abadie. Jackson: University Press of Mississippi, 1989. 124–47.

———. "Faulkner and Love: The Question of Collaboration." *Faulkner at One Hundred: Retropsect and Prospect: Faulkner and Yoknapatawpha, 1997.* Ed. Donald M. Kartiganer and Ann J. Abadie. Jackson: University Press of Mississippi, 2000. 188–95.

———. "Faulkner's Fictional Photographs: Playing with Difference." *Out of Bounds: Male Writers and Gender(ed) Criticism.* Amherst: University of Massachusetts Press, 1990. 290–315.

———. Introduction. *Vision in Spring.* By William Faulkner. Austin: University of Texas Press, 1984. ix–xxviii.

———. *The Origins of Faulkner's Art.* Austin: University of Texas Press, 1984.

———. "Pierrot and the Marble Faun: Another Fragment." *Mississippi Quarterly* 32 (Summer 1979): 473–76.

———. "Pop Culture Invades Jefferson: Faulkner's Real and Imaginary Photographs of Desire." *Faulkner and Popular Culture: Faulkner and Yoknapatawpha, 1988.* Ed. Doreen Fowler and Ann J. Abadie. Jackson: University Press of Mississippi, 1990. 110–41.

———. "Who Wears the Mask? Memory, Desire, and Race in *Go Down, Moses.*" *New Essays on* Go Down, Moses. Ed. Linda Wagner-Martin. Cambridge: Cambridge University Press, 1996. 101–27.

———. "William Faulkner, Poet to Novelist: An Impostor Becomes an Artist." *Creative Biography: Proceedings of a Conference at the Chicago Institute for Psychoanalysis, 1982.* New York: International University Press, 1984. 305–46.

Simpson, Lewis P. "Isaac McCaslin and Temple Drake: The Fall of New World Man." *Nine Essays in Modern Literature.* Ed. Donald E. Stanford. Baton Rouge: Louisiana State University Press, 1965. 88–106.

———. "Sex and History: The Origins of Faulkner's Apocrypha." *The Maker and the Myth: Faulkner and Yoknapatawpha, 1977.* Ed. Evans Harrington and Ann J. Abadie. Jackson: University Press of Mississippi, 1978. 43–70.

Singal, Daniel. "William Faulkner and the Discovery of Evil." *The War Within: From Victorian to Modernist Thought in the South, 1919–1945.* Chapel Hill: University of North Carolina Press, 1982. 153–97.

———. *William Faulkner: The Making of a Modernist.* Chapel Hill: University of North Carolina Press, 1997.

Skei, Hans H. "'Faulkner Before Faulkner': The Early Career as a Construction in Retrospect." *Faulkner at One Hundred: Retropsect and Prospect: Faulkner and Yoknapatawpha, 1997.* Ed. Donald M. Kartiganer and Ann J. Abadie. Jackson: University Press of Mississippi, 2000. 193–99.

Slabey, Robert M. "Faulkner's *Sanctuary.*" *Explicator* 21 (January 1963): item 45.

———. "Myth and Ritual in *Light in August.*" *Texas Studies in Literature and Language* 2 (Autumn 1960): 328–49.

Slatoff, Walter J. *Quest for Failure: A Study of William Faulkner.* Ithaca: Cornell University Press, 1960.

Slaughter, Carolyn N. "*Absalom, Absalom!:* 'Fluid Cradle of Events (Time).'" *Faulkner Journal* 6 (1991): 65–84.

———. "*As I Lay Dying:* Demise of Vision." *American Literature* 61 (1989): 16–30.

Smith, Henry Nash. *Virgin Land: The American West as Symbol and Myth.* Cambridge: Harvard University Press, 1950; reissued 1970.

Snead, James A. *Figures of Division: William Faulkner's Major Novels.* New York: Methuen, 1986.

Sollors, Werner. "Ethnicity." *Critical Terms for Literary Study.* Ed. Frank Lentricchia and Thomas McLaughlin. Chicago: University of Chicago Press, 1990. 288–305.

Sommers, Pamela. "Fascinated by Faulkner: In 'Bicycle,' Three Women and a Man of Letters." *Washington Post,* 6 November 1995: D5.

Spiegel, Alan. *Fiction and the Camera Eye: Visual Consciousness in Film and the Modern Novel.* Charlottesville: University Press of Virginia, 1976.

Srikanth, Rajini. "Why I, a Woman of Color from India, Enjoy Teaching William Faulkner." *Mississippi Quarterly* 49 (Summer 1996): 441–56.

Stam, Robert, Robert Burgoyne, and Sandy Flitterman-Lewis, eds. *New Vocabularies in Film Semiotics: Structuralism, Post-Structuralism and Beyond.* New York: Routledge, 1992.

"Stamp to Honor Novelist William Faulkner." *Washington Post Weekend,* 10 July 1987: 45.

Stavrou, C. N. "Ambiguity in Faulkner's Affirmation." *Person* 40 (Spring 1959): 169–77.

Stevens, Wallace. *The Necessary Angel: Essays on Reality and the Imagination.* New York: Vintage, 1942.

Stimpson, Catharine R. "Feminist Criticism." *Redrawing the Boundaries: The Transformation of English and American Literary Studies.* Ed. Stephen Greenblatt and Giles Gunn. New York: The Modern Language Association of America, 1992. 251–70.

Stonum, Gary Lee. "Faulkner's Last Phase." *Faulkner: New Perspectives.* Ed. Richard Brodhead. Englewood Cliffs, NJ: Prentice Hall, 1983. 195–207.

———. "Visionary Poetics." *Faulkner's Career: An Internal Literary History.* Ithaca: Cornell University Press, 1979. 41–60.

Straumann, Heinrich. "An American Interpretation of Existence: Faulkner's *A Fable.*" *William Faulkner: Three Decades of Criticism.* Ed. Frederick J. Hoffman and Olga W. Vickery. East Lansing: Michigan State University Press, 1960. 349–72.

Strong, Amy Lovell. "Machines and Machinations: Controlling Desires in Faulkner's *Sanctuary.*" *Faulkner Journal* 9 (1994): 69–82.

Sugarman, Helen Lynne. "'He Was Getting It Involved with Himself': Identity and Reflexivity in William Faulkner's *Light in August* and *Absalom, Absalom!*" *Southern Quarterly* 36.2 (Winter 1998): 95–102.

Sundquist, Eric J. *Faulkner: The House Divided.* Baltimore: Johns Hopkins University Press, 1983.

Swisher, Clarice, ed. *Readings on William Faulkner.* San Diego: Green Haven Press, 1998.

Tangum, Marion. "Rhetorical Clues to *Go Down, Moses:* Who is Talking to Whom?" *Heir and Prototype: Original and Derived Characterizations in Faulkner.* Ed. Dan Ford. Conway: University of Central Arkansas Press, 1987. 8–21.

Tanyol, Denise. "The Two-Way Snake Bite: The Dead Doctor Wounds His Son in William Faulkner's *The Wild Palms.*" *Mississippi Quarterly* 50.3 (1997): 465–75.

Tao, Jie. "Growing Up in the South: Faulkner's *Intruder in the Dust.*" *William Faulkner: Achievement and Endurance.* Ed. Jie Tao. Proceedings of the International Faulkner Symposium at Bejing University. Bejing: Bejing University Press, 1998.

Tate, Allen. *The Language of Poetry.* New York: Russell and Russell, 1960.

Taylor, Carole Anne. "*Light in August:* The Epistemology of Tragic Paradox." *Texas Studies in Language and Literature* 22 (1980): 48–68.

Taylor, Walter. *Faulkner's Search for a South.* Urbana: University of Illinois Press, 1983.

Tebbetts, Terrell L. "Dilsey and the Compsons: A Jungian Reading of Faith and Fragmentation." *Publications of the Arkansas Philological Society* 21.1 (1995): 78–98.

———. "Giving Jung a Crack at the Compsons." *Approaches to Teaching* The Sound and the Fury. Ed. Stephen Hahn and Arthur Kinney. New York: Modern Language Association of America, 1996. 79–83.

———. "'I'm the man here': *Go Down, Moses* and Masculine Identity." *Faulkner and Postmodernism: Faulkner and Yoknapatawpha, 1999.* Ed. John N. Duvall and Ann J. Abadie. Jackson: University Press of Mississippi, 2002. 81–94.

———. "Shadows of Jung: A Psychological Approach to *Light in August.*" *Southern Literary Journal* 22 (1989): 80–95.

———. "Tense Unresolve: Ending a Course on Faulkner." *Teaching Faulkner: Approaches and Methods.* Ed. Stephen Hahn and Robert W. Hamblin. Westport, CT: Greenwood Press, 2001. 191–200.

Thompson, Lawrance. "Mirror Analogues in *The Sound and the Fury.*" *English Institute Essays.* Ed. Alan Downer. New York: Columbia University Press, 1954. 29–56. Reprinted in *William Faulkner: Three Decades of Criticism.* Ed. Frederick J. Hoffman and Olga W. Vickery. New York: Harbinger, 1963. 211–25.

———. *William Faulkner: An Introduction and Interpretation.* 2nd ed. New York: Holt, Rinehart and Winston, 1967.

Tobin, Patricia. "'The Shadowy Attenuation of Time': William Faulkner's *Absalom, Absalom!*" *Time in the Novel.* Princeton, NJ: Princeton University Press, 1978. 107–32.

Torgovnick, Marianna. "Story-Telling as Affirmation at the End of *Light in Augus*t." *Closure in the Novel.* Princeton, NJ: Princeton University Press, 1981. 157–75.

Towner, Theresa M. *Faulkner on the Color Line: The Later Novels.* Jackson: University Press of Mississippi, 2000.

———. "Unsurprised Flesh: Color, Race, and Identity in Faulkner's Fiction." *Faulkner and the Natural World: Faulkner and Yoknapatawpha, 1996.* Ed. Donald M. Kartiganer and Ann J. Abadie. Jackson: University Press of Mississippi, 1999. 45–65.

Trezise, Simon. "The Making of Dickens: Aspects of Biographical Criticism." *Dickens Quarterly* 11.1 (1994): 26–35.

Trilling, Lionel. "The McCaslins of Mississippi," *Nation,* 30 May 1942: 632–33.

Tucker, John. "William Faulkner's *As I Lay Dying:* Working Out the Cubist Bugs." *Texas Studies in Language and Literature* 26 (1984): 388–404.

Turner, Darwin T. [with Shelby Foote and Evans Harrington]. "Faulkner and Race." *The South and Faulkner's Yoknapatawpha: The Actual and the Apocryphal: Faulkner and Yoknapatawpha, 1976.* Ed. Evans Harrington and Ann J. Abadie. Jackson: University Press of Mississippi, 1977. 86–103.

———. "Faulkner and Slavery." *The South and Faulkner's Yoknapatawpha: The Actual and the Apocryphal: Faulkner and Yoknapatawpha, 1976.* Ed. Evans Harrington and Ann J. Abadie. Jackson: University Press of Mississippi, 1977. 62–85.

Turner, Frederick Jackson. *The Frontier in American History.* 1920. New York: Holt, Rinehart and Winston, 1962.

Turner, Joseph W. "The Kinds of Historical Fiction: An Essay in Definition and Methodology." *Genre* 12 (Fall 1979): 333–55.

Urgo, Joseph R. "*Absalom, Absalom!:* The Movie." *American Literature* 62.1 (March 1990): 56–73.

———. *Faulkner's Apocrypha:* A Fable, Snopes, *and the Spirit of Human Rebellion.* Jackson: University Press of Mississippi, 1989.

———. "Menstrual Blood and 'Nigger' Blood: Joe Christmas and the Ideology of Sex and Race." *Mississippi Quarterly* 41 (1988): 391–401.

———. "Postvomiting: *Pylon* and the Faulknerian Spew." *Faulkner and Postmodernism: Faulkner and Yoknapatawpha, 1999.* Ed. John N. Duvall and Ann J. Abadie. Jackson: University Press of Mississippi, 2002. 124–42.

———. "Where Was That Bird? Thinking *America* through Faulkner." *Faulkner in America: Faulkner and Yoknapatawpha, 1998.* Ed. Joseph R. Urgo and Ann J. Abadie. Jackson: University Press of Mississippi, 2001. 98–115.

Urgo, Joseph R., and Ann J. Abadie, eds. *Faulkner in America: Faulkner and Yoknapatawpha, 1998.* Jackson: University Press of Mississippi, 2001.

Vanderveen, Arthur A. "Faulkner, the Interwar Gold Standard, and Discourses of Value in the 1930s." *Faulkner Journal* 12.1 (1996): 43–62.

Vaughn-James, Martin. *The Cage: A Visual-Novel.* Toronto: Coach House Press, 1975.

Végos, Roland. "'Let me play a while now': The Hermeneutics of Heritage and William Faulkner's *Absalom, Absalom!*" *Amerikastudien* 42 (1997): 625–36.

Vickery, John B. "Ritual and Theme in Faulkner's 'Dry September.'" *Arizona Quarterly* 18 (Spring 1962): 5–14.

Vickery, Olga W. *The Novels of William Faulkner: A Critical Interpretation.* 1959. Baton Rouge: Louisiana State University Press, 1992.

Volpe, Edmund L. *A Reader's Guide to William Faulkner.* New York: Farrar, Straus, and Giroux, 1964.

Wachholz, Michael. "Marginality and William Faulkner's *Light in August.*" *Cultural Difference and the Literary Text: Pluralism and the Limits of Authenticity in North American Literatures.* Ed. Winfried Siemerling. Iowa City: University of Iowa Press, 1996. 130–41.

Wadlington, Warwick. *Reading Faulknerian Tragedy.* Ithaca, NY: Cornell University Press, 1987.

Waggoner, Hyatt H. *William Faulkner: From Jefferson to the World.* Lexington: University of Kentucky Press, 1959.

Wagner-Martin, Linda, ed. *New Essays on* Go Down, Moses. Cambridge: Cambridge University Press, 1996.

Waid, Candace. "The Signifying Eye: Faulkner's Artists and the Engendering of Art." *Faulkner and the Artist: Faulkner and Yoknapatawpha, 1993.* Ed. Donald M. Kartiganer and Ann J. Abadie. Jackson: University Press of Mississippi, 1996. 208–49.

Wall, Carey. "*Go Down, Moses:* The Collective Action of Redress." *Faulkner and Cultural Studies.* Spec. issue of *Faulkner Journal* 7.1–2 (Fall 1991/Spring 1992): 151–74.

Warren, Marsha. "Time, Space, and Semiotic Discourse in the Feminization/Disintegration of Quentin Compson." *Faulkner Journal* 4.1–2 (Fall 1988/Spring 1989): 99–111.

Warren, Robert Penn. "Cowley's Faulkner." *New Republic,* 12 August 1946: 176–80; 26 August 1946: 234–7.

———. "William Faulkner." *The Forms of Modern Fiction: Essays Collected in Honor of Joseph Warren Beach.* Ed. William Van O'Connor. Minneapolis: University of Minnesota Press, 1948. 125–43.

———. "William Faulkner." *William Faulkner: Three Decades of Criticism.* Ed. Frederick J. Hoffman and Olga W. Vickery. New York: Harcourt, Brace, 1963. 109–24; Reprinted from *New Republic,* 12 August 1946: 176–80.

———, ed. *Faulkner: A Collection of Critical Essays.* Englewood Cliffs, NJ: Prentice-Hall, 1966.

Watson, James G. "'But Damn Letters Anyway': Letters and Fictions." *New Directions in Faulkner Studies: Faulkner and Yoknapatawpha, 1983.* Ed. Doreen Fowler and Ann J. Abadie. Jackson: University Press of Mississippi, 1987. 228–53.

———. "Carvel Collins's Faulkner: A Newly Opened Archive." *Library Chronicle of the University of Texas* 20.4 (1990): 17–35.

———. "Faulkner's 'What is the Matter with Marriage.'" *Faulkner Journal* 5 (Spring 1990): 69–72.

———. "'My Father's Unfailing Kindness': William Faulkner and the Idea of Home." *American Literature* 64.4 (December 1992): 749–61.

———. "New Orleans, *The Double Dealer,* and 'New Orleans.'" *American Literature* 56.2 (May 1984): 214–26.

———. *William Faulkner, Letters and Fictions.* Austin: University of Texas Press, 1987.

———. *William Faulkner: Self-Presentation and Performance.* Austin: University of Texas Press, 2000.

———, ed. *Thinking of Home: William Faulkner's Letters to His Mother and Father, 1918–1925.* New York: Norton, 1992.

Watson, Jay. "Faulkner's Forensic Fiction and the Question of Authorial Neurosis." *Faulkner and Psychology: Faulkner and Yoknapatawpha, 1991.* Ed. Donald M. Kartiganer and Ann J. Abadie. Jackson: University Press of Mississippi, 1994. 165–88.

———. *Forensic Fictions: The Lawyer Figure in Faulkner.* Athens: University of Georgia Press, 1993.

———. "Overdoing Masculinity in *Light in August;* Or, Joe Christmas and the Gender Guard." *Faulkner Journal* 9.1–2 (1993–1994): 148–77.

———. "Writing Blood: The Art of the Literal in *Light in August.*" *Faulkner and the Natural World: Faulkner and Yoknapatawpha, 1996.* Ed. Donald Kartiganer and Ann J. Abadie. Jackson: University Press of Mississippi, 1997. 66–97.

Watson, Neil. "The 'Incredibly Loud . . . Miss-fire': A Sexual Reading of *Go Down, Moses.*" *Faulkner Journal* 9 (1994): 113–24.

Watt, Ian. "Impressionism and Symbolism in *Heart of Darkness.*" *Joseph Conrad: A Commemoration: Papers from the 1974 International Conference on Conrad.* Ed. Norman Sherry. London: Macmillan, 1976. 37–53.

Weinstein, Arnold L. *Vision and Response in Modern Fiction.* Ithaca, NY: Cornell University Press, 1974.

Weinstein, Philip M. *Faulkner's Subject: A Cosmos No One Owns.* Cambridge: Cambridge University Press, 1992.

———. "'If I Could Say Mother': Construing the Unsayable about Faulknerian Maternity." *Faulkner's Discourse: An International Symposium.* Ed. Lothar Hönnighausen. Tübingen: Max Niemeyer Verlag, 1989. 3–15.

———. "Meditations on the Other: Faulkner's Rendering of Women." *Faulkner and Women: Faulkner and Yoknapatawpha, 1985.* Ed. Doreen Fowler and Ann J. Abadie. Jackson: University Press of Mississippi, 1986. 81–99.

———. "'No Longer at Ease Here': Faulkner in the New Millennium." *Teaching Faulkner: Approaches and Methods.* Ed. Stephen Hahn and Robert W. Hamblin. Westport, CT: Greenwood Press, 2001. 19–30.

———. "Postmodern Intimations: Musing on Invisibility: William Faulkner, Richard Wright, and Ralph Ellison." *Faulkner and Postmodernism: Faulkner and Yoknapatawpha, 1999.* Ed. John N. Duvall and Ann J. Abadie. Jackson: University Press of Mississippi. 2002. 19–38.

———. "Teaching *The Sound and the Fury* in the Context of European Modernism." *Approaches to Teaching Faulkner's* The Sound and the Fury. Ed. Stephen Hahn and Arthur Kinney. New York: Modern Language Association of America, 1996. 108–13.

———. *What Else but Love? The Ordeal of Race in Faulkner and Morrison.* New York: Columbia University Press, 1996.

———, ed. *The Cambridge Companion to William Faulkner.* Cambridge: Cambridge University Press, 1995.

Wenska, Walter. "'There's a Man with a Gun Over There': Faulkner's Hijackings of Masculine Popular Culture." *Faulkner Journal* 15 (Fall 1999/Spring 2000): 35–60.

Werlock, Abby H. P. "Victims Unvanquished: Temple Drake and Women Characters in William Faulkner's Novels." *Women and Violence in Literature: An Essay Collection.* Ed. Katherine Anne Ackley. New York: Garland Publishing, 1990. 3–49.

Werner, Craig. "Beyond Realism and Romanticism: Joyce, Faulkner, and the Tradition of the American Novel." *Centennial Review* 23 (1979): 242–62.

———. "Minstrel Nightmares: Black Dreams of Faulkner's Dreams of Blacks." *Faulkner and Race: Faulkner and Yoknapatawpha, 1986.* Ed. Doreen Fowler and Ann J. Abadie. Jackson: University Press of Mississippi, 1987. 35–57.

———. *Paradoxical Resolutions: American Fiction Since James Joyce.* Urbana: University of Illinois Press, 1982.

West, Ray B., Jr. "Atmosphere and Theme in 'A Rose for Emily.'" *Readings on William Faulkner.* Ed. Clarice Swisher. San Diego: Green Haven Press, 1998. 65–73.

Weston, Jessie L. *From Ritual to Romance.* Garden City, NY: Doubleday Anchor, 1957.

Widmaier, Beth. "Black Female Absence and the Construction of White Womanhood in Faulkner's *Light in August.*" *Faulkner Journal* 16.3 (Fall 2000/Spring 2001): 23–40.

Wilde, Meta Carpenter, and Oren Borsten. *A Loving Gentleman: The Love Story of William Faulkner and Meta Carpenter Wilde.* New York: Simon and Schuster, 1976.

Williams, David. *Faulkner's Women: The Myth and the Muse.* Montreal: McGill–Queen's University Press, 1977.

Williams, Ora G. "The Theme of Endurance in *As I Lay Dying.*" *Louisiana Studies* 9 (1970): 100–104.

Williamson, Joel. "A Historian Looks at Faulkner." *Faulkner and the Artist: Faulkner and Yoknapatawpha, 1993.* Ed. Donald M. Kartiganer and Ann J. Abadie. Jackson: University Press of Mississippi, 1996. 3–21.

———. *William Faulkner and Southern History.* Oxford: Oxford University Press, 1993.

Wilson, Charles Reagan. "Our Land, Our Country: Faulkner, the South, and the American Way of Life." *Faulkner in America: Faulkner and Yoknapatawpha, 1998.* Ed. Joseph R. Urgo and Ann J. Abadie. Jackson: University Press of Mississippi, 2001. 153–66.

Wilson, Charles Reagan, and William Ferris, eds. *Encyclopedia of Southern Culture.* Chapel Hill: University of North Carolina Press, 1989.

Wilson, Deborah. "'A Shape to Fill a Lack': *Absalom, Absalom!* and the Pattern of History," *Faulkner Journal* 7.1–2 (Fall 1991/Spring 1992): 61–81.

Wilson, Edmund. *The Wound and the Bow.* Boston: Houghton Mifflin, 1941.

Wilson, Rob. "Producing American Selves: The Form of American Biography." *Contesting the Subject: Essays in the Postmodern Theory and Practice of Biography and Biographical Criticism.* Ed. William H. Epstein. West Lafayette, IN: Purdue University Press, 1991. 167–92.

Witemeyer, Hugh. *The Future of Modernism.* Ed. Hugh Witemeyer. Ann Arbor: University of Michigan Press, 1997.

Wittenberg, Judith Bryant. *Faulkner: The Transfiguration of Biography.* Lincoln: University of Nebraska Press, 1979.

———. "Gender and Linguistic Strategies in *Absalom, Absalom!*" *Faulkner's Discourse: An International Symposium.* Ed. Lothar Hönnighausen. Tübingen: Max Niemeyer Verlag, 1989. 99–108.

————. "*Go Down, Moses* and the Discourse of Environmentalism." *New Essays on* Go Down, Moses. Ed. Linda Wagner-Martin. Cambridge: Cambridge University Press, 1996. 49–71.

————. "Race in *Light in August:* Word-symbols and Obverse Reflections." *The Cambridge Companion to William Faulkner.* Ed. Philip M. Weinstein. Cambridge: Cambridge University Press, 1995. 146–67.

————. "Teaching *The Sound and the Fury* with Freud." *Approaches to Teaching Faulkner's* The Sound and the Fury. Ed. Stephen Hahn and Arthur Kinney. New York: Modern Language Association of America, 1996. 73–78.

————. "Temple Drake and *La parole pleine.*" *Mississippi Quarterly* 48 (1995): 421–41.

————. "William Faulkner: A Feminist Consideration." *American Novelists Revisited: Essays in Feminist Criticism.* Ed. Fritz Fleischmann. Boston: G. K. Hall, 1982. 325–38.

————. "The Women of *Light in August.*" *New Essays on* Light in August. Ed. Michael Millgate. New York: Cambridge University Press, 1987. 103–22.

Wittig, Monique. *The Straight Mind and Other Essays.* Boston: Beacon Press, 1992.

Wood, Amy Louise. "Feminine Rebellion and Mimicry in Faulkner's *As I Lay Dying.*" *Faulkner Journal* 9.1–2 (Fall 1993/Spring 1994): 99–112.

Woodbery, Bonnie. "The Abject in Faulkner's *As I Lay Dying.*" *Literature and Psychology* 40.1 (1994): 26–42.

Woolf, Virginia. "Mr. Bennet and Mrs. Brown." *Virginia Woolf: Collected Essays.* Vol 1. New York: Harcourt, 1967. 319–37.

————. *To the Lighthouse.* 1927. San Diego: Harcourt, Brace, 1981.

Wright, Elizabeth. *Psychoanalytic Criticism: Theory in Practice.* New York: Methuen, 1984.

Wyatt, David. "Faulkner and the Reading Self." *Faulkner and Psychology: Faulkner and Yoknapatawpha, 1991.* Ed. Donald M. Kartiganer and Ann J. Abadie. Jackson: University Press of Mississippi, 1994. 272–87.

————. *Prodigal Sons: A Study in Authorship and Authority.* Baltimore: Johns Hopkins University Press, 1980.

Yeats, William Butler. *A Collection of Poems of W. B. Yeats.* New York: Macmillan, 1903.

Yellin, David G., and Marie Connors, eds. *Tomorrow and Tomorrow and Tomorrow.* Jackson: University Press of Mississippi, 1985.

Yonce, Margaret. "'Shot Down Last Spring': The Wounded Aviators of Faulkner's Wasteland." *Mississippi Quarterly* 31 (1978): 359–68.

Young, James Dean. "Quentin's Maundy Thursday." *Tulane Studies in English* 10 (1960): 143–51.

Young, R.V. "The Old New Criticism and Its Critics." *First Things* 35 (1993): 38–44.

Zacharasiewicz, Waldemar, ed. *Faulkner, His Contemporaries, and His Posterity.* Tübingen: A. Francke, 1993.

Zeitlin, Michael. "Faulkner and Psychoanalysis: The *Elmer* Case." *Faulkner and Psychology: Faulkner and Yoknapatawpha, 1991.* Ed. Donald M. Kartiganer and Ann. J. Abadie. Jackson: University Press of Mississippi, 1994. 219–41.

————. "The Passion of Margaret Powers: A Psychoanalytic Reading of *Soldiers' Pay.*" *Mississippi Quarterly* 46 (1993): 351–72.

————. "Returning to Freud and *The Sound and the Fury.*" *Faulkner Journal* 13.1–2 (1998): 57–76.

———. "Versions of the 'Primal Scene': Faulkner and *Ulysses.*" *Mosaic* 22.2 (1989): 63–77.

Zender, Karl F. *The Crossing of the Ways: William Faulkner, the South, and the Modern World.* New Brunswick, NJ: Rutgers University Press, 1989.

———. *Faulkner and the Politics of Reading.* Baton Rouge: Louisiana State University Press, 2002.

———. "Faulkner at Forty: The Artist at Home." *Southern Review* 17.2 (1981): 288–302.

———. "'That Evening Sun': Marginality and Sight." *William Faulkner's Short Fiction: An International Symposium.* Ed. Hans H. Skei. Proceedings from the 1995 International Faulkner Symposium. Oslo, Norway: Solum, 1997. 253–59.

Zink, Karl E. "Flux and Frozen Moments." *PMLA* 71 (1956): 285–301.

Index

Items in **bold face** appear in the glossary. References to works of other authors appear under that author's name.

Desire, 22, 94, 172, 176, 180, 184–85, 187,
    197, 210
De Spain, Major, 45
Desvergues, Alain, 269
Detective, detective fiction, 37, 262, 265–66,
    273–74
Deviant, deviance, 172
Devil, *See* Satan
"Dial, The," 273
Dialogism, dialogic, 58–60
Díaz-Diocaretz, Myriam, 222
Dichotomy, 156, 177
Dickens, Charles, 10, 98, 133, 175
Dickerson, Mary Jane, 7, 317, 334n14
Dickinson, Emily, 324
Diegetic, 106
Dietician (Miss Atkins), 150
Dignity, 51
Dillon, George L., 244–45
Dilsey, 93, 176, 208, 247, 312. *See* Gibson
Discipline/disciplinarity, 168, 170, 181
Discourse, 45, 55, 59–60, 63n8, 164–65,
    168, 171–72, 175, 189–92, 322, 333
Dispossessed, dispossession, 21, 135
Disrupt, disruption, 61, 100
Doctor, the, 182
Donaldson, Susan V., 37, 174–75, 178–79,
    192, 193n10, 208, 226–28, 292–93,
    302n65, 330, 337n50
Dondlinger, Mary Jo, 44
Dos Passos, John, 269
Dostoyevsky, Fyodor (and works), 269
Double Dealer, The, 87
Douglas, Harold J., 331
Douglass, Paul, 118n2, 120n23
Doyle, Don H., 33–34, 42, 326, 336n35
Drake, Judge, 142–44; Temple, 7, 10, 12, 60,
    142–43, 152, 171, 175–77, 207, 210,
    221–22, 231, 266, 269, 286, 291, 300n41,
    302n59, 312
Dream(s), 22, 24, 197–98, 291
Dreamwork, 197
Dreiser, Theodore, 268
Drinking, 68, 73, 82, 89, 93–94. *See* alcohol
"Dry September," 7, 39, 179, 250, 252,
    254–55, 311
Duclos, Donald P., 79, 338n61
During, Simon, 164, 192n1
Duvall, John N, 52–53, 57, 62n4, 63n7, 115,
    124n70, 126, 141, 143, 151–52, 209, 217,
    222, 229–30, 255
Duvert, Elizabeth, 36
Dynasty, 308

Eagleton, Terry, 95, 131
Earl (The Sound and the Fury), 133
Early, James, 293, 299n29
Easter, 14–15, 106, 133, 135–36
Ebony, 194n25
Eby, Cecil D., 7
Eco, Umberto, 235, 246, 248
Economy, economic, 58, 60, 98, 131, 139,
    141, 152–56, 164, 166, 180, 189, 216,
    228, 230, 263
Eddy, Charmaine, 211
Eden, edenic, 7, 13, 14, 21–22, 42, 266
Editorial theory, 280, 283, 288
Edmonds, 327; Cass, 26n24, 158, 304n75;
    Roth, 78, 141, 156–60
Eighties (1980s), 39, 77–81, 83, 86, 88
Einstein, Albert, 103
Eisenhower, Dwight D., 31, 310
Eisenstein, Sergei, 188
"Elder Watson in Heaven," 35
Eliot, T. S., 1–5, 7–9, 17, 24, 25n1, 61, 67,
    71, 76, 109, 113, 236, 245, 337n47
"Elmer," 206
Elmore, A. E., 118n1
Elnora, 179
Emerson, Caryl, 59
Emerson, O. B., 246
Emerson, Ralph Waldo, 324
Emotion, emotional, 51, 83
Empathy, empathic, 189
Endore, Guy, 183
Endurance, endure, 318
English, English Department(s), 165–66,
    168, 286, 322, 325
Enlightenment, the, 138, 152, 193n13
Environment(al), 44, 58
Epic, 1, 7–8, 20
Episcopal, 338n53
Epistemological loss, 100
Epstein, William, 98
Erase, erasure, 187, 191
Erikson, Erik, 82
Eros, 273
Escape, 183, 188, 194n23
Essays, Speeches, & Public Letters, 246
Essentialism, 153–54
Ethnicity, 38, 40–42, 138
Europe, European, 22, 41, 131, 176, 189,
    191, 242, 264–65
Eve, 14
Everyman, 333, 338n63
Evil, 3, 11, 13, 16, 133, 144, 160, 169, 284
Exegesis, exegetical, 103

About the Editors and Contributors

THE EDITORS

Charles A. Peek is Martin Professor of English, University of Nebraska (Kearney). Co-editor (with Robert W. Hamblin) of *A William Faulkner Encyclopedia* (Greenwood Press, 1999) and of the *Teaching Faulkner* newsletter. He has published articles on Faulkner and been invited to present papers at international conferences on Faulkner, Hemingway, and Cather. In 2000, he was awarded the Pratt-Heins Excellence in Teaching Award and has presented "Teaching Faulkner" sessions for the University of Mississippi SAKS Fellows and (for 13 years) at the annual Faulkner and Yoknapatawpha Conference. He serves as president-elect of the Nebraska Center for the Book and on the Board of Governors of the Willa Cather Pioneer Memorial and Educational Foundation.

Robert W. Hamblin is professor of English and director of the Center for Faulkner Studies, Southeast Missouri State University, Cape Girardeau, Missouri. In addition to editing *A William Faulkner Encyclopedia* (Greenwood Press, 1999) and the *Teaching Faulkner* newsletter, he is associate editor of *The Cape Rock* (poetry journal), poetry editor for *Aethlon: The Journal of Sport Literature,* and co-editor (with Louis Daniel Brodsky) of the five-volume *Faulkner: A Comprehensive Guide to the Brodsky Collection.* In addition to authoring numerous Faulkner books and articles, he has published 2 books of poetry and is widely sought as a speaker on Faulkner and the South.

THE CONTRIBUTORS

Caroline Carvill is professor of American Literature, Rose-Hulman Institute of Technology, Terre Haute, Indiana. Her interests include Southern writers, service-learning, and Modern American Literature. She contributed to *A William Faulkner Encyclopedia* and is a regular participant at the Faulkner and Yoknap-atawpha conferences.

Philip Cohen is dean of the Graduate School, vice provost for Academic Affairs, and professor of English, University of Texas at Arlington. He is the editor of *Devils and Angels: Textual Editing and Literary Theory* and *Texts and Textuality: Textual Instability, Theory, and Interpretation* and has published widely on American Literature, William Faulkner, and on the relationship between literary studies and textual scholarship and editorial theory. His scholarly work has been supported by a summer stipend and travel grants from the National Endowment for the Humanities.

Doreen Fowler is professor of English, University of Kansas, Lawrence, Kansas. She is the author of *Faulkner: The Return of the Repressed* and more than 30 journal articles on Faulkner and other authors. She is also co-editor of nearly a dozen collections of essays on Faulkner. Currently, she is working on a book tentatively titled, *Making a Difference: Writing Race,* a psychoanalytic interpretation of the construction of racial difference in the works of William Faulkner, Richard Wright, Flannery O'Connor, and Toni Morrison.

M. Thomas Inge is Robert Emory Blackwell Professor of English and Humanities at Randolph-Macon College in Ashland, Virginia, where he teaches American studies, interdisciplinary humanities, and Asian literature. He lectures on and writes about Southern literature and culture, American humor and comic art, and William Faulkner. Recent publications include *William Faulkner: The Contemporary Reviews, Conversations with William Faulkner,* and new editions of Mark Twain's *A Connecticut Yankee in King Arthur's Court* and Sam Watkins's memoir of the Civil War, *Company Aytch.* He is senior editor of the four-volume reference work *Greenwood Guide to American Popular Culture.*

Pamela Knights is senior lecturer in English and American Literature, University of Durham, England, and National Teaching Fellow. She has published numerous articles on Faulkner, Wharton, and others, and edited a critical anthology of Kate Chopin for Oxford World's Classics. She is currently working on a series of articles on regionality in fiction.

Amy E. C. Linnemann is a doctoral student at Indiana University, Bloomington. Her research interests include nineteenth- and twentieth-century fiction and the philosophy of literature. She is currently working on a critical examination of childbirth in twentieth-century American literature, as well as on Simone de Beauvoir and Emmanuel Levinas.

Peter Lurie has taught in the History and Literature concentration at Harvard University and has been research fellow in Film Studies at Oxford University. He has published articles on Faulkner in *American Literature* and in the proceedings of the International Faulkner Symposium at the University of Rennes, Rennes, France. His book, *Vision's Immanence: Faulkner, Film, and the Popular Imagination,* will be published in 2004.

Kevin Railey is professor and chair of English, Buffalo State College, Buffalo, New York. His work on Faulkner has appeared in the *Arizona Quarterly,* the *Faulkner Journal,* and in the Faulkner and Yoknapatawpha volume, *Faulkner in a Cultural Context.* His book, *Natural Aristocracy: History, Ideology and the Production of William Faulkner,* was published in 1999. He is currently guest editing a volume of the *Faulkner Journal* about Faulkner and ideology.

D. Matthew Ramsey is assistant professor of American Literature and Film, Denison University, Granville, Ohio. He received his Ph.D. from Ohio State University, where he developed his current interests in Faulkner and film, adaptation theories, detective fiction, horror films, and conspiracy theory. He is currently working on a book on adaptation and authorship and an article on a locked-room mystery story by Melville Davisson Post.

Debrah Raschke is associate professor of English, Southeast Missouri State University, Cape Girardeau, Missouri. She has published numerous essays on modern and contemporary British literature and literary theory and is working on a book manuscript titled *Modernism, Metaphysics, and Sexuality.*

Terrell L. Tebbetts is Brown Professor of English, Lyon College, Batesville, Arkansas, where he chairs the Language and Literature Division. His research, focused on twentieth-century American writers and especially William Faulkner, has appeared in *Philological Review, New Orleans Review, Southern Literary Journal, South Central Review, Approaches to Teaching* The Sound and the Fury, *Teaching Faulkner,* and *Faulkner and Postmodernism.* He was also a contributor to *A William Faulkner Encyclopedia.*

Theresa M. Towner teaches literary studies at the University of Texas at Dallas. She has published *Faulkner on the Color Line: The Later Novels* and essays on Faulkner, African American literature, and theory, and the connections between them.